# THE ROUTLEDGE (
## TO PHILOSOPHY OF SOCIAL SCIENCE

*The Routledge Companion to Philosophy of Social Science* is an outstanding guide to the major themes, movements, debates, and topics in the philosophy of social science. It includes thirty-seven newly written chapters, by many of the leading scholars in the field, as well as a comprehensive introduction by the editors. Insofar as possible, the material in this volume is presented in accessible language, with an eye toward undergraduate and graduate students who may be coming to some of this material for the first time. Scholars too will appreciate this clarity, along with the chance to read about the latest advances in the discipline. *The Routledge Companion to Philosophy of Social Science* is broken up into four parts:

- Historical and Philosophical Context
- Concepts
- Debates
- Individual Sciences.

Edited by two of the leading scholars in the discipline, this volume is essential reading for anyone interested in the philosophy of social science, and its many areas of connection and overlap with key debates in the philosophy of science.

**Lee McIntyre** is a Research Fellow at the Center for Philosophy and History of Science at Boston University. He has previously taught philosophy at Harvard University, Colgate University, Tufts Experimental College, Simmons College, and Boston University. McIntyre is the author of *Respecting Truth: Willful Ignorance in the Internet Age* (Routledge, 2015); *Dark Ages: The Case for a Science of Human Behavior* (2006); and *Laws and Explanation in the Social Sciences: Defending a Science of Human Behavior* (1996).

**Alex Rosenberg** is the R. Taylor Cole Professor of Philosophy at Duke University. He has held fellowships from the National Science Foundation, the American Council of Learned Societies, the Guggenheim Foundation, and the National Humanities Center. In 1993 Rosenberg received the Lakatos Award in the philosophy of science. He was the Phi Beta Kappa-Romanell lecturer for 2006–7. Rosenberg is the author of twelve books in the philosophy of science, two novels, and about 200 papers.

# ROUTLEDGE PHILOSOPHY COMPANIONS

*Routledge Philosophy Companions* offer thorough, high-quality surveys and assessments of the major topics and periods in philosophy. Covering key problems, themes and thinkers, all entries are specially commissioned for each volume and written by leading scholars in the field. Clear, accessible and carefully edited and organised, *Routledge Philosophy Companions* are indispensable for anyone coming to a major topic or period in philosophy, as well as for the more advanced reader.

The Routledge Companion to Aesthetics, Third Edition
*Edited by Berys Gaut and Dominic Lopes*

The Routledge Companion to Philosophy of Religion, Second Edition
*Edited by Chad Meister and Paul Copan*

The Routledge Companion to Philosophy of Science, Second Edition
*Edited by Martin Curd and Stathis Psillos*

The Routledge Companion to Twentieth Century Philosophy
*Edited by Dermot Moran*

The Routledge Companion to Philosophy and Film
*Edited by Paisley Livingston and Carl Plantinga*

The Routledge Companion to Metaphysics
*Edited by Robin Le Poidevin, Peter Simons, Andrew McGonigal, and Ross Cameron*

The Routledge Companion to Nineteenth Century Philosophy
*Edited by Dean Moyar*

The Routledge Companion to Ethics
*Edited by John Skorupski*

The Routledge Companion to Epistemology
*Edited by Sven Bernecker and Duncan Pritchard*

The Routledge Companion to Philosophy and Music
*Edited by Theodore Gracyk and Andrew Kania*

For a full list of published *Routledge Philosophy Companions*, please visit https://www.routledge.com/series/PHILCOMP.

**Forthcoming:**

# PRAISE FOR THE SERIES

*The Routledge Companion to Aesthetics*

"This is an immensely useful book that belongs in every college library and on the bookshelves of all serious students of aesthetics."—*Journal of Aesthetics and Art Criticism*

"The succinctness and clarity of the essays will make this a source that individuals not familiar with aesthetics will find extremely helpful."—*The Philosophical Quarterly*

"An outstanding resource in aesthetics … this text will not only serve as a handy reference source for students and faculty alike, but it could also be used as a text for a course in the philosophy of art."—*Australasian Journal of Philosophy*

"Attests to the richness of modern aesthetics … the essays in central topics—many of which are written by well-known figures—succeed in being informative, balanced and intelligent without being too difficult."—*British Journal of Aesthetics*

"This handsome reference volume … belongs in every library."—**CHOICE**

"The *Routledge Companions* to Philosophy have proved to be a useful series of high quality surveys of major philosophical topics and this volume is worthy enough to sit with the others on a reference library shelf."—*Philosophy and Religion*

*The Routledge Companion to Philosophy of Religion*

"… a very valuable resource for libraries and serious scholars."—**CHOICE**

"The work is sure to be an academic standard for years to come … I shall heartily recommend *The Routledge Companion to Philosophy of Religion* to my students and colleagues and hope that libraries around the country add it to their collections."—*Philosophia Christi*

*The Routledge Companion to Philosophy of Science*

A **CHOICE** Outstanding Academic Title 2008

"With a distinguished list of internationally renowned contributors, an excellent choice of topics in the field, and well-written, well-edited essays throughout, this compendium is an excellent resource. Highly recommended."—**CHOICE**

"Highly recommended for history of science and philosophy collections."—*Library Journal*

"This well conceived companion, which brings together an impressive collection of distinguished authors, will be invaluable to novices and experienced readers alike."—*Metascience*

### The Routledge Companion to Twentieth Century Philosophy

"To describe this volume as ambitious would be a serious understatement. ... full of scholarly rigor, including detailed notes and bibliographies of interest to professional philosophers. ... Summing up: Essential."—**CHOICE**

### The Routledge Companion to Philosophy and Film

"A fascinating, rich volume offering dazzling insights and incisive commentary on every page ... Every serious student of film will want this book. ... Summing Up: Highly recommended."—**CHOICE**

### The Routledge Companion to Philosophy of Psychology

"This work should serve as the standard reference for those interested in gaining a reliable overview of the burgeoning field of philosophical psychology. Summing Up: Essential."—**CHOICE**

### The Routledge Companion to Metaphysics

"The *Routledge Philosophy Companions* series has a deserved reputation for impressive scope and scholarly value. This volume is no exception. ... Summing Up: Highly recommended."—**CHOICE**

### The Routledge Companion to Nineteenth Century Philosophy

A **CHOICE** Outstanding Academic Title 2010

"This is a crucial resource for advanced undergraduates and faculty of any discipline who are interested in the 19th-century roots of contemporary philosophical problems. Summing Up: Essential."—**CHOICE**

### The Routledge Companion to Ethics

"This fine collection merits a place in every university, college, and high school library for its invaluable articles covering a very broad range of topics in ethics[.] ... With its remarkable clarity of writing and its very highly qualified contributors, this volume is must reading for anyone interested in the latest developments in these important areas of thought and practice. Summing Up: Highly recommended."—**CHOICE**

### The Routledge Companion to Philosophy and Music

"Comprehensive and authoritative ... readers will discover many excellent articles in this well-organized addition to a growing interdisciplinary field. Summing Up: Highly recommended."—**CHOICE**

"… succeeds well in catching the wide-ranging strands of musical theorising and thinking, and performance, and an understanding of the various contexts in which all this takes place."
—*Reference Reviews*

### The Routledge Companion to Phenomenology

"Sebastian Luft and Søren Overgaard, with the help of over sixty contributors, have captured the excitement of this evolving patchwork named 'phenomenology'. *The Routledge Companion to Phenomenology* will serve as an invaluable reference volume for students, teachers, and scholars of phenomenology, as well as an accessible introduction to phenomenology for philosophers from other specialties or scholars from other disciplines."—**International Journal of Philosophical Studies**

### The Routledge Companion to Epistemology

A **CHOICE** Outstanding Academic Title 2011.

"As a series, the *Routledge Philosophy Companions* has met with near universal acclaim. The expansive volume not only continues the trend but quite possibly sets a new standard. … Indeed, this is a definitive resource that will continue to prove its value for a long time to come. Summing Up: Essential."—**CHOICE**

### The Routledge Companion to Philosophy of Language

"This collection presents more than 65 new essays by prominent contemporary figures working in the philosophy of language. Collectively, they represent the cutting edge of philosophical research into issues surrounding the use, understanding, and study of language. … [T]he book constitutes an invaluable current resource for students and scholars alike. It will appeal to anyone interested in the current state-of-play within this important area of philosophical research. Summing Up: Highly recommended."—**CHOICE**

### The Routledge Companion to Social and Political Philosophy

"This 15th book in the *Routledge Philosophy Companions* series is also the most comprehensive, both chronologically and conceptually. … The polish and high quality of the essays provide a multifaceted mirror of the passions and interests of contemporary academic Anglophone philosophy. Summing Up: Highly recommended."—**CHOICE**

### The Routledge Companion to Ancient Philosophy

"This excellent reference will be useful to faculty and students alike… . The essays are of uniformly high quality."—**CHOICE**

# THE ROUTLEDGE COMPANION TO PHILOSOPHY OF SOCIAL SCIENCE

*Edited by*
*Lee McIntyre and Alex Rosenberg*

LONDON AND NEW YORK

First published 2017 by Routledge

2 Park Square, Milton Park, Abingdon, Oxfordshire OX14 4RN
52 Vanderbilt Avenue, New York, NY 10017

*Routledge is an imprint of the Taylor & Francis Group, an informa business*

First issued in paperback 2019

*Library of Congress Cataloging in Publication Data*
A catalog record for this book has been requested

ISBN: 978-1-138-82575-8 (hbk)
ISBN: 978-0-367-87157-4 (pbk)

Typeset in Goudy
by Out of House Publishing

# CONTENTS

# CONTENTS

# CONTENTS

# NOTES ON CONTRIBUTORS

**Kenneth Baynes** is Professor of Philosophy at Syracuse University. He is the author of many articles in social and political philosophy and, most recently, of *Habermas* (Routledge, 2015).

**Cristina Bicchieri** is the S. J. P. Harvie Professor of Philosophy and Psychology at the University of Pennsylvania. She works on social norms and behavioral ethics.

**Sharon Crasnow** is Distinguished Professor of Philosophy, Emerita, Norco College, California and an Associate of the Centre for Humanities Engaging Science and Society (CHESS) at Durham University. Her research interests are methodological issues in philosophy of social science and feminist epistemology.

**Justin Cruickshank** has research interests in critical realism, Popper, pragmatism, and the sociology of knowledge. His publications include critiques of critical realism in *Philosophy of the Social Sciences* and the *Sociological Review*, and discussion of Popper and Rorty in *Social Epistemology*.

**Janette Dinishak** is an Assistant Professor of Philosophy at the University of California, Santa Cruz. She works primarily in the philosophy of psychiatry, the philosophy of psychology, Wittgenstein, and the epistemology of other minds. She has published papers on Wittgenstein, philosophical questions concerning autism and perception, and deficit views of human differences.

**Stephen M. Downes** is Professor of Philosophy at the University of Utah. His research interests are in philosophy of biology, specifically in biological approaches to explaining human behavior. He also has broader interests in philosophy of science, including an interest in the role of models in science and the place of biology in the social sciences. His work is published in journals such as *Philosophy of Science*, *Biology and Philosophy*, *Studies in History and Philosophy of Science*, and *Philosophy of the Social Sciences*. He is co-editor (with Edouard Machery) of *Arguing about Human Nature* (Routledge, 2013).

**David Eck** is a Professor in the Philosophy Department at Cañada College, California. His research interests concern the social dimensions of knowledge, with an emphasis on the relationship between cognitive science and social epistemology.

**Brian Epstein** is Associate Professor of Philosophy at Tufts University. His research interests include philosophy of social science, metaphysics, and philosophy of language. Epstein is the author of *The Ant Trap: Rebuilding the Foundations of the Social Sciences* (2015).

**Brian Fay** is William Griffin Professor of Philosophy, Emeritus, Wesleyan University, Middletown, Connecticut. He was editor of *History and Theory*, 1991–2011. He is author of *Social Theory and Political Practice*, *Critical Social Science*, and *Contemporary Philosophy of*

*Social Science: A Multicultural Approach*; editor of *Louis O. Mink: Historical Understanding* and *History and Theory: Contemporary Readings*; and author of numerous scholarly essays.

**Steve Fuller** is Auguste Comte Professor of Social Epistemology at the University of Warwick. The author of more than twenty books, he recently completed a trilogy on the idea of 'Humanity 2.0'. His latest book is *Knowledge: The Philosophical Quest in History* (Routledge, 2015).

**Vincent Guillin** is Associate Professor in the Philosophy Department at the Université du Québec à Montréal and a member of CIRST (Montréal). His current research focuses on the history and philosophy of the human sciences, and most notably on the works of Auguste Comte and John Stuart Mill. He is also interested in the use of comparison and experimentation in social science and the various models of scientific governance.

**Randall Harp** is an Associate Professor of Philosophy at the University of Vermont. His interests include the philosophy of action, moral psychology, and philosophy of social science. His work is published or forthcoming in *Journal of Moral Philosophy*, *Theoria*, and *The Routledge Companion to Free Will*.

**Conrad Heilmann** is an Assistant Professor of Philosophy at Erasmus University Rotterdam, where he is also a co-director of the Erasmus Institute for Philosophy and Economics (EIPE). His work focuses on the philosophy of economics, with particular interests in intertemporal choice, behavioral economics, and measurement.

**David Henderson** is the Robert R. Chambers Distinguished Professor of Philosophy at the University of Nebraska, Lincoln. His interests include explanation and the relation between it and interpretation in the social sciences. His most recent work focuses on norms and their explanatory place in the social sciences. He also works in epistemology and has come to be interested in the idea that epistemic norms can be understood in terms of social norms and the kinds of cooperation and coordination they afford in epistemic communities.

**Kevin D. Hoover** is Professor of Economics and Philosophy at Duke University. He is editor of *History of Political Economy* and past co-editor of the *Journal of Economic Methodology*.

**Marianne Janack** is Professor of Philosophy at Hamilton College in Clinton, New York.

**Marija Jankovic** is an Assistant Professor of Philosophy at Davidson College, North Carolina. Her areas of specialization are philosophy of language and philosophy of mind.

**Tuukka Kaidesoja** is University Researcher at the Academy of Finland Centre of Excellence in the Philosophy of the Social Sciences (TINT) at the University of Helsinki. Kaidesoja is the author of *Naturalizing Critical Realist Social Ontology* (2013) and several articles on philosophy of the social sciences and sociological theory.

**Kareem Khalifa** is an Associate Professor of Philosophy at Middlebury College, Vermont. His interests include general philosophy of science, epistemology, and philosophy of social science. He has published articles in *British Journal for the Philosophy of Science*, *Journal of Economic Methodology*, *Philosophy of Science*, *Philosophy of the Social Sciences*, *Social Epistemology*, *Synthese*, and *Theoria*, among others. He is currently completing a book on scientific understanding.

**Harold Kincaid** is Professor of Economics at the University of Cape Town, Visiting Professor at the Finland Centre of Excellence in the Philosophy of the Social Sciences at the University of Helsinki, and the author of multiple books and many journal articles and book chapters on issues in the philosophy of social science.

**Jaakko Kuorikoski** is currently a Professor in Social and Moral Philosophy at the University of Helsinki and a Research Fellow at the Academy of Finland Centre of Excellence in the Philosophy of the Social Sciences (TINT). He has published on explanation, models and simulations, mechanisms, and causality in, among others, *British Journal for the Philosophy of Science*, *Erkenntnis*, *Philosophy of Science*, *Philosophy of the Social Sciences*, and *Synthese*.

**Daniel Little** is a philosopher of social science who writes on social explanation, social ontology, and methodological issues in sociology. His most recent books include *New Contributions to the Philosophy of History* (2010) and *New Directions in the Philosophy of Social Science* (2016). He serves as Chancellor of the Dearborn campus of the University of Michigan, where he is a Professor of Philosophy; he also serves as Professor of Sociology at the University of Michigan-Ann Arbor.

**Kirk Ludwig** is Professor of Philosophy at Indiana University, Bloomington. He works in the philosophy of mind and action, philosophy of language, epistemology, and metaphysics. He is co-author (with Ernie Lepore) of *Donald Davidson: Meaning, Truth, Language and Reality* (2005) and *Donald Davidson's Truth-Theoretic Semantics* (2007). He is co-editor with Marija Jankovic of the forthcoming *Routledge Handbook on Collective Intentionality* and author of two books on collective action with Oxford University Press: *From Individual to Plural Agency: Collective Action 1* (2016) and *From Plural to Institutional Agency: Collective Action 2* (2017).

**Lee McIntyre** is a Research Fellow at the Center for Philosophy and History of Science at Boston University and an Instructor in Ethics at Harvard Extension School. He has previously taught at Colgate University, Boston University, Tufts Experimental College and Simmons College, and was Executive Director of the Institute for Quantitative Social Science at Harvard University. He is the author of *Laws and Explanation in the Social Sciences: Defending a Science of Human Behavior* (1996); *Dark Ages: The Case for a Science of Human Behavior* (2006); and *Respecting Truth: Willful Ignorance in the Internet Age* (Routledge, 2015). He is the co-editor of several anthologies in the philosophy of social science and the philosophy of chemistry.

**Eleonora Montuschi** is an Associate Professor of Philosophy in the Department of Philosophy and Cultural Heritage at the Ca' Foscari University of Venice and Senior Research Fellow at the London School of Economics. Her research and teaching areas are the philosophy of science and social science, scientific and social objectivity, the theory and practice of evidence, and methodological issues in the social sciences.

**Nico Orlandi** is Assistant Professor of Philosophy at the University of California, Santa Cruz. Nico's main areas of specialization are philosophy of mind, philosophy of psychology, and epistemology.

**Julian Reiss** is Professor of Philosophy at Durham University and Co-Director of the Centre for Humanities Engaging Science and Society. His writings are in the philosophy of science, especially in philosophy of economics and of medicine, and include the books *Error in Economics* (2008); *Philosophy of Economics: A Contemporary Introduction* (2013); and *Causation, Evidence, and Inference* (2015).

**Mark Risjord** is a Professor of Philosophy at Emory University and the University of Hradec Králové, Czech Republic. His books include *Woodcutters and Witchcraft: Rationality and Interpretive Change in the Social Sciences* (2000) and *Philosophy of Social Science* (Routledge, 2014). He edited *Naturalism and Normativity in the Philosophy of the Social Sciences* (Routledge, 2016).

**Michael Root** is an Emeritus Professor of Philosophy at the University of Minnesota and writes about the use of race as a variable in population-level studies in the social and biomedical sciences as well as race as a basis for diagnosis or treatment in the clinic.

**Alex Rosenberg** is R. Taylor Cole Professor of Philosophy (as well as Biology and Political Science) at Duke University. He is the author of more than a dozen books in the philosophy of biology and social science, and about 200 articles, especially on causation, economics, and reductionism in these disciplines. He won the Lakatos Award in 1993, was the national Phi Beta Kappa-Romanell lecturer in 2006–7, and has held fellowships from the Guggenheim Foundation, the American Council of Learned Societies, and the National Humanities Center. He is also the author of two historical novels.

**Don Ross** is Professor of Economics at the University of Cape Town, and Program Director for Methodology at the Center for Economic Analysis of Risk at Georgia State University. His main current areas of research are the philosophy of economics, experimental economics of risk and time preferences, gambling addiction and related public health problems, strategic aspects of human socialization, and scientific metaphysics. He is the author or editor of thirteen books and numerous articles.

**Paul A. Roth** is Distinguished Professor in the Department of Philosophy at the University of California, Santa Cruz. He has published widely on subjects including the philosophy of history (primarily historical explanation), philosophy of social science, naturalized epistemology, and Quine.

**Warren Schmaus** is Professor of Philosophy at the Illinois Institute of Technology in Chicago. He conducts research on the history and philosophy of science in nineteenth- and twentieth-century France, and has published two monographs on Emile Durkheim: *Durkheim's Philosophy of Science and the Sociology of Knowledge* (1994) and *Rethinking Durkheim and His Tradition* (2004).

**Jeremy Shearmur** was educated at the London School of Economics, where he also worked for eight years as assistant to Karl Popper. He taught philosophy at the University of Edinburgh, political theory at the University of Manchester, and both subjects at the Australian National University, where he is currently an Emeritus Fellow. He is the author of *Hayek and After* and *The Political Thought of Karl Popper*, and joint editor of Popper's *After the Open Society* and of *The Cambridge Companion to Popper*.

**Giacomo Sillari** is Senior Lecturer in the Political Science Department at the LUISS Guido Carli in Rome. He has previously taught at Scuola Normale Superiore in Pisa, Italy and at the University of Pennsylvania. His interests and research are in behavioral economics, game theory, and the philosophy of social sciences.

**David Livingstone Smith** is Professor of Philosophy at the University of New England in Biddeford, Maine. His most recent book, *Less Than Human: Why We Demean, Enslave, and Exterminate Others*, was winner of the 2012 Anisfield-Wolf award for non-fiction.

**Stephen Turner** is Distinguished University Professor in Philosophy at the University of South Florida. His writings on cognitive science and social science are largely collected in *Brains/ Practices/Relativism: Social Theory after Cognitive Science* (2002) and *Understanding the Tacit* (2014).

**Thomas Uebel** is Professor of Philosophy at the University of Manchester. He has published widely in the history of philosophy of science and on logical empiricism. Among his books are *Empiricism at the Crossroads: The Vienna Circle's Protocol-Sentence Debate* (2007) and *The Cambridge Companion to Logical Empiricism* (edited with Alan Richardson, 2007).

**Bruno Verbeek** is Director of the Centre for Political Philosophy at Leiden University and Senior Lecturer in the Institute for Philosophy of Leiden University, where he coordinates the MA Program in Philosophy of Political Science. He has worked on the application of rational choice theory (in particular game theory and decision theory) to issues in ethics, political philosophy, and legal theory. He is the author of *Moral Philosophy and Instrumental Rationality: On the Virtues of Cooperation* (2002) as well as several articles on social norms, conventions, and the rationality of pre-commitment strategies in bargaining and other contexts. Currently, he is working on questions concerning the authority of norms (e.g. legal norms). In addition, he has been thinking hard about questions regarding the justice of taxation.

**Gregory Wheeler** is Assistant Professor of Philosophy at the Munich Center of Mathematical Philosophy at the Ludwig Maximilian University of Munich. His research focuses on formal, social, and computational epistemology and the foundations of probability and statistics. He has published over forty articles that have appeared in journals such as *Noûs*, *Mind*, *Philosophy and Phenomenological Research*, *Philosophy of Science*, *British Journal for the Philosophy of Science*, *Erkenntnis*, *Synthese*, *Journal of Philosophical Logic*, and *Studia Logica*. He is editor of *Minds and Machines*, and he has previously held positions at Carnegie Mellon University, the Max Planck Institute for Human Development, and the Center for Artificial Intelligence Research at the New University of Lisbon.

**K. Brad Wray** is a Professor of Philosophy at the State University of New York, Oswego. He is the author of *Kuhn's Evolutionary Social Epistemology*, published by Cambridge University Press in 2011. He has published numerous articles on Kuhn, the social epistemology of science, and the realism/antirealism debate in philosophy of science.

**Petri Ylikoski** is Professor of Science and Technology Studies at the University of Helsinki. His research interests range from sociological theory to core issues in philosophy of science. Most recently he has been working on philosophical foundations of analytical sociology.

**Julie Zahle** is Associate Professor in the Section of Philosophy, at the Department of Media, Cognition and Communication, University of Copenhagen and Research Fellow at the Academy of Finland Centre of Excellence in the Philosophy of the Social Sciences (TINT), University of Helsinki. Her research focuses on various topics within the philosophy of the social sciences including the individualism–holism debate, theories of practice, qualitative methods, and values in the social sciences.

# INTRODUCTION

## Lee McIntyre and Alex Rosenberg

The philosophy of social science has long been the younger sibling of the philosophy of natural science, living in its shadow in much the same way that the social sciences have historically measured their success against the natural sciences. As a branch of the philosophy of science, we often find issues in the philosophy of social science covered in one or two entries on "individual sciences" in the larger anthologies, along with the philosophy of physics, biology, and—more recently—chemistry. This is welcome but, given the scope of the social sciences and the important philosophical issues they raise, insufficient. You hold in your hands the solution: *The Routledge Companion to Philosophy of Social Science.*

The diversity of issues raised by the philosophical study of social scientific inquiry cannot help but mirror the wide range of subjects and methodological approaches that are pursued by the individual sciences in question: economics, psychology, history, anthropology, sociology, and political science. But there is one philosophical issue that has ranged across these sciences that is in some ways the defining issue that brought the philosophy of social science into being. How is the study of human behavior, human action, and human affairs in general like or unlike the study of natural phenomena?

This question—with its requisite focus on the problem of explanation—led to an enormously fruitful period in the philosophy of science, when the logical positivists were first attempting to show that there was a strict method of demarcation between science and non-science, and that the social sciences could be on the right side of this, if only they agreed to employ exclusively empirical methods and give up any sort of speculation about meaning or values. To say that this was a heavy lift would be an understatement. Even for those social scientists who sought to live up to this ideal there were serious problems, given the eventual collapse of logical positivism in its own failure to outline a workable verification criterion that was capable of demarcating between meaningful and meaningless statements. If there were no criteria by which even natural scientific theories could be privileged, what hope was there for the social sciences?

This did not, however, deter many of those who had already been bitten by the bug of putting more "science" in the social sciences. For even if the logical positivists failed in their task, weren't the natural sciences still sciences? Weren't they somehow privileged and special in their empirical approach? Maybe the positivists had merely mischaracterized what was distinctive about science. And, if so, couldn't the social sciences still hitch their wagon to that star?

Thus the philosophy of social science (which was born alongside the discipline of sociology with the work of Comte, Mill, and Durkheim) was ushered into the modern era, as a full-fledged branch of the philosophy of science. Quick on the heels of the demise of logical positivism, a group of philosophers of science (Carl Hempel, Ernest Nagel, Herbert Feigl, etc.) gave up on trying to solve the positivists' problem of "empirical meaning" and instead focused on the more salient problem of "method," which was to become the hallmark of "logical empiricism." This, however, immediately led to another question. Could the method of inquiry in the social sciences be the same as that in the natural sciences?

Now the terms of debate were clear, for—as at its founding—the question of social scientific method was again in full focus. Clearly, the method that was being pursued in the natural sciences was successful; it led not only to ever-deeper realms of theoretical understanding in such fields as physics and biology, but also to a technological revolution the likes of which the world had never seen. And, if they were ostensibly pursuing this same method, why were the social sciences such comparative failures?

Predictably, different answers to this question were given by different sides in the debate. Those who embraced logical empiricism felt that it was because "the social sciences were not working hard enough to follow proper method" or that they were "still too young." Critics of logical empiricism, on the other hand, argued that "the subject matter of the social sciences is fundamentally unlike that of the natural sciences, and therefore needs its own method."

One now understands why the next fifty years of the philosophy of social science was dominated by arguments about law-like explanation in the social sciences, whether social entities and processes could be explanatorily reduced to individuals and their behavior, and whether human action or behavior was predictable.

As the philosophy of science itself evolved during this period, however, the terms of debate began to shift. Especially with the emergence of Thomas Kuhn's work in the 1960s, philosophers began to question whether even "science" was science—whether one could actually say that the thing that made scientific inquiry unique (if anything could) was its method. Did science even follow some "objective" method? Were theories chosen uniquely on the basis of their empirical evidence? And what was the role of social factors in influencing scientific change? Now the door was wide open for social scientists to rethink their own role. No longer merely an afterthought of the natural sciences, the social sciences began to assert their own power as an alternative way of understanding, following a different model of what it meant to "explain." Perhaps the interpretation of meaning of social events to the agents who participated in them was a legitimate (or perhaps the only appropriate) form of inquiry. Maybe beliefs and desires were ineliminable in explanation and irreducible to the explanans that natural science countenanced.

It is important not to overplay this scenario. During the heyday of logical empiricism, there were plenty of critics of the idea of "unified science," which came as a holdover from logical positivism in recommending identical methods of inquiry across the natural and social sciences. Likewise, during the post-Kuhnian birth of interpretivism, critical theory, and social constructivism there were plenty of empiricists who sought to defend the idea that science was special and worthy of being emulated. But the point is that the central question of philosophy of social science was now in full view. Could (and should) the social sciences try to be more like the natural sciences? What about the stubborn fact that humans are a conscious subject matter, who possibly have free will and a subjectively self-aware ability to understand (and guide) their own actions?

The chapters in this volume do an excellent job of examining the four corners of this debate from its historical roots right up to today's cutting-edge issues of social ontology and behavioral economics. Of course, the philosophy of science has not itself remained stagnant, and neither has the philosophy of social science. Yes, the philosophy of social science is still dominated by questions of explanation, but this is an enormously rich area, encompassing issues in epistemology, ontology, meaning, and values. Students, teachers, and scholars who come to this volume will gain a rich appreciation of the individual debates and controversies within this field, from both a historical and theoretical perspective. This volume is a collection of short, focused chapters on leading concepts and debates, written by many of the preeminent researchers in the field. The coverage is fairly comprehensive, with just enough overlap to show continuity between the issues. The volume as a whole takes no position on the important debates within the discipline, but we have given the authors a free hand to indicate their own views, within the context of full coverage of both sides of any given debate. The outcome, we feel, is a great advantage for both students and scholars alike. Students will be treated to entries that are written in intelligible language by leading scholars, while seasoned researchers will surely be curious to see what their colleagues have said in providing a survey of their favorite topics.

The volume is broken up into four parts:

I  Historical and Philosophical Context
II  Concepts
III  Debates
IV  Individual Sciences.

In Part I, we focus on the deepest historical roots of social inquiry in the 18th century, right up through the development and evolution of logical empiricism and its critical aftermath, to the present day "counter-revolution" of empirical methods.

In Part II, we focus on the bread-and-butter conceptual issues that would be a part of any analysis of the study of human action and behavior. The issues of explanation, reduction, emergence, methodological individualism, functionalism, and naturalism would be found in any anthology in the philosophy of social science going all the way back to the 1960s, but are here presented in contemporary context. These are joined by a sampling of some new concepts that limn the four corners of the present-day field.

In Part III, we turn to some of the most contentious contemporary debates in the philosophy of social science. Some, as we'll see, are long-standing (such as the debate about laws), and some are brand new (such as machine epistemology and big data).

In Part IV, we have focused on those philosophical issues raised by individual social sciences. It is important to note that we have aimed here for the widest possible coverage and not neglected those disciplines (namely sociology, anthropology, and political science) that are seldom covered in volumes such as this. Indeed, in the case of the philosophy of political science, one of us has tried—in collaboration with a scholar in this philosophically neglected field—to ask why not all of the individual social sciences *have* a specialized discipline. In much the same way that the philosophy of chemistry was ignored for decades in favor of the philosophy of physics and biology, we have sought to do justice to the idea that the philosophy of social science should have something of interest for sociologists, anthropologists, and political scientists alike.

We hope that readers will appreciate the easy availability of these three dozen newly written papers that now fill a long-standing gap in the Routledge Companion series. When Michael Martin and Lee McIntyre's *Readings in the Philosophy of Social Science* appeared with MIT Press in 1994, it was the first comprehensive anthology in the field since May Brodbeck's *Readings in the*

*Philosophy of the Social Sciences* (1968) and Leonard Krimerman's *The Nature and Scope of Social Science* (1969). The MIT Press volume exploited a wave of new interest in the philosophy of social science, collecting together many of the classic papers—along with new scholarship—so that teachers would have an updated resource and scholars would have a handy reference for their ongoing work. That volume marked the beginning of a twenty-year renaissance of interest in the philosophy of social science that saw the emergence of many new textbooks and anthologies, and a spate of scholarship that led to new topics which now join the old. As such, for the present volume we had the luxury of commissioning new essays from this fresh-flowing stream—trusting that the classic papers are still out there for those who wish to find them. In any case, with the death of our friend Michael Martin in 2015, the old MIT volume is never going to see a second edition and the need for a new teaching volume seems pressing.

The current Routledge Companion volume came together fairly quickly (as these things go), but was still over two years in the making. We would like to thank Martin Curd for his excellent advice on the entire undertaking; Brian Fay, Harold Kincaid, Dan Little, Mark Risjord, Paul Roth, and Brad Wray for their specific advice on the best topics and contributors; Tom McCarthy and Georgia Warnke for their advice when we needed it; and the entire team at Routledge (especially Andy Beck, our editor) for seeing us the whole way through.

Most of all we wish to thank our stellar list of contributors, who produced excellent work and were a pleasure to work with as well.

# Part I
# HISTORICAL AND PHILOSOPHICAL CONTEXT

1

# COMTE AND THE POSITIVIST VISION

## *Vincent Guillin*

A spectre has long been haunting the philosophy of social science—the spectre of positivism. Once the dominant view on the nature and prospects of scientific inquiry and its application to the study of social phenomena, it gradually appeared obvious to many that this conception failed to capture the defining characteristics of science, so much so that the very label "positivism" has become "a term of abuse" (Giddens 1977, 29). Yet, despite its demise, that positivist view of science still remains influential today, albeit in a somewhat paradoxical manner, to the extent that it provides a convenient representation of an obsolete methodological ideal that generally serves as a foil for social science and the different disciplines it encompasses (for a classic formulation of that position, see Hayek 1979). It is important to point out, however, that "logical positivism," the modern incarnation of the positivist idea—which has been rightfully criticized for its uncritical reliance on the analytic-synthetic distinction, its unsatisfactory verification criteria for cognitive meaningfulness, and its inability to come up with a clear theory of the confirmation of empirical statements—is a far cry from the original vision entertained by Auguste Comte, the very philosopher to whom it owes its name.

Unfortunately, contemporary critics of positivism tend to overlook such a distinction and think of positivism as one monolithic view. Accordingly, the "positivist persuasion" (Alexander 1996, 649) is often condensed as a few guiding principles held to mark out and govern the scientific enterprise as a whole. Applied to the study of social reality, these principles are generally summarized as follows (for convergent accounts of that methodological paradigm, see Blaikie 2004 and Williams 2006):

- The scientific study of social phenomena must emulate the approach and methods successfully developed in the natural sciences.
- Just as there are laws of natural phenomena, there are laws of social phenomena, conceived as general statements specifying the existence of constant conjunctions between kinds of events or entities.
- The discovery of these laws depends primarily on observation, both as the source of data from which nomological generalizations are derived and as the empirical benchmark against which to test for their truth or falsity.

- Mathematical tools are given pride of place in the formalization of social data, whilst quantitative methods play a crucial role in the verification, experimental and non-experimental, of social scientific statements.
- Scientific progress is gauged both by reference to the subsumption of individual instances under general laws, and to the gradual reduction of the specific laws governing the diversity of social facts to a limited set of higher-level lawlike statements, the derivation of the latter from the most fundamental biological and physical laws of nature being regarded as a heuristic standard, if not a practical possibility.
- Any statement, hypothesis, or theory that cannot be reduced to observational terms or assessed factually is deemed unscientific; accordingly, since normative statements are not amenable to verification because of their lack of empirical content, they are to be excluded from the purview of scientific discourse.

In other words, a positivist social science is naturalistic in approach, committed to empiricism, driven by a search for general laws, mathematically informed and quantitatively oriented, longing for nomological reduction or at least theoretical unification, and axiologically neutral.

Now, what is striking about that so-called "positivist" conception of social science is the extent to which it diverges from the views actually advocated by Auguste Comte. Of course, some key tenets of the "positivist persuasion" were indeed present in Comte's Positive Philosophy, primarily those bearing on the general aspects of scientific investigation (the importance of observation, the pursuit of nomological knowledge). But this modern-day version of positivism sits ill with many of the most distinctive aspects of Comte's views on the nature and methods of social science, a whole field he not only provided with its name—the barbarous but now time-proven "sociology"—but which he also almost singlehandedly attempted to establish theoretically and methodologically. Accordingly, in what follows, after a quick perusal of Comte's general philosophy of science—perhaps the only part of his intellectual inheritance reclaimed by other positivists such as Mill, Spencer, or the logical empiricists—I will draw attention to the most original dimensions of his philosophical and methodological contributions to social science, namely his intellectualism, his historicism, his holism, his refusal to apply mathematics to social phenomena, his anti-reductionism, and his axiologically laden conception of social science. As I hope to show, in many respects, Auguste Comte was not exactly your regular type of positivist.

## 1 "Treating Politics in a Scientific Manner": Naturalism and Social Science

A former student of the prestigious *École Polytechnique*, where he had been introduced to the latest developments in both the mathematical and physical sciences—the teaching of the former providing him with his only and somewhat precarious means of subsistence for most of his life (on Comte's biography, see Pickering 1993–2009)—Auguste Comte, who was also well acquainted with recent advances in biology and medicine, can undoubtedly be counted amongst those who were convinced, in the first half of the 19th century, that science had become the one and only source of genuine knowledge about the world. Yet he also acknowledged that a whole domain of reality had so far eluded the reach of scientific investigation, namely social phenomena. And if science really aimed at universality, the only way to achieve it was by "complet[ing] the system of observational sciences by the foundation of social physics" (Comte 1988, 1st Lesson, 13) or, as he would later dub it, sociology (Comte 1975, II, 47th Lesson, 88).

Such a project, which Comte had entertained as early as his 1822 *Plan des travaux scientifiques nécessaires pour réorganiser la société*, a programmatic sketch in which he first ventured "to treat politics in a positive manner" by raising it "to the rank of the sciences of observation" (Comte 1998, 86 and 81), took its definitive shape in his monumental six-volume *Cours de philosophie positive* (1830–42), the "first purpose" (Comte 1988, 1st Lesson, 13) of which was the foundation of sociology (for general accounts of Comte's sociology, see Gane 2006 and Wernick 2001). There, Comte appeared straightforwardly naturalistic: drawing on a philosophical appraisal of the history of mathematics, astronomy, physics, chemistry, and biology, which occupied the first three volumes of the *Cours* and which spelled out how the scientific mind had approached the various kind of phenomena and the different methods it relied upon for doing so, Comte then extended—in the last three volumes—the methodological bounty he had harvested from his patient survey of the natural sciences to the study of social phenomena. Yet, right from the start, Comte had a pretty good idea of what the scientific or positive spirit consisted in: "recognizing the impossibility of obtaining absolute truth, [it] gives up the search after the origin and hidden cause of the universe and a knowledge of the final causes of phenomena"; it endeavours "only to discover, by a well-combined use of reasoning and observation, the actual laws of phenomena— that is to say, their invariable relations of succession and likeness"; finally, it constantly tends, "although in all probability it will never attain such a stage," towards the establishment of a system in which "we could look upon all the different observable phenomena as so many particular cases of a single general fact" (Comte 1988, 1st Lesson, 2–3). Such was the "positive method" sociology had to take up if it wanted to become a science worthy of that name.

In many respects, Comte's famous "law of the three states" offered a prime example of the way the positive method applied to social phenomena. For, Comte claimed, that sociological generalization about human intellectual development, which stated that "each branch of our knowledge ... passes in succession through three different theoretical states"—"the theological or fictitious state, the metaphysical or abstract state and the scientific or positive state"—resulting in "three methods of philosophizing, whose characters are essentially different and even radically opposed to each other" (Comte 1988, 1st Lesson, 1–2), was clearly vindicated by different kinds of empirical facts. On the one hand, Comte argued, "its accuracy [was] immediately verified by all those who are fairly well acquainted with the general history of the sciences," which plainly evidenced how, in the theological state, the human mind primarily "directs its researches mainly toward the inner nature of beings, and towards the first and final causes of all the phenomena it observes" and "represents these phenomena as being produced by the direct and continuous action of more or less supernatural agents," before it replaces, in the metaphysical state, "the supernatural agents ... by abstracts forces, real entities or personified abstractions, inherent in the different beings of the world," which give "rise by themselves to all phenomena observed," eventually reaching the positive state in which all phenomena are considered "subject to invariable natural laws," the "discovery of these laws and their reduction to the least possible number constitut[ing] the goal of all our efforts" (Comte 1988, 1st Lesson, 2 and 8). On the other hand, Comte continued, since "the starting point [is] necessarily the same in the education of the individual as in that of the species," the observation of the "development of the individual intelligence" bears witness that "each of us ... has been successively—as regards the most important ideas—a theologian in childhood, a metaphysician in youth, and a natural philosopher in manhood." "This verification of the law," Comte concluded, "can easily be made by all who are on a level with their era" (Comte 1988, 1st Lesson, 4). Everything considered, it seems that Comte's major—by own lights—empirical contribution to sociology complied with the demands of his very definition of the positive method: the "law of the three states" was an informative generalization accounting for the evolution of human ideas globally, both at the level of the species (historically) and the individual (genetically, so to speak), thereby explaining a wealth of heterogeneous facts; different sources of evidence (based on historical and psychological observation) were invoked for its corroboration; and it even licensed some definite instances of rational prediction that could confirm its exactitude (the advent of sociology itself serving, in a somewhat paradoxical manner, as a crucial test of the validity of its first law).

## 2 A Qualified Empiricist: Intellectualism and Historicism in Comte

Yet, in the process of assessing the plausibility of that law, Comte insisted on one consideration that seriously qualified his endorsement of empiricism. For, as he himself underlined, what the law of the three states also revealed was that there existed a "logical necessity" (Comte 1988, 1st Lesson, 5) according to which observation must depend on a theoretical framework that defines, among the indefinite number of empirical facts available, those that are epistemologically relevant, which in turn explained why the human mind first adopted "theological philosophy," the only intellectual scheme that precisely addressed "the most insoluble questions—such as the inner nature of objects, or the origin and purpose of all phenomena ... [it] proposes to itself, in preference to all others, in its primitive state" (ibid.). More generally, Comte argued, this showed that theories could not be derived inductively from mere observations, but that they necessarily preceded them, since the former made possible the latter in the first place: "[f]or if, on the one hand, every positive theory must necessarily be founded upon observations, it is, on the other hand, no less true that, in order to observe, our mind has need of some theory" (ibid.). In other words, Comte was no doubt an empiricist in matters of verification (see Comte 1975, I, 28th Lesson, 456–64, for his "Fundamental theory of hypotheses"), but he surely was no inductivist as to theory construction, especially in sociology, and clearly endorsed the view that observations are necessarily theory-laden. Hence Comte's dissatisfaction with the work of historians, who had so far contented themselves, as the *Plan* claimed, with compiling "*annals*, that is to say descriptions and chronological arrangements of a certain sequence of particular facts," whereas "true *history*, conceived in a scientific spirit," should consist in "the investigation of the laws governing the social development of the human race," that is "proceed from the general to the particular" (Comte 1998, 142) and not the other way round.

But, if so, what was the theoretical framework appropriate to a positive sociology? The *Plan* made it clear that the positivization of the study of social phenomena required both the acknowledgment that "social organization [is] intimately tied to the state of civilization [i.e. the advancement of knowledge] and determined by it" (Comte 1998, 90) and the endorsement of the idea that "the progress of civilization develops according to a necessary law" (93), a view that was both given content to and corroborated by the law of the three states. In other words, for Comte, positive sociology was both "intellectualistic," to the extent that it assumed that the primary explanatory factor of human progress was the development of the mind, and "historicist" (in the sense of Popper 1957), since it presumed that this intellectual development necessarily consisted in a long-term historical trend that could be captured by laws similar to those governing natural phenomena. As Comte himself pointed out, the elaboration of that conceptual scheme both demanded that, from a historical point of view, social phenomena had reached a stage of their development advanced enough as to display clearly the progressive nature of their evolution (a threshold definitively crossed, according to Comte, with the advent of the French Revolution), and, from an epistemological perspective, that the human mind had matured enough so that it could deal positively with those phenomena, drawing on the decisive contributions of Aristotle (whose empirical investigations of the constitution of the Greek *polis* privileged observation over imagination), Montesquieu (who, in the *Esprit des lois*, distinctly conceived "political phenomena as being necessarily subjected to invariable natural laws" [Comte 1975, II, 47th Lesson, 85]), and Condorcet (who saw clearly that "civilization is subjected to a progressive course all of whose stages are rigorously connected to each other according to natural laws which can be unveiled by philosophical observation of the past" [Comte 1998, 116]). Now that history was ripe and human intelligence had reached its positive state, sociology could truly become scientific.

Of course, the intellectualism and historicism characteristic of Comte's sociology, which he not only considered empirically vindicated but also as the very assumptions the study of society could not dispense with, have never been accepted as such even by self-proclaimed positivists, much less by the majority of practitioners of social science. For the former, because the claim that "the world is governed and overturned by ideas, or, in other words, that the whole social mechanism rests finally on opinions" (Comte 1988, 1st Lesson, 28) unduly narrowed the range of possible causal relations existing among social phenomena. For the latter, because it turned the methodologically driven quest for empirical laws into a metaphysically loaded kind of historical determinism. Now, one might still argue that Comtean positivism nonetheless had the methodological resources to cope with Comte's own pronouncements about the nature and course of evolution, since it put a premium on the verification of scientific statements, a test on which one could rely to demonstrate the unwarranted character of Comte's most provocative claims. In perfect accordance with the positivist creed, observation would, in that respect, serve as the ultimate umpire of the truth or falsity of sociological propositions. Unfortunately, Comte's very conception of the spirit and methods of positive sociology seriously constrained the scope and objectivity of such an empirical appraisal.

## 3 Holism and the Synthetic Perspective.

As emphasized above, Comte fully endorsed the thesis of the theory-ladenness of scientific observations. What was distinctive about his position was the content and status of the theoretical assumptions he considered necessary for carrying out the search for sociological laws, which he carefully expounded in four lessons of the *Cours* (48 to 51) that served as a methodological preamble to the detailed description of the historical transition of mankind from the theological state (52–54), through the metaphysical (55), to the positive state (56–57). Accordingly, in the 48th Lesson, which was dedicated to the "Fundamental Characteristics of the Positive Method as Applied to the Rational Study of Social Phenomena," Comte introduced his readers to the theoretical framework that would guide sociological inquiry. Borrowing a distinction from the biological domain, Comte claimed that sociology consisted in both the "fundamental study of the conditions of existence of society" and of "the laws of its continuous motion" (Comte 1975, II, 48th Lesson, 109), the former concentrating on "social statics," that is the consideration of social structures, whilst the latter focused on "social dynamics," that is the description of their evolution through time, "order" and "progress" being the two complementary dimensions of any social reality. But Comte also took pain to underline that any sociological investigation, be it static or dynamic, had to be informed by the thought that what distinguished social phenomena was their synthetic nature, the fact that there existed among the various elements composing social systems and the various phases of their development a connectedness that was even more striking than the wholeness typical of living beings. This holistic perspective, which had been already adopted in the most advanced biological studies, imposed itself even more forcefully on sociologists, who, because they were dealing with phenomena more complex than those biologists considered, had to give precedence to the consideration of the whole over the examination of the parts, thereby privileging synthesis over analysis, the approach that has far dominated in the inorganic sciences. As Comte put it, "since social phenomena are indeed thoroughly connected, their real study should never be rationally separated, hence the permanent obligation ... to always consider simultaneously the various social aspects, either in social statics or ... in social dynamics" (119).

The principle of the "fundamental co-relation of [social] phenomena," which Comte promoted as the "primary guide in their direct exploration" (120), directly governed the manner in which sociological observation was to be carried out. On the one hand, it prompted social statics to become "the positive study, both experimental and rational, of the mutual actions and reactions the various parts of the social system exert on one another" (111), a study that clearly demonstrated, according to Comte, "the fundamental solidarity existing between all the possible aspects of the social organism" (112). More precisely, Comte argued, this "social consensus," which was the "key idea of social statics" (118), amounted to acknowledging the present "state of the integral development of mankind, considered in all its various modes of activity, be they intellectual, moral or physical" as connected to the current "political institutions and social mores" (114) and dictated that sociology regard as the "true social unit," not the individual, since "any system [has to be] necessarily made out of elements that are essentially homogeneous to it" (50th Lesson, 183), but the family, because one could discern in it the seed of the various features—purposiveness, hierarchy, specialization—that would reach their full extent in the human association at large. In other words, social statics was both heuristically and ontologically holistic. But social dynamics, on the other hand was no less synthetic, since it also emphasized the continuity inherent in the various stages of the evolution of mankind considered as a single entity that had been exposed to "the consecutive social modifications actually observed among distinct populations (48th Lesson, 123). Once again drawing on a biological analogy, Comte conceived of social dynamics, which he himself regarded as the real improvement brought about by positive sociology in the understanding of social phenomena, as the search for the laws of development of mankind, "the true general spirit of dynamic sociology [consisting] in conceiving each of these successive social states as the necessary result of the previous one and the indispensable force behind the next" (ibid.). And just as the "law of the three states" offered an insight that captured this fixed pattern of succession, the sociological lessons of the *Cours* aimed at documenting precisely the course of that progressive evolution.

Yet, as already pointed out with respect to his intellectualism and his historicism, Comte's emphasis on the connectedness—both diachronic and synchronic—characteristic of social phenomena, and the synthetic outlook he accordingly advocated for their positive study, is hardly reconcilable with some of the central heuristic tenets of the "positivist persuasion," namely its nominalism and its atomism (Blaikie 2004, 836). On the one hand, Comte's holism and his tendency to treat society as a unified being within which the various parts primarily exist in relation to their contribution to the whole that they form has been generally regarded with great suspicion by modern-day positivists to the extent that they saw in them the remnants of an archaic organicist conception which postulates the existence of abstract entities (such as "society" itself or "social states") and reifies them unwarrantedly. On the other hand, Comte's radical exclusion of the individual from social science is utterly at odds with the atomist approach often favored by later positivists, who start from the analysis of the various social agents' values, desires, and beliefs to explain the social outcomes resulting from the aggregation of their actions. In this last respect, Comte's stubborn refusal to acknowledge the scientific status of both psychology— discarded either as a theological relic in its rationalist version or as a metaphysical vestige in its empiricist manifestations (on Comte and psychology see Scharff 1995, ch. 1)—and political economy, blamed, among many other reasons, for its analytic bent and its individualistic model of the *homo œconomicus* (on Comte and political economy, see Weinberg 1982, Part II, ch. 2), might well have served as a definitive *reductio ad absurdum* of his sociological views.

## 4 Positive Methods in Sociology and the Proscription of Mathematics.

Comte's synthetic perspective did not merely infuse the most general assumptions of sociology; for it also directly affected his account of the methods most suited to sociological inquiry. First of all, Comte argued, "the universal connectedness of the various social aspects" (Comte 1975, II, 48th Lesson, 142) would give observation, especially the collection of facts practiced by historians and ethnographers, its scientific justification, since "the immediate inspection or direct description of all sorts of events" and "the consideration of what might appear the most insignificant customs, the appreciation of all sorts of monuments, the analysis and comparison of languages, etc." (141–42) would now be integrated in a theoretical framework within which they would contribute to a better understanding of the conditions necessary for both "order" and "progress." As for experimentation, although the sheer complexity and connectedness of social phenomena severely restricted its use, it still could be relied upon under the form of "natural experiments," such as revolutions or social upheavals, that could indicate more or less precisely the limits of variation to which the social order could be exposed. The comparative method could also be relevant to sociology, since it allowed for the comparisons of the various ways in which the different groups that constitute humanity developed; but, since it restricted itself to synchronic or geographic comparisons, it had to be supplemented by what Comte held to be the properly sociological procedure, namely the "historical method" (148), which aimed at "forming the whole of human events into coordinated series that clearly show their gradual sequence" (150). In line with his verificationist bent, Comte made clear that sociological generalizations— such as the claim that the course of history was clearly marked by the progressive subordination of temporal powers to spiritual ones or by the continuous decline of the military spirit and the correlative development of industrial dispositions—would have to withstand the test of empirical evidence either as postdictions or predictions, whilst also acknowledging that such corroborations (which would mostly concern historical tendencies) would not be as precise as those carried out in the natural sciences.

What is undoubtedly most striking in Comte's methodological discussion is his radical proscription of mathematics from the sociological toolbox. A professional mathematician himself, Comte nonetheless argued that social phenomena, precisely because of their connectedness and historicity, exceeded the analytic resources of mathematical theories. Taking stock of the attempts of Bernoulli, Condorcet, and, more recently, Laplace, he specifically targeted the "chimerical subordination" of sociological studies to "the illusory theory of chances" (49th

Lesson, 168), "a philosophical monstrosity" (58th Lesson, 704) that "directly amount[ed] to giving our real personal ignorance as the natural measure of our opinions' degree of likelihood" (49th Lesson, 169), thereby negating the very idea that deterministic laws governed social phenomena. Accordingly, if positivism is defined as "the position that social facts can be reliably measured" (Abbott 2004, 252) or as the claim that "scientists only deal in those things that are measurable" (Williams 2006, 231), the positivism of Comte, who suspected that "mathematical analysis" might serve "to conceal, under an imposing gibberish, the inanity of conceptions" (Comte 1975, II, 48th Lesson, 152), surely has nothing in common with what we now call "sociological positivism."

## 5 Unification vs. Reductionism: Positivism and Materialism

Comte surely believed that the increasing number of phenomena to be subsumed under laws and the subsumption of these specific laws under a limited set of higher-level general statements were distinct indicators of the advance of knowledge, since "the real philosophic purpose of all science" is to try "to diminish as far as possible the number of general laws necessary for the positive explanation of natural phenomena" (Comte 1988, 1st Lesson, 32), a goal that no doubt extended to social phenomena. Yet, Comte also stressed that the attempt, characteristic of positive philosophy, at "sum[ming] up, in a single body of homogeneous doctrine, the aggregate of acquired knowledge relating to the different orders of natural phenomena" (31) was not to be conflated with the "chimerical ... attempts at the universal explanation of all phenomena by a single law," both because "the resources of the human mind are too feeble" and because "the universe is too complicated to admit of our ever attaining such scientific perfection" (ibid.). This last feature, coupled with the idea that there exist "different orders of reality," indeed prompted Comte to build the *Cours* around a "classification" or a "hierarchy of the sciences." According to that scheme, the different sciences had evolved more or less rapidly towards positivity depending on the degree of simplicity and generality of the phenomena they studied. Hence the resulting "scale of the sciences," which put mathematics first, followed in orderly fashion by astronomy, physics, chemistry, and biology. And since sociology had to deal with the most complex and special kind of facts, it was no surprise that it "necessarily progressed more slowly than all the preceding orders" (2nd Lesson, 12) of phenomena.

Comte's classification offered a very original view of the architectonics of the positive sciences that stressed both their "encyclopedic" dependence and their epistemological autonomy. As to the former, Comte argued, since there existed an objective dependence between the various kinds of phenomena (for example, certain astronomical, physical, and chemical conditions had to be realized for life to appear), the higher a science was located in the scale, the greater its dependence on the laws and methods of the preceding sciences. As for epistemological autonomy, Comte maintained that, since each order of reality displayed specific features (for instance only living beings reproduced and fell ill), each fundamental science needed to elaborate its own specific methods and concepts so as to be able to discover the various original laws proper to the phenomena it studied. Accordingly, for Comte, unification was primarily a methodological and explanatory issue, and his scientific pluralism clearly made him an opponent of ontological reductionism or, as he would call it, "materialism," that is the "continuous tendency to degrade the most noble speculations by assimilating them to the most common ones" (Comte 1929, 1, 50). This also explained why Comte always insisted on having elaborated a "philosophy of the sciences" in the plural, and would have considered the very idea of "a philosophy of science," as entertained by later positivists, an outright subversion of the encyclopedic ideal.

In Comte's eyes, sociology was undoubtedly the most perfect example of the way encyclopedic dependence and epistemological autonomy were enforced through the classification of the sciences. On the one hand, because social phenomena were the most complex and least general of all, the laws of astronomy, physics, and chemistry, which "accounted for the external conditions of human existence," and those of biology, which provided "the real laws of human nature" (Comte 1975, II, 49th Lesson, 156), necessarily had to be included in sociological explanations and serve as checks on sociological generalizations. On the other hand, because neither the inorganic sciences nor biology were equipped to take into account the properly historical dimension of human phenomena, the originality of the latter guaranteed the encyclopedic position of sociology as an autonomous science of the social. Yet, it must also be emphasized that Comte did not always stick to his professed anti-reductionism in matters sociological (as illustrated by his biological reductionism with respect to gender equality; see Guillin 2009) and that, as already evidenced by his holism and his use of the static/dynamic distinction, Comte's sociology relied heavily on a biologically inspired scheme that, for instance, conceived of social evolution as a mere development, an understanding which precluded the very possibility of the historical emergence of any novelty whatsoever.

## 6 Positive Sociology and Positive Politics

But encyclopedic dependence was also supposed to have a feedback effect on the sciences of the classification. For if the full development of the positive spirit had only been achieved by the coming of age of the study of social phenomena, then sociology, because its account of human evolution also provided, as its key element, a rationale for scientific progress and its conditions, would have to exert a "necessary philosophical reaction … on all the preceding sciences" (Comte 1975, II, 49th Lesson, 170). According to Comte, the beneficial effects of that final encyclopedic primacy of sociology would be manifold: first, it would lead to a more positive conduct of future scientific inquiry, based on a reliable knowledge of human cognitive capacities and of the respective domain of each science, going so far as to render "scientific discoveries … amenable to a true rational prevision, by way of an exact appraisal of the previous movements of science, duly interpreted in accordance with the fundamental laws of the real course of the human mind" (172) and paving the way for "some sort of rational theory" of discovery that would "usefully direct the instinctive efforts of individual genius" (173); second, it would have "the social point of view" (58th Lesson, 707) prevailing over all scientific investigations, thereby ensuring that they would indeed cater to the real needs of mankind instead of pandering to theological or metaphysical illusions. In other words, because usefulness was an essential aspect of positivity, sociology was here to remind us that "the true necessary destination of our sound speculations [was] the continuous improvement of our actual condition, individual or collective, rather than the futile satisfaction of a barren curiosity" (Comte 2003, 121).

There was more than meets the eye in this last dimension of the "reaction" of sociology over the encyclopedic scale. For it did not merely reveal the pragmatic element present in Comte's positivism, together with his belief that scientific knowledge provided the best means of bettering the human lot: as Comte famously put it, "from science comes prevision; and from prevision comes action" (Comte 1988, 2nd Lesson, 38). It also pointed towards the genuinely political nature of Comte's overall project, which was already apparent in the very title of his 1822 pamphlet and stated again at the outset of the *Cours*: "the foundation of social physics," the "first and special object" (1st Lesson, 13–14) of that treatise, would promote "positive philosophy" as "the only solid basis for the reorganization that must terminate the crisis in which the most civilized nations have found themselves for so long" (28). More precisely, since he diagnosed the ongoing state of political and social crisis plaguing post-revolutionary societies as resulting from the absence of a shared system of beliefs that would replace the outdated theological and metaphysical principles, Comte naturally turned to sociology as the only appropriate remedy to that intellectual anarchy: because it had identified the static and dynamic laws of society, the positive study of social phenomena could now become the basis of a "Positive Politics" (which would eventually give rise to a "religion of humanity," as the subtitle of Comte's later *Système de politique positive* made clear [Comte 1929]) that would protect mankind from the arbitrariness of rulers; but it would also foster among the ruled a sense of order—thereby deterring them from any form of dissent, violent or not—whilst clearly indicating the possible avenues for improvement compatible with the existing social structures and their patterns of historical development (on the articulation of Positive Philosophy and Positive Politics, see Guillin 2015). Accordingly, a positive sociology was not merely a scientifically sound sociology; it was also, and perhaps primarily, a politically driven sociology that was meant to deliver the ideological and practical means of furthering at once "order" and "progress." In other words, the methodologically motivated attempt at insulating the study of social phenomena from values by restricting it to the consideration of facts and its normative corollary, the ideal of an axiologically neutral social science, would have simply appeared to Auguste Comte utterly incompatible with a properly positive sociology. So much for the fact–value distinction .... As I hope is now clear, such a stance, combined with the intellectualism, the historicism, the holism, the distrust of mathematical methods, and the anti-reductionism characteristic of his philosophical views, marks out Comte as a very peculiar positivist.

# References

Abbott, A. (2004) *Methods of Discovery. Heuristics for the Social Sciences*. New York and London: Norton.

Alexander, J. C. (1996) "Positivism," in A. Kuper and J. Kuper (eds.), *The Social Science Encyclopedia*, 2nd edn. London and New York, Routledge, 649–50.

Blaikie, N. (2004) "Positivism," in M. S. Lewis-Beck, A. Bryman, and T. Futing Liao (eds.), *The Sage Encyclopedia of Social Science Research Methods*. London: Sage, vol. 2, 836–38.

Comte, A. (1929) *Système de politique positive, ou Traité de sociologie instituant la religion de l'Humanité*, 4 vols. Paris: Au siège de la Société Positiviste.

———. (1975) *Cours de philosophie positive*. Ed. Michel Serres et al., 2 vols. Paris: Hermann.

———. (1988) *Introduction to Positive Philosophy*. Trans. Frederick Ferré. Indianapolis: Hackett Publishing Company.

———. (1998) *Early Political Writings*. Trans. H. S. Jones. Cambridge: Cambridge University Press.

———. (2003) *Discours sur l'esprit positif*. Introduction and notes A. Petit. Paris: Vrin.

Gane, M. (2006) *Auguste Comte*. London: Routledge.

Giddens, A. (1977) "Positivism and its Critics," in A. Giddens, *Studies in Social and Political Theory*. London: Hutchinson, 29–89.

Guillin, V. (2009) *Auguste Comte and John Stuart Mill on Sexual Equality. Historical, Methodological and Philosophical Issues*. Leiden and Boston: Brill.

————. (2015) "The Rule of Sociological Method. Auguste Comte's Positive Politics before the *Système de Politique Positive*," in K. N. Demetriou and A. Loizides (eds.), *Scientific Statesmanship, Governance, and the History of Political Philosophy*. New York: Routledge, 226–41.

Hayek, F. V. (1979) *The Counter-Revolution of Science. Studies on the Abuse of Reason*. 2nd edn. Indianapolis: The Liberty Fund.

Pickering, M. (1993–2009) *Auguste Comte. An Intellectual Biography*. Cambridge: Cambridge University Press, 3 vols.

Popper, K. R. (1957) *The Poverty of Historicism*. London: Routledge and Kegan Paul.

Scharff, R. C. (1995) *Comte after Positivism*. Cambridge: Cambridge University Press.

Weinberg, A. (1982) *The Influence of Auguste Comte on the Economics of John Stuart Mill*. London: E. G. Weinberg.

Wernick, A (2001) *Auguste Comte and the Religion of Humanity. The Post-Theistic Program of French Social Theory*. Cambridge: Cambridge University Press.

Williams, M. (2006) "Positivism," in V. Jupp (ed.), *The Sage Dictionary of Social Research Methods*. London: Sage, 229–31.

# 2
# DURKHEIM AND THE METHODS OF SCIENTIFIC SOCIOLOGY

## Warren Schmaus

### Introduction

Social scientists writing about Emile Durkheim (1858–1917) typically put him to some rhetorical use, either as a founder of the discipline of sociology or anthropology, to whom one can appeal in the justification of one's own methodology, or as a whipping boy to punish for all that is seen as wrong with the social sciences. He has been attacked for trying to model the social sciences on the natural sciences and for employing a functionalist model of explanation that provides a theoretical justification for the status quo and conservatism. Others have accused him of deviating in his empirical studies from his professed methodology in *The Rules of Sociological Method* (1895a)[1] or have argued that he was constantly changing his methods over the course of his career. Rarely has the aim of the social science literature on Durkheim been to give a careful exegesis of his works. In Anglophone social sciences, the problem has been compounded by theorists building on unreliable translations, which sometimes go so far as to translate a French term with its exact opposite in English. Durkheim has been made out to be such an incoherent and unattractive thinker—at least in Anglophone sociology—that one can only wonder how he managed to be included in the Holy Trinity of founding fathers: Marx, Durkheim, and Weber.

Some of the problems of interpretation can be explained at least in part by ambiguities in Durkheim's methods. In order to evaluate Durkheim's social science methodology, we need to keep several cross-cutting and overlapping distinctions in mind. First of all, we need to distinguish methods of investigation, methods of persuasion, and methods of explanation. By methods of investigation, I mean the ways in which he analyzed empirical data and used it to support his theories. His methods of persuasion have to do with how he argued that his theories were superior to alternative theories in the field. His methods of explanation are those by which he accounted for social phenomena. Second, we need to distinguish his professed methodology in *The Rules* from his actual working methods in his empirical studies. *The Rules* covers primarily his methods of investigation and explanation, whereas his substantive works like *The Division of Labor in Society* (1893b), *Suicide* (1897a), and *The Elementary Forms of Religious Life* (1912a) make use of methods of persuasion. Also, the order in which he presented his results in these works is not necessarily either the temporal order in which he arrived at them or the logical order in which he derived them. Finally, the methods by which he explained the phenomena may not be exactly what he prescribed in *The Rules*.

A third set of distinctions has more to do with the meanings of the terms Durkheim used. Durkheim was educated as a philosopher and he used philosophical terms in his sociological works. These terms often had different meanings in French philosophy during his lifetime than the meanings they have taken on in more recent social sciences. These terms can also have a third sense in philosophy today. For instance, philosophers approaching the sociological literature on Durkheim for the first time will be surprised to find Durkheim, with his rich ontology of collective representations, social forces, and suicidogenic currents, described as a "positivist."

These distinctions should be kept in mind when evaluating the charge that Durkheim's substantive works deviated from his expressed methodology. Durkheim never intended *The Rules* to be a text about argument strategies. When he criticized his opponents' theories for things like ambiguity, inconsistency, question-begging, unwarranted ad hoc assumptions, and methodological weaknesses, he simply took it for granted that these criticisms are generally accepted modes of argument in academic discourse that need no special defense. Keeping these distinctions in mind will also facilitate determining whether, and in what sense, Durkheim's methods may have changed over the course of his career.

## Durkheim's Reception in the Social Sciences

Durkheim's works have been put to different uses according to country and discipline. He is considered a founding father in both anthropology and sociology, but the boundaries between these disciplines are drawn differently in the United States, Europe, and Latin America.

In France, Durkheim's *Elementary Forms*, along with other works by Durkheim, Marcel Mauss, Henri Hubert, and Lucien Lévy-Bruhl, gave rise to a tradition of ethnological research that continued after Durkheim's death up through the work of Claude Lévi-Strauss. This tradition was characterized by a method of tracing concepts and social practices from their supposedly "elementary" forms in early societies to their more complex forms in more advanced societies. Social structures and functions were important explanatory concepts. Durkheim's *Suicide*, on the other hand, was relatively ignored in France.

British social anthropologists such as Bronislaw Malinowski, Alfred Radcliffe-Brown, and E. E. Evans-Pritchard who developed structural functionalism were influenced by this French tradition. The *Elementary Forms* was the first of Durkheim's major works to be translated into English, in 1915. Subsequently, Durkheimian-inspired anthropology crossed the Atlantic, with Malinowski bringing it to Yale and Lévi-Strauss bringing it to the University of São Paolo. More recently, however, anthropologists have moved away from structural functionalism and questioned the assumption that some present-day cultures represent the way other present-day cultures were in the past. They have also criticized Durkheim for relying on questionable ethnographies.

American sociologists, on the other hand, were attracted to Durkheim's earlier works. *The Division of Labor* and *The Rules* were first translated into English in the 1930s, around the time that Talcott Parsons published *The Structure of Social Action* (1937), drawing heavily on

Durkheim. *Suicide* was translated into English in 1951 and inspired a generation of quantitative work in sociology, despite Durkheim's unsophisticated statistical methodology. Parsons interpreted Durkheim's methods of explanation as having moved from an original "positivism" through "voluntarism" to "idealism" over the course of his career. Voluntarism corresponds to Parsons' own approach, in which the behavior of social actors is explained through postulating internalized norms and values. However, sociologists such as Whitney Pope (1973) and Stephen Turner (1986) have since shown that Durkheim never used this method of explanation.

Also, Parsons used the term "positivism" in quite a different sense than it had in Durkheim's time. For Parsons, it meant explaining social actors' actions in terms of their rational responses to conditions in the external environment, as if their relation to it were like that of natural scientists (1937, 61, 67, 438). Although the term positivism had taken on many different meanings in Durkheim's day through the works of Comte, Spencer, Mill, Bain, Mach, Avenarius, Ostwald, and others, no one at that time used it in Parsons' sense. For Durkheim, positivism appears to have meant treating moral philosophy as a natural science. In the original introduction to *The Division of Labor*, Durkheim had said that the aim of a "positive science of morality" is to arrive at general moral principles from the study of moral facts (1893b, 20). In this work, he sought to determine whether increasing specialization is morally desirable by comparing its causes and effects to those of other morally desirable phenomena (1902b, xxxvii, 4).

## Social Facts

One thing on which everyone seems to agree is that Durkheim defended the autonomy of sociology by arguing that there is a distinct class of phenomena that constitute its field of study: social facts. He defined them as ways of thinking and acting that constrain individuals and that are external to each individual consciousness, taken singly (1895a, 6ff.; 1897a, 356). Scholars such as Steven Lukes have complained that Durkheim equivocated with regard to the meaning of constraint through the examples he provided, from performing duties prescribed by custom or law to having to use the national language (1973, 12–13). But these different examples could all be regarded as but the effects or visible signs of an underlying social reality that constrains individuals. Similarly, things like suicide statistics or codes of law are often taken to be Durkheim's social facts, but they are again only their external or observable signs.

Originally, Durkheim characterized this underlying social reality as residing in the collective consciousness. This soon led to charges of his having postulated a group mind. But for Durkheim, there was no such thing, especially no conscious entity that exists over and above individuals. Sociology required no ontological substance or substratum other than "that which forms through the uniting of all the individual consciousnesses" (1897a, 361) or "the whole of associated individuals" (1898b, 38–39). Society existed for Durkheim only in and through individual consciousnesses (1912a, 299). To avoid the group mind objection, Durkheim abandoned the term "collective consciousness" and wrote instead about collective representations, the constitutive elements of the collective consciousness. He explained that there are two kinds of mental representation in each individual mind: individual and collective representations. The latter are initially formed from the fusion of individual representations in periods of "collective effervescence," such as during religious festivals. Fusion occurs when individuals recognize that others share the same representations. The resulting collective representations have greater force or power than individual representations, which explains the coercive or constraining power of social facts, which they exert unconsciously over individual minds (1912a, 297; 1955a, 173; 1902b, 67). To be sure, Durkheim did not shrink from taking a realist interpretation of collective representations, as well as social forces and suicidogenic currents. But these entities did not exist independently of the minds of individuals.

## Methods of Inquiry

It is also generally recognized that Durkheim advised sociologists to consider social facts as things, that is, as just as real as things in the material world (1895a, xi, 20). This has been interpreted in several ways, concerning both methods of inquiry and methods of explanation. With regard to the former, it has been read as endorsing a form of naïve inductivism and empiricism. This reading is reinforced by Durkheim's criticism of those who would proceed from ideas to things, rather than from things to ideas, and then, sounding a bit like Bacon, his advice to discard all prenotions or preconceptions and to define groups of social phenomena in terms of their external characteristics (1895a, 20ff.).

In the passages in question, Durkheim was simply arguing that sociology is an empirical science and not just a form of social theory that proceeds by analyzing our ordinary notions of things and then turns to the facts only as illustrations or confirmations. Often what went under the name of sociology at that time—such as the works of Comte and Spencer—looked more like philosophy than science. Similarly, Durkheim saw political economy as more ideological than empirical, claiming that even the law of supply and demand had never been experimentally confirmed (1895a, 31–34). For Durkheim, mathematics is the only science that can proceed through mental analysis alone, since we construct its objects ourselves; sociology must use the empirical methods of physics, chemistry, and physiology (1895a, xi–xiii).

The naïve inductivist and empiricist interpretation is just as wrong for Durkheim as it has proven to be for Bacon. The kind of induction Durkheim endorsed was eliminative, not enumerative induction, that is, a method of eliminating putative causal explanations and not one of simply generalizing from particular experiences. Durkheim explicitly criticized approaches that seek exhaustive detailed accounts of every society, and argued that what sociology should seek instead are what Bacon called "decisive or crucial facts" (1895a, 98), that is, the kinds of facts that can decide between competing hypotheses in a crucial experiment. In *The Elementary Forms*, he called this a "well-made experiment" (1912a, 135, 593). In this work, Australian religions provided the crucial test for whether totemism, animism, or naturism is the earliest form of religion. According to Durkheim, only the totemistic hypothesis could explain the origins of the distinction between the sacred and the profane as well as the origins of the ideas of souls, sacred beings, and religious forces. Far from generalizing from facts, Durkheim was not above "correcting" the facts. For instance, he "inferred" that despite the lack of evidence, Australians must have had totems for phratries as well as for clans, like the Amerindians do (1912a, 157).

After all, how else would Durkheim have been able to arrive at unobservable entities such as collective representations except through the method of hypothesis and test? One cannot get there by simple induction and generalization from observations. Nor can collective representations be known through introspection, as they work unconsciously. Collective representations and the relations among them must be postulated in hypotheses. Durkheim argued that what gives sociology the status of a science like the natural sciences is the use of hypotheses about unobservable entities in an "unknown world" to explain the phenomena (1897a, 349, 351; cf. 1912a, 597; 1898b, 33). It is true that Durkheim often used "hypothesis" as a term of abuse when attacking his opponents. But this was in the context of criticizing people like Spencer who would borrow hypotheses from other sciences such as biology without verifying them in sociology (1895d, 608).

Durkheim's method of hypothesis and test is not quite the more current concept of hypothetico-deductivism, in which test consequences are derived from hypotheses in conjunction with statements of initial conditions. Rather, Durkheim seems to have thought that effects may be derived directly from their causes. Disconfirmation was more important to him than confirmation: although several corroborating facts will not prove a hypothesis, a single fact may suffice to refute it (1895a, 163), assuming that the disconfirming fact is reliable (1888c, 265–66; 1895d, 608) and does not allow for alternative interpretations (1912a, 515), and the hypothesis is not confirmed by many other facts (1902a(i), 321). He also stressed the importance of defining terms in one's hypothesis clearly in terms of observable characteristics in order to be able to tell whether facts indeed confirm it (1895a, 43–44, 54).

Durkheim thought one could not actually perform experiments in sociology (1895a, 159). But instead, one can appeal to ready-made experiments provided by statistical, historical, and cross-cultural comparisons. For Durkheim, the logic of the experimental method was captured by Mill's canons of induction. Of Mill's methods, the method of concomitant variation was the most useful for sociology (1895a, 158ff.). Durkheim used this method for testing causal hypotheses, not for mechanically generating laws from observations (1895a, 161). He never sought precise mathematical laws where one value varied as a function of the other. For two phenomena to vary in direct or inverse proportion was sufficient to indicate a causal relationship for him. Durkheim showed no knowledge of developments in statistical methods by mathematicians such as Adolphe Quetelet and Francis Galton.

However, Durkheim recognized that the presence of a concomitance will not alone prove a causal relationship. He stipulated that it is better to have not just one but a series of concomitant variations for comparison, from the same society, from other societies of the same type, and from other types of societies (1895a, 165–69; 1909e, 156). For example, if we were to find an inverse relationship between the size of families and suicide rates, we should investigate whether this also holds in countries other than our own. On the other hand, his arguments against factors like alcoholism or climate as possible causes reveal that he thought the absence of a concomitance could disprove a hypothesis. A hypothesis can also be rejected if it says nothing about a concomitance or if an alternative provides a better fit. *Suicide* adds three further conditions on the acceptability of a causal hypothesis: there must be a sufficient number of facts so as not to be attributable to accidental circumstances, the facts must not allow of some alternative explanation, and the hypothesis must not be contradicted by other facts (1897a, 71–80).

Durkheim actually did little original empirical work himself. *Suicide* contains some previously unpublished evidence, but also draws on published works by criminologists such as Enrico Morselli's *Il suicido* of 1879. Durkheim obtained 26,000 dossiers from Gabriel Tarde at the French Bureau of Legal Statistics and thanked Mauss for sorting them by age, sex, marital status, and number of children (1897a, xi, n. 2). *Suicide* uses a crude version of the method of concomitant variation that proceeds by grouping and averaging. For example, to investigate the effects of family size, he classified the eighty-two departments of France into six groups according to suicide rates, and then compared the average family size for each group (1897a, 209). Some other classification of the eighty-two departments would not necessarily have yielded the same neat results. Of course, to question his use of suicide data is not to refute his theory of suicide, but only to leave it unconfirmed. (One could make a similar point about his use of unreliable ethnographic reports in *The Elementary Forms*.)

*The Division of Labor* and *The Elementary Forms* draw on published sources only. In the first work, Durkheim also used a form of the method of concomitant variation. One variable was the position of a society on a scale from primitive to modern, which Durkheim assumed reflected the degree of specialization of labor in that society. The other variable was the relative proportion of retributive law versus restitutive law, which for Durkheim indicated the relative strength of mechanical versus organic solidarity. The idea was to show that organic solidarity was replacing mechanical solidarity in modern society. Of course, there are other possible explanations of the differences Durkheim found in societies' codes of law.

After *The Division of Labor* and *Suicide*, cross-cultural comparisons took on more importance than the method of concomitant variations. *The Elementary Forms* employs a method of historical analysis, which he had characterized in *The Rules* as a method of sociological proof (1895a, 166ff.). In this method he arranged societies on a scale from simplest to most complex, and then traced the development of some social fact or institution throughout the entire series, as it adds elements becoming more complex. He thought that this method allowed one to analyze a social fact into elements that could not otherwise be easily distinguished (1912a, 4; 1888c, 264–65; 1909e, 153). This method of arranging things in series according to degree of complexity is traditionally French, going back at least to Descartes. Indeed, Durkheim called it a "Cartesian principle" that the first link in the chain plays an important role in getting at the real explanatory essence of something (1912a, 5). (Hence the title of Durkheim's methodological work, which alludes to Descartes's *Rules for the Direction of the Mind*.) Whether Durkheim followed the Cartesian model to the extent of accepting a classification of societies into linear series is not clear. At times, he disavowed the linear model in favor of an arboreal one for the evolution of human societies (e.g. 1901a(i), 245–46). Yet he appears to have assumed a linear classification of societies in both *The Elementary Forms* and *The Division of Labor*.

## Methods of Persuasion

Durkheim began each of his substantive works with a preliminary definition of the social phenomenon in question, such as suicide or religion, in terms of its external, observable characteristics. Then he sought the real essence of this phenomenon, which will provide the causes of its observable characteristics. Along the way, he compared his theory with his competitors' alternative explanations, arguing that his own theory has wider explanatory scope and provides the best explanations of the phenomena in question.

Durkheim's method of comparative theory evaluation thus resembles the logic of crucial experiments, but is broader in scope. Competitors' theories are rejected not only when they are contradicted by the facts, but when they say nothing at all about them. They are also rejected for generating unsolved problems that Durkheim's theory does not face. For instance, Durkheim argued that the hypothesis that collective totems derive from individual totems has problems that his own hypothesis does not have to solve (1912a, 253). Alternative theories are criticized for conceptual as well as empirical problems. In *Suicide*, he rejected the hypothesis that the suicide rate varies with race because of the ambiguity of the concept of race (1897a, 54–68) and the insanity hypothesis for not being falsifiable (1897a, 21ff.). Durkheim also rejected explanations that made use of ad hoc hypotheses, such as Lévy-Bruhl's conjecture that primitives have an alternative logic (1912a, 342).

*The Elementary Forms* provides perhaps the clearest example of Durkheim's procedure. It begins with a preliminary definition of religion expressed in terms of a distinction between the sacred and the profane, which is maintained by an institution such as a church. To find the essential nature of religion, it turns to what he took to be the earliest form of religion, represented by Australian totemism. He then defended the hypothesis that this was the earliest form of religion against the alternative hypotheses that either animism or naturism were the earliest form, as described above. Durkheim then explained the sacred character attached to certain totemic objects in terms of the social forces that are experienced in periods of collective effervescence during the performance of religious rites. Finally, he generalized this conclusion to include contemporary religions, maintaining that the feelings of well-being to which they give rise are but the result of social forces. What people take to be their religious experiences are in fact caused by an underlying reality of social forces, much as our sensory experience of colors is caused by an underlying reality of different wavelengths of light (1912a, 597).

## Methods of Explanation

Durkheim's concept of explanation combines explaining the meaning of a concept with explaining a fact by subsuming it under a general expression, such as a causal law. In fact, he did not seem to distinguish definitions from explanatory generalizations, as he wrote about definitions in terms appropriate for empirical hypotheses, such as the verification of definitions and the ability of definitions to account for the facts (1902b, 73, 52, 32). Ultimately, to explain a social fact was to provide its underlying real essence, which one could only gradually approach and never completely arrive at, and which would define the fact and furnish its cause and function. To be sure, he clearly stated that the knowledge of laws was the goal of sociology, for instance when he said: "There is a whole part of sociology that should investigate the laws of collective ideation and that still entirely remains to be done" (1898b, 47, n. 1). These laws of collective ideation were supposed to explain how collective representations can give rise to other collective representations. However, it is not clear that he ever discovered any such laws, and the explanations he gave appear to involve the deduction of effects directly from postulated causes, rather than from laws and statements of initial conditions.

A second ambiguity in his method of explanation concerns causes and functions. Durkheim denied the possibility of a plurality of causes for the same effect (1895a, 155ff.), although he introduced a distinction between normal and pathological cases to deal with exceptions to this principle, that is, where the same effects appear to have resulted from different causes. But in the normal course of events, causes are both necessary and sufficient for their effects, and effects are not only logically necessary conditions of their causes, but sufficient indicators of their presence, making causes difficult to distinguish from effects. Since the function of a social fact is to be found among its effects, Durkheim's functional explanations are often mistaken for causal explanations, in spite of his warnings in *The Rules* against confusing causal with functional explanations.

For instance, *The Division of Labor* has been construed as showing that specialization is caused by increasing social, moral, or "dynamic" density, that is, the density of interpersonal relationships, which in turn results from increasing physical population density. Alternatively, Durkheim could be interpreted as having claimed that the specialization of labor is an adaptation to increasing dynamic density rather than a result of it. The latter reading is suggested by Durkheim's reference to Darwin's principle of the divergence of character, according to which specialization is an adaptation to minimize competition with similar organisms. Similarly, the division of labor among humans could minimize competition among them (1902b, 248ff.). Durkheim is quite explicit that without the interpersonal relationships that make up social density, people could respond to increasing population density simply by dispersing (1902b, 270–71; 1895a, 115). The function of specialization is to maintain those interpersonal bonds, so that individuals continue to see themselves as members of the same society and stay together. As a result, population density may then increase. One could argue that Durkheim wrote *The Rules* precisely in order to try to defend *The Division of Labor* against the charge that it explains specialization ultimately in terms of physical causes. In *The Rules* he argued that the physical population density may serve as the means to measure the dynamic density, as they march together in lock step, but that it is not an exact measure (1895a, 140 and n. 1). However, that leaves the question of what gets the whole process started unexplained, that is, what causes the dynamic density to increase.

Sometimes Durkheim himself appears to have been led astray by the confusion of causes with functions, as in his theory of the categories in *The Elementary Forms*. The problem is only compounded by an ambiguity between the categories and their collective or cultural representations. Durkheim attempted to identify them, but this would be like confusing numbers with numerals. He seems to have wanted *The Elementary Forms* to be read as showing that the categories have social causes. But what he succeeded in showing is that the categories have important social functions and that their collective representations have social causes or at least social models. According to Durkheim, all societies appear to use the same categories of space, time, causality, and class because these categories have necessary social functions. For example, all societies need some way of communicating about spatial directions. However, different societies need not all represent space in the same way. Each society may have its own system of representing the categories. These representations make explicit what are already implicit in people's minds. Durkheim claimed that individuals have no more need than an animal does of a conceptual representation of space and time in order to orient itself and satisfy its individual needs (1912a, 632).

Although Durkheim's causal and functional explanations may not have always been distinct from each other, he was clear about distinguishing functional explanations from explanations in terms of intentions, goals, or purposes. For Durkheim, the function of some social phenomenon has nothing to do with anything that people may have intended. Facts about groups of individuals cannot be explained in terms of facts about the individuals that make up the group, especially not facts about their intentional behavior. To explain social phenomena in terms of individual intentions would be to mistakenly give them a psychological explanation. Sociology is an autonomous science for Durkheim, as social phenomena such as social suicide and homicide rates are not reducible to individual psychology.

## What is Problematic about Durkheim's Methods

Durkheim's assumption that sociology must have its own, real theoretical entities in order to be considered a genuine science is problematic on several levels. He was modeling sociology on the direction in which he saw the natural sciences moving in his day. But history suggests that positing theoretical entities and taking a realist stance towards them is not always the only or even the best way to go. Also, physics, chemistry, and molecular biology today all share the same fundamental entities, and the idea of ascribing causal powers to them in this stochastic universe is questionable. It may be that twentieth-century social scientists did not take Durkheim's ontology of collective representations, social forces, and suicidogenic currents seriously, focusing their attention instead on things like suicide statistics and population density in his works, precisely because they were more positivist in the philosophical anti-realist sense than Durkheim ever was.

There are further problems with collective representations. It is not clear how an unconscious mental representation can be the bearer of meaning, and even the identification of meanings with conscious mental representations faces philosophical difficulties. Yet Durkheim appears to have been closed to new ways of thinking about meaning, as he strongly defended the traditional concept of ideas representing reality against William James's pragmatic approach to meaning and truth (1955a). In all fairness, however, there is an alternative approach that is at least implicit in Durkheim's works, in which the meanings of collective representations can be defined in terms of their functions, their causes, and their relationships with other collective representations.

Durkheim thought he needed to posit collective representations in order to explain what he took to be the ideas that held a society together, thus making the Comtean assumption that it is shared ideas that accomplish this task. Perhaps the difficulty Durkheim experienced in finding any such shared ideas in contemporary society explains the fact that he subsequently turned his attention to the study of simpler societies such as the Australian totemists.

## What is Valuable in Durkheim's Methodology

Perhaps Durkheim's most valuable contribution was his defense of a holist or collectivist alternative to methodological individualism in the social sciences. He demonstrated that there is a distinct class of social phenomena that cannot be completely explained in terms of individual behavior. Specifically, he argued that no account in terms of individual psychology can explain how different social groups have different suicide and crime rates, which goes a long way towards illuminating how *Suicide* became a classic and a model in American sociology. However, Durkheim perhaps did not quite see that this methodological principle does not depend on any ontology specific to sociology. This could be explained through an analogy with biology. Although biological organisms are nothing but physical and chemical entities, there are biological explanations that employ concepts like function and adaptation that cannot be reduced to physics and chemistry. Similarly, although there is no social entity over and above the individuals that constitute a society, the reason some cities have higher homicide rates than others cannot be explained in terms of individual psychology.

Durkheim also gave valuable advice about avoiding common-sense terms and concepts. That is, to really understand social phenomena such as suicide or religion, we must step back from our ordinary notions of these things, which may simply reflect cultural and other biases. For instance, we should not define religion in terms of beliefs in gods or other supernatural entities, as that privileges certain religions over others. Also, the fact that suicide may be viewed negatively while self-sacrifice may be viewed positively should not blind us to the possibility that what looks to be a suicide bombing from one society's point of view may appear to be the noble act of a martyr to another.

One could object that Durkheim could not explain the social meaning of suicide and say that it was inappropriate for him to treat social facts in a natural scientific sort of way. However, there is no reason to think that sociology cannot concern itself with both meanings and causes. Durkheim at least attempted to combine the two; whether he was successful, of course, is a separate question. But one can ask just how successful other social theorists have been in trying to distinguish an "interpretive" from an "explanatory" social science. Often the arguments turn on contrasting the social sciences with an unrealistic picture of the natural sciences. For instance, Dilthey's hermeneutic method involves making an hypothesis about the whole in order to interpret its parts, and then using these interpretations to modify our original hypothesis about the whole, and endlessly repeating this cycle (Anderson 2003). But at a general enough level, this could describe the method of any science, natural or social, including Durkheim's sociology. Durkheim's hypothesis about religion is used to interpret different sorts of rites and practices, which reflects back on his concept of religion as a whole to form a new tentative hypothesis. There appears to be no set of methods that is specific to the social sciences that distinguishes them from the natural sciences, or set of methods that is common to all but only the natural sciences.

## Note

1  I cite the original French versions of Durkheim's works, providing my own translations, since the available English translations are not always reliable. The reference numbering system is that originally established by Steven Lukes (1973) and subsequently updated by Robert Alun Jones and Daniela Barberis at http://durkheim.uchicago.edu/.

## References

Anderson, R. L. (2003) "The Debate over the *Geisteswissenschaften* in German Philosophy," in T. Baldwin (ed.), *The Cambridge History of Philosophy 1870–1945*. Cambridge: Cambridge University Press, 221–34.

Durkheim, E. (1888c) "Introduction à la sociologie de la famille [Introduction to the Sociology of the Family]," *Annales de la Faculté des Lettres de Bordeaux* 10: 257–81. Repr. in 1975a, vol. 3, 9–34.

——— (1893b) *De la division du travail social: étude sur l'organisation des sociétés supérieures [The Division of Labor in Society: A Study of the Organization of Higher Societies]*. Paris: Alcan. The pages from the introduction to the first edition that were removed in subsequent editions have been reprinted in 1975a, vol. 2, 257–88.

——— (1895a) *Les règles de la méthode sociologique [The Rules of Sociological Method]*, 8th edn. Paris: Alcan, 1927.

——— (1895d) "L'origine du mariage dans l'espèce humaine d'après Westermarck [The Origin of Marriage in the Human Species According to Westermarck]," *Revue Philosophique* 40: 606–23. Repr. in 1975a, vol. 3, 70–92.

——— (1897a) *Le suicide: étude de sociologie [Suicide: A Study in Sociology]*, Paris: Alcan. New edn., Paris: PUF, 1930, repr. 1986. The preface to the first edition that was removed in subsequent editions is reprinted in 1975a, vol. 1, 43–48.

——— (1898b) "Représentations individuelles et représentations collectives [Individual and Collective Representations]," *Revue de Métaphysique et de Morale* 6: 273–302. Repr. in 1924a, *Sociologie et philosophie*. Paris: PUF, 13–50.

——— (1901a(i)) "Deux lois de l'évolution pénale [Two Laws of Penal Evolution]," *L'Année Sociologique* 4: 65–96. Repr. in 1969c, 245–73.

——— (1902a(i)) "Sur le totemisme [On Totemism]," *L'Année Sociologique* 5: 82–121. Repr. in 1969c, 315–52.

——— (1902b) *De la division du travail social* [*The Division of Labor in Society*], 2nd edn. Paris: Alcan. Repr. Paris: PUF, 1986.

——— (1909e) "Sociologie et science sociale [Sociology and Social Science],"in H. Bouasse (ed.), *De la méthode dans les sciences.* Paris: Alcan, 259–85. Repr. in 1970a, J.-C. Filloux (ed.), *La science sociale et l'action.* Paris, PUF, 137–58.

——— (1912a) *Les formes élémentaires de la vie religieuse* [*The Elementary Forms of Religious Life*]. Paris: Alcan. Fourth edn., Paris: PUF, 1960; repr. 1985.

——— (1955a) *Pragmatisme et sociologie* [*Pragmatism and Sociology*]. Paris: Vrin.

——— (1969c) *Journal Sociologique,* J. Duvignaud (ed.). Paris: PUF.

——— (1975a) *Textes,* V. Karady (ed.). Paris: Les Éditions de Minuit.

Lukes, S. (1973) *Emile Durkheim: His Life and Work.* New York: Penguin Books.

Parsons, T. (1937) *The Structure of Social Action.* New York: Free Press, 1968.

Pope, W. (1973) "Classic on Classic: Parsons' Interpretation of Durkheim," *American Sociological Review* 38: 399–415.

Turner, S. (1986) *The Search for a Methodology of Social Science: Durkheim, Weber, and the Nineteenth-Century Problem of Cause, Probability, and Action.* Dordrecht, the Netherlands: Reidel.

# Further Reading

Durkheim, E. *The Rules of Sociological Method and Selected Texts on Sociology and its Method,* S. Lukes (ed.), W. D. Halls (trans.) (New York: Free Press, 1982) is the better of two English translations of Durkheim (1895a) and contains useful translations of other of Durkheim's essays relevant to his methodology.

Jones, R. A. *The Development of Durkheim's Social Realism* (Cambridge: Cambridge University Press, 1999) also interprets Durkheim's work in historical context to provide a provocative alternative to standard sociological readings of Durkheim.

Lukes, S. *Emile Durkheim: His Life and Work* (New York: Penguin Books, 1973) is the most complete intellectual biography of Durkheim.

Schmaus, W. *Durkheim's Philosophy of Science and the Sociology of Knowledge: Creating an Intellectual Niche* (Chicago: University of Chicago Press, 1994) and *Rethinking Durkheim and His Tradition* (Cambridge: Cambridge University Press, 2004) interpret Durkheim's thought in the context of the philosophical and intellectual traditions of his time.

# 3

# VERSTEHEN AND THE REACTION AGAINST POSITIVISM

## Brian Fay

### I A Broad Account of *Verstehen*

"*Verstehen*" is German for "to understand." In the context of the philosophy of social science, the term has a more specific meaning, namely, to grasp the meaning of the behavior, relations, psychological processes, utterances, and cultural products such as rituals or artworks, for those who create and act in terms of them. The term was first used in this sense by the nineteenth-century German historian Johann Droysen to differentiate between natural and social science: the natural sciences *explain* ("*erklären*") natural phenomena, whereas the social sciences *understand* the meaning of ("*verstehen*") the phenomena they study.[1] But it was only in the late nineteenth-century German idealist thinking of Wilhelm Dilthey that *verstehen* became prominent in the philosophy of the social sciences and a fully worked out account of it appeared.[2] Later thinkers, such as Max Weber, Alfred Schutz, Martin Heidegger, Hans Gadamer, Peter Winch, Jürgen Habermas, and many others, have provided further accounts of *verstehen* and employed the concept, if not the term, in their philosophies of social science.[3] To this day the term "*verstehen*" is used even in English to refer to the task of uncovering the meaning of an action, practice, institution, social relation, cultural object, or psychological state.[4]

The emergence of *verstehen* bespoke a reaction against the positivism that dominated thinking among nineteenth-century philosophers and practitioners of the newly emerging social sciences. Positivists wanted to make the study of humans and their societies properly scientific, to sever its connection with literature and ethics by adopting the same attitudes and methodologies that led the study of natural phenomena out from under the thumb of theology and metaphysics. Thinkers such as Comte and Mill urged a "positive science of man," one that consisted in descriptions rooted in strict observations of publicly observable facts, and causal explanations that were verifiable on the basis of predictions assessable by means of shared evidence. But a problem for this program is that human behavior is characteristically meaningful: actions are undertaken for reasons; social practices follow rules;

utterances signify or express something other than themselves; as a result, the descriptions of this behavior typically comprise intentional terms that pick out an action, relation, or psychological state in terms of their meaningfulness. Thus, people are not just *moving* in some observable fashion; in so doing they are *voting* or *exchanging money* or *marrying* or *praying* (or they are *pretending* to do so, or *rehearsing* to do so, or *parodying* doing so, and so forth—the permutations are virtually endless). Deciding what they are doing and why they are doing it thus seems to require interpreting the *meaning* of their observable movements, and this necessitates that sociologists, economists, and anthropologists attempt to understand (*verstehen*) them. It would therefore seem that as long as humans are taken to be symbol-users whose behavior expresses their intentions and bespeaks the cultural context in which they live—which is to say, are subjects fit for study by the social sciences—the study of them must include a role for *verstehen*.

It is thus that those labeled "anti-positivists" or "humanists" (or, sometimes, "idealists") have united around the centrality of *verstehen* in the social sciences. Despite any differences they might have regarding the nature of *verstehen*, they all agree that it consists in ferreting out the meanings of social behavior and mental states, and of cultural objects and social practices, and that such ferreting is essential to the study of the doings, relatings, and experiencings of human beings. But beyond this simple basic claim and bare-bones account, exactly of what *verstehen* consists is a difficult question that has prompted a rich tradition of reflection and a contentious set of answers to it. These differences center around the questions of how meaning should be understood and how it is best ascertained—questions that have sparked quite different answers among those who insist on the importance of *verstehen* in the human sciences.

One way to usefully divide these various answers is to put them into two broad categories, the *intentionalist* and the *holist*. Intentionalists typically interpret meaning to be a function of the intentions of individual meaning-makers, whereas holists characteristically interpret meaning in terms of social rules and practices. According to intentionalists, *verstehen* involves discovering the psychological processes that undergird the actions and relations of intentional agents; in the words of H. P. Rickman, commenting on the philosophy of Dilthey, "*verstehen* is the comprehension of some mental content—an idea or intention or feeling—manifested in empirically given expressions such as words or gestures."[5] According to holists, *verstehen* consists of deciphering the sense of publicly available symbol systems; in the words of Clifford Geertz, the anthropologist most responsible for initiating the so-called "interpretive turn" in anthropology:

> To say that culture consists of socially established structures of meaning in terms of which people do such things as signal conspiracies and join them or perceive insults and answer them, is no more to say that it is a psychological phenomenon, a characteristic of someone's mind, personality, cognitive structure, or whatever, than to say that Tantrism, genetics, the progressive form of the verb, the classification of wines, the Common Law, or the notion of a "conditional curse" ... are.[6]

A question for *intentionalists* is how individuals can—and indeed must—understand the thoughts and feelings of one another in order to live in society and to live a recognizably human life. Intentionalists put this down to certain skills that render human beings agents and communicators in a highly distinctive way, such as the ability to classify, to form and follow rules, and to express their beliefs and desires so that others will know how they wish these others to act having acquired this knowledge. On this view, meaning derives from the ability of agents to form and act on intentions, and ascertaining the meaning of actions and relations, and the products of these, consists in discovering the intentions that are expressed in them.

Given this account of meaning, the goal of social analysis is, not surprisingly, to uncover the inner processes that are at work in various behaviors and relations and that are revealed in and through them. These processes consist of agents' motives, perceptions, beliefs, desires, and other mental phenomena that underwrite their behavior, as well as the products of this behavior such as social institutions and cultural expressions. Sometimes these processes are short-handedly summarized by the term "reason," as in the question, for what reason do the Melanesians engage in cargo cults? On this account, understanding the meaning (*verstehen*) of people's actions and relations and the cultural objects that they produce is thus grasping the reasons that are at work in them.

How are social analysts supposed to accomplish this task? Intentionalists have given a number of different answers to this question, but all of them place the subjective experience of particular agents at the center of things. People view the world differently from one another, and have different ways of being, acting, and relating as a result, such that to understand them requires that one appreciate how *they* perceive and relate to their world. What do *they* mean when they utter the sounds they do, or engage in the behaviors they perform, or produce the artifacts they do? However, how to determine the subjective experience of agents is a matter of debate. Some theorists have said that to discover the intentions of those being interpreted, interpreters must *relive* or *simulate* their experiences (relive or simulate in the sense that observers so empathetically identify with those being studied that what takes place in the observer's mind mirrors what takes place in the minds of those under study).[7] Other theorists have argued that in order to capture the experiences of others, it is not necessary to empathetically have them oneself but rather to *reconstruct* the lives of others in the sense of unearthing the content of the beliefs and desires that undergird their behavior.[8] Such a reconstruction involves determining what others think and feel, how they put their thoughts and feelings together, and how they express them in their actions and relations. On the reliving/simulation view of ascertaining meaning, *verstehen* consists of empathetic transposition in which analysts come to have exactly the same experiences as those under study, at least in their imaginations. On the reconstruction view, *verstehen* consists of a psychological interpretation in which agents' beliefs, desires, and actions are fit together in a way that makes sense of them.

No matter how the intentionalist construal of *verstehen* is parsed, if the goal is to ascertain the intentions that lie behind behavior and that are at work in various relations and cultural productions, the question arises whether ascertaining these intentions is a form of causal explanation or not. Put succinctly: are reasons causes of action? This question has generated an enormous literature, some claiming that reasons are not causes but account for actions in their own *sui generis* way;[9] others have asserted they are straightforwardly causal in kind;[10] still others have maintained that reasons, although not causes, can help in the discovery of causes; and still others have argued that reasons are a special type of cause that renders them unlikely subjects for a general science of human beings.[11] The first and fourth of these responses contribute to the idea that *verstehende* sciences are different in kind from sciences of the natural world and are irreducible to them, whereas the second and third responses attempt to show that despite the centrality of *verstehen*, the social sciences can be of a piece with the natural sciences.

In opposition to all this, *holists* reject the idea that *verstehen* is about uncovering the intentions of agents. As holists see it, the problem with any approach to meaning that sees it as resulting from individual consciousness is that it misinterprets something that is inherently social and public as something individual and private. Take, for example, an account of linguistic meaning that sees it as stemming from the intentions of individual speakers; the problem with this account of intentionality is that one can have intentions only because one is already situated within a web of meaning provided by one's language and the culture within which one resides, and the meanings of one's utterances are a function of their role within this cultural web. Far from linguistic meaning deriving from one's intentionality and subjectivity, the opposite is the case. Moreover, what applies to linguistic meaning applies equally to the meaning of behavior and even mental processes.

In the English-speaking world, the philosopher most responsible for arguing for the essentially social and public character of meaning is Wittgenstein of the *Philosophical Investigations*.[12] Thus, for example, in the so-called private-language argument, Wittgenstein argued that even with regard to one's own inner conscious states, an isolated subject could not construct a meaningful language to describe them. Language requires rules, and rules require others as checks to ensure they are being followed. Thus meanings do not exist within the minds of individual egos, but are located in the shared domains of activity on the basis of which human beings act and relate to one another (what Wittgenstein called "forms of life").

But this means that the focus of social investigation must move away from the consciousness of the individual (his or her intentions and reasons) to the broader social world and its history, on which the individual draws in order to be conscious and intentional in the first place (at least insofar as consciousness involves sense-making). This cultural world consists of language, social rules and institutions, cultural objects like houses and city streets and artworks, ideologies, and so forth, all of which are situated within ongoing historical traditions. On this view, meaning is a broadly historico-cultural phenomenon, not an individual psychological one, and the interpretation of meaning (and the search for its source of meaning) must turn from the minds of people to the historically situated public world of their shared practices.[13]

The relevance of all this for *verstehen* should be obvious: in a holist approach, understanding meaning is parsed not in terms of ferreting out the intentional psychological states of individual actors but rather in terms of placing their activities, relations, and products within their larger sociohistorical context, which is what gives them meaning. On this view, *verstehen* consists not in uncovering individual intentions but instead in interpreting the sense of actions, relations, and practices, in a way akin to interpreting the meaning of a poem or painting, or in translating utterances from one language to another.

## II Some Common But Mistaken Definitions of *Verstehen*

In light of the previous section, one should be able to see that each of the following five well-known definitions of *verstehen* is deeply problematic.

1. *Verstehen* is said to consist of "*understanding the meaning of action from the actor's point of view.*" But this can't be what *verstehen* consists of, for the simple reason that social scientists write for audiences that are typically different from their subjects, so that they are required to translate the actions and thoughts of the observed into the language of their audience, and thus to go beyond the actor's point of view. Moreover, and more important, social scientists often adopt a perspective that is different from that of their subjects, bringing to bear considerations that are intended to reveal what their subjects are doing more accurately and vividly than the subjects

can do themselves. This is especially evident in cases in which their subjects systematically misunderstand what they are doing, feeling, or how they are relating to one another. In these cases, to understand them from their point of view would in fact be to misunderstand them!

Of course, in trying to understand others, social scientists must learn what their subjects do by their own lights, and therefore must unearth the conceptual schemes that underlie their actions and relations. To fail to do this is a form of ethnocentrism. A great danger in trying to understand others is to assume that they are just like us, and so to inadvertently interpret them by means of concepts that fail to capture the distinctiveness of their lives. So interpreters can't ignore the point of view of others in trying to understand them. But this doesn't mean that interpreters are *limited* to this point of view. To think this is to be ethnocentric, but in reverse.

2. *Verstehen* is said to consist of *"entering into the shoes of the other."* In some ways this is a version of #1, but it brings out more sharply an important mistake often found in writings about *verstehen*, namely, the failure to distinguish between *being* an *x* and *understanding* an *x*. Just because I am a Catholic does not mean that I thereby understand what it means to be a Catholic, any more than having the feelings I do *ipso facto* entails that I understand the meaning of these feelings. I can be myself but not understand myself. Generalizing from this fact, even if a social scientist were to so fully enter the shoes of another that he or she became this other, this wouldn't thereby mean that he or she thereby knew the meaning of the other's acts or feelings. Indeed, it might well be the case that only by being different from the other is an interpreter able to understand what the other is up to, precisely because this difference allows the interpreter to see aspects of the other's life that the other cannot see for him- or herself.

3. *Verstehen* is said to be *"an intuitive doctrine or method of interpreting human culture especially in its subjective motivational and valuational aspects."* The problem with this is that *verstehen* isn't any more (or less!) "intuitive" than any other form of cognition. Interpreters might have a "feeling in their bones" as to the meaning of what others are doing, and might even have great confidence in this feeling, but to claim to understand others involves subjecting these intuitions to public tests to ascertain whether the proffered interpretation in fact actually reveals what an action or relation means. Does the interpretation jibe with the larger context within which the act or relation is situated? How, exactly? Does the interpretation reveal aspects of the act or relation that otherwise would remain opaque or mysterious? Does it do these things better than its competitors? In asking and answering these questions, interpreters are forced to go far beyond their initial intuitions.

Nor does *verstehen* necessarily focus on the "subjective motivational" aspects of the lives of those it studies. In the first place, *verstehen* often addresses public phenomena such as rites, rituals, laws, artworks, ceremonies, written documents, buildings, and the like, and these aren't "subjective" in any meaningful sense. Determining the meaning of a tribal dance involves determining the point of the dance by placing it into its broader cultural context, and doing this isn't about the subjective states of its performers but about the public meaning of what they do. In this case, meaning isn't private at all; in the striking catchphrase of Hilary Putnam, "meaning just ain't in the head."[14] In the second place, to label psychological states like motives, beliefs, and desires "subjective" is already to buy into a dualist understanding of what such states are, and there is no reason why *verstehen* should necessarily be aligned with, or saddled with, such dualism. Many philosophers, from Dewey to Wittgenstein to Quine, have argued against seeing mental states as "inner" or "subjective."

It is by rejecting the idea that meaning and/or psychological states are private that Geertz could argue that understanding isn't about entering into a realm that is subjective and inner, but is instead

> like trying to read (in the sense of 'construct a reading of') a manuscript—foreign, faded, full of ellipses, incoherencies, suspicious emendations, and tendentious commentaries, but written not in conventionalized graphs of sound but in transient examples of shaped behavior.[15]

The point here is *not* that Geertz or Putnam is correct, but rather that *verstehen* shouldn't be defined in a way that renders it incompatible with their accounts simply as a matter of definition.

4. *Verstehen* is said to consist of "*the empathetic understanding of human behavior.*" To understand the meaning of a ritual, say, do anthropologists need to empathize with its performers—need, that is, to at least imaginatively share the same feelings they have, or believe what they believe, or suffer along with them? Those who adopt a reliving or simulation approach to uncovering meaning evidently think the answer to this question is yes, but there are too many counterexamples to this idea for it to be persuasive. The private notebooks of the father of social anthropology, Bronislaw Malinowski, reveal that anthropologists may not only not share much with their subjects, they may actually find them off-putting or offensive, as Malinowski did the Trobriand Islanders even as he successfully understood (*verstehen*) the ceremonial exchange of shells throughout eastern New Guinea in his classic *Argonauts of the Western Pacific* (1922).[16] Another example is Alexis de Tocqueville, who arguably provided the most acute understanding of what democracy in America means even though he was a French aristocrat out of sympathy with the Americans he encountered. As he wrote in his masterwork, "The spectacle of this universal uniformity saddens me and chills me and I am tempted to regret a society that is no more."[17]

Malinowski's methodological slogan was "participant observation," and Tocqueville successfully interacted with Americans of all walks of life in his nine-month visit to the United States, so one might find their personal reactions to those they studied to be surprising; but, on second thought, it shouldn't be so: one can participate in the life of a group of people even if one despises them, and one can understand them even if one finds them odd or strange or even repulsive. To unearth the meaning of the Nazi swastika, an investigator needn't suffer with the Nazis, or sympathize with their goals, or share their ideology. In fact, it is probably the case that those who are unsympathetic to Nazism are best suited to understanding its meaning just because Nazism involved systematic self-delusion. Thus, *verstehen* simply is not, nor does it require having, an "empathetic feeling" for one's subjects.

5. It is said that with *verstehen* "*individuals are seen to create the world by organizing their own understanding of it and giving it meaning.*" Even though sociologists who tout the importance of *verstehen* in the social sciences often claim this about human culture, it is a mistake to identify *verstehen* with this claim. A simple argument shows the problems of doing so. If *verstehen* involves understanding what others think and feel, then it must include understanding what they think and feel about the source of meaning in their lives. But then consider the case in which a certain class of agents assumes that the meaning in their lives is *given* to them by something other than themselves (by God; Reality; the Holy Spirit; Nous; Tao; Reason), a meaning that they do not create but rather discover; in this case, to assume that understanding subjects entails viewing them as creators of the meanings by which they live their lives would ironically require interpreters to go well beyond understanding (*verstehen*) this class of people to critiquing their beliefs

about the nature of their beliefs. One thus needs to distinguish between *understanding the meaning of* what others do and *assessing the source of this meaning*. These are two different enterprises of which only the first is assignable to *verstehen*.

## III  The Positivist Reply to *Verstehen*

Committed to seeing the social sciences as of a piece with the natural sciences, positivists (or, more broadly, naturalists) have always been suspicious of *verstehen*. After all, there's nothing like it in the sciences that study natural phenomena—no appreciating how a plant views its world or how a planet feels about its orbit. Furthermore, the kinds of tests typical of the natural sciences and that positivists see as essential for ferreting out truth and eliminating error—principally predictions (or retrodictions) whose accuracy can be verified by observation—don't fit the case of *verstehen*, no matter how it is construed. Anthropologists don't assess accounts of the meaning of the cockfight in Balinese society on the basis of whether these accounts predict publicly observable events.

A standard positivist response to *verstehen* is that though it may be a way to *discover* a hypothesis about some social phenomenon or other, it is not a way to *validate* it. In short, it might be a tool in the context of discovery, but it is inappropriate in the context of justification. Thus, though *verstehen* might well have a role in the generation of a social-scientific theory, it must be abandoned when science gets down to the brass tacks of assessing whether a theory is worthwhile or not.[18]

If *verstehen* is interpreted as empathetic intuition, it's not hard to see why positivists would think this. For how would investigators know whether their intuitions about others were veridical or not? Presumably whether they were sufficiently like the state of those being studied. But to determine whether this obtains, scientists would already have to know the nature of this state, and this they could not do on the basis of other intuitions, because then the same question about sufficient similarity would just arise again in this context. This means that there must be some means other than empathy to determine subjects' inner states, thereby rendering empathy redundant. Moreover, it doesn't appear that there is any reliable way to assess whether empathetic identifications are accurate or not. Because they are strongly held, or vivid, or of long standing, bears no weight in determining whether they are true; and being essentially private, it's hard to see how they can be subjected to public testing. In short, *verstehen* understood as empathetic intuition appears to be both otiose and unreliable.

But there is a problem with this argument against *verstehen*, namely, that it rests on conceiving *verstehen* as empathetic intuition, and we've already seen that *verstehen*, understood as uncovering the meaning of actions, relations, and cultural products, need not be cashed out in terms of intuition or empathy. *Verstehen* is more like deciphering the sense of the Rosetta Stone than it is like transporting oneself into the mind of another. Of course, assessing whether a particular interpretation is accurate involves tests different from those typically at play in the natural sciences, but these tests can be as rigorous, public, and dispositive as the latter.

The fundamental problem with the positivist idea that *verstehen* is only a heuristic device is that it misses the central point that the identification of social events necessarily depends on understanding the meanings they have for those engaged in them and that make them count as the events they are. If putting a marked ballot in a box is to count as a political act, the agent has to have known what voting is and how to participate in it, and the act has to be part of a larger system of rules that give it its meaning. Simply marking a piece of paper without any understanding of how this is connected to choosing a leader, or doing so in an inappropriate context, is not voting, and it would be a mischaracterization of the act if a political scientist were to count it as such, and to include it in a study of political behavior. What is true of voting is true of the full range of intentional actions, relations, and cultural products that are the objects of study in the human sciences.

Some naturalists have recognized the force of this point and so have adopted another tack to avoid *verstehen*: to radically reconceive the social sciences in a way that eliminates from them any and all descriptions and explanations that require *verstehen*. One variant of this approach is behaviorism, which seeks to redefine intentional terms in purely behavioral terms. Another, more promising, variant is well captured in the title of the classic book by Alexander Rosenberg, *Sociobiology and the Preemption of the Social Sciences*.[19] This book argues that if the social sciences are to become properly scientific (which includes being able to generate laws that underwrite causal explanations of a general sort), they will have to replace the vocabulary of current social science—that is, its intentional idiom that speaks of beliefs, desires, motives, reasons, and the like: the idiom that requires *verstehen* to function—with that derived from population and evolutionary biology in which *verstehen* plays no role.

Whether the sociobiological or behaviorist project is viable is beyond the scope of this essay,[20] but it is worth noting that both pay a backhand compliment to *verstehen* by tacitly acknowledging that it plays an essential role in the social sciences as they are currently practiced, that is, employing an intentional idiom. Thus, talk of winnowing *verstehen* out of these sciences is wishful thinking unless one is willing to substantially change their nature.

## IV Beyond *Verstehen*

But just as positivists have undersold *verstehen*, some of its proponents have oversold it. That is, so impressed by its ubiquity and power, they have defined social science entirely in terms of understanding (*verstehen*). This is so-called *verstehende* or interpretive social science. According to this view, social science is exclusively concerned with the meaning of social actions, relations, and cultural products, and thus with discovering how those who perform these actions, engage in these relations, or create these products understand them. On this view, a sharp divide exists between the natural sciences (devoted as they are to casual *explanations* and the discovery of general laws) and the social sciences (devoted to interpretive *understandings* of the meaning of social phenomena for those engaged in them).

But the analogy "natural science is to social science as explanation is to understanding" breaks down once one thinks further about the questions social science is apt to ask, even assuming that unearthing the meaning of social phenomena by means of *verstehen* must play a fundamental role in it. Thus, even if social scientists can't approach the subjects they study without understanding what these subjects mean when they act, relate to one another, speak, produce artworks, engage in social practices, and so on, such understanding does not, by itself, constitute a full explanation for why they occur. To know that a particular event is a rain dance, one needs to know the meaning of the movements involved; but knowing this meaning isn't sufficient to know why the dance is performed in its present social setting, or the conditions that gave rise to it, or that keep the practice alive, or that potentially undermine it. In general, when social scientists investigate why structures of rules, values, beliefs, and the like emerged in one sort of social setting but not another, or why certain conditions produce or foster various institutions or ways of interacting, they are asking causal questions whose answers require going beyond the self-understandings required of those engaged in them. For example, why did capitalism emerge when it did, and what conditions must obtain for it to remain successful? People living in capitalist systems, even successful ones, need not be able to answer these questions—indeed, they may be peculiarly misplaced to do so in just the way that a fish is peculiarly misplaced to realize that he lives in water.

Moreover, in addition to the causes of intentional actions and practices, social sciences are also interested in patterns of the *unanticipated* consequences of actions and relations. A graphic example of this is the so-called paradox of savings: in a capitalist system, increased savings can lead to a weakening of aggregate demand and, through this, to a decline in the national product and a subsequent reduction of personal income, and thus to a drop in savings. Here, saving more leads to saving less. This paradox occurs despite the fact that no one in the system need intend it or even be aware of it. It is for the social scientist to look beyond the intentions of those being studied to ascertain the unforeseen consequences of this behavior (which, in this case, is a type of self-undermining behavior). There are countless examples of social analysis in which social scientists have discovered unintended consequences of actions that have a significant role to play within particular social settings—discoveries of which require that the social scientist go beyond *verstehen* in order to detect them.

In short, social science is an explanatory enterprise as well as an interpretive one, and because it is, its theories typically go beyond the intentions of those being studied—and therefore what is discoverable by means of *verstehen*—to include wide-ranging causal theories that seek to comprehend the conditions that give rise to, and result from, these intentions. Kinship theory in anthropology, exchange theory in sociology, the theory of transformational grammar in linguistics, modernization theory in political science, and cognitive dissonance theory in psychology are a few examples of the theoretical dimension in modern social science that transcends *verstehen* even as each of them envisions a role for *verstehen* within them.

Indeed, even within the confines of *verstehen* itself, social-scientific theorizing that goes beyond the conceptual horizon of those being studied is often called for. For intentional actions, a distinction can be drawn between the *competence* of agents and their actual *performances*; the former concerns the capacities agents must have in order to engage in a certain sort of behavior, whereas the latter refers to the actual execution of this behavior. Agents' competence might consist in their mastery of certain grammatical rules or certain norms of rationality, for instance, where their performance of actions in accord with these rules might or might not conform to these norms. For example, Chomskian linguists have tried to model the set of skills that enable a speaker to create and understand well-formed sentences in a language (indeed, in any language that is recognizable as such), a type of theorizing that, while it clearly involves *verstehen* (how else to tell whether a sentence is well formed or not?), goes well beyond anything that *verstehen* can itself yield. Rational choice theory and game theory are additional *competence theories* that have an important place in modern social-scientific analysis that, while dependent on unearthing the meanings of actions through *verstehen*, goes beyond such unearthing.[21]

In yet another way social science often is called on to transcend *verstehen* even as it employs it, namely, when people's motives, wants, values, beliefs, and ideology—indeed, their entire way of looking at the world—mask social reality as much as reveal it. This can occur when people's self-understandings are at variance with their actual social behavior; or when actors' ideas and feelings are joined in ways that they are not aware of, and that lead them to act in patterns that they don't recognize and would resent if they did; or where a specific belief and action system is incompatible with other norms of a culture; or where there are deep incoherencies within the conceptual scheme that underlies a particular social formation; or where people maintain beliefs that are at variance with evidence that they themselves accept as determinative; and so on. In these cases social scientists must confront the fact that meanings in a society can be *illusions* that can underwrite forms of behavior that would be adjudged irrational and/or self-defeating and/or objectionable by the agents themselves if they knew about them. In these circumstances, social scientists are called on to view structures of meaning as deceptive as well as revelatory, and to discover the causes of such a system of illusory meanings, the conditions in which such meanings become illusions, and the conditions that must be changed to enlighten those in the grip of such illusions. In short, this sort of analysis calls for a *critical theory* that seeks to provide an account of a form of living that goes beyond the self-understandings of those engaged in this form—indeed, that often goes beyond that which is envisioned by the worldview they share. Marxism and Freudian theory are vivid examples of such a theory, as are some feminist theories. Here again *verstehen* plays a role in such analyses, which must in the first instance be grounded on how those being studied understand what they are doing, but they must proceed far beyond this understanding to reveal the ways this understanding hides what is actually occurring even as it underwrites it.

To sum up, then: while *verstehen* may be a necessary component of any social science that takes those it studies to be intentional beings whose behaviors, relations, and cultural products are meaningful, it isn't sufficient in itself to answer certain questions that social scientists will want to ask about them: what are their causes? What are their effects? What are the competences that underwrite them? In what ways do they mask social reality as well as reveal it (if they indeed do)? Besides *verstehen*, then, social science must also include causal theories, competence theories, and critical theories in its toolbox. *Verstehen* may be a necessary element in the social sciences, but it is not sufficient in itself.

## Notes

1 J. G. Droysen, *Grundriss der Historik* [1858]. There is no good English translation of this work. Available online is an 1882 edition published by Verlag Von Veit in Leipzig: https://archive.org/stream/grundriss derhist00droyuoft#page/n3/mode/2up (accessed January 24, 2015).

2 See Wilhelm Dilthey, *Introduction to the Human Sciences*, trans. Raymond J. Betanzos (Detroit: Wayne State University Press, 1988); H. A. Hodges, *Wilhelm Dilthey. An Introduction* (London: Routledge, 1944); and the English translation in H. P. Rickman, *Pattern and Meaning in History. Wilhelm Dilthey's Thoughts on History and Society* (London: George Allen and Unwin, 1961). A projected six-volume edition of *Wilhelm Dilthey: Selected Works*, ed. Rudolf Makkreel and Frithjof Rodi, by Princeton University Press is in the making. The first four volumes are available; these are those of most relevance to the topic of *verstehen*: I: *Introduction to the Human Sciences* (1991); II: *Understanding the Human World* (2010); III: *The Formation of the Historical World in the Human Sciences* (2010); and IV: *Hermeneutics and the Study of History* (2010). For a full-scale, authoritative, account of Dilthey's philosophy, see Rudolf Makkreel, *Dilthey: Philosopher of the Human Studies* (Princeton, NJ: Princeton University Press, 1993); H. P. Rickman, *Wilhelm Dilthey. Pioneer of the Human Studies* (Berkeley: University of California Press, 1979); and Theodore Plantinga, *Historical Understanding in the Thought of Wilhelm Dilthey* (Toronto: University of Toronto Press, 1980).

3 See Alfred Schutz, *The Phenomenology and the Social World*, trans. George Walsh and Frederick Lehnert (Evanston, IL: Northwestern University Press, 1967); Martin Heidegger, *Being and Time* (especially

sections 31 and 32), trans. John Macquarrie and Edward Robinson (New York: Harper and Row, 1962); Hans Gadamer, *Truth and Method*, trans. Joel Weinsheimer and Donald G. Marshall, 2nd edn. (New York: Crossroads, 1992); Peter Winch, *The Idea of a Social Science and its Relation to Philosophy* (London: Routledge and Kegan Paul, 1958); Jürgen Habermas, *Knowledge and Human Interests*, trans. Jeremy J. Shapiro (Boston: Beacon Press, 1971), and *On the Logic of the Social Sciences*, trans. Shierry Weber Nicholson and Jerry A. Stark (Cambridge, MA: MIT Press, 1988).

Of particular note in the development of the idea of *verstehen* are the methodological writings of Max Weber. (See Max Weber, *The Methodology of the Social Sciences*, ed. and trans. Edward Shils and Henry A. Finch [Glencoe, IL: Free Press, 1948], and *Economy and Society. An Outline of Interpretive Sociology*, ed. and trans. Guenther Roth and Claus Wittich [Berkeley: University of California Press, 1978].) Weber offered a sophisticated analysis purporting to show how understanding the meaning of human behavior and psychology should be factored into the study of human life—sophisticated because Weber sought to show that understanding meaning, and explanation by means of causes, were compatible with one another and required one another. Weber's account became quite important, even though his thinking about *verstehen* and causality is notoriously complex—not to say confused—partly because of his prominence as a historical sociologist. For a brilliant discussion of Weber's views, see W. G. Runciman, *A Critique of Max Weber's Philosophy of Social Science* (Cambridge: Cambridge University Press, 1972).

4 William Outhwaite, in his book about *verstehen* in the social sciences (*Understanding Social Life. The Method Called Verstehen* [London: George Allen and Unwin, 1975]), translates the term to mean "interpretive understanding." Other, particularly excellent accounts of *verstehen* are: G. H. von Wright, *Explanation and Understanding* (Ithaca, NY: Cornell University Press, 1971); Dan Little, *Varieties of Social Explanation* (Boulder, CO: Westview Press, 1990); and Michael Martin, *Verstehen. The Uses of Understanding in Social Science* (New Brunswick, NJ and London: Transaction Publishers, 2000). Exceptional collections of essays about the topic are Paul Rabinow and William Sullivan, *Interpretive Social Science. A Second Look* (Berkeley: University of California Press, 1988), and Fred Dallmayr and Thomas McCarthy, *Understanding and Social Inquiry* (South Bend, IN: University of Notre Dame Press, 1978).

5 H. P. Rickman, "Wilhelm Dilthey," *Encyclopedia of Philosophy*, ed. Paul Edwards (New York: Macmillan and The Free Press, 1967), 405.

6 Clifford Geertz, "Thick Description" in *The Interpretation of Culture* (New York: Basic Books, 1973), 12–13.

7 In Dilthey's pithy phrase, "Understanding is the rediscovery of the I in the Thou" (quoted in Hodges, *Wilhelm Dilthey. An Introduction*, 114). Collingwood famously claimed that historical events must be understood from the inside and that this entailed that historians *rethink* the thoughts of historical actors; see *The Idea of History* (Oxford: Oxford University Press, 1956), 213. This approach has been updated in Simulation Theory that roots the similarity between interpreter and interpreted in a shared biology and evolutionary history or in historical continuity. See the collection *Folk Psychology*, ed. Martin Davies and Tony Stone (Oxford: Blackwell, 1995), which contains a number of important essays exploring Simulation Theory, and also the excellent collection of more recent essays examining simulation as a method in the social sciences edited by Hans Herbert Kögler and Karsten R. Steuber, *Empathy and Agency. The Problem of Understanding in the Human Sciences* (Boulder, CO: Westview, 2000).

8 As William Dray put it in *Laws and Explanation in History* (Oxford: Clarendon Press, 1957), 122: "What we very often want is a reconstruction of the agent's calculation of means to be adopted toward his chosen end in the light of the circumstances in which he found himself."

9 See Winch, *The Idea of a Social Science*.

10 Carl G. Hempel, *Aspects of Scientific Explanation, and Other Essays in the Philosophy of Science* (New York: Free Press, 1965).

11 Donald Davidson, "Actions, Reasons, and Causes" and "Mental Events," both republished in Donald Davidson, *Actions and Events* (Oxford: Clarendon Press, 1980); and "Thinking Causes," in J. Heil and A. Mele (eds.), *Mental Causation* (Oxford: Clarendon Press, 1993), 3–17.

12 Ludwig Wittgenstein, *Philosophical Investigations*, trans. G. E. M. Anscombe (Oxford: Blackwell, 1953), especially the opening sections (1–88), those devoted to analyzing what following a rule consists of, and to the famous private language argument (sections 172–280). For a powerful exegesis

of these sections, see Saul Kripke, *Wittgenstein on Rules and Private Language* (Cambridge, MA: Harvard University Press, 1982). For a profound account of linguistic meaning in particular, and normativity in general, along broadly—though substantially enriched—Wittgensteinian lines, see Robert Brandom, *Making It Explicit* (Cambridge, MA: Harvard University Press, 1994). According to Brandom's *inferential semantics*, conceptual contents are to be understood in terms of the formally and materially valid inferences they underwrite, not the intentions of utterers. To understand, according to this view, means to be able to aptly use a concept as both a conclusion and a premise in ongoing reasoning processes. A concept should not therefore be understood as a representation of its object but as set of possible legitimate moves in an ongoing conversational exchange. The meaning of a predicate assigned to an object is thus not like a word picture of it, but instead results from the inferences that this concept licenses. The concept, so to speak, *channels* those legitimate inferences that comprise a part of the entire system of inferential relationships into a particular situation of its applicability. Needless to say, this is a holist view in that meaning derives from a concept's role in a system of possible inferences.

Two of the most insightful presentations of the holist approach to *verstehen* are those of Winch, *The Idea of a Social Science*, and Charles Taylor, "Interpretation and the Sciences of Man," originally published in the *Review of Metaphysics*, 25, 1 (September, 1971): 3–51, and reprinted in Charles Taylor, *Philosophical Papers 2: Philosophy and the Human Sciences* (Cambridge: Cambridge University Press, 1985), 15–58.

13 The philosopher in the so-called Continental Tradition who first developed these ideas was Martin Heidegger in *Being and Time*, especially sections 31 and 32, 182–95. The philosopher who developed these ideas into a full-fledged philosophy of understanding, and indeed a philosophy of human being, is Hans Gadamer; see especially his masterwork, *Truth and Method*, which offers the deepest and most complete statement of a holist construal of *verstehen* in our time.

14 Hilary Putnam, "The Meaning of 'Meaning'," *Philosophical Papers*, vol. 2: *Mind, Language, and Reality* (Cambridge: Cambridge University Press, 1975).

15 Geertz, "Thick Description," 10.

16 Bronislaw Malinowski, *A Diary in the Strict Sense of the Term* (London: Routledge, 1967).

17 Alexis de Tocqueville, *Democracy in America*, ed. Eduardo Nolla, trans. James T. Schleifer (Indianapolis: Liberty Fund, 2012), 1281.

18 The *locus classicus* of the positivist response is Theodore Abel, "The Operation Called *Verstehen*," *American Journal of Sociology*, 54 (1948): 211–18. This essay is reprinted in Dallmayr and McCarthy, *Understanding and Social Inquiry*, 81–92. See also Richard Rudner, *Philosophy of Social Science* (Englewood Cliffs, NJ: Prentice Hall, 1966), especially 71–73.

19 Alexander Rosenberg, *Sociobiology and the Preemption of the Social Sciences* (Baltimore and London: Johns Hopkins University Press, 1980).

20 See Thomas Nagel, *Mind and Cosmos: Why the Materialist Neo-Darwinian Conception of Nature Is Almost Certainly False* (Oxford and New York: Oxford University Press, 2012).

21 See Noam Chomsky, *Aspects of a Theory of Syntax* (Cambridge, MA: MIT Press, 1969), especially ch. 1.

# 4

# THE DEVELOPMENT OF LOGICAL EMPIRICISM

## Thomas Uebel

Logical empiricism—also known as logical positivism or neopositivism (there is no princi-pled distinction to be drawn here, see below, section 3)—was a philosophical movement that spanned less than half of the 20th century but left a lasting if controversial legacy. Originating in the 1920s in the Vienna Circle around Moritz Schlick and in the Berlin group around Hans Reichenbach, logical empiricism sought an understanding of the nature of modern science after the revolutionary developments in mathematics and physics that culminated in Einstein's theo-ries of relativity, an understanding that neither traditional empiricism nor transcendental ideal-ism was held to be able to supply. In doing so, logical empiricists built to varying degrees on the pioneering works of Gottlob Frege, Bertrand Russell, and Ludwig Wittgenstein in logic and of Ernst Mach, Henri Poincaré, and Pierre Duhem in philosophy of science. Exiled from Central Europe by National Socialism, by the 1940s prominent logical empiricists like Rudolf Carnap, Herbert Feigl, C. G. Hempel, and Reichenbach himself were able to establish themselves at North American universities and, along with like-minded native and former visitors like Ernest Nagel and W. V. O. Quine, started to influence a new generation of philosophers. (Schlick was murdered in 1936 in Vienna.) While most of the solutions proposed by logical empiricists no longer command acceptance, many of the problems they identified continue to define the field of philosophy of science.

Logical empiricism is best known for the claim that much of what passed for knowledge in ordinary life, science, and philosophy was in fact meaningless because it had no tangible con-sequences by which to assess whether it was true. For the social sciences this meant the denial of their principled separation from the natural sciences as demanded by idealist social thinking long dominant in Germany, but not the denial of any methodological differences. Since formu-lating the decisive meaning criterion by which all discourse was to be regimented proved dif-ficult (see below, section 1), it is often asserted that logical empiricism failed, full stop. However, what has been shown to have failed was mainly its British empiricist (phenomenalist) redux in A. J. Ayer's *Logic, Truth and Language* (1936) and the Cold War North American variant which, stripped of the socio-political context of the original, had descended into an arid for-malism whose relevance for understanding science as practiced was highly questionable (see below, section 6). Whatever the original intentions of logical empiricism may have been, its fall from favor in the 1960s was widely received as a liberation for the social sciences. Reporting on the historical record of logical empiricism therefore demands not only a list of already well-chronicled failings but also the peeling back of layers of misapprehension that prevent recognition of its unfulfilled potential—or better: of the potential that it once possessed but that nowadays is realized independently in different quarters. To this end this chapter discusses the doctrines and development of logical empiricism by building on recent scholarship that corrected long-standing misconceptions.

# 1

Logical empiricism's core conception consisted of the fundamental assumption that the only propositions that are cognitively significant are those whose truth or falsity makes a difference that is discernible, at least in principle and however fallibly, and the sharp and exclusive distinction between propositions that are synthetic in nature and justifiable only *a posteriori* and propositions that are analytic and justifiable only *a priori*, with the former assigned to the empirical sciences and the latter to logic and mathematics. Logical empiricists therefore rejected the idea that there could be *a priori* knowledge of synthetic truths like those of physics or that empiricism could account for knowledge of necessary truths like those of arithmetic. Instead they embraced versions of logicism and held, with Hume, that all necessity was verbal necessity. Most spectacularly they denied that philosophy possessed the means to achieve any metaphysical knowledge over and above scientific knowledge: any such claims were not false but cognitively meaningless.

The qualifier is important here. Other forms of meaning ("emotive") were recognized but held to be irrelevant for the purpose at hand. As philosophers of science, logical empiricists were not concerned to develop a theory of linguistic meaning in full generality but to circumscribe the boundaries of scientific discourse. They agreed with Mach that "where neither confirmation nor refutation is possible, science is not concerned" (1883/1960, 587). This readily translates into a criterion of testability by evidence which can find expression in subtly distinct conceptions such as verifiability, falsifiability, confirmability, disconfirmability, or outright probabilism. Once it is allowed that different types of sciences have different ways of establishing the probity of their findings it is difficult to consider such verificationism to be other than common sense. Yet trouble arose with attempts to formulate the criterion in exact logical terms so as to adduce necessary and sufficient conditions for cognitive significance. Once a criterion was put through the logical paces of permutation and inference, it turned out to be either too narrow (it excluded high-level scientific theories) or too broad (it allowed in statements like "The absolute is all-present"). Despite repeated attempts that varied both in strength and modality (whether it applied to terms or statements, needed to be conclusive or not, and appealed to physical or logical possibilities of testing) it has not been possible to formulate such a criterion for natural language discourse (see Hempel 1965). (What is often overlooked, however, is that the development of such a criterion for constructed languages remains under discussion (see Justus 2014).)

Since verificationism was the fulcrum for the logical empiricists' novel attack on metaphysics, this negative result caused considerable embarrassment. But it is worthwhile to consider the motivation behind it. In their time and day, the demand that factual discourse be perspicuous and its claims testable had clear socio-political implications. As regards social thought, it meant opposition to the supra-individual holism that was peddled by the ideologues of fascism and Nazism. Even today a criterion of cognitive significance can be argued to be of vital importance. So it is only fair to note that the result that (formal languages aside) such a criterion can only be understood in contextual pragmatic terms, not in abstract logical-semantic ones, is due largely to the efforts of logical empiricists to prove otherwise—and that on their pragmatist wing (see below, section 3) this result came to be recognized.

## 2

That the glass is only half-empty encourages a closer look at the movement. As indicated, significant differences obtained with regard to how the principle of empirical significance was to be understood. These differences spilt over into the question of what remained of philosophy. For some, post-metaphysical philosophy simply reduced to epistemology while allowing for scientific realism, for others it became an investigation into the constitutive powers of language, for yet others it offered comprehensive if deflationary reflection on science by scientific means, yet others followed wherever Wittgenstein led. Logical empiricism was far from monolithic.

A common view of the development of logical empiricism recognizes three successive phases: an initial one marked by naïve enthusiasm, a middle one of successive disillusionments, and a final one of its remaining potential being exhausted by sober professionalism. Like all received views, this one is not wholly mistaken, but hopelessly oversimplified. It is not just that what is naïve for some may appear bold to others, nor that it tells a tale, all too familiar in the profession, of thwarted ambition. It is rather that, as received views do, it plots the development in a far too streamlined fashion and overlooks the variation that the core conception of logical empiricism allowed. It would not be much of an exaggeration to add that what had exhausted itself in the final period had little to do, beyond the core conception, with what started so brightly.

What exhausted itself were indeed "ideas which restated the foundationalist epistemology of British empiricism in linguistic, as opposed to psychological terms"—a characterization by Richard Rorty of "the ideas which make up what we now call 'logical positivism' or 'logical empiricism'" (1999, 1). That Rorty, in the same breath, endorses Ayer's shilling shocker *Language, Truth and Logic* as the authentic expression of logical empiricism both explains and invalidates his description. It is not that no form of logical empiricism is foundationalist, but that only some are (though by far not as many as may be thought). What is still more important is the nature of the anti-foundationalist variant of logical empiricism thereby overlooked. In its best moments it offers a philosophically deflationary metatheory of science that complements second-order inquiries of a formal-logical nature with second-order inquiries of an empirical kind and so avoids much of the criticism that was leveled at the logical empiricism that had exhausted itself by the late 1960s.

That the kind of logical empiricism that was overlooked turns out to be not only very different but also very much more interesting than its Ayerian variant is surely one of the more notable discoveries of the history of philosophy of science. In early logical empiricism we find *inter alia* a variant of modernist thought that was indeed as science-centered as any positivism can be, but also more anti-foundationalist than previous philosophies had been. Influenced by French conventionalism, it resolved to be thoroughly constructivist in its approach to the philosophical concepts and categories with which it sought to resolve the Kantian problematic of objectivity that earlier empiricisms did not recognize. This variant of logical empiricism was not yet exhausted of its potential when the so-called "received view" of scientific theories began to fall into disrepute, but had only been lost from view (for a variety of reasons too complex to go into here). That it got lost while Carnap was still practicing may seem puzzling at first but stops being so once it is noted that the turbulence of the Kuhnian revolution (amidst which it seemed to disappear) precluded paying any attention to the question of what someone perceived as "old guard" might really have had in mind, especially when that veteran showed no inclination to campaign on his own and his movement's behalf.

## 3

To see the alternative emerging, it must be noted that logical empiricism did not start from a fixed program but rather from the recognition of a pressing intellectual need (to understand modern science) and the conviction that traditional means (existing philosophies) were incapable of meeting it. What are known as programs of the movement typically were occasional pieces and featured early and still speculative interim results that were not shared across the movement. (Already *The Scientific Conception of the World: The Vienna Circle* [Carnap, Hahn, and Neurath 1929] contained modifications and revisions of views previously published by members of the Circle: it was not a founding document but a post-hoc declaration seeking to forestall the defection of its nominal leader.) It is more instructive to judge logical empiricism in terms of its more sophisticated expressions than to regard its development as the progressive weakening of unrealistic goals, for despite appearances some of the later versions were also philosophically more radical in having shed residual traditionalisms. (Carnap is a case in point: see below.) And as has often been noted, the repeated admissions that earlier formulations of their doctrines were inadequate and demanded further development were prompted by discoveries made mostly by members of the movement itself. The process of clarification was self-propelled and fueled by internal criticism. (Consider Hempel's critiques of the meaning criterion [1950, 1951].)

Another point to bear in mind is that logical empiricism comes in two varieties. The best known one may be called "formalist" and presents the approach to the problems of philosophy of science associated with the work of Carnap in devising logico-linguistic frameworks for scientific theories and Hempel in confirmation theory. It proceeded by providing logically perspicuous delineations of necessary and sufficient conditions of contested concepts and (ideally) axiomatized recastings of the empirical theories at issue. The lesser known one may be called "pragmatist" and sought understanding by considering the sciences as practiced from a historical and social perspective. It was, of course, the former variant of logical empiricism that achieved dominance in philosophy of science after World War II and it is only in retrospect that the pragmatist variant, represented previously by Otto Neurath and after his death by Philipp Frank, has come to be recognized again.

Then there are the different dynamics of the two centers of early logical empiricism, the Vienna Circle and the Berlin group, that must be recognized. Relations between them were not always easy and this left marks on the historiography of the movement itself. The persistent myth about the Vienna Circle's supposedly phenomenalist "logical positivism" having been overcome only by Reichenbach's realist "logical empiricism" is owed to this rivalry (see Uebel 2013). To be sure, Reichenbach pioneered scientific realism, but it wasn't he who rescued the Circlists nor is it clear that they needed rescuing. To begin with, apart from Feigl and Blumberg who coined "logical positivism" for the purpose of marketing the ideas of their *Doktorvater* and his associates in North America in (1931), no one back in Vienna liked the term very much (not even Schlick himself) and already in the same year

Neurath argued against the epistemology there outlined (1931a) and instead proposed the name "logical empiricism" (1931b). Moreover, by the time Reichenbach introduced his own term "logistic empiricism" (1936) no one in Vienna still adhered to the type of reductionism he castigated—nor indeed did Carnap, even in his *The Logical Construction of the World* (1928a, hereafter *Aufbau*), pursue the foundationalist ambitions that Reichenbach attributed to him (much like Quine later on) in his begrudgingly late review of that book. It need not be denied that around 1930 Carnap was temporarily seduced by the foundationalist vision of a psychologized *Tractatus* (supplemented by the constitutional theory of the *Aufbau*), but this reading of his methodological solipsism was soon given up again under the influence of Neurath. And when Carnap finally banned all traditional epistemology as psychologistic from his own preferred form of the successor discipline to traditional philosophy, namely "logic of science" (1934, §72), his ban included the concern with skepticism that Reichenbach's conception of philosophy as "analysis of science" still countenanced (1938).

Finally, there are the internal dynamics within each of the two groups. In the Vienna Circle the tensions between different wings pulling their developing philosophies of science (as we would say nowadays) into different directions were most pronounced. There they found expression, for instance, in the so-called protocol-sentence debate about the form, content, and status of observation statements which saw its participants Neurath, Carnap, and Schlick articulate contrasting epistemologies (see Uebel 2007). Along with different reactions to Wittgenstein and his perceived strictures against metalinguistic discourse, this debate helped to consolidate a "left" as distinct from a "more conservative right" wing of the Circle (Carnap 1963, 57), with Neurath, Carnap, Frank, and Hahn defining the former and Schlick and Waismann the latter. (It may be noted that the left wing split equally between practitioners of the formalist and the pragmatist variety.)

So logical empiricism was a highly varied movement. Occasionally, some variants ran into conflict with each other (like Reichenbach's and Carnap's conceptions of philosophy or Neurath's and Schlick's analyses of evidence), while on yet other occasions different variants suggested compatibility (like some representatives of the formalist and pragmatist variants). At all times, however, logical empiricist formulations, even of the core conception (though not the core conception itself), were meant to reflect the latest advance—meaning that they were provisional.

It is sometimes held to be supremely ironic that Kuhn's *The Structure of Scientific Revolutions* (1962) was first published as no. 2 of vol. 2 of the series *International Encyclopedia of Unified Science* founded by Neurath and edited with Carnap and Charles Morris, since *Structure* more than any other work is generally credited as instrumental for the decline of logical empiricism. As a matter of fact, however, Carnap welcomed Kuhn's contribution (see Reisch 1991) some aspects of which can, after all, be aligned with the pragmatist variant of logical empiricism promoted in North America by the somewhat marginalized Frank (who once told of what we now know of as "Kuhn loss" in a lecture attended by young Tom). There's undeniably irony to be discerned in the relation with Kuhn, but the joke is not on logical empiricism. Nor is this the only instance where logical empiricism still pointed forward while falling out of favor in the profession. Whether they are always recognized as such by contemporary practitioners, there are at least three live legacies that logical empiricism left for posterity. Carnap and Hempel inaugurated formal epistemology and philosophy of science, Neurath and Frank pioneered naturalistic philosophy of science, and Reichenbach and Feigl promoted scientific realism—all three of these research programs continue to hold considerable interest nowadays.

# 4

So then, how is the development of logical empiricism better characterized? The following periods can be distinguished, as it were, "extensionally."

(i) The pre-formation period: this includes the pre-World War I discussion group with Frank, Hahn, and Neurath; Schlick's *General Theory of Knowledge* (1918) and his analysis of the epistemological basis of general relativity (1917–22); Schlick's debate in correspondence with Reichenbach in 1920; the Erlangen conference of 1922 convened by Carnap and Reichenbach.

(ii) The pre-public period: this includes the formation of the discussion group around Schlick in Vienna, its early readings of Wittgenstein's *Tractatus* (1922), and the entry of Reichenbach into the Berlin Society of Empirical Philosophy and his assumption of its leadership in 1927–28.

(iii) The public Central European period: this includes the inauguration of the Verein Ernst Mach in 1928; the Conferences for the Epistemology of the Exact Sciences in 1929 in Prague (at which *The Scientific World Conception* was unveiled) and in 1930 in Königsberg (where Gödel's incompleteness result was first reported); the name-change to "Society of Scientific Philosophy" initiated by the Berlin group; the beginning of the publication of the journal *Erkenntnis* edited by Reichenbach and Carnap, of the book series "Writings on the Scientific World Conception" edited by Schlick and Frank, and of the series of shorter writings "Unified Science" edited by Neurath.

(iv) The period of (increasing) internationalization: this includes the Congresses for the Unity of Science, starting with a preparatory meeting in Prague in 1934 and continuing through 1939 with yearly meetings in Paris (twice), Copenhagen, Cambridge in England and Cambridge, Massachusetts (and a small last one in Chicago in 1940); the closing down of *Erkenntnis* in Germany in 1938 with a brief respite in Holland until 1940; the flight and/or emigration of most important members of the Circle and the Berlin group ultimately either to England or the USA; the deaths of Hans Hahn (1934), Schlick (1936), Walter Dubislav (1937), Kurt Grelling (murdered in Auschwitz, 1942), Edgar Zilsel (1944), and Neurath (1945).

(v) The North American period: a period of dominance during which, following earlier advocacy of related points of view by former visitors like Quine (before his apparent apostasy) and Nagel and other sympathetic contributors to the series "International Encyclopedia of Unified Science," Carnap, Reichenbach, Feigl, and Hempel become recognized as leading practitioners of the philosophy of science, writing some of the standard essays, monographs, anthologies, and textbooks by which logical empiricism came to be widely known. (Despite or because of A. J. Ayer's *Language, Truth and Logic* of 1936 England proved less hospitable.)

(vi) The period of decline: this set in with the reception of Thomas Kuhn's *The Structure of Scientific Revolutions* of 1962, Paul Feyerabend's critical essays of the 1960s, and methodological generalizations derived from Quine's earlier rejection of the analytic/synthetic distinction (1951). Thus it was in reaction to logical empiricism's perceived Cold War orthodoxy of formalist abstraction that the Kuhnian revolution stressed the inescapable historical and social embedding of all of the sciences.

To be sure, there's some inevitable overlap between stages (iii) and (iv) and between (v) and (vi), but these two distinctions do help to clarify the dynamic of the development of logical empiricism. (Talk of the "unified science movement" picks out stage [iv], but not stage [iii], while talk of the "received view" of scientific theories picks out what is shared by stages [v] and [vi].)

Giving a unified "intensional" characterization of these periods or the development of logical empiricism generally is far more difficult—precisely because of the cross-cutting complications noted above. The problem is not so much difficulties like that of locating Carnap's *Aufbau*—how much of it belongs in stage (i) and how much in stage (ii)?—whereas, by contrast, Schlick's "Experience, Cognition, Metaphysics" (1926) and Carnap's "Pseudoproblems in Philosophy" (1928b) can be assigned to stage (ii) without any problems. It is rather that the fates of the different variants of logical empiricism do not follow the same course and so resist subsumption under one covering description. (For instance, as already hinted at, even though he served as the motor of the unified science movement, Neurath and the pragmatist conception of logical empiricism disappeared from view after his death in 1945, with Frank unable to generate much interest in their socio-historical analyses of scientific practice.)

There is, of course, the towering figure of Carnap and it might be wondered whether he did not provide for the continuity required to tell a convincing story. Indeed, having lived through stages (ii) through (vi) with major contributions in each, Carnap is very much the poster boy for characterizations of logical empiricism such as those drawn by Rorty and Quine and Putnam. But the Carnap drawn by them is a very much reduced philosopher compared to the Carnap to be found when his own writings are considered. While Rorty is right that there is no more to Ayer's logical positivism than the addition of the logico-linguistic dimension to British empiricism, he is badly mistaken about Carnap. To begin with, Carnap was steeped in neo-Kantian thought early on (as his *Aufbau* still shows) and his later rejection does not betoken ignorance but that he had come to think better of it. But not only the early Carnap, also the later Carnap was much different from how he was described. To be sure, he was the foremost representative of the formalist variant of logical empiricism, but his enthusiasm for logical engineering and language construction was not a quixotic hunt for an ideal language by means of which to capture reality once and for all, but a sober search for piecemeal improvements of clarity in our means of thought. Moreover, Carnap always expected his investigations of the possibilities for expression in his "logic of science" to be complemented by investigations of the practical possibilities for solutions of the demands that science as practiced faced (as pursued once by Neurath and Frank). So not only were both the early and the late Carnap different philosophers than imagined by the mistaken standard descriptions of logical empiricism, but it is also very much to be doubted whether it was Carnap's own conception of logical empiricism that the Kuhnian revolution had shown to be untenable.

## 5

Consider now the movement's standard conception of scientific theories (for a critical overview see Suppe 1977). Logical empiricist philosophy of science distinguishes sharply between propositions concerning observable data and their regularities from propositions that are purely theoretical. Its understanding of the concept of a scientific theory as a finitely axiomatized set of propositions applies primarily to the latter (and extends only derivatively to the former). Many have questioned the sharpness of the observational–theoretical distinction (Putnam 1962), but it is important to note that except in some early formulations no epistemologically foundationalist ambitions attended the drawing of the distinction and that, in any case, empiricism demands some such distinction.

Concerning the development of logical empiricism's so-called two-languages model of scientific theories, the prominent role of Schlick must be mentioned, whose *General Theory of Knowledge* (1918, 2nd edn. 1925) introduce it to a wider readership. (Schlick took Hilbert's axiomatization of geometry as his model, but other precursors of the two-languages model can be found in the work of the French conventionalists Poincaré, Duhem, and Rey, as Frank had noted still earlier.) According to the two-languages model, scientific theories comprise an observational part formulated with observational predicates as customarily interpreted, in which observations and experiential laws were stated, and a theoretical part which consisted of theoretical laws or law-like statements the terms of which merely implicitly defined, namely, in terms of the roles they played in the laws in which they figured. Both parts were connected in virtue of a correlation that could be established between selected terms of the theoretical part and observational terms.

In the later 1920s Schlick's model was challenged by a more streamlined conception of scientific theories with just one system of concepts along lines as suggested by Carnap's *Aufbau* (1928a). The difficulties of defining dispositional terms (let alone fully theoretical terms) explicitly in observational terminology led to the return to the two-languages model and ultimately to the conception of scientific theories as uninterpreted calculi connected to observation by potentially complicated correspondence rules (Carnap 1939). According to this "received view," theoretical concepts in use were considered to be only partially interpreted, unlike observational ones, but the resultant dependence of the meaning of the former on the synthetic axioms of the theory rendered the analytic–synthetic distinction problematical.

The final step in this development links logical empiricism somewhat tenuously to contemporary debates. From about 1958 Carnap sought to conceive of the asymmetry between observational and theoretical in terms of Ramsey's method for regimenting scientific theories by replacing the theoretical terms of finitely axiomatized theories by bound higher-order variables. The resulting Ramsey-sentence featured only observational terms but retained the explanatory and predictive power of the original theory. Unlike contemporary structural realists who seek in ramseyfications a middle path between entity realism and instrumentalism, Carnap was attracted by it for its presumed help in retaining the analytic–synthetic distinction for the theoretical language and sustaining his abstention from ontological quarrels (Carnap 1963, §24). Meanwhile other logical empiricists, like Feigl, had begun to explore "semantic realism" (1950) or, like Hempel, prepared to abandon the analytic–synthetic distinction and embraced a moderate version of holism (1951).

Given the predominance of the formalist variant as represented by the received view, it is easy to mistake a further restriction of its theorizing as essential to logical empiricism as such. Building on the distinction between investigations of the context of the discovery and of the context of the justification of a scientific hypothesis, Reichenbach (1938) declared concern with the latter to be the sole business of philosophy of science. Now as long as scientific knowledge claims and their justifications are thought of entirely in abstract terms, it also makes sense to assign only logic and probability theory to their investigation and bar empirical sciences like psychology and sociology. In this Reichenbach's "analysis of science" agreed with Carnap's "logic of science" and furnished the blueprint for the mainstream of logical empiricism, but not for all of it. In recognition of the social and historically conditioned nature of the scientific enterprise, Neurath and Frank also allowed history and the empirical sciences to inform the investigation of justificatory practices—while continuing to distinguish between descriptive and properly philosophical, normative inquiries. (Their so-called "pragmatics of science" was to complement Carnap's logic of science.)

Two more standard features of logical empiricist doctrine must be mentioned before we can turn to its bearing on the philosophy of social science. The first is the thesis of the unity of science. The thesis was originally put forward as the denial of the claim, prominent in German philosophy since the second half of the 19th century, that the natural sciences and the sciences of the human world (*Geisteswissenschaften*, *Kulturwissenschaften*) were of a radically different nature both ontologically and epistemologically. Later on one also distinguished between the thesis as pertaining to the unity of method, the unity of language, and the unity of laws across all the sciences. The standard picture of the unity of science as consisting of a reductive pyramid of scientific disciplines with physics as its basis was still propagated as a "working hypothesis" in the 1950s (Oppenheim and Putnam 1958) but already in the later 1930s its viability was gently questioned by Carnap, who considered the reductive unity of all scientific laws to be at best a goal for the distant future—a goal that nowadays has been widely abandoned. By contrast, the thesis of the unity of the language of science, postulating the translatability of the languages of all disciplines into that of physics, fared somewhat better. Understood by Carnap originally as tied to the language of mathematical physics (1932), "physicalism" has long since morphed into a variety of related standard ontological stances (but that was not Carnap's intention). Later relaxed to require only non-eliminative "reduction sentences" relating scientific statements to the observational "thing-language" (Carnap 1936–37), physicalism came to coincide with the methodological claim to unity characteristic of empiricism: that all claims of the non-formal sciences had to be empirically testable at least in principle. (Beyond that no identity of investigative methods was prescribed to the different disciplines.)

The other feature that looms large here is Hempel's model of deductive-nomological explanation. According to it, a scientific explanation is a deductive argument with one or more universal statements representing laws and a statement of initial conditions as premises and a singular statement representing a predicted or retrodicted outcome as conclusion (Hempel 1942; I neglect the inductive variants later supplied). Famously, the social sciences and especially history resisted the recasting of their explanations that this model seemed to require. While this was at first thought to reflect rather badly on these disciplines, ultimately it was Hempel's model that was discarded as unduly schematic and restrictive (see Salmon 1989). A pattern of liberation was set that the social sciences happily embraced.

# 6

Mathematical physics served as the paradigm for the reconstruction of scientific theories in orthodox logical empiricism. Neurath voiced opposition already during the interwar years, but after World War II no leading member of the movement took his place. This is not to say that Hempel and Nagel did not do valuable work on functional and teleological explanation and investigated subjectivism and the value dimension of social science (see Nagel 1961 and Hempel 1965), but they did not question the primacy of the model of scientific theories focused on physics. Richard Rudner's 1966 textbook *Philosophy of Social Science* can be considered as representative for orthodox logical empiricism in its late stage.

Rudner's first proper chapter, "The Construction of Social Theory," starts by defining "theory" in abstract terms as a "systematically related set of statements, including some lawlike generalizations, that is empirically testable," proceeds to explain the concepts of deductive, formal, interpreted, and axiomatic systems, and discusses different forms of term introduction and the difficulties caused by dispositional and theoretical terms, adding that while "these problems are not peculiar to the philosophy of social science" their import there "is especially exacerbated by the lesser degree of formalization of theories characteristic of the social sciences" (23). That the social sciences fall "considerably short of full formalization" (ibid.) is noted with regret but Rudner continued to rely on this ideal when he explained models as alternative interpretations of the axioms and theorems of a theory, elaborated the notions of definitional and classificatory schemata and typologies, and judged that "almost all typologies that occur in the literature [of social science] have failed to provide the explicit theoretical framework that such systems of ordering require for rigor" (38) because their "ordering-relation concepts" are missing. (Thus the concept of an open society was dismissed as at best heuristic on account of providing no measure of whether one that censors only movies is more or less open than one that censors only comic books.) For Rudner, the lack of quantification and metrical typologies showed that "the social sciences are poor in theory" (40). Unsurprisingly, after explaining the notions of a theory's power and simplicity as applicable to formalized systems, he concluded that they are "scarcely employable in the social sciences" (46). Discussing the fallback notion of partial formalization in terms of systematic presuppositions, quasi-deductions, and relative primitives even led him to the admission that the "nonexistence of an adequate criterion for deciding what constitutes an appropriate degree of formalization" shows that this "aspect of scientific method" is "itself scientifically 'out of control'" (53). Given that by then Rudner had nearly reached the half-way mark in his monograph, one may rightly fear for the rest: true to form, the next chapter disposes of Weber's ideal types as inadequate by the standards of "theoretical idealizations" in physics (62) before discussing the Hempelian logic of explanation in abstract or natural scientific terms. Matters improve somewhat in the next chapter, if only because there at least arguments by other *philosophers* of social science are critically discussed—though Weber, for one, continues to be read most unsympathetically. Rudner's book then closes with a short chapter on the standard topic of "Functionalism and Other Problems of Teleological Inquiry."

It is difficult to disagree with Daniel Little's assessment (2009) of "how foreign this approach is to actual theoretical work by social scientists": "this approach proves to be singularly unhelp-ful when it comes to actually understanding and criticizing the social sciences as they actually exist." Three key errors are diagnosed: first, that all the sciences have the same fundamental logic (namely that of the "received view"); second, that the investigation of the central con-cept of rationality employed in the explanation of social action is unduly reduced to a matter of concept formation; third, that it is overlooked that social science's "theories of the middle range" typically are not systematizations of the same generality as physics and so need different standards of evaluation.

7

It remains to see whether Rudner's book really should count as "an exceptionally clear exposi-tion and development of the central ideas of logical positivism in application to social-scientific theorizing," as Little has it. That the interwar years offered alternative fare was first suggested by Hempel (1969), who recalled Neurath's vigorous and politically motivated crusade against ideal-istic obscurantism in the human sciences while bemoaning his lack of logical finesse. What must be added is that Neurath was not just sloppy but also already in his day argued against the reduc-tionist version of the unified science program. In particular, contrary to Rudner's prescriptions,

Neurath did not require that social science be conducted just like natural science: "The programme of unified science does not presuppose that physics can be regarded as an example for all the sciences to follow" (1937a, 78).

Long thought to signify reductionism at its most rabid, Neurath's use of the slogan "physicalism" actually hides doctrines of quite different intent. For our purposes we can distinguish between three: the epistemological, the metalinguistic, and the nomological conception of physicalism. The first represents what is nowadays called "epistemological naturalism," the denial of epistemological aprioricism. Roughly, such a position seeks to explain—and legitimate—scientific knowledge claims in a scientific manner. (As noted, Neurath pursued scientific metatheory of an empirical kind: the pragmatics of science.) The second conception of physicalism was closely linked to the idea of empiricist significance as the availability of intersubjective evidence (he rejected the possibility of private languages already in 1931). Importantly, Neurath's basic language in which such evidence was phrased was not the theoretical language of physics itself, but the "physicalistically cleansed" everyday language. And even though he spoke of "individual and social behaviourism," his metalinguistic physicalism is best read as in intention a form of what nowadays is called "non-reductive physicalism" (without its ontological dimension): his "universal slang" did not exclude the intentional idiom. The third aspect of Neurath's physicalism bears on the supposed reducibility of the laws of the various individual sciences to those of physics and throws into relief his non-standard conception of the idea of the unity of science itself: "According to physicalism, sociological laws are not laws of physics applied to sociological structures, but they are also not unproblematically reducible to laws about atomic structures" (1933, 106). Noting that "social behaviourism establishes laws of its own kind" (1932/1983, 75), Neurath stressed the conceptual autonomy of social science. Accordingly, his claim for unified science was minimalist: "All laws of unified science must be capable of being linked with each other, if they are to fulfill the task of predicting as often as possible individual events or groups of events" (68).

Neurath died in 1945 and his views did not win the day. In fact, from the mid-1940s onward he stood accused of having misunderstood the scientific method as such when in fact he anticipated the pluralist trend in contemporary philosophy of social science. Tellingly this criticism which Neurath received from Popper—an arch-opponent of logical empiricism who shared many of its views but elected to stress his differences—reflects a similar assumption to that powering Rudner's prescriptions: that the scientific method holds similar prescriptions for all the sciences not only with regard to testability in principle, but with regard to how their theories are structured. Popper charged Neurath with mistaking the nature of theoretical science by allowing social science to aim for generalizations that only hold "within 'the present cosmological period'" (Popper 1944–45/1961, 103). The quotation is not exact, but Popper's attached footnote correctly refers to Neurath's paper containing the claim that "most sociological regularities that support the deduction of predictions are formulated in such a way that they are valid only for relative complex structures of certain geographical regions and historical periods" (1936/2004, 506). This was enough for Popper to count Neurath as a historicist by hankering after what might be called "soft" historical laws. To start with, the laws in question were not intended to be laws of history, but sociological and/or economic laws that were relativized to certain historical periods and types of social structures. Yet that is not the worst of Popper's mistakes: he wrote, "It would not be a sign of laudable scientific caution if we were to add such a condition, but a sign that we do not understand scientific procedure. For it is an important postulate of scientific method that we should search for laws with an unlimited realm of validity" (1944–45/1961, 103; the quotation contains a footnote reference to "historicists" like Neurath). That it is "an important" task to find exceptionless laws does not mean, however, that it is the only task for science. Nowadays, of course, theorists argue persuasively that universal laws are by no means the exclusive aim of social science (e.g. Kincaid 1990). Evidently Neurath was of the same view.

That Neurath adopted such heterodox positions may seem surprising, given that he was the chief propagandist of the unified science movement, but his opposition becomes readily intelligible once we note again that he was a social scientist himself. His economics, moreover, were far from what might be expected of a positivist and deserve reassessment. As an opponent of Mises and Hayek in the socialist calculation debate he pioneered incommensurability arguments against the monetarization of non-market goods that have become standard fare in ecological economics (1925). As a theorist of real income, he not only questioned the use of concepts like gross domestic product, but also worked towards the development of measures of well-being that, he insisted, had to be in-kind and multi-dimensional (1937b), foreshadowing more recent developments in welfare economics. To be sure, Neurath was an outlier in several respects. But his example—like that of the later Carnap and Frank—shows that, as long as we align we ourselves with critical Enlightenment values, we discard the entirety of logical empiricism at our peril.

# References

Ayer, A. J. (1936) *Language, Truth and Logic*. London: Gollancz (2nd edn. 1946).

Blumberg, A. and Feigl, H. (1931) "Logical Positivism." *Journal of Philosophy* 28: 281–96.

Carnap, R. (1928a) *Der logische Aufbau der Welt*. Berlin: Bernary. Trans. *The Logical Structure of the World*. Berkeley: University of California Press, 1967. Repr. Chicago: Open Court, 2003

Carnap, R. (1928b) *Scheinprobleme in der Philosophie*. Berlin: Bernary. Trans. "Pseudoproblems in Philosophy," in *The Logical Structure of the World*. Berkeley: University of California Press, 1967, 301–43. Repr. Chicago: Open Court, 2003.

Carnap, R. (1932) "Die physikalische Sprache als Universalsprache der Wissenschaft." *Erkenntnis* 2: 432–65. Trans. *The Unity of Science*. London: Kegan, Paul, Trench Teubner & Co., 1934.

Carnap, R. (1934) *Logische Syntax der Sprache*. Vienna: Springer. Rev. edn. trans. *The Logical Syntax of Language*, London: Kegan, Paul, Trench Teubner & Cie, 1937. Repr. Chicago: Open Court, 2002.

Carnap, R. (1936–37) "Testability and Meaning." *Philosophy of Science* 3: 419–71 and 4: 1–40.

Carnap, R. (1939) *Foundations of Logic and Mathematics*. Chicago: University of Chicago Press.

Carnap, R. (1963) "Intellectual Autobiography" and "Comments and Replies," in P. A. Schilpp (ed.) *The Philosophy of Rudolf Carnap*. LaSalle, IL: Open Court, 3–84 and 859–1016.

Carnap, R., Hahn, H., and Neurath, O. (1929) *Wissenschaftliche Weltauffassung—Der Wiener Kreis*. Vienna: Wolf. Trans. in F. Stadler. T. Uebel (eds.) *Wissenschaftliche Weltauffassung—Der Wiener Kreis*. Vienna: Springer, 2012, 75–116.

Feigl, H. (1950) "Existential Hypotheses: Realistic vs. Phenomenalistic Interpretations." *Philosophy of Science* 17: 32–62.

Hempel, C. G. (1942) "The Function of General Laws in History." *Journal of Philosophy* 39: 35–48. Repr. in Hempel, *Aspects of Scientific Explanation and Other Essays*. New York: Free Press, 1965, 231–44.

Hempel, C. G. (1950) "The Empiricist Criterion of Meaning." *Revue Internationale de Philosophie* 4: 41–63. Repr. in A. J. Ayer (ed.), *Logical Positivism*. New York: Free Press, 1959, 108–27.

Hempel, C. G. (1951) "The Concepts of Cognitive Significance: A Reconsideration." *Proceedings of the American Academy of Arts and Sciences* 80: 61–77.

Hempel, C. G. (1965) "Empiricist Criteria of Cognitive Significance: Problems and Changes," in Hempel, *Aspects of Scientific Explanation and Other Essays*. New York: Free Press, 101–21.

Hempel, C. G. (1969) "Logical Positivism and the Social Sciences," in P. Achinstein, S. F. Barker (eds.) *The Legacy of Logical Positivism*. Baltimore: John Hopkins Press, 163–94.

Justus, J. (2014) "Carnap's Forgotten Criterion of Cognitive Significance." *Mind* 123: 415–36.

Kincaid, H. (1990) "Defending Laws in the Social Sciences." *Philosophy of the Social Sciences* 20: 56–83.

Little, D. (2009) "Neopositivist Philosophy of Social Science," at http://understandingsociety.blogspot. co.uk/2009/09/neo-positivist-philosophy-of-social.html (accessed October 20, 2015).

Mach, E. (1883) *Die Mechanik in ihrer Entwicklung*. Leipzig: Brockhaus. Trans. *The Science of Mechanics*, LaSalle, IL: Open Court, 1960.

Nagel, E. (1961) *The Structure of Science: Problems in the Logic of Scientific Explanation*. New York: Harcourt, Brace and World. Repr. Indianapolis: Hackett, 1979.

Neurath, O. (1925) "Sozialistische Nützlichkeitsrechnung und kapitalistische Reingewinnrechnung." *Der Kampf* 18: 391–95. Trans. "Socialist Utility Calculation and Capitalist Profit Calculation," in Neurath, *Economic Writings. Selections 1904–1945*, ed. T. Uebel and R. S. Cohen. Dordrecht: Kluwer, 2004, 466–72.

Neurath, O. (1931a) "Physikalismus." *Scientia* 50: 297–303. Trans. "Physicalism," in Neurath, *Philosophical Papers 1913–1946*, ed. R. S. Cohen and M. Neurath. Dordrecht: Reidel, 1983, 52–57.

Neurath, O. (1931b) "Physicalism: The Philosophy of the Vienna Circle." *The Monist* 41: 618–23. Repr. in Neurath, *Philosophical Papers 1913–1946*, ed. R. S. Cohen and M. Neurath. Dordrecht: Reidel, 1983, 48–51.

Neurath, O. (1932) "Soziologie im Physikalismus." *Erkenntnis* 2: 393–431. Trans. "Sociology in the Framework of Physicalism" in Neurath, *Philosophical Papers 1913–1946*, ed. R. S. Cohen and M. Neurath. Dordrecht: Reidel, 1983, 58–90.

Neurath, O. (1933) "Das Fremdpsychische in der Soziologie" [unsigned abstract]. *Erkenntnis* 3: 105–6.

Neurath, O. (1936) "Soziologische Prognosen." *Erkenntnis* 6: 398–405. Trans. Sociological Predictions" in Neurath, *Economic Writings. Selections 1904–1945*, ed. T. Uebel and R. S. Cohen. Dordrecht: Kluwer, 2004, 506–12.

Neurath, O. (1937a) "Prognosen und Terminologie in Physik, Biologie, Soziologie," in *Traveaux du IXème Congrès International de Philosophie. IV. L'Unité de la Science: La Méthode et les Méthodes*. Paris: Herman & Cie., 77–85.

Neurath, O. (1937b) "Inventory of the Standard of Living." *Zeitschrift für Sozialforschung* 6: 140–51. Repr. in Neurath, *Economic Writings. Selections 1904–1945*, ed. T. Uebel and R. S. Coheno, Dordrecht: Kluwer, 2004, 513–26.

Oppenheim, P., and Putnam, H. (1958) "The Unity of Science as a Working Hypothesis," in H. Feigl, G. Maxwell, and M. Scriven (eds.) *Minnesota Studies in the Philosophy of Science 2*. Minneapolis: University of Minnesota Press, 3–36.

Popper, K. (1944–45) "The Poverty of Historicism." *Economica* 11: 86–103, 11: 119–37, and 12: 69–89. Rev. and repr. *The Poverty of Historicism*. London: Routledge and Kegan Paul, 1961.

Putnam, H. (1962) "What Theories Are Not," in E. Nagel, P. Suppes, and A. Tarski (eds.) *Logic, Methodology and Philosophy of Science*. Stanford: Stanford University Press, 240–51. Repr. in Putnam, *Philosophical Papers Vol. 1*. Cambridge: Cambridge University Press, 1978, 215–27.

Quine, W. V. O. (1951) "Two Dogmas of Empiricism." *Philosophical Review* 60: 20–43. Repr. in Quine, *From a Logical Point of View*. Cambridge, MA: Harvard University Press, rev. edn. 1980, 20–46.

Quine, W. V. O. (1969) "Epistemology Naturalized," in Quine, *Ontological Relativity and Other Essays*. New York: Columbia University Press, 69–90.

Reichenbach, H. (1936) "Logistic Empiricism in Germany and the Present State of its Problems." *Journal of Philosophy* 33: 141–60.

Reichenbach, H. (1938) *Experience and Prediction*. Chicago: University of Chicago Press. Repr. Notre Dame: University of Notre Dame Press, 2006.

Reisch, G. (1991) "Did Kuhn Kill Logical Empiricism?" *Philosophy of Science* 58: 264–77.

Rorty, R. (1999). "Introduction," in W. Sellars, *Empiricism and the Philosophy of Mind*, ed. R. Brandom. Cambridge, MA: Harvard University Press, 1–12.

Rudner, R. (1966) *Philosophy of Social Science*. Englewood Cliffs, NJ: Prentice Hall.

Salmon, M. (1989) "Four Decades of Scientific Explanation," in P. Kitcher and W. Salmon (eds.) *Scientific Explanation*. Minneapolis: University of Minnesota Press. Repr. separately, Minneapolis: University of Minnesota Press, 1990.

Schlick, M. (1917–22) "Raum und Zeit in der gegenwärtigen Physik." *Die Naturwissenschaften* 5: 161–67, 177–86. Enlarged edn. Berlin: Springer, 1919, 4th rev. edn. 1922. Trans. "Space and Time in

Contemporary Physics," in Schlick, *Philosophical Papers Vol.1 (1909–1922)*, ed. H. L. Mulder and B. van de Velde-Schlick. Dordrecht: Reidel, 1979, 207–69.

Schlick, M. (1918) *Allgemeine Erkenntnislehre*. Berlin: Springer, 1918, 2nd rev. edn. 1925. Trans. *General Theory of Knowledge*. LaSalle, IL: Open Court, 1974.

Schlick, M. (1926) "Erleben, Erkennen, Metaphysik." *Kantstudien* 31: 146–58. Trans. "Experience Cognition, Metaphysics," in Schlick, *Philosophical Papers Vol. 2 (1925–1936)*, ed. H. L. Mulder and B. van de Velde-Schlick. Dordrecht: Reidel, 1979, 99–111.

Suppe, F. (1977) "The Search for a Philosophical Understanding of Theories," in F. Suppe (ed.) *The Structure of Scientific Theories*, 2nd edn. Urbana, IL: University of Illinois Press, 3–241.

Uebel, T. (2007) Empiricism at the Crossroads: The Vienna circle's Protocol-Sentence Debate, Chicago: Open Court.

Uebel, T. (2013) "'Logical Positivism'—'Logical Empiricism': What's in a Name?" *Perspectives on Science* 21: 58–99.

# Further Reading

The considerable growth of literature on logical empiricism in recent decades was spearheaded by A. Coffa, *The Semantic Tradition from Kant to Carnap. To the Vienna Station*, ed. L. Wessels (Cambridge: Cambridge University Press, 1991), the essays by M. Friedman collected in *Reconsidering Logical Positivism* (Cambridge: Cambridge University Press, 1999), and the work of R. Haller, translated in T. Uebel (ed.) *Rediscovering the Forgotten Vienna Circle. Austrian Studies on Otto Neurath and the Vienna Circle* (Dordrecht: Kluwer, 1991). Detailed history and bibliographical resources are provided by F. Stadler in *The Vienna Circle. Studies in the Origins, Development and Influence of logical Empiricism* (Vienna and New York: Springer, 2001, 2nd edn. 2015). Recent assessments of the great variety of topics raised by and concerning logical empiricism are given in A. Richardson and T. Uebel (eds.) *The Cambridge Companion to Logical Empiricism* (Cambridge: Cambridge University Press, 2007), and in R. Creath and M. Friedman (eds.) *The Cambridge Companion to Carnap* (Cambridge: Cambridge University Press, 2007). Further concise overviews of the doctrines of the "Vienna Circle" and "Logical Empiricism" are given by Uebel in *The Stanford Encyclopedia of Philosophy* (internet resource) and M. Curd and S. Psillos (eds.) *The Routledge Companion to the Philosophy of Science* (London: Routledge, 2008, 2nd edn. 2013), respectively. For more detailed discussions of Neurath's philosophy of social science see T. Uebel, "Philosophy of Science in Early Logical Empiricism: The Case of Radical Physicalism," in Richardson and Uebel, *Cambridge Companion to Logical Empiricism*, 250–77, of the development of his economic thought see the "Introduction," in Neurath, *Economic Writings*, ed. T. Uebel and R. S. Cohen (Dordrecht: Kluwer, 2004), 1–108, and of the lasting impact of his economics see J. O'Neill and T. Uebel, "Analytical Philosophy and Ecological Economics," in J. Martinez-Alier and R. Muradian (eds.) *Handbook of Ecological Economics* (Cheltenham: Edward Elgar, 2015). All the above provide ample further references.

# 5
# POPPER'S INFLUENCE ON THE SOCIAL SCIENCES

*Jeremy Shearmur*

## 1 Introduction

Karl Popper had distinctive views on social philosophy and the philosophy of the social sciences, and also on epistemology and the philosophy of science. Both areas are of importance for the social sciences. Despite the fact that his major appointment was at the London School of Economics, his ideas have not been as influential on the social sciences as one might have expected. Aside from a few figures who wrote directly in the elaboration and defense of his views such as Joseph Agassi, Ian Jarvie, and John Watkins, his influence is also not always easy to identify.[1] There are, I think, three reasons for this. They relate to his philosophy of science, his philosophy of social science, and also to certain sociological factors concerning his career.

## 2 The Philosophy of Science

Popper's views on epistemology and the philosophy of science were distinctive. (For a brilliant introduction which brings this out well, see Hacohen 2016.) Popper was a product of Vienna in the inter-war period. While he was not a Kantian, he was influenced by his early work in psychology and by the naturalized Kantianism of the Würzburg School, whose members included Karl Bühler, and also by the biological approach of Otto Selz (ter Hark 2004). Popper was also influenced by discussions with Julius Kraft of issues in Leonard Nelson, Fries, and Kant, and also by discussions with Heinrich Gomperz. All this meant that, while he had many interests in common with the members of the Vienna Circle, his underlying approach to philosophy was very different from their empiricism.

A further complication related to the development of his work, and to its publishing history. Popper initially wrote *Die beiden Grundprobleme der Erkenntnistheorie*, which was only published as Popper 1979, 2009. In 1934, he published *Logik der Forschung* (Popper 1934, 1959), which was in part a highly abbreviated—but in certain respects more developed—treatment of issues discussed at much greater length in *Die beiden Grundprobleme*, but which also contained a lot of new material on technical issues in the theory of probability and quantum theory. It was published in a series associated with the Vienna Circle. Popper, while he was conscious of holding metaphysical views—and was critical of the positivists' dismissal of metaphysics as meaningless—was also conscious of not having an account of how metaphysical theories could be appraised. In both *Die beiden Grundprobleme* and *Logik der Forschung*, he avoided metaphysics—suggesting, indeed, that metaphysical theories should be re-interpreted as 'methodological rules'. More generally, his approach treated what was open to rational appraisal as the formal (mathematics and logic), the empirical, and methodological proposals.

Methodological proposals were to be appraised in terms of their usefulness in helping us towards the aims of science. About these, Popper's views were distinctive, and it is important to understand them if one is to understand his approach. Popper, as is well known, argued that universal scientific theories could not be verified, but that they could be falsified relative to the scientific community's acceptance of 'basic statements'. (Here, his approach stressed tentative, but inter-subjectively accepted, statements about the results of experiments, rather than individuals' sensations.) Popper stressed knowledge as involving conjectures and refutations, in which induction (and, thus, the problems raised by Hume about induction) played no role. Popper was well aware of 'conventionalism'. Conventionalists had stressed the way in which our ideas function as a system, and that, in the event of our experiencing a problem about our existing ideas (by way of the discovery of a contradiction, or by way of an empirical refutation), it was open to us to choose which element of our knowledge we should modify, as a way of dealing with the problem. In Popper's view, the approach to this problem which the conventionalists themselves took—to be guided by considerations of simplicity and to make the minimum changes necessary to deal with the problem—was perfectly feasible. It was striking, however, that at the time this had been used to defend older approaches to science against Einstein's innovations. Popper, by contrast, identified strongly with the kind of revolutionary approach exemplified by Einstein's work. Popper favored intellectual boldness, and—although he would only put it in such terms later—a view which was realist and fallibilist: which saw our knowledge as aspiring to understand the structure of the world. In pursuit of this goal, he favored methodological rules which encouraged us to choose theories, and modifications of our existing ideas, which were bold and testable. All this meant that at the heart of his presentation of his views in *Logik der Forschung*, his exposition of his own views constituted a response to what has often been advanced as a key objection (the conventionalist objection) to his ideas. He also offered an analysis of explanation as involving the proffering of testable statements of laws and initial conditions, from which a description of what one wished to explain could be deduced.

His *Logik der Forschung* formed the background to his *Open Society* (Popper 1945) and *The Poverty of Historicism* (Popper 1944–45, 1957), in which he discussed issues of social and political philosophy and the methodology of social science. This is important because, from the 1950s, significant changes took place in Popper's views. In particular, he developed some (modest) ideas about how metaphysical theories could be critically appraised *qua* solutions to the problems that they were attempting to resolve. He also offered ideas about the role of metaphysical ideas as 'research programs' for science. Already in *Logik der Forschung*, he had referred to the positive role that some metaphysical ideas had played in the development of science. But now he stressed not only their historical role, but also that there could be rational assessment of such competing ideas. He even developed his own ideas about how a metaphysic of probabilistic dispositions, i.e. 'propensities', could serve as a research program for the future development of science. Popper had also become convinced that some ideas introduced by Alfred Tarski enabled one to avoid problems that he thought had affected the kind of common-sense or 'Aristotelian' correspondence theory of truth that he favored.

Popper also became more explicit about favoring what might be called an 'aspirational realism' as an aim for science: science was seen as potentially grasping for an understanding not just of truth, but also for a knowledge of structures behind the appearances of things. At the same time, Popper's approach was firmly fallibilistic: however successful our theories, we could not be sure that they were the last word, and might not in time be superseded. In addition, in the 1960s he readily accepted the suggestion made by William Bartley, that his approach replaced the aim of justification, by openness to criticism.

I have, in the foregoing, referred to Popper's first published book as *Logik der Forschung*. The reason for this was to implicitly stress the fact that this book was not translated into English until 1959 (Popper 1959). While *Logik der Forschung* had been well received on its appearance, what was distinctive about Popper's work was not well appreciated in the English-speaking world. In addition, his later ideas were intended to form part of a "Postscript" to the translation of *Logik der Forschung*, which he had hoped would appear in 1954. But the *Postscript* only appeared as (Popper 1982–83). One result of all this was that Popper's ideas were typically known in the English-speaking world only from shorter statements, addresses, and essays. And, for example, it was simply not appreciated—other than by a few of Popper's colleagues who had discussed these issues with him, or who read the proofs of the *Postscript*—just how different from logical empiricism his approach was, and that his treatment of 'metaphysical research programs' offered a more rationalistic alternative approach to many of the issues with which Kuhn was concerned in *The Structure of Scientific Revolutions*.

## 3  Philosophy of Social Science

In his mid-teens, Popper was a Marxist, and worked in the office of the Austrian Communist Party (Bartley 1989; Hacohen 2000). As he has often described, Popper was led to question his attachment to Marxism when a demonstration organized by the communists led to the death of some working people. He became critical not just of the cogency of communist claims to intellectual leadership, but also of many aspects of the Marxism which influenced not just the Austrian Communists but also the Social Democrats. His ideas about this were set out, in some detail, in the discussion of Marx in his *Open Society*. Popper became critical, however, of the more general ideas which he referred to as 'historicism'. This term—which Popper coined for the purpose—covered a variety of themes. Popper was critical of the view that there was a trajectory to history, and that the task of the social sciences was to understand this trajectory scientifically. He was also critical, however, of broader Hegelian-influenced and religious ideas about there being a 'plot' to history, and of historical periodization. Historicism, however, was wider even than this in its scope. Popper was at odds with moral and aesthetic futurism, and in fact, while he does not discuss this, with the kinds of ideas which had influenced theological modernism and theological liberalism, too. Popper developed a battery of arguments against a whole range of these ideas. But his presentation in *The Poverty of Historicism* and *The Open Society* was in some ways handicapped by the fact that, at the time, his view about the scope of what was open to rational argument was limited.

Popper's views about the methodology of social science were strongly influenced by his more general ideas about the philosophy of science. But there were other significant aspects to his ideas about the social sciences.

First, while Popper was critical of Marxism, it also influenced his positive views. While Popper favored 'methodological individualism', he was critical of what he called 'psychologism'. In the first paragraph of chapter 14 of his *Open Society* he refers to, and endorses, Marx's opposition "to the plausible doctrine that all laws of social life must be ultimately reducible to the psychological laws of human nature," citing Marx's epigram: "It is not the consciousness of man that determines his existence—rather, it is his social existence that determines his consciousness." In addition, when he is giving an account of scientific objectivity, Popper stresses inter-subjectivity and offers a critique of the idea of science as something that could be undertaken by Robinson Crusoe; he also suggests that 'reasonableness' could be understood in a similar way. While objectivity understood in terms of inter-subjectivity in Popper is also a theme which he draws from Kant's *Critique of Pure Reason* (cf. Popper 1959, section 8), on this occasion Popper refers by contrast to Crusoe's approach to the "social ... character of scientific method" (1945, ch. 23, text before n. 9). The use of Crusoe to draw a contrast between individual and social forms of production is a theme in Marx's *Capital*, vol. 1 (Troels Eggers Hansen has suggested that Karl Bühler 1922 may be important here.).

Second, Popper had discussions with Karl Polanyi in Vienna in 1924–25. Polanyi, at the time, was giving a seminar to a small number of socialist students about issues concerning economic calculation under socialism (Schaffer 2006, 329). (It is worth noting that Popper does not seem to have been concerned with this question, and while he later referred to some of Hayek's work on this theme, and to Hayek's ideas about the methodology of economics, it is important to differentiate between Popper and those like Hayek and Machlup who were involved in discussions with Ludwig von Mises about the philosophy of social science.) What seem to have made an impression on Popper were private conversations with Polanyi. The first touched on how Marx's work might be understood (Popper 1945, ch. 14, n. 11): He credits to Polanyi the idea that it was Marx who first conceived social theory as the study of the unwanted social repercussions of nearly all our actions.

The second conversation related to essentialism and 'methodological nominalism'. As Popper wrote in his *Open Society* (Popper 1945, ch. 3, n. 30):

> The theory that while the physical sciences are based on a methodological nominalism, the social sciences must adopt essentialist ('realistic') methods, has been made clear to me by K. Polanyi (in 1925); he pointed out, at that time, that a reform of the methodology of the social sciences might conceivably be achieved by abandoning this theory.

What Popper criticized as 'essentialism' again involved several different ideas. In part, he was critical of the view that there was some essence to, say, the state, which was to be studied as the key to its various manifestations. In part, he was critical of the idea that there were essences which could be grasped intuitively, where this intuitive grasp gave us reliable knowledge which we did not need to put to empirical test. In part, however, as in some of his comments about Marx, by 'essentialism' he also sometimes means the idea that there were structures to be grasped behind the phenomena which we are studying. This last view, however, is one which Popper himself came to endorse—albeit when it was understood in a fallibilistic manner—when he indicated that he was not unhappy with the description of 'modified essentialism' for the views that he later put forward in contradistinction to instrumentalistic views about the character of natural science (Popper 1963, ch. 3; 1974, 1114–116).

Popper's writing on the methodology of the social sciences started with his work on "The Poverty of Historicism." (Popper 1976a, ch. 24, mentions that *The Open Society* grew out of his work on chapter 10 of *The Poverty*; it was initially called "Marginal Notes on the History of Historicism."[2]) In a historical note to the 1957 book edition of *The Poverty*, Popper says that the idea "that the belief in historical destiny is sheer superstition, and that there can be no prediction of the course of human history by scientific or any other rational methods—goes back to the winter of 1919–20" (Popper 1957, iv). In the historical note, Popper also refers to the main outline having been completed in 1935, with first presentation of "The Poverty of Historicism" as having taken place in Brussels in January or February 1936. He says, there, that Karl Hilferding made some important contributions to the discussion, while in *Unended Quest* (ch. 24) he explains that these consisted of links that Hilferding made to Popper's analysis of causal explanation in *Logik der Forschung* (*The Logic of Scientific Discovery*). It would seem to me plausible that this related to Popper's having argued that explanation must involve universal laws and also initial conditions—and thus that the thrust of Popper's early presentations of *The Poverty of Historicism* is likely to have involved a criticism of the unconditional character of historicist prophecy.

Popper and Hayek both grew up in Vienna. But Popper met Hayek for the first time in London in 1935. They seem to have got on well, and Hayek invited Popper to deliver a paper—on "The Poverty of Historicism"—to a seminar that he and Morris Ginsberg were running, on the methodology of social science. Popper took "The Poverty" to New Zealand, where he had discussions about methodology with the economist Harold Larsen and subsequently with Colin Simkin, who has reported that work on *The Poverty* was put on the back burner while Popper worked on *The Open Society*. A version of *The Poverty* was submitted to, but rejected by, *Mind*. Popper worked further on the paper, expanding it, and it was eventually published in *Economica*, which Hayek was then editing, in 1944 and 1945. Popper had also been reading, and refers to, work by Hayek on the methodology of economics. In addition, as I have described elsewhere (Shearmur 1998), Popper re-wrote the final part of the paper in the light of his reading of Hayek's "Scientism and the Study of Society." In addition, because there were paper shortages, Hayek cut *The Poverty* for its *Economica* publication. He had Popper's permission to do so, but was not able to consult him about what was cut.[3]

Popper has described his ideas about the methodology of the social sciences as an attempt "to generalize the method of theoretical economics" (Popper 1994, 155), and he also noted (Popper 1994, 181) that he was "particularly impressed by Hayek's formulation that economics is 'the logic of choice'." This, and his more general discussion of his methodology of social science in "Models, Instruments and Truth" (Popper 1994, ch. 8), has led some authors to see Popper, with his stress on methodological individualism, rationality, and situational logic, as having offered an early formulation of the program of rational choice theory (Hedström et al. 1998). This is a reasonable view to take. But at the same time, one must not overlook the aspect of Popper's approach which he took over from Marx, where his anti-psychologism and his stress on the social contrast with economics-inspired rational choice theory. Indeed, Popper was himself—for example in the papers which form chapters 3 and 4 of his *Objective Knowledge* (Popper 1972)— to offer his own approach to hermeneutics. Popper also refers to his 'logic of the situation' "as embrac[ing], for example, the logic of choice and the logic of historical problem situations" (Popper 1994, 181, n. 1).

In his *Karl Popper: The Formative Years* (Hacohen 2000, 362–65) Malachi Hacohen has discussed the fact that Popper took Felix Kaufmann's *Methodenlehre der Sozialwissenschaften* with him to New Zealand, and corresponded with Kaufmann about it, during the course of 1937 (Kaufmann 1936, 2014). While at times he found Kaufmann's work hard going, Hacohen reports that Popper found the second part of it useful as a guide to material with which he then took issue, in his own methodological writings.

An interesting influence on Popper's methodological views in the social sciences was his reading of Max Weber's work. In *The Poverty of Historicism* and *The Open Society*, he refers both to Weber's *Wissenschaftslehre* and to his *Wirtschaft und Gesellschaft*. (I recall Popper mentioning to me that he sometimes found Weber's German difficult to understand—he commented that the translation in *The Methodology of the Social Sciences* [Weber 1949] was much clearer than Weber's German!)

There is also a more general problem—in considering Popper's influence—posed by some wider resemblances between Popper's and Weber's views. Popper refers to Weber's ideas about history in both *The Open Society* and *The Poverty of Historicism*. While he is not in full agreement with Weber, their views are very close (compare Popper's reference to aspects of Weber's views as being "the closest anticipation that I know to the analysis offered here" [Popper 1957, 145]). Popper differs from Weber because of his own views about causal explanation. But what Popper has to say about the role of 'points of view' in historical interpretation in *The Open Society* is very close to Weber's reaction to issues about history raised by Rickert. In addition, Popper refers to Weber in connection with the idea that "psychological analysis of an action in terms of its (rational or irrational) motives presupposes ... that we have previously developed some standard of what is to be considered as rational in the situation in question" (Popper 1945, ch. 14, text to n. 14). This is important for two reasons: on the one hand, Popper and Weber share an anti-psychologistic approach to social explanation.[4] On the other, they both favor explanations in terms of what Popper refers to as 'situational logic';[5] and Popper notes that Weber is, in fact, in agreement with him that appeals to intuitive understanding have to be assessed by ordinary empirical methods (Popper 1945, ch. 11, n. 44). Popper is critical of what he discerns to be elements of essentialism in Weber, and differs from him because Popper wishes to stress commonalities between the methods in the natural and the social sciences.

What was characteristic of Popper's own approach to the methodology of social science, was that he emphasized the idea of the unity of *method* between natural and social science, but where this was interpreted in terms of his own distinctive views about the natural sciences. He stressed the significance of fallibilism and the importance of testing, and his ideas about explanation. While he was critical of the idea that the social sciences had distinctive methods, his own approach there endorsed an emphasis on rationality and the 'situational logic' of individuals, which was compatible with what was being stressed by those who argued for the distinctive character of the social sciences and humanities. Popper, though, was happy to extend the method of sympathetic understanding to the natural sciences, too.

The problem that I have stressed, in interpreting the influence of Popper, comes about just because Popper's own version of methodological individualism, situational analysis, and the rationality principle, in which claims about intuitive understanding need to be independently assessed, looks very much like Weberian analysis (but also, seen in another way, like rational choice theory). It seems to me that unless people are concerned with the specifically philosophical aspects of Popper's analysis, it will not be obvious by which account they will have been influenced. While the use that is made of Popper in connection with testability is often not differentiated from similar points made in the work of logical empiricists. In addition, it is worth noting that in Weber's critical analysis of the (older) historical school of economics (Weber 1976), he was taking issue with an important exemplar of what Popper was to criticize as 'historicism'. A Weberian view of history (or one influenced by Rickert, more generally), would be at odds with all 'historicist' tendencies—although Popper had some worries about Weber's 'ideal types'.[6] All told, as Hacohen brings out (Hacohen 2000, 476), Popper did not appreciate just how close he and Weber were.

## 4 Some Sociological Issues

Popper had felt very isolated in New Zealand, and was delighted when Hayek assisted him to obtain an academic position at the London School of Economics. However, Hayek was himself to leave the LSE a few years after Popper arrived. Popper was also a somewhat isolated figure in British philosophy. While his *Open Society* had been received well, he came to Britain at a point when the influence of the later Wittgenstein was on the rise, and British 'linguistic philosophy' was influential. Popper had most in common with the small group interested in the philosophy of science, and played a leading role in the formation of the British Society for the Philosophy of Science.

At the LSE, Popper was particularly concerned with the philosophy of natural science. He was gradually joined by John O. Wisdom, John Watkins, William Bartley, and subsequently Imre Lakatos (while Ernest Gellner held a position in the Department of Sociology). This meant that while there was a lively group of people sympathetic to Popper's concerns, and undergraduate teaching was offered over quite a range of philosophical topics, and there was a regular research seminar, there was not, initially, a department as such, and undergraduates were able to study philosophy only as part of the B.Sc. (Econ.) degree (although a degree in economics and philosophy was subsequently introduced). Popper had a number of graduate students; but Popper's position in British philosophy (and the fact that the discipline was dominated by Oxford and Cambridge), meant that both he and his students were marginalized.

Popper had written—in *The Poverty of Historicism* and *The Open Society*—about issues in the philosophy of social science. But after he arrived at the LSE, he did little further work in this field. (His main subsequent pieces were, first, a re-statement of his views in a symposium with Adorno at the German Sociological Association in 1961 [Popper 1976b contained a revised version of his piece; Popper 1992, ch. 5 restored a text closer to the original German], which in a sense started off a rather unproductive exchange which became known as the 'Positivismusstreit'. Second, there was a refinement and development of his views—with discussion about the role of models—in his "Models, Instruments and Truth" [Popper 1994, ch. 4]. There was also an interview and a paper relating to his ideas about the philosophy of history. [See Popper 1994, ch. 7; 2008, ch. 21.])

During the 1950s, there was discussion of Popper's work at the LSE (de Marchi 1988)[7] and elsewhere, and there was extensive discussion in print of his ideas about 'Methodological Individualism' (e.g. O'Neill 1973). But Popper himself was not involved in this. A key role was played, rather, by his colleague John W. N. Watkins, and by Popper's graduate students (and also assistants), Joseph Agassi and Ian Jarvie. In addition, while on many substantive issues their views differed, Ernest Gellner, who held a position in the Department of Sociology, championed a broadly Popperian approach to the social sciences.[8] However, with the exception of Jarvie, who worked in anthropology, neither Popper nor his graduate students were themselves involved closely in the social sciences.

There is not, on the present occasion, space for me to engage in detailed analysis and critical assessment of Popper's philosophy of social science. For this I am happy to refer the reader to work by Ian Jarvie (2016), Noretta Koertge (1975), Bruce Caldwell (1991) and William Gorton (2006).

I would, however, make one comment about it. In the field of the natural sciences Popper, in addition to developing his own detailed philosophical and methodological ideas, was deeply engaged with substantive discussion about science and its history. Those studying philosophy as undergraduates were required to undertake a course in the history of (natural) science; while at an MA level, we were expected to undertake primary research in the history of science as part of our training. Popper himself wrote extensively about quantum theory, the arrow of time, and also about issues to do with invariants in science. By contrast with this, we were not expected to have any particular knowledge of the history of the social sciences. There was, when I was at the LSE, a seminar in the philosophy of social science; but it was somewhat jejune and formulaic, and, above all, disconnected from the history of, and from current theoretical disputes in, the social sciences. (Ian Jarvie—who had left the LSE Philosophy Department long before I arrived—was one glorious exception to this; Spiro Latsis worked on detailed issues in the methodology of economics, but his approach was Lakatosian rather than Popperian [Latsis 1972]; see also Shearmur 1991.) In addition, the *kind* of engagement with contemporary issues which had fired Popper's own work had become less pressing. For the interpretation of Marxism with which he engaged itself disappeared in the late 1960s and 1970s. It is striking that, in some reflections on the occasion of Popper's death in *Radical Philosophy*, the then-editor of *New Left Review*, a leading Marxist intellectual journal, *welcomed* Popper's critique of the older-style Marxism to which they were also opposed (Blackburn 1995).

## 5 Conclusion

Popper's work relating to the social sciences is interesting and deserves more attention than it has attracted to date, as does the issue of his influence and the debates about his work. Of the greatest value, in my judgment, is his more general epistemological approach. Here, a key role could, I think, be played in part by his emphasis on the importance of the critical assessment of our theories (and on the need for tests which all involved in the field, not just a theory's supporters, think would be worthwhile). In addition, a key role could and should be played by his ideas about 'metaphysical research programs'. These offer an alternative to a Kuhnian perspective, but, as opposed to Kuhn, stress the importance of ongoing critical dialogue about metaphysical and methodological issues between those who favor different approaches, as well as the importance of a degree of self-awareness about what plays a key role in one's approach—and thus of the significance to one's program of breaking with such assumptions.

Popper's more specific ideas on the philosophy of social science seem to me of less importance. This is not to say that, for example, there is not a lot of historicism around today which deserves to be combated. (In addition, it would be worth people appreciating that the alternative to Marxism is not a choice between postmodernism or rational choice theory.) But because of the relatively impoverished view of the scope of what was open to reason which Popper had when he wrote *The Open Society* and *The Poverty of Historicism*, it seems to me that his account was less expansive than it could have been. It was also, in my view, a shame that he was not able to engage more substantively with the ideas of the older Frankfurt School. For a key problem about their work was the role played by what looked like a ghost of a Hegelian view of 'Reason'. Just what its character and status were, and the grounds that we had to take it seriously, cried out for a Popperian approach. Popper was in no position to undertake such work himself, and his position at the LSE meant that he had relatively few graduate students who were able to undertake this kind of work.

In my view, the most important thing that a 'Popperian' approach could contribute would not be to stress the respects in which it is akin to rational choice theory. It would, rather, be critical engagement with substantive issues in the theoretical and empirical social sciences. For, as Popper's own work in the philosophy of natural science made clear, a 'critical rationalist' approach repudiates the idea that philosophy's concerns should be 'second order' or simply technical. In this context, Ian Jarvie's *The Revolution in Anthropology* (Jarvie 1964) was particularly important as indicating the *kind* of work which might be undertaken.[9] It was interesting that some of those reviewing his book called for further work to be undertaken exploring his approach. It would seem to me a shame that his work in this field did not lead to a flourishing critical Popperian school of critical reflection on the social sciences. Perhaps it is not too late.

## Notes

1 There has also been an important influence on writers on the methodology of economics, such as Marc Blaug, Lawrence Boland, Bruce Caldwell, and Wade Hands, but I cannot discuss their interesting work here, for reasons of space.
2 See Colin Simkin, "The Birth of *The Open Society*," Appendix 1 to his 1993, 185.
3 The material that was cut is reproduced in Shearmur 1998.
4 Popper's anti-psychologism, however, does not derive from Weber: Popper's approach was systematically anti-psychologistic, after he made his own shift from psychology to philosophy.
5 The resemblances, however, are closer in Weber's methodological writings than they are in some of Weber's actual sociology. Compare Beetham 1985.
6 See Popper 1945, ch. 11, n. 44 and also Watkins 1952.
7 From what Richard Lipsey has written, it would seem as if LSE economists' interest in Popper was as an alternative to Lionel Robbins's account of the methodology of economics: Lipsey 1997, ix.
8 I would like to thank Joseph Agassi for a conversation about this in September 2015, and Ian Jarvie for some important criticisms and for stressing to me the importance of Michael Banton as a sociologist influenced by Popper (compare Barnton 2015).
9 See also Jarvie and Agassi's work on the issue of the rationality of magic, e.g. the papers in Agassi and Jarvie 1987.

## References

Agassi, J. and I. Jarvie (eds.) (1987) *Rationality: The Critical View*. Dordrecht, etc: Nijhoff.
Barnton, M. (2015) "John Rex's Main Mistake," *Ethnic and Racial Studies*, 38, 8, 1369–381.
Bartley, W. (1989) *Rehearsing a Revolution*, available at: http://bartleyinstitute.org/shelf/page/3/.
Beetham, D. (1985) *Max Weber's Theory of Modern Politics*. Cambridge: Polity.
Blackburn, R. (1995) "Popper and the New Left," *Radical Philosophy* 70 (March/April), 8.
Bühler, Karl, *Die geistige Entwicklung des Kindes*, Jena: Gustav Fischer.
Caldwell, B. (1991) "Clarifying Popper," *Journal of Economic Literature*, 29, 1, 1–33.
de Marchi, N. (1988) "Popper and the L.S.E. Economists," in de Marchi (ed.), *The Popperian Legacy in Economics*. Cambridge: Cambridge University Press, 139–66.
Gorton, W. (2006) *Karl Popper and the Social Sciences*. Albany, NY: SUNY Press.
Hacohen, M. (2000) *Karl Popper: The Formative Years*. Cambridge: Cambridge University Press.
Hacohen, M. (2016) "The Young Popper, 1902–1937: History, Politics and Philosophy in Interwar Vienna," in Shearmur and Stokes, *Cambridge Companion to Popper*, 30–68.
ter Hark, M. (2004) *Popper, Otto Selz, and the Rise of Evolutionary Epistemology*. Cambridge: Cambridge University Press.
Hedström, P., R. Swedberg, and L. Udéhn (1998) "Popper's Situational Analysis and Contemporary Sociology," *Philosophy of the Social Sciences*, 28, 3, 339–64.
Jarvie, I. (1964) *The Revolution in Anthropology*. London: Routledge.
Jarvie, I. (2016) "Popper's Philosophy and the Methodology of Social Science," in Shearmur and Stokes, *Cambridge Companion to Popper*, 284–317.

Kaufmann, F. (1936) *Methodenlehre der Sozialwissenschaften*. Vienna: Springer.

Kaufmann, F. (2014) *Felix Kaufmann's Theory and Method in the Social Sciences*, ed. R. Cohen and I. Helling. Cham, etc: Springer International.

Koertge, N. (1975) "Popper's Metaphysical Research Program for the Human Sciences," *Inquiry* 18, 437–62.

Latsis, S. (1972) "Situational Determinism in Economics," *British Journal for the Philosophy of Science* 23, 3, 207–45.

Lipsey, R. (1997) *Macroeconomic Theory and Policy*. Cheltenham: Edward Elgar.

O'Neill, J. (ed.) (1973) *Modes of Individualism and Collectivism*. London: Heinemann Educational.

Popper, K. (1934) *Logik der Forschung: Zur Erkenntnistheorie der modernen Naturwissenschaft*. Vienna: Julius Springer.

Popper, K. (1944–45) "The Poverty of Historicism," *Economica*, 11, 42, 86–103; 11, 43, 119–37; 12, 46, 69–89.

Popper, K. (1945) *The Open Society and its Enemies*. London: Routledge and Kegan Paul.

Popper, K. (1957) *The Poverty of Historicism*. London: Routledge and Kegan Paul.

Popper, K. (1959) *The Logic of Scientific Discovery*. London: Hutchinson.

Popper, K. (1963) *Conjectures and Refutations*. London: Routledge and Kegan Paul.

Popper, K. (1972) *Objective Knowledge*. Oxford: Clarendon Press.

Popper, K. (1974) *The Philosophy of Karl Popper*, ed. P. A. Schilpp. La Salle, IL: Open Court.

Popper, K. (1976a) *Unended Quest*. London: Fontana.

Popper, K. (1976b) "The Logic of the Social Sciences," in T. Adorno et al., *The Positivist Dispute in German Sociology*. London: Heinemann Educational, 87–104.

Popper, K. (1979 [1930–33]) *Die beiden Grundprobleme der Erkenntnistheorie*, ed. Troels Eggers Hansen. Tübingen: Mohr.

Popper, K. (1982–83) *Postscript to The Logic of Scientific Discovery*, ed. W. W. Bartley (1982: *The Open Universe*. London: Hutchinson; 1982: *Quantum Theory and the Schism in Physics*. London: Hutchinson; 1983: *Realism and the Aim of Science*. London: Hutchinson).

Popper, K. (1992) *In Search of a Better World*. London: Routledge.

Popper, K. (1994) *The Myth of the Framework*, ed. M. Notturno. London: Routledge.

Popper, K. (2008) *After the Open Society*, ed. J. Shearmur and P. Turner. London: Routledge.

Popper, K. (2009) *The Two Fundamental Problems of the Theory of Knowledge*, ed. T. Hansen. London: Routledge.

Schaffer, F. (2006) "Vorgartenstrasse 203: Extracts from a Memoir," in Kenneth McRobbie and Karl Polanyi Levitt (eds.), *Karl Polanyi in Vienna*, 2nd edn. Montreal, etc.: Black Rose, 328–46.

Shearmur, J. (1991) "Popper, Lakatos and Theoretical Progress in Economics," in *Appraising Modern Economics. Studies in the Methodology of Scientific Research Programmes*, ed. M. Blaug and N. de Marchi. Cheltenham: Edward Elgar, 35–52.

Shearmur, J. (1998) "Popper, Hayek and the Poverty of Historicism Part I," *Philosophy of the Social Sciences*, 28, 3, 434–50.

Shearmur, J. and G. Stokes (eds.) (2016) *The Cambridge Companion to Popper*. Cambridge: Cambridge University Press.

Simkin, C. (1993) *Popper's Views on Natural and Social Science*. Leiden, etc: Brill.

Watkins, J. (1952) "Ideal Types and Historical Explanation," *British Journal for the Philosophy of Science* 3, 9, 22–43.

Weber, M. (1949) *The Methodology of the Social Sciences*, trans. E. Shils and H. Finch. Glencoe, IL: Free Press.

Weber, M. (1976) *Roscher and Knies: The Logical Problems of Historical Economics*, trans. G. Oakes. New York: Free Press.

# 6
# KUHN'S INFLUENCE ON THE SOCIAL SCIENCES

## *K. Brad Wray*

Perhaps no philosopher has had a greater influence on the social sciences than Thomas Kuhn. This is ironic because in *Structure of Scientific Revolutions* Kuhn set out to develop an understanding of the nature of scientific knowledge and scientific inquiry in the natural sciences. He did not discuss the social sciences at all, except to note in the Preface that it was while working at the Center for Advanced Studies in the Behavioral Sciences surrounded by social scientists that he hit upon the "paradigm concept," noting that paradigms are largely absent in the social sciences (see Kuhn 2012, xlii). But with its many suggestive metaphors *Structure* resonated with social scientists, providing exciting insights into their own fields of study.

On the one hand, Kuhn's influence on the social sciences has been quite pronounced. In some social sciences *Structure* is on Ph.D. reading lists (see Walker 2010, 434), and much of the language Kuhn used to characterize the epistemic culture of the natural sciences has been adopted and applied widely by social scientists to their disciplines. On the other hand, the influence that Kuhn's work has had on the social sciences has sometimes been rather unfruitful, even pernicious at times. And many of the adaptations of Kuhn's views are based on misunderstandings of his views.

## Kuhn's *Structure*

Kuhn's influence on the social sciences is due, almost exclusively, to the publication of *Structure of Scientific Revolutions* (see Kuhn 1962/2012). Both Kuhn's earlier historical work, including *The Copernican Revolution*, and his later work, including the essays in *The Road since Structure*, have had a negligible impact on the social sciences. Because of the influence of *Structure* on the social sciences, it is worth briefly outlining the main themes in the book, highlighting those that caught the interest of social scientists.

*Structure* presents a theory of scientific knowledge and inquiry. The view it presents is meant to be contrasted with a popular positivist view of science. The positivists were alleged to maintain that the growth of scientific knowledge is cumulative, without interruptions or setbacks of any significance. Scientists are guided by a method that, in conjunction with careful attention to data, ensures that when they are confronted by a choice between competing theories they can unequivocally determine which theory is the superior theory, that is, which theory is closest to the truth. Kuhn's account of science is a reaction to this particular view. Whether or not anyone actually held this view is beside the point.

Kuhn notes that during his training as a physicist he uncritically accepted this positivist view of science. But when he looked at the history of science he saw things quite differently. Contrary to what the positivists suggest, the growth of science is not a continuous march closer and closer to the truth. Instead, periods of rapid growth are interrupted by revolutionary changes of theory. These revolutionary changes of theory are disruptive, and often lead to a loss of knowledge in some areas. Further, Kuhn did not believe that there was anything like a scientific method that could unequivocally resolve disputes between proponents of competing theories. Instead, looking at the historical record, Kuhn came to believe that scientists were rather dogmatic, uncritically accepting the theory they were taught. This observation, though, was not meant as a criticism of science. Rather, Kuhn believed that the dogmatism that characterizes science explains scientists' success in accomplishing their research goals. By uncritically accepting the theory they were taught, scientists have the determination to make nature fit the conceptual boxes or categories that the accepted theory provides. The constraints supplied by the accepted theory provide scientists with the focus to resolve challenging research problems, to solve the puzzles of "normal science." Only in times of crises, when persistent anomalies begin to turn up in a scientific field, do scientists begin to consider alternative theories. And such innovations are often initially met with considerable resistance.

Kuhn also claims that scientists working in the same scientific field do not necessarily share a common understanding of the accepted theory, nor are they bound together by a set of explicit methodological rules. Rather, according to Kuhn, more fundamental are the paradigms, or exemplars, accepted in a field. Exemplars are widely accepted solutions to research problems, solutions that provide insight into solving related research problems. These exemplars play a crucial role in the socialization of young scientists-in-training. Laboratory exercises are designed to force students to learn to apply exemplary solutions to other related scientific problems. In fact, Kuhn believes that scientists learn the key concepts of their field by solving problems in the laboratory, not through a close study of a theory. For example, it is in modeling a solution to a problem in a physics lab that a student learns the concepts of mass, velocity, momentum, and the like.

Kuhn describes competing theories as providing scientists with incommensurable world views. Because of the incommensurability of competing paradigms or theories a change of theory in a field can be quite complicated. Scientists working with competing theories may not fully understand each other. Nor are they apt to agree about which scientific problems in their field are most significant. Thus, incommensurability can pose a significant challenge to theory change. At times incommensurability can even *seem* to threaten the rationality of theory change.

## Initial Reactions to *Structure*: Some Archival Evidence

Right from the beginning *Structure* attracted the attention of social scientists. This was somewhat unexpected as Kuhn was only professing to be providing an account of scientific change for the *natural sciences* (see Kuhn 2000, 307). Most of the historical examples in *Structure* are drawn from physics, chemistry, and astronomy. None are drawn from the social sciences. Still *Structure* resonated with social scientists from a variety of disciplines.

The Thomas S. Kuhn Archives at the Massachusetts Institute of Technology (MIT) contain a vast store of letters that Kuhn received following the publication of *Structure*. Many are fan mail, expressing enthusiasm for the book, and a significant number were from social scientists. Two economists who would later be honored with Sveriges Riksbank Prizes in Economic Sciences in Memory of Alfred Nobel, the so-called "Nobel Prizes in Economics," were among those who contacted Kuhn about *Structure* and its implications for their field, namely, Wassily Leontief and George Stigler. On the one hand, Stigler describes *Structure* as "a splendid book" and compliments Kuhn for arousing him "from his customary lethargy" (see Stigler, March 14, 1963, in Box 4: Folder 15, *Structure of Scientific Revolutions*, Correspondence S, Thomas S. Kuhn Archives). On the other hand, Stigler questions the extent to which Kuhn's theory of science describes economics. Specifically, Stigler questions whether Kuhn's view of scientific revolutions matches what occurred with "the marginal utility revolution of the 1870s, [and] the Richardian revolution" in economics (see Stigler in Box 4: Folder 15, *Structure of Scientific Revolutions*, Correspondence S, Thomas S. Kuhn Archives). Leontief was left with a different impression after reading *Structure*. He claims that "what [Kuhn] said about the Natural Sciences certainly applies to Economics too" (see Leontief, February 24, 1964, in Box 4: Folder 11, *Structure of Scientific Revolutions*, Correspondence K–L, Thomas S. Kuhn Archives). Significantly, Leontief recognizes that Kuhn's book is about the natural sciences.

Kuhn's reply to Stigler is noteworthy. Kuhn claims that though he knows "nothing about economics" he has "long been one of [Stigler's] distant admirers" (see Kuhn 1963, in Box 4: Folder 15, *Structure of Scientific Revolutions*, Correspondence S, Thomas S. Kuhn Archives). Consequently, Stigler's "letter meant a great deal to [Kuhn]" (see Kuhn 1963, in Box 4: Folder 15, *Structure of Scientific Revolutions*, Correspondence S, Thomas S. Kuhn Archives). But Kuhn suggests that the alleged counter-examples Stigler cites from economics do not differ from the examples of theory change that Kuhn is more familiar with in physics. He suggests to Stigler that his alleged counter-examples may in fact qualify as scientific revolutions, provided the changes "demanded some reconstruction of the older theory" because the "proposed innovations were incompatible with parts of the [accepted theories]" (see Kuhn 1963, in Box 4: Folder 15, *Structure of Scientific Revolutions*, Correspondence S, Thomas S. Kuhn Archives).

## The Scientific Status of the Social Sciences

Many social scientists did exactly what Stigler and Leontief did, reflect on whether Kuhn's theory of scientific knowledge and scientific inquiry were relevant to their own discipline. Indeed, there is a substantial body of scholarly literature by social scientists seeking to determine how well Kuhn's theory of science fits their discipline.

Eckberg and Hill (1979) suggest that Kuhn's *Structure* fueled a long-standing preoccupation of sociologists to reflect on the scientific status of sociology and the social sciences in general (see Eckberg and Hill 1979, 933). On the one hand, sociologists tend to compare the social sciences to the natural sciences and regard any differences between the two as indicating that the social sciences are falling short and are not fully scientific (see Eckberg and Hill 1979, 934). On the other hand, given Kuhn's description of the natural sciences, sociologists began to think that the social sciences have as much of a claim to being scientific as do the natural sciences (see Eckberg and Hill 1979, 934). That is, given the apparent sordid side of research practices that

Kuhn describes in the natural sciences, some social scientists were less self-conscious about what they had taken to be failings in their own fields.

Political scientists were also inspired to reflect on their discipline. In his Presidential Address to the American Political Science Association (APSA), David Truman (1965) raised doubts about whether political science ever had a paradigm. Rightly, Truman notes that "a crucial feature of a true paradigm is its precision ... precision in the paradigm permits the investigator to know when something is wrong" (Truman 1965, 866). Political science, though, lacked precise theories and paradigms. Truman notes that until recently individual textbooks in political science often even lacked consistency in the way they employed theories and background assumptions between chapters (see Truman 1965, 870). A year later, in his Presidential Address to the APSA, Gabriel Almond (1966) argued that political science did have a paradigm, but his description of the discipline leaves one wondering what it is. Both Truman and Almond seem to assume that ideally all political scientists will be united by a single paradigm. Both seem to regard paradigms that are unique to sub-specialties within political science as divisive and fractious. This, though, was not Kuhn's view.

Jerone Stephens notes that some political scientists even thought that a paradigm could be imposed on a research community (see Stephens 1973, 482–83, and Walker 2010, 440). In this way, a field like political science could be set on a clear path to being a science. Stephens, though, rightly notes that this was not Kuhn's view, nor is it a practical means for a field to become scientific (see Stephens 1973, 483).

## Social Scientific Paradigms: Their Ubiquity and their Relevance

There has been a lot of confusion about what Kuhn meant by the term "paradigm." Margaret Masterman famously counted twenty-one different uses of the term in *Structure* (see Masterman 1970). It took Kuhn some time to determine what exactly he meant by "paradigm." Until around 1970, Kuhn used the term "paradigm" to refer to a variety of different things: (1) sometimes "paradigm" meant theory, as in the Copernican paradigm; (2) sometimes "paradigm" meant disciplinary matrix, that is, the combination of theory, goals, and standards, as in the reigning paradigm in 18th-century physics; and (3) sometimes "paradigm" meant exemplar, as in Kepler's mathematical model of the orbit of Mars (see Wray 2011, ch. 3). It is the latter meaning that Kuhn ultimately settled on.

Despite this ambiguity, or perhaps because of it, the term "paradigm" is now thoroughly integrated into the vocabulary of scientists, both natural and social. Recently, Shiping Tang (2011) has argued that there are "only 11 foundational paradigms in [the] social sciences" (see Tang 2011, 211). Whether or not Tang's claim would stand up to the critical scrutiny of social scientists across the disciplines need not be settled here. The point is that social scientists are now quite comfortable thinking in terms of the paradigms of their disciplines. In this respect, Kuhn has had a wide-ranging, though perhaps shallow, impact on the social sciences.

Social scientists are divided on what the correct level of analysis is with respect to finding paradigms in the social sciences. Many sociologists identify what they take to be paradigms of the whole discipline, such as functionalism, or conflict theory, theoretical orientations that are used by many sociologists working on different research topics (see Eckberg and Hill 1979, 935). But Eckberg and Hill (1979) claim that this is a mistake. Nothing worth calling a paradigm, they claim, cuts across the whole discipline of sociology. Instead, they believe sociologists should be looking for paradigms specific to much smaller research areas. Thus, we should expect to find paradigms specific to research on the sociology of age and aging, or research on the sociology of political movements.

For example, in the 1980s and 1990s sociologists concerned with the study of political stability and instability discussed the new "elite paradigm" (see Field and Higley 1980, and Cammack 1990). The level of analysis in this case is a very specific research topic, political stability and instability, and the elite paradigm is presented as an alternative to existing paradigms in the sub-field. Similarly, Baltes and Nesselroade (1984) discuss the paradigms operative in the sub-field of life-span developmental psychology, an interdisciplinary field that cuts across sociology and psychology. They note that sociologists and psychologists researching in this area may need different paradigms, as psychologists tend to be more concerned with the biological basis of life-span development than sociologists, who are principally concerned with the social dimensions of life-span development. The level of specificity in these examples is closer to the sort of thing that Kuhn had in mind when he equated paradigms with exemplars.

George Ritzer (1981) offers an alternative perspective. He does not think that sociologists should follow Kuhn slavishly. Instead, he claims that sociologists should refashion the "paradigm" concept to fit the needs of the discipline. Ritzer claims that the notion of a paradigm as an exemplar offers little insight into sociology. Instead, he thinks the notion of a paradigm as a disciplinary matrix is more relevant to sociology (see Ritzer 1981, 245).

Incidentally, textbooks in sociology have also adopted the language of paradigms. John Macionis's *Sociology* presents students with the "three major theoretical paradigms" (see Macionis 1997, 16–22). These are (1) the Structural-Functional Paradigm associated with Emile Durkheim, (2) the Social-Conflict Paradigm associated with Karl Marx, and (3) the Symbolic-Interaction Paradigm associated with Max Weber. Aside from mentioning Kuhn's name when the term "paradigm" is first introduced, there is no mention of the specifics of Kuhn's view.[1]

Indeed, it is now quite common for Kuhn not to be cited when sociologists discuss paradigms (see, for example, Cammack 1990, and Field and Hilberg 1980). This is what Robert K. Merton meant by "obliteration by incorporation" (see Merton 1988, 621). Sociologists no longer seem to think it is necessary to alert readers to Kuhn's earlier analysis of the notion of a paradigm. The concept is fully integrated into the research literature.

Economists, too, have raised questions about whether the paradigm or theory is the appropriate unit of analysis for understanding changes in their field. Axel Leijonhufvud (1976), for example, claims that "the 'doctrines' and 'schools' of economics are not all animals of the same species as ... Ptolemaic and Copernican astronomy or the Phlogiston and Oxygene [*sic*] theories of combustion; nor ... do they very often succeed each other in such clear-cut fashion" (Leijonhufvud 1976, 68). Leijonhufvud claims that often "in economics ... several analytical traditions [survive] side-by-side" (75). Thus, as far as he is concerned, in economics there is no reigning paradigm as Kuhn suggests there is in the natural sciences. Instead, paradigms or "analytical traditions" are more like tools in a toolbox that can be used separately or together, as the task at hand demands.

Alternatively, A. W. Coats (1969) suggests that "economics may ... [have] been dominated throughout its history by a single paradigm—the theory of economic equilibrium via the market mechanism" (Coats 1969, 292).

Political scientists also embraced the notion of paradigms. As noted above, in both 1965 and 1966 the presidents of the APSA drew on Kuhn's *Structure* for insight into the nature of their discipline in their presidential addresses (see Stephens 1973, 476–78). Stephens (1973) provides a comprehensive overview of the scholarly literature in political science that sought to draw insight from Kuhn's *Structure*. Stephens argued that the "paradigm" concept added nothing new to analyses in political science (Stephens 1973, 467). The way political scientists use the term "paradigm," Stephens explains, is more or less equivalent to the way they use the term "theory." Consequently, the paradigm concept sheds no new light on debates in political science about the discipline, its internal dynamics, or its research practices. Indeed, Stephens even doubts whether Kuhn provides an accurate account of the natural sciences (see Stephens 1973, 467).

Stephens also argues that there are important differences in how political scientists and natural scientists are trained. Whereas in the natural sciences there is a single relatively uniform curriculum taught in a field at any given time, as Kuhn notes, Stephens argues that students in political science are presented with the views of competing schools. In fact, "diverse points within schools are presented to students as legitimate ways of studying politics, and they are introduced to this inter- and intra-school diversity through readings of original research reports" (see Stephens 1973, 483). So there is no consensus about the single best theory or theoretical framework in political science, unlike what Kuhn describes in the natural sciences.

In a 2010 survey article intended to halt appeals to Kuhn and paradigms, Thomas Walker argues that the "paradigm mentality based on normal science and incommensurability has been widely employed, if not internalized, by political scientists" (Walker 2010, 436). But, as Walker rightly notes, the notion of paradigm employed by political scientists is "drawn only loosely from Kuhn's work" (433). Walker argues that appeals by political scientists to Kuhn have been unfruitful, and the discipline would be better served by drawing on Karl Popper's work (see Walker 2010, 434). Popper, after all, explicitly wrote on the social sciences, whereas Kuhn was concerned narrowly with the natural sciences. Contrary to what Walker seems to imply, Popper had a rather negative view about the social sciences (see Popper 1970, 58).

Walker raises two types of concerns with the way Kuhn's work has been used by political scientists, and scholars in international relations in particular. First, he does not think that a single theory or paradigm dominates in this research sub-field in political science. Second he believes that if political scientists tried to emulate natural scientists, as described by Kuhn, it would lead to the suppression of alternative theories and hypotheses (see Walker 2010, 434). Guided by Kuhn, Walker believes that political scientists will be led to "engage in hostile zero-sum turf wars" in their efforts to ensure that their own paradigm is not displaced by an alternative paradigm (ibid.). Walker argues that the "misappropriation of [Kuhn's model] of science … encourages hyper-specialized tribalism within subfields and furthers the Balkanization of political science as a discipline" (ibid.).[2]

A number of issues arise out of social scientists' analyses of the paradigm concept. The following questions are still worth reflecting on:

- How many paradigms are there in a social scientific field or specialty at any one time?
- Can competing and incompatible paradigms be used in a social scientific field, and if so, what does it say about the social sciences?
- What is the relevant social group in the social sciences that shares a paradigm?

## The Place of Revolutionary Changes of Theory in the Social Sciences

There is another question that has occupied social scientists since the publication of Kuhn's *Structure*: Are there revolutionary changes of theory in the social sciences as there are in the natural sciences?

Economists have had more to say on this issue than other social scientists. Coats (1969) was struck by the fact that revolutionary changes of theory of the sort that Kuhn describes in *Structure* are not at all common in economics. On the one hand, Coats claims that "the most striking example of paradigm-change in economics, the Keynesian revolution of the 1930's [*sic*], possessed many of the characteristics associated with Kuhn's 'scientific revolutions'" (Coats 1969, 293). On the other hand, he argues that "it is now clear that the Keynesian paradigm was not 'incompatible' with its predecessor" (ibid.). Coats suggests that there is a reason for this difference between economics and the natural sciences. He suggests that "economic theories … are usually less rigid and compelling than their natural science equivalents" (ibid.). Consequently, he believes that we should not be surprised to discover that "the structure of scientific revolutions is much less discernible in economics than in the natural sciences" (ibid.).

Coats also notes that the practice of "normal science" is different in the social sciences than in the natural sciences. According to Coats,

> economists … have enjoyed considerable success in two phases of the 'normal' scientific activity of actualizing the promise inherent in their paradigm, i.e. extending knowledge of 'relevant' facts, and improving the 'articulation' of the paradigm itself. However, their efforts to improve the match between the facts and the paradigm's predictions have met with only limited success.
>
> (Coats 1969, 292)

Prediction seems to play a less significant role in the social sciences, Coats suggests. Coats's assessment is a bit misleading. Social scientific theories enable social scientists to predict *patterns*, even if they do not enable them to make precise predictions of singular events (see Hayek 1964, 344–45). This may be a consequence of the nature of the objects studied, rather than an indication that social scientific theories are deficient in some way.

Mark Blaug (1976) also argues that disruptive revolutionary changes have had little or no role in economics. He argues that Imre Lakatos's theory of scientific change provides a more accurate description of key changes in economic theory. In all fairness to Kuhn, Blaug attributes views to him that he does not accept. For example, Blaug emphasizes the inability to communicate across theoretical lines, suggesting that incommensurability undermines the possibility for a *rational evaluation* of competing theories. Blaug also claims Kuhn believes that external factors like personal influence determine which theory is ultimately accepted. This is a caricature of Kuhn's view. Incommensurability, as far as Kuhn is concerned, is an impediment to effective communication across theoretical lines, and it makes it challenging to compare competing theories. But Kuhn believed that the problem of theory choice is ultimately resolved on the basis of epistemic factors. Kuhn is thus an internalist (see Wray 2011, ch. 9).[3]

Anthropologists have also focused on the issue of whether or not there are revolutions in their discipline. Archaeologists in particular have debated whether or not a scientific revolution occurred in their discipline in the 1960s. Paul Martin, for example, argues that there was a revolution. Until the early 1960s American archaeologists had aligned themselves and their discipline with history, and were concerned primarily with cataloguing and classifying artifacts. By the 1960s, Martin claims, a new paradigm was emerging (Martin 1971, 3). Archaeologists now identified themselves with anthropologists, and thus identified themselves with social scientists. Working within the new paradigm, they now consciously set out to develop a general theory of cultural change (see Martin 1971, 1–2). Like other scientists, they aimed "to establish general laws covering the behavior of the observed events or objects" (5).

By the end of the 1970s, some archaeologists and anthropologists were becoming disenchanted with attempts to understand their discipline through a Kuhnian framework. David Meltzer (1979), for example, took issue with the uncritical and reckless application of Kuhn's framework (Meltzer 1979, 644; also 649). Further, he insisted that there was little evidence to support the popular claim that there was a revolution in archaeology in the 1960s. Metzer grants that there were significant *methodological* changes introduced into the discipline. But he rightly notes that methodological changes do not constitute a revolution in Kuhn's sense (see Meltzer 1979, 653). Revolutions essentially involve a change of theory.

There is one noteworthy feature of the discussion of Kuhn's views in archaeology. The debate took place in a national context, specifically in *American* archaeology (see both Martin 1971 and Meltzer 1979). This seems to be one respect in which the social sciences do differ from the natural sciences. Theoretical orientations are not tied to different nations in the natural sciences. That is not to say that the training and practices of the natural sciences do not differ from country to country. But the same theories are accepted in different nations in the natural sciences. Social scientists, though, are generally more concerned with issues of national concern, which may in fact lead to the acceptance of different theories in different nations in the social sciences (see, for example, Akers 1992).

## The Elephant in the Room: The Sociology of Scientific Knowledge (SSK)

Sociology of science is the specific sub-field in the social sciences in which Kuhn has had the greatest influence. Indeed, Barry Barnes's book *Kuhn and Social Science* is almost exclusively concerned with Kuhn's influence on the sociology of science (see Barnes 1982, ix).

Barnes reads Kuhn's *Structure* as offering a sociological account of science. To a large extent this is correct (see Wray 2011 and Wray 2015). Much of what Kuhn says in *Structure* is about the social structure of scientific research communities, the units that create scientific knowledge and validate knowledge claims. He describes the various social changes that a research community undergoes in its efforts to address the challenges encountered in the course of pursuing its research goals. Kuhn also draws attention to the important role that socialization plays in scientific training, including the processes by which scientists-in-training learn to perceive, which essentially involves learning to attend to the relevant similarities and differences in the phenomena. Importantly, the notion of "relevant similarities" is relative to a theory or conceptual scheme. Barnes rightly notes that Kuhn made valuable contributions to our understanding of science in these areas even if he failed to provide empirical support for some of his claims.

But Kuhn was dismayed at the direction sociology of science developed, especially with the emergence of the Strong Programme of Sociology of Scientific Knowledge (see Kuhn 1977, xxi; and 2000, 316–17). The Strong Programme, largely based in Britain, developed in response to Kuhn's *Structure*, and in reaction to Merton's approach to the sociology of science. Merton and his students worked within a functionalist framework, and often conducted quantitative studies of science. The Strong Programme, on the other hand, conducted qualitative studies, including historical studies of scientific controversies and ethnographic studies of specific scientific research settings. The proponents of the Strong Programme identified themselves as Kuhnians of sorts, despite Kuhn's own misgivings.

The proponents of the Strong Programme are finitists, arguing that every act of classification is underdetermined by logic and observation (see Barnes 1982, 27–35). Finitism is an extreme form of nominalism. Barnes believes that Kuhn is a finitist, though the commitment of the proponents of the Strong Programme to finitism is not in any way dependent on Kuhn endorsing finitism (see Barnes 1982, 34–35).

Indeed, this is one of the key differences between Kuhn's own view and the view of the Strong Programme. Contrary to what is implied by finitism, Kuhn believes that once a research community is committed to a particular conceptual framework or theory, how specific things are to be classified is determined, at least for the most part (see Wray 2011, ch. 9). Normal science involves the commitment to a conceptual framework, which in turn provides clear criteria for classifying the phenomena. Those phenomena that defy straightforward classification are anomalies, on Kuhn's view. In periods of crisis, though, Kuhn believes that the criteria for classifying phenomena are relaxed and often called into question. Indeed, a scientific revolution gives rise to a new conceptual scheme that will inevitably lead scientists to classify things in new ways. Copernicus' planets are different from Ptolemy's planets. The term "planet" acquires a new intension and a new extension after the Copernican Revolution in astronomy. Whereas for Ptolemy planets were wandering stars, contrasted with the fixed stars, and the earth did not count as a planet, for Copernicus planets are satellites of the sun, and the earth clearly was a planet (see Kuhn 2000, 312).

Kuhn's chief complaint against the Strong Programme and post-*Structure* sociological studies of science in general is that they fail to explain what role nature plays in scientific disputes (see Kuhn 2000, 317). Instead, they tend to focus on "negotiation." To some extent this is not a fair assessment of the Strong Programme. Though the proponents of the Strong Programme emphasize the role of interests and negotiation in determining the outcome of scientific disputes, Barnes is quite explicit that scientists' interests include the "interest in prediction and control" (see Barnes 1982, 110).

Kuhn's own views about the sociology of science were quite similar to Merton's (see Kuhn 1977, xxi). Like Merton, Kuhn offered a functionalist account of scientific research communities and research practices.

## Kuhn and the Social Sciences: A Coda

Steve Fuller (2000) has famously argued that Kuhn's influence is due, to a large extent, to the fact that he did not fully understand what he was saying. Others read into *Structure* many interesting things that were no part of Kuhn's intentions.

But there is another side to the story that has emerged in this survey of Kuhn's influence on the social sciences, which is that Kuhn is misunderstood. Kuhn is misunderstood, to a large extent, because many people did not bother to take the time to listen to what he was saying. Caught up by his engaging writing, including his many vivid metaphors, many saw in *Structure* things that pleased them, even if they were not the sorts of things that Kuhn had intended.

## Acknowledgements

I thank Lee McIntyre and Lori Nash for constructive feedback on an earlier draft. I also thank David Andrews for his feedback and especially for assistance in navigating through the literature on economics. I thank the staff at the Institute Archives and Special Collections at the

Massachusetts Institute of Technology Libraries, especially Nora Murphy. I thank MIT for grant-ing me permission to access the material in the Thomas S. Kuhn Archives. Finally, I thank the State University of New York, Oswego, for supporting two trips to the Archives at MIT.

## Notes

1 Sharer and Ashmore (2003) provide a brief discussion of Kuhn's view and the role of paradigms in archaeology, in their textbook *Archaeology: Discovering our Past*. They define a paradigm as "an overall strategy with its unique research methods, theory, and goals" (see Sharer and Ashmore 2003, 109), and suggest that the field of prehistoric archaeology "consists of three research traditions, each of which has evolved under different circumstances, defining its own problems for investigation and the set of data it considers relevant to such problems" (109–10).
2 Specialization came to play an important role in Kuhn's later philosophy. Crises are sometimes resolved not only by revolutionary changes of theory, but also by the creation of new scientific specialties (see Wray 2011, ch. 7).
3 Coats was writing in the late 1960s, and Blaug was writing in the mid-1970s. This was before the rise of behavioral economics. One could debate whether behavioral economics constitutes a revolution-ary change of theory or not. On the one hand, Herbert Simon saw his work, which replaced the ideal rational agent with "a restricted rational agent," as overturning the accepted theory of mainstream eco-nomics (see Sent 2004, § 2 and p. 754). On the other hand, Daniel Kahneman's work on bounded rationality is seen as a refinement of, and thus continuous with, the neoclassical approach to economics (see Sent 2004, 749; see also Kahneman 2003).

## References

Akers, R. L. (1992) "Linking Sociology and Its Specialties: The Case of Criminology," *Social Forces*, 71: 1, 1–16.
Almond, G. A. (1966) "Political Theory and Political Science," *American Political Science Review*, 60: 4, 869–79.
Baltes, P. B., and J. R. Nesselroade (1984) "Paradigm Lost and Paradigm Regained: Critique of Dannefer's Portrayal of Life-Span Developmental Psychology," *American Sociological Review*, 49: 6, 841–47.
Barnes, B. (1982) *T. S. Kuhn and Social Science*. New York: Columbia University Press.
Blaug, M. (1976) "Kuhn versus Lakatos, or Paradigms versus Research Programmes in the History of Economics," in S. J. Latsis (ed.), *Method and Appraisal in Economics*. Cambridge: Cambridge University Press, 149–80.
Cammack, P. (1990) "A Critical Assessment of the New Elite Paradigm," *American Sociological Review*, 55: 415–20.
Coats, A. W. (1969) "Is There a 'Structure of Scientific Revolutions' in Economics?" *Kyklos: International Zeitschrift für Sozialwissenschaften*, 22: 2, 289–96.
Eckberg, D. L., and L. Hill, Jr. (1979) "The Paradigm Concept and Sociology: A critical Review," *American Sociological Review*, 44: 925–37.
Field, G. L., and J. Higley. (1980) *Elitism*. London: Routledge and Kegan Paul.
Fuller, S. (2000) *Thomas Kuhn: A Philosophical History for Our Times*. Chicago: University of Chicago Press.
Hayek, F. (1964) "The Theory of Complex Phenomena," in M. A. Bunge (ed.), *The Critical Approach to Science and Philosophy*. Glencoe, IL: Free Press, 332–49.
Kahneman, D. (2003) "Maps of Bounded Rationality: Psychology for Behavioral Economics," *American Economic Review*, 93: 5, 1449–475.
Kuhn, T. S. (1962/2012) *Structure of Scientific Revolutions*, 4th edn. Chicago: University of Chicago Press.
Kuhn, T. S. (1963) "Letter to George Stigler," Thomas S. Kuhn Archives. MC240. Box 4: Folder 15, *Structure of Scientific Revolutions*, Correspondence S. Institute Archives and Special Collections, MIT Libraries, Cambridge, MA.

Kuhn, T. S. (1977) "Preface," in Kuhn, *Essential Tension: Selected Studies in Scientific Tradition and Change.* Chicago: University of Chicago Press, ix–xxiii.

Kuhn, T. S. (2000) "A Discussion with Thomas S. Kuhn," in Kuhn, *The Road since Structure: Philosophical Essays, 1970–1993, with an Autobiographical Interview,* ed. J. Conant and J. Haugeland. Chicago: University of Chicago Press, 255–323.

Leijonhufvud, A. (1976) "Schools, 'Revolutions,' and Research Programmes in Economic Theories," in S. J. Latsis (ed.), *Method and Appraisal in Economics.* Cambridge: Cambridge University Press, 65–108.

Leontief, W. (1964) "Letter to Thomas Kuhn," Thomas S. Kuhn Archives. MC240. Box 4: Folder 11, *Structure of Scientific Revolutions,* Correspondence K–L. Institute Archives and Special Collections, MIT Libraries, Cambridge, MA.

Macionis, J. J. (1997) *Sociology,* 6th edn. Upper Saddle River, NJ: Prentice Hall.

Martin, P. S. (1971) "The Revolution in Archaeology," *American Antiquity,* 36: 1, 1–8.

Masterman, M. (1970) "The Nature of Paradigms," in I. Lakatos and A. Musgrave (eds.), *Criticism and the Growth of Knowledge: Proceedings of the International Colloquium in the Philosophy of Science, London, 1965, vol. 4.* Cambridge: Cambridge University Press, 59–89.

Meltzer, D. J. (1979) "Paradigms and the Nature of Change in American Archaeology," *American Antiquity,* 44: 4, 644–57.

Merton, R. K. (1988) "The Matthew Effect in Science, II: Cumulative Advantage and the Symbolism of Intellectual Property," *Isis,* 79: 4, 606–23.

Popper, K. R. (1970) "Normal Science and its Dangers," in I. Lakatos and A. Musgrave (eds.), *Criticism and the Growth of Knowledge: Proceedings of the International Colloquium in the Philosophy of Science, London, 1965, vol. 4.* Cambridge: Cambridge University Press, 51–58.

Ritzer, G. (1981) "Paradigm Analysis in Sociology: Clarifying the Issues," *American Sociological Review,* 46: 2, 245–48.

Sent, E.-M. (2004) "Behavioral Economics: How Psychology Made Its (Limited) Way Back Into Economics," *History of Political Economy,* 36: 4, 735–60.

Sharer, R. J., and W. Ashmore (2003) *Archaeology: Discovering our Past,* 3rd edn. New York: McGraw-Hill.

Stephens, J. (1973) "The Kuhnian Paradigm and Political Inquiry: An Appraisal," *American Journal of Political Science,* 17: 3, 467–88.

Stigler, G. (1963) "Letter to Thomas Kuhn," Thomas S. Kuhn Archives. MC240. Box 4: Folder 15, *Structure of Scientific Revolutions,* Correspondence S. Institute Archives and Special Collections, MIT Libraries, Cambridge, MA.

Tang, S. (2011) "Foundational Paradigms of Social Sciences," *Philosophy of the Social Sciences,* 41: 2, 211–49.

Truman, D. B. (1965) "Disillusion and Regeneration: The Quest for a Discipline," *American Political Science Review,* 59: 4, 865–73.

Walker, T. C. (2010) "The Perils of Paradigm Mentalities: Revisiting Kuhn, Lakatos, and Popper," *Perspectives on Politics,* 8: 2, 433–51.

Wray, K. B. (2011) *Kuhn's Evolutionary Social Epistemology.* Cambridge: Cambridge University Press.

Wray, K. B. (2015) "Kuhn's Social Epistemology and the Sociology of Science," in William J. Devlin and Alisa Bokulich (eds.), *Kuhn's Structure of Scientific Revolutions: 50 Years On.* Boston Studies in the Philosophy of Science 311. Dordrecht: Springer Verlag, 167–84.

## Archival Sources

Thomas S. Kuhn Archives. MC240. Box 4: Folder 11, *Structure of Scientific Revolutions,* Correspondence K–L. Institute Archives and Special Collections, MIT Libraries, Cambridge, MA.

Thomas S. Kuhn Archives. MC240. Box 4: Folder 15, *Structure of Scientific Revolutions,* Correspondence S. Institute Archives and Special Collections, MIT Libraries, Cambridge, MA.

# 7

# INTERPRETIVISM AND CRITICAL THEORY

## Kenneth Baynes

## 1 Introduction

Interpretive social science (or interpretivism) and critical theory, despite important differences, converge on the view that the human or social sciences are "autonomous" and cannot be unified with or subsumed under the natural sciences. This is because the social sciences, as part of their object-domain, must take into consideration the meanings or "self-interpretations" of the social actors themselves in a way that is not true for the natural sciences. Arguments for the autonomy of the social sciences on these grounds extend back to debates in the late 19th century but they continue to surface in some of the most recent debates about the aims of social inquiry (Roth 2003).

Interpretivism as a distinct approach in the social sciences can be traced back at least to the work of Wilhelm Dilthey. In response in particular to the positivism of J. S. Mill and Auguste Comte, Dilthey argued that there was a centrally important distinction between the *Naturwissenschaften* (natural sciences) and the *Geisteswissenschaften* (human or cultural or social sciences): whereas the former searched for universal laws and causal explanations, the latter were primarily concerned with isolating the meaning of particular historical events. One of Dilthey's principal contributions to the social sciences was his claim that they depended upon a re-identification of the "lived experience" of the social actors themselves and that this precluded subsuming them under causal laws (Beiser 2011, 333). Though he is sometimes misunderstood on this point, the social theorist Max Weber agreed with Dilthey on the importance of what he called "subjective meaning" of the actors involved in circumscribing the object-domain for the social sciences. In contrast to Dilthey, however, he was more optimistic about the possibility of finding general laws and causal explanations. Rather, he insisted on the double criteria of "adequacy of meaning" and "causal adequacy" (or the confirmation of probable interpretations of meaning via generalized causal explanations) (Weber 1978, 11–12). Other interpretivists have challenged Weber's own identification of meaning with "subjective" (or psychological) states of individual actors and argued that the meaning relevant for the social sciences is public in character and located in the symbolic expressions and/or rule-governed behavior of the social actors (Winch 1958). This latter view was given further impetus by the later work of Ludwig Wittgenstein and has given rise to extensive debates about the concept of rule-following.

Critical theory also traces its origins back to the 19th century in the writings of Karl Marx and Friedrich Engels. Although the focus on social meaning differs from interpretive social science, it is no less important. Initially, Marx and Engels focused on the experience of alienation (*Entfremdung*) within the working class and for them the point of social inquiry was to criticize the failure of political economy to explain this general feature of social life at the time. Later critical theory in the work of Georg Lukács and then the "Frankfurt School" (Max Horkheimer, Theodor Adorno, Herbert Marcuse, et al.) expanded its aims to include an explanation of why an oppressed class might nonetheless fail to discern the specific causes of its own oppressed condition. In contrast to versions of Marxism that focused primarily on the economy or "material conditions" of life, the later tradition of critical theory also paid more attention to cultural and political institutions and, like interpretivism, this requires greater attention to the meanings that practices and institutions have for the participants themselves. In more recent developments in critical theory, this has also included a renewed attention to the nature of social practices and the possibilities of critique made available by them (Iser forthcoming). It is thus interesting, but not completely surprising, to find that there is a great deal of convergence in much recent work in interpretive social science and critical theory about the nature of social practices and about the "autonomy" of social science and its position relative to new accounts of naturalism (Rouse 2006).

## 2 Interpretivism

An early and extremely influential text defending interpretivism in the English-speaking world was Peter Winch, *The Idea of a Social Science and its Relation to Philosophy* (1958). Though he was also influenced by R. G. Collingwood and the German tradition of *Verstehen*, including Weber, Winch was among the first to draw out some of the implications of Wittgenstein's philosophy for the social sciences. In particular Winch challenged the dominant view of the time, which was a form of positivism according to which there are no significant differences between the natural and social sciences. Rather, the goal of all science—whether natural or social—is a model of explanation that sought to explain phenomena by bringing them under general laws—the so-called "deductive-nomological" model of explanation. According to this view, exemplified, for example, by Hempel, the objectivity of science was preserved through a strong separation between fact and values and the success of explanation was identified with successful prediction. For Winch, by contrast, this model of explanation rested on a fundamental misunderstanding of the goal of the social sciences, which is to understand the meaning of the institution and practices in question from the point of view of the participants themselves. Although this did not exclude the use of generalizations or statistical data, it did place an important constraint on them. In a sense Winch reversed the priority suggested by the positivists: whereas for Hempel participants' meaning might be a helpful (though not necessary) heuristic for the development of generalizations, they should not play any role in their confirmation (Hempel 1965, 258). Winch, by contrast, argued for exactly the opposite position: without an adequate interpretation of meaning, statistical support would add nothing to the confirmation of an interpretation (Winch 1958, 113). Nothing could support (or undermine) the adequacy of an interpretation short of another interpretation.

Although Weber had made more or less the same claim about the need for an adequate interpretation of action from the participant's perspective, he nonetheless insisted on the importance
of causal adequacy as well. Winch therefore apparently embraces a more radical position and it
is important to see why. For Winch all meaningful action is rule-governed and these rules were
in turn "constitutive" for a given "form of life." A set of rules is thus relative to a given form of
life and it follows that to understand the meaning of social action requires recovering or reconstructing the rules specific to a given form of life. This makes the social sciences importantly
different from the natural sciences: "for whereas in the case of the natural scientist we have to
deal with only one set of rules, namely those governing the scientist's investigation itself, here
what the sociologist is studying, as well as his study of it, is a human activity and is therefore carried on according to rules. And it is these rules, rather than those which govern the sociologist's
investigation which specify what is to count as 'doing the same kind of thing' in relation to that
kind of activity" (Winch 1958, 86–87). This is what Anthony Giddens would later refer to as
the "double hermeneutic" and, according to him as well, it distinguishes the social sciences from
the natural sciences. The primary task of social inquiry is to elucidate the implicit rules that are
constitutive for a given practice or form of life. At one point, Winch suggests that this makes
the task of inquiry much more like the work of philosophical inquiry (Winch 1958, 114); it is,
to borrow Brian Fay's description, a kind of "conceptual anthropology" rather than an empirical
science. What makes Winch's claim more radical than Weber's, however, is his assumption that
interpretive understanding requires relinquishing, or at least temporarily suspending, the rules
constitutive for one's own practices and immersing oneself in the practices or form of life that is
the object of inquiry. Winch's criticism of Lévy-Bruhl and other anthropologists who refuse to
make this step is that their interpretations will invariably be ethnocentric and result in a failure
of understanding.

A number of issues are at stake in Winch's claim and it is important to consider them for an
assessment of his position. First, as noted, Winch assumes that social action is rule-governed and
that, when it concerns the motives for action, these rules take the form of reasons. This leads
him to conclude that, since reasons cannot be causes, what the sociologist is looking for are not
causal generalizations but an identification of the rules that "rationalize" the agent's actions.
But here Winch's conclusion may go further than his argument permits. The claim that reasons
cannot be causes relies on a debatable claim that since the relation between a reason for action
and the action performed is "internal" or conceptual, reasons cannot properly be part of a causal
explanation of the action. However, this so-called "logical connection argument" has been decisively challenged (Davidson 1980; Rosenberg 2016). Further, even if Winch is correct that all
rational action is rule-governed, it does not seem to follow that rational interpretations that
appeal to rules obviate the need for any causal claims. Consider, for example, a case in which
there may be more than one reason either of which would be sufficient for the agent to act, or
the case of two individuals both of whom have the same reason but one acts and the other does
not. Such cases would seem to require the ability to distinguish those situations in which a given
reason is causally efficacious and one in which it was not (see MacIntyre 1971, 215f.). They
thus also suggest that reasons and causes are not mutually exclusive in the way that the logical
connection argument supposes and that in some cases identifying the actual reason will require
citing the cause of the action as well.

A second set of concerns about Winch's view are found in the so-called rationality debates
of the 1960s and the question of relativism (Wilson 1970; Hollis and Lukes 1982). Winch's
claim that understanding requires "going native" or a complete immersion in the other's form

of life, together with his assumption that the criteria of intelligibility or rationality of action are relative to a form of life, entails that no cross-cultural judgments about the rationality of action or forms of life can be made. We can say, of course, that the Azande are not being scientific (according to our criteria), but we cannot say that they are being irrational or "illogical" as such. As Alasdair MacIntyre and many others have argued, this leads to a form of relativism this is arguably not even coherent (MacIntyre 1971). Winch modified his position somewhat in a response—claiming that criteria of rationality are not closed or static—but it is not clear he adequately addressed the challenge (Winch 1970). A third set of concerns—which will be discussed further in connection with Taylor's position below—has to do with the nature of rule-following. Here it can simply be noted that Winch makes the controversial assumption that all (rational) action consists in the following of a rule or convention that either is or could be made explicit to the participants.

In a number of influential works, Charles Taylor also defends an interpretivist position in the social sciences. He has been especially critical of the extension of the natural sciences into the domain of the social sciences. In fact, it is fair to say that he considers this spread of an "absolute" or "objectivist" perspective to be an unfortunate legacy of the Enlightenment. In "Interpretation and the Science of Man" (1970), Taylor, like Winch, claims that the primary aim of the social sciences is to understand social practices from the perspective of the participants themselves and that this can come about only through a grasp of the "experiential meanings" of those actors (Taylor 1985, 23). Like Winch, he also claims that these meanings are not simply subjective psychological states; rather, they are "intersubjective meanings" which are contained in the practices themselves. Drawing on the work of Wittgenstein and John Searle concerning "constitutive rules," Taylor speaks in terms of "constitutive practices" that make the behavior in question the kind of action that it is—raising a hand, for example, counts as a vote in the context of a certain practice (Taylor 1985, 34). Understanding requires a grasp of these constitutive rules and practices, and the attempt to provide a "brute data" description—one that avoids any reliance upon a contestable interpretation—would simply amount to a failure to understand the action or practice in question (Taylor 1985, 41). For Taylor, there is simply no way to avoid the conflict of interpretations.

Nonetheless, Taylor seeks to avoid the relativism often associated with this position. He describes his own view as "evaluative realism," by which he means that there are better or worse, even correct or incorrect, interpretations where the aim is to describe accurately the desirability-characterizations the actors themselves employ (or those they would employ upon a more fully reflective formulation) (1981, 192). Accordingly, an agent's own self-description is not incorrigible and, somewhat paradoxically, though we are constituted through our self-interpretations, we can be mistaken in our own attempts to interpret ourselves or describe the reasons for our action (Baynes 2010). Moreover, for Taylor, the aim of inquiry is not a "value-free" description as the positivist hoped to achieve; rather, Taylor speaks of the development of "perspicuous contrasts" between and among different forms of life and the search for a "fusion of horizons" in which each perspective might learn something new about itself and the other (Taylor 2011, 32). However, no description is neutral or "value free"; nor is it "absolute" or beyond contestation. For him, this approach is preferable not only to the relativism frequently associated with Winch but also to one which denies there is any sense to the idea of radically different cultures or worldviews or one that too quickly assumes there cannot be different views about rationality at stake (Taylor 2011, 35; Taylor 1985, ch. 5: "Rationality").

Taylor also addresses a deep controversy in the rule-following literature—precisely where are the rules to be found, and just how are they to be characterized. In summarizing the debate, Taylor describes two different positions: On the one hand, to follow a rule may bottom out as a descriptive claim about how individuals behave. This is what Brandom describes as "regularism" and it suggests that rule-following is in the end a causal affair. On the other hand, to claim that such a *de facto* description of a practice does not exhaust all that can be said about a correct or incorrect application of a rule is what Brandom refers to as "regulism" (Brandom 1994, 28). Taylor is equally explicit about the alternatives: "This first [regularism] would interpret … the connections that form our background as just *de facto* links, not susceptible of any justification. For instance, they are imposed by our society; we are conditioned to make them …. The second interpretation takes the background as really incorporating understanding; that is, a grasp on things which although quite unarticulated may allow us to formulate reasons and explanations when challenged" (Taylor 1995, 167–68). The challenge for most interpretivists, including Taylor, is to provide a convincing defense of this second view. However he rejects Brandom's own proposal and suggests that in the end there is something mysterious about how language works. There is, for Taylor, a sense in which the disclosive power of language—its ability to provide resources for articulation—exceeds our individual capacity to give or respond to reasons and in fact it is this power of language that makes possible any individual capacity (Taylor 2011, ch. 3: "Language not Mysterious?"). Taylor grants that this may leave some feeling deeply unsatisfied as an account of interpretation, but he seems to regard the desire for more to be another symptom of the excesses of the Enlightenment. Faced with the same choice between regularism and regulism as accounts of rule-following, others have concluded either that there is no such thing as shared or common meaning (Turner 2010) or that language in this sense does not exist (Davidson 1986).

Clifford Geertz, a cultural anthropologist who had a long career at the Institute for Advanced Study in Princeton, has also done much to promote an interpretive approach within the social sciences. It would be difficult to overestimate his influence not only within anthropology but also in popularizing an interpretive approach within the social sciences more widely (see Ortner 1984). *The Interpretation of Cultures* (1973) developed many of the same themes and concerns found in the work of Taylor—especially the overconfidence of a scientific (functionalist) approach to the study of cultures—but also provided many concrete examples of his interpretive perspective. "Deep Play: Notes on a Balinese Cockfight" is a frequently anthologized essay in which Geertz defends a "semiotic" approach in his field. "The culture of a people is an ensemble of texts, themselves ensembles, which the anthropologist strains to read over the shoulders of those to whom they properly belong" (452). Geertz notes his indebtedness to Wittgenstein and others, but locates his interpretive approach in the broader tradition of Weberian sociology: "Believing, with Max Weber, that man is an animal suspended in webs of significance he himself has spun, I take culture to be those webs, and the analysis of it to be therefore not an experimental science in search of law but an interpretive one in search of meaning" (5). Like Taylor and Winch, Geertz argues that a social science that attempts to avoid the interpretation of "thick description" would miss what is most central to the objects of study—namely, how the world is for those participating in it. Much as the reading and re-reading of *Macbeth* helps us to discover something about our own subjectivity, the enactment and re-enactment of the cockfight enables the Balinese discover something about themselves.

> Attending cockfights and participating in them is, for the Balinese, a kind of sentimental education. What he learns there is what his culture's ethos and his private

sensibility (or anyway, certain aspect of them) look like when spelled out externally in a collective text; that the two are near enough alike to be articulated in the symbolics of a single such text; and—the disquieting part—that the text in which this revelation is accomplished consists of a chicken hacking another mindlessly to bits.

(Geertz 1973, 449)

The vocabulary of "discovery" and "revelation" is somewhat misleading, however, as Geertz's claim seems to be that the Balinese are constituted or constructed through their enactment and interpretation of these symbolic forms (451).

As several critics have pointed out, Geertz's rich descriptions can sometimes leave the reader uncertain as to claims concerning the significance of the cockfight: Is Geertz's claim that the cockfight is about domesticating violence as Paul Rabinow and William Sullivan's therapeutic reading suggest, or is it a surrogate for the struggle between good and evil as Daniel Little suggests, or is Geertz's claim that the cockfight is (for the Balinese) about something else? (Martin 1999, 192–93). It is difficult to see how to judge among these competing interpretations. Indeed, as Crapanzano argues, it is not at all clear that there is a single meaning that the cockfight has for the Balinese (Crapanzano 1986). Geertz also appears to be uncertain about what form or degree of rationality should be ascribed to social actors, as evidenced in his remarks on the debate between Marshall Sahlins and Gananath Obeyesekere on Captain Cook's fateful voyage to the Hawaiian Islands (Geertz 2000, 98–107). Finally, in his review of the rationality debates, Geertz defends a more modest form of relativism or, at the least, argues that the dangers of relativism have been greatly overstated by anti-relativists (Geertz 2000, ch. 3). This position too unfortunately leaves rather unclear how competing interpretations of the social actors' interpretations are to be adjudicated.

## 3 Critical Theory

The connection between interpretive social science and critical theory can be initially framed in connection with Hegel's idea of a "reason in history": reason is not outside or beyond history (as in traditional metaphysics from Plato to Kant) but is rather to be found in history—that is, in the social and cultural products of rational human activity. The traces of reason in history, however, are not always clearly visible or on the surface since the consequences of human action can have unintended consequences and can unleash forces that operate against that very reason (see Honneth 2009, ch. 3). Initially, the ambition of the Frankfurt School was the development of a coordinated program of interdisciplinary social research in which the reason in history that had become stilted and/or misdirected under the exponential growth of capitalism might be recovered. The broad outlines of this project can be found in the early writings of its members, and especially Max Horkheimer's programmatic essay, "Traditional and Critical Theory" (Horkheimer 1972; Hoy and McCarthy 1994). However, as Horkheimer and Adorno made clear in *The Dialectic of the Enlightenment*, the rise of fascism, the Holocaust, and World War II, led to much greater pessimism on their part with respect to possibilities for a more rational society. Indeed, reason had evidently unleashed its opposite. Despite this, and despite the much more enigmatic position adopted by Adorno in the 1950s and 1960s, in his writings on the social sciences, he remained committed to a (still broadly Weberian) position that sought to integrate both an interpretivist and causal (or functional) approach to society. This view is especially evident in Adorno's participation in the "positivist dispute" in the early 1960s, even as the language he employs is that of Hegel's logic with its dialectical opposition and mediation of subject (agency) and object (structure) (Adorno et al. 1976; Benzer 2011). But it was Adorno's erstwhile assistant at the Institute, Jürgen Habermas, who would eventually articulate in a more ambitious—and more optimistic—form the outline of a critical theory of society. In this sense, *The Theory of Communicative Action* signals a return to the idea of interdisciplinary social research initially described by Horkheimer and his associates.

Habermas's contributions to debates about the nature of social inquiry are vast and cover a long period, from his own participation with Adorno in the "positivist dispute" in the early 1960s. This sketch must be limited and will focus on his later theory. It should be noted, though, that from his early debate with Hans-Georg Gadamer and in his influential work *Knowledge and Human Interests*, Habermas has always entertained a hybrid approach at the level of methodology: one that, like Weber, would seek to integrate interpretive and (broadly) causal (or functionalist) elements (Habermas 1988; Baynes 2015). As importantly, however, like Taylor, Habermas has always been equally suspicious about attempts to replace interpretation with a thorough-going naturalistic description of human activity. It is such a hybrid view that nonetheless gives priority to interpretation—or the participant's perspective—that is presented in *The Theory of Communicative Action* (TCA; 1984/1987).

Like Weber, who began by introducing a distinction between formal and substantive (or value) rationality (and action), Habermas also begins with a set of metatheoretical reflections that yields a typology of action. His basic distinction is between communicative (or "consent-oriented") and instrumental action. Whereas the aim of the latter is to intervene in the world or influence others, communicative action constitutes an independent and distinct type of social action. The goal or telos of communicative action is not expressed in an attempt to influence others, but in the attempt to reach an agreement or mutual understanding (*Verständigung*) with one or more actors about something in the world (TCA 1, 86). While all action is goal-oriented in a broad sense, in the case of communicative action any further ends the agent may have are subordinated to the goal of achieving a mutually shared definition of the agent's life-worldly situation through a cooperative process of interpretation. It is this latter notion of communicative action based on (either a "traditionally-secured" or "discursively-achieved") consensual agreement that lies at the core of his theory. In acting communicatively, individuals more or less naïvely accept as valid the various claims raised with their utterance or action and mutually suppose that each is prepared to provide reasons for them should the validity of those claims be questioned. In a slightly more technical (and controversial) sense, and one tied more specifically to modern structures of rationality, Habermas also holds that individuals who act communicatively at least tacitly aim at reaching understanding about something in the world by relating their interpretations to three general types of validity claims that are constitutive for three basic types of speech acts: a claim to truth raised in constative speech acts, a claim to normative rightness raised in regulative speech acts, and a claim to authenticity or truthfulness raised in expressive speech acts (TCA 1, 319f.).

At a methodological level, this analysis of social (or communicative) action underscores the need for an interpretive or *verstehende* approach in the social sciences. The requirement of *verstehen* arises because the objects that the social sciences study—actions and their products—are embedded in "complexes of meaning" that can be understood by the social inquirer only as he or she relates them to his or her own pre-theoretical knowledge as a member of the lifeworld. This, in turn, gives rise to the "disquieting thesis" that the interpretation of action cannot be separated from the interpreter's taking a position on the validity of the claims explicitly or implicitly connected with the action (*TCA* 1, 107). The process of identifying the reasons for an action unavoidably draws one into the process of assessment in which the inquirer must adopt the perspective of an (at least virtual) participant. Understanding the reasons for action requires taking a position on the validity of those reasons according to our own lights, and that means (at least initially) setting aside an external or "third-person" perspective in favor of an internal or "first-person" perspective in which both actor and interpreter belong to the same "universe of discourse." It is in this way that Habermas is able to connect the notion of social rationality more generally with his specific claim that reason is (most fundamentally) a dispositional property of agents to challenge and negotiate the claims to validity raised in their speech and action. To speak of a "reason in history" is thus, in the final instance, to make a claim about the rational capacities of speaking and acting subjects or, to use slightly different terms, it is to make a claim about the normative statuses the social actors—as well as their interpreters—must mutually ascribe to one another.

Despite this emphasis on social (or communicative) rationality with its ties to criticizable validity claims, Habermas does not think that society can simply be viewed as a sort of large-scale debating club. Actors' interpretations are generally taken for granted and form part of an implicit background of knowledge and practices that constitute what he calls (following Edmund Husserl) the "lifeworld." Though this background is therefore in some sense common or shared, it is not always (or even for the most part) the product of a discursively achieved agreement. It may also be the result of a more traditionally secured agreement (as when norms are more or less passively accepted) or the result of a disturbance to the communicative structure in which one or more actors are coerced or, at least, in which they are caused to act in ways which do not coincide with the reasons they would otherwise have endorsed. This claim of course raises many difficult questions with respect to an agent's reasons for action and for the possibility of critique. But this intimate relation between lifeworld and communicative action is crucial for Habermas's account:

> Subjects acting communicatively always come to an understanding in the horizon of a lifeworld. Their lifeworld is formed from more or less diffuse, always unproblematic, background convictions. This lifeworld background serves as a source of situation definitions that are presupposed by participants as unproblematic.
>
> (*TCA* 1, 70)

Habermas's treatment of the lifeworld is greatly indebted to the phenomenological analysis of Alfred Schutz and Thomas Luckmann, which emphasizes its fundamentally implicit or taken-for-granted character, its holistic structure, and the fact that it does not stand at the conscious disposition of actors but remains in the background as a pre-interpreted horizon (*TCA* 2, 131ff.). So understood, the lifeworld forms a "vast and incalculable web of presuppositions" against which particular actions and utterances acquire their meaning. Furthermore, in stressing its holistic character, he suggests that the lifeworld cannot in its entirety become problematic or a topic of debate; at most, it can fall apart (*TCA* 2, 130). Rather, it is only specific themes or aspects of an action situation that are open to problematization by social actors.

Social actors make use of the lifeworld as a resource that provides cultural knowledge, legitimate orders, and acquired competences; at the same time, the symbolic reproduction of the lifeworld depends on the interpretive accomplishments of its members across these institutional domains.

> While the segment of the lifeworld relevant to the situation encounters the actor as a problem which he has to solve as something standing as it were in front of him, he is supported in the rear by the background of his lifeworld. Coping with situations is a circular process in which the actor is two things at the same time: the initiator of actions that can be attributed to him and the product of traditions in which he stands as well as of group solidarities to which he belongs and processes of socialization and learning to which he is subjected.
>
> (TCA 2, 135)

However, he also warns that this description of a circular process should be accepted with caution: actors are not products of the lifeworld in a way that renders them passive nor should the lifeworld be regarded as a self-perpetuating process—a macro-subject—that has a life of its own. Rather, it is individuals (and groups) who reproduce the lifeworld through their communicative action and the lifeworld is "saddled upon" the interpretive accomplishments of its members (TCA 2, 145). Or, to express the same point in somewhat different terminology, reference to the sociality of the agent (and her reasons)—as a "product" of the lifeworld—must not be at the expense of her status as a rational and accountable agent, but rather must be seen as a central condition or feature of that agency. Habermas's model of social agency thus makes it possible to avoid the extremes of treating agents as "cultural dopes" who passively reproduce their lifeworld, on the one hand, or as individual utility-maximizers who despite their situation always act (insofar as they are rational) to maximize their own self-interest, on the other. Neither of these extremes captures adequately the idea that actors are both deeply embedded in and indebted to the lifeworld *and* accountable agents who reproduce through their interpretive accomplishments—that is, the give and take of reasons (Habermas 1992, 43; Grannoveter 1985).

Finally, though his reasons for this can't be pursued here, Habermas claims that this "interpretive" approach to society as "lifeworld" which gives prominence to the idea of communicative action must be supplemented with the concept of society as "system." This permits the theorist to describe society from an "observer's perspective" rather than from the (interpretive) perspective of a participant. It further allows for the claim that social integration can in large measure also be achieved when the task of coordinating action is shifted to mechanisms that do not depend directly on the intentions of actors (consider, for example, Smith's "invisible hand" of the market). In those cases what Habermas calls "systems integration" refers to the way that a society (or one of its subsystems) can be stabilized not through the consensual agreement of social actors but through the outcomes or consequences of their decisions. Habermas's introduction of a "two-level" concept of society—his distinction between society as lifeworld and society as system—is done in order to secure access methodologically to this dominant feature of modern societies. It is, however, in keeping with his earlier description in *On the Logic of the Social Sciences* of his own approach as "a hermeneutically enlightened and historically oriented functionalism" (Habermas 1988, 187).

Despite some of the difficulties and challenges confronting it (see Honneth and Joas 1991; and Baynes 2015), Habermas has continued to insist upon the relevance of this two-level concept of society—one that combines both interpretive social science and functionalist or systems-theoretic perspective—for his model of a critical social theory. Working solely from the internal perspective of the participant—and thus treating action and their products as tied to the domain of reasons—the social inquirer (as a virtual participant) is unable to perceive systemic causes of distortions to the structures of communication as such.

> A *verstehende* sociology that allows society to be wholly absorbed into the lifeworld ties itself to the perspective of self-interpretation of the culture under investigation; this internal perspective screens out everything that inconspicuously affects a sociocultural lifeworld from the outside.
>
> (*TCA* 2, 150)

At the same time, systemic disturbances to the communicative infrastructure of the lifeworld cannot be identified exclusively from an external or observer's perspective since, as we have seen, the structures of the lifeworld (and, by extension, the types of collective learning processes connected to them) are only accessible through a reconstructive analysis that begins with the member's intuitive knowledge (*TCA* 2, 151). This emphasis on the need to begin with an interpretive approach also reveals the limits of a theoretical approach that relies solely on an external perspective (McCarthy 1991, 122). If communicative disturbances and their systemic causes are to be identified, the critical theorist must be able to work simultaneously with an internal (participant's) and external (observer's) perspective—that is, with an analytic perspective on society as lifeworld and system.

Habermas's sketch of a critical social theory would seem to go a long way toward addressing some of the shortcomings of interpretivism while preserving its important insights. On the one hand, it gives priority to a description of the object-domain (society as lifeworld) from the participant's perspective as emphasized by interpretivists. Society consists primarily in the network of practices and institutions that constitute the social meanings of the actors involved and these networks are reproduced through the "interpretive achievements" of those actors. Actors are not conceived as "cultural dopes" who are simply shaped by—or caused to act in conformity with—those networks. At the same time, actors are not conceived "atomistically" or in an excessively "individualistic" manner. Rather, they are conceived "relationally" and their interpretive accomplishments depend upon both the recognition of their status by others and the contexts of social meaning provided by the lifeworld they inhabit (Haslanger 2015).

Habermas's conception also avoids some of the more convincing criticisms of interpretivism. Its aims are not too restricted (Martin 1999) since it does not limit social inquiry exclusively to the interpretation of meaning and permits both causal and functional explanations as well. It also stakes out an initially plausible position with respect to the rationality debates and the question of relativism. Social inquirers must take a position (at least virtually) with respect to the rational acceptability of the claims made by participants in their object-domain, while at the same time acknowledging that constructing rational interpretations and, beyond that, offering social explanations when rational interpretations fail, is an extremely difficult task fraught with all sorts of risk and danger. (For some examples of these risks and dangers, see Fricker 2007; and Stoljar 2014.)

Nonetheless, serious criticisms and challenges remain for interpretivists and critical theorists insofar as both insist upon the autonomy of the social sciences. Various theorists from very different perspectives continue to question whether a case for the existence of shared or common or intersubjective meaning can be made. For example, Stephen Turner and Paul Roth have suggested that there is little to be said in support of this widely shared assumption. If their objections are sustained, the claim that such meanings constitute the object-domain of the social sciences will be less convincing (Turner 2010; Roth 2003). Relatedly, even if the existence of shared social meanings strike many as a reasonable assumption to make (see Haslanger 2015), there is still the question of how different interpretive frameworks or schemes or (in Habermas's case) "lifeworlds" are individuated. Clearly there must be allowance for a great deal of fluidity and flexibility with respect to them, whether one is describing the "thicker" contexts of action or even the more general features of societies and social institutions. But if appeal to the social "background" or "lifeworld" or "habitus" is to be assigned a significant role in social inquiry, much more needs to be said about how they are specifically identified and distinguished from one another. Further, in both interpretivism and critical theory there is a renewed attention to the question of social practices (see Rouse 2006 for an extensive and detailed overview). Some of the earlier debates about structure vs. agency re-emerge in these discussions, as do also new perspectives on the earlier debate on rule-following. Though Habermas's description of the "circular process" in which actors draw upon the resources of the lifeworld while they at the same time reproduce it through communicative action represents one position in the discussion, many issues have been raised that deserve more attention than they have received thus far. Finally, even in recent discussions in the loosely defined "Frankfurt School" tradition of critical theory, the question of how practices are best conceived and what resources they offer for the possible critique of those practices has been approached from a variety of perspectives, some of which depart significantly from Habermas's position as it has been outlined here (Honneth 2009; de Bruin and Zurn 2009; Celikates 2006; Iser forthcoming).

# References

Adorno, Theodor et al. 1976. *The Positivist Dispute in German Sociology*. New York: Harper and Row.

Baynes, Kenneth. 2010. "Self, Narrative and Self-constitution: Revisiting Taylor's 'Self-interpreting Animals'," *Philosophical Forum* 41: 441–58.

Baynes, Kenneth. 2015. *Habermas*. New York: Routledge.

Beiser, Frederick. 2011. *The German Historicist Tradition*. New York: Oxford.

Benzer, Matthias. 2011. *The Sociology of Theodor Adorno*. New York: Cambridge University Press.

Brandom, Robert. 1994. *Making It Explicit: Reasoning, Representing, and Discursive Commitment*. Cambridge, MA: Harvard University Press.

Celikates, Robin. 2006. "From Critical Social Theory to a Social Theory of Critique," *Constellations* 13: 21–40.

Clifford, James and George Marcus, eds. 1986. *Writing Culture: The Poetics and Politics of Ethnography*. Berkeley: University of California Press.

Crapanzano, Vincent. 1986. "Hermes' Dilemma," in Clifford and Marcus, *Writing Culture*, 51–76. Davidson, Donald. 1980. "Actions, Reasons, and Causes," in *Essays on Actions and Events*. New York: Oxford University Press, 3–19

Davidson, Donald. 1986. "A Nice Derangement of Epitaphs," in *Truth and Interpretation*, ed. Ernie Lepore. Oxford: Blackwell, 433–46.

de Bruin, Boudewijn and Chris Zurn, eds. 2009. *New Waves in Political Philosophy*. London: Palgrave Macmillan.

Fay, Brian. 2000. "Winch's Philosophical Bearings," *History of the Human Sciences* 13: 50–62.

Fricker, Miranda. 2007. *Epistemic Injustice*. New York: Oxford University Press.

Geertz, Clifford. 1973. *The Interpretation of Cultures*. New York: Basic Books.

Geertz, Clifford. 2000. *Available Light: Anthropological Reflections on Philosophical Topics*. Princeton, NJ: Princeton University Press.

Giddens, Anthony. 1976. *New Rules for Sociological Method*. New York: Basic Books.

Grannoveter, Mark. 1985. "Economic Action and Social Structure: The Problem of Embeddedness," *American Journal of Sociology* 91: 481–510.

Habermas, J. 1984/1987. *The Theory of Communicative Action*. Boston: Beacon Press.

Habermas, J. 1988. *On the Logic of the Social Sciences*. Cambridge, MA: MIT Press.

Habermas, J. 1992. *Postmetaphysical Thinking*. Cambridge, MA: MIT Press.

Haslanger, Sally. 2015. "Social Structure, Narrative, and Explanation," *Canadian Journal of Philosophy* 45: 1–15.

Hempel, Carl. 1965. *Aspects of Scientific Explanation*. New York: Free Press.

Hollis, Martin and Steven Lukes, eds. 1982. *Rationality and Relativism*. Cambridge, MA: MIT Press.

Honneth, Axel. 2009. *Pathologies of Reason*. New York: Columbia University Press.

Honneth, Axel and Hans Joas, eds. 1991. *Communicative Action: Essays on Jürgen Habermas's The Theory of Communicative Action*. Trans. J. Gaines and D. Jones. Cambridge: Polity Press.

Horkheimer, Max. 1972. *Critical Theory*. New York: Seabury Press.

Horkheimer, Max and Theodor Adorno. 1987. *Dialectic of Enlightenment*. Ed. G. Schmid Noerr. Stanford, CA: Stanford University Press.

Hoy, David and Thomas McCarthy. 1994. *Critical Theory*. New York: Blackwell.

Iser, Mattias. Forthcoming. *Indignation and Progress*. New York: Oxford University Press.

McCarthy, Thomas. 1991. "Complexity and Democracy," in Honneth and Joas, *Communicative Action*, 119–39.

MacIntyre, Alasdair. 1971. *Against the Self-Images of the Age*. Notre Dame: University of Notre Dame Press.

Martin, Michael. 1999. *Verstehen: The Uses of Understanding in Social Science*. New Brunswick, NJ: Transaction Books. Ortner, Sherry. 1984. "Theory in Anthropology since the Sixties," *Comparative Studies in Science and Society* 26.1: 126–66.

Rosenberg, Alexander. 2016. *Philosophy of Social Science*. Boulder, CO: Westview Press.

Roth, Paul. 2003. "Beyond Understanding: The Career of the Concept of Understanding in the Human Sciences," in *The Blackwell Guide to the Philosophy of the Social Sciences*, ed. Stephen Turner and Paul Roth. Malden, MA: Blackwell, 311–33.

Rouse, Joseph. 2006. "Practice Theory," in *Handbook of the Philosophy of Science*, ed. Stephen Turner and Mark Risjord. Dordrecht: Elsevier, 639–82.

Stoljar, Natalie. 2014. "Autonomy and Adaptive Preference Formation," in *Autonomy, Oppression, and Gender*, ed. Andrea Veltman and Mark Piper. New York: Oxford University Press, 227–52.

Taylor, Charles. 1981. "Explanation and Understanding in the Geisteswissenschaften," in *Wittgenstein: To Follow a Rule*, ed. S. Holtzman and C. Leich. Boston: Routledge, 191–210.

Taylor, Charles. 1985. "Interpretation and the Sciences of Man," in *Philosophical Papers Vol. 2*. New York: Cambridge University Press, 15–57.

Taylor, Charles. 1995. *Philosophical Arguments*. Cambridge, MA: Harvard University Press.

Taylor, Charles. 2011. *Dilemmas and Connections*. Cambridge, MA: Harvard University Press.

Turner, Stephen P. 2010. *Explaining the Normative*. Cambridge: Polity Press.

Weber, Max. 1978. *Economy and Society*. Ed. G. Roth and C. Wittich. Berkeley: University of California Press.

Wilson, Bryan, ed. 1970. *Rationality*. Oxford: Basil Blackwell.

Winch, Peter. 1958. *The Idea of a Social Science and its Relation to Philosophy*. London: Routledge and Kegan Paul.

Winch, Peter. 1970. "Understanding a Primitive Society," in Wilson, *Rationality*, 78–111.

# 8

# THE EMPIRICAL COUNTER-REVOLUTION

## Jaakko Kuorikoski[1]

Methodological anti-naturalism is dead—at least in contemporary philosophy of science. Winchian arguments claiming that explanation of human action and social phenomena is a conceptual impossibility, an illegitimate application of the grammar of the natural sciences to the normative sphere of rule-governed meaning, have not gained much traction in contemporary philosophies of language, mind, or explanation. Arguments from the centrality of free agency in the understanding of human experience, sometimes combining existential phenomenology and philosophical anthropology with hermeneutic ideas, seem similarly limited in appeal. These arguments have been unable to move the compatibilist consensus in philosophy of science, which regards the inconsistency of free will and causal explanation as a naïve conceptual confusion and leaves no room for any residual notion of agent causation. The apparent lack of strict laws of human behavior and societies (see Reiss this volume) is no longer seen as an insurmountable obstacle for causal explanation. The causalist consensus is now further bolstered by the currently popular theories of causal explanation and discovery which are not founded upon a nomothetic ideal of science. Also the locality and contextuality of social knowledge that motivated Clifford Geertz's anti-naturalism is now being tackled with these new ideas of causality, mechanisms, and extrapolation. Even the inherently value-laden nature of social science has now been accommodated within broader conceptions of scientific objectivity capable of acknowledging the fact that scientific knowledge in general is a fundamentally human product and thus its production and even evaluation are legitimately subject to various social and political considerations. Finally the old accepted truism that social sciences are necessarily non-experimental has been rendered decidedly obsolete by the widespread adoption of laboratory and field experiments.

Besides such purely philosophical arguments, anti-naturalist positions can also be motivated by practical empirical concerns. Whereas the philosophically motivated anti-naturalisms based on *a priori* arguments from the nature of human action, experience, or sociality have been, more or less, refuted by other philosophical arguments, empirically motivated skepticism against the possibility of a truly "scientific" social science can only be met with examples of empirically successful "scientific" social science. In this chapter I will highlight some relatively recent methodological trends within the social sciences that arguably exemplify the way in which empirical research fulfilling the epistemological criteria of the methodological naturalist is possible in practice. These trends are the rise of experimental social science, the methodological debate on causal inference in case studies, big coordinated interdisciplinary research projects utilizing various empirical methods, and the promises of Big Data. These trends by no means exhaust empirically successful and self-consciously "scientific" social science. Other notable methodological developments include the theoretical and formal advances in causal inference from statistical data, which are covered in this book (Kaidesoja's contribution, see also Morgan and Winship 2007), and the methodological reform movement of analytical sociology, which emphasizes various empirical methodologies, such as empirically calibrated agent-based models and experimentation.

But perhaps the most important *scientific* development in favor of the naturalist is the naturalization of folk-psychology itself. Automatic attributions of mental states as causes of behavior and the broader narrative practices constituting the intentionality of human behavior are no longer seen as a conceptually (and possibly *a priori*) necessary bedrock of understanding, but as important empirical phenomena to be scientifically explained.[2] Despite the experimental demonstrations of the fallibility of these interpretive practices, few would be ready to predict that the social sciences will do away with intentional psychology as an important explanatory resource, and there is much philosophical work to be done in reconciling our empirical understanding of folk-psychology with our social scientific explanatory practices. I will therefore end by arguing that the project of defending methodological naturalism has led philosophy of science to be almost exclusively focused on the kinds of empirical methods presented here, while leaving unanswered pressing methodological questions related to interpretive methods as topics to be dealt exclusively within methodological anti-naturalist frameworks or within "philosophies" of science developed within the social sciences. Philosophically motivated methodological naturalism should be more concerned with practical methodological issues related to interpretive empirical methods.

## Experimenting with the Social

It is generally accepted that the experimental method is the most reliable way of confirming causal claims, and the perceived impossibility of experimentation in the social sciences has historically been an important motivation for methodological anti-naturalism. The common conviction that meaningful social scientific experimentation is impossible has many roots: the lack of social laws, the contextuality of social action, the holistic nature of meaning, the openness of social systems in the wild, and freedom of will. And even if single people or small groups could be experimented upon, as is routinely done in psychology and social psychology, surely it is impractical to carry out experiments at the societal level.

Yet the growing acceptance of experimentation across the social sciences is one of the clear methodological trends of the last two decades. Social behavior is orderly and predictable, at least in the aggregate, and theoretically important behavioral and cognitive phenomena can be experimentally investigated in the laboratory. Most philosophical attention has been devoted to behavioral economics (see Heilmann's chapter in this volume) and more broadly game-theoretical experimental designs used in political science, social psychology, and even anthropology. For example, one of the biggest and surely most-debated anthropological projects in recent years has been the cross-cultural experimental comparison of fairness norms funded by the MacArthur Foundation. The research program saw a group of anthropologists subject people from diverse cultural backgrounds to a standardized battery of ultimatum and public goods games. The guiding idea was that these standardized games would act as devices for measuring culture-specific social preferences (concern for others' well-being or overall fairness) (Guala 2008). The overall result of the first part of the program was that, contrary to what might be expected, such social preferences seemed to be correlated with how well the tested culture was integrated into market economies (Henrich et al. 2004). The upshot seems to be that markets do not render people selfish rational agents, but the other way round. The second phase of the project (Ensminger and Henrich 2014) added a third-party punishment game and concentrated on probing this preliminary finding and on testing alternative hypotheses that might explain the observed patterns in the cross-cultural findings. The results also show that high offers are also associated with belonging to a monotheist world religion and punishment of unfair behavior is associated with community size.

The methodology and the implications of this research program are highly contentious. What became apparent was that the interpretation of the experimental results required understanding of the social norms through which the subjects viewed the rather alien experimental situation. For example, the ostensibly bizarre behavior of accepting unfair offers but rejecting (and thus altruistically punishing) excessively fair offers observed among the Au and Gnau of New Guinea could be made sense of only against the backdrop of a highly regimented social norm dictating reciprocity for all gifts. When such norms hold, it is sensible to avoid situations in which one would be left indeterminably in debt, such as an outwardly altruistic offer in an ultimatum game. These studies therefore not only demonstrate that meaningful measurement of social behavior is possible cross-culturally, but also highlight the necessity of contextual interpretive knowledge in such an enterprise.

Not all laboratory experimentation in the social sciences is designed around a strategic anonymous decision problem using explicit monetary incentives. Although most economists may scoff at such designs, many behavioral and psychological assumptions underlying theories of social phenomena can be studied experimentally without implementing these strict idealizing procedures. For example, Centola, Miller, and Macy (2005) used a computational model to suggest that the emergence of unpopular norms could be explained by the use of "false" enforcement of a norm as a signaling device for sincerity. Two crucial assumptions of the model, that conformity to an unpopular norm can lead to false enforcement and that false enforcement is an effective signal of apparent sincerity, were then tested in a set of further experiments. For example, the latter assumption was tested with a design in which the subjects were asked to read an unintelligible academic text, allegedly written by a respected academic. The subjects were then told that someone had stated publicly that the unintelligible text was clear. Some were told that the person in question had also publicly reprimanded people who disagreed with the evaluation whereas others were not. Those who were told of the enforcement were more likely to accept the evaluation as sincere (Willer et al. 2009).

Laboratory experiments, especially those in the style of behavioral economics, do not even remotely resemble any social situation in the wild, because the idea is to isolate theoretically important tendencies in social behavior. This means that even if the experiment is internally valid, inferring from the results to the wild is often problematic, because the stability of the investigated tendency is uncertain and the tendency may not be empirically observable in the wild because of other pre-empting causes. For example, even if altruistic punishment of unfair behavior were a deep-rooted tendency made manifest in ultimatum experiments, it is debatable whether it can sustain co-operation in the wild (Guala 2012).

A way of circumventing these external validity worries is to conduct the experiment directly in the population and context of interest. Because other confounding factors cannot be experimentally controlled in the wild, field experiments, almost by definition, rely on randomization. For example, a series of field experiments has estimated the degree of racial discrimination in the US labor market. Because of many potential and plausible confounders, simply looking at the unemployment rates of different ethnic groups or comparing the group-specific probabilities for successfully applying for a similar position are not sufficient for reliably estimating the effect of outright discrimination. An ingenious way around these problems was to randomly assign otherwise identical job applications with either a "white-sounding" or a "black-sounding" name. Because of randomization, any difference in the success rate of these otherwise identical applications would have to be due to the inferred ethnicity of the applicant. In a related study, white and black actors with similar qualifications were randomized for different job interviews. Not surprisingly, these field experiments revealed a significant amount of racial bias in the US labor market (Bertrand and Mullainathan 2004).

Field experiments are important especially when what is at stake is a possible policy intervention. In such cases, the reliability of our knowledge of the causal efficacy of the contemplated policy is more important than theoretical considerations concerning the underlying mechanisms of social behavior. Because of this, field experiments have become increasingly prominent in fields such as development economics. Proponents of evidence-based policy place great weight on field experiments, which are seen as the gold standard for causal knowledge, much as randomized controlled trials are seen as absolutely essential in medicine. Needless to say, many questions remain open concerning the utility and scope of application of both laboratory as well as field experiments. The extent to which social interaction can be broken down into stable independent components that can be studied in isolation is an open question. One of the most heated recent debates in the social sciences concerns the replicability of social psychological experiments: many laboratory phenomena that were thought to be robust and stable have been proven to be much more fragile and ephemeral than previously thought. As much as three-quarters of generally accepted experimental results in social psychology turned out to be impossible to replicate (Open Science Collaboration 2015). Moreover, rendering experimental knowledge of our cognitive processes truly explanatorily relevant for group- and social-level phenomena is not as straightforward in practice as it may appear for the naturalistically minded philosopher. There is also a danger that the emphasis on experiments, for example due to demands of evidence-based policy, may end up crowding out other sources of evidence and limit the kind of research published and funded.[3] For further worries and considerations related to experimentation in the social sciences, see Crasnow's contribution to this volume.

## Case Studies and Process Tracing

Another recent development in line with methodological naturalism is that the causal ambitions of case-based qualitative research are now taken seriously in the methodological discussion within the social sciences. Especially in fields like international relations, in which the sample sizes are bound to be small but the aim of inquiry is nevertheless knowledge for use and intervention, principles of *process tracing* for (mostly within-case) causal inference are being formulated and debated. In broad strokes, process tracing refers to a set of methodologies for tying detailed observations of token events, together with background knowledge, into a causal chain linking a putative cause to its putative effect. In political science more broadly, the debate over process tracing was, by and large, launched in the wake of the influential methodological treatise by King, Keohane, and Verba (1994). King, Keohane, and Verba tried to unify qualitatively oriented case studies and quantitative statistical studies under a single logic of inference. This meant that in case studies, too, the logic of causal inference is similar, except that the sample size is one. Although many were sympathetic to the general outlook of methodological naturalism and with the view that social science should become more "outcome oriented," i.e. concerned with causal questions, the prospects for the evidential value of case studies looked bleak. The process-tracing literature is an attempt to rescue case studies from the fate of simply being (literally) impoverished cousins of proper statistical studies, something of a last resort when "proper" quantitative methods of causal inference are unavailable.

Andrew Bennett and Alexander George (1997) viewed process tracing as a theoretically structured method for colligating empirical observations. They distinguished two types of process tracing. Process verification is a theory-first procedure in which observations are matched to predictions from a theory which already has independent empirical support. Process induction is a more inductive procedure of linking observations into hypothetical causal chains which can then be generalized and tested against other cases. In both cases, warrant that the links between observed events are actually causal cannot come from the observations themselves, but from a more general theory. An important restriction placed by Bennett and George is that the observed chain of events must be "continuous," i.e. each observed link should conform to the predictions of the general theory.

Also within philosophy of science, case study methodology is now mostly discussed in terms of process tracing. This means that the aim of case studies is the establishment of objective knowledge of the causal process and mechanisms operating within the investigated setting. The general idea is that in-depth longitudinal investigation of single social settings can provide reliable evidence of intermediate steps in the process hypothesized to mediate the influence of the cause unto its effect. Here the concept of social mechanism can have some traction on the general evidential problem in process tracing. Daniel Steel has argued that the concept of mechanism can be used to explain the epistemic added value of process tracing: evidence for causal relations between parts (between events in the process) can be easier to come by than direct evidence (such as field experiments or statistical studies controlling for all possible confounders) for the causal relation of interest (Steel 2004, 2008). Parts of social mechanisms are usually taken to be decisions, practices and habits of actors, norms, and sometimes other social institutions. The idea is not that mechanistic evidence would be somehow a different *kind of* evidence,[4] only that thinking in terms of mechanisms is a way of relating evidence from other sources, such as experimental evidence from psychology and social psychology, as well as context-specific social observations obtained by participant observation, to bear on the case in hand.

Despite this common understanding of the goals of case-based inquiry, and of the need for formulating stronger epistemic principles for fulfilling those goals, the logic of process tracing has not really advanced in ways that would have provided new practicable methodologies. As Attilia Ruzzene notes (2013), there is thus far little agreement on what the exact criteria for successful process tracing are and whether process tracing should be assigned a more important role than as a "heuristic" tool, short of proper warrant. Moreover, many proposed applications of process tracing are historical, and the utilization of experimental and ethnographic methods to the study of the parts of historical processes and mechanisms faces obvious problems. Ruzzene argues that case-based process tracing cannot be taken as a reliable method for causal inference on its own, but it can be effectively used in tandem with other, direct methods of casual inference in eliminating alternative causal hypotheses.

## Coordinated Empiricism

Radical anti-naturalist arguments imply that "positivist" and interpretive methods are fundamentally incompatible: either social research aiming at objective causal explanation is a fundamentally confused enterprise to begin with or, at least, the knowledge interests of "the positivist" are fundamentally different from producing meaningful understanding, and possibly emancipation. Many methodological treatises in the social sciences have reinforced this conception by arguing that different "etic" (referring to third-person, objectivist perspective) and "emic" (first-person, subjectivist perspective) research traditions form different and incommensurable paradigms of social research (e.g. Burrell and Morgan 1979) with little or no potential for cross-communication or cross-validation. Such views are extremely counterproductive for the scientific understanding of society.

As the example of cross-cultural evaluation of economic experiments already demonstrated, scientific understanding of complex social phenomena requires both "interpretive" methods as well as quantitative analysis (with some experimentation thrown in for good measure). Other good examples of the necessity of multiple perspectives and methods are ambitious, coordinated multi-method research projects, such as the Project on Human Development in Chicago Neighborhoods (PHDCN) and Understanding Autism. PHDCN was a massive coordinated longitudinal study of urban segregation, inequality, and how families, schools, and neighborhoods affect child and adolescent development.[5] Urban ethnographic studies have traditionally emphasized neighborhoods' effects on the fortunes of people living in them, but statistical analyses have had a hard time quantifying or even establishing the existence of these effects. The project used community surveys about all things possibly relevant to neighborhood effects, such as organizational and political structures, cultural values, information and formal social control, and social cohesion. More innovatively, the project produced something they called Systematic Social Observations. The researchers drove around Chicago block by block and videotaped the entirety of the neighborhoods studied. Then researchers studied the tapes and meticulously noted down observations on variables such as drinking establishments, recreational facilities, street conditions, the number of security persons, children, and teenagers visible, traffic, the physical condition of buildings, cigarettes and cigars on the street or in the gutter, empty beer bottles visible on the street, tagging graffiti, condoms on the sidewalk, and intoxicated people. The project also crucially relied on interviews of residents and community leaders. The project also included a field experimental component: in their "lost letter experiment" researchers distributed stamped and addressed envelopes in neighborhoods across the city and measured the rate of return. Rates of return correlated with the rate at which people in the area had reported willingness to help an injured unknown person.

One of the key take-home results of this study was that social cohesion of a neighborhood (or "collective efficacy"), rather than, e.g., social ties as such, is an important determinant of neighborhood disadvantage. Moreover, black neighborhoods are doubly disadvantaged in that even those white neighborhoods which score low on collective efficacy are usually bordered by "better" neighborhoods and can thus free ride on social cohesion.

Social and psychological conditions involving both biological causes as well as complex social feedback mechanisms form an important area of research in which a coordinated multi-method approach is necessary for disentangling such causal complexities. The last four decades have seen a roughly tenfold increase in autism diagnoses, especially in the USA. The increase is alarming and there is much talk about "the autism epidemic" in the press, but the crucial unanswered question is to what extent the epidemic is a matter of an increase in certain kinds of developmental disorders and to what extent only an increase in diagnoses. Understanding such a complex phenomenon involving both social and "biological" causes requires creatively combining various methods, theoretical approaches, and sources of data.

The Understanding Autism project, based in the Interdisciplinary Center for Innovative Theory and Empirics (INCITE) at Columbia University, analyzed various sources of data about the spatial distribution and changes in incidence of autism diagnoses in California, together with life-history surveys mapping individual trajectories from perceived childhood developmental problems to an autism-spectrum diagnosis as well as early evaluations of individual children.[6] A careful analysis of changes in the spatial distribution of diagnoses, simulation modeling of the structure of social networks, and a statistical decomposition of incidence rates into age, period and cohort effects, have together suggested that the autism-spectrum diagnoses seem to be contagious through social networks and that (at least) approximately half of the epidemic is explainable as an increase in such socially transmitted willingness to "search for" a positive diagnosis. The majority of the "epidemic" is thus due to changes in diagnoses, not in the rate of developmental disorders as such. Using annual evaluations of diagnosed children carried out on most Californian children diagnosed, six different subgroups with different trajectories were also identified, thus increasing our understanding of the considerable diversity in the disorder. Work is currently under way in building more empirically calibrated simulation models as well as in analyzing the life histories of parents of autistic children with the aim of uncovering the social mechanisms influencing diagnoses as well as individual developmental trajectories.

Understanding the experiences of the parents of autistic children is not only important for understanding the actual risk factors and the social drivers of autism diagnoses. Despite overwhelming scientific consensus, public belief in the link between autism diagnosis and the MMR vaccine remains strong. Especially in California, vaccination denialism represents a new form of public mistrust of science by well-educated and socioeconomically well-off citizens. Understanding the social reality of the afflicted children and their parents is therefore not just important for understanding the social mechanisms influencing the developmental trajectories of neurally atypical children, but also for managing the disconnect between the lived social reality and the scientific consensus (Bearman 2010).

## Big Data

For many, the dawning era of Big Data holds great promise for a truly scientific empirical social science. More and more of our daily activities are now leaving a digital trace. Our social life seems to have relocated itself to the Internet, much of our consumption is purchased with credit cards or online, and we communicate with devices that not only record whom we are talking to, but also track our whereabouts when doing so. Such masses of data cannot be handled manually, but require computational methods to search for potentially meaningful patterns. Simple correlations between variables are one thing, but theoretically more interesting possibilities lie in the application of network theories to such masses of data. Moreover, some forms of Big Data, such as huge corpuses of conversation in internet forums, require algorithms that are sensitive to semantic content.

At the same time as these new sources of data necessitate new methods for mining them, these new methods can also revitalize existing repositories of data. For example, massive archives, such as the collected transcripts of the Supreme Court decisions in the USA or the archived records of the East India Trade Company, just to name a few examples, become possible objects of knowledge in exciting new ways.

The epistemological promise of Big Data is to render social science more empirical. Social science based on Big Data can be purely inductive—free from empirically vacuous social theory, prejudiced *a priori* selection of variables, and the overly constraining and hollow statistical construct of "the average man" coupled with a random error term (Lee and Martin 2015). According to its advocates, hypothetico-deductivism is ill-suited to the social sciences because either available theory is simply not strong enough or theoretically informed hypotheses illegitimately limit the sociological imagination. Proponents talk of a paradigm shift from an ill-conceived statistics of causal validation to the more flexible logic of machine learning. As Paul DiMaggio describes this attitude, "The computer-science perspective is liberating, as it forces us to recognize real interpretive uncertainty and seek out appropriate and substantively relevant forms of validation fitted to specific research goals" (DiMaggio 2015). The ultimate hope is that if there is enough data, it will speak for itself—as long as it is probed with the right algorithm.

But the social scientific significance of Big Data cannot be realized solely on the basis of clever algorithms. Big Data is usually "found" as it is, instead of being intentionally produced in order to answer some specific question, and there are major worries related to the epistemology of using such found data. Found data is usually subject to activity bias and cannot therefore be treated as representative of any kind of consensus. Also in virtue of being big, almost all findings from Big Data are bound to be statistically significant in the standard statistical sense, whether or not they are significant in any substantial scientific sense (McFarland and McFarland 2015). However, the real challenges of Big Data are not really technical, but theoretical. Machine learning can uncover interesting patterns and sometimes unexpected social phenomena, but not explanations. Data-mining is also inherently local, and any results require meaningful integration with some more general sociological theory in order to have any external validity.

## Throwing the Interpretive Baby Out with the Normative Bathwater

Important as the developments laid out above are, it is arguable that the topics in current philosophy of social science provide a somewhat distorted view about the prominence of these "new" empirical methods and sources of data. Perhaps in an effort to provide counter-examples to the philosophical anti-naturalist arguments, much of the philosophical discussion has centered on these avenues or research (although not much attention has thus far been given to Big Data). Nevertheless, a randomly sampled social scientist would unlikely find these examples very representative of her own research. Consequently, much of recent philosophical work, important as it has been, is directly methodologically relevant for only a minority of social scientists. The conceptual underpinnings of behavioral economics and the foundations of casual discovery algorithms are also easily accessible for the philosopher and they can be meaningfully discussed relatively free from the mundane practicalities of their empirical implementation. And let us not even get started on the amount of philosophical attention given to formal modeling in the social sciences.

Hence, even though the *a priori* philosophical arguments in favor of methodological anti-naturalism should be left firmly in the dustbin of history, more philosophical attention should be devoted to methodological issues related to the interpretation of action and varieties of meaning-concepts attributed to broader social phenomena. Even though much of the social sciences are now more explicitly and, more importantly, methodologically reflectively engaged in empirical causal research and the theoretical study of social mechanisms, the empirical study of these causal relations and mechanisms almost always has to include a strong interpretive component. Social action is influenced by the meanings that the actors attribute to their surrounding events and institutions and social institutions themselves arguably partly constituted by these meanings and normative practices. And the empirical study of these meanings and normative practices is fraught with philosophical issues largely untouched by current mainstream philosophy of science (however, see Kincaid 1996, ch. 6; and Risjord 2000). Beyond simple causalism, how exactly should the relationship between folk-psychological attribution of intentional states and causal explanation be understood? How can the reliability of these attributions, both those made by the researcher and those made by the studied subjects, be measured and improved? How should we understand the explanatory role of the various meaning-concepts routinely attributed to larger social units, such as practices, rituals, and other social institutions? In what way can such attributions be seen as objective and how should we evaluate their reliability? What ethical and political considerations should we take into account when moving beyond the self-attributed folk-psychological explanations of those studied? These are all important questions that should also interest the methodological naturalist.

## Notes

1 The author would like to thank Caterina Marchionni and Petri Ylikoski for their valuable comments. The writing of the chapter was supported by the Academy of Finland.
2 This naturalist stance should be applied to any putative "bedrock" or "baseline" for understanding human behavior—rational choice theory being one prominent example (Ylikoski and Kuorikoski 2016).
3 This concern has been raised about criminology in the USA.
4 Russo-Williamson thesis claims that there are two distinct kinds of evidence, mechanistic evidence and evidence of difference-making, and that both are required in warranting causal claims (Russo and Williamson 2007). For a defense of the view that mechanistic evidence can also be analyzed as being evidence of difference-making, albeit at a different level, see Claveau 2012.
5 See www.icpsr.umich.edu/icpsrweb/PHDCN/ and Sampson 2012.
6 See www.incite.columbia.edu/understanding-autism.

## References

Bennett, A. and George, A. 1997. "Process Tracing in Case Study Research." MacArthur Foundation Workshop on Case Study Method, New York.
Bearman, P. 2010. "Just-So Stories: Vaccines, Autism, and the Single Bullet Disorder." *Social Psychology Quarterly* 20: 1–4.
Bertrand, M. and Mullainathan, S. 2004. "Are Emily and Greg More Employable Than Lakisha and Jamal? A Field Experiment on Labor Market Discrimination." *American Economic Review* 94(4): 991–1013.
Burrell, G. and Morgan, G. 1979. *Sociological Paradigms and Organisational Analysis.* London: Heinemann.

Centola, D., Willer, R., and Macy, M. 2005. "The Emperor's Dilemma: A Computational Model of Self-Enforcing Norms." *American Journal of Sociology* 110(4): 1009–40.

Claveau, F. 2012. "The Russo–Williamson Theses in the Social Sciences: Causal Inference Drawing on Two Types of Evidence." *Studies in History and Philosophy of Science Part C* 43: 806–13.

DiMaggio, P. 2015. "Adapting Computational Text Analysis to Social Science (and Vice Versa)." *Big Data and Society* 2(2) doi: 10.1177/2053951715602908.

Ensminger, J. and Henrich, J. (eds.). 2014. *Experimenting with Social Norms: Fairness and Punishment in Cross-Cultural Perspective*. New York: Russell Sage Foundation.

Guala, F. 2008. "Paradigmatic Experiments: The Ultimatum Game from Testing to Measurement Device." *Philosophy of Science* 75: 658–69.

Guala, F. 2012. "Reciprocity: Weak or Strong? What Punishment Experiments Do (and Do Not) Demonstrate." *Behavioral and Brain Sciences* 35: 1–15.

Henrich, J., Boyd, R., Bowles, S., Camerer, C., Fehr, E., and Gintis, H. (Eds.). 2004. *Foundations of Human Sociality: Economic Experiments and Ethnographic Evidence from Fifteen Small-Scale Societies*. Oxford: Oxford University Press.

Kincaid, H. 1996. *Philosophical Foundations of the Social Sciences: Analyzing Controversies in Social Research*. Cambridge: Cambridge University Press.

King, G., Keohane, R., and Verba, S. 1994. *Designing Social Inquiry. Scientific Inference in Qualitative Research*. Princeton, NJ: Princeton University Press.

Lee, M. and Martin, J.-L. 2015. "Coding, Counting, and Cultural Cartography." *American Journal of Cultural Sociology* 3: 1–33.

McFarland, D. and McFarland, R. 2015. "Big Data and the Danger of Being Precisely Inaccurate." *Big Data and Society* 2(2) doi: 10.1177/2053951715602495.

Morgan, S. and Winship, C. 2007. *Counterfactuals and Causal Inference: Methods and Principles for Social Research*. Cambridge: Cambridge University Press.

Open Science Collaboration. 2015. "Estimating the Reproducibility of Psychological Science." *Science* 349 doi: 10.1126/science.aac4716.

Risjord, M. 2000. *Woodcutters and Witchcraft: Rationality and Interpretive Change in the Social Sciences*. New York: SUNY Press.

Russo, F. and Williamson, J. 2007. "Interpreting Causality in the Health Sciences." *International Studies in the Philosophy of Science* 21(2): 157–70.

Ruzzene, A. 2013. "Process Tracing as an Effective Epistemic Complement." *Topoi* 33(2): 1–12.

Sampson, R. 2012. *Great American City: Chicago and the Enduring Neighborhood Effect*. Chicago: University of Chicago Press.

Steel, D. 2004. "Social Mechanisms and Causal Inference." *Philosophy of the Social Sciences* 34(1): 55–78.

Steel, D. 2008. *Across the Boundaries: Extrapolation in Biology and Social Science*. Oxford: Oxford University Press.

Willer, R., Kuwabara, K., and Macy, M. 2009. "The False Enforcement of Unpopular Norms." *American Journal of Sociology* 115(2): 451–90.

Ylikoski, P. and Kuorikoski, J. 2016. "Self-Interest, Norms, and Explanation," in Risjord, M. (ed.) *Normativity and Naturalism in the Philosophy of the Social Sciences*. Abingdon: Routledge.

# Part II
# CONCEPTS

# 9
# EXPLANATION
## *David Henderson*

### Introduction

When thinking about scientific and social scientific explanation, one cannot simply reflect on the common use of terms such as 'explanation' and 'explains'. Doing so may afford some perspective, but scientific explanations would turn out to be a special class of what passes for explanation in common and wide usages. Such terms are very flexible or diverse in their usage. One plausible understanding of them is that they mark out what counts as satisfactory answers to a rather diverse set of questions. One can *explain why something happened*, of course; and this prominently includes some scientific explanations—those explaining why some event occurred or why some regularity obtains. But one can also *explain why it is good or right* to do some act—and while scientific results may be relevant there, such are not of themselves scientific explanations. One can explain *how some item* (perhaps an organ) *functions within a system* (perhaps that which maintains blood sugar in a certain range). Again, this includes some scientific explanations. But one can also explain how one is thinking—and here an adequate explanation of how one is thinking is one that merely communicates the content of one's thoughts. Related terms, such as 'understanding', are similarly broad and flexible (see, for example, Grimm 2014).

In giving an account of scientific (and social scientific) explanations, one does better reflecting on the more restrictive evaluation of "explanations" within the sciences and on the kinds of information that the sciences can and sometimes do afford for answering the restricted class of explanation-seeking questions. Plausibly, the social sciences afford information of a sort like that of the sciences generally—information affording explanatory practices that are rather like those in the sciences generally.

Here is a leading idea: scientific work provides general, empirically tested and testable, information that allows one to understand why certain events and regularities obtain. One *explains why* certain composite materials (with certain properties) form in certain settings. One explains why folk punish norm violators. In both cases, one appeals to general information about some of the items—atoms and humans, and systems composed of these things. One *explains how* certain systems work in terms of the organized interaction of their parts—machines and their parts, physiological systems and their organs, minds and their neurons and transmitters, groups and their agents. There certainly seem to be deep parallels in some of the explanations and explanatory information found there.

This chapter focuses on two issues:

First, what is the place of laws, or special classes of empirically supported generalizations, in social scientific explanation? Insofar as the social sciences are sciences, there is at least a very strong presumption that many explanations there should be recognizable as instances of what amounts to explanation in the sciences generally. A central question in the philosophy of science generally has been the place of laws (or special classes of empirically supported generalizations) in scientific explanation. On this matter, how uniform are the sciences generally, the special sciences, and the social sciences specifically? It is common to write of the explanation supporting generalities as *laws*. Yet some philosophers have worried that too many unrealistic requirements have come to be associated with talk of "laws," and that one would do better abandoning talk of laws (Woodward, as discussed below, pursues this line).

Second, what is the cognitive achievement that constitutes (scientific) explanation? What is the cognitive itch that explanation scratches? Is it best understood as some distinctive unified understanding? Or is it an identification of certain dependencies in the phenomena or events of interest? What is the character of explanatory dependencies?

Obviously, the two questions are intimately related—answers to the one constrain and inform answers to the other. In effect, we seek to understand the character of the cognitive achievement that the relevant generalizations afford. One may seem to have enough of a sense for answers to one of the questions—perhaps the first—that one reasonably seeks to root one's account there. But, if this leads to persistent tension with what sense one has for the other question, one has a real problem. Perhaps one has rooted a weed with useless or inadequate fruit. One needs coordinated answers to the two questions.

## The Place for Laws in Explaining Why

The contemporary discussion of scientific explanation takes its departure from Hempel's classic (1965) formulation of an empiricist model. On Hempel's account, a scientific explanation is an argument; its conclusion characterizes the "phenomena to be explained" (the explanandum), while its premises (the explanans) include a law (or laws) and related initial conditions. The law must be essential to the derivation of the explanandum—not mere fluff thrown in among the premises. On this central deductive-nomological (or DN) model, the explananda is shown to be a deductive consequence of the law(s) and initial conditions. To allow for explanations that turn on irreducibly probabilistic laws, Hempel also envisioned inductive-statistical (or IS) explanations. These required statistical generalizations that also were laws. Hempel's account has been particularly influential. For a reflection of many of the twists and turns in the subsequent discussion, see Salmon (1989) and Woodward (2014b).

A lot here seems to rest on the idea of a nomic generalization—a law. So satisfactory development turned on explicating this notion. A central idea is that some generalizations represent mere accidental regularities, while others—the laws—are not so accidental. But it is not at all easy to make this distinction precise. At least as a starting place one might suggest that laws are true, exceptionless, universal generalizations, and that they mention factors that make a difference in the course of events. The idea that laws mention factors that make a difference is particularly interesting. Given Humean scruples shared by Hempel and his fellow empiricists, many philosophers of science were at least uncomfortable with modalities (characterizing what "would" happen had the world been different, rather than simply what does happen—a regularity in the world as it is).[1] Yet, it was taken to be diagnostic of laws that they support counterfactual conditionals. Laws allowed us to understand how things would have been different in certain respects had various initial conditions been different. Applied to cases, they allow one to isolate factors on which the explanandum depended—factors that were necessary for the explanadum in the conditions obtaining, or perhaps sufficient. They characterized patterns of dependence in the relevant physical, chemical, biological, or social setting.

This much seems important: that certain regularities in certain domains have empirically proven pretty robust, and that these are then supposed or deployed when evaluating modal claims about (for example) what "would" or "had to" happen were various conditions to have obtained. The importance of generalizations accurately capturing such patterns of dependency seems to be central to explanation, even for philosophers who are ready to abandon talk of laws—for Woodward (2000, 2003), explanatory generalizations allow one to answer *what-if-things-had-been-different* questions.

Note that Hempel's account of scientific results—laws—is fitting to his account of what it is to explain: explanations answer the why-question by showing that the explanandum was to be expected, given the initial conditions. In the case of DN explanations, the initial conditions are those that the true universal conditional characterizes as nomically sufficient for the explanandum (Hempel 1965, 337). In the case of IS explanation, one explains by showing that the explanandum was highly probable. In some cases, we might need to make do with incomplete information that nevertheless allows one to answer why-questions in a way that is informed by approximations to laws—generalizations that are not strictly true universal generalizations free of spatial and temporal restrictions and of *ceteris paribus* qualifications. Hempel allows that such partial explanatory understanding may result from something short of a law deployed in what is an "explanation sketch" (Hempel 1965, 423). There is a sense in which one has an explanation here, if an explanation is an answer to the relevant why-question and if partial answers are answers of sorts.

Many philosophers have thought that Hempel's account of laws is overly demanding—that either the laws that science affords commonly meet fittingly less demanding conditions or something less than laws are adequate to scientific explanation. As will be discussed below, Woodward (2000) argues that generalizations with a significant degree of invariance can explain—and that this is typically what the sciences yield. Woodward feels no need to make a case for thinking that these generalizations are laws, and indeed is disinclined to so label them.

In any case, there are telling problems with the idea that one explains simply by subsuming an explanandum event, state-of-affairs, or phenomenon under some universal generalization. For example, the height of a flagpole, the elevation of the sun at some time, and the law-like rectilinear propagation of light may explain the length of the pole's shadow at that time. But one could just as well deduce the height of the pole from the length of the shadow—and this would not explain the height of the pole! Such asymmetries in explanation suggest that explanation must somehow fill one in on dependencies that need not be evident from at least some nomic generalizations. Further support for such concerns is provided by the observation that, even were it a law that one who takes birth-control pills will not get pregnant, one could not explain Jim not getting pregnant on the basis of his having taken birth-control pills. Salmon (1989, 46ff.) discusses many such problems and suggestions. It seems right to conclude that, insofar as it does not require, or provide the resources for, sorting out asymmetrical causal dependencies in events and processes, the covering law account with its account of laws as simply true universal generalizations is too thin. Nomic expectability, as understood there, may readily fall short of explanation.

A richer account of explanation and explanatory information is apparently needed, and there have been numerous suggestions. For example, Salmon (1971) initially tried to provide the resources for making the relevant distinctions by attention to regularities that still do not invoke causality—relying instead on the still austere notion of statistical dependency. Salmon (1984) subsequently abandoned this approach, proposing what he termed the Causal Mechanical (or CM) Model. The basic idea of this model is that one's scientific generalizations should characterize processes of a distinctive sort. These are processes that can "transmit a mark"—their parameters may be changed by interaction with other processes, and these parameters then tend to be conserved or to develop in generalizable ways. Notice that both the matters of "marking a process" and the "transmission of a mark" are understood in terms of counter-factual conditionals—of how things would have been different were certain things not to occur, or were certain things to occur. The interaction of such processes are causal interactions. Generalizations regarding such processes and their interactions carry information about causal dependencies. Thus, the CM model seems a move in a helpful direction. However, as it was developed, it seems to be subject to some of the problems that it was intended to solve (for a concise summary, see Woodward (2014b, 37–43). It is particularly significant for purposes of the philosophy of the social science that Salmon's characterization of causal processes applies most naturally to simple continuous physical systems. Its application is tenuous in connection with the special sciences in which one is commonly dealing with complex, composite, processes extended in space and time.

Kitcher (1981, 1989) suggested a different way of enriching the covering law model. He proposed that many explanations be understood as a matter of deploying patterned structures of argument—explanation schemata. In effect, these are schematic exemplars for the explanation of significant ranges of phenomena. Here, explanations continue to be understood as arguments that account for their explananda. An explanation schema provides a framework for fitting such phenomena into a patterned set—for example, a set of evolutionary arguments drawing on similar classes of initial conditions. This is admittedly laudable. On the other hand, Kitcher does not build causal notions into his account—and this seems a limiting feature. For a development of such concerns regarding Kitcher's Explanation Schemata (or ES) Model, see Woodward (2003, ch. 8).

The general philosophical accounts of scientific explanation and laws discussed to this point confront additional misgivings when thinking about the special sciences generally, and in the social sciences in particular. These have to do with several common general ideas about laws that would seem to make laws (and, on these accounts, explanations) impossible to come by in the special and social sciences. Central here is the idea that laws are true exceptionless generalizations unrestricted with respect to time and place. This is a lot to ask, and it seems clearly too much to ask when studying those complex, contingent, evolving systems that are the subject of biology, psychology, and the social sciences.

The idea that laws are universal generalizations has sometimes been taken to require that they not mention specific times and places. It may, for example, be a true universal generalization that all coins in my pocket on July 12, 2015 are silver in color. On no plausible account would this be the kind of universal generalization that makes for a law. But, if strictures against being spatially or temporally restricted are understood to prohibit generalizations treating of contingent, spatially and temporally located systems, then the special sciences can have no laws. After all, both biological systems and species, and social systems and entities, are undeniably transient, spatially and temporally located entities. It seems that one must recognize that, while the relevant biological or social scientific generalization make no explicit reference to times and places, some of the concepts and terms featured there have reference to historically specific entities—for example, species as populations of organisms with certain features that evolved at a time and place, or groups organized in terms of certain classes of norms which again are historically specific. The empirically supported generalizations of the special sciences deal with kinds and entities that arise contingently. Significantly, in various degrees, the systems of interest in the special sciences do have a significant persistence—and thus, subject to a range of background conditions, one can generalize about regularities in those systems.

Parallel points pertain to the idea that laws are exceptionless generalizations. The special sciences deal with populations, commonly organized into complex systems—and the individuals within the relevant population are not utterly homogeneous. One atom (of a particular isotope) of an element may behave pretty much like any other, but one instance of a species or one tallgrass prairie ecosystem, or one member of a tribe of hunter-gatherers, need not behave exactly like any other. (Indeed, the point is important for the theory of evolution and for some theories of cultural change.) Given such variations, exceptionless generalizations are hard to come by in the special sciences. There have been a range of responses to this point.

One family of responses takes its departure from the idea of a *ceteris paribus* generalization—a universal generalization with a *ceteris paribus* clause that might serve as a place-holder for refinements yet to come. One version of this idea is that the *ceteris paribus* clause represents one's inarticulate and commonly incomplete understanding of a law that is yet to be fully grasped. On this view, it would be natural to say that such *ceteris paribus* generalizations can feature in something short of an explanation, but rather like an explanation (recall Hempel's "explanation sketches"). Again, on such an account, the explanation itself would require us to eliminate the *ceteris paribus* clauses, turning the fleshed out generalization into a law. This view holds on to the connection between explanations and laws, while allowing for partial answers to explanation-seeking why-questions in terms of an incomplete grasp of a law. On this view, the special sciences have yet to provide an explanation, for they have yet to find a law, but they have sketched many approximations affording partial answers to why-questions.

The whole tenor of this appeal to explanation sketches rooted in *ceteris paribus* approximations to laws seems misguided for a simple reason: the reasons for laws being hard to come by in the special sciences are themselves reasons to think that the class of *ceteris paribus* conditions are diverse and unmanageable at the level of the special sciences. There are too many variations on being a grizzly bear, rooted in both genetics, grizzly life histories, and ecological (including *in utero*) conditions to accommodate when generalizing about grizzly bears—and there will always be more conditions waiting in the wings. Similarly for humans—and human psychology. Similarly for human norm and norm following. If *ceteris paribus* generalizations are not laws, there likely are no laws to be discovered in the social sciences.

More revisionary responses have either (a) allowed that *ceteris paribus* generalizations are not laws and yet can provide explanations—answers to explanation-seeking why-questions (for example), or (b) allow that *ceteris paribus* generalizations can be laws. The first response abandons the law/explanation connection—the second adopts a less demanding account of laws. Kincaid (1990) and McIntyre (1996) pursue the second option, defending the place for laws—*ceteris paribus* laws—in the special and social sciences.

Woodward (2000, 2003) has developed an influential account along the first lines. Although Woodward does not write of ceteris paribus generalizations, he focuses on generalizations with a significance but limited range or "domain of invariance." Woodward is concerned to articulate the features of certain generalizations in virtue of which those generalizations can foster explanations and serve as themselves explanatory. Here are some leading ideas:

First, the generalizations that support the prominent class of explanations are those that would allow us to answer a range of what Woodward terms "what-if-things-had-been-different questions." This is to say that, not only can an appropriate generalization be used in connection with information about initial conditions to show the explanandum was to be expected, as the traditional DN model demands, but it can also provide an understanding of how the explanandum variable would be different were the explanans variables to take a range of different values. In the terms used above, the generalization allows one to appreciate the patterns of dependency involving the parameters mentioned in the generalization.

Second, whether or not a generalization can be used to explain has to do with whether it is significantly *invariant rather than with whether it is lawful* (as judged using traditional measures). The idea of an invariant generalization turns on the idea of an *intervention*.

The idea of *an intervention* involves an idealization of an experimental situation—but one that need not be done by humans or planned (there are "natural experiments"): "an intervention on some variable $X$ with respect to some second variable $Y$ is a causal process that changes $X$ in some appropriately exogenous way, so that if a change in $Y$ occurs, it occurs only in virtue of the change in $X$, and not as a result of some other set of causal factors" (Woodward 2000, 200). An *invariant generalization* describing a relationship between two or more variables *is invariant if it would continue to hold—would remain stable or unchanged—as various other conditions change* as the result of interventions. The set or range of changes over which a relationship is invariant is its *domain of invariance*.

One can distinguish two sorts of changes that are relevant when thinking of invariance:

1. Changes "that we would intuitively regard as the background conditions to some generalization—changes that affect other variables besides those that figure in the generalization itself" (Woodward 2000, 205). (The gravitational inverse square law is untouched by the Dow Jones average, or by the temperature of objects, for example.)
2. Changes in those variables that figure explicitly in the generalization itself.

"For a generalization to count as invariant, there must be some interventions ... for variables figuring in the relationship for which it is invariant" (Woodward 2000, 206). This does not require that it is invariant across all such changes. The ideal gas law, $PV = nRT$, is famously invariant only under some range of interventions on temperature, for example. Invariance is a matter of degree—as a generalization may hold under a more of less wide range of interventions.

Woodward's approach provides a particularly congenial framework for thinking about much explanation in the special science, including the social sciences. One can arrive at generalizations that characterize regularities in complex, contingent, evolving systems that are the subject of biology, psychology, and the social sciences. Some of these generalizations will characterize dependencies within the system that might in principle be investigated experimentally—by intervening (or watching for natural interventions). Some of these generalizations will have a significant domain of invariance. With a more or less articulate sense for this domain of invariance, we can use the relevant generalizations to answer what-if-things-had-been-different questions, grasping dependencies, and explaining what transpires.

Woodward's account is probably a largely adequate account of an important class of explanation in the social sciences. In particular, it accounts for how the kind of generalizations afforded by the special sciences can explain why certain events or regularities obtain. This amounts to a qualified recommendation: Woodward's account is recommended as a largely adequate account of *one* important class of explanations. To see the significance of this qualification, recall that there are at least two constraints on (or resources in) understanding explanation in the sciences. First, one has some sense for the place of laws, or special classes of empirically supported generalizations, in scientific, including social scientific, explanation. Developing on this sense has been the central pursuit in what has transpired to this juncture. We have discussed Hempel's classical, mid-twentieth-century, attempt to say what the generalizations would need to be like, and surveyed various misgivings and alternatives. We arrived at a seemingly superior account. All this should be understood in light of the second matter: what is the cognitive achievement that constitutes scientific explanation? What is the cognitive itch that explanation scratches? The explanations on which we have to this point focused provided answers to questions regarding why some event (or phenomena) occurred (or occurs), in contrast to some other event (or phenomena). In Woodward's terms, this is a matter of answering what-if-things-had-been-different questions. One grasps such patterns of dependency in light of generalizations having significant invariance.

## Functional Explanations as How-Explanations

In addition explanation-seeking questions concerning why various events or phenomena obtained, there are other kinds of explanation-seeking question asked and answered in the sciences. Sometimes, one seeks to understand or explain *how* certain systems work. Commonly we do this by analyzing the organized interaction of the components of the system. For example, we might explain how humans and related animals maintain blood glucose levels within certain ranges by an analysis of the system. Here we would characterize the components of the system (the liver, the pancreas) and their dispositions to react to certain states of their environment (by releasing certain hormones such as insulin or glucagon, for example). We trace how such responses act on other components of the system (prompting glucose/glycogen inter-conversion, for example). The dispositions of the relevant components, and the mechanisms of the processes making for these dispositions, are, of course, understood in terms of significantly invariant generalizations. So our analytical understanding of *how* the system managed to do what it does (for example, its capacity for maintaining blood glucose homeostasis) meshes well with the kinds of causal explanations discussed already. Still, while related to causal explanations, the explanation provided by the analysis of the system itself is different. It affords an analytical answer to *the question of how* the system does what it does. (For a developed version of this example, see Rosenberg 1985, ch. 3.)

Cummins (1975, 1983) develops an account of "functional analysis" in which functions are causal roles in a system. One can analyze the relatively sophisticated capacity of a complex system—a computer, a radio receiver, a cognitive agent, a hunting party, an economy—into the organized workings of a set of simpler capacities. These simpler capacities are "functions" or causal roles performed by system components. Here there need be no suggestion that the disposition of the whole system is desirable or good—although the related talk of a capacity might suggest otherwise. Cummins (1975) discusses how characterizing such functions-as-causal-roles in an organized system provides explanation of the sophisticated causal disposition of the system. Call this the Analytical Functional Model of explanation (AF). On this AF model, the functional understanding of *how* a system works is distinct from an explanation of why there is a system (or a component) with such dispositions capacities—although this explanatory analysis of how a system works can often be used in a further explanation of why there are such systems.

Arguably, talk of functions and functional explanation is ambiguous. For there is a common type of explanation, itself associated with talk of functions, that does seek to explain *why* there are systems with particular dispositions of the sort Cummins discusses. On the account of functional explanation articulated by Wright (1976) a function is a capacity (in effect a function as understood by Cummins) that has a significant role in a *selection explanation* of the items having that capacity. Having the ability to maintain body temperature within a certain range may give individuals with that ability (or proto-ability) an evolutionary advantage. Similarly, by way of example, in much recent social scientific work on norms, there is the idea that the ability to coordinate on the provision of certain kinds of public goods may give a competitive advantage to certain groups, and that this may have given some advantage to individuals with certain social sentiments and dispositions. Such explanations would envision selection at multiple levels, rooted in various dispositions that constitute functions in Cummins's AF sense (see Sober and Wilson 1998; and Boyd and Richerson 1985; J. Henrich et al. 2004; N. Henrich and Henrich 2007; Richerson and Boyd 2005).

## Explanatory Information in Forms Other Than Generalizations?

Let us again focus on causal explanations of why some event obtained. Why did the members of the tribe punish the agent who failed to participate in the hunt? Why did the punishment take the form and severity that it did? We have seen that explaining such matters involves the grasp of how things would have been different in the relevant respects had things been different in the antecedents.

I have suggested that explanations of particular events or particular phenomena can depend on generalizations with a fitting degree of invariance. Some of the relevant generalizations deal with the social psychology *of humans*—thus having application to a delimited class of systems. This befits many invariant generalizations in the special sciences. Further, many of these generalizations would only hold within certain ranges of conditions, and this is in keeping with the idea of a domain of invariance for a given generalization. Here are some of the relevant generalizations: Certain primates feel uncomfortable excitement when seeing other critters in pain—again within limits and contexts. That is, they tend to have various empathetic and social sentiments. They tend to bob, dodge, or wince in ways that parallel what they might do were the relevant misfortune happening to them instead. These crude generalizations can be refined (see the literature discussed in Goldman 2006). In empirically refining these generalizations, we come to better understand some of the empathetic processes that are important for human coordination and cooperation. Various other relevant generalizations have to do with the human psychology of choice between alternatives. For example, people in an economy and political/social system will be more responsive to situations framed in terms of risks than to the parallel situation framed in terms of opportunities. Some of their choices will be managed by quick heuristics rather than slower algorithmic processes. Again, this can be refined (Kahneman 2011; Kahneman, Slovic, and Tversky 1982). There do seem to be real differences in kinds of closeness of social relationships, and these can be relevant when explaining episodes of human cooperation. Again, these are matters subject to further study and evolutionary explanation (J. Henrich and Boyd 2001; N. Henrich and Henrich 2007). So, we do have invariant generalizations (in various stages of development) that afford us social scientific explanation of phenomena such as that mentioned above.

At the same time, a strong case can be made for the claim that we humans also have a differently based ability to understand and explain each other's actions, choices, beliefs, and desires (individually and in combination)—an ability that sometimes provides explanations that go beyond those explanations we can underwrite by scientifically tested generalizations with fitting degrees of invariance: humans have some capacity for understanding and explaining one another by using our own cognitive and conative processes (with some set up) to simulate others.

As writers like Goldman (2006) and Stueber (2006) characterize these simulation-based explanations, they proceed in three phases: First, there is the *matching phase* in which one assembles a set of pretend-beliefs and pretend-desires on which to deploy one's cognitive processes. One might understand pretend-beliefs and pretend-desires as beliefs that one adds to one's own set of standing beliefs and desires. One will commonly need to prevent certain beliefs or desires that as a matter fact one possesses from having a role in the processing to come—as the subject of one's simulation may lack that information or those desires. Second, the *simulation phase*, in which one's cognitive process are put to work employing the content (the make-beliefs, make-desires, attitudes, and likely observations) assembled in the matching phase. This is the phase in which one determines where such content would lead (assuming an agent were using processes relevantly similar to one's own). Third, an *attribution phase*, in which what transpired in the simulation phase serves as a basis for the attribution of lines of thought and thus dependencies in thought to one's subject.

Call this the Simulation Model of explanation (SM). It has clear connections with models of empathetic understanding and one may want to compare other contributions to this volume—on *verstehen* and interpretation and critical theory, for example.

The whole has something of a hypothetical character: if the cognition occurring in us plausibly yields the beliefs, desires, and decisions that obtained in the episode in question—the explananda—and if we have consistent successes in our related simulations, then we have some basis for confidence that we are accurately simulating the others' thoughts and dependencies in those thoughts.

Henderson (1996, 2011) argues that simulation-based explanations are like the explanations invoking invariant generalizations in that they answer to why- or what-if-things-had-been-different questions. But, the answer here is not arrived at by subsuming the events or processes under moderately invariant generalizations characterizing regularities. Instead they are arrived at by way of putting in play in us cognitive processes that are rather like the processes in play in the others. One's sense for the dependencies in the cases, for how things would have been different were certain conditions different, comes by way of making things different in one's pretense. But for this to reveal dependencies in the other's cognition, one's processes must be relevantly similar to those processes in play in the agents simulated. Here there is room for a lot of interpenetration of simulation and propositional understandings in the form of more or less invariant generalizations (Henderson 2011).

We began this chapter by noting that while 'explanation' is a rather flexible term—explanations as they feature in science is a rather more specific or delimited matter. In one central class of cases, scientific explanation turns on providing answers to why-questions or what-if-things-had-been-different questions. Such answers afford an understanding of patterns of dependency in the course of events, or in the relations between phenomena. In paradigmatic scientific explanation, this is provided by the application of generalizations with a significant degree of invariance. Whether or not one terms these generalizations "laws" is perhaps a matter of taste. In a second class of cases, scientific explanation turns on providing answers to how-questions, exhibiting how some disposition or "capacity" of a system arises out of the structure and capacities of components of the system (explaining how neurons can think, for example, or groups can pursue public goods). Again, this is managed in terms of generalizations concerning the organization of specific classes of systems and the causal regularities involving their constituents. Now we have come upon this twist: It seems to be the case that some answers to why- or what-if-things-had-been-different questions are afforded by using ourselves to simulate the other. Such simulation may be conditioned by much background propositional information, including more or less invariant generalizations. Such information may inform how we set up our simulation (the matching phase) and our confidence that we have succeeded (the attribution phase). But its core, the simulation phase itself, is not a matter of propositional derivation from background generalizations.

What we get by simulation then answers what-if-things-had-been-different questions, and qualifies as explanation. In an important sense, it is the same sort of explanation as the kind of explanation afforded by subsuming events and phenomena under invariant generalizations. But, one may wonder whether, or in what sense, it constitutes a form of scientific explanation.

If the question is whether it is a *distinctively* scientific form of explanation, the answer clearly is no—it is not distinctive of scientific explanation in the sense of being largely restricted to work in the sciences. It is found across in much of everyday human interpretive and explanatory practice. But note, the same can be said of those answers to what-if-things-had-been-different questions that draw on more or less invariant generalizations. When one explains the window's breaking by it being struck by a rock, one explains in terms of very moderately invariant generalizations involving common glass and hard objects. What is distinctive about the scientific explanation involving invariant generalizations is not the use of generalizations to answer what-if-things-had-been-different questions, but the typical empirical depth and precision of the generalizations (and the use of predicates that have undergone greater empirical selection).

One might wonder whether there is a difference in the extent to which simulation explanations are subject to being refined in the way in which scientific explanations relying on invariant generalizations are. Here there is likely a mixed picture. First, there is little reason to think that the matching cannot be better informed as we obtain better information about diversity in human cognitive and cultural processes. Further, there is reason to think that the attribution phase might be informed by refined information about cultural and cognitive differences and the limits of agents' cognitive plasticity. But, it is plausible that the heart of simulation, one's own processes and the limits of their momentary plasticity, may limit the refinement of simulation in a way that has no general scientific parallel (see Henderson 2011).

It is certainly the case that simulation plays an important role in social scientific practice. Consider a work such as N. Henrich and Henrich (2007), in which the authors look to explain the tight, but varying, cooperation within an ethnic community within Detroit—and to use this to support explanations of human cooperation within communities generally. Here, generalizations at many levels (evolutionary, psychological, anthropological) are clearly in play in overlapping ways. At the same time, in gathering their quantitative and qualitative data, the authors make use of close field observation and interviews. Arguably, in many instances, they rely on simulation for understanding what is presented to them.

These remarks on simulation and explanation relate to a thought regarding disciplinary variation in explanatory aspirations. Woodward (2014a, 210) notes that highly general models such as the covering law, unification, causal-mechanical, or interventionist models have a "universalist aspiration" of providing a one-size-fits-all account. He continues, "Such models should reveal commonalities across disciplines; but they should also enable us to see why explanatory practice varies as it does across disciplines and the significance of such variation." Biologists, for example, may be particularly concerned to analyze mechanisms, thereby tracking causal processes underlying their analyzed capacities. Functional analysis may then play a larger role in biology than in physics. Social scientists may have parallel concerns, in keeping with the kinds of special systems that are their subject of study. They may also use simulation at important junctures.

# Note

1 It is safe to say that over the last forty years philosophers have come to be increasingly comfortable with such modalities.

# References

Boyd, Robert, and Richerson, Peter J. (1985). *Culture and the Evolutionary Process*. Chicago: University of Chicago Press.

Cummins, Robert. (1975). "Functional Analysis." *Journal of Philosophy* 72, 741–65.

Cummins, Robert. (1983). *The Nature of Psychological Explanation*. Cambridge, MA: MIT Press.

Goldman, Alvin I. (2006). *Simulating Minds: The Philosophy, Psychology, and Neuroscience of Mindreading*. Oxford and New York: Oxford University Press.

Grimm, Stephen R. (2014). *Understanding as Knowledge of Causes Virtue Epistemology Naturalized: Bridges between Virtue Epistemology and Philosophy of Science*. Dordrecht: Springer Netherlands.

Hempel, Carl G. (1965). *Aspects of Scientific Explanation, and Other Essays in the Philosophy of Science*. New York: Free Press.

Henderson, David. (1996). "Simulation Theory vs. Theory Theory: A Difference without a Difference in Explanation." *Southern Journal of Philosophy* 34, 65–94.

Henderson, David. (2011). "Let's be Flexible." *Journal of the Philosophy of History* 5, 261–99. doi: 10.1163/187226311X582347.

Henrich, J., and Boyd, R. (2001). "Why People Punish Defectors: Weak Conformist Transmission can Stabilize Costly Enforcement of Norms in Cooperative Dilemmas." *Journal of Theoretical Biology* 208, 79–89.

Henrich, J., Boyd, R., Bowles, S., Camerer, C., Fehr, E., and Gintis, H. (eds.). (2004). *Foundations of Human Sociality: Economic Experiments and Ethnographic Evidence from Fifteen Small-Scale Societies*. Oxford and New York: Oxford University Press.

Henrich, Natalie, and Henrich, Joseph Patrick. (2007). *Why Humans Cooperate: A Cultural and Evolutionary Explanation*. Oxford and New York: Oxford University Press.

Kahneman, Daniel. (2011). *Thinking, Fast and Slow*. New York: Farrar, Straus and Giroux.

Kahneman, Daniel, Slovic, Paul, and Tversky, Amos. (1982). *Judgment under Uncertainty: Heuristics and Biases*. Cambridge and New York: Cambridge University Press.

Kincaid, Harold. (1990). "Defending Laws in the Social Sciences." *Philosophy of the Social Sciences* 20(1), 56–83.

Kitcher, Philip. (1981). "Explanatory Unification." *Philosophy of Science* 48, 507–31.

Kitcher, Philip. (1989). "Explanatory Unification and the Causal Structure of the World." *Scientific Explanation XI*. Minneapolis: University of Minnesota Press, 410–504.

McIntyre, Lee. (1996). *Laws and Explanation in the Social Sciences: Defending a Science of Human Behavior.* Boulder, CO: Westview.

Richerson, Peter. J., and Boyd, Robert. (2005). *Not by Genes Alone: How Culture Transformed Human Evolution.* Chicago: University of Chicago Press.

Rosenberg, Alexander. (1985). *The Structure of Biological Science.* Cambridge and New York: Cambridge University Press.

Salmon, Wesley C. (1971). "Statistical Explanation." in W. C. Salmon, R. C. Jeffrey and J. G. Greeno (Eds.), *Statistical Explanation and Statistical Relevance.* Pittsburgh: University of Pittsburgh Press, 29–87.

Salmon, Wesley C. (1984). *Scientific Explanation and the Causal Structure of the World.* Princeton, NJ: Princeton University Press.

Salmon, Wesley C. (1989). *Four Decades of Scientific Explanation.* Minneapolis: University of Minnesota Press.

Sober, Elliott, and Wilson, David Sloan. (1998). *Unto Others: The Evolution and Psychology of Unselfish Behavior.* Cambridge, MA: Harvard University Press.

Stueber, Karsten R. (2006). *Rediscovering Empathy: Agency, Folk Psychology, and the Human Sciences.* Cambridge, MA: MIT Press.

Woodward, James. (2000). "Explanation and Invariance in the Special Sciences." *British Journal for the Philosophy of Science* 51(2), 197–254.

Woodward, James. (2003). *Making Things Happen: A Theory of Causal Explanation.* New York: Oxford University Press.

Woodward, James. (2014a). "Explanation." in M. Curd and S. Psillos (Eds.), *The Routledge Companion to Philosophy of Science*, 2nd edn. New York: Routledge, 203–13.

Woodward, James. (2014b). "Scientific Explanation." *The Stanford Encyclopedia of Philosophy*, Edward N. Zalta (Ed.) (Winter). Accessed August 10, 2015. http://plato.stanford.edu/archives/win2014/entries/scientific-explanation/.

Wright, Larry. (1976). *Teleological Explanations: An Etiological Analysis of Goals and Functions.* Berkeley: University of California Press.

# 10
# REDUCTIONISM

## *Harold Kincaid*

My mandate in this chapter is to write about reductionism in the social sciences. Given this task my focus is on how reductionism plays out in actual social research. This does not mean that I am not going to discuss reductionism in the philosophy of the social sciences. On my naturalist Quinean view (Kincaid 1996), philosophy of social science and social science are continuous in a strong sense. Arguments in the philosophy of social science ultimately have to be tied to empirical social science; empirical social science in turn often invokes many philosophical arguments.

Questions of reductionism—the idea that theories about social entities can be translated into theories that are only about individual behavior—are live, substantive issues in contemporary social science. The purpose of this chapter is fourfold: to clarify the various different theses that fall under the reductionist rubric, to look at more philosophical arguments that want to decide the issues in general terms, to point to the real empirical issues that are involved, and to say something about where the weight of the evidence lies. However, since there are multiple independent reductionist claims being debated and since the claims ultimately turn on empirical details, no overall assessment of reductionism in the social sciences would make sense.

The chapter begins in section 1 with strict reductionist versions of methodological individualism. It will be argued that there is not much reason to think these versions have much applicability, and standard philosophical arguments both for and against try to show more than can be demonstrated on purely conceptual grounds. However, methodological individualism as a claim about theory reduction continues to have its defenders and moreover the presupposed model of intertheoretic reduction involved provides a clear baseline against which to compare other, logically weaker individualist accounts. Sections 2 and 3 look at versions of reductionism that do not require eliminativist theory reduction, with section 2 examining currently widespread claims that reductionist mechanisms are necessary and section 3 looks at the extent to which social phenomena can be captured in individualist terms without invoking explanations in terms of social entities. Section 4 concludes with a brief listing of other reductionist issues that space precludes me from discussing.

## 1 Prospects for Theory Reduction

A standard version of reductionism in the social sciences is methodological individualism. Apparently, the term was coined my Schumpeter in the early 1950s. It has had a steady stream of advocates from at least then up until the present, though advocates have not generally been careful to state exactly what their version of the doctrine entails. However, the repeated claim has been that all social phenomena should be explained in terms of individual behavior. So Watkins (1955) says "large-scale social phenomena … should be explained in terms of the situations, dispositions and beliefs of individuals." Fifty-eight years later we get a sociologist saying the same thing: "a social fact of any kind must be explained by direct reference to the actions of its constituents [individuals—HK]" (Demeulenaere 2013, Kindle 182).

The claim that all social explanations can be captured in individualist terms can be read as a thesis about theory reduction. The positivists, especially Nagel (1979), developed a fairly clear account of the idea that one theory can be reduced to another as part of their general project of formalizing theories and of promoting the unity of science. The basic requirements they described for reducing one theory to another were (1) two formulated theories, (2) a set of bridge laws linking their basic categories or terms in a lawlike way with each other, and (3) a demonstration that the explanations of the theory to be reduced could be derived from the reducing theory. The bridge laws are required because (and to the extent that) the different theories describe the world in different terms; the laws allow us to substitute the terms of one theory for another in a systematic way.

A classic case of such reduction is supposed to be exemplified by the relation of the gas laws of chemistry to the laws of statistical mechanics of physics. A bridge law, for example, equates the chemical notion of temperature to the physics concept of the mean kinetic energy of the particles in a gas. With the help of that bridge law and others, the laws relating temperature, pressure, and volume should be derivable from Newton's laws applied to gas particles. The explanations of the gas laws should then be able to be fully explained in terms of the physics of the particles composing gases.

This sort of reductive relation is one way of understanding methodological individualism: explanations in social terms should be derivable from explanations in entirely individualist terms. Assuming that parsimony and unification with more fundamental theories is an important scientific goal (and that explanations in terms of individuals are more fundamental), then social explanation should be in terms of individuals.

Several caveats need to be noted about this formulation of methodological individualism to ensure we do not bias the case against that doctrine. The reductionist claim does not have to hold for social theories that are not well supported—there is no requirement to reduce bad social science. The reductionist version of individualism also does not have to claim that we can currently reduce all social explanations. The argument is that this is in principle achievable and a desirable scientific goal. Of course if the claim is so in principle that only God could do it, then methodological individualism would stop being much of a methodological claim about real social science.

How are we to assess this version of reductionism in the social sciences? Philosophers and social scientists on both sides of the issues have thought that some very general conceptual considerations settle the issue.

A standard argument for methodological individualism is that since society is composed of individuals, and no social phenomena happen independently of them, it must be the case that we can explain everything about the social in terms of individuals. Thus Demeulenaere (2013, Kindle 182) says that "1. Social life only exists in virtue of the actors who live it. 2. Consequently a social fact of any kind must be explained by direct reference to the actions of its constituents," quite explicitly claiming that composition entails some kind of reducibility.

So an ontological claim about society is supposed to entail an explanatory claim about the explanatory power of our theories of individual behavior to explain social phenomena. The ontological claims can be made more precise if that seems desirable: social entities are composed solely of individuals and once all the facts about individuals are set, so too are the facts about social phenomena (in standard philosophical terminology social facts supervene on individual facts).

Another standard argument *against* methodological individualism also appeals to some very general ontological facts about society. The argument is that the attitudes and behavior of individuals in society are influenced by their membership in social groups, their social roles, the general organization of society, etc. Social wholes influence individuals. So we cannot explain everything about social wholes in terms of individuals.

Though both of these arguments have long been made and continue to be made for and against reductionist versions of methodological individualism, there are quite compelling reasons to think that they fail. The basic reasons they do so were given some time ago. The basic problem is that there is no entailment from the way the world is made to what our explanatory resources can handle. So take the ontological argument for individualism first. From the fact—if it is one—that social entities are composed of individuals and that social facts supervene on individual facts (see Epstein 2015 for doubts about the latter), it does not follow that we can reduce social explanations to explanations in terms of individuals. Reduction requires bridge laws that allow us to replace higher-level explanations with lower-level explanations.

Yet it is possible that social categories are brought about in indefinitely many ways by groupings of individual behaviors—they are "multiply realized"—and that our explanations of individual behavior presuppose rather than eliminate appeals to social entities and facts. So though there may be indefinitely many ways a corporation can be "realized" or organized in terms of individual behaviors and the relations between them, all the while corporations still share common characteristics as social entities such as profit maximizing. Explanations of the behaviors of individuals in corporations may be about individuals in a sense, but the explanations may invoke facts about norms and organizational structures and incentives.

If either condition holds, then the bridge laws necessary for reduction fail. If social phenomena are multiply realized, then there is no one-to-one equation of them with individual phenomena. If explanations in terms of individuals depend on background social facts, then those explanations do not eliminate the social. These possibilities may be enough to show that composition and supervenience do not entail reducibility.

The arguments just given against reduction have a long philosophical pedigree. The multiple realizations argument goes back to Fodor's (1974) general defense of the autonomy of the non-physical sciences (and more rigorously outlined in Hellman and Thompson 1975). The problem that individual explanations presuppose social context goes back at least to Mandelbaum (1955).

I think there is a general consensus that these arguments are serious obstacles to strict reductionist versions of individualism. Yet there are certainly dissenters. Some have doubted that multiply realizable categories can be legitimate scientific categories at all (Papineau 2009; see Khalidi 2013 for a response). Zahle (2007) raises doubts about arguments that explanations in terms of individuals presuppose social explanations.

The argument against reductionist versions of individuals from downward causation are similarly suspect. It may well be that individual behavior is influenced by the social entities such as organizations that they belong to. From that it does not follow that those social influences could never be cashed out in terms of the individual behaviors making up those social entities; in fact, this is just what the methodological individualist claims. Again, it seems that the ontological facts do not tell us what our explanations can do.

If the multiple realizations and presupposing social explanation arguments are compelling, then arguments for or against reductionist versions of methodological individualism will have to be empirical: they will have to show that issues such as multiple realizability or the presupposing of social information are or are not real-world possibilities. Or, put in other terms, they will have to show that real parts of social science have been reduced or that they are in the process being reduced. The holist will have to give reasons to think that multiple realizations and presupposing social facts when explaining in terms of individuals are likely scenarios.

I know of no individualist successes or near-success in current social science that provide actual individualist reductions in the strict sense. Neoclassical microeconomics or current New Keynesian macroeconomics might be thought to be possible success stories; economists certainly paint them as showing how social phenomena can be explained in terms of constrained individual maximizing. However appearances are deceiving. Microeconomics is generally about the behavior of firms and households, not individuals. Current macroeconomics is about collective entities called representative agents where all consumers or firms are treated as a unitary entity. Even if these accounts are well confirmed—and arguably much microeconomics is and most of contemporary macroeconomics is not—then they do not explain in terms of the traits of individuals but of collective social agents.

There may also be good reasons to think that multiple realization type phenomena occur in the social sciences. For example, many collective social entities are the product of selective processes: firms exist and have the characteristics they do because they survive in a competitive race with other firms and the same probably holds for civil society organizations and even for states. However, selective processes do not "care" how entities organize themselves to win competitions; it is the traits that hold of the collective entity that matter, not how those collective traits are brought about by the organization of individuals making up the collective entity. So diversity in how individual behavior brings about organizational behavior may be likely.

I will argue in the next section that presupposing social facts in the process of explaining individual behavior also is a common situation. Thus on my view strict reductionist versions of individualism are not currently very important issues in the social sciences.

However, there are other considerably more open and live issues surrounding reduction in the social sciences to which I turn now, starting with questions about how individualist we can be or how holist we must be.

## 2 How Individualist Can We Be and How Holist Must We Be?

The strict reductionist vision of individualism is an all or nothing picture: either social phenomena are fully explainable in individualist terms or they are not. Yet there is no reason the issues should be so black and white. Social explanations may invoke social factors to a greater or lesser degree in various senses. I would argue that a number of lively contemporary empirical issues in the social sciences are precisely about how individualist or how holist we must be (Kincaid 2014, 2015).

How could we rank explanations in terms of how individualist they are? While these are not precise metrics by any means, rough rankings can be gotten in part by looking at several different kinds of factors/questions. It is helpful first to make some distinctions between different kinds of "social factors" that we might appeal to in explanations. The clearest cases of social factors are social entities that are, in philosophical terminology, concrete particulars—organized collective social entities that have an identifiable existence over time. So organizations such as corporations, national governments, NGOs, and so on are prime examples. In an intuitive sense these are more social than what are often labeled as institutions. Norms and social roles are examples of institutions; they are social for sure, but it might be argued that they are properties of individuals, something that cannot be said of organizations. So with that distinction in mind we can ask whether an explanation:

- may invoke a richer set of social entities vs. a thinner set
- may give the social entities invoked more or less causal importance relative to individual factors
- makes more reference to organizations relative to institutions.

Each of these elements is independent and I do not pretend that there is any way to determine how exactly they should be traded off to get an overall measure. However, they are enough to make some rough judgments.

So examples of ongoing empirical debates in the social sciences which are about how individualist we can be (or how holist we must be) are:

1. Debates in contemporary experimental and behavioral economics over "other regarding preferences" (Bowles 2006; Binmore 2007) are a controversy over how much extra-individual information we need. The evidence from various experimental games shows that individuals sometimes benefit others at their own expense. Bowles and others think this evidence shows that individuals have innate (in exactly what sense is not clear) preferences for the well-being of others, distastes for inequality, and other such social preferences. This explanation of individual prosocial behavior is more individualist compared to the sort of explanation given by Binmore and others. They argue that norms, the sanctions enforcing them, and the existence of organizations that ensure individuals play repeated games with each other lead individuals to develop—to learn—reciprocating strategies. Individuals in games show other-regarding preferences because they bring them from the institutions and organizations that structure their lives. This is an ongoing debate, and it concerns whether we need to invoke institutions and organization in explaining individual behavior.

2. Smith (2008) suggests that it is an interesting open question to what extent market coordination is the result of individual rationality versus the result of the kind of market institutions they participate in. Gode and Sunde (1993), for example, seem to show that in auctions even quite stupid agents will reach competitive equilibrium. Thus Smith (65) says the issue is "How much of the performance properties of markets are due to characteristics of the individual, and how much to those of institutions?" This is asking how individualist we can be in the sense of whether we need to invoke institutions over and above individual preferences and beliefs to explain economic outcomes.

3. Smith's point here builds on earlier work by Becker. Becker (1962) showed that the aggregate law of downward-sloping demand curve—the law that when prices increase, demand declines—would still hold even if individuals chose randomly, given sufficiently tight budget

constraints and relative prices. The latter will cause decreasing purchases with increasing prices for whatever choices are made, since increasing prices change what can be bought. We do not have to assume much about individuals to explain this aspect of aggregate market behavior and in that sense do not have to be very individualist.

4. Aspects of the debate over the reality of race also turn in important ways on how individualist and holist we should be. The issue here is not the biological reality of race but rather how much our racial categories are due to historically contingent institutional and organizational practices or how much is due to deep-seated individual traits. Of course the two interact. Yet it is an open question whether individual traits that exist across a range of different institutional arrangements and history contribute to the construction of racial categorizations. Mallon and Kelly (2012) show that there is social-psychological and neurobiological evidence that ingroup favoritism and outgroup biases are common. Here is a case where we have to be individualist in ways holists are naturally inclined to reject.

5. Yet on the other side of the racism story is a debate that suggests that we can only be so individualist. Schelling (1969) famously showed that we could explain segregation by only invoking relatively mild individual preferences for living with others of the same race. Using an early form of agent-based simulation, he showed that there were tipping-point phenomena that could produce racial residential segregation. However, the key point here is that Schelling described what could happen. Showing what is possible in a model is not necessarily showing what happens in reality. Research after Schelling demonstrated that the practices of banks and government agencies played a crucial role in American segregation (Massey and Deaton 1996). In this case we cannot be as individualist as Schelling imagined.

6. A long-standing debate in the social sciences concerns the nature of social class (Lareau and Conley 2008; Crompton 2008; and Wright 2005). The current debate in large part resolves around the question of whether social classes are best conceived of as sets of types of individuals or as concrete social entities (Kincaid 2016). Thinking of social classes as types of individuals means looking at characteristics of individuals that sort them into different groups. Income levels and occupations are prime examples. Classes as concrete social entities are macrosociological aggregations that have sufficient structure to be considered particulars. There is good evidence that in the United States there exists a ruling elite that has a complex and dense set of interconnections and organizational elements (Domhoff 2014). That is evidence that the ruling elite is a class in the sense of a concrete individual. When classes are best thought of as types of individuals, then we have a relatively more individualist account. It is relatively individualist in that social elements are still involved: classes as occupational types still presuppose the social organization of work, even if class in this sense is not a concrete particular. Appeals to classes as real collective social entities is obviously a more holist account. The classic Marxist tradition asserts that there is a working class that is a concrete social entity in the same way that the ruling elite in the USA is; on my view the evidence is fairly strong that the Marxist view has been wrong at most points in history and that there are rather working classes in the sense of employment relations and occupations. Thus this debate is an instance of the question of how individualist or holist we should be.

7. A debate related to that over classes concerns the causes of poverty. Such debates have to be careful not to over-generalize: a major part of poverty in India concerns the situation of small-scale rural farmers, while in the USA low-wage urban jobs are much more important. However, focusing on just the USA, a long-standing debate in the social sciences

asks whether poverty results from individual deficits such as lack of skills, education, work ethic and even IQ or rather whether the causes of poverty are low-paying jobs, antiunion policies, taxation policies, the extent of the social safety net, and other macrosociological factors. Of course, the two kinds of explanations are not mutually exclusive. However, there is a real debate in the social sciences over which of these two kinds of factors are most important, which is again a debate over how individualist or holist we should be. On my view at least, we need to be fairly holist (see Royce 2015 for a detailed defense of this claim).

8. Developments in multilevel statistical modeling (Luke 2004)—statistical models that use data about individuals and the groups they belong to—provide ways of answering the question of whether social or individual factors are more important. That question has long looked misplaced in much the same way as the question of whether nature or nurture is more important. However, if we have clearly specified causal models in the right situation the relative size of causal effects can be made sense of. So IQ, school quality, and neighborhood characteristics are variables that can be put into a causal model. Their relative importance can then can be estimated by structural equation modeling techniques. There are complications involved in the statistics, but Shipley (2009) describes promising tests of multilevel causal models by examining the dependencies and independencies among variables in the data that are implied by a possible multilevel causal model. These types of models and empirical investigations are asking how individualist and holist we should be.

## 3 Mechanisms and Reduction

There has been a recent sustained body of literature defending individualism on the grounds that social explanations need mechanisms (see, for example, Demeulenaere 2013). There is a booming philosophical literature on mechanisms (Craver and Darden 2013). However, there are multiple notions of mechanisms and multiple rationales for why they are needed, leaving the debate susceptible to arguments at cross purposes (Kincaid 2012). Thus it is useful to clarify debates over mechanisms in general before turning to the demand for individualist mechanisms.

We need to distinguish at least the following ideas about mechanisms, viz. that they:

- are needed to explain versus to confirm
- are horizontal—mediating connections—or vertical—grounding or composing—in nature
- are essential or just useful.

These are different senses of mechanisms and there is no reason they should all play the same role.

Elster (1983) has claimed that mechanisms are needed to eliminate spurious causes; that is a claim about confirmation. However, others say that accounts are incomplete without mechanisms—that is a claim about explanation.

Much of the mechanisms literature is about the role of compositional detail in explanations. Such mechanisms are "vertical" in that they are about how higher-level processes and capacities are brought about by realizing compositional detail. At other times advocates of mechanisms wants them to remove explanatory gaps between causes and effects, and that concern suggests they want mechanisms in terms of intervening causes, which I label horizontal.

Finally, there is ambiguity about how strongly we need mechanisms. Can we only confirm or explain if we have mechanisms? Or, are our explanations and evidence enhanced—stronger—if we can supply mechanisms?

These are not the only possible dimensions: mechanisms might have different imports depending on the kinds of empirical methods we are using, whether we want theoretical explanations or want to intervene, are identifying causal effects or causal effect sizes, and more. However, just sticking to the three different dimensions mentioned above, it is obvious that there are at least nine different possible theses about the need for mechanisms which need not stand or fall together.

With these distinctions in hand we can now point to some further complications in the need for individualist mechanisms. Nothing in the various claims about mechanisms on their own entails that the mechanisms must be in terms of individuals or at least solely in terms of individuals. There are complications from above and below individuals, as it were. Some good social science supplies mechanisms, but it is not mechanisms in terms of individuals. For example, aggregate market phenomena—total demand and supply—as well as macroeconomic relationships such as that between employment level and government spending—might be explained in terms of corporations and households as the realizing vertical mechanisms. Horizontal mechanisms in macroeconomics can be other macroeconomic variables. From the other direction— from below—mechanisms for social phenomena may be subpersonal (Ainsley 2014). Economic models, for example, sometimes invoke subpersonal agents whose bargaining produces individual behavior. Whether any of these accounts is well confirmed is of course an open question. The point, however, is that mechanisms can be given at multiple levels and that it takes an argument to show that even if we need mechanisms, they must be in terms of individuals.

I think it is implausible to think in general that mechanisms, either horizontal or vertical, are always essential to confirm or explain, though there is a lively debate (Russo and Williams 2007). A problem with thinking that mechanisms are essential is that causal relations between medium-sized objects provide compelling instances where we seem to have well-confirmed causal explanations without either providing underlying detail or a full accounting of all intermediate causes (it is not clear what "all" means here). Much of structural and civil engineering is based upon and provides evidence for such causal claims; so does much of planetary science. So a building collapses because the load of the floor is more than the supporting pillars can take; the position of the moon and the force of gravity cause the tides. All of these explanations can be confirmed without accounts of underlying molecular detail and without giving all the steps between cause and effect.

So a key question is whether the social sciences can provide such aggregate causal explanations. I think sometimes they can. For example, we have some relatively well-confirmed causal accounts of the relations between household and firm behavior in markets. Thus the basic idea that social science can explain at the macrosociological level is not incoherent; the question is just when and where the social sciences can produce similar results, something which is a matter of ongoing controversy.

In macroeconomics, for example, there has been a long debate over what is called "microfoundations" (Hoover 2010). A significant proportion of the economics profession believes that no models can be well confirmed unless they are "grounded" in the constrained maximizing decisions of individuals. This claim is both ambiguous and dubious in at least one sense. It is ambiguous because being "grounded in" individualist mechanisms is not a clear notion. On one reading grounding requires derivability from individual decision making; this is a reductionist thesis. On another reading "grounded in" should be taken as "not inconsistent with." Macroeconomic claims about the causal relation between aggregates such as interest rates and unemployment can potentially be confirmed by ordinary statistical methods that look for correlations when potential confounders are held constant; these are precisely the general types of methods that can be used in confirming the causal relations between medium-sized objects mentioned earlier. These relations can be established and can be explained independently of their being derived from individual behavior.

In the macroeconomics case and in social science in general it would seem that aggregate claims are suspicious—both in terms of how well confirmed they are and how well they explain—if they seem to make assumptions about individual behavior that we know are implausible (this is just an instance of the total evidence requirement for confirmation). So if macroeconomic models assume that individuals are systematically stupid or fooled, that surely counts against them. "Grounding" in this weaker sense of "consistent with" seems a quite reasonable reductionist requirement.

It is also reasonable to think that providing information about how the behavior of individuals brings about aggregate social phenomena adds to our explanatory power. Consider the explanations I cited above in reference to the question of how individualist or holist we should be. In every case there was a tie of some sort to individual behavior. There is a wealth of evidence that success in science in general comes from providing integrated accounts of parts and wholes and of theories at different levels (Kincaid 1997). Those integrations generally leave roles for higher-level or aggregative accounts and are in that sense nonreductionist. It seems plausible that this picture is the way forward for the social sciences as well.

## 4 Other Issues

There certainly are other reductionist issues in the social sciences that have not been covered here due to space restrictions, the expertise of the author, and the coverage of other chapters in this volume. In the latter category fall debates over collective intentionality—debates over the extent to which it is reasonable to treat groups as having intentions that are not simply the sum of individual intentions (see the chapter by Epstein in this volume). Other debates of interest include issues related to sociobiology and evolutionary psychology and general debates about physicalism and causation that have relevance to the social sciences.

The question raised earlier about "how individualist can we be" was put in terms of how much social explanation must be added to individualist explanations. But that question can also be framed as one roughly about how individualist can we be in terms of explaining via innate individual processes. There is a lively debate in the social and behavioral sciences and in the philosophy of social science concerning how much of individual behavior can be explained in terms of evolutionarily selected innate psychological mechanisms—the antireductionist in the social sciences will argue that the answer is little (see Rosenberg 2012 for a good overview). The debates here are many, with special attention to the kind of evidence given for evolutionary explanations and the extent to which evolution would hardwire specific behaviors.

A related debate conceptually pits the approaches of economics versus that of other social and behavioral sciences. Economics tends to work with models in which individuals have fixed preferences; that working assumption seems quite dubious to social psychologists, who often doubt that individuals have any fixed preferences at all. The issues here are quite complicated (see Ross 2014 for a good review).

Finally, another ongoing debate relevant to reductionism in the social sciences concerns the extent to which real causal efficacy can be ascribed to anything but fundamental particles. Some versions of physicalism—the view roughly that everything in the world is composed of the basic particles of physics and does not act independently of them—seem to entail that there are no real causal relations above the level of fundamental particles (see Kim 1993 for an early statement and McDonald 2010 for more recent discussions). I am suspicious that there is illegitimate philosophical legislating of what science can do in these arguments (Kincaid 1996), but there is certainly lively ongoing debate over the issue.

# References

Ainsley, G. 2014. *Picoeconomics: The Strategic Interaction of Successive Motivational States within the Person.* Cambridge: Cambridge University Press.

Becker, G. 1962. "Irrational Behavior and Economic Theory." *Journal of Political Economy* 70(1): 1–13.

Binmore, K. 2007. *Does Game Theory Work? The Bargaining Challenge.* Cambridge: MIT Press.

Bowles, S. 2006. *Microeconomics: Behavior, Institutions, and Evolution.* Princeton, NJ: Princeton University Press.

Craver, C. and Darden, L. 2013. *In Search of Mechanisms.* Chicago: University of Chicago Press.

Crompton, Rosemary. 2008. *Class and Stratification.* Cambridge: Polity.

Demeulenaere, P. 2013. *Analytical Narratives and Social Mechanisms.* Cambridge: Cambridge University Press.

Domhoff, G. William. 2014. *Who Rules America? The Triumph of the Corporate Rich*, 7th edn. New York: McGraw-Hill.Elster, J. 1983. *Explaining Technical Change: A Case Study in the Philosophy of Science.* Cambridge: Cambridge University Press.

Epstein, B. 2015. *The Ant Trap.* Oxford: Oxford University Press.

Fodor, J. 1974. "Special Sciences: or, the Disunity of Science as a Working Hypothesis." *Synthese* 28: 77–115.

Gode, D. and Sunder, S. 1993. "Allocative Efficiency of Markets with Zero Intelligence Traders." *Journal of Political Economy* 101: 119–37.

Hedström, P. and Bearman, P. eds. 2009. *The Oxford Handbook of Analytical Sociology.* Oxford: Oxford University Press.

Hellman, G. and Thomson, F. 1975. "Physicalism: Ontology, Determination and Reduction." *Journal of Philosophy* 72: 551–64.

Hoover, K. 2010. "Microfoundational Programs." SSRN Working Paper, January 2010.

Khalidi, M. 2013. *Natural Categories and Human Kinds.* Cambridge: Cambridge University Press.

Kim, J. 1993. *Supervenience and Mind.* Cambridge: Cambridge University Press.

Kincaid, H. 1996. *Philosophical Foundations of the Social Sciences: Analyzing Controversies in Social Research.* Cambridge: Cambridge University Press.

Kincaid, H. 1997. *Individualism and the Unity of Science: Essays on Reduction, Explanation, and the Special Sciences.* Lanham, MD: Rowman and Littlefield.

Kincaid, H. 2012. "Mechanisms, Causal Modeling, and the Limitations of Traditional Multiple Regression," in H. Kincaid, ed., *Oxford Handbook of the Philosophy of the Social Sciences.* Oxford: Oxford University Press, 46–64.

Kincaid, H. 2014. "Dead Ends and Live Issues in the Individualism–Holism Debate," in J. Zahle and F. Collin, eds., *Rethinking the Individualism–Holism Debate: Essays in the Philosophy of Social Science.* Dordrecht: Springer, 139–52.

Kincaid, H. 2015. "Open Empirical and Methodological Issues in the Individualism–Holism Debate." *Philosophy of Science* 82(5): 1127–138.

Kincaid, H. 2016. "Debating the Reality of Social Classes." *Philosophy of Social Science* 46(2): 189–209.

Lareau, Annette and Conley, Dalton. eds. 2008. *Social Class: How Does It Work?* Thousand Oaks, CA: Sage.

Luke, D. 2004. *Multilevel Modeling*. Thousand Oaks, CA: Sage.

McDonald, C. and McDonald, G. 2010. *Emergence in Mind*. Oxford: Oxford University Press.

Mallon, R. and Kelly, D. 2012. "Making Race Out of Nothing: Psychologically Constrained Social Roles," in Kincaid, *Oxford Handbook*, 507–33.

Mandelbaum, M. 1955. "Societal Facts." *British Journal of Sociology* 6(4): 305–17.

Massey, Douglas S. and Denton, Nancy A. 1996. *American Apartheid: Segregation and the Making of the Underclass*. Cambridge, MA: Harvard University Press.Nagel, E. 1979. *The Structure of Science: Problems in the Logic of Scientific Explanation*. Indianapolis: Hackett.

Papineau, D. 2009. "Physicalism and the Human Sciences," in C. Mantzavinos (ed.), *Philosophy of the Social Sciences: Philosophical Theory and Scientific Practice*. Cambridge: Cambridge University Press, 103–24.

Rosenberg, A. 2012. *Philosophy of the Social Sciences*. Boulder, CO: Westview Press.

Ross, D. 2014. *Philosophy of Economics*. London: Palgrave.

Royce, Edward. 2015. *Poverty and Power: The Problem of Structural Inequality*. Lanham, MD: Rowman and Littlefield.

Russo, F. and Williamson, J. 2007. "Interpreting Causality in the Health Sciences." *International Studies in the Philosophy of Science* 21(2): 157–70.

Schelling, T. 1969. *Models of Segregation*. Santa Monica, CA: Rand Corporation.

Shipley, Bill. 2009. "Confirmatory Path Analysis in a Generalized Multilevel Context." *Ecology* 90(2): 363–68.

Smith, V. 2008. *Rationality in Economics*. Cambridge: Cambridge University Press.

Watkins, J. 1955. "Methodological Individualism: A Reply." *Philosophy of Science* 22: 58–62.

Wright, Erik Olin. 2005. *Approaches to Class Analysis*. Cambridge: Cambridge University Press.

Zahle, J. 2007. "Holism and Supervenience," in S. Turner and M. Risjord, eds., *Handbook of Philosophy of Science: Philosophy of Anthropology and Sociology*. Elsevier: Amsterdam, 311–43.

# 11
# EMERGENCE

## Julie Zahle

There are multiple notions of emergence. They have in common the idea that emergent phenomena (properties, patterns, etc.) arise from, or depend for their occurrence on, more basic phenomena. They differ as to the further conditions that phenomena must meet in order to qualify as emergent. Traditional specifications stress that, relative to the more basic phenomena from which they arise, emergent phenomena are irreducible, unexplainable, novel, and/or unpredictable. More recent definitions also point to, and emphasize, alternative features as being constitutive of emergence.

Theories of emergence have been advanced within a wide range of disciplines and in relation to a variety of phenomena. The focus of this chapter is theories of *social* emergence as advanced within the social sciences and the philosophy of the social sciences. These theories hold that *social* phenomena, such as universities, traffic jams, wealth distributions, residential segregations, firms, and social norms, constitute an important subset of emergent phenomena and that they depend for their occurrence on more basic phenomena typically in the form of individuals. Moreover, like other theories of emergence, accounts of social emergence point to further—and oftentimes different—features as being defining of emergent phenomena. Most, if not all, theories of social emergence agree that just as some social phenomena are emergent relative to more basic phenomena typically in the form of individuals, the more basic phenomena are, or may be, emergent relative to even more basic phenomena, some of which are, or may be, emergent relative to yet more basic phenomena, and so on. Still, social accounts of emergence tend to pay rather little attention to phenomena below the level of individuals.

The first comprehensive treatments of emergence go back to the tradition of British Emergentism that came into existence around the 1850s while lasting well into the 1920s (McLaughlin 1992). It was one of its representatives, G. H. Lewes, who coined the term "emergence." The British Emergentists did not take an interest in social emergence. Other theorists, however, did. For example, Durkheim's work around the turn of the 19th century is often regarded as containing an early discussion of social emergence though he did not explicitly use the term "emergence" (Sawyer 2005, 100). Somewhat later, the idea of social emergence is invoked by theorists like Talcott Parsons, George Homans, and Peter Blau (see Parsons 1968 [1937]; Homans 1950; Blau 1964). Still, it is probably not until the 1990s that it is possible to talk about the existence of a more sustained and widespread interest in social emergence. Among other things, the 1990s were characterized by discussions of social emergence by proponents of Critical Realism, who were following up, and elaborating on, Roy Bhaskar's seminal work in this respect (see Bhaskar 2000 [1979]). Likewise, the use of Agent-Based Computational Modeling really took off during this period and reflections on this method involved accounts of social emergence. Since then, the idea of social emergence has been widely explored—and debated.

In the following, three recent and influential theories of social emergence are examined. The first is representative of a relational conception of social emergence, whereas the second advocates a supervenience-based account of social emergence. Both accounts spell out emergence as a synchronic dependency relation: Emergent social phenomena *co-occur* with the more basic phenomena, typically individuals, from which they emerge. Different from this, the third account of social emergence regards emergence as a diachronic dependency relation: Emergent social phenomena arise, *over time*, from more basic phenomena mainly in the form of individuals. The third account presents a generative conception of emergence.

The distinction between emergence as a synchronic and diachronic dependency relation is useful from the perspective of classifying notions of emergence. Another helpful distinction is that between ontological and epistemic notions of emergence. Ontological notions regard emergence as a genuine feature that phenomena may have. As such, phenomena qualify as emergent independently of meeting any criteria that relate to our knowledge of the phenomena. In contrast, epistemic notions view emergence as a feature that phenomena have relative to our limited knowledge with respect to these phenomena, as when emergent phenomena are defined as phenomena that we are *not* in a position to explain or predict by appeal to our complete theories about the more basic phenomena from which they somehow arise. The three accounts of social emergence to be examined below exemplify ontological notions of emergence.

Commonly, accounts of social emergence are linked to, or taken to have implications for, positions within the longstanding methodological individualism–holism debate. One version of this dispute is the dispensability debate: Methodological individualists insist that the social sciences should offer individualist explanations only, that is, explanations focusing on how individuals, their actions, beliefs, etc. bring about various events. Holist explanations—that is, explanations centered on social phenomena as bringing about various events—should be dispensed with. In contrast, methodological holists typically maintain that the social sciences should put forward both individualist and holist explanations: In some cases individualist explanations, in other cases holist explanations, are in order. The three theories of social emergence considered below are widely regarded, whether by their proponents or by others, as bearing on the dispensability debate. This aspect of discussions of social emergence is briefly covered, too.

## Relational Emergence

Theories of relational emergence have been offered within different disciplines and in relation to diverse phenomena. Within the social sciences and their philosophy, accounts of social phenomena as relationally emergent phenomena have been developed too. Most notably, different versions of relational accounts of social emergence have been offered by critical realists like Roy Bhaskar, Margaret Archer, and Dave Elder-Vass (Bhaskar 1982, 2000 [1979]; Archer 1995; Elder-Vass 2010, 2014). Also, another important advocate of this approach is Mario Bunge (Bunge 2003). In the following, Elder-Vass's version of the relational conception of social emergence is examined. His account is both very clear and well developed.[1]

A good place to start is by looking at Elder-Vass's notion of social entities. He explicates these as relatively enduring wholes that are composed of interrelated parts in the form of individuals.

Sometimes social entities have material things as their parts too (Elder-Vass 2010, 157). Still, Elder-Vass does not make much of this insight so, for the sake simplicity, it is ignored in the following. One notable kind of social entity is organizations like firms, schools, households, and religious associations. Social entities like these have social properties. Like other properties, these properties are defined by being causally effective. For this reason Elder-Vass talks interchangeably about the properties and causal powers of social entities.

On this basis, Elder-Vass's theory of social emergence may be specified as an account concerned with social entities as having emergent social properties. He defines emergent social properties as the properties/powers that a social entity has in virtue of (some of) its parts, viz. individuals, standing, at that moment, in certain relations to each other. In this formulation, "at that moment" is meant to signal that emergence is a synchronic dependency relation: The emergent social properties co-occur with the individuals from whom they emerge. The characterization brings out what is distinctive about relational understandings of emergence: It is taken that an entity's properties qualify as emergent if they are the result of the entity's parts being, at that moment, suitably *related*. Moreover, Elder-Vass's notion of emergence is ontological: The criteria that social properties must meet in order to qualify as emergent are ontological; they do not make any reference to our knowledge, or lack of same, with respect to these properties.

Elder-Vass distinguishes between two types of emergent social properties. On the one hand, there are emergent social properties that are ascribed to social entities as wholes. These are exemplified by a country's power to go to war, a government's power to introduce a new tax, and a barbershop quartet's "ability to produce [... a] harmonized performance" (Elder-Vass 2010, 154). On the other hand, there are emergent social properties that are delegated, and as such ascribed, to individuals who form part of social wholes. Despite being ascribed to individuals, these properties qualify as social properties because they are powers that individuals have in virtue of being, at that moment, interrelated with other individuals who form part of a given social entity. Examples of delegated emergent social properties are an individual's power to fire, to hire, to vote, and to grade. In virtue of their emergent social powers, social entities may not only have a causal impact on other social entities. Also, they may have a downward causal influence on their parts as when a company assigns a different range of tasks to an employee and hereby brings it about that the employee changes her work routines.

Elder-Vass holds that, in addition to emergent social properties, social entities possess resultant or aggregative properties. As Elder-Vass explains it, these are the properties of social entities that their parts, viz. individuals, would also possess in isolation or as elements in an unstructured collection of parts. For example, the power to shout is a resultant social property when ascribed to a kindergarten since the children making up the kindergarten would also have this property in isolation. Other examples of resultant social properties are the power to eat or to walk fast as ascribed to social entities. Resultant social properties clearly differ from the emergent social ones: Social entities' emergent social properties are never possessed by their parts either in isolation or as elements in an unstructured collection of parts (see Elder-Vass 2010, 16ff.).

In the introduction, it was noted that emergent phenomena are sometimes defined by being irreducible, unexplainable, novel, and/or unpredictable. Elder-Vass does not appeal to any of these notions in his relational specification of emergence. Still, without regarding these features as being constitutive of emergence, he discusses whether emergent social phenomena are irreducible and unexplainable. In one sense of the term, he points out, emergent social properties are irreducible: They are causally effective in their own right. The reason is, he explains, that "relationally emergent causal powers cannot be eliminatively reduced: these powers would not exist if the whole did not exist, and thus they are ultimately powers of the whole and not of the parts" (Elder-Vass 2014, 8). In another sense of irreducible, though, emergent social properties are *not* irreducible: Elder-Vass stresses the importance of explanations that trace the way in which emergent social properties are the result of their parts, viz. individuals, being suitably interrelated. These explanations, he contends, are always possible in principle (ibid.). Since emergent social properties may be thus explained, they are perfectly reducible in an explanatory sense. Hence, the view that emergent phenomena are unexplainable may be dismissed.

Relational accounts of social emergence are often used as basis for a defense of the holist position within the individualism–holism debate on dispensability. Elder-Vass is no exception in this regard: He makes it clear that his account lends support to the view that both holist and individualist explanations are indispensable within the social sciences. He takes it that holist explanations are ones that describe how social entities, in virtue of their *social* properties, partially brought about some events. In contrast, individualist explanations focus on *individual* properties, that is, the properties that individuals have independently of being, at that moment, part of a given social entity. The explanations specify how individuals, in virtue of these properties, partially brought about some event.

Now, Elder-Vass contends that whenever a holist explanation appeals to resultant social properties, the explanation may be replaced by a corresponding individualist explanation. For instance, if some event is explained by reference to the noise made by a kindergarten, this event may equally well be explained by pointing to, and enumerating, the noise made by each of the children making up the kindergarten. The situation is different whenever a holist explanation refers to an emergent social property. In this case, the explanation cannot be substituted by an individualist explanation because an individualist explanation, remember, refers only to individual properties and these are unable to produce the effect of an emergent social property. To see this, consider the claim that John is out of work because he was fired by his (now former) boss. The power to fire is an emergent social property of the boss and whatever the boss's individual properties, these do not add up to this property of being able to fire employees. Consequently, individual properties cannot be mentioned in place of an appeal to the power to fire in an explanation of why it is that John is now out of work. Thus, holist explanations that refer to emergent social properties are indispensable. In this fashion, Elder-Vass's notion of social emergence serves as basis for his defense of methodological holism.

A number of criticisms have been raised against Elder-Vass's account. For instance, Anthony King has disputed Elder-Vass's claim that suitably interrelated individuals form social entities that have their own irreducible causal powers (King 2007). King contends that it constitutes a misrepresentation of social reality to hold that there are such ontologically distinct social entities. There is nothing more to social reality than "all the social relations between its members taken together" (215). Coming from a different direction, Douglas Porpora has objected to Elder-Vass's account on the ground that it fails to acknowledge that when individuals stand in various relations, the relations may have their "own distinct causal effects" (Porpora 2007, 196). It is typically these relations, or relational properties, rather than the emergent properties, Porpora states, that should be the focus of analysis. Finally, Julie Zahle has pointed out that Elder-Vass works with a very narrow conception of individualist explanations compared to that advocated by methodological individualists. Accordingly, she argues, methodological individualists are likely to reject Elder-Vass's reasons in support of methodological holism since these trade on his narrow conception of individualist explanations (Zahle 2014).

## Supervenience-Based Emergence

In the 1960s and 1970s, philosophers of mind began to argue that mental properties are realizable by multiple physical properties (see Putnam 1967 and Fodor 1974). Somewhat later, in the 1980s, philosophers began to explore the idea of supervenience as a way to specify the dependency relation between mental and physical properties, and other pairs of properties. Both multiple realization and supervenience became popular notions that were also taken up in the analysis of social phenomena. Keith Sawyer's influential account of social emergence exemplifies this development: It relies on both these notions. Sawyer's account may be characterized as a supervenience-based theory of social emergence.

Sawyer's discussion rests on a distinction between social and individual properties. Social properties, he specifies, are properties of constellations of individuals. They are exemplified by the property of being a church, a family, a collective movement, a meeting of a reading club, and an institution. By comparison, individual properties are properties of individuals in the form of their observable actions and their beliefs, desires, and the like (Sawyer 2002, 555, n. 8).

The first step in Sawyer's theory of social emergence is the contention that the relationship between social and individual properties is one of supervenience: Social properties supervene on individual ones and this means that whenever two constellations of individuals have the same individual properties, they have identical social properties, too. As such, there can be no change in social properties unless there is a change at the level of individual properties (Sawyer 2002, 543). The individual properties fix the social properties, as it is also sometimes put. As an illustration of this idea, consider individuals with various beliefs, practices, etc. who form a constellation with the social property of being a church. Since "being a church" is a supervenient social property, any other constellation of individuals with similar beliefs, practices, etc. likewise has this property. Also, a constellation of individuals cannot cease to be a church unless the individuals change some of the beliefs, practices, etc. that "being a church" supervenes on.

The next step in Sawyer's account is the observation that social properties being supervenient is compatible with their being realizable by different combinations of individual properties. For example, the property of being a church is multiply realizable in this sense: "Being a church," Sawyer states, "can be realized by a wide range of organizational structures, cultural practices, and individual beliefs and dispositions" (Sawyer 2002, 545). Further, Sawyer continues, and this is the last step in his account of social emergence, it is possible for supervenient social properties to be multiply realizable in a wildly disjunctive manner. This is the case when the combinations of individual properties that may realize a social property differ significantly from each other or when the number of the possible realizing combinations of individual properties is large or even endless (see Sawyer 2005, 67). According to Sawyer, it is this subset of supervenient social properties, viz. ones that are not simply multiply realizable, but wildly so, that qualify as emergent social properties. As he puts it, a "social property may be said to be emergent when it is multiply realized in wildly disjunctive systems of individuals" (Sawyer 2005, 72).

As these considerations bring out, Sawyer's theory of social emergence has as its focus emergent social properties. Since "supervenience" refers to a synchronic dependency relation and since relations of emergence are a subset of supervenience relations, it follows that emergence, too, is a synchronic dependency relation. It is exactly because Sawyer's account has it that emergent social properties are supervenient properties of a special kind that his approach may be characterized as a supervenience-based theory of social emergence. Also, his notion of social emergence is ontological: Supervenient social properties are emergent if they meet the ontological criteria of being multiply realizable and this in a wildly disjunctive manner. Finally, note how Sawyer's and Elder-Vass's accounts diverge. Sawyer takes it as defining of emergent social properties that they are supervenient and wildly multiply realizable, whereas Elder-Vass specifies emergent social properties as properties that social entities have in virtue of their parts being, at that moment, suitably interrelated. The two characterizations hold that completely different conditions must be met in order for a social property to qualify as emergent.

This clarified, it may be wondered whether Sawyer also discusses the features of being irreducible, unexplainable, novel, and unpredictable that are sometimes used to characterize emergent phenomena. Sawyer focuses on one of these features. He stresses repeatedly that emergent social properties are irreducible to the more basic properties from which they emerge, viz. individual properties. By this he means that an emergent social property is not identical to a *single* combination of individual properties. The reason behind this ontological claim has already been rehearsed above: Due to their being wildly multiply realizable, emergent social properties must be identified with a disjunction of different combinations of individual properties.

Within philosophy, it is common to use reflections about properties as being supervenient and multiply realizable as a basis for claims to the effect that explanations which refer to these properties are indispensable. Sawyer does so too. His reasoning along these lines amounts to a defense of methodological holism. The core of his argument is the claim that social laws are irreducible to individual laws. Social laws, he makes it clear, are ones that refer to *social* properties in their antecedent whereas individual laws are ones that refer to *individual* properties in their antecedent. Further, drawing on a common interpretation of Nagel's model of intertheoretic reduction, Sawyer maintains that in order to reduce social laws to individual laws, bridge laws must be provided. These link *each* description of a social property with a *single* description of a combination of individual properties while expressing that the social property is identical to the combination of individual properties (see Sawyer 2002, 548). The bridge laws make it possible to replace each description of a social property with a corresponding description of individual properties such that the social laws may be replaced by corresponding individual laws. The point is now, Sawyer states, that bridge laws cannot be advanced when social laws refer to emergent social properties in their antecedent because, due to their being wildly multiply realizable, these properties cannot be identified with *single* combinations of individual properties. This means that whenever a social law refers to an emergent social property in its antecedent, it is irreducible; it cannot be replaced by an individual law. It is exactly because emergent social properties figure in such irreducible laws, Sawyer insists, that they qualify as causally effective properties (Sawyer 2005, 71–72, see also his 2003).

There is only a small step from the finding that there are irreducible social laws to the conclusion that holist explanations are indispensable. Sawyer favors the covering law model of explanation which has it that explanations must include laws. Moreover, he regards explanations that involve social laws as holist explanations and explanations that include individual laws as individualist explanations. Against this background, consider holist explanations that appeal to social laws which antecedent refers to an emergent social property. Because these laws are irreducible, holist explanations that appeal to them cannot be replaced by individualist explanations that refer to corresponding reducing individual laws. This shows that holist explanations are indispensable. In this manner, Sawyer's account of social emergence serves as ground for his defense of methodological holism: It is exactly when explanations make appeal to social laws that refer to an emergent social property in their antecedent that they, viz. the explanations, cannot be dispensed with in favor of corresponding individualist explanations.

Sawyer's account of social emergence has given rise to debate. According to Greve, Sawyer must take it that social laws sometimes link an emergent social property with a disjunction of different combinations of individual properties (Greve 2012). Yet, Greve continues, because Sawyer regards laws of this disjunctive sort as acceptable, he cannot at the same time maintain that bridge laws are unacceptable if they link a description of a social property with a disjunction of different combinations of individual properties. Due to this inconsistency, Greve argues, Sawyer has not mounted a convincing defense of downward causation understood as the claim that there are social laws linking emergent social properties with combinations of individual properties (Greve 2012). (See also Sawyer's response [Sawyer 2012] and Greve's rejoinder to it [Greve 2013].) Another line of criticism has been presented by Elder-Vass, who concentrates on Sawyer's position as to when supervenient social properties count as being wildly multiply realizable (Elder-Vass 2014). For instance, one criterion has it that supervenient social properties are wildly multiply realizable when they are realizable by a large number of combinations of individual properties. But why, Elder-Vass asks, does the sheer number of realizing combinations of individual properties matter? And exactly how many combinations of individual properties does it take for the number of realizations to qualify as being large? Since Sawyer does not answer these questions, Elder-Vass concludes, this aspect of Sawyer's account of social emergence is unsatisfying. Lastly, Petri Ylikoski has pointed out that both Nagel's model of intertheoretic reduction and the covering law model of explanation have been heavily criticized within philosophy of science (Ylikoski 2009). Accordingly, Ylikoski maintains, it is problematic for Sawyer's defense of methodological holism that it rests on these two models.

## Generative Emergence

Within the social sciences, agent-based computational (ABC) modeling is used to study how the actions of numerous interdependent agents may generate various social phenomena. An early example of the approach is Thomas Schelling's work, from the late 1960s and the 1970s, on the way in which segregated neighborhoods may arise from the interdependent actions of individuals who would actually prefer to live in mixed neighborhoods (see Schelling 1978). Still, it was not until the 1990s when it became possible to use computers for the purposes of ABC modeling that the method really gained ground. As part of their reflections on the method, ABC modelers invoke the idea of social emergence. In this section, Joshua Epstein's generative account of social emergence, as it may be called, is examined. Epstein is a founder and influential proponent of ABC modeling.

Epstein's focus is on a specific kind of social phenomena, namely macroscopic patterns or regularities. These are exemplified by traffic jams, wealth distributions, price distributions, migrations, civil wars, economic classes, norm distributions, and military tactics. Social phenomena or properties like these, Epstein contends, are emergent when "arising from local agent interactions" (Epstein 2006, 38, the definition is taken over from Epstein and Axtell 1996, 35). That is, macroscopic patterns are emergent when generated as the result of agents' interactions, over time, with other agents to whom they are somehow connected or close. Because the emergent macroscopic patterns are said to be produced as the result of basic phenomena, in the form of agents, engaging in interactions *over a period of time*, this account depicts social emergence as a diachronic dependency relation. Further, the notion of emergence is ontological: The criteria that macroscopic patterns must meet in order to qualify as emergent do not relate to our knowledge, or lack of same, with respect to these patterns.

The way ABC modelers study the generation of emergent social phenomena is by creating artificial societies in which artificial agents produce artificial emergent social phenomena. As Epstein explains it, the building of an ABC model involves an initial specification of the artificial agents in terms of the rules they follow and in terms of other properties with which they are equipped. An initial specification is always such that the artificial agents are autonomous, that is, "as a matter of model specification, no central controllers or other high authorities are posited *ab initio*" (Epstein 2006, 6). Moreover, the artificial agents are typically made heterogeneous: They are not all endowed with the same properties. For instance, they may differ with respect to their preferences, physical abilities, social roles, and the like. Further, the rules are specified so that the agents interact with other close-by agents or with other agents to whom they are somehow connected. For this reason, their actions qualify as local. Finally, Epstein explicates, it is common to offer initial specifications that make the artificial agents have bounded rationality. This means that the artificial agents are modeled such that they can only obtain incomplete information about their artificial society. For instance, they may only be equipped with the ability to see things at a certain limited distance with the result that they have only imperfect information about their surroundings. Also, their having bounded rationality means that the artificial agents are only equipped with bounded computational powers in the sense that they are made to act in accordance with rather simple rules (ibid.). An example of a rule of this sort might be the rule to go to the nearest unoccupied spot with the most food available. In addition to an initial specification of the artificial agents, the environment in which the artificial agents are to "live" must also be built by stipulating its properties and the rules according to which it develops.

Once an initial specification of the artificial agents and their artificial environment has been provided, the model may be run by letting the artificial agents act in accordance with their rules in the artificial environment. Eventually, the repeated applications of the rules result in the generation of an artificial emergent social phenomenon. Epstein describes this as the growing of a "macroscopic regularity from the bottom up" (Epstein 2006, 7). He goes on to state that when an initial specification has been shown to result in an artificial macroscopic regularity, it may be regarded as a candidate, i.e. a possible, explanation of the corresponding real-life emergent social phenomenon. In fact, Epstein insists, in order even to qualify as a candidate explanation of an actual emergent social phenomenon, it must have been established that if the explanation is turned into an initial specification and run, it results in the generation of an artificial version of the phenomenon. Epstein summarizes this point by saying that "[i]f you didn't grow it, you didn't explain its emergence" (8).

Against this background, some of Epstein's further reflections on the notion of emergence may briefly be noted. Among other things, he comments that the definition of emergent phenomena as being unexplainable makes no sense in the context of agent-based modeling. ABC modelers take it to be possible in principle to explain emergent social phenomena: This assumption underlies their efforts to find initial specifications that may generate, and as such serve as candidate explanations of, emergent social phenomena (Epstein 2006, 36). In a similar spirit, Epstein points out that insofar as explanations based on ABC models are regarded as a kind of reduction, the position that emergent phenomena are distinguished by being irreducible must also be rejected in the context of agent-based modeling. Finally, he emphasizes that because there are a host of different accounts of emergence, ABC modelers should consider not using the notion or, at least, they should always be careful to explicate what they mean by emergence.

Within discussions of ABC modeling, it is common to find comments to the effect that ABC modeling is representative of, or necessarily goes hand in hand with an endorsement of, methodological individualism (see, e.g., Macy and Flache 2009, 248; Wan 2011, 188). In order to examine this view, consider an ABC model in which the artificial agents are individual human beings who follow various rules in an artificial environment. An initial specification along these lines may, without difficulty, be turned into a candidate individualist explanation that states how individuals, acting according to various rules, etc., brought about an emergent social phenomenon. Moreover, based on further empirical investigation, it may be determined that the explanation in question is in fact the actual individualist explanation of the emergent social phenomenon. In this manner, ABC models may indeed serve as basis for the advancement of individualist explanations.

However, this is not the same as granting that ABC modelers must necessarily subscribe to the thesis of methodological individualism. As Epstein (2006) also points out, the artificial agents in ABC models need not be regarded as representative of individual human beings (7). It is perfectly possible to identify the artificial agents in an ABC model with, say, firms or households. In these cases, the initial specifications may not be turned into candidate— and actual—individualist explanations. Instead, they may serve as basis for candidate—and actual holist—explanations that show how social phenomena, like firms or households, bring about various effects. Further, and though Epstein does not explicitly say this, his reflections bring out another reason why ABC modeling is compatible with the rejection of methodological individualism. The thesis states that individualist explanations *alone* should be advanced within the social sciences. Yet, the use of ABC modeling is perfectly compatible with holding, as Epstein does, that explanations other than ones based on these models are sometimes in order, too. Accordingly, there is also room for holding that these alternative explanations should sometimes be holist ones. The upshot of these considerations is that ABC modelers may, but need not, subscribe to methodological individualism (on this point, see also Marchionni and Ylikoski 2013).

In response to Epstein's account, it may be noted that ABC modelers disagree about the right way in which to define social emergence. For instance, another proponent of ABC modeling, Peter Hedström, maintains that emergent social phenomena are "brought about by the actions of individuals" (Hedström 2005, 75). Moreover, he specifies, emergent social phenomena are such that they "cannot, in practice, be predicted by knowing everything there is to know about the pre-emergent properties of the parts" (74). Thus, differently from Epstein, Hedström regards unpredictability in practice as a constitutive feature of emergence and as such he subscribes to an epistemic notion of emergence. Moreover, as an example of a criticism of Epstein's theory, Macy and Flache's reflections on ABC modeling and explanation may briefly be noted. They point out that in order to be able to grow a macroscopic pattern, ABC modelers may end up with a highly elaborate initial specification (Macy and Flache 2009, 263). However, if an initial specification is so complex that it is difficult to see how the artificial social phenomenon in question emerged from it, then the specification loses its explanatory potential. Accordingly, they propose, Epstein's motto that if a social phenomenon has not been grown, its emergence has not been explained needs to be supplemented by another slogan: "If you don't know *how* you grew it, you didn't explain it" (ibid.—italics in the original).

## Conclusion

In the foregoing, three accounts of social emergence have been examined. The relational and the supervenience-based account regard social emergence as a synchronic dependency relation. They represent competing views of social emergence. By contrast, the generative account conceives of social emergence as a diachronic dependency relation. Due to its concern with what happens over time, it does not conflict with any of the synchronic accounts. That is, it is possible to hold both that there are social phenomena that emerge from, in the sense of co-occur with, more basic phenomena, and that there are social phenomena that emerge from, in the sense of arise over time from, more basic phenomena. All three theories are influential ontological notions of social emergence. Yet, they are by no means the only available accounts. There is still an ongoing debate about the right understanding of social emergence and on the possible linkages between such accounts and the individualism/holism debate.[2]

## Notes

1 This section draws, and expands, on Zahle 2014.
2 I would like to thank Tuukka Kaidesoja, Lee McIntyre, and Petri Ylikoski, as well as Jan Faye and Klemens Kappel, for their helpful comments on earlier versions of this chapter.

## References

Archer, M. (1995) *Realist Social Theory: The Morphogenetic Approach*. Cambridge: Cambridge University Press.
Bhaskar, R. (1982) "Emergence, Explanation, and Emancipation," in P. F. Secord (ed.) *Explaining Social Behavior*. Beverly Hills: Sage, 275–310.
Bhaskar, R. (2000 [1979]) *The Possibility of Naturalism* (3rd edition). London: Routledge.
Blau, P. M. (1964) *Exchange and Power in Social Life*. New York: John Wiley.
Bunge, M. (2003) *Emergence and Convergence*. Toronto: University of Toronto Press.
Elder-Vass, D. (2010) *The Causal Power of Social Structures: Emergence, Structure, and Agency*. Cambridge: Cambridge University Press.
Elder-Vass, D. (2014) "Social Emergence: Relational or Functional?" *Balkan Journal of Philosophy* 1: 5–16.
Epstein, J. M. (2006) *Generative Social Science. Studies in Agent-Based Computational Modeling*. Princeton, NJ: Princeton University Press.
Epstein, J. M. and Axtell, R. (1996) *Growing Artificial Societies: Social Science from the Bottom Up*. Washington, DC: Brookings Institution Press.
Fodor, J. A. (1974) "Special Sciences (Or: The Disunity of Science as a Working Hypothesis)," *Synthese* 28(2): 97–115.
Greve, J. (2012) "Emergence in Sociology: A Critique of Nonreductive Individualism," *Philosophy of the Social Sciences* 42(2): 188–223.
Greve, J. (2013) "Response to Keith Sawyer," *Philosophy of the Social Sciences* 43(2): 246–56.
Hedström, P. (2005) *Dissecting the Social: On the Principles of Analytical Sociology*. Cambridge: Cambridge University Press.
Homans, G. C. (1950) *The Human Group*. New York: Harcourt, Brace & World.
King, A. (2007) "Why I Am Not an Individualist," *Journal for the Theory of Social Behaviour* 37(2): 211–19.

McLaughlin, B. P. (1992) "The Rise and Fall of British Emergentism," in A. Beckman, H. Flor, and J. Kim (eds.) *Emergence or Reduction? Essays on the Prospects of Nonreductive Physicalism.* Berlin: Walter de Gruyter, 49–93.

Macy, M. and Flache, A. (2009) "Social Dynamics from the Bottom Up. Agent-Based Models of Social Interaction," in P. Hedström and P. S. Bearman (eds.) *The Oxford Handbook of Analytical Sociology.* Oxford: Oxford University Press, 245–68.

Marchionni, C. and Ylikoski, P. (2013) "Generative Explanation and Individualism in Agent-Based Simulation," *Philosophy of the Social Sciences* 43(3): 323–40.

Parsons, T. (1968 [1937]) *The Structure of Social Action.* New York: The Free Press.

Porpora, D. (2007) "On Elder-Vass: Refining a Refinement," *Journal for the Theory of Social Behavior* 37(2): 195–200.

Putnam, Hilary (1967) "Psychological Predicates," in W. H. Capitan and D. D. Merrill (eds.) *Art, Mind, and Religion.* Pittsburgh: University of Pittsburgh Press, 37–48.

Sawyer R. K. (2002) "Nonreductive Individualism: Part I—Supervenience and Wild Disjunction," *Philosophy of the Social Sciences* 32(4): 537–59.

Sawyer, R. K. (2003) "Nonreductive Individualism: Part II—Social Causation," *Philosophy of the Social Sciences* 33(2): 203–24.

Sawyer, R. K. (2005) *Social Emergence: Societies as Complex Systems.* Cambridge: Cambridge University Press.

Sawyer, R. K. (2012) "Response to 'Emergence in Sociology'," *Philosophy of the Social Sciences* 42(2): 270–75.

Schelling, T. C. (1978) *Micromotives and Macrobehavior.* New York: W. W. Norton & Co.

Wan, P. Y.-Z. (2011) "Emergence à la Systems Theory: Epistemological *Totalausschluss* or Ontological Novelty," *Philosophy of the Social Sciences* 41(2): 178–210.

Ylikoski, P. (2009) "Review of *Social Emergence* by R. Keith Sawyer," *Philosophy of the Social Sciences* 39(3): 527–30.

Zahle, J. (2014) "Holism, Emergence, and the Crucial Distinction," in J. Zahle and F. Collin (eds.) *Rethinking the Individualism–Holism Debate: Essays in the Philosophy of Social Science.* New York: Springer, 177–96.

# Further Reading

Bedau, M. A. and P. Humphreys (eds.). *Emergence. Contemporary Readings in Philosophy of Science* (Cambridge, MA: MIT Press, 2008) is a useful selection of papers on emergence in general.

Kaidesoja, Tuukka. *Naturalizing Critical Realist Social Ontology* (London: Routledge, 2013) offers an examination, and discussion, of critical realist notions of emergence.

# 12
# METHODOLOGICAL INDIVIDUALISM

## Petri Ylikoski

Ideas about social scientific explanation lie at the core of debates about methodological individualism (MI). The spirit of MI is captured in a definition by Jon Elster:

> [A]ll social phenomena—their structure and their change—are in principle explicable in ways that only involve individuals—their properties, their goals, their beliefs and their actions.
>
> (Elster 1985, 5)

For many individualists, like Elster, the basic idea of MI, when properly understood, is obvious and almost trivial. However, in equal measure, for many opponents the doctrine is an obviously wrong and unnecessary limitation for social scientific theorizing. The main task of this chapter is to explain how this state of affairs is possible. Much hangs on how MI is formulated. It might be that David Ruben is still right:

> [M]ethodological individualism has never been stated with enough clarity and precision to permit proper evaluation.
>
> (Ruben 1985, 13)

However, there is much more at stake than abstract issues about social explanation. Strong emotions are associated with the label 'methodological individualism'. It is connected to other highly charged but obscure notions like reductionism and political individualism. Reductionism is often believed to have strong implications for disciplinary autonomy and is thus highly loaded with disciplinary politics. For some social sciences 'methodological individualism' (without any precise definition) has become a part of disciplinary identity. In economics, a denial of methodological individualism simply signals lack of understanding of economics. In contrast, for many sociologists, supporting methodological individualism still signals an anti-sociological attitude that overlooks many crucial aspects of social reality. Politics proper come into the picture, as it is often suspected that methodological debates about individualism are covert means to challenge or push political views like Marxism or liberalism. While the issues of identity and politics are important for understanding the debates about MI, I will set them aside in this chapter and focus on philosophical issues at the core of the debate.

# 1 The Many Faces of Methodological Individualism

The debates about methodological individualism started in the 1950s. However, the term is a bit older. It was introduced by Joseph Schumpeter in 1908 to distinguish individualism as a methodological approach in economics from individualism as a political position. It is notable that Schumpeter did not present MI as a general principle that applies to all social explanation, but as a special method used in theoretical economics (Udéhn 2001, 104–6). Methodological individualism became a general thesis about social explanation through the work of J. W. N. Watkins. Inspired by Max Weber, Friedrich von Hayek, and Karl Popper he formulated and defended MI as a general doctrine about social ontology and explanation that received a lot of attention. The starting points of both Schumpeter's and Watkins's discussions were Max Weber's writings, but as soon as the debate started this connection was severed and methodological individualism came to be discussed as a general idea about social explanation.

Watkins originally formulated MI quite loosely:

> All social phenomena are, directly or indirectly, human creations. ... [T]he social scientist can continue searching for explanations of a social phenomenon until he has reduced it to psychological terms.
>
> (Watkins 1952, 28–29)

It is quite clear that Watkins thought the latter claim about explanation to be a simple implication of the first claim about ontology and that the whole principle is rather trivial. It turned out that he was only half right. Hardly anyone would dispute the first claim about ontology. It is the second claim that turned out to be controversial. Although Watkins talks about reduction and psychology, his real claim (inspired by Max Weber) is that social phenomena are "only *explained* by being are shown to be the resultants of individual activities" (1952, 29). Thus the central claim seems to be that only the individual attributes, like "dispositions, beliefs, and relationships of individuals" (ibid.) are doing any real explanatory work in the social sciences. This is the core issue. While most critics do not deny that individual attributes have a role in social explanation, they challenge the idea that individual attributes are sufficient. We will come back to this core issue, but let us first put Watkins's claim in some context.

Five years later Watkins articulates an important background assumption:

> If methodological individualism means that human beings are supposed to be the only moving agents in history, and if sociological holism means that some superhuman agents or factors are supposed to be at work in history, then these two alternatives are exhaustive.
>
> (Watkins 1957, 106)

This implies that an important motivation for MI is to keep scientifically or philosophically suspicious explanatory factors out of the social sciences. For Watkins, Weber, and other methodological individualists, human intentional agents are the only irreducible source of teleology in the social world. Thus teleological historical laws that override or outflank individual agency are out (Watkins 1957; Pettit 1993, ch. 3). Similarly suspicious are uncritical attributions of goals, interests or actions to nations, classes, and other social wholes.

Already these two quotations from Watkins show that from the beginning MI has been a confusing mix of quite different issues. Depending on whether one focuses on Watkins's definitions, his examples, or on the views he aims to criticize, one gets a very different idea of the key issue. Furthermore, when Watkins and other individualists responded to these criticism, they often reformulated MI, which in turn led to a new cascade of criticisms, defenses, and reformulations. Thus there are many different streams of debate about MI (Udéhn 2001), for example:

1. There is a debate about the scope of rational choice methodology in the social sciences. Watkins's first paper discusses and defends Max Weber's reconstruction of model-building strategy employed by economists. In this strategy you explain social phenomena as outcomes of rational and self-interested actions by agents who are characterized by preferences stipulated by the theorist and who are facing a certain kind of social situation. It is clear from Watkins's later writings that he intended MI to be a much more general thesis about social explanation, but the association between MI and rational choice methodology remains strong. The connection is very clear in economics, but also in sociology, where MI is often just an alternative label for rational choice inspired approaches. This is natural, as this is precisely the methodology that Schumpeter originally baptized 'methodological individualism'.

2. There is a debate about the reducibility of social concepts. Watkins's original definition talked about the reduction of social phenomena to individual dispositions. This was taken in the 1950s and 60s to imply that the meanings of social concepts should be defined in terms of individual predicates. The idea was that a person being a bank-teller is not a fact about that particular individual, but presupposes the existence of the social institution "bank." As these social facts cannot be reduced to individual psychological facts—because the social concepts cannot be translated without residue to individual concepts—the critics of MI suggested that explanatory reduction also fails (Mandelbaum 1955). This debate about semantic individualism was important in the first decades of MI, but of late it has become less and less relevant. Most people accept some sort of meaning holism (Pettit 1993, ch. 4), but do not regard it as relevant to the MI debate about explanation.

3. There is a debate about the scientific status of Marxist social theory. Watkins was a student of Popper and Marxist social theory was one his main targets. He was especially suspicious of Marx's philosophy of history and his treatment of classes as subjects of historical processes. Given the prominence of Marxism in the second half of the 20th century, it is no wonder that the most heated debates about MI were around this. It is notable that what started as an outside criticism transformed, with time, into an internal debate within Marxism when Jon Elster and other analytical Marxists attempted to reconstruct Marxist theory without teleology or functionalist thinking (Elster 1985; Wright, Levine, and Sober 1992).

I will not discuss these themes more extensively in this chapter. In the following, the focus will be on understanding the core assumptions of MI: the ontological primacy of individual action and the explanatory implications of this idea.

## 2 The Dialectics of the Debate

One of the most surprising features of the MI debate is that many of the participants treat their position as obvious and find any opposition hard to understand. For people like Watkins and

Elster, MI is almost trivially true once it is properly understood. At the same time, opponents like Steven Lukes and Geoffrey Hodgson find the doctrine highly implausible once the distinction between ontological and explanatory doctrines is properly recognized. The difference in focus explains this puzzling discrepancy.

For most advocates of MI, the main motivation is purging suspicious explanatory factors from the social sciences. They are quite clear about what they oppose:

> Methodological collectivism ... assumes that there are supra-individual entities that are prior to individuals in the explanatory order. Explanation proceeds from the laws either of self-regulation or of development of these larger entities, while individual actions are derived from the aggregate pattern.
>
> (Elster 1985, 6)

In other words, methodological individualists want to rule out historical or functional laws that are incompatible with individual agency, attribution of agency or other psychological attributes to loose collective entities like nations or classes, and functional explanations that are not supported by underlying causal mechanisms. For them, the definition of MI is mainly a tool for ruling out these dubious ideas about social explanation. More generally, methodological individualism is regarded as a useful antidote against fuzziness and general conceptual obscurity. (Recall that MI-inspired analytical Marxism was also called non-bullshit Marxism.) Given this background, it not a surprise that they find it hard to believe that there would be any serious scientific opposition to their view.

The critics of MI mostly focus on the formulations of the doctrine. Very few of them defend any positive program of collectivism, holism, or organicism. Nor do they defend intellectual obscurantism. (It might be that methodological holism is a philosophical ideal type like skepticism in epistemology: it is a recognizable philosophical position, but very hard to find in real life.) What anti-individualists find objectionable are implications of the individualist doctrine as it is formulated. For them, MI is either trivial or too restrictive. When formulated too broadly, the doctrine accommodates everything that a sensible anti-individualist would want. In this case, it is hard to see what all the fuss is about. On the other hand, if the doctrine is formulated too strictly, it will rule out perfectly sensible social explanations, deem useful and unproblematic social scientific concepts illegitimate, and leave important parts of the social world unexplained. This is what anti-individualists are primarily motivated to defend.

Hodgson (2007) articulates this trivial or wrong dilemma clearly (for an alternative formulation see Lukes 1968). According to him, there are two ways to formulate MI:

> (a) social phenomena should be explained entirely in terms of individuals alone; or
>   (b) social phenomena should be explained in terms of individuals plus relations between individuals.
>
> (Hodgson 2007, 220)

Version (a) is a strong and interesting claim. However, it is difficult to see how one would practically implement such a program. Furthermore, most individualists from Watkins to Elster have formulated MI in a way that allows relations between individuals. They are not atomists who deny the importance of relations and interactions between individuals (Wright, Levine, and Sober 1992, 109–13). Furthermore, they do not deny the role of social processes in the formation of individuals. For them social influences on individual beliefs, desires, dispositions, or opportunities are completely acceptable as long as they happen through interactions with other individuals. According to Hodgson, this move already trivializes MI, by creating a backdoor which makes institutions and social structures acceptable explanatory factors. He argues that in modern social theory, social structures are usually conceived as sets of interactive relations between individuals, while social institutions are regarded as special sorts of social structures that involve widely observed rules. Thus, if MI legitimizes social structures and institutions, it is easy to accept but it is difficult to see what the fuss is about.

It is not difficult to see how individualists would reply. They would point out that Hodgson has all too optimistic a view of modern social theory: there is a lot of obscure social theorizing in which the connections between postulated structures, mentalities, discourses, etc. and individuals and their relations are not as unproblematic as Hodgson suggests. So, while the original targets of MI have vanished, there is still enough obscurity around to make MI relevant. This is the rhetorical setting of the debate: both parties provide only two options to choose from, but also argue that the opposition is posing a false dilemma.

## 3 The Difficulty of Being Precise

At the heart of MI is the idea that explanations in terms of individuals and their actions are somehow privileged. Making this claim more precise, we need a general consensus on how individual and non-individual social properties are demarcated, a common idea of explanation, and an articulation and justification for the assumption of explanatory privilege. The problem is that there is no consensus on these issues.

The formulation of MI presupposes that we can say which properties are individualistically acceptable, but the demarcation between individual and non-individual social properties is highly controversial. Given the centrality of this issue, it is surprising that the issue has not received more attention. For example, no one has provided a detailed account of social relational properties, although we have seen their relevance for the debate. Similarly, a systematic taxonomy and analysis of various sorts of macro social concepts found in the social sciences (Ylikoski 2012) is missing from the discussion. Kincaid's observation that "the individualism–holism debate has been long on rhetoric and short on clarity" (Kincaid 1997, 13), seems to be correct. Thus typically individualists operate with some intuitive set of individualistically acceptable properties and anti-individualists accuse them of cheating. Individualists are either defining individual properties so broadly that there is no difference from a moderate holist position, or they conveniently forget structural/institutional presuppositions of their allegedly individualistic explanations.

A similar observation holds for explanation. It is quite common to base the argumentation on some intuitions about social explanation. People have different intuitions about explanation, so it is no wonder that they might reach different conclusions. In the case of explanation, we also have a lot of explicit theories. In fact, the last six decades of MI debate have been very productive in terms of theories of explanation (Salmon 1989; Woodward 2003). The problem is that no general consensus has emerged about the right theory of explanation. Thus while the DN (deductive-nomological) account that Watkins utilized in his arguments has pretty much lost its appeal, it is unclear what the replacement should be. While most people would go for some sort of causal theory of explanation, the details matter. Different theories of explanation produce different results with respect to MI. For example, if explanation involves statements of causal or counterfactual dependence (Woodward 2003), various institutional and structural facts can easily be shown to be explanatory. They are causal difference-makers, so why can't they be fully legitimate explanatory causes? However, individualists might not be satisfied with this. For example, they could distinguish between mere causal claims and explanations proper. While it might be true that one can have sensible causal claims involving macro variables, these are not sufficient for explanation. Many individualists find mechanism-based theories of explanation appealing (Elster 1985, 2007; Hedström and Ylikoski 2010). Thus, they could argue that full mechanistic explanation would include individuals and thus justify their belief that individual agency has a crucial role in all social explanation.

A popular strategy among philosophers of science has been to deploy conceptual tools from philosophy of mind to resolve the individualism–holism debate. The idea has been to view the problem as analogical to the mainstream way of conceiving the relation between the physical and the mental (Currie 1984; Pettit 1993; Kincaid 1997; Zahle 2006; Sawyer 2005; List and Spiekermann 2013). Anti-individualists have been excited about the possibility of presenting arguments that are similar to the arguments for non-reductive materialism. The idea is to have individualistically acceptable ontology without losing explanatory autonomy of non-individual social properties. The appeal of this strategy is based on the belief that the ideas of supervenience and multiple realization provide a neat way to argue against reductionism. The basic idea of supervenience is that higher-level properties can be multiply realized by lower-level properties, but once the lower-level properties are fixed, the higher-level properties are fixed as well. There can be no difference in supervenient properties without a difference in subvenient properties. Multiple realizability is assumed to block any reduction of social properties to individual properties while realization guarantees that nothing ontologically spooky is happening.

The problem with this approach is that although it has brought more technical sophistication to the debate, it has not really resolved the issue. The first problem is that while the early enthusiasm over supervenience was based on the vision of non-reductive materialism, the relation between supervenience and reduction has become quite unclear. There is no consensus on how to understand the idea of reduction: the results depend on how you understand reductive explanation. So, this strategy does not bypass the problem of having agreement about theories of explanation. The second problem is that this strategy also presupposes a solution to the demarcation problem between individual and social properties. As long as there is general disagreement about individualistically acceptable properties, the philosophy of mind strategy cannot resolve the issue. In fact, without agreement about individual properties one cannot even evaluate the claim that social properties supervene on individual properties. The third problem is that this approach introduces a strong but possibly highly misleading metaphysical idea of levels to the debate. For philosophers it might be natural to talk about individual and social levels, but it is questionable how well this scheme—and the analogy with mind–brain relations—applies to the social sciences. As I argue elsewhere (Ylikoski 2014) the metaphor of levels might be a highly misleading way to conceive of social scientific micro–macro relations. Finally, this approach is methodologically quite sterile. The philosophical debate takes an end-of-science perspective that considers relations between future well-confirmed social and individual theories. This is an in-principle debate about reductive relations between imaginary theories without a proper theory of reductive explanation. The practical methodological implications of this highly abstract debate can be expected to be quite sparse.

It seems that we have to tolerate some uncertainty and ambiguity on the questions of explanation and demarcation of individual properties. Without clear answers to these questions, we will not have a determinate philosophical solution to the debate. Some progress might still be possible by focusing on the idea of explanatory privilege. The claim that individual properties are explanatorily privileged can be understood at least three different ways. First, we have a strong formulation:

**S-IM**: All non-individual properties are not explanatory.

This claim straightforwardly denies any explanatory relevance to non-individual social properties. This blunt thesis is the usual target of critics of MI. However, it is unclear whether individualists really subscribe to this principle. Starting from Watkins (1957, 106), individualists have contrasted unfinished or half-way explanations of everyday social science with ideal rock-bottom explanations. For example, Elster writes that:

> In principle, explanations in the social sciences should refer only to individuals and their actions. In practice, social scientists nevertheless refer to supra-individual entities such as households, firms, or nations, either as a *harmless shorthand* or as a *second-best approach* forced upon them by lack of data or of fine-grained theories.
>
> (Elster 2007, 13)

Thus it seems that Elster would subscribe to a less harsh thesis:

**E-IM**: Non-individual properties can be derivatively explanatory and placeholders for proper individualistic explanations.

This is one way to interpret the idea of half-way explanation. It saves the critic's intuition that non-individual properties are explanatory and is compatible with everyday explanatory practices of the social sciences, but still retains a strong commitment to the idea of explanatory privilege. However, there is also another way to reconstruct the idea of rock-bottom explanation:

**W-IM**: Non-individual properties are explanatorily legitimate as long as they have satisfactory microfoundations in acceptable individual explanatory factors.

The differences between these formulations are significant, but they all capture the idea that everything is ultimately explainable in terms of individual properties. In the case of S-IM this happens directly, while in W-IM this happens through chains of explanatory presupposition: non-individual properties are explanatory, but only if they can be given acceptable microfoundations. E-IM is a compromise between the two, but it is based on a rather vague idea of placeholder explanation. Given this difficulty, accepting W-IM makes more sense. Notice that W-IM might also be acceptable to most anti-individualists, depending on how the idea of microfoundations is understood. If the demand of microfoundations is understood as reduction, anti-individualists would leave the boat, but if it only signals that it must be explicable how social wholes are constituted by individuals, their mental states, relations, and material resources, most would probably be ready to buy the argument. This is not a problem; there is no reason to assume that MI has to be a controversial doctrine. However, we still have not answered the question of why individual properties are explanatorily privileged.

## 4 Methodological Individualism in Action

The study of abstract principles does not take us far. One of the major problems in philosophical debates about MI is the rarity of real examples. So it makes sense to take a brief look at methodological individualism in practice. Game theory is often cited as MI in action. Thus we can assume that it gives us a pretty good idea what these individualists think MI would look like in practice.

Game theory studies strategic interactions by modeling them as games in which the agents are facing a choice between different behaviors whose consequences depend on the choices of other agents. For our purposes, the most relevant part of this setting is the rules of the game. They determine what strategies are open to agents, how information and resources are distributed to agents, and how individual payoffs (and other outcomes) are generated. The formal description of the game does not usually involve references to social structures and institutional rules, which may give an appearance that the model does not involve these things. However, this impression is simply wrong. While some of the rules may be interpreted as a description of the physical situation in which the individual players interact, the rest of them describe exogenous institutions (Janssen 1993, 36). Thus it seems that in practice game theorists (and individualists) do not find social structures and institutions problematic as background factors for their models.

Furthermore, these factors seem to be central explanatory variables in game-theoretical models. If this sounds strange, consider the following observations. Game theory operates with rational choice theory, which is not a very rich or empirical account of individual agents. The strong assumptions about rationality and knowledge are justified by their analytical convenience: the results of interesting models would remain robust even if these assumptions were relaxed. Game theory is not really focused on studying individuals' mental life. Rather, it is analysis of situations of strategic interaction. Furthermore, it is not primarily in the business of making point predictions, but that of comparative statics that study how changes in game parameters change players' behavior and collective outcomes. In other words, the attention is on how changes in the rules change the agents' choices (and thus outcomes). If the key explanatory variables in a study are those that are systematically varied and whose consequences are observed, then we can conclude that social structures and institutions are among the key explanatory variables in game theoretical social science. Furthermore, it is hard to believe that the explanatory power of game theory would increase if these facts were reconstructed, assuming that it were possible even in principle, in some "individualistic" vocabulary. Rather, the models would just get more complicated, without additional insights provided about the issues of interest.

These structural presuppositions have not gone unnoticed by the critics of MI and they have raised the accusation that individualists do not practice what they preach (Kincaid 1997). However, it is hard to believe that people would be this massively misguided about their own activities. Maybe the core of MI is having individual agency rather than reducing all properties to individual properties? Thus structural and institutional facts are allowed as long as they do not involve any dubious collective agency and they can be explained in a way that is compatible with the ontological requirements of individualism. In other words, institutional and structural facts are acceptable in explanations as long as they do not have problematic explanatory presuppositions and the explanations involve individual agency. This sounds much like W-IM and is compatible with what sociologists like Siegwart Lindenberg, James Coleman, and Peter Hedström characterize as 'structural individualism' (Udéhn 2001, 318–19).

Game theory provides another surprising observation: agents in game theoretical models are not necessarily individuals. Economists and political scientists seems to accept firms, households, states, and other organizations as agents in their models, and individualists don't complain about this. Furthermore, it is ironic that rational choice theory seems to apply better to corporate agents like firms and parties than to proper individuals like consumers and voters (Satz and Ferejohn 1994). What this suggests is that MI is not so much about purity about individual properties, but about agency. Firms, states, and households are corporate agents with legal status and defined responsibilities. They are not persons, but their inner workings are assumed to be well understood in terms of individual actions. Thus they seem to be legitimate agents for the purpose of studying structures of strategic interaction. Again, this seems to be compatible with the W-IM interpretation of explanatory privilege.

Basically the same observations also apply to agent-based simulation models in the social sciences. Agent-based simulation methodology has been heralded as an implementation of MI that is more flexible than rational choice theory (Macy et al. 2011). It allows detailed bottom-up modeling of micro–macro dynamics and it is not confined to assumptions about homogeneity or the rationality of agents. However, we have exactly the same thing: the rules of the simulation may reflect exogenous structural and institutional facts, some of the central explanatory variables are structural, and the agents may well be corporate agents. These things are typically not found to be problematic, so it is safe to conclude that they do not challenge the basic individualist commitment. What the agent-based simulations do show is that micro–macro dynamics are messy and that understanding them is a substantial cognitive challenge that cannot be resolved simply by appealing to abstract ontological principles like MI.

## 5 The Primacy of Agency

If the argument of the previous section is right, MI is really about agency. But what makes individual agency so special? The underlying motivation for MI is the idea of the ontological primacy of individual agency. While the social world contains all kinds of things—such as meanings, institutions, collective agents, social structures, etc.—none of these things would exist or operate without individual intentional agency. From this generally accepted ontological idea individualists infer that the operation of these things cannot be understood without understanding their relation to individual action. In other words, purely holistic explanations would miss something essential about the way in which the social world works. On this interpretation individualists are not denying the existence of these things, nor are they denying that they can engage in causal relations. What they are claiming is that explanatory understanding of these things requires connecting them to human agency.

This observation explains why so many individualistically oriented social scientists find the idea of mechanism-based explanation so appealing (Elster 2007; Hedström and Ylikoski 2010). In this view the task of explanation is to open the black box of social processes and show the cogs and wheels that make it work. MI can be understood in this context as a claim that intentional individual agency is an important cog that cannot be ignored in any social explanation. On this interpretation households and corporate agents can be regarded as relatively well-understood compound components and there is no need to dissect them to their constituents for most purposes. In other words, their behaviors are assumed to be safely rooted in individual intentional action.

Anti-individualists may not dispute these points. They might agree about the ontological primacy, and also about what a full mechanism-based social explanation would involve. However, they might object that the mechanistic ideal is too demanding: it should be allowable to abstract away from individual agency. If this is the only disagreement, the debate about MI is really about the pragmatics of explanation: is it legitimate to explain without spelling out the mechanisms by which the non-individual social causes bring about their effects (Kincaid 1997)? This is a perennial issue related to mechanism-based explanation, but it has no special connection to individual agency. However, individualists might be committed to additional ideas about the explanatory primacy of intentional individual action.

One of these ideas is *intentional fundamentalism*. According to this view the understanding provided by intentional (rational) action has some special qualities that set it apart from all other causal explanations. The roots of this view can be traced to Max Weber's claim that for sociological purposes "collectivities must be treated as *solely* the resultants and modes of organization of the particular acts of individual persons, since these alone can be treated as agents in a course of subjectively understandable action" (Weber 1968, 13). This is often interpreted as Weber's statement of MI, but here the most relevant part is the reference to subjectively understandable action. One interpretation is that Weber takes intentional explanation to have some special qualities that make it somehow privileged. In the same spirit, many social scientists, especially those inspired by rational choice theory, describe rational explanations as 'rock bottom', 'especially satisfactory', or not requiring further explanation (Ylikoski 2012).

Intentional fundamentalism can be used as a basis for a regress argument for MI. This argument starts with the (often implicit) premise that a genuine explanation requires that the *explanans* is itself explained or is inherently intelligible. Following this principle, explanations referring to supra-individual social facts would only be explanatory when they themselves are explained by facts about individuals. Of course, this opens up a possibility of regress that will continue until fundamental physics, or even infinitely. (This regress argument is often raised against mechanism-based accounts of explanation.) Here the special status of rational explanation comes to the rescue: because it has the special character of being "subjectively understandable" it stops the regress and provides genuine explanation. As there is no similar special character for supra- or sub-individual explanatory factors, we would now have a unique justification for MI.

The problems with this regress argument are multiple (Ylikoski 2012). First, the premise of explanatory regress is based on a misunderstanding. An explanation only presupposes that the *explanans* is true, not that it is explained. The explanation of the *explanans* is a separate question. The second problem is that the idea of special understanding provided by intentional explanation does not go well with a more general idea of mechanism-based explanation. Although there are evolutionary reasons for the cognitive salience of folk-psychological explanatory schemes, they do not provide the basis for explanatory privilege. Folk psychology might be indispensable in the social sciences, but there is no reason to turn it into a virtue. Rather, we should constantly pay attention to its limitations. Intentional fundamentalism also makes it difficult to recognize that not all social scientific explanatory mechanisms involve intentional action. For example, some sub-personal psychological mechanisms might be highly relevant for social scientific explanations (e.g. stereotype threat). Similarly, some mechanisms might not involve individual or rational agents (e.g. selection mechanisms in organizational ecology). Thus it makes sense to think of intentional action as a (non-rigid) disciplinary stopping point for the social sciences rather than a privileged explanatory level.

Given the non-viability of intentional fundamentalism, the best strategy for individualists to defend MI is to appeal to the ontological primacy of intentional action, the need for deeper mechanism-based explanations, and the typical obscurity of social theorizing that does not take ontological primacy seriously. This does not imply a philosophical vindication of MI, but it might justify the heuristic idea of social theorizing: all or most credible social scientific explanations have intentional agents as their basic building blocks. Thus it would make sense as a heuristic principle to focus on individual agents and the situations they face, because this is the most reliable way to get a hold on relevant social mechanisms. Of course, this way of conceiving of MI may be too much for critics. After all, most of the controversial content is gone and it is hard to see what is at stake anymore. However, this reflects the historical development of the MI debate: modern versions of MI, like structural individualism, have become so close to moderate holism that the positions are difficult to distinguish from one another by their commitments (Udéhn 2001). There probably are some differences between the positions, but they are so small that they are made invisible by the variance within each camp and general imprecision of the formulations.

## 6  Conclusion

Methodological individualism could be more properly called explanatory individualism. Also the emphasis on individuals might be partly misleading, as the real issue for many individualists seems to be agency rather than individuality as such. The long and unresolved history of MI is mostly explained by the ambiguity of more basic notions involved in its formulation. Thus, people have very different views about the content of MI. Most of the dragons that the original MI supporters fought are dead, so it is worth considering whether we should retire the notion of MI altogether. If MI is motivated by something like intentional fundamentalism, it is a form of hermeneutic romanticism that should be given up. If MI is a tool for fighting against obscurantism in social theory, it is probably too imprecise for that. Explanatory obscurity is best fought directly rather than by appealing to highly abstract philosophical principles. And finally, while MI has played a major role in highlighting the complexities of micro–macro relations in the social sciences—for example in relation to collective action—these issues are highlighted more effectively by addressing the empirical and theoretical challenges directly rather than by focusing on vague philosophical doctrine. Of course, the retirement of the MI does not mean that all involved issues have been solved. It simply means that these issues are better discussed directly.

## Acknowledgment

The author has received funding from the European Research Council under the European Union's Seventh Framework Programme (FP7/2007–2013) / ERC grant agreement no. 324233 and Riksbankens Jubileumsfond (DNR M12-0301:1).

## References

Currie, G. (1984). "Individualism and Global Supervenience." *British Journal for the Philosophy of Science* 35: 345–58.

Elster, J. (1985). *Making Sense of Marx.* Cambridge: Cambridge University Press.

Elster, J. (2007). *Explaining Social Behavior: More Nuts and Bolts for the Social Sciences.* Cambridge: Cambridge University Press.

Hedström, P., and Ylikoski, P. (2010). "Causal Mechanisms in the Social Sciences." *Annual Review of Sociology* 36: 49–67.

Hodgson, G. M. (2007). "Meanings of Methodological Individualism." *Journal of Economic Methodology* 14(2): 211–26.

Janssen, M. (1993). *Microfoundations: A Critical Inquiry*. London: Routledge.

Kincaid, H. (1997). *Individualism and the Unity of Science: Essays on Reduction, Explanation, and the Special Sciences*. Lanham, MD: Rowman & Littlefield.

List, C., and K. Spiekermann. (2013). "Methodological Individualism and Holism in Political Science: A Reconciliation." *American Political Science Review* 107(4): 629–43.

Lukes, S. (1968). "Methodological Individualism Reconsidered." *British Journal of Sociology* 19(2): 119–29.

Macy, M.,Centola, D.,Flache, A.,de Rijt, A., and Willer, R. (2011). "Social Mechanisms and Generative Explanations: Computational Models with Double Agents." In *Analytical Sociology and Social Mechanisms*, ed. P. Demeulenaere. Cambridge: Cambridge University Press, 250–65.

Mandelbaum, M. (1955). "Societal Facts." *British Journal of Sociology* 6 (4): 305–17.

Pettit, P. (1993). *The Common Mind: An Essay on Psychology, Society and Politics*. Oxford: Oxford University Press.

Ruben, D.-H. (1985). *The Metaphysics of the Social World*. London: Routledge.

Salmon, W. (1989). *Four Decades of Scientific Explanation*. Minneapolis: University of Minnesota Press.

Satz, D., and Ferejohn, J. (1994). "Rational Choice and Social Theory." *Journal of Philosophy* 91: 71–87.

Sawyer, R. K. (2005). *Social Emergence: Societies as Complex Systems*. Cambridge: Cambridge University Press.

Udéhn, L. (2001). *Methodological Individualism: Background, History and Meaning*. London: Routledge.

Watkins, J. W. N. (1952). "Ideal Types and Historical Explanation." *British Journal for the Philosophy of Science* 3 (9): 22–43.

Watkins, J. W. N. (1957). "Historical Explanation in the Social Sciences." *British Journal for the Philosophy of Science* 8 (30): 104–17.

Weber, M. (1968). *Economy and Society*. Berkeley: University of California Press.

Woodward, J. (2003). *Making Things Happen: A Theory of Causal Explanation*. Oxford: Oxford University Press.

Wright, E. O., Levine A., and Sober E. (1992). *Reconstructing Marxism: Essays on Explanation and the Theory of History*. London: Verso.

Ylikoski, P. (2012). "Micro, Macro, and Mechanisms." In *The Oxford Handbook Of Philosophy of the Social Sciences*, ed. H. Kincaid. Oxford: Oxford University Press, 21–45.

Ylikoski, P. (2014). "Rethinking Micro–Macro Relations." In *Rethinking the Individualism–Holism Debate: Essays in Philosophy of Social Science*, ed. Finn Collin and Julie Zahle. Berlin: Springer, 117–35.

Zahle, J. (2006). "Holism and Supervenience." In *The Handbook of Philosophy of Science: Philosophy of Anthropology and Sociology*, ed. S. P. Turner and M. Risjord. Amsterdam: Elsevier, 311–41.

# 13
# FUNCTIONALISM

## *Alex Rosenberg*

Functionalism as an explanatory strategy is fairly obvious and common, both in ordinary life and in biology. We often explain something's character or even its very existence by citing the function it serves. The functions something serves are one or more of its effects, or the effects of its presence and behavior. The presence or operation of something has indefinitely many effects, but only a few of them are among its functions. Thus, among the effects of my pressing the accelerator pedal on my car is to burn more gasoline, raise the RPM of the engine, to increase the battery's charge, and perhaps to attract the attention of the police. But none of these effects is its function—speeding the car up. Citing this function—speeding the car up—explains why I pressed the gas pedal, of course.

Along with common sense, biology also explains the occurrence of events, the persistence of states, the onset of processes, and most of the properties of organisms and their parts by appeal to their functions.

The strategy of explaining human norms, rules, roles, practices, institutions, and artifacts by their function has also been an explicit strategy in the social sciences. Thus, for example, the jury system is identified in ordinary life and the law as the institution (in nations employing English common law) that has the function of determining matters of fact in legal proceedings. But this may be quite a superficial functional analysis, one that obscures some other, deeper functional role or disguises that the jury system shares with other institutions in countries without juries at all. Both of these possibilities are important because identifying "deeper" functions or wider functional categories is essential to the development of explanatory theories in the social sciences. Thus, some sociological analysis may hold that the real function of the jury system is *ideological*—to encourage public acceptance of decisions made elsewhere on the basis of class interests instead of on the basis of real guilt or innocence. The institution of the jury system is thus to be explained in terms of its "real function," that of sustaining other institutions—e.g. private property. Alternatively, if the jury system's role is really one of "peaceful conflict resolution," then it will be classified together with other social institutions having the same role. A functionalist theory may then seek to explain its emergence and persistence because it has this conflict-resolving function.

The difference between apparent and real functional roles is often described in terms of the distinction between *latent* and *manifest* functions. The manifest functions of a social institution are those that it was, as it were, intentionally designed to accomplish and/or that it is recognized by its participants as accomplishing. Latent functions are those it serves unwittingly, without the recognition of its participants. Such unnoticed functions are often held to be more important and more systematically significant than the manifest functions of the institution.

For instance, the manifest function of marriage is to legalize domestic and sexual relations and regularize the duties and rights associated with them. According to the founder of functionalism, Emile Durkheim (1897), however, marriage has more important latent functions. Its latent function is that of maintaining the optimal degree of social integration. In that respect, it is to be grouped with other social institutions that may seem quite different from it: the jury system, for example, or the institutions of the Catholic parish.

Identifying things by their functional role may also enable us to recognize the artificiality of distinctions between social institutions. For example, the functions of the police as the agency of law enforcement, and of the courts as the agency of adjudication in legal questions, may seem quite distinct. Yet the Marxian sociologist who views the jury system as an institution for enforcing class interests may bring the jury system together with the police into one category of institutions with a single latent function. That sociologist may argue that the institution operates effectively by making it appear as though both its components have distinct identities and separate functions.

Individuating social institutions by function and framing explanatory theories about them are intimately associated. Just to identify something as an instance of a functional category is already to advance a generalization about it. To identify marriage as a socially integrating institution involves asserting that marriage encourages social integration. That is a generalization as well as a classification. It enables us to lump marriage together with other such institutions and then to see whether we can frame hypotheses about them. For instance, we may consider the generalization that certain institutions reduce the individual's probability of suicide. In fact, Durkheim's claim that there are three different types of suicides—egoistic, altruistic, and anomic—is based on a prior classification of social institutions into functional types that protect against too much social egoism, too much social altruism, or social anomie. Durkheim's classification of suicides was based on an examination of the consequences of three different ways that institutions can break down, failing to fulfill their function of maintaining an optimal degree of social integration.

For a period in twentieth-century social science, the methodology of seeking functions for features of human affairs was also called *structural functionalism*. Among its other advocates were European anthropologists such as Maus, Malinowski, and Lévi-Strauss, and the American sociological theorist Talcott Parsons. In this context *structuralism* suggests that there are social structures that are necessary for a society's persistence, its character or identity that are not intentionally constructed or even noticed by its participants, that therefore these structures can't be reduced to or explained in terms of the behavior or the thoughts of individuals and groups of them, and that their functions need to be identified by the social scientist.

As an explicit analytical strategy functionalism is no longer explicitly and widely endorsed in social science. It is however difficult to avoid, even by those who repudiate it or otherwise deny that identifying socially significant matters must invoke their functions. The reason becomes clear when we consider the taxonomies, the typologies, the systems of classification, categorization, and identification of social, political, economic, anthropological, and cultural phenomena that are of interest to the social scientist.

## Functional Analysis

Almost everything of interest in the social sciences is defined, identified, individuated, and distinguished by its function. The reasons for this are obvious. First, most of the nouns in ordinary language are functional—i.e. their definitions are given mainly in terms of their effects, and in particular their effects on us, as opposed to their structures or composition. This is particularly obvious for nouns that name artifacts, things humans make. Second, what makes a social phenomenon one that social scientists notice, what brings it to their attention, is its effects on individuals and groups. And for those effects to last long enough to be of interest, they will have to be functions, as we shall see—though often not functions intended by any individual or group. Third, the ameliorative interests of social scientists motivate them to focus on identifying the effects on people and groups of persistent social norms, roles, practices, institutions. As we shall shortly see, the effects that most interest social scientists are their functions—intended or unintended by the individuals who embrace the norms, participate in the practices, sustain the institutions.

The idea that almost everything of interest to social scientists has functions may seem dubious at first blush. That sounds like an idea worthy of Pollyanna or Voltaire's Dr. Pangloss, who thought that the bridge of the nose was there to rest eyeglasses on. Indeed one of the chief objections that undermined functionalism as advanced by Durkheim and his followers was the charge that its taxonomic and explanatory strategy is unwarrantably conservative and complacent. If every norm, role, practice, institution of interest in societies has functions—i.e. effects that meet needs, confer benefits, are adaptations or otherwise advantageous—then few if any should be tampered with on pain of harming the society whose needs they meet. A functionalist might argue that even if we don't know the function of an institution such as the patriarchy, we should not seek to abolish it unless and until we can be sure that whatever benefit it accords society can still be met by other means. This is a prescription for complacency that few reformist or radical agents of social change will accept. An analytical method that warrants such a prescription is unlikely to be accepted.

This charge against functionalism, however, rests on a serious mistake or oversight that the early functionalist made. Once it is recognized, functional analysis in the social sciences becomes much more compelling. The error functionalists made, which made their view sound so implausible, was to mis-identify the *beneficiaries* of the functions that roles, norms, practices, institutions, and organizations fulfilled. They assumed, quite myopically and wrongly, that the function of institutions, practices, organizations, was to fulfill the needs of individual people and social groups. But it's obvious that many institutions, practices, organizations are in fact harmful to people, confer no net advantage or benefit on them, for instance most religions, or Chinese foot-binding, or tobacco smoking.

Only in the late 20th century did it become apparent that in these and other cases, a change in perspective—a *Gestalt switch*—would enable us to see what was not previously apparent: the relevant beneficiaries of institutions, practices, organizations that are harmful to people were the institutions themselves, the practices, organizational structures that parasitize human hosts. Many institutions, organizations, and practices prey on people and groups, treat them as niches, environments to be exploited. Think of how and why heroin addiction persists and spreads: the practice has several effects on people that ensure the practice's persistence. These effects of heroin addiction "perform" functions for the practice; the practice persists because it has these functions.

Chinese foot-binding is a nice example of how this works. Foot-binding persisted for about 1,000 years in China. It got started because women with bound feet were more attractive as wives. Bound feet functioned in part as a signal of wealth, since only rich families could afford the luxury of preventing daughters from working. Other functions of bound feet were to make it easier to keep track of girls, and ensure their virginity. So, at first, when the practice arose, foot-bound girls had more suitors. Pretty soon every family that could afford it was binding daughters' feet to ensure they'd get married. Result: when every girl's feet were bound, foot-binding no longer provided an advantage in the marriage market, and all foot-bound girls were worse off because they couldn't walk, suffered other health effects, etc. Foot-binding starts out conferring a benefit on some families, or even some girls. By the time it becomes really widespread and fixed, it has lost its original function (of giving a few girls an advantage in the marriage market) and acquired another one (making a girl marriageable at all), even though it is actually harmful to every foot-bound girl's health and welfare. But once everyone was doing it, no one could get off the foot-binding merry-go-round. Anyone who stopped binding daughters' feet condemned them to spinsterhood. That is why foot-binding persisted despite its harmful effects (Mackie 1996). For whom or for what did its features have functions? For itself, for the practice, norm, institution of foot-binding! The practice persisted, like any parasite, because some of its effects function for it, exploiting the "weaknesses" of humans and their institutions—marriage, the desire for virgin brides and large dowries, the desire to control women before and after marriage.

Once we widen our focus, the claim that almost everything of interest to social scientists in human affairs has functions becomes far less Panglossian. Functional analysis—identifying kinds, categories, types of social significance by identifying the needs, benefits, or advantages they confer, is indispensable to a social science with any chance of practical application to the amelioration of human affairs. But doing so is a far trickier matter than merely trying to figure out what benefit a rule, a role, a practice, an institution confers on the people who participate in it. It may not have any benefit for them at all: its function may include harming people, even though they don't recognize it.

## Functional Taxonomies and Functional Explanation

Taxonomizing or classifying social phenomena by function goes hand in hand with explaining the emergence and persistence of social phenomena by appeal to their functions. If most matters in the domain of the social sciences have functions, then this cannot be a coincidence: explaining the emergence of norms, roles, rules, practices, institutions with functions will have to appeal to the fact that they have functions.

The need for functional explanations in the social sciences is powerfully illustrated by a trio of examples from the discipline that has most firmly resisted such explanations: economics. The preferred explanatory strategy of economics is one that employs rational choice theory, explaining aggregate outcomes as the result of rational choices by utility- or preference-maximizing agents. But there are several economic institutions that fulfill crucial economic functions but which cannot be explained as the intended outcomes of individual rational choice.

Consider three central economic facts: the ubiquity of markets, the emergence of money, and the existence of firms. Each of these institutions fulfills an important *need* individuals have. None emerged as the intended outcome of a rational choice process. It was the Nobel Prize-winning economist Friedrich Hayek who earliest and most clearly recognized the problem facing economic theory of explaining the emergence of economic institutions. He called it the problem of 'spontaneous order'. But that is just to label the problem, as we'll see.

In the case of the firm the human need is to solve a transaction cost problem, as Ronald Coase first noticed only in 1937. Without a solution to this problem, the division of labor must come to a standstill and with it almost all the productivity increases humans have contrived since the

Middle Ages. No rational agent recognized what the problem was that everyone faced, no one decided to invent the firm in order to solve this problem. It emerged "spontaneously" to "order" exchanges between individuals in ways that solved a transaction-cost problem. The firm is an example of "spontaneous order." The firm did not originate as a conscious contrivance, nor was it the gift of a benevolent deity. Its emergence and persistence demands explanation. And the fact that it fills an important function cannot be incidental to the explanation of its emergence and persistence.

Money solves the biggest problem of barter: what the economists call the double coincidence of wants. Without money if I want oranges and have only bananas, I need to find someone who wants bananas and has oranges. What's more, since we can't divide and store bananas and oranges, I'll need to find someone who wants to trade in exact whole numbers of bananas and oranges that match up with the amounts I am prepared to trade. This is a problem that becomes intractable very early in human exchange. How does it get solved? Several times in distant cultures the same solution was hit upon: the emergence of a commodity with common features: portability, divisibility, durability, utility or widespread desirability, and short-term limits on its quantity. When money emerged no one consciously recognized that it would have to have these features. No one intentionally, rationally chose to adopt some commodity owing to its having the features that solved the problem of the double coincidence of wants.

The emergence of money requires that agents solve another problem, one of coordination. Sooner or later they must all converge on the same commodity to serve as money. People must solve a "common knowledge" problem. Somehow each agent must be willing to adopt a certain commodity as money and must come to believe that everyone else will adopt the same commodity, and must believe that everyone else will be confident that every other agent has adopted the same commodity. You can see that this is a set of problems that can't be solved by individual rational choice, nor can it be solved by some explicit social contract. The institution of money is another example of order emerging without any one intending it or taking steps to bring it about. Of course to say that money emerged spontaneously is simply to label the problem. To model the acceptance among large numbers of rational individuals of a commodity as the *numeraire*, or as the optimal solution to a cooperative game, is not to solve this problem but to structure it in a way that cries out for functional explanation: an account of the emergence and persistence of money that gives its function a crucial causal role in its emergence and persistence, independent of whether people designed or even recognized the real need for money.

The third example, Hayek's example, the system of market prices, is the most important illustration of the need for functional explanations of the "spontaneous order" in human institutions. The unsolvable problem of socialist central planning is informational. Central planning faces the mathematical problem of converting a list of available inputs and a list of desired outputs into a list of production orders, and then continually updating this list as input availability changes and desired outputs change. Central planning faces the further problem of sending information about each of the changes in inputs and outputs only to those who need to have this information in order to make their production plans. The central planner can't send the changes to everyone: we'd have to spend the better part of every day just trying to find the information we need from a daily massive data dump. But the central planner can no more figure out to whom exactly to send the updated information than it can figure out the initial production order. Updating this order as circumstances change is still another challenge beyond the powers of rational, intentional choice and planning implementation. These are all what mathematicians call NP-hard problems ("nondeterministic polynomial-time hard problems"). There is no known algorithmic, computerizable solution to such problems, and a good chance than none exists. This is the fundamental reason the Soviet economies collapsed. Even a society composed exclusively of exemplars of New Socialist Man would not be able to solve the relevant NP-hard problem.

Yet the problem is solved all day, everyday, instantaneously by the system of market prices. The market price system is an information storage, retrieval, and calculation system—a vast virtual computer—that provides the closest approximation to mathematically correct solutions to the central planners' calculation problems and at no cost whatever.

The market price system performs a function indispensable not just to modern life, but to all human life since the Pleistocene. It meets a need that cannot have been foreseen by humans, no matter how rational. It is a solution to that need that no human or coalition of humans could have filled by intentional design and contrivance. Indeed it is a solution that rational choice would have led individuals to try to undermine or subvert in their own interests. But the solution to the problem people face is so ingenious it automatically and successfully responds to such subversion attempts. Even the strongest exponents of rational choice theory have recognized this feature of markets: their prescription for the elimination of monopoly, externalities, insider trading, and other "market failures" is to leave them alone. The excess "rents" these failures produce send price signals to the rest of the rational agents in the economy that will change their behavior and compete away the rents and the market failures.

The market price system operates continually to meet a need that no human or set of humans could fulfill by intentional and deliberate action. The function served by the market price system cannot be met by people, no matter how rational they are, and no matter how powerful and inexpensive their information storage, retrieval, and computational resources are. And the market price system emerged, like money, spontaneously, independently, repeatedly and without malice of human forethought throughout human history, everywhere, across the globe.

These three examples highlight the economist's version of a problem facing all social sciences. This is Hayek's problem of spontaneous order: How is it that a large number of social practices and institutions that fulfill functions have emerged and persisted? It can't be a coincidence that most practices and institutions of interest to social scientists fulfill functions (though recall, not always for people or groups). Science cannot accept the occurrence of coincidence on so massive a scale. It demands an explanation for these institutions that treats their fulfillment of functions as part of the causal process of their emergence and persistence. Nothing less will dispel the unacceptable possibility of coincidence.

## Functionalism's Problem of Teleology

Satisfying this demand that functions be part of the scientific, causal, law-governed empirically testable explanation for the emergence and persistence of social phenomena, is the hard problem of functionalism.

How could the function an institution fulfills be part of the causal explanation of its emergence and persistence? We can immediately exclude at least two "scenarios": divine benevolence/malevolence, and future causation. If an omnipotent, omniscient or at least very powerful and knowledgeable agency designed and constructed human institutions in order to attain its aims or objectives, then it would be no surprise that such institutions do so. We may exclude this possibility without further discussion. If the fulfillment of future needs or benefits could bring about past histories of the emergence and persistence of institutions, then our problem would also be solved. This possibility too can be excluded owing to the fact that the future outcomes cannot bring about past events. The idea that nature is intrinsically purposive, that the past is somehow organized to aim at and attain future outcomes, as ends, goals, objectives, was expunged from physics in the 17th century, from chemistry in the 18th, and from biology with Darwin's theory of natural selection in 1859. It would be an embarrassment were the social sciences to cling to such notions, especially in light of their physical impossibility.

Of course, if human institutions were, like artifacts, the result of conscious, deliberate human design, there would be no mystery about the role of their functions in their emergence. Just as a knife functions to cut because it was designed by people to do so, a consciously constructed institution such as the UN Declaration of Human Rights or the US Constitution owes its existence and its function to the designs of the humans who brought it into existence. But in fact few important human institutions are artifacts—products of intentional human design. Recall the examples of the firm, money, and the market.

Once we have excluded divine benevolence, future causation, immanent teleology, or human design, it's hard to see how the function of a social institution can play a role in its emergence and persistence. As the 17th-century Dutch philosopher Benedict Spinoza pointed out, for something's effects—even its useful, beneficial, advantageous effects to explain its existence is to reverse the order of nature—to make the future bring about the past.

Notice that biology has the same problem as the social sciences: It explains the emergence and persistence of biological traits by identifying their functions. The classical example exploits William Harvey's discovery in the 17th century that the function of the heart is to pump the blood. Ever since then the explanation of why organisms have hearts is "in order to pump the blood." Before Darwin this explanation worked because it was underwritten by theism: the omnipotent benevolent deity designed vertebrates to have hearts and implemented his design. Once God is excluded from the domain of scientific explanation, such "teleological" (goal-directed, purposive) explanations become, to say the least, problematical. Goals, ends, purposes in the future cannot cause processes, events, or states in the past that bring them about, since they don't yet exist when the events, states, and processes occur that will attain them. If purposes, goals, ends can't cause their means, they can't figure in the scientific, causal explanation of the occurrence of their means of attainment.

Darwin's theory of natural selection solved this problem for biology. Consider, of all the different effects on the body of having a heart, what makes pumping blood its function? The function of the heartbeat—to circulate the blood—is its function because, over the course of evolution, random variations in heart configurations that fostered circulation were selected for because of their contribution to the fitness of the animals with those variations. The selection of successive variations produced hearts of the current adapted design. Thus, a heart that circulates the blood is an adaptation. Functional claims in biology turn out to be only apparently about future effects when they are really about prior causes in the long evolutionary past.

Thus, in biology, claims of the form the function of x is to F are invariably backed up by an *etiology*—a history of heritable blind variations that the local environment filters for fitness, or adaptedness, for having more or better F-capabilities. This persistent cycle of variation and filtering produces a succession of increasingly adapted x-like structures that eventuate into x's that do F. So in biology, to attribute a function to a biological trait is usually to commit oneself to a Darwinian process as the etiology of how the trait came about.[1]

The process of blind variation and natural selection that Darwin discovered provides a purely causal mechanism that produces the appearance of purpose-driven, goal-directed processes in which the means are explained by the ends. But it is mere "appearance." The process that produces biological functions, adaptations, traits that meet needs, confer benefits, secure advantages to organisms in the struggle for survival, is blind, random, passive, and utterly undirected, just as the rest of science requires.

## Challenges for a Darwinian Vindication of Social Functions

Well, why can't sociological functionalism take a page out of biology's book? Why can't it help itself to a Darwinian theory of the natural selection of societies and their traits—their roles, practices, institutions? Such a theory might go something like this: blind variation produces a variety of social institutions with diverse effects for their societies. Among the various institutions that spring up, some were adaptive for the societies in which they arose, some were maladaptive, and others were neutral. The fitter among competing norms, rules, roles, practices, institutions were selected for, i.e. in some cases multiplied, in others persisted, in still others expanded their domains, or all three. Societies with adaptive institutions flourished, those with maladaptive were extinguished, and those with adaptively neutral institutions were overwhelmed in competition with societies with the better-adapted ones. By a succession of refinements through the mechanism of variation and selection, there arose the institutions we recognize today, since all these institutions are adaptive in the societies where they occurred. And this entirely Darwinian causal account underwrites functional explanations in the social sciences.

In the first three-quarters of the twentieth century, hardly any social scientists were tempted to offer such a Darwinian theory for the existence and character of social institutions, the social facts about these institutions, and their relationship to one another. Very few social scientists, including functionalists, ever took the Darwinian theory seriously. However, few social scientists ever seem to express disquiet about the absence of an explanation even for why social institutions with functions are widespread, or for that matter even possible.

One reason few social scientists were prepared to take Darwinian theory seriously for social science was the widespread belief that, as a theory about genetically fixed, hardwired traits, it had no relevance to human affairs. Almost nothing of interest in human affairs seems to be hardwired and genetically encoded; human societies and their components are so different from one another, while human genetic inheritance is so similar, that it's obvious the latter could not explain the former. Culture and civilization, it was confidently held, is a matter of nurture and not nature. Much of it is the product of cognitive processes that are themselves acquired by learning, that is, are transmitted by linguistic and other culturally dependent processes. Thus, the very idea that a Darwinian theory of natural selection might be relevant to human affairs was considered laughable when it was not stigmatized as dangerous. It was viewed as dangerous, since theories of human cultural differences as genetically hardwired were convenient beliefs for racists, sexists, and xenophobes.

There was a further and much more powerful reason why Darwinian theory was long deemed of no relevance to human affairs and therefore unable to provide any support for a functional theory of social institutions. The most important feature of human society is the fact that people cooperate, that they behave in accordance with moral norms that prevent people from acting selfishly, egotistically, and without regard for their fellow creatures. Admittedly, these norms are sometimes enforced only within groups and not across them, and there are always a handful of individuals who flout these rules. But no society could function without substantial cooperation among its members; no social institutions could long exist without all participants sharing the burdens of its maintenance; and there would be no social facts about institutions to explain without human cooperation. But Darwin's theory apparently could not explain cooperation among humans. Indeed, it would lead us to expect that there is no cooperation among egoistic fitness-maximizers. The evident falsity of this seeming implication long made Darwinian processes completely unavailable for any account of function in social science.

Closely coupled with Darwinian theory's apparent difficulty of explaining social cooperation by individual fitness-maximizers was its perceived resistance to group selection. This is the claim that besides individuals, group traits are subject to shaping into adaptations by a process of random variation and natural selection operating at a level distinct from, and in opposition to the selection of, adaptations of individuals or their genes. Insofar as social functions are group-level traits, any difficulty in identifying Darwinian processes operating above and in different directions from individual selection made the process unavailable as a way of providing the causal mechanism functional explanation requires.

Owing to a range of developments in behavioral biology and ecology, evolutionary anthropology, game theory, and experimental economics over the course of the second half of the 20th century, biology was able to solve the problem of how social cooperation could have evolved by natural selection among individual egoistic fitness-maximizing organisms. It was also able to reconcile individual and group selection as compatible Darwinian processes (Okasha 2009). In doing so, these disciplines gave new impetus to attempts to extend the Darwinian account of biological function to social institutions. In particular they motivated the development of models and theories in the social science that provided a completely non-genetic, non-hereditary mechanism for Darwinian cultural evolution. These developments raised again, especially among philosophers of social science and philosophers of biology, the question of whether there is scope for a literal, and not a merely metaphorical, Darwinian approach to cultural evolution. This question is of great interest independent of any vindication of functionalism, but it is indispensable for the claim that the emergence and persistence of social institutions is due to their functions.

Whether there is real, non-metaphorical, literal scope for Darwinian processes in a domain is widely held to require something equivalent to biological genes to act as replicators-units of transmission, and to build interactors with traits that are selected, pass through an environmental filter, reproduce, or become extinct. Like genes social replicators will have to store and transmit traits faithfully enough and long enough for environmental filtration to shape their social effects into adaptations and to maintain them as adaptations. In the biological domain these replicators are the genes. The equivalent replicators in the social domain came to be called 'memes', following usage invented by Richard Dawkins (1976).[2]

The most forceful argument against Darwinian cultural evolution holds that there are no memes. There is nothing that transmits social practices and packages of them with enough copy-fidelity among individuals and groups to be shaped by any environmental process of selection. People influence people, they don't faithfully transmit traits to one another. Variation in practices is continual, not a matter of occasional mutation. Social change is nothing like biological evolution. No memes, *ergo* no Darwinian processes. (See Sperber 2000 for the origin of this widely mooted argument.)

The issue is serious for Darwinian social science. That natural selection is an attractive metaphor in the description of human affairs is both unexceptional and uninteresting. The issue is whether it is more than a metaphor. Are all, most, many social process literally, actually, really matters of blind variation and environmental filtration? That is the issue. If a real Darwinian process requires actual replicators, then the no-memes critique must be addressed. It can be.

Darwinian social scientists and defenders of functionalism respond to this objection in several ways. To begin with, it is obvious that the literal application of Darwinian theory to a domain does not require that the domain contain gene-like replicators. Biological replicators—genes—did not predate Darwinian processes, they were produced by it. Natural selection presumably got its start prior to the emergence of these replicators, and for that matter, prior to the emergence of any recognizable very high-fidelity informationally rich replicators. Moreover, natural selection is likely to produce replicators of the sort that the genes constitute only when environments change slowly, when evolution is extremely gradual, cumulative, and atomistic in its shaping of individual traits, one by one, for adaptations. When one or more of these conditions do not obtain, adaptive evolution may employ replicators and processes of replication quite unlike genes.

Following Richerson and Boyd (2006), defenders of Darwinian approaches to culture have also argued that cultural replicators need not have the high-fidelity features of genes, since there are a variety of practices, norms, and institutions in human culture which have emerged as adaptations precisely because they preserve the adaptive informational content of replicators even under conditions of low copy fidelity. (See Driscoll 2008 for a useful discussion.)

It may be granted that Darwinism about human affairs does require cultural replicators, probably a variety of quite different kinds of replicators, and some of them may be gene-like.

But the trouble with the no-memes argument is that it rests on an idea of what genes are and how they work that was obsolete about a hundred years ago. This is the one trait-one gene idea, the notion that most or many significant observed inherited traits are controlled by a single gene.

There are only a small number of such traits in any mammal, and in humans only about seven such traits are known. For example, tongue rolling or the widow's peak. All other inherited traits in humans, like eye and skin color, even sexual characteristics, are each the result of the inheritance of many and in some cases a huge number of genes. In fact, genes don't really transmit or control the appearance of any of the biological traits common sense and folk biology think they do. Each gene controls the production of a protein or other large molecule. There are 25,000 of these genes, switched on and off in every cell of our bodies. It's the protein molecules they code for and the order in which the proteins are produced by the genes that build and operate biological machinery. Many different traits that don't have anything to do with each other are built or controlled by the same gene; many traits that look to us absolutely the same across individuals—say eye color—are the result of different sets of different genes in different people. And when we actually locate the genes inside the nucleus of our somatic cells, and in the sperm and egg that develop into our bodies when they combine, these genes can differ from one another substantially without that difference making any difference for the proteins they produce.

The moral for memes is obvious: if memes are like genes then any single meme will by itself almost never either control the appearance of a behavior or action or anything else that common sense or even sophisticated social science is interested in. It will take many, many memes working together to produce anything of interest to the human sciences, and we may never be able to detect or identify memes by doing anything like garden-variety sociology, economics, anthropology, or even psychology. Whatever memes are, they are going to be as complicated and hard to identify as genes are, or even more so!

If memes are anything like genes, it is going to be very hard to identify them, isolate or individuate them, and learn the details of how they work. Doing any of these things will be orders of magnitude more difficult than what a century of molecular biology has done for genetics. This is not an argument for the existence of memes. At most it is a well-grounded explanation for why social and behavioral scientists are unlikely to find them, an excuse erected on the criticism of a bad argument against the very possibility of memes. If there are memes, then regularities about their transmission, mode of action, and realizations in the brain, will be complex, short-lived, and completely beyond the reach of any hypothesis-testing in the social sciences. So, if we can't identify them, why suppose that there are any memes?

The real argument for memes, or something very like them, is twofold: first, almost all significant features of human affairs—historical actions, events, processes, norms, organizations, institutions, etc.—have functions; second, functions can only arise as adaptations, and the only source of adaptation in nature—including human affairs—are Darwinian processes of blind variation and environmental filtration.

Functionalism in social science is unavoidable and it requires a Darwinian mechanism of cultural evolution.

## Notes

1 Sometimes functional analysis in biology and especially in physiology does not explicitly presuppose Darwinian etiologies of blind variation among heritable traits and successive rounds of environmental filtration that sculpts them. Sometimes to attribute a function to something is simply to assert that what it does contributes to the capacity of some larger structure containing it to behave in a certain way. Thus to say that the function of the iris is to modulate the amount of light falling on the retina has no explicit implication that it was selected for exactly this and only this effect, or that it was a single trait or feature of the eye selected for at all. When "function" is used in this "causal role" (Cummins 1975) sense in biology, it seems free from any explicit suggestion of why the trait or its function is advantageous for any biological entity at all. However, when function is used in social science, there is always this suggestion of benefit conferred or adaptation. So this "causal role" account of how the concept of function sometimes works in biology has little relevance to the present problem.

2 At about the same time Dawkins coined the term, E. O. Wilson (Lumsden and Wilson 1980) introduced the word 'culturgen' to name whatever fills the replicator role in culture. Had things turned out differently, Wilson's term would have become the meme for 'memes' instead.

## References

Coase, R. H. (1937) "The Nature of the Firm," *Economica* 4: 386–405.

Cummins, R. (1975) "Functional Analysis," *Journal of Philosophy* 72: 741–60.

Dawkins, R. (1976) *The Selfish Gene*. Oxford: Oxford University Press.

Driscoll, C. (2008) "The Problem of Adaptive Individual Choice in Cultural Evolution," *Biology and Philosophy* 23: 101–13.

Durkheim, E. (1897/1951) *Suicide: A Study in Sociology*. New York: The Free Press.

Hayek, F. (1945) "The Use of Knowledge in Society," *American Economic Review* 35: 519–30.

Mackie, G. (1996) "Ending Footbinding and Infibulation: A Convention Account," *American Sociological Review* 61: 999–1017.

Okasha, S. (2009) *Evolution and the Levels of Selection*. Oxford: Oxford University Press.

Richerson, P., and Boyd, R. (2006) *Not by Genes Alone*. Chicago: University of Chicago Press.

Sperber, D. (2000) "An Objection to the Memetic Approach to Culture," in Robert Aunger ed., *Darwinizing Culture: The Status of Memetics as a Science*. Oxford: Oxford University Press, 163–73.

Lumsden, C., and Wilson, E. O. (1980) *Genes, Mind, and Culture*. Cambridge, MA: Harvard University Press.

# 14
# NATURALISM
## *David Livingstone Smith*

## Introduction

Naturalism can be roughly characterized as the view that philosophy is, in some sense, continuous with science. There are probably very few philosophers working today who would not describe their position as, in some sense, "naturalistic." However, this seeming unity conceals a great deal of diversity (Kitcher 1992; Rosenberg 1996; Flanagan 2008). I will not attempt to tease out, motivate, or criticize the various strands of contemporary and classical naturalism in this chapter—a task that would far exceed the space available. Instead, I will concentrate on the relevance of the two main kinds of naturalism—ontological naturalism and methodological naturalism—to the philosophy of social science. Then, extrapolating from work in the philosophy of psychology, I will focus on a problem that any naturalistically inclined philosopher of social science must grapple with: the problem of whether and how intentionalistic explanations of social phenomena can be brought into relation with non-intentionalistic ones.

## Philosophical Background

According to one very influential view, to explain a phenomenon scientifically is to subsume it under a law (Hempel 1965)—a spatiotemporally unrestricted, exceptionless generalization with modal force. On this view, part of the scientist's job is to describe the constituents of the world in such a way as to distinguish those kinds of things that feature in law-like generalizations from those that cannot. Included in the latter category is the kind "armchair." There are no laws of armchairs—that is, laws that describe the behavior of armchairs as such ("armchair" is not normally included in indices of physics textbooks). Armchairs are a kind, but they are not a natural kind. They are human contrivances—living-room furniture rather than parts of the furniture of the world. They are created rather than discovered, and their very existence is dependent upon human social practices. There are no laws of armchairs, because the category "armchair" is orthogonal to physical and chemical categories—categories like "polymer" and "iron" that describe the materials from which (some) armchairs are constructed. The causal properties of any given armchair are deducible only insofar as it is described as a complex physical object possessing paradigmatically physical and chemical properties (for example, a certain mass and chemical composition). Unlike what is the case for paradigmatic natural kinds such as chemical elements or elementary particles, what makes something an armchair is nothing more than the purpose that it is intended to serve.

Of course, a description specifying only physical and chemical properties does not exhaust the properties of armchairs, and does not address those properties of armchairs that are normally most interesting to us. Properties like *being comfortable* or *having a pleasing shape* are irreducible to physical properties (there are no non-disjunctive, exhaustively physical predicates that capture them). All the more, there are no purely physical predicates that capture the function of armchairs, their economics, or their cultural significance in American households, all of which fall under the purview of the social sciences.

The armchair example suggests that there is a big difference between the natural and social sciences. The natural sciences are concerned with features of the material world, the properties of which are independent of the meanings that human beings assign to them. Our beliefs about gold have no impact on the fact that it is dense and ductile, soluble in aqua regia, and melts at 1,948° Fahrenheit. The social sciences are concerned with the products of human agency (artificial kinds)—or the social uses of natural kinds (for example, the value that we attach to gold, its symbolic and monetary significance).

Natural science has formulated laws that allow us to explain and predict events with astonishing precision. And even disciplines like biology, which do not have strict laws, make use of highly resilient empirical generalizations that permit powerful inductions. In consequence, natural science has empowered us to shape our world by harnessing these empirical regularities. And because scientific knowledge is cumulative, scientific progress enables us to become more successful at explaining, predicting, and intervening as time goes by. In stark contrast, the empirical yield from the social sciences has been meager at best. Its predictive power lags well behind even seventeenth century natural science. As Rosenberg (2012, 19) remarks:

> Why have the social sciences not provided increasing amounts of cumulative scientific knowledge with technical payoff for predicting and controlling social processes? The social sciences have failed, despite long attempts, because they have not uncovered laws or even empirical generalizations that could be improved in the direction of real laws about human behavior and its consequences. This diagnosis calls for both an explanation of why no laws have been discovered and a proposal about how we can go about discovering them.

Several hypotheses can be offered as to why the gap between the natural and social sciences has not only persisted, but has widened with each passing year. One possibility is that social systems are far more complex than paradigmatically physical systems, and it will therefore take longer for the social sciences to approximate the degree of precision that is characteristic of the natural sciences, which progress more rapidly on account of the relative tractability of their subject matter. Another possibility is that physics and chemistry do not provide a model of explanation that is appropriate to the social sciences. This response bifurcates into two intellectual streams: either the social sciences are not sciences at all, but are instead interpretive disciplines (Taylor 1971), or they are genuine sciences that do not conform to the nomological-deductive approach. The interpretive or "hermeneutic" tradition in the social sciences goes back to the work of Wilhelm Dilthey in the nineteenth century. The basic idea is if we wish to comprehend the social sphere, we need to consider the *meaning* of human action. To do this, we need to think of human beings as rational agents rather than as physical objects subject only to causal laws.

With regard to the second option, there has been a great deal of work in the philosophy of science since the 1970s challenging the hegemony of physics as a normative model for science. Philosophers of biology have argued that biological regularities, however robust, are local and contingent rather than universal and necessary (Beatty 1993), that classical genetics now appears to be irreducible to molecular genetics (Kitcher 1984), and the view that species are natural kinds has been subject to critical scrutiny (Ghislin 1974; Hull 1978). These developments, in conjunction with the ascendency of evolutionary thinking in psychology, economics, anthropology, suggest that natural and social science may not be as remote from one another as has hitherto been assumed (Wilson 1998).

## Ontological Naturalism

There are two main varieties of naturalism: ontological naturalism and methodological naturalism. I will first discuss ontological naturalism, as applied to the social sciences, and then go on to address the more contentious subject of methodological naturalism.

Ontological naturalism is the view that only natural things exist. But for this claim to be contentful, we need some reasonably clear notion of what it is for something to be natural, and some criteria for differentiating things that are from things that are not. John Stuart Mill pointed out that the word "natural" has two meanings. "Nature," in the broadest sense, denotes "everything which is." In a second, narrower, sense it refers to everything that has not been modified by human intervention (Mill 1874, 12). Social science cannot but be naturalistic in the first sense. If everything that exists is part of nature, then social norms, institutions, and practices are all natural. Economic behavior is as natural as the migratory behavior of salmon, and religious institutions are as natural as carbon dioxide. But in the second, narrower sense, neither economic behavior nor religious institutions are natural.

One weakness of this account is that it fails to capture the distinction between "natural" and "supernatural" that is often invoked by philosophers who identify naturalism with antisupernaturalism (Stroud 2004). If miracles occur, then (according to the view presented in the preceding paragraph) they are natural in both broad and narrow senses. They are natural in the broad sense simply in virtue of existing, and they are natural in the narrow sense in virtue of not being products of *human* agency. To rule out supernaturalism, we can stipulate that everything that is natural (in the broad sense) is physical, and go on to say that anything that is natural, in the second sense, is not the product of agency. Ontological naturalism, in the most inclusive sense, entails that all agents and the things that they fashion are physical. In the more restricted sense, it entails that things are non-natural just in case they have been fashioned by agents. Given that supernatural beings are, by definition, non-physical, this leaves us with idea that all non-natural things are physical things that have been fashioned by human agents. The subject matters of the social sciences are ontologically non-natural in this sense only.

Ontological naturalism per se is not a matter of controversy in philosophy of the social sciences. For the most part, even those social scientists who countenance the possibility that non-physical things exist are not inclined to regard these things as playing any role in the subject matter of social science (see Flanagan 2008). Importantly, ontological naturalism does not have any substantive implications for the *practice* of social science. One can accept that all things are physical—or, more restrictively, that social science deals only with physical things—while denying that social scientists should use methods derived from or modeled upon those used in the natural sciences to study these things.

## Methodological Naturalism

Methodological naturalism is roughly the view that social phenomena are best understood by means of the investigative methods that are used by natural scientists. Whereas virtually all philosophers of the social sciences are ontological naturalists, it is not the case that virtually all (or even most) of them are methodological naturalists. Methodological naturalism is far more controversial than its ontological counterpart, and evaluating its prospects requires one to engage with some difficult philosophical problems.

Controversies about methodological naturalism turn on disagreements about the relation, if any, between social scientific and natural scientific explanations. It is a truism in the philosophy of science that theories are underdetermined by data—that any phenomenon or class of phenomena is consistent with any number of explanations of those phenomena (Duhem 1954). Science proceeds by winnowing contending explanations by devising experiments or making observations that allow one to make an *inference to the best explanation*. This procedure is applicable only with respect to *competing* explanations. Competing explanations are explanations at the same metaphysical "level"—paradigmatically, explanations that cite different causes for the same phenomena. Two or more explanations compete if the truth of one entails the falsity of the others.

Philosophers of social science are confronted with the task of determining the relations between non-competing explanations at *different* metaphysical levels. More specifically, they must address the problem of giving an account of the relationship between explanations of behavior that cite intentional states and those that do not. That explanations of behavior that cite intentional states do not compete with those that cite subintentional processes such as neuron firings is vouchsafed by the fact that explanations *for the same phenomenon* of the former sort and of the latter sort can both be true. To illustrate, your act of reading these words can be explained by your desire to find out what I have to say about methodological naturalism, and it can also be explained as the result of a complex sequence electrochemical events occurring in your central nervous system. Assuming the truth of ontological naturalism, any explanation of the first sort entails the truth of *some* explanation of the second sort.

When we look around the world, we find that certain things, and not others, behave in ways that we can explain by attributing intentional states to them. Such things are called *intentional systems* (Dennett 2009). Human beings are paradigmatic intentional systems, but they are not the only ones. We also describe aggregates of human beings using the intentional idiom (we claim that Iran has nuclear *aspirations* or that the Catholic Church *disapproves* of abortion), not to mention non-human animals and chess-playing computer programs (Dennett 1989). When we think of something as an intentional system, we consider it to be categorically rational—that is, we think of it as having reasons for what it does. These need not be good reasons. An intentional system can behave irrationally (for example, by acting in a manner that is contrary to its own best interests), but it cannot (*qua* intentional system) behave non-rationally. Reasons for actions can be cashed out with reference to the agent's beliefs and desires. To say that a person's action was brought about by a certain reason is just to say that the person had a certain desire and that she believed that she could satisfy that desire by performing certain actions.

Dennett (1987, 17) describes intentional systems as systems whose behavior can be explained and predicted by taking a certain stance, which he calls the "intentional stance." When we take the intentional stance to a system, we treat it as if its behavior is explained by its having reasons for behaving thusly.

> Here is how it works: first you decide to treat the object whose behavior is to be predicted as a rational agent; then you figure out what beliefs that agent ought to have, given its place in the world and its purpose. Then you figure out what desires it ought to have, on the same considerations, and finally you predict that this rational agent will act to further its goals in the light of its beliefs. A little practical reasoning from the chosen set of beliefs and desires will in most instances yield a decision about what the agent ought to do; that is what you predict the agent will do.

Notice that I said that we treat it "as if" its behavior is explicable in this way. Dennett's account does not commit one to the view that if something is an intentional system then it *really* has reasons for its behavior, although his account is obviously compatible with such a claim. Dennett contrasts the intentional stance with the design stance and the physical stance. When we take the design stance towards a thing, we consider it in light of what it is for—i.e. what it has been designed to do—and when we take the physical stance towards a thing we consider it in light of the causal properties of its physical constituents. Dennett does not make any claims about conceptual connections between explanations at the three levels, but his approach suggests that the sorts of explanations that we give when we take the intentional stance towards a thing are not reducible to design-stance or physical-stance explanations. Put somewhat differently, on Dennett's analysis, the fact that the behavior of a thing is amenable to the intentional stance says nothing substantive about either its design or its physical constitution. I will refer to explanations framed at the latter two levels as *subintentional* explanations.

Social scientists study intentional systems. As Rosenberg (2012, 21) points out:

> [S]ince the very beginnings of philosophy of social science in the late nineteenth century, it has been argued by important social scientists and philosophers that these disciplines must invoke the same framework of explanatory concepts that people use in everyday life to explain their own and other people's actions—the categories of beliefs, desires, expectations, preferences, hopes, fears, wants, that make actions *meaningful* or *intelligible* to ourselves and to one another.

Sometimes this strategy is explicit, as when psychologists investigate human behavior, and sometimes it remains implicit, as when economists use an intentional idiom to describe the behavior of economic systems. The fact that ontological naturalism allows for multiple, non-competing explanations of the behavior of intentional systems presents an opportunity as well as a problem for methodological naturalists. Explaining the behavior of intentional systems as a function of the behavior of their subintentional parts may make it possible for social scientists to emulate the precision and predictive power of the mature natural sciences, but this cannot be achieved unless one understands the relations that obtain between intentional and subintentional explanations. The problem of determining these relations is known as the *interface problem* (Bermúdez 2005). The discussion that follows is strongly influenced by Bermúdez's analysis of the interface problem and his account of the ways that philosophers have attempted to address it.

One approach, sometimes called *interpretivism*, denies that the interface problem can be solved. Interpretivists hold that there is an unbridgeable gap between intentional and subintentional idioms, and that this makes it impossible establish any principled relation between them. Donald Davidson has championed this approach most effectively. Davidson (1980) argued that when we attribute intentional states to a person, we interpret her behavior in such a way as to "make sense" of it, and that this is fundamentally different from the methods used in the natural sciences. To bring out this difference, contrast the way that we go about explaining human actions with the way neuroscientists explain why a certain neuron fired when it did. In the first case, we attribute reasons to the person such that her action was intelligible in light of those reasons. But it would be ridiculous to try to explain the behavior of neurons in this way. There are, to be sure, reasons why the neuron fired, but these were not the *neuron's reasons* for firing.

According to interpretivist approaches, intentional and subintentional accounts of the behavior of intentional systems are incommensurable, because the "norms of rationality" that we bring to bear in the former case have "no echo in physical theory" (Davidson 1980, 231). Furthermore, the vocabulary that we use to describe intentional states is so different from the vocabulary used in the natural sciences that intentional terms cannot be slotted into nomological generalizations. So, there are no laws of intentional psychology, and no laws connecting intentional and subintentional states. This does not prevent methodological naturalists from approaching the objects of their study from a subintentional perspective, but it does entail that knowledge about subintentional processes cannot be incorporated into intentionalistic accounts of social phenomena.

A different approach to the interface problem has it that intentional states have subintentional counterparts, and this makes it possible to build bridges between intentional and subintentional characterizations of intentional systems. A group of approaches known as "functionalism" have offered the most influential solutions to the interface problem along these lines. One of these, often referred to as "common-sense functionalism" (also called "philosophical functionalism") identifies intentional states with *causal roles*. Causal roles are jobs that parts of systems do that enable the system to exercise some capacity. Applied to human psychology, common-sense functionalism has it that beliefs, desires, hopes, fears, and other intentional states are what brains *do* to produce rational behavior. So, for example, the state characterized as "hoping to spot a porcupine" is realized by whatever brains do to cause one to perform actions like purchasing a copy of *How to Spot a Porcupine*, searching through the woods with a pair of binoculars, uttering sentences like "I hope that I see a porcupine today," and so forth.

In common with other versions of functionalism, common-sense functionalism makes a distinction between causal roles and the realizers of those roles. The realizer of a causal role corresponding to an intentional state is a subintentional physical process that produces the effect specified by the role. In the example given above, the realizers of the causal role characterized as "hoping to spot a porcupine" are sequences of neuron firings that produce hoping-to-spot-a-porcupine-type behaviors. Causal roles are multiply realizable—that is, they can have many different realizers. Whatever goes on in my brain that realizes the hoping-to-spot-a-porcupine role need not be the same thing that realizes the same role in your brain (or even in my brain on a different occasion).

Common-sense functionalism can be applied to any intentional system. If the behaviors of a system are aptly characterized in intentional terms, there must be some subintentional processes that realize the intentional states underpinning the behaviors. However, this form of functionalism does not seem adequate to achieve the goals that methodological naturalists strive to attain.

Knowing that the behavior of a system, characterized intentionally, must (ultimately) have subintentional realizers does not yield the robust empirical generalizations, because (thanks to the principle of multiple realizability) one cannot "read off" the realizers of causal roles from the roles themselves. Common-sense functionalism therefore provides only cold comfort to those methodological naturalists who hope to emulate the precision and predictive power afforded by natural science.

A different form of functionalism, "homuncular functionalism" (also called "psychological functionalism"), relies on a procedure called "functional decomposition" to bridge the gap between intentional and subintentional explanations. Starting with the behavior of an intentional system, homuncular functionalists determine what processes need to occur in the system in order to produce that behavior. They do this by identifying the sequence of sub-tasks that need to be executed in order for the behavior to occur, and match these with subsystems that execute them. The subtasks and subsystems are then further broken down into their constitutive components, and the procedure is iterated until one has decomposed the system into very simple, subintentional elements. As applied to psychological states, the functional decomposition of an intentional state might terminate at the level of neural systems or the firing of individual neurons, depending on one's explanatory aims.

Psychological functionalism looks like a promising strategy for tackling the interface problem in the psychological sphere. However, when it is applied to the behavior of larger social systems, functional decomposition is unlikely to lead to the sorts of results that methodological naturalists are aiming at. To see why, we need to briefly discuss the distinction between holistic and individualistic accounts of social facts. Methodological individualism (or "individualism" for short) is the thesis that social facts are reducible to facts about individual human beings. As John Stuart Mill (1865, 464), himself an advocate of individualism, put it:

> The laws of the phenomena of society are, and can be, nothing but the laws of the actions and passions of human beings united together in the social state. Men, however in a state of society, are still men; their actions and passions are obedient to the laws of individual human nature. Men are not, when brought together, converted into another kind of substance, with different properties; as hydrogen and oxygen are different from water .... Human beings in society have no properties but those which are derived from, and may resolved into, the laws of nature of individual man.

In contrast, the holistic view states that social facts are constitutive of facts about the behavior of individuals. The intentional behavior of individuals cannot be pried away from the large social systems in which these individuals dwell. As Rosenberg (2012, 173) vividly describes it:

> Consider the example of my cashing a check. How is such behavior explained? In order not to miss aspects of this explanation suppressed because of their banality and obviousness, imagine explaining this behavior to someone who does not understand the concept of money. To do that I need to explain the significance of my action to me and the teller, and that brings in the entire monetary and banking system. The teller and I are operating under rules—enforced by society—that give the exchange its meaning. But the rules are unintelligible except against the background of rules with compliance conditions, that is institutions of persuasion and enforcement .... If reference to social facts is unavoidable in describing individual facts, they can hardly

be composed of or dependent on them. Social facts must have a separate and distinct existence. So the argument goes.

Psychological functionalism presents difficulties both for individualists and for holists. According to individualism, functional decomposition of a social system should terminate in individual human beings, because individual human beings are the basic units from which social systems are composed. But if that is the case, then the functional decomposition of social systems never reaches the subintentional level. To paraphrase the punch-line of an old joke, it's intentional systems all the way down. To get at the subintentional level of analysis, the individualist must press the decomposition further, to the level of neural processes occurring in the brains of individual human beings. But it seems doubtful that claims about aggregates of neuron firings can provide foundations for empirical generalizations about large-scale social processes.

Holists who are tempted to pin their hopes to homuncular functionalism face a different and even less tractable problem. If social facts are partly constitutive of facts about individuals, then the whole project of decomposing social systems seems profoundly misguided. From this perspective, decomposing large-scale social processes into smaller functional units amounts to changing the subject. Consider Rosenberg's example of the act of cashing a check, quoted above. From a holistic perspective, the notion that the behavior of the banking system can be decomposed into the behaviors of individual actors (tellers, customers, bank managers, and so on) is *unintelligible*.

Each of the approaches to the interface problem that I have discussed so far has taken the intentional stance as its point of departure. But suppose that one analyzes intentional systems entirely in terms of subintentional processes, and dispenses with the intentional strategy entirely? Perhaps the intentional idiom is obfuscating, and prevents us from properly grasping the causal processes that drive social systems and the sooner we dispense with it, the sooner we will arrive at a mature, empirically powerful social science. This approach to the interface problem is known as *eliminativism*, because it counsels us to banish intentionally infused discourse from the vocabulary of the social sciences. Rather than talk about social systems in the language of belief and desire, we should confine ourselves to describing the non-intentional, causal processes that drive the behavior of such systems.

The eliminativist program has been worked out in detail in the context of the philosophy of mind. According to Paul Churchland, a prominent contemporary eliminativist, intentional psychology (also known as "folk psychology" [FP]) has "not advanced sensibly in two or three thousand years."

> The FP of the Greeks is essentially the FP we use today, and we are negligibly better at explaining human behavior in its terms than was Sophocles. This is a very long period of stagnation and infertility for any theory to display …. Perfect theories, perhaps, have no need to evolve. But FP is profoundly imperfect. Its failure to develop its resources and extend its range of success is therefore darkly curious, and one must query the integrity of its basic categories …. FP is a stagnant or degenerating research program, and has been for millennia.
>
> (Churchland 1981, 74–75)

If we look at the history of science, we find that stagnant theories, and the explanatory terminologies that come with them, are often abandoned wholesale when better theories come along.

Perhaps this is the appropriate fate of the intentional idiom in social science. As Churchland (1981, 76) goes on to point out:

> FP suffers explanatory failures on an epic scale, that it has been stagnant for at least twenty-five centuries, and that its categories appear (so far) to be incommensurable with or orthogonal to the categories of the background physical science whose long-term claim to explain human behavior seems undeniable. Any theory that meets this description must be allowed a serious candidate for outright elimination.

It may be that intentionalistic accounts of social systems are ripe for elimination in virtue of their explanatory deficits. However, the examples from the history of science that are standardly invoked by proponents of eliminativism are disanalogous with the challenges faced by philosophers of social science grappling with the interface problem. In the historical cases—for example, the replacement of the 18th-century phlogiston theory of combustion by modern accounts—a theory is displaced by a competing theory. But, as I mentioned earlier, intentional and subintentional accounts of the behavior of intentional systems do not compete. If intentionalistic explanations of social phenomena are eliminated, it will not be because subintentional accounts are more effective at performing the *same* explanatory task. Rather, it will be because such explanations are regarded as without value. This presupposes that what we want from social science explanations is empirical power rather than rational understanding, but this only begs the question against hermeneutic approaches. If, as many social scientists believe, the intentional idiom is a non-negotiable component of our very conception of a social system, then eliminativism is not a live option.

## Conclusion

Social science compares very unfavorably with natural science along a number of dimensions. Despite over a century of sustained efforts by social scientists, we are unable to make inferences about social processes that are anywhere near the level of precision and reliability of those routinely made by physicists, chemists, and biologists. The reasons for this are still in dispute, but it is plausible to suppose that part of the problem turns on the difficulty of determining the relation between intentional and subintentional explanations. Methodological naturalists are committed to the view that social scientists should emulate the investigative methods that are used by natural scientists. Although laudable, this program cannot be put into effect without addressing a range of very difficult conceptual issues. Natural scientists do not have to contend with these philosophical conundrums, but social scientists, it seems, cannot avoid doing so.

## References

Beatty, J. (1993) "The Evolutionary Contingency Thesis," in G. Wolters and J. G. Lennox (eds.), *Concepts, Theories, and Rationality in the Biological Sciences*, Pittsburgh: University of Pittsburgh Press, 45–82.

Bermudez, J. L. (2005) *Philosophy of Psychology: A Contemporary Introduction*, New York: Psychology Press.

Churchland, P. M. (1981) "Eliminative Materialism and the Propositional Attitudes," *Journal of Philosophy* 78(2): 67–90.

Davidson, D. (1970) "Mental Events," in L. Foster and J. Swanson (eds.), *Experience and Theory*, London: Duckworth, 79–101.

Davidson, D. (1980) *Essays on Actions and Events*, Oxford: Clarendon Press.

Dennett, D. (1987) *The Intentional Stance*, Cambridge, MA: MIT Press.

Dennett, D. C. (1989) "True Believers: The Intentional Strategy and Why It Works," in *The Intentional Stance*, Cambridge, MA: Bradford Books, 13–42.

Dennett, D. C. (2009) "Intentional Systems Theory," in A. Beckerman, B. P. McLaughlin, and S. Walter (eds.), *The Oxford Handbook of Philosophy of Mind*, Oxford: Oxford University Press, 13–42.

Duhem, P. (1954) *The Aim and Structure of Physical Theory*, trans. from 2nd edn. by P. W. Wiener, Princeton, NJ: Princeton University Press.

Flanagan, O. (2008) "Varieties of Naturalism," in P. Clayton (ed.), *The Oxford Companion to Religion and Science*, Oxford: Oxford University Press, 43–52.

Ghiselin, M. (1974) "A Radical Solution to the Species Problem," *Systematic Zoology* 23: 536–44.

Hempel, C. (1965) *Aspects of Scientific Explanation and Other Essays in the Philosophy of Science*, New York: Free Press.

Hull, D. (1978) "A Matter of Individuality," *Philosophy of Science* 45: 335–60.

Kitcher, P. (1984) "1953 and All That: A Tale of Two Sciences," *Philosophical Review* 93(3): 335–73.

Kitcher, P. (1992) "The Naturalists Return," *Philosophical Review* 101(1): 53–114.

McIntyre, L. (1999) "Davidson and Social Scientific Laws," *Synthese* 120(3): 375–94.

Mill, J. S. (1865) *A System of Logic, Ratiocinative and Inductive*, vol. II, 6th edn., London: Longmans, Green, and Co.

Mill, J. S. (1874) *Nature, the Utility of Religion, Theism, Being Three Essays on Religion*, London: Longman, Green, Reader, and Dyer.

Rosenberg, A. (1996) "A Field Guide to Recent Species of Naturalism," *British Journal for the Philosophy of Science* 47(1): 1–29.

Stroud, B. (2004) "The Charm of Naturalism," in M. De Caro and D. MacArthur (eds.), *Naturalism in Question*, Cambridge, MA: Harvard University Press, 21–35.

Taylor, C. (1971) "Interpretation and the Sciences of Man," *Review of Metaphysics* 25: 3–51.

Wilson, E. O. (1998) *Consilience: The Unity of Knowledge*, New York: Alfred A. Knopf.

# Further Reading

Bermudez, J. L. (2005) *Philosophy of Psychology: A Contemporary Introduction*, New York: Psychology Press. This is the best guide to the interface problem, and the various ways that philosophers of psychology have tried to solve it.

Chant, S. R., Hindricks, F., and Preyer, G. (eds.) (2014) *From Individual to Collective Intentionality: New Essays*, Oxford: Oxford University Press. This is an excellent collection of papers dealing with the notion of aggregate intentions.

De Caro, M., and MacArthur, D. (eds.) (2004) *Naturalism in Question*, Cambridge, MA: Harvard University Press. This collection of essays by leading philosophers critically interrogates the naturalistic turn in philosophy.

Richie, J. (2008) *Understanding Naturalism*, Stocksfield, UK: Acumen. This is useful primer on some of the main arguments for naturalism in 20th- and 21st-century philosophy.

Rosenberg, A. (2012) *Philosophy of Social Science*, Boulder, CO: Westview Press. This introductory text by a leading contemporary methodological naturalist provides an accessible introduction to the naturalism/anti-naturalism debate in the philosophy of social science.

# 15
# GAME THEORY

*Cristina Bicchieri and Giacomo Sillari*

Game theory studies situations of strategic interaction. An interaction between two or more players is said to be strategic when the outcomes do not depend on the individual actions of the agents involved, but rather on the joint actions of the agents involved. Chess is a typical example, in which the choice to make a specific move depends on strategic considerations about what the other player is going to do, as the outcome of the game will depend on both players' moves. Other typical examples of strategic interactions include firms competing for business, politicians competing for votes, animals fighting over prey, bidders competing in an auction, threats and promises in long-term relationships, (be they between spouses, parents and children, co-workers or nuclear super-powers), and so on. Game theory studies the strategic decisions of players. Players can be profit-maximizing firms, expected utility rational maximizers, but also animals, computer-generated artificial agents, or, in evolutionary game theory, entities that lack any natural or artificial rational ability, such as genes. In more recent years, behavioral game theory (Camerer 2003) has emerged to study the behavior of boundedly rational, flesh-and-bone agents.

The relevance of game theory for social science and for the philosophy of social science is multifarious. The first philosophical contribution in which game theory plays a fundamental role is Lewis (1969), in which a philosophical account of social convention is offered in game-theoretic terms. Lewis's book has become seminal in several fields: his game-theoretic account of social conventions was further developed to deal with norms by Ullman-Margalit (1977/2016), Sugden (1986/2005) and Bicchieri (2006); his definition of common knowledge was formalized by Aumann (1976) and played a major role in contributions to the philosophy of social sciences exploring the interplay between coordination and rationality as in Bicchieri (1993). Important applications of game theory and evolutionary game theory to the philosophy of social science and to political philosophy are found in Skyrms (1996, 2004) and Binmore (1994, 1998, 2005).

This chapter is divided into five sections. In the first section we introduce strategic games and discuss dominance, best replies, focal points, mixed strategies and Nash equilibrium. In the second, we introduce sequential games and discuss backwards induction and subgame perfection. In the third, we apply the theory to Bicchieri's account of social norms. In the fourth, we review basic notions about the epistemic foundations of game theory, while in the fifth and last section we discuss repeated games.

## 1 Normal Form Games

Any strategic interaction involves two or more decision-makers (players) each with two or more ways of acting (strategies), such that the outcome depends on the strategy choices of all players. Each player, furthermore, has well-defined preferences over all possible outcomes, enabling corresponding utility functions determining payoffs to be assigned. If players are allowed to enter binding agreements before the game is played, we say that the game is *cooperative*, otherwise that it is *non-cooperative*. In this chapter, we concentrate on non-cooperative game theory.

In a so-called *normal form game*, it is made explicit who the players are, what strategies are at each player's disposal and what the payoffs are for each player in each outcome. More formally, a game structure in normal form is a triple containing:

- A list of $N$ players $I = \{1,...,N\}$.
- For each player $i \in I$, a finite set of pure strategies $S_i = \{s_1,...,s_n\}$.
- For each player $i \in I$, a payoff (utility) function from the set of all strategy profiles (outcomes of the game) to the real numbers $u_i : S_1 \times ... \times S_N \rightarrow \mathbb{R}$.

It is convenient to represent the three elements above in a *matrix*, for instance, in Figure 15.1 we represent the well-known *prisoner's dilemma*. Two prisoners are interrogated separately. This reflect the fact that, in game theory, each player picks a strategy independently from the other players. Each prisoner can implicate the other (defect) or they can keep mum (C). The outcome of the game is represented in terms of players' payoffs and is the joint product of the two strategies chosen. If both prisoners keep mum, they will be free relatively quickly (payoff of 2 in the upper left corner of the matrix), while if they implicate each other, they will have to serve more time (payoff of 1 in the lower right). The best case is the one in which one player implicates the other, but the other does not. In such a case, the former player will get out of prison immediately (payoff of 4) while the other will have to serve a long sentence (payoff of 0).

A normal form game is often understood as a situation in which players choose simultaneously. This temporal interpretation, although intuitive, is not quite correct. Since the normal form is not supposed to yield any information about the sequential order of play, it is best understood as a list of outcomes, one for each combination of strategies players might choose.

The game in Figure 15.1 is a game of complete information, in that the players are assumed to know the rules of the game, that is the game structure above, including other players' strategies and payoffs. Next to this assumption, it is also assumed that players are rational (utility maximizers). More precisely, it is standard to assume that there is *common knowledge* among all players of both

(CK1) the structure of the game, including players' strategy sets and payoff functions;
(CK2) players' rationality.

The concept of common knowledge, introduced by Lewis (1969) and formalized by Aumann (1976), denotes the epistemic state in which everyone in a group G knows $p$, everyone in G

| | C | D |
|---|---|---|
| C | 2,2 | 0,4 |
| D | 4,0 | 1,1 |

*Figure 15.1* Prisoner's Dilemma

knows that everyone knows $p$, everyone in G knows that everyone knows that everyone knows $p$ and so on, *ad infinitum*.

How are rational players supposed to choose their strategies under assumptions CK1 and CK2? In the case of the prisoner's dilemma, the two assumptions lead to a precise prediction of play. Notice that in the game in Figure 15.1, each player is better off defecting *no matter* what the other player does. For example, if Column cooperates, Row gets a payoff of 4 by defecting and a payoff of 2 by cooperating, whereas if Column defects, Row gains a payoff of 1 by defecting and of 0 by cooperating. When, regardless of what other players do, a strategy yields a player a payoff strictly inferior to some other strategy, it is called a *strictly dominated* strategy. More formally, $s_i$ is strictly dominated for player $i$ if there exists an $s_i' \in S_i$ such that

$$u_i\left(s_i', s_{-i}\right) > u_i\left(s_i, s_{-i}\right) \quad \text{for all } s_{-i} \in S_{-i},$$

where $s_{-i}$ denotes the strategies chosen by all players excluding player $i$.

As pointed out above, a simple inspection shows that C is strictly dominated by D. Hence, rational players will never choose to cooperate. CK1 and CK2 are thus sufficient to predict the rational outcome of the game. Notice that players would *jointly* prefer to cooperate, however they *individually* prefer to defect. This tension between individual rationality and joint outcome is the essence of the dilemma and of its relevance for philosophy of social science. We will come back to this when dealing with repeated games.

Sometimes, however, CK1 and CK2 are not sufficient to predict what rational players will do. Consider the game represented in Figure 15.2. In this game players want to *coordinate* their actions, in that their interests are aligned and therefore their preferences are, unlike in the prisoner's dilemma, conditional on the other player's choice of strategy. The game in Figure 15.2 is often called the "driving game," since, on the road, we prefer to keep right of left depending on whether incoming traffic is keeping right or left. In other words, L is a *best reply* to the other player's choice of L, while R is a best reply to R.

When, in general, all players are choosing mutual best replies, they are content with their choices, meaning that they would not want to unilaterally change their action if they had a chance. They decline to unilaterally change because, since each player is playing a best reply to the other players' actions, no player could improve by changing her action. Thus, all players are maximizing their payoff given what others are doing and when players are jointly maximizing their payoffs they are playing the *Nash equilibrium* of the game. Informally, a Nash equilibrium specifies actions and beliefs such that (i) each player's action is optimal given her beliefs about others' choices and (ii) players' beliefs are correct. In other words, an outcome that is not a Nash equilibrium requires either that some players be irrational or that some players "misperceive" the situation. More formally, a Nash equilibrium is a vector of strategies $\left(s_1^*, \ldots, s_N^*\right)$, one for each of the N players in the game, such that each $s_i^*$ is optimal given (i.e. is a best reply to) $s_{-i}^*$. That is

$$u_i\left(s_i^*, s_{-i}^*\right) > u_i\left(s_i, s_{-i}^*\right) \quad \text{for all } s_i \in S_i.$$

|  | L | R |
|---|---|---|
| L | 1,1 | 0,0 |
| R | 0,0 | 1,1 |

*Figure 15.2* The Driving Game

Notice that optimality is only conditional for a given $s^*_{-i}$, not for all possible $s_{-i}$. That is to say that a strategy that is optimal against $s^*_{-i}$ may fare poorly against a different strategy combination.

There are (Binmore 1994, 1998, 2005) two main reasons why Nash equilibria are important. First, ideally rational players reaching Nash equilibrium will play it, as it maximizes their payoffs. Second, if play is shaped by evolutionary pressures, such pressures will yield when players are in equilibrium. Notice, however, that CK1 and CK2, above, do not allow players (or theorists) to predict rational play in the game of Figure 15.2 (Bicchieri 1993), since in the game there are two equilibria $((L,L)$ and $(R,R))$ and rationality remains silent as to which one to select, failing to solve the "problem of equilibrium selection" (Harsanyi and Selten 1988). Let us consider a further example of a game with multiple equilibria: Suppose two players need to divide \$100 between them. They must restrict their proposals to integers and each has to independently propose a way to split. If the total proposed equals or is less than \$100, the players get what they claimed, otherwise they get nothing. This game has 101 equilibria (all pairs of claims summing up to 100), so is there a way to predict which one will be chosen, if any? Behavioral game theory may observe a modal 50/50 split. Many players would reason that it is the simple, fair and equitable solution to the game. In the words of Thomas Schelling, it is a *focal point* (Schelling 1960).

The idea of focal points as strategies or combinations of strategies that are salient under some respects and hence likely to be chosen by players who are trying to coordinate their action, is at the core of David Lewis's account of *convention* (Lewis 1969; Rescorla 2007; Sillari 2013). According to Lewis, a convention is a solution to a recurrent coordination problem. The conventional solution is salient because it has worked in the past and thus, by force of precedent acquires the status of a focal point. Classical game theory, however, filters out any social or cultural information regarding choice of strategy, so that players can only rely on CK1 and CK2 to coordinate their action. But CK1 and CK2 are of no help in the case of multiple equilibria. To solve the problem of equilibrium selection one can take one of two avenues. One is to study populations of players subject to some kind of evolutionary pressures: the evolutionary dynamics may solve indeterminacy (for a critique of the approach, see Sugden 2001.) The other is to consider the set of equilibria and eliminate some of them because they are in some sense unreasonable, hence strengthening the rationality requirement. This is the approach taken by the *refinement* of Nash equilibrium program (Kohlberg 1990; van Damme 1987).

We have seen a game with a unique equilibrium (mutual defection in the prisoner's dilemma of Figure 15.1) and a game with multiple equilibria (driving to the right or to the left in the driving game of Figure 15.2). We show now that there exist games in which there are no equilibria in pure strategies. In the *zero-sum* game depicted in Figure 15.3, each player has a coin and shows one side of it. Row wins 1 if both players show heads or both players show tails and loses 1 otherwise, and vice versa for Column. There are no combinations of best replies: If Row shows heads, then Column's best reply is to show tails, but Row's best reply to that is to show tails, to which Column's best reply is to show heads. Nash has however demonstrated that all games possess at least one equilibrium. Nash's result holds because a player may choose to play a pure strategy, or, instead, she may choose to randomize over her pure strategies; a probability distribution over pure strategies is called a *mixed strategy* and is denoted by $\sigma_i$. Each player's randomization is assumed to be independent of that of his opponents, and the payoff to a mixed strategy is the expected value of the corresponding pure strategy payoffs.

In a Nash equilibrium in mixed strategies, the equilibrium strategy of each player makes the other player indifferent between their strategies. Suppose that, in the game in Figure 15.3, Row player chooses $\sigma_i = (.5H, .5T)$, that gives equal probability to $H$ and $T$. Then if Column plays

| | H | T |
|---|---|---|
| H | 1,−1 | −1,1 |
| T | −1,1 | 1,−1 |

*Figure 15.3* Matching Pennies

$H$, she will lose with probability .5 when Row plays H and win with probability .5 when Row plays $T$. The expected payoff of 0 would be the same if Column played $T$ or any of her mixed strategies. Thus, Column is indifferent and all her strategies are (weak) best replies. Since the game is symmetrical, $\sigma_j = (.5H, .5T)$ chosen by Column makes Row indifferent, hence $(\sigma_i, \sigma_j)$ is a Nash equilibrium in mixed strategies. An equilibrium in mixed strategies always exists and is always weak, in that unilateral deviation does not induce a loss, although it does not induce a gain either.

## 2 Extensive Form Games

Games can be represented in a different and possibly richer way, called the *extensive form*. In the extensive form more elements of play are specified: besides the finite set of players, we specify the order of moves, players' choices at each move, and the information that players possess when she is called to choose. The sequence of play is represented by a game tree $T$, understood as a finite set of partially ordered nodes $t \in T$ satisfying a precedence relation <. A *subgame* is a collection of branches of a game such that they start from the same node and the branches and the node together form a game tree by itself. A tree representation is sequential, because it shows the order in which actions are taken by the players. It is intuitively appealing to think of the sequentiality in the extensive form representation as introducing a temporal element that was lacking in the normal form. However, what matters is the information that players have about other players' actions when they are called to choose. Such information is not represented in the normal form, while it is in the extensive form. This is the reason why a normal form game could represent one of several extensive form ones. When the order of play is irrelevant to a game's outcome, then restricting oneself to the normal form is justifiable. When the order of play is relevant, however, the extensive form must be specified.

In an extensive form game, the information a player has when she is choosing an action is explicitly represented using *information sets*, which partition the nodes of the tree. If an information set contains more than one node, the player who has to make a choice at that information set will be uncertain as to which node she is at. Not knowing which node one is at means that the player does not know which action was chosen by the preceding player. If a game contains information sets that are not singletons, the game is one of *imperfect information*. Consider for instance the game shown as Figure 15.4.

In the prisoner's dilemma, players make their choices in the ignorance of the other player's choice. This is reproduced in Figure 15.4 by introducing the *information set* that contains player 2's nodes. The information set represents player 2's ignorance about player 1's move at the previous node: player 2 cannot distinguish between the left and the right node or, in other terms, she does not know whether player 1 has chosen C or D.

The notion of strategy in an extensive game is that of a *complete plan of action* that specifies, for each node of the tree, what action a player is to choose. Note that a strategy can therefore specify moves at nodes that will never be visited.

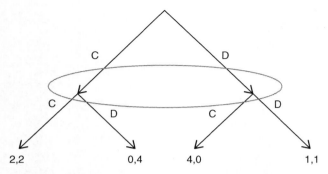

*Figure 15.4* The Prisoner's Dilemma in Extensive Form.

Consider the game in Figure 15.5. Player 1 is called to play at the first and last nodes. Thus the strategies at her disposal are all the possible combinations of actions at both nodes: *Ax*, *Ay*, *Dx* and *Dy*. Notice that if player 1 plays *D* at her first node, the game ends there and so she will never get to play *x* or *y*. A strategy is a fully contingent plan of action, that cannot be changed during the course of the game. The game in Figure 15.5 has two equilibria: (*Dx*,*a*) and (*Dy*,*d*): is there a way to solve the selection problem? If player 1 were to play in the third node, she would prefer *x* to *y*, since the former yields her a payoff of 4 and the latter of only 2. Knowing this, and knowing that player 1 is rational, at the second node player 2 will choose *d*, netting a payoff of 2 rather than *a*. At the first node, knowing that player 2 is rational and that she knows that player 1 is rational as well, player 1 will prefer to play *D* (for a payoff of 1) than *A* (for a payoff of 0). Thus, even if (*Dy*,*a*) is an equilibrium, it seems to be an unreasonable one, as it requires player 1 to choose against her own best interest at the last node. The reason why it is an equilibrium is that, actually, the last node will never be reached in equilibrium, so player 1 can be indifferent between *Dx* and *Dy*.

The sequential procedure we have used to conclude that only (*Dx*,*d*) is a reasonable solution is known as *backward induction*. In finite games of perfect information with no ties in payoffs, backward induction always identifies a unique equilibrium. The premise of the backward induction argument is that mutual rationality and the structure of the game are common knowledge among the players. It has been argued by Binmore (1987), Bicchieri(1989, 1993), and Reny (1992) that under certain conditions common knowledge of rationality leads to inconsistencies. For example, if player 2 were to reach her decision node, would she keep thinking that player 1 is rational? How would she explain 1's move? If 1's move is inconsistent with common knowledge of rationality, player 2 will be unable to predict future play; as a corollary, what constitutes an optimal choice at her node remains undefined. As a consequence of the above criticisms, the usual premises of backward induction arguments have come to be questioned (cf. Pettit and Sugden 1989; Basu 1990; Bonanno 1991).

The earliest refinement proposed to rule out implausible equilibria in extensive games of perfect information is *subgame-perfection* (Selten 1965). A Nash equilibrium is subgame-perfect if its component strategies (when restricted to any subgame) remain a Nash equilibrium of the subgame. The equilibrium (*Dy*,*d*) is not subgame-perfect: in the subgame starting at the last node, *y* is a dominated strategy. Note that the backward induction equilibrium is always subgame-perfect.

Consider now the *ultimatum game*, introduced by Güth et al. (1982). In this game two players, the proposer and the respondent, are to divide $10 between them. The proposer offers an allocation of the $10 between her and the respondent. If the responder accepts the allocation,

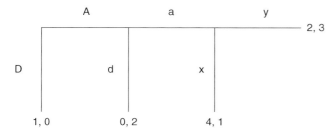

*Figure 15.5* An Extensive-Form Game.

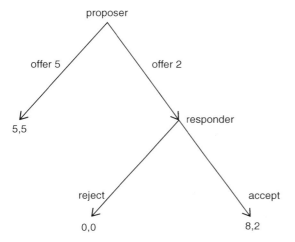

*Figure 15.6* The Mini-Ultimatum Game.

the money is divided as the proposer indicated. If the responder rejects the allocation, the two players get nothing. We consider here a simplified version of the game (Figure 15.6), sometimes called the "mini-ultimatum" game, in which the proposer can only allocate in two ways: 8 for her and 2 for the responder, or 5 for each. The responder always accepts the latter division, while she can reject the former.

There are two equilibria for this game: (*offer 2, accept*) and (*offer 5, reject*). However, backwards induction only identifies one equilibrium: at her node, if reached, the responder will *accept*, as 2 > 0. But then, knowing that, the proposer will *offer 2*, ruling out the second equilibrium listed above. While the first equilibrium is yielded by backward induction, and hence it is subgame-perfect, in experiments of one-shot ultimatum games the modal offer is around the 50 percent split. The result carries over to the mini-ultimatum game of Figure 15.5 as well. A typical explanation of such behavior is given in terms of social norms (see Bicchieri 2006). In the following section, we show how game theory can apply to social norms and the ultimatum game.

## 3 Games and Norms

The norm-based utility function introduced by Bicchieri (2006) tries to capture, through a game-theoretic model, the idea that when a norm exists individuals will show different 'sensitivities' to it, and this should be reflected in their utility functions (cf. also Bicchieri and Chavez 2010; Bicchieri and Sontuoso 2014). Consider a typical $n$-person (normal-form) game. For the sake of formal treatment, we represent a norm as a (partial) function that maps what the player expects other players to do into what the player "ought" to do. In other words, a norm regulates behavior conditional on other people's (expected) behaviors. Denote the strategy set of player $i$ by $S_i$, and let $S_{-i} = \prod_{j \neq i} S_j$ be the set of strategy profiles of players other than $i$. Then a norm for player $i$ is formally represented by a function $N_i : L_{-i} \rightarrow S_i$, where $L_{-i} \subseteq S_{-i}$. Two points are worth noting. First, given the other players' strategies, there may or may not be a norm that prescribes how player $i$ ought to behave. So $L_{-i}$ need not be—and usually is not—equal to $S_{-i}$. In particular, $L_{-i}$ could be empty in the situation where there is no norm whatsoever to regulate player $i$'s behavior. Second, there could be norms that regulate joint behaviors. A norm, for example, that regulates the joint behaviors of players $i$ and $j$ may be represented by $N_{i,j} : L_{-i,-j} \rightarrow S_i \times S_j$. Since we are concerned with a two-person game here, we will not further complicate the model in that direction.

A strategy profile $s = (s_1, \ldots, s_n)$ instantiates a norm for $j$ if $s_{-j} \in L_{-j}$, that is, if $N_j$ is defined at $s_{-j}$. It violates a norm if for some $j$, it instantiates a norm for $j$ but $s_j \neq N_j(s_{-j})$. Let $\pi_i$ be the payoff function for player $i$. The norm-based utility function of player $i$ depends on the strategy profile $s$, and is given by

$$U_i(s) = \pi_i(s) - k_i \max{}_{s_{-j} \in L_{-j}} \max{}_{m \neq j} \{\pi_m(s_{-j}, N_j(s_{-j})) - \pi_m(s), 0\},$$

where $k_i \geq 0$ is a constant representing $i$'s sensitivity to the relevant norm. Such sensitivity may vary with different norms; for example, a person may be very sensitive to equality and much less so to equity considerations. The first maximum operator takes care of the possibility that the norm instantiation (and violation) might be ambiguous in the sense that a strategy profile instantiates a norm for several players simultaneously. We conjecture, however, that this situation is rare, and under most situations the first maximum operator degenerates. The second maximum operator ranges over all the players other than the norm violator. In plain words, the discounting term (multiplied by $k_i$) is the maximum payoff deduction resulting from all norm violations.

In the ultimatum game, the norm we shall consider is the norm that prescribes a fair amount the proposer ought to offer. To represent it we take the norm functions to be the following: the norm function for the proposer, $N_1$, is a constant $N$ function, and the norm function for the responder, $N_2$, is nowhere defined. If the responder (player 2) rejects, the utilities of both players are zero.

$$U_{1reject}(x) = U_{2reject}(x) = 0.$$

Given that the proposer (player 1) offers $x$ and the responder accepts, the utilities are the following:

$$U_{1accept}(x) = M - x - k_1 \max(N - x, 0)$$
$$U_{2accept}(x) = x - k_2 \max(N - x, 0),$$

where $N$ denotes the fair offer prescribes by the norm, and $k_i$ is non-negative. Note, again, that $k_1$ measures how much the proposer dislikes to deviate from what he takes to be the norm. To obey a norm, 'sensitivity' to the norm need not be high. Fear of retaliation may make a proposer with a low $k$ behave according to what fairness dictates but, absent such risk, her disregard for the norm will lead her to be unfair.

Again, the responder should accept the offer if $U_{2accept}(x) > U_{2reject} = 0$, which implies the following threshold for acceptance: $x > k_2N/(1 + k_2)$. Obviously the threshold is less than $N$: an offer more than what the norm prescribes is not necessary for the sake of acceptance.

For the proposer, the utility function is decreasing in $x$ when $x \geq N$, hence a rational proposer will not offer more than $N$. Suppose $x \leq N$. If $k_1 > 1$, the utility function is increasing in $x$, which means that the best choice for the proposer is to offer $N$. If $k_1 < 1$, the utility function is decreasing in $x$, which implies that the best strategy for the proposer is to offer the least amount that would result in acceptance, i.e. (a little bit more than) the threshold $k_2N/(1 + k_2)$. If $k_1 = 1$, it does not matter how much the proposer offers provided the offer is between $k_2N/(1 + k_2)$ and $N$.

It should be clear at this point that the $k$'s measure people's sensitivity to various norms. Such sensitivity will usually be a stable disposition, and behavioral changes may thus be caused by changes in focus or in expectations. A theory of norms can explain such changes, whereas a theory of inequity aversion *à la* Fehr and Schmidt (1999) does not.

## 4 Epistemic Foundations

As we have seen, game theory is intertwined with aspects related to players' knowledge and beliefs about one another and the situation they find themselves in. Since Aumann's pioneering work on common knowledge (Aumann 1976), game theorists have paid more and more attention to the evaluation of solution concepts based on the epistemic assumptions and hypotheses from which they can be derived (see Battigalli and Bonanno 1999; Aumann and Brandenburger 1995; for a behavioral approach, see Devetag et al. 2013). For instance, one does not need the full force of CK1 and CK2 to identify the unique equilibrium of the prisoner's dilemma of Figure 15.1: once players know the structure of the game, and they are rational, they will not play their dominated strategy. Thus, we do not need CK2 (common knowledge of rationality), but the mere fact of rationality, with no epistemic structure on top of it. Such epistemic hypotheses can be mathematically analyzed in the formal framework provided by *interactive epistemology* (Aumann 1999).

An intuitive understanding, dating back to Leibniz, of the epistemic state in which an agent knows that "It is sunny in Philadelphia" is that the agent thinks that in all possible worlds that she cannot distinguish from the actual world, it is sunny in Philadelphia. Formally, we have a space set whose points are worlds and over which we define *events* and an *information function* that partitions the space set. The partition is such that an agent cannot distinguish the worlds belonging to the same cell of the partition. Thus, the intuition above can be made more precise by saying that in a possible world $\omega$, player $i$ knows an event $E$ if and only if the set $E$ (of possible worlds in which $E$ obtains) includes the cell of her information partition containing $\omega$. It is possible to define a knowledge function $K_i$ for each player $i$ so that, when given $E$ as an argument, it returns as a value the set of those worlds such that, for each one of them, the cell of $i$'s information partition which contains it is a subset of $E$. That is to say, $K_iE$ is the event that $i$ *knows* $E$. Knowledge can be given various axiomatic properties (see Fagin et al. 1995; Meyer and van der Hoek 1995/2004) such as, e.g., that $K_iE$ be a subset of $E$, tantamount to requiring that what players know is actually true (this property typically distinguishes between knowledge and belief).

Knowledge functions can be iterated, thus they can represent mutual and higher-order knowledge, and Aumann (1976) provides a mathematical definition of the idea of common knowledge in the setup sketched above. A proposition $p$ is *common knowledge* between, say, two players $i$ and $j$ if and only if the set of worlds representing $p$ includes the cells of $i$'s and $j$'s partitions *meet* which contain $p$, where the *meet* of two partitions is the finest common coarsening of them. An application of the definition is the theorem proven in the same article, in which it is shown that if players have common priors, and their posteriors are common knowledge, then the posteriors are equal, even if the players derived them by conditioning on different information. Or, in other words, that one cannot "agree to disagree." While Aumann (1976) formalizes Lewis's definition of common knowledge, it is debated whether Aumann's seminal definition is a faithful rendition of Lewis's informal characterization of common knowledge (cf. Vanderschraaf 1998; Cubitt and Sugden 2003; Sillari 2005, 2008b; Paternotte 2011; Vanderschraaf and Sillari 2014).

It is often argued that these models pertain to idealized agents, and that they fail to adequately capture the epistemic attitudes of realistic agents. On this issue, the interested reader can consult Sillari (2006, 2008a), where a solution based on so-called *awareness structures* is examined from both a philosophical and logical point of view. In a nutshell, game theoretic models enriched with (un)awareness represent how individual players *perceive* the game: it could be, for instance, that player $j$ is not simply uncertain as to whether $i$'s strategy set includes strategy $s_i$, but in fact is entirely in the dark about the very availability of such a $s_i$ for $i$. This naturally would be a very important aspect of the interaction, from a strategic point of view. Awareness, thus, allows one to represent strategic interactions more realistically. The large literature on the application of *awareness structures* to game theory is well summarized in Schipper (2014).

In such a framework it is possible to investigate which strategy profiles are compatible with certain epistemic assumptions about the players. For example, CK1 and CK2 from section 1 above imply that players would never choose strictly dominated strategies. The first contributions in this sense are Pearce (1984) and Bernheim (1984), in which a procedure is devised to eliminate players' strategies that are not *rationalizable*, i.e. not supported by internally consistent beliefs about other players' choices and beliefs. In general, certain epistemic conditions may be proven to justify all the strategy profiles yielded by a certain solution concept, and only those, hence providing *epistemic foundation* for that solution concept. For example, in Aumann and Brandenburger (1995) it is proven that, for two-person games, mutual knowledge (i.e. first-order knowledge among all the players) of the structure of the game, of rationality, and of the players' strategies imply that that the strategies constitute a Nash equilibrium of the game.

## 5 Repeated Games

Despite the observation, made in section 1, that rational players always defect rather than cooperate in prisoner's dilemma-like games of cooperation, game theory is ideally suited to study issues of cooperation and reciprocity. We have already seen in section 2 how in game theory we find a framework to precisely reason about norms and normative behavior. Moreover, while cooperation is irrational in the one-shot prisoner's dilemma (what is there for me to be gained by trusting or cooperating with a stranger that I will never meet again?), it need not be so if the interaction is *repeated*. In fact, there are rational, cooperative solutions to cooperation games if such games are repeated. The idea, intuitively, is that if by cooperating today, I may bring about your cooperation tomorrow, then it may make sense for me to cooperate today. What this entails is that there must be a "tomorrow": if the game horizon is finite, then, again, no cooperative solution is viable. To see this, we can use a backward induction argument. If the horizon of the interaction is finite, then, at the last round of interaction, players will not have any incentive to cooperate, since cooperation only makes sense when it can bring about cooperation in the future. But then players have no reason to cooperate at the round just before the last one, as they know that in the last round the other player will defect. and so on, to find out that players will defect at each round.

A repeated game has an element of sequentiality to it, so it is helpful to think of it in extensive form. We know from section 2 that in extensive forms, strategies determine a contingent plan of action. Hence, in repeated games a strategy determines what a player will do in all iterations. The payoffs will be given by the sum of the payoff for each repetition of the game, suitably discounted. If players always defect in the finitely repeated dilemma, there are myriad cooperative equilibria in the infinitely or indefinitely repeated dilemma. As long as there is *some* positive probability that the game will continue, cooperation is self-sustainable in the game. Whether cooperation will be sustained in equilibrium will depend on the probability of future play.

As an example, consider the following strategy for the indefinitely repeated prisoner's dilemma, traditionally called *grim trigger*. The player adopting the trigger strategy begins by cooperating at stage one, and she cooperates at each round if she has observed her opponent cooperate in the previous round. Were the opponent ever to defect, the trigger strategy switches to defection and never contemplates cooperation again. What happens if a player using the trigger strategy meets another player adopting the same strategy? They both start off by cooperating, and, since cooperation is observed at each round, they continue cooperating at each subsequent iteration of the stage game. Is this sustainable for rational players? It depends on the probability that the game will end at each stage. If the probability is sufficiently high that the sum of the future discounted payoff of mutual cooperation is greater than the current payoff of free-riding defection, then rational players will continue to cooperate. Moreover, all payoff combinations are feasible that players could have agreed upon if pre-play bargains were enforceable, a result known as the Folk Theorem of game theory. What is irrational in a one-shot interaction may be rational in a repeated one, provided certain conditions are met. The conclusion we may draw is that phenomena such as cooperation, reciprocation, honoring commitments, and keeping one's promises can be explained as the outcome of rational, self-interested choices. In repeated interactions, even a person who cares only about material, selfish incentives can see that it is in his interest to act in a cooperative way.

## References

Aumann, R. (1976). "Agreeing to Disagree." *Annals of Statistics* 4: 1236–239.

Aumann, R. (1999). "Interactive Epistemology I: Knowledge." *International Journal of Game Theory* 28: 263–300.

Aumann, R., and Brandenburger, A. (1995). "Epistemic Conditions for Nash Equilibrium." *Econometrica* 63: 1161–180.

Basu, K. (1990). "On the Non-existence of a Rationality Definition for Extensive Games." *International Journal of Game Theory* 19: 33–44.

Battigalli, P., and Bonanno, G. (1999). "Recent Results on Belief, Knowledge and the Epistemic Foundations of Game Theory." *Research in Economics* 503: 149–226.

Bernheim, B. (1984). "Rationalizable Strategic Behavior." *Econometrica* 52: 1007–28.

Bicchieri, M. C. (1989). "Self-Refuting Theories of Strategic Interaction: A Paradox of Common Knowledge." *Erkenntnis* 20: 69–85.

Bicchieri, M. C. (1993). *Rationality and Coordination*. Cambridge: Cambridge University Press.

Bicchieri, M. C. (2006). *The Grammar of Society*. Cambridge: Cambridge University Press.

Bicchieri, C., and Chavez, A. (2010). "Behaving as Expected: Public Information and Fairness Norms." *Journal of Behavioral Decision Making* 23(2): 161–78. Repr. in M. Baurmann, G. Brennan, R. E. Goodin, and N. Southwood (eds.), *Norms and Values. The Role of Social Norms as Instruments of Value Realisation*. Baden-Baden: Nomos Verlag.

Bicchieri, C., and Sontuoso, A. (2014). "I Cannot Cheat on You After We Talk." In M. Peterson (ed.), *The Prisoner's Dilemma*. Cambridge: Cambridge University Press.

Binmore, Ken G. (1987). "Modeling Rational Players: Part I." *Economics and Philosophy* 3(02): 179–214.

Binmore, Ken G. (1994). *Game Theory and the Social Contract: Playing Fair*. Vol. 1. Cambridge, MA: MIT Press.

Binmore, Ken G. (1998). *Game Theory and the Social Contract: Just Playing*. Vol. 2. Cambridge, MA: MIT Press.

Binmore, Ken G. (2005). *Natural Justice*. Oxford: Oxford University Press.

Bonanno, G. (1991). "The Logic of Rational Play in Games of Perfect Information." *Economics and Philosophy* 7: 37–61.

Camerer, C. (2003). *Behavioral Game Theory*. Princeton, NJ: Princeton University Press.

Cubitt, R., and Sugden, R. (2003). "Common Knowledge, Salience, and Convention: A Reconstruction of David Lewis's Game Theory." *Economics and Philosophy* 19: 175–210.

Devetag, G., Hosni, H., and Sillari, G. (2013). "You Better Play 7: Mutual versus Common Knowledge of Advice in a Weak-Link Experiment." *Synthese* 190(8): 1351–381.

Fagin, R., Halpern, J., Moses, Y., and Vardi, M. Y. (1995). *Reasoning about Knowledge*. Cambridge, MA: MIT Press.

Fehr, E., and Schmidt, K. M. (1999). "A Theory of Fairness, Competition, and Cooperation." *Quarterly Journal of Economics* 114(3): 817–68.

Güth, W., Schmittberger, R., and Schwarze, B. (1982). "An Experimental Analysis of Ultimatum Bargaining." *Journal of Economic Behavior and Organization* 3(4): 367–88.

Harsanyi, J. C., and Selten, R. (1988). *A General Theory of Equilibrium Selection in Games*. Cambridge, MA: MIT Press.

Kohlberg, E. (1990). "Refinement of Nash Equilibrium: The Main Ideas." In T. Ichiischi, A. Neyman, and Y. Tauman (eds.), *Game Theory and Applications*. San Diego: Academic Press.

Lewis, D. K. (1969). *Convention*. Cambridge, MA: Harvard University Press.

Maynard Smith, J., and Price, G. R. (1973). "The Logic of Animal Conflict." *Nature* 146: 15–18.

Meyer, J.-J., and van der Hoek, W. (1995/2004). *Epistemic Logic for AI and Computer Science*. Cambridge: Cambridge University Press.

Nash, J. (1996). *Essays on Game Theory*. Cheltenham, UK: Edward Elgar.

Paternotte, C. (2011). "Being Realistic about Common Knowledge: A Lewisian Approach." *Synthese* 183(2): 249–76.

Pearce, D. (1984). "Rationalizable Strategic Behavior and the Problem of Perfection." *Econometrica* 52: 1029–50.

Pettit, P., and Sugden, R. (1989). "The Backward Induction Paradox." *Journal of Philosophy* 4: 1–14.

Rescorla, M. (2007). "Convention." In Edward N. Zalta (ed.), *The Stanford Encyclopedia of Philosophy* (Summer 2015 Edition), http://plato.stanford.edu/archives/sum2015/entries/convention/, accessed August 10, 2016.

Reny, P. (1992). "Rationality in Extensive Form Games." *Journal of Economic Perspectives* 6: 429–47.

Schelling, T. (1960). *The Strategy of Conflict*. Cambridge, MA: Harvard University Press.

Schipper B. C. (2014). "Awareness." In H. van Ditmarsch, J. Y. Halpern, W. van der Hoek, and B. Kooi (eds.), *Handbook of Epistemic Logic*. London: College Publications.

Selten, R. (1965). "Spieltheoretische Behandlung eines Oligopolmodels mit Nachfragetragheit." *Zeitschrift fur die gesamte Staatwissenschaft* 121: 301–24.Sillari, G. (2005). "A Logical Framework for Convention." *Synthese* 147: 379–400.

Sillari, G. (2006). "Models of Awareness." In G. Bonanno, W. Van Der Hoek, and M. Wooldridge (eds.), *Proceedings of the 7th Conference on Logic and the Foundations of Game and Decision Theory (LOFT)*. Amsterdam: Amsterdam University Press.

Sillari, G. (2008a). "Quantified Logic of Awareness and Impossible Possible Worlds." *Review of Symbolic Logic* 1(4): 514–29.

Sillari, G. (2008b). "Common Knowledge and Convention." *Topoi* 27(1–2): 29–39.

Sillari, G. (2013). "Rule-Following as Coordination: A Game-Theoretic Approach." *Synthese*, 190(5), 871–90.

Skyrms, B. (1996/2014). *Evolution of the Social Contract*. Cambridge: Cambridge University Press.

Skyrms, B. (2004). *The Stag Hunt and the Evolution of Social Structure*. Cambridge: Cambridge University Press.

Sugden, R. (1986/2005). *The Economics of Rights, Co-operation and Welfare*. Oxford: Basil Blackwell.

Sugden, R. (2001). "The Evolutionary Turn in Game Theory." *Journal of Economic Methodology* 8(1): 113–30.

Ullmann-Margalit, E. (1977/2015). *The Emergence of Norms*. Oxford: Oxford University Press.

Van Damme, E. (1987). *Stability and Perfection of Nash Equilibria*. Berlin: Springer.

Vanderschraaf, P. (1998). "Knowledge, Equilibrium, and Convention." *Erkenntnis* 49: 337–69.

Vanderschraaf, P., and Sillari, G. (2014). "Common Knowledge." In E. N. Zalta (ed.), *The Stanford Encyclopedia of Philosophy* (Spring 2014 Edition), http://plato.stanford.edu/archives/spr2014/entries/common-knowledge/, accessed August 10, 2016.

# 16

# SITUATIONAL ANALYSIS

## Kevin D. Hoover

## 1 Origins and Nature of Situational Analysis

*Situational analysis* is a term popularized by Karl Popper. It is sometimes also referred to as *situational logic*, *logic of situations*, or the *logic of the situation*. Situational analysis and its synonyms have been used for over a century in a variety of fields from military strategy, to psychology, to sociology—sometimes in senses closely related to Popper's usage (see e.g. Mannheim 1936 [1997], 95), sometimes in quite different senses. Our concern here is principally with situational analysis as it has derived from Popper.

Popper first deployed the idea of situational analysis in an early draft of the *Poverty of Historicism*, which was ultimately published in 1957 (see Popper 1982). There, Popper attacked the idea that history could be understood as the working out of universal laws (such as Marx's laws of historical materialism) analogous to the laws of physics or as expressions of transindividual "spirits of the age." Historical laws cannot serve as the focus of a theoretical science, as the only plausible candidates are "trivial and used unconsciously" (Popper 1957, 150). The goal of historical explanation, in contrast to theoretical explanation, is to account for singular outcomes; and singular outcomes depend on a complex of partial causes and initial conditions that run into the remote past, most of which are of little interest. Historical interpretation for Popper is a matter of adopting a "point of view" (Popper 1957, 151). Situational analysis might provide the basis for such an interpretation, tracing the interaction of a dominant motivation with principal constraints. The constraints, in fact, provide most of the explanatory force. Because of the limited point of view and the focus on singular outcomes, such accounts, which are sometimes wrongly mistaken for theories, rarely result in testable hypotheses and, therefore, while valuable nonetheless, cannot be regarded as scientific.

Popper subsequently came to view situational analysis as more than a strategy of historical interpretation, but rather as the basis for a theoretical and scientific social science. The method of situational analysis "was an attempt *to generalize the method of economic theory (marginal utility theory) so as to become applicable to the other theoretical social sciences*" (Popper 1982, 117–18; see also 1976, 102–3). Here Popper echoes the now dominant definition of economics, due to Lionel Robbins (1932, 15): "Economics is the science which studies human behaviour as a relationship between ends and scarce means which have alternative uses." The vision can be stated quite generally as the idea that economics is the science of optimization under constraints.

A typical explanation based on "marginal utility theory," supposes that consumers gain utility from goods at decreasing rates. Then, a consumer with a fixed budget would allocate consumption in such a way that an additional (i.e. marginal or infinitesimal) unit of any good would add to utility at the same rate per dollar.[1] A situational analysis using this apparatus supposes a simplified or idealized consumer motivation: consume in such a way that one can reach the highest feasible utility given the situation (i.e. for the available budget).

Even without knowing the exact way in which consumption of different goods translates into utility, the assumption that every good faces diminishing marginal utility is enough to demonstrate that, *ceteris paribus* real income, the demand curve for a good slopes downward with respect to its own price. Stronger assumptions—i.e. more detailed descriptions of the situation—result in stronger conclusions. Thus, for example, if a consumer could be assigned a concretely parameterized utility function, then the demand curve itself, rather than just its generic character, could be derived.

David Hume famously denied that *is* implies *ought*. No descriptive fact about the world logically implies a normative claim. The most characteristic methodological move in economics constructs the explanations of economic behavior by imputing a dominant goal or motive to individuals and then figuring what their optimal choices would be in the circumstances in which they find themselves. For the economist, Hume's dictum is thus turned on its head: *what ought to be* implies what *is*. This is the mode of explanation that Popper advocates generalizing throughout the social sciences.

Popper describes situational analysis as

> *a purely objective method* in the social sciences … [that] consists in analysing the social *situation* of acting men sufficiently to explain the action with the help of the situation, without any further help from psychology. Objective understanding consists in realizing that the action was objectively *appropriate to the situation* …. [T]he situation is analyzed far enough for the elements which initially appeared to be psychological (such as wishes, motives, memories, and associations) to be transformed into elements of the situation.
>
> (Popper 1976, 102)

The assumption that people in fact act appropriately to the situation as they see it—that is, the inversion of Hume's dictum, so characteristic of economics—is what Popper calls the *rationality principle*.

Noretta Koertge has reconstructed Popper's argument as follows:

1. *Description of the Situation*: Agent A was in a situation of type C.
2. *Analysis of the Situation*: In a situation of type C, the appropriate thing to do is *x*.
3. *Rationality Principle*: Agents always act appropriately to their situations.
4. *Explanandum*: (Therefore) A did *x*.

> (Koertge 1979, 87)

Koertge's reconstruction captures nicely two key features of situational analysis: first, it is meant to be an application of methodological individualism—ultimately, it is to individual behavior that social science must look for its explanations; and, second, that, while eschewing psychological explanations, it analyzes human behavior as goal-directed or intentional. There is, however, a third feature of Popper's analysis that Koertge's reconstruction overlooks: Popper sees situational analysis as typically deployed in support of type-level explanations and not as an account of singular explanations. Koertge's quantifier "always" in the rationality principle must be softened to *generally* or *typically*. It is the shift from singular to type-level explanations that most likely accounts for the shift in Popper's early presentation of situational analysis as an interpretive methodology of history to his later claim that it constitutes an objective, scientific methodology of social explanation. We consider these features in turn.

## 2  The Methodology of Situational Analysis

In rejecting a law-based account of history, Popper explicitly and fully appealed to the individual as the motive force behind not only history but social interactions more generally. He embraced methodological individualism. Yet, Popper did not conceive of social interaction as always accountable through the *direct* interaction of intentional agents. Methodological individualism would have to explain the way that ideas spread, traditions are created, and institutions are formed and break down, and these may be the unintended consequences of individual social interaction (Popper 1957, 149; 1950, 288–89). The institutions may then, in turn, form some of the constraints that define the situation in which intentional agents act. The complexity and particularity of such institutional settings, on the one hand, militates against lawlike historical explanation and, on the other, suggests situational analysis as an effective alternative. Situations transcend individuals; nevertheless, the situations are traceable to individuals, and the motivations of individuals are the ultimate engine of social behavior.

An important justification for the rejection of internal psychology as the basis for explanation is that, once we have even a very broad-brush notion of a goal, the relevant human behavior is often more driven by the constraints than by the fine details of the psychology. Herbert Simon (1959) draws an analogy with pouring molasses into a bowl: if all one wants to know is the equilibrium depth of the molasses, the physical properties, beyond the fact that it is a fluid, do not matter to our accurately predicting the outcome. Simon (1996, 51–54) similarly suggests that, despite our ignorance of the physiology of an ant's nervous system or the various confounding perceptions an ant may receive along the way, a good explanation of the ant's path on a beach could be cashed out in terms of a simple ascription of motivations (e.g. that the ant aims to carry food back to the anthill) and the constraints (e.g. the location of the anthill and the landscape of the beach).

Spiro Latsis (1976, esp. 19–23) argues, against the broad applicability of situational analysis as dominated by constraints, that it applies only to single-exit situations. Single-exit situations are ones in which, given the motivation and the constraints, only one outcome is possible. In economics, optimization problems with a unique solution would be single-exit situations; while, in contrast, those with multiple solutions or multiple equilibria would be multi-exit situations. Multi-exit situations may be regarded as "situationally open" (19). Latsis argues that "[i]n multiple-exit situations the agent's internal environment, i.e. his psychological characteristics, etc. become central components in the explanation" (16).

To the degree that multiple-exit situations are common and Latsis's criticism of situational analysis is correct, situational analysis would not be the unique method of explanation in the social sciences but would apply to a limited domain. In some sense, Popper anticipates the objection with the suggestion that the domain of explanation is limited in social science in any case. For Popper, social science is mainly interested in type-explanation rather than singular explanation. Explanations in the social sciences are rarely about individuals but about groups or tendencies. Demand curves in economics are generally not individual, but rather market, demand curves. A good deal of the plausibility of Popper's claim that the situational constraints can be adequately specified and that personal psychology can be ignored results from the assumption that the social scientist targets typical or group behavior to which, for example, statistics might apply.

History aims at singular explanation. Popper does not reject a psychological point of view as a basis for historical interpretation *tout court*; yet he generally supposes that situational analysis explains more, and more convincingly, even when it is not falsifiable—and, therefore, by his lights, not scientific (1957, 151). This is not to say that situational analysis of history necessarily does not generate testable hypotheses, but only that it may not do so and may nonetheless have interpretive value (see also Popper 1982, 118). In contrast to the historian, the social scientist aims at type-explanations—in particular, with the construction of models of typical situations (Popper 1967 [1983], 357). Such explanations are, then, "explanations in principle" rather than "explanations in detail" (358). Situational analysis provides the basis for testable hypotheses (Popper 1982, 118).

Typical situations are often captured in models; and, in this regard, the social sciences and the natural sciences rely on similar strategies. Popper gives the example of the natural scientist who wants to explain recurring eclipses (1967 [1983, 358]). A very rough model, consisting of a lamp to represent the sun and a larger and a smaller ball to represent the earth and the moon, can easily demonstrate that a full moon is a necessary but not sufficient condition of eclipses. If our explanation is left as generic, we need very little more detail about the parts of the model, but what we must have is some idea of the typical movement of the earth relative to the sun and of the moon relative to the earth. That is, we require an additional element—namely, a specification of what it is that "*animates*" the model. How much detail we need in terms of accurate representation of sizes, relative initial positions, and laws of motion depends on exactly what level of predictive or explanatory precision we seek.

Popper suggests that the same strategy of modeling the principal parts and their relationship (the constraints) can be applied to social sciences. The animating principle—analogous in the eclipse model to Newton's laws of motion plus the law of gravity—is the rationality principle. The rationality principle, as stated, for example, in Koertge's reconstruction, is broad—more similar to "lower mass bodies orbit higher mass bodies in elliptical orbits" than to the complete Newtonian account of planetary motion. But for certain kinds of explanation, the very crude model of the lamp and balls is perfectly adequate, and for certain kinds—indeed, Popper would argue, for most kinds of social explanation—the broad animating principle expressed in the rationality principle will be adequate.

Popper's central idea here is that the key to explanation in social science, like the key to predicting Simon's ant's path, is to understanding the constraints in such detail that a very coarse animating principle—namely, that the "various person's or agents involved act *adequately, or appropriately*, that is to say, in accordance with the situation" (Popper 1967 [1983], 359). The necessary concreteness and detail of the animating principle is inversely proportional to the concreteness and detail included in the model, for a given required precision of explanation. For that reason, "the principle of acting appropriately to the situation … [is] clearly an *almost empty* principle" (359). The methodological strategy is that "we should pack or cram our whole theoretical effort, our whole explanatory theory, into an analysis of the situation: into the *model*" (ibid.).

Whether derived from Popper or not, the economists Gary Becker and George Stigler in a famous paper, "De Gustibus Non Est Disputandum" (1977), embrace Popper's methodological strategy. The animating principle in microeconomic explanations is to *maximize utility*. Becker and Stigler suggest giving all agents in a model the same utility function, which amounts to relying on only the broadest characteristics of preference maximization, and distinguishing one agent from another through the detailed descriptions of the constraints that they face (Popper's "situation"). As for Popper, the animating principle is nearly empty: *agents consistently choose what they prefer from the feasible options*. And, as with Popper, the degree to which their account supports precise explanation is made to depend on the concreteness and detail of the specification of the constraints. Such an approach may well flounder in the attempt ɟo predict any individual's detailed behavior, but it is really aimed at successfully predicting either the coarse behavior of individuals (as with Simon's ant) or the more precise *statistical* behavior of collections of individuals.

## 3 Situational Analysis and the Methodology of the Natural Sciences

In emphasizing the parallel between model-based explanation in the physical and the social sciences, Popper underlines his commitment to the unity of science, as well as to his famous *demarcation criterion*—namely, that propositions are scientific only if they are falsifiable and that *the* method of science is to seek out such falsifications in the process that he characterizes as "conjectures and refutations." There is, however, a line of criticism that suggests that Popper sees natural and social sciences as having fundamentally different methodologies, to the point that D. Wade Hands argues that we should label Popper's methodology of the natural sciences $P_N$ and his methodology of the social sciences $P_S$ (see also Koertge 1979, esp. 83–84, 92–95; Caldwell 1991, 17–22). Popper encourages this interpretation through his choice of examples drawn from the social sciences as his prime illustrations of unfalsifiable pseudo-science: Marx's theory of history, Freud's psychoanalysis, and Adler's individual psychology (1972, 33–65, esp. 34–39). The gravamen of this line of criticism is that Popper takes the rationality principle (in the context of situational analysis) to be *the* method of the social sciences and, at the same time, to be unfalsifiable, which would either undercut the unity of science or require him to re-evaluate the scientific status of the theories of Marx, Freud, and Adler, having judged them by the wrong criterion.[2]

It would be implausible to explain away the putative dilemma as Popper having changed his mind about the nature of science; for, once he had articulated the notion that situational analysis is the method of social science, he frequently reasserts both the criterion of falsification and the unity of science in close conjunction with restatements of the role of situational analysis. He writes, for instance:

> The method of the social sciences, like that of the natural sciences, consists in trying out tentative solutions to certain problems: the problems from which our investigations start and those which turn up during the investigation.
>
> Solutions are proposed and criticized. If a proposed solution is not open to pertinent criticism, then it is excluded as unscientific ….
>
> If the attempted solution is open to pertinent criticism, then we attempt to refute it; for all criticism consists of attempts at refutation.
>
> (Popper 1976, 89)

Despite these assertions of the unity of science, the charge of inconsistency gains traction and plausibility from Popper's own words. Commenting on his own statement of the rationality principle, "Agents always act in a manner appropriate to the situation in which they find themselves," Popper notes that individual agents, driven by other motives, may sometimes act inappropriately (1982, 361). He continues:

> But a principle that is not universally true is false. Thus the rationality principle is false. I think there is no way out of this. Consequently, we must deny that it is *a priori* valid.
>
> Now if the rationality principle is false, then an explanation which consists of the conjunction of this principle and a model must also be false, even if the particular model in question is true.
>
> But can the model be true? Can any model be true? I do not think so. Any model, whether in physics or in the social sciences, must be an oversimplification. It must omit much, and it must overemphasize much.
>
> (Popper 1982, 361)

Yet, Popper does not retract the rationality principle or situational analysis.

A principle of charitable interpretation—even of one's own beliefs and works—is to prefer the account that maximizes their consistency. Neither Popper's critics nor Popper himself have interpreted situational analysis sufficiently charitably. Models are not propositions; in themselves, they cannot be true or false. They may, of course, be used to make claims that can be true or false despite simplifications and omissions. Popper falls into a common trap, not only of regarding models as themselves bearers of truth values, but of assuming that the only model that could bear the value *true* is one that was a one-to-one recapitulation of the world. But such a model is not a model; it is the world. A genuine model can be used to make falsifiable claims about the world—true when accurately asserted—within specific domains and up to explicitly or implicitly specified degrees of precision (cf. Popper 1976, 101, 103).

When seen in the context of models, the rationality principle—despite the grammar of its statement—should not be regarded as a declarative proposition. The "always" is not a universal quantifier in a factual proposition but a universal injunction in an imperative statement, namely, an instruction on how to construct models—a methodological rule. Popper embraces the economists' inversion of Hume's dictum: build your models such that what is optimal within the model (i.e. *what ought to be* in the model's delimited world) implies what the model asserts is the case (i.e. what *is* in the model's world). Even on this construal, the model is not itself a truth bearer with respect to the actual world, though it can be used to construct falsifiable propositions when the actual world is asserted to be like the model world in particular respects and to particular degrees.

One advantage of treating the rationality principle as a methodological injunction is that it is consistent with the unity of science, as it makes claims about modeling generally and not about the social sciences in particular. Situational analysis for Popper arises naturally in the social sciences but also in other cases in which the appropriate account must be highly localized and non-universal. As we saw earlier, Popper first presents situational analysis as a non-scientific method of historical explanation. It was non-scientific because in the complex and unique circumstances that generate particular historical events, he believed that falsification of an explanation would not typically be possible. Nevertheless, it was possible that different points of view could be illuminating, even if not falsifiable. Rejecting the logical positivists' contrary view, Popper neither treats *meaningful* and *scientific* as synonyms, nor does he equate metaphysics with nonsense. When applied to the social sciences, Popper sees the hypotheses generated through the application of situational analysis as sometimes falsifiable and, hence, scientific in the same sense that the hypotheses of physics are scientific (1967 [1983], 360).

Natural history poses much the same problem for Popper as human history—it is highly complex and local. The circumstances that generate a particular species with very specific characteristics are probably unique, and an evolutionary explanation, down to the last detail, is unlikely to be falsifiable (Popper 1982, ch. 37). Popper sees Darwinian evolution as not "a testable scientific theory, but a *metaphysical research programme*—a possible framework for testable scientific theories" (1982, 168; see also 1979, 67–72). Darwin's account of evolution can be seen as species themselves pursuing a program of conjectures (mutations) and refutations (failures to survive). And the characteristic mode of explanation follows the same situational logic (Popper 1982, 168; see also 1979, 167). Some applications of situational analysis to history may be testable, while others are only interpretive. Situational analysis amounts to a conjecture based on "an idealized reconstruction of the *problem situation*"—what Popper elsewhere called a "model": "the explanatory theory of action will, in the main, consist of a conjectural reconstruction of the problem and its background. A theory of this kind may well be testable" (1979, 179).

The appeal of situational analysis for Popper is that he sees it as the most effective way of generating testable hypotheses. Far from standing in conflict with falsifiability as the criterion demarcating the scientific from the nonscientific, Popper sees situational analysis as the way in which social sciences, history, and natural history can meet the demarcation criterion and become scientific. The unfalsifiability of the rationality principle is a red herring. Even in his original account of science in *The Logic of Scientific Discovery* (1959), Popper does not require that every statement that is useful in science be falsifiable, but only that every truly scientific theory deliver hypotheses that could be falsified in principle.[3] As an opponent of foundationalism, Popper goes out of his way to reject the idea that each and every element of theories be empirically grounded. To try to ground each element would result in an infinite regress or a vicious circularity (Popper 1959, 87, n. *1, 93–94, 104–5). Rather he holds that some important elements are maintained conventionally, and some can be best described as metaphysics (not a pejorative term for Popper), and these elements are not themselves testable (sections 11, 29).

When situational analysis and the rationality principle are properly understood, the supposed tension between them and Popper's falsification criterion vanishes. Situational analysis stands in a difficult relationship to another of Popper's well-known views. Drawing on Reichenbach's (1938, 382) distinction between the "logic of justification" and the "logic of discovery," Popper denies that discovery has any logic:

> The initial stage of conceiving or inventing a theory, seems to me to call for neither logical analysis nor to be susceptible of it. The question of how a new idea occurs to a man—whether it is a musical theme, a dramatic conflict, or a scientific theory—may be of great interest to empirical psychology; but it is irrelevant to the logical analysis of scientific knowledge.
>
> (Popper 1959, 31)

Science proceeds by a process of conjectures and refutations, though the provenance of the conjectures stands outside the methodology of science. Yet, situational analysis amounts to a preferred methodology for generating conjectures. Situational analysis revolves around the normative claim that the formulation of conjectures should be based on an application of the rationality principle to a rational reconstruction or idealized model of the situation. Is not the implied methodology a logic of conjecture formulation—a logic of scientific discovery? That must hinge on exactly what is meant by "a logic."

If "logic" meant only a demonstratively valid pattern of inference, then the same type of argument that Popper makes against the existence of an inductive logic, could be brought to bear on any logic of discovery (1959, section 1). This is the way that Popper is most frequently read. But logic can have other meanings. For example, Popper indicates that *situational logic* refers to the assumption that the actors in a model "act within the terms of the model, or that they 'work out' what was implicit in the situation" (1967 [1983], 359). Similarly, situational analysis supplies a normative model of the practice of social science: apply the rationality principle to suitably idealized models. Acting within the terms of that model, working out the implications of the rationality principle in the cognitive situation amounts to a "methodological logic" in the same sense that situational analysis itself is an object level logic. Inasmuch as the role of situational analysis is to provide a mechanism for generating falsifiable hypotheses, it would appear to provide a logic of scientific discovery. And inasmuch as Popper advocates situational analysis as the premier methodology of the social sciences, he can hardly consistently deny that the context of discovery is part of the social sciences—and, indeed, part of any science for which it proves fruitful—or that it constitutes a logic.

## Notes

1 Popper invokes the notion of marginal utility, which is the original way that these ideas were developed in the 19th century. Modern microeconomics, however, does not assume that consumers have measurable utility, but only that they have well-ordered preferences that allow them to rank bundles of goods with respect to each other. Then the optimal position can be stated as, consume in such a way that the marginal rate of substitution between any pair of goods is equal to the relative price of the two goods.

2 Even in its own terms, this argument is not watertight, as it attacks only the uniqueness of Popper's falsificationist demarcation criterion. It assumes that situational analysis sets up a second, social-scientific demarcation criterion: consistency with situational analysis. The theories may fail to fulfill the natural-science criterion and still not fulfill the social-science criterion.

3 Popper 1959 is the English translation with revisions of his German original, *Logik der Forschung* (1935).

## References

Caldwell, Bruce J. (1991) "Clarifying Popper," *Journal of Economic Literature* 29(1), 1–33.

Hands, D. Wade. (1985) "Karl Popper and Economic Methodology," *Economics and Philosophy* 1(1), 83–99.

Koertge, Noretta. (1979) "The Methodological Status of Popper's Rationality Principle," *Theory and Decision* 10(1), 83–95.

Latsis, Spiro. (1976) "A Research Programme in Economics," in Spiro Latsis, ed. *Method and Appraisal in Economics*. Cambridge: Cambridge University Press, 1–42.

Mannheim, Karl. (1936 [1997]) *Ideology and Utopia*, repr. in *Ideology and Utopia: Collected Works*, vol. 1. London: Routledge, 1997.

Popper, Karl R. (1935) *Logik der Forschung*. Berlin: Springer.

Popper, Karl R. (1950) *The Open Society and Its Enemies*. Princeton, NJ: Princeton University Press.

Popper, Karl R. (1957) *The Poverty of Historicism*. Boston: Beacon Press.

Popper, Karl R. (1959) *The Logic of Scientific Discovery*. London: Hutchinson.

Popper, Karl R. (1967 [1983]) "The Rationality Principle," in David Miller, ed. *A Pocket Popper*. London: Fontana, 1983, 357–65.

Popper, Karl R. (1972) *Conjectures and Refutations: The Growth of Scientific Knowledge*, 4th edn. London: Routledge and Kegan Paul.

Popper, Karl R. (1976) "The Logic of the Social Sciences," in Theodor Adorno et al., *The Positivist Dispute in German Sociology*, trans. Glyn Adey and David Frisby. New York: Harper and Row, 87–104. Popper, Karl R. (1979) *Objective Knowledge*, rev. edn. Oxford: Oxford University Press.

Popper, Karl R. (1982) *Unended Quest*. LaSalle, IL: Open Court.

Reichenbach, Hans. (1938) *Experience and Prediction: An Analysis of the Foundations and Structure of Knowledge*. Chicago: Chicago University Press.

Robbins, Lionel. (1932) *The Nature and Significance of Economic Science*. London: Macmillan.

Simon, Herbert A. (1959) "Theories of Decision-Making in Economics and Behavioral Science," *American Economic Review* 49(3), 253–83.

Simon, Herbert A. (1996) *Sciences of the Artificial*, 3rd edn. Cambridge, MA: MIT Press.

Stigler, George A. and Gary S. Becker. (1977) "De Gustibus Non Est Disputandum," *American Economic Review* 67(2), 76–90.

# 17
# BIAS IN SOCIAL SCIENCE EXPERIMENTS

## *Sharon Crasnow*

No method has come to be so closely identified with modern science as experimental method. Nonetheless, until the second half of the 20th century experiments were rare in the social sciences. Experimental method first came to prominence in psychology. More recently there has been a marked increase in the use of experimental methods in the other social sciences, most notably economics and political science. Rebecca B. Morton and Kenneth C. Williams, authors of a key text for experimental method in political science, outline the key reason for this turn to experimentation: "nonexperimental methods have failed to answer some significant research questions, particularly causal ones" (Morton and Williams 2010, 260).

In this chapter, I address the question of bias in experimental research, drawing a distinction between value bias—the way values might distort scientific findings—and inferential and methodological bias. I argue that while two features of experimental research—randomization and masking—do contribute to stronger causal inference, neither fully eliminates two sources of inferential bias that also affect observational research: omitted variable bias and selection problems. Moreover, I argue that the new experimental turn suffers from what might be called "methodological bias": the belief that a particular method—in this case experiments—should be preferred, perhaps even to the exclusion of others, to address the fundamental and elusive problems of causal inference. I conclude with a plea for methodological pluralism.

## Evidence for Causation in Social Science

To see why experimental methods are thought to provide better evidence for causes than observational (non-experimental) methods, let us start with the underlying idea behind experiment captured in John Stuart Mill's Method of Difference.

> If an instance in which the phenomenon under investigation occurs, and an instance in which it does not occur, have every circumstance in common save one, that one occurring only in the former; the circumstance in which alone the instances differ, is the effect, or the cause, or a necessary part of the cause, of the phenomenon.
>
> (Mill 1843a, 455)

Two circumstances are compared, one in which B occurs and one where it does not. If the two circumstances are the same in all respects except one, A, then we can conclude that A is the cause or part of the cause of B. Thus finding or creating two such circumstances is a way of generating evidence for a causal claim.

But Mill believed that experiments could not be used to study the social realm. He offers two reasons for this:

> The first difficulty which meets us in the attempt to apply experimental methods for ascertaining the laws of social phenomena, is that we are without the means of making artificial experiments. Even if we could contrive experiments at leisure, and try them without limit, we should do so under immense disadvantage; both from the impossibility of ascertaining and taking note of all the facts of each case, and because (those facts being in a perpetual state of change) before sufficient time had elapsed to ascertain the result of the experiment, some material circumstance would have ceased to be the same.
>
> (Mill 1843b, 540)

Mill identifies the inability of the researcher to isolate and manipulate a suspected causal factor separately from all other factors as an insurmountable problem. Without a way to solve this problem, we cannot be sure that we have eliminated all other possible causes. But even were we to be able to do so the second problem would remain. The social world is in flux in ways that could continually disrupt whatever causal principle experiments might seem to discern. Thus the nature of the social prevents researchers from establishing what Mill takes to be two key requirements of experimental method. His conclusion is a strong one: experimental method is not possible in the social sciences.

And yet the pattern of reasoning behind the Method of Difference offers an ideal towards which to strive and much observational research in the social sciences is therefore modeled on approximating this ideal. For example, comparative case studies focus on the similarities and differences between the cases so as to isolate causal factors. However, in comparing cases researchers can, at best, control for some of the dimensions on which they might vary; a host of unknown or unobservable factors remain potential confounders of the causes investigated. Efforts to deal with such confounders—factors that have the potential to interact with or be screened off from the investigated, possible causes—have involved using increasingly sophisticated statistical techniques, most notably multiple regression analysis, in an effort to approximate experiments and isolate causes. Critiques of such approaches have come from several different quarters, however. For example, the statistician David A. Freedman has argued that such approaches require assumptions that have uncorroborated empirical content (Collier, Sekhon, and Stark 2010, xiii–xvi). Angus Deaton in economics has cast doubt on the widespread use of instrumental variables to produce "quasi-experiments" through statistical means (Deaton 2010). These kinds of worries are part of the motivation for the turn to experiment.

## Randomized Controlled Experiments: An Ideal

R. A. Fisher first advocated for randomized controlled experiments in the context of agriculture in his *The Design of Experiments* (1935/1971). The basic features of the design conform to Mill's Method of Difference. For randomized design, two groups are compared: one group that receives the "treatment" or "intervention" and one that does not. The treatment is the one factor that differs between the two groups. The "difference" discerned is the difference in the average effect on the outcome variable of interest between the two groups. The means of holding all other factors constant—controlling for them—is through random assignment of the members to the treated and non-treated groups. Alan S. Gerber and Donald P. Green note in their textbook on field experiments that "Random allocation is the dividing line that separates experimental from non-experimental research in the social sciences" (Gerber and Green 2012, 8). It is random allocation of treatment that is most closely identified with experiment in the social sciences.

The argument that random allocation addresses Mill's concern about identifying all other possible causal factors depends on there being an equal chance of each individual landing in either group. If so, then all factors—both known and unknown, observed and unobserved—are accounted for. If the difference in outcome between the two groups is significant—the average effect for the treatment group shows a significant difference from the average effect for the control group—then the conclusion that the treatment caused the difference is supported.

But random allocation only addresses one of Mill's concerns: that the design controls for all possible confounds except the treatment. The changeable nature of the social world was his second. There are several ways in which this is a worry. First there is the problem of transportability (generalizability) of results. While we might establish that a cause was operating locally—at a particular place and time—the flux of the social world prevents us from concluding that any causal principle established through an experiment would be like those in the natural sciences—transportable beyond the particular case. This is often referred to as the problem of external validity.

But there are other features of the social world to which Mill's remarks apply. Because the social sciences are *human* sciences and experimentation in human realms involves intervention into the lives of the subjects, social science experiments give rise to worries about psychological features of human beings that might affect the results of the experiment. When subjects become aware that they are being observed it may affect their behavior. Ian Hacking refers to such interactions as "looping effects." Looping effects result because the objects of study in the social sciences are what Hacking calls "interactive kinds" as opposed to the "indifferent kinds" investigated in the natural sciences (Hacking 1999, 108). The nature of social kinds as interactive kinds is one way that they present a moving target.

Experimental design can address some known looping effects through concealing the results of the random allocation from researchers so that they will not implement the experiment or interpret the data in some way that is more likely to support their preferred outcome. When possible, the identity of the groups should be masked for the participants as well. For example, a placebo control—a similar but inactive treatment that further disguises which group is getting the treatment—can be used if possible. The Hawthorne effect—changes in the behavior of individuals due to the fact that they know they are being observed—can be mitigated if subjects are screened from the knowledge that they are observed (although ethical concerns about informed consent can sometimes make this difficult). Randomized controlled experimental design generally includes such techniques to address at least some looping effects.

## The Virtues of Experimental Method

"Bias" typically has a negative connotation when used in relation to scientific research. It suggests that the research has missed its mark—that it is skewed or slanted away from an accurate account of the portion of reality it ought to describe. Missing the mark could be due to a failure to properly weight evidence because of holding a particular point of view, values or beliefs, or ideological commitments. But, as Miriam Solomon points out "Social epistemologists such as Goldman, Kitcher and Hull have already shown that factors such as competitiveness and desire for credit … can be conducive to scientific progress" (Solomon 2001, 53). These analyses indicate that science need not be value-free in order to be good and so such biases need to evaluated case by case in order to determine if their effect is negative or positive.

I will refer to this sort of bias as *value bias*. Value biases do the work of shaping research at each stage: the questions that we ask; the framing of the question; the conception of the objects of inquiry; decisions about what types of data to collect; data-generating procedures; analysis of data; decisions about when to stop collecting data; and drawing and reporting conclusions from the data (Anderson 2004, 11). Problems arise not *because* biases are operating but rather because of *how* they are operating. For example, Solomon argues that value factors can be problematic if they are not balanced with empirical factors (Solomon 2001). Elizabeth Anderson argues that they are problematic when they are held dogmatically and not responsive to empirical evidence (Anderson 2004).

It is beyond the scope of this chapter to develop a full account of value bias. In virtue of being human, observers have points of view—beliefs, interests, and desires. All of these can affect the choices that they make about what sorts of things to observe, what they take to be important about those subjects, their interpretation of their observations, their consideration of alternative hypotheses, and thus ultimately the conclusions that they draw. Good researchers are sensitive to these concerns and engage in their research in ways that guard against pernicious biases—for example, seeking alternative hypotheses, testing hypotheses against empirical evidence, and adopting ways of collecting observational data that are as transparent as possible. Given that there are so many entry points for value bias in the research process, I suggest that transparency of method is good practice to facilitate evaluation of the role of values in science; I return to this issue below.

The other types of bias that are particularly relevant for a discussion of experiment are varieties of *inferential bias* and I focus on them here. These are biases that affect the strength of the inference drawn. Again, they are not in themselves negative, since all estimates of the nature of reality drawn on the basis of evidence will differ to some extent from that reality. Biases are negative when they result from bad practice (systematic error). The specific forms of inferential bias that I will focus on are: (1) omitted variable bias—failure to take into account factors that may have an influence on producing or preventing the production of the effect (also referred to as "confounders" and (2) selection bias—errors resulting in over-representation of one or more factors in the comparison groups (or in samples).

Observational research most intractably suffers from a problem that takes us back to Mill's concern about identifying all the facts: the problem of confounders. Known confounders might be addressed in observational research through techniques known as matching or balancing. But experiments appear to provide a cleaner alternative, with random allocation eliminating the need for identifying confounders at all.

Does randomized controlled experimental design deliver on this promise? I offer two kinds of considerations to aid in answering the question. First, John Worrall (2002) has challenged arguments that randomized controlled trials are the means to achieve this goal. Second, the actual practice of social scientists doing experimental research clearly indicates that simple randomized control design is just one element of generating data to support causal inference and must be supplemented.

Worrall considers several arguments for the necessity of randomization in the context of medical trials, but the arguments are relevant for the social sciences as well (Worrall 2002, S320–S328). The first is Fisher's argument that significance testing requires random allocation. Fisher argued that significance testing is meaningless unless it is equally probable for any individual to have landed in either the control or the experimental group (random allocation). But, as Worrall notes, the argument loses some of its force since the question of whether significance testing has epistemic validity is disputed. First, the level at which a difference is significant is conventional and hence arbitrary. Second, what counts as a significant difference may vary depending on the context. The second of these concerns indicates that pragmatic considerations can come into play when evaluating significance levels. For example, a preference for Type 1 errors (claiming a significant difference when the difference is not significant) as opposed to Type 2 errors (failing to detect a significant difference) can affect judgments about what is an appropriate level of significance. Significance level is thus worth investigating as a site of value bias, but more relevant to the present concern about inferential bias.

A second argument for randomized controlled design is that random allocation controls for all confounders (omitted variables), including not only those that are known but those that are unknown as well. This idea seems to allow one of Mill's concerns to be addressed. It also appears to be one of the ways in which experimental methods are distinguished from observational methods in the social sciences. Worrall counters, "This claim is of course, if taken literally, trivially unsustainable. It is perfectly possible that a properly applied random process might 'by chance' produce a division between control and experimental groups that is significantly skewed" (Worrall 2002, S322). While the theoretical underpinnings of random allocation in principle support that omitted variable bias can be eliminated, in practice it is quite possible that a random allocation to experimental and control groups results in unbalanced groups. Repeated draws diminish the problem, but in practice experiments are not typically done with repeated draws. Such imbalances may also be addressed through matching or balancing the groups or adjusting the data *ex post*, but then random allocation is no longer doing the work of controlling for confounders.

Worrall considers the possibility that claims for random allocation could be interpreted more weakly. Perhaps the correct interpretation of the claim is that random allocation *tends* to balance the control and experimental groups on all potential causal factors. But this solution is not completely satisfying. "Even if there is only a small probability that an individual factor is unbalanced, given that there are indefinitely many possible confounding factors, then it would seem to follow that the probability that there is some factor on which the two groups are unbalanced (when remember randomly constructed) might for all anyone knows be high" (Worrall 2002, S324).

The third argument that Worrall examines is that random allocation eliminates selection bias. Worrall accepts that this is a good argument; however, he points out that it is not the random allocation per se, but rather the concealment and masking made possible through the random allocation that are doing the work.

Worrall draws the conclusion that while randomized controlled experimental design is a valuable inferential tool, it is not clear that it is superior to carefully conducted observational research in this regard. The design does not eliminate omitted variable bias and thus is not the methodological panacea that it is often claimed to be.

In addition to these problems, there are of course a number of ways in which actual social science experiments differ from the ideal model. As noted, experiments often include balancing or matching of the control and experimental group and so statistical techniques that are more sophisticated and often more controversial than the means squared tests used for significance testing in basic experimental design. Random allocation also often involves "blocking" or "stratified" sampling where participants are selected to represent particular previously known characteristics of the population (rather than simple randomization). Furthermore, actual experiments often involve variations of the treatment over more than two groups—multilevel and multitreatment experiments. All of these characteristics of actual experiments highlight the fact that experiments are not conducted in a knowledge vacuum—experimental design and interpretation of data frequently depend on other background knowledge or assumptions.

Morton and Williams make this clear. "Too often researchers focus on only one estimation strategy to establish causality. Given the conditional nature of causal estimates and the implicit and untested assumptions that most of these procedures make, use of a variety of procedures can help mitigate concerns about the robustness of the analysis" (Morton and Williams 2010, 179). While such techniques are needed to address problems of bias not eliminated through random allocation, they shift design away from the ideal and in doing so introduce new avenues through which biases may occur. The legitimacy of such adjustments needs to be argued for. Background beliefs and assumptions—including methodological assumptions—need to be clearly presented and supported—in effect, making an argument that important features of the ideal are still in place and that adjustments are warranted. In this respect, experimental method does not differ from other research methods.

## In the Laboratory and in the Field

Experiments come in many varieties. Here I focus on laboratory and field experiments. Laboratory experiments offer the maximum control over the environment, but because laboratory conditions may bear little resemblance to real world situations, the results of such experiments may not travel beyond the laboratory.

Laboratory experiments intended to test general theories only need to show that there are cases that do not conform to that theory. However, experiments used to support the development of positive theories are more problematic. For example, Joseph Heinrich, Stephen J. Heine, and Ara Norenzayan have argued that many social science experiments recruit subjects from a fairly specific population—undergraduates at universities in the industrialized northern and western hemispheres. They claim that these participants in laboratory experiments are predominantly WEIRD—Western, Educated, Industrialized, Rich, and Democratic—and thus outliers in relation to the majority of the world's population. Experiments conducted with such outliers as participants may not be generalizable. They support this conclusion with empirical findings from tests of "the Ultimatum Game and other related experimental tools across thousands of subjects randomly sampled from 23 small-scale human societies, including foragers, horticulturalists, pastoralists, and subsistence farmers, drawn from Africa, Amazonia, Oceania, Siberia, and New Guinea …. Three different experimental measures show that people in industrialized societies consistently occupy the extreme end of the human distribution" (Heinrich, Heine, and Norenzayan 2010, 65). Thus they argue that the human behavior examined through such experiments is highly dependent on environment and culture and so such experiments do not support universal conclusions.

The ability to transport the results from the experimental sample to the target depends on the extent to which the laboratory circumstances resemble the real world or the extent to which the potential effects of the controlled factors are fairly well known. However, it may also sometimes depend on the representativeness of the randomly allocated sample population, something that is not supposed to matter with experiments. Random allocation is not always able to sufficiently "wash out" the selection bias inherent in the sample, and when it cannot the ability of the evidence to support generalization is compromised. While conclusions about local populations do not suffer from this worry—political science experiments on voting behavior, for example—caution when making universal claims is warranted.

Transportability of findings from an experiment is often described as a question of external validity. The distinction between internal and external validity is generally attributed to Thomas D. Cook and Donald T. Campbell (Cook and Campbell 1979). Roughly, an experiment is internally valid if the experimental design supports the causal inference in the experiment. An experiment is externally valid if the results apply outside of the experimental context.

Field experiments are sometimes claimed to have greater external validity because they are conducted in real-world settings. Morton and Williams define a field experiment as one in which "the researcher's intervention takes place in subjects' natural environments and the researcher has only limited control beyond the intervention conducted" (Morton and Williams 2010, 46). Data that supports causal inference in such a setting is more likely to be generalizable to other natural settings. However, this argument depends on important additional assumptions about similarities between the circumstances under which the experiment is carried out and the external circumstances to which its results are extrapolated.

Interestingly, some advocates of experiments—particularly field experiments –have argued that their greatest virtue is not their external validity but their replicability (Duflo and Banerjee 2012). The meaning of "replication" is ambiguous in the literature. It might mean: re-analysis of the original data from an experimental study using the same assumptions; same data but different assumptions; similar experiment in the same place; or similar experiment in a different place. Replication is also used to mean replication of something considered to be the same phenomenon. This is how Francesco Guala uses the term, for example: "Genuine replications … usually involve some (minor or major) modification of the original design. Another way to put it is that scientists usually aim at reproducing experimental phenomena rather than the experiments themselves" (Guala 2005, 14). This last seems most close to what Duflo and Banerjee mean.

Similar experiments run at different times and locations or multiple experiments run at the same time with varying treatments provide additional ways to test the relationship between the independent and dependent variable. The slight variations in background condition also aid in affirming the robustness of the findings. Varying treatment is an additional way of controlling for suspected confounders. Replicability reflects the iterative nature of knowledge production and helps to establish phenomena under investigation as robust. It also provides a way of recognizing unwarranted assumptions behind faulty generalization.

Much observational research does not appear to be replicable—ethnographic research, for example—but other observational research is less subject to these worries. The in-depth research that goes into case studies can, at least in principle, be replicated through researchers recovering original data sources—contemporaneous newspaper accounts and document archives, for example. Databases constructed from observations and quantitative results obtained with them can be exactly reproduced when the databases and the coding rules through which they were established are transparent and publicly accessible. This is increasingly the expectation. Recent efforts to create qualitative data repositories challenge some of these claims of experimental difference (see the Qualitative Data Repository at https://qdr.syr.edu/). Thus it is not clear that the differences between observational and experimental research are that significant with respect to replication.

## Methodological Bias

The previous two sections have argued that issues of inferential bias—specifically omitted variable bias and selection bias—cannot be addressed solely by randomized controlled experimental design but require supplemental arguments, many of which may involve reference to data generated through non-experimental research. Philosophy of science literature that acknowledges the role of values in science frequently calls for transparency of such assumptions to facilitate evaluation of the support for the theory (hypothesis) acceptance (i.e. Longino 1990; Harding 1991; Solomon 2001). Thus as with all causal reasoning in science, analysis of reasoning that relies on experimental data generation should also involve an examination of such contextual elements, background knowledge, and auxiliary assumptions.

Gerber, Green, and Kaplan (hereafter GGK) have argued that while the need for such information is particularly pressing for observationally generated data, it is less so for data derived from experiments. In relation to the use of observationally generated data with multiple regression analysis they argue that "[t]o estimate the parameters that govern cause and effect, the analyst of observational data must make several strong assumptions about the statistical relationship between observed and unobserved causes of the dependent variable. To the extent that these assumptions are unwarranted, parameter estimates will be biased" (Gerber, Green, and Kaplan 2004, 251). In their view, this results in two kinds of uncertainty present in observational research: statistical uncertainty because of the assumptions made; and a theoretical uncertainty about the model under which those assumptions were made. Experimental research reduces the risk of bias due to incorrect parameter assumptions through random assignment—the parameters that govern cause and effect have been accounted for. The uncertainties in observational research mean that we can never know the degree to which our observational data are biased. Thus we never know what weight to give observational evidence and consequently GGK argue that observational data are useless in updating beliefs.

GGK's argument depends on considering experiments as ideal experiments. As noted in the discussion of Worrall, random allocation does not ensure an experiment cannot be biased, but the potential sources of bias are thought to be clearer and can be assessed and adjusted for in ways not possible in observational research. GGK appear to be confident that the conventional econometric models through which non-ideal experiments are adjusted are reliable.

There are also implications for resource allocation. Because of the prevailing uncertainty in observational research, GGK argue that funds are better spent on experiments. While they do not deny that it might be possible to learn some things through observational research, the circumstances under which such learning can be achieved are limited (Gerber, Green, and Kaplan 2004, 267–68). While experiments (particularly field experiments) can sometimes be expensive, because of the uncertainty in observational studies and correspondingly better evidence generated through experiments, the latter are more cost effective given external validity—they inform policy.

In effect GGK give an argument that methodological bias for experimental research is justified—both epistemically and financially—and consequently the argument is one that can be evaluated both for inferential bias and value bias. I explore the question of inferential bias first.

Arguments for the value of experimental method focus on ideal experiments, but, as noted at several different points in the previous sections, actual experiments are not ideal experiments. Random allocation for any given experiment can result in unbalanced groups in which potentially important causal factors are over-represented. There are conventional econometric techniques that test for or correct imbalance; however, employing such methods requires justifying assumptions.

This is not an idle worry. For example, consider two recent replications (Aiken et al. 2015 and Davey et al. 2015) of Edward Miguel and Michael Kremer's influential 2004 experimental study of the effect of deworming on education in Kenya. The first of these is a "pure replication," using the original data, assumptions, and methods. While it largely supports many of the original findings, the authors report, "Our most important finding was that after correction of coding errors in the original authors' analysis files, there was little evidence for previously described 'positive externalities' (or indirect effects) from the deworming intervention on school attendance in untreated schools" (Aiken et al. 2015, 1579). But it was exactly these findings about positive externalities that have most influenced policy, and their sensitivity to features such as coding errors speaks to the concern about evaluation of assumptions.

The second replication (Davey et al. 2015) re-analyzes the original data but uses different methods and assumptions. While some findings are consistent with the original findings, they note, "In our re-analysis, the strength of evidence that the deworming intervention improved school attendance was dependent on analytical choices, some of which are at risk of bias" (Davey et al. 2015, 1591). Again, methodological choices matter and need justification.

The need for statistical analyses that require assumptions with empirical implications is particularly acute for field experiments. There are additional sources of bias that result from the difficulty of controlling the experimental environment. For example: it is difficult to ensure that all who receive the treatment receive it in the same way; members of the treatment group may fail to comply with the treatment (rejecting it or not following protocol); there can be spill-over effects—members of the control group may note that their neighbors appear to be benefiting from some intervention that they do not receive and may alter their behavior accordingly, or alterations in the behavior of the treatment group may affect the behavior of the control group; attrition (drop outs); missing data. Any of these or perhaps other "disruptions" to the ideal experiment—one where all factors are accounted for or controlled for—might require techniques for adjustment. Assumptions made in the implementation of those techniques need to be justified.

These are epistemic considerations, but they ultimately affect the financial considerations that GGK raise as well. Since many methodological assumptions have empirical implications, justifying such assumptions is necessary as part of the argument that the data supports the claimed causal conclusions. While adjustments to parameters and variations in research design can aid in testing such empirical assumptions, conducting replications of experiments means raising the cost of research. GGK's cost–benefit analysis no longer appears so decisive.

A further value consideration comes from the methodological bias for experimental research. As economics and political science have come to embrace experimental method, there is publication bias for experimental work in top journals and consequently greater pressure on those in the discipline to do experiments. But questions of external validity involve assessing the relevant similarities and differences between the site of the experiment and potential targets for effective treatment. We need to know facts on the ground in order to do so. This is where observational research—case studies and process tracing, particularly—excels. Pressure to train experimental researchers often comes with a cost—a lack of available training in other methods. This is a cost to social science disciplines and future knowledge production.

Cartwright and Hardie argue that knowledge of effectiveness or evidence for use requires knowledge of the support factors (Cartwright and Hardie 2012). Experiments may give us evidence that a particular treatment works *there*—wherever it is that the experiment was done—but the argument that it works *here* depends on the presence of the same or sufficiently similar supporting factors. While a good randomized experimental design can tell us that there is a causal relationship between A and B—that there is a causal mechanism operating—it cannot tell us *what* that mechanism is. That means we do not know all the support factors through which the effect comes about from experiment alone. Observational methods—particularly qualitative methods such as case studies and process tracing—are the sorts of methods that traditionally provided the detailed on-the-ground evidence that I have argued must go into experimental design, evaluation, and assessment of external validity. If methodological bias for experimental method prevents resources from going into the training in non-experimental methods or discourages the publication of work that currently employs such methods, a crucial resource for the social sciences may be lost. This would indeed be a negative result of value bias.

## Conclusions

In summary, worries about bias do not appear to be solved solely through experimental design. All methods rely on background knowledge and both empirical and methodological assumptions in order to provide evidence. Experiments are a particularly elegant design and a valuable part of the social science methods toolbox. However, there are good reasons to think that they are not the only approach to social science research. Future work should look closely at the ways in which observational research and social science research can be integrated, and so I conclude with a plea for methodological pluralism, a view that I have argued for elsewhere (Crasnow 2015). I have argued here that experiment does not eliminate all sources of bias—either value bias or inferential bias. An uncritical belief that it can is a kind of wishful thinking—the desire for a method that can be a talisman protecting us from error in reasoning. Experiments are a good method, but it is unlikely that any method could fulfill such a wish.

## References

Aiken, A. M., C. Davey, J. R Hargreaves, and R. J Hayes (2015) "Re-analysis of Health and Educational Impacts of a School-Based Deworming Programme in Western Kenya: A Pure Replication," *International Journal of Epidemiology* 44: 1572–580.

Anderson, E. (2004) "Uses of Value Judgments in Science: A General Argument, with Lessons from a Case Study of Feminist Research on Divorce," *Hypatia: A Journal of Feminist Philosophy* 19: 1–24.

Cook, T. D. and D. T. Campbell (1979) *Quasi-experimentation: Design and Analysis for Field Settings.* Boston: Houghton Mifflin.

Cartwright, N. and J. Hardie (2012) *Evidence-Based Policy: A Practical Guide to Doing It Better.* Oxford: Oxford University Press.

Collier, D., J. Sekhon, and P. Stark (2010) "Editors' Introduction: Inference and Shoe Leather," in D. Collier, J. Sekhon, and P. Stark (eds.) *Statistical Models and Causal Inference: A Dialogue with the Social Sciences,* Cambridge: Cambridge University Press.

Crasnow, S. (2015) "Feminism, Causation, and Mixed Methods Research," in S. N. Hesse-Biber and R. B. Johnson (eds.) *The Oxford Handbook of Multimethod and Mixed Methods Inquiry*. Oxford: Oxford University Press.

Davey, C., A. M. Aiken, R. J. Hayes, and J. R. Hargreaves (2015) "Re-analysis of Health and Educational Impacts of a School-Based Deworming Programme in Western Kenya: A Statistical Replication of a Cluster Quasi-randomized Stepped-Wedge Trial," *International Journal of Epidemiology* 44: 1581–592. doi: 10.1093/ije/dyv128.

Deaton, A. (2010) "Instruments, Randomization, and Learning about Development," *Journal of Economic Literature* 48: 424–55.

Duflo, E. and A. Banerjee. (2012) "The Experimental Approach to Developmental Economics," in D. L. Teale (ed.) *Field Experiments and Their Critics: Essays on the Uses and Abuses of Experimentation in the Social Sciences*. New Haven: Yale University Press.

Fisher, R. A. (1935/1971) *The Design of Experiments*, 8th edn. New York: Hafner Publishing Company.

Freedman, D. A. (2004) "Sampling," in M. S. Lewis-Beck, Alan Bryman, and Tim Futing Liao (eds.) *Encyclopedia of Social Science Research Methods*. Thousand Oaks, CA: Sage Publications, Inc.

Guala, F. (2005) *The Methodology of Experimental Economics*. Cambridge: Cambridge University Press.

Gerber, A. S. and D. P. Green (2012) *Field Experiments: Design, Analysis, and Interpretation*. New York: W. W. Norton and Company.

Gerber A. S., D. P. Green, and E. H. Kaplan (2004) "The Illusion of Learning from Observational Research," in I. Shapiro, R. M. Smith, and T. E. Masoud (eds.) *Problems and Methods in the Study of Politics*. Cambridge: Cambridge University Press.

Hacking, I. (1999) *The Social Construction of What?* Cambridge, MA: Harvard University Press.

Harding, S. (1991) *Whose Science? Whose Knowledge? Thinking from Women's Lives*. Ithaca, NY: Cornell University Press.

Heinrich, J., S. J. Heine, and A. Norenzayan (2010) "The Weirdest People in the World?" *Behavioral and Brain Sciences* 33: 61–135.

Longino, H. E. (1990) *Science as Social Knowledge: Values and Objectivity in Scientific Inquiry*. Princeton, NJ: Princeton University Press.

Mill, J. S. (1843a) *A System of Logic, Ratiocinative and Inductive, Being a Connected View of the Principles of Evidence, and the Methods of Scientific Investigation, vol. I*. London: John W. Parker, West Strand.

———. (1843b) *A System of Logic: Ratiocinative and Inductive, Being a Connected View of the Principles of Evidence, and the Methods of Scientific Investigation, vol. II*. London: John W. Parker, West Strand.

Morton, R. B., and K. C. Williams (2010) *Experimental Political Science and the Study of Causality: From Nature to the Lab*. Cambridge: Cambridge University Press.

Solomon, M. (2001) *Social Empiricism*. Cambridge, MA: MIT Press.

Worrall, J. (2002) "What Evidence in Evidence-Based Medicine?" *Philosophy of Science* 69(S3): S316–S330.

# 18
# CAUSAL INFERENCE AND MODELING

## Tuukka Kaidesoja

### Introduction

One of the core challenges in all social sciences is to produce causal understanding of social phenomena. Despite its importance, there is no consensus about the best way to address this challenge in empirical social research. Rather, there have been various approaches to causal inference and causal modeling whose underlying assumptions are quite different. Although I focus here on sociology, because it is the discipline I know the best, many of the issues addressed are common to the other social sciences as well. This chapter then provides understanding of the basic issues and philosophical assumptions concerning how statistical and theoretical models are used in making causal inferences in sociological research.

I begin by discussing statistical approaches to causal inferences and modeling that have dominated methodological discussions in sociology. Then I move on to consider the theoretical modeling approaches to causal inference and explanation that are often contrasted to the research practices where causal inferences are exclusively made by using statistical models (e.g. Little 1991; Hedström 2005; Goldthorpe 2001, 2007). My aim is to describe the basic ideas about how causal inferences are made in each approach. I also discuss philosophical assumptions about causation and mechanisms related to these approaches as well as briefly evaluate their strengths and weaknesses. Nevertheless, I do not deal here with the issues concerning the operationalization of theoretical concepts and their measurement, nor do I discuss the specific statistical assumptions associated with different kinds of statistical models and techniques. I also ignore the distinction between probabilistic and deterministic theories on causation. In these respects the chapter somewhat simplifies the issues.

### The Robust Dependence View on Causal Inference

Starting from the 1950s, statistical methods and causal inferences have been closely connected to each other in sociology (Lazarsfeld 1957; Blalock 1961; Abbott 1998). The object of explanation in studies using statistical techniques has often been the observed variation in some variable representing some sociologically interesting property of a population of individuals (e.g. education, attitudes, values, or rates of criminal behavior). Statistical explanations for this variation have in turn been formulated in terms of some other variables (e.g. family background, gender, ethnicity, or residential area). In addition, many studies of this kind use non-experimental survey data about a sample of individuals that has been selected from a larger population using statistical sampling techniques (e.g. randomized sampling).

In studies like this, sociologists typically build and evaluate statistical models on the basis of observed correlations between the values of variables in their data-set. Pearson correlation is commonly used as a measure for the strength of linear co-variation of two standardized variables of interest. To take a simple example, we may have a variable X that represents years of formal education and a variable Y that represents monthly income. By analyzing our sample, we may observe that these continuous variables correlate in the sense that high levels of education are associated with high levels of income. This is an example of positive correlation, meaning that we can say, for each individual in our sample, that a high value of X raises the probability of (or "predicts") the high value of Y. Nevertheless, sociologists are not interested in the statistical properties of their sample only. They rather want to make inferences concerning the population that the sample represents. In order to justify inferences of this kind, they use specific sampling and estimation techniques that are discussed in textbooks on statistical methods.

It is generally acknowledged that the observed correlation between two variables as such is not a causal relation. This is because the observed correlation may turn out to be an accidental relation or it may have been produced by some confounding variable. Sociologists use various tests for statistical significance to evaluate the probability that the correlation is an accidental relation. In the case of non-accidental relations between two variables, something more is required for a relation to be causal than just the observed correlation between them. In textbooks on statistical analysis (in nonexperimental contexts), these extra requirements often include at least the following:

(i)  The values of the independent variable X for all units of analysis can be considered as being temporally prior to the values of the dependent variable Y.

(ii)  There are no confounding variables $Z_1, \ldots, Z_n$ that have produced the observed correlation between the variables X and Y.[1]

Now, according to what Goldthorpe (2001) calls *the robust dependence* interpretation of causation, we have a causal relation between the correlating variables X and Y once these two conditions are met. In this view, then, causation is understood in terms of non-spurious correlations between observable variables (e.g. Lazarsfeld 1957, 124–25). This view is often associated with the Humean regularity theory of causation.

To continue the previous example, it is reasonable to assume that a person usually spends time in formal education before he or she starts working regularly. This means that the correlation between our variables X (representing years of formal schooling) and Y (representing monthly incomes) can be plausibly assumed to fulfill the condition (i). Note that this assumption is not based on statistical analysis of our sample but in common-sense (or "theoretical") assumptions about our variables. In order to control the effects of confounding variables, we can analyze what happens to the correlation between X and Y when we hold the values of the test variable $Z_i$ (e.g. age or gender or ability) constant. If the correlation between X and Y does not disappear when the variable $Z_i$ is conditioned on (i.e. when the values of $Z_i$ are held constant), then we can say that the correlation is robust (or non-spurious) with respect to the variable $Z_i$. If the correlation disappears in all classes of the variable $Z_i$ (i.e. when $Z_i$ takes different values), then we may contend that there is no direct statistical link between X and Y, and that the variable $Z_i$ that correlates with both X and Y explains the observed correlation between X and Y. This means that the correlation between X and Y turns out to be spurious and that they are not therefore causally related. It is also possible that the observed correlation significantly changes (either decreases or increases) when we consider it in different classes of the variable $Z_i$. In cases like this, the variable $Z_i$ is said to moderate the statistical association between the variables X and Y. We may also find that there is some variable $Z_i$ (e.g. representing the effect of the father's occupation to the choice of his son's occupation) in the causal path between the variables X and Y that partly mediates the relation between X and Y. The *intervening variables* of this kind are sometimes called "mechanisms," but, as we shall see later, this is not the only way of using the concept of mechanism in sociology. In these latter two cases, we have specified how X and Y are causally related.

The previous paragraph describes the basic idea of the procedure that is sometimes called *elaboration* (e.g. Lazarsfeld 1957). This procedure consists of the conditioning of different "test variables" that may confound the observed correlation between two variables. What variables should then be included in the set of our test variables? There is no general rule for making this choice. In practice the answer depends on our substantial (or "theoretical") assumptions about the plausible relations among the variables that we have constructed and measured. Nevertheless, once we have taken into account all confounding variables, advocates of the robust dependence view on causation hold that reliable inferences about how the analyzed variables cause variation in the dependent variable Y can be made by means of elaboration. This view on causation is not limited to the relations between two variables but it has also been applied in the context of multivariate models (i.e. models that include more than one independent variable).

Though the robust dependence view of causation has been influential in statistically oriented sociology, it has also been heavily criticized by sociologists and philosophers of social science (e.g. Little 1991; Abbott 1998; Goldthorpe 2001; Woodward 2003; Hedström 2005, ch. 5). The core problem of this view is that, in nonexperimental contexts, we can never be sure whether we have conditioned all confounding variables (or even the most important of them) in our study. For this reason, the causal inferences that we have drawn on the basis of our elaborations (or regression models) alone may simply be incorrect and completely misleading insofar as there remains one or more unobserved and/or unknown confounding variable(s). Despite this problem, the core idea of elaboration is important in other views on statistical causal inference as well.

The other problem with the robust dependence view is that it tends to equate causal analysis with correlational analysis, meaning that substantial theoretical considerations play a minor role in causal analysis (e.g. Goldthorpe 2001, 3–4; Hedström 2005, ch. 5). The critics consider this problematic because the observed correlations between variables as such do not tell us anything about how the correlations in the data-set (including the robust ones) have been generated by the actions and interactions of human agents (and organized groups) acting in specific contexts. In addition, the critics indicate that this view of causal analysis conflates the practices of prediction and causal explanation, which should be kept separate. Because of these kinds of problems, the robust dependence view of causation is seldom explicitly advocated in current sociology.

## The Potential Outcome Model and the
## Manipulationist View of Causal Inference

In recent decades, the most popular alternative to the robust dependence view in sociology has been the *potential outcome model of causation and causal inference* (e.g. Sobel 1996; 2000; Morgan and Winship 2007; Gangl 2010). Since this view is based on experimentation practices in medical and agricultural sciences, its basic ideas can be best explained by considering randomized controlled experiments.

In medical experiments of this kind, the experimenter randomly assigns the subjects into the test group and control group. Then she changes the value of independent variable X (e.g. a dichotomous variable representing the presence or absence of some medical treatment) in the test group (where X = 1) and leaves it the same as before in the control group (where X = 0). During the experiment, the experimenter either controls the potentially confounding variables $Z_i$ in both groups or assumes that their effects are randomly distributed between the groups. At the end of the experiment, she measures the values of the dependent variable Y (e.g. representing some medical condition that the treatment is supposed to affect) in each subject and compares their means with the means of the earlier values of Y that were measured before the treatment. If the experimenter can assume that the responses are on average the same in all subjects and that the treatments of different subjects are independent of each other, then she can legitimately infer that the difference in the averages of the measured changes with respect to the variable Y between these two groups was caused by the manipulated change of the value of the independent variable X (i.e. whether the subjects got the treatment or not).

Now, taking its cue from experimentation practices of this kind, the potential outcome model holds that we should be able (at least in principle) to manipulate the potential causes of the variation in the dependent variable if we want to make reliable causal inferences about the effects of these causes (e.g. Sobel 1996; Goldthorpe 2001; Gangl 2010). Hence, there is a close link between the potential outcome model and the manipulationist view of causation. More generally, the potential outcome model conceives causal relations in counterfactual terms. This means that if we consider the relation between the values of variables X and Y with respect to a particular unit of analysis, then we can in principle determine whether the measured variables are causally related by *comparing* how the value of the dependent variable Y with respect to the unit of analysis would have changed (or not changed) between two *hypothetical* situations: In the first situation, the unit is exposed to the treatment (i.e. it is assigned to the test group). In the second situation, the unit is not exposed to the treatment (i.e. it is assigned to the control group). The causal effect of the dichotomous independent variable X can then be written $y_t - y_c$ where $y_t$ is the value of variable Y in the case of treatment (x = 1) and $y_c$ is the value of variable Y in the case of non-treatment (x = 0) of the unit. Since it is not possible for the same unit of analysis (e.g. a person) to be treated and not-treated (or belong to the test and the control group) at the same time, this characterization of causation is counterfactual. In the potential outcome model, randomized controlled experiments are then understood as *approximations* to the counterfactual situations of this kind since they enable us to estimate *the average effects of* X.

Accordingly, this model considers causal inference as "an effort to use observable data as a valid substitute to the unobservable (counterfactual) outcome information in order to estimate the causal effect of interest" (Gangl 2010, 25). When applied in nonexperimental contexts, this approach suggests that we should try to imitate experimental settings as far as possible by using suitable research designs and statistical techniques. For example, in some sociological studies it is possible to utilize "naturally occurring experiments" or to study the effects of policy interventions that take place in the specific "test population" which is compared to a similar "control population" where the intervention did not take place (e.g. Morgan and Winship 2007; Gangl 2010). I will not discuss these quasi-experimental research designs (where the treatment of subjects is not randomly assigned) or the statistical techniques related to them (e.g. matching, sensitivity analysis, and partial identification approaches) here any further since my focus is on the basic assumptions underlying each of the approaches to causal inference.

Woodward's (2003) manipulationist theory of causation can be seen as the most sophisticated philosophical theory of causation that is largely based on the potential outcome model. According to Woodward (15, 43), causal relations should be understood in terms of the relations of dependence between variables that remain invariant under interventions. He writes that the intuitive idea of the manipulationist theory is "that an intervention on [the variable] X with respect to [the variable] Y changes the value of X in such a way that if any change occurs in Y, it occurs only as a result of the changes in the value of X and not from some other source" (14; see also 98). This applies only in cases where the intervention is not correlated "with other causes of Y except for those causes of Y (if any) that are causally between the intervention and X or between X and Y, and that the intervention not affect Y via a route that fails to go through X" (14). He further specifies that causal relations between the values of variables are usually invariant with respect to a specific range of interventions, not with respect to all conceivable interventions. These views then imply that a generalization G describes causal relation between the values of variables X and Y, if (and only if) "G would continue to hold under some intervention that changes the value of X in such a way that, according to G, the value of Y would change—'continue to hold' in the sense that G correctly describes how the value of Y would change under this intervention" (15). It is important to add that Woodward (2003) argues that his view of causation can be generalized to nonexperimental contexts. For this reason, he seeks to detach his theory of causation and causal explanations from the actually conducted experiments by introducing the notions of hypothetical experiment and ideal intervention.

I think that it cannot be denied that Woodward's account of causal relations and specification of the meanings of different kinds of cause concepts is very precise and closely connected to the actual practices of experimentation and statistical analysis in the sciences. Like the potential outcome model, it also provides a practical criterion to decide which of the two variables one is the cause and which the effect, since only the manipulation of the causes influences their effects, not vice versa. The manipulationist view of causation also enables us to make a clear conceptual distinction between the spurious correlations and causal relations between the values of variables since only causally related variables are linked by the objective relation that remains invariant under (a certain range of) manipulations. Accordingly, this view is clearly different from the robust dependence view on causation that is restricted to the actual (or factual) causes of the variation in a dependent variable. By contrast, Woodward (2003, 11) emphasizes that knowledge about causal relations provides us with counterfactual information about *potential outcomes* that enables us to answer "what-if-things-had-been-different" questions.

Before moving on to consider multivariate statistical models, I will briefly mention three general objections that have been often raised against application of the potential outcome model of causal inference and the manipulationist views of causation in the context of nonexperimental sociology. First, it has been argued that these views problematically deny that the so-called intrinsic variables (i.e. those variables that are part of the constitution of units of analysis) can be among the causes of social phenomena, because such variables cannot be manipulated, i.e. they cannot take different values (e.g. Goldthorpe 2001, 6–7). Second, even though the manipulationist view on causation is built upon the practice of experimentation that involves intentional actions by the experimenter, critics have argued that it does not do justice to the intentional actions and interactions of people who bring about the effects of manipulations in nonexperimental settings that are typical to sociological studies. Rather, it runs into difficulties, for example, in situations where individuals' responses to the actual manipulations, such as policy interventions, involve purposive human agency (Goldthorpe 2001, 7–8; see also Hedström 2005, ch. 5). This is because people typically are both aware of these policy interventions and their beliefs about them may significantly modify the results of these interventions, meaning that they do not only passively respond to them but may, for example, intentionally act to counter the aims of the policy intervention. Finally, if we assume the notion of hypothetical manipulation, the manipulationist view on causation is perfectly compatible with sociological explanations in which the variation in some macro variable (e.g. economic inequality between countries) is causally explained in terms of the values of other macro variables (e.g. levels of government corruption, taxation, and education) rather than in terms of the interactions of entities with causal powers (e.g. individuals and organizations) in specific contexts. In this respect, these views alone do not give us any conceptual tools for criticizing explanations that lack *causal depth*, i.e. do not provide a proper account of causal processes that underlie the statistical associations of macro variables (e.g. Little 1991, ch. 8; Hedström 2005, chs. 2 and 5; cf. Gangl 2010, 40–41).

Hence, though the majority of sociologists and philosophers of social science would probably admit that the manipulationist approach is a step forward from the robust dependence view of causation and causal inference, it is an open question how adequate and useful it turns out to be in the context of sociological research.

## Multivariate Models and Causal Inference

The relations between variables in sociological studies are often more complicated than those that can be described by using just two variables. This is one of the reasons why sociologists use multivariate statistical models. In this section, I will very briefly consider some basic ideas of multiple regression models and structural equation models. My focus will be on how these models have been used in making causal inferences from the viewpoint of the potential outcome model.

Here is the general form of the linear regression model:

1. $Y = \alpha + \beta_1 X_1 + \beta_2 X_2 + [\ldots] + \beta_n X_n + \varepsilon$.

It consists of a constant $\alpha$, regression coefficients $\beta_1, \beta_2, \ldots, \beta_n$ connected to independent variables $X_1, X_2, \ldots, X_n$ and an error term $\varepsilon$. Sociologists typically interpret the estimated regression coefficients in terms of the relative weights of the respective independent variables in accounting for variance in the dependent variable Y. In the causal interpretation of the model, the estimated coefficient $\beta_1$ linked to the variable $X_1$ is interpreted as the change in value of the dependent variable Y associated with the change of one unit in the variable $X_1$ when the values of other independent variables (i.e. $X_2, \ldots, X_n$) are conditioned. For our purposes, the error term $\varepsilon$ can be said to represent the variance in Y that is not captured by the independent variables included in the model. Sociologists typically evaluate the fit between their regression model and data by counting the coefficient of variation $R^2$ that roughly describes how much observed variance in the data-set their model accounts for.

Regression models of this kind can be used for descriptive purposes without any attempt to make inferences about causal relations between variables. But a common justification for the uses of the linear type of regression models to make causal inferences has been to claim that they are useful tools for controlling the effects of potentially confounding variables as well as estimating the relative size of the effects of different independent variables (e.g. Sørensen 1998, 243). According to the potential outcome model, regression models can provide us with counterfactual information about what would have happened to the value of the variable Y if we had manipulated the value of some $X_i$ while conditioning the other X-variables. It is important to note that making causal inferences of this kind requires that the possible (or plausible) confounding variables are included in the model, in which case the error term should only contain the effects of such variables that do not correlate with the independent variables included in the regression model. Otherwise the model is likely to be seriously biased. The problem with regression models is that unknown confounding variables may generate serious biases when the models are used in making causal inferences even though there are certain statistical techniques that can be used to control the effects of unknown confounders (see e.g. Gangl 2010).

Though regression models are still often used in sociology, recent methodological discussions on causal inference by means of statistical models have nevertheless revolved around the structural equation models (e.g. Pearl 2000; Morgan and Winship 2007; Kincaid 2012). Models of this kind are based on systems of equations that aim to account for causal relations between many variables. In building models of this kind, sociologists select suitable variables and specify the structural constraints of the model (i.e. hypothesized relations between variables) on the basis of their antecedent theoretical assumptions (or causal models) and then test the structural equation model by using a suitable estimation technique. Since they use many equations to specify the relations among many variables, structural equation models enable sociologists to study not only the direct influences of many variables but also indirect and latent influences. Hence, models of this kind can be used to represent more complex causal structures between variables when compared to elaboration and simpler regression models. Nowadays, structural equation models are often represented in the form of directed acyclic graphs that connect many variables and, thereby, specify the causal paths through which variables are assumed to affect each other (e.g. Morgan and Winship 2007; also Kincaid 2012).

Though it is not possible to do justice to these discussions here, I will end this section by highlighting two important features of Woodward's (2003, ch. 7; cf. Pearl 2000) causal interpretation of structural equation models that are largely shared by counterfactual approaches on causal inference in current sociology (e.g. Morgan and Winship 2007). The key component of Woodward's (2003) causal account of these models is his concept of a causal mechanism that refers to the relations of dependence underlying the arrows in the path diagram that are drawn on the basis of a structural equation model under investigation. According to his view, causal mechanisms of this kind are invariant and modular: They are invariant in the sense that the equations related to the specific causal paths in the true model are assumed to describe how manipulation of the values of the independent variable would change the values of the dependent variable of the equation (319). They are modular in the sense that "it is possible to disrupt or replace (the relationship represented by) any one of the equations in the system [e.g. structural equation model, T. K.] by means of an intervention on (the magnitude corresponding) the dependent variable in that equation, without disrupting any of the other equations" (48).

Though these ideas seem to work pretty well in more mechanistic contexts, it is debatable whether these two conditions of causal mechanisms needed in making causal inferences by means of structural equation models are too restricted for the purposes of developing and testing causal models about *social processes and mechanisms that involve complex social interactions* (e.g. Cartwright 2007; also Gangl 2010, 40–41; Kincaid 2012). It is precisely processes of this kind that have been the focus of interest in theoretical modeling tradition.

## Theoretical Modeling and the Generative Account of Causation

Despite the impressive developments of statistical methods in recent decades, a number of sociologists and philosophers of social science have criticized the practice of statistical causal modeling in nonexperimental sociology. Their main worry is that the connection between the practices of statistical causal modeling and substantial sociological theories has remained very thin, resulting in the formulation of causal models that are sociologically implausible (e.g. Little 1991, 1998; Abbott 1998; Hedström and Swedberg 1998; Sørensen 1998; Goldthorpe 2001, 2007; Hedström 2005; Manicas 2006). Critics have also indicated that new statistical techniques have not much changed how causal inferences are made in the actual research practices of sociology. For one thing, it has been argued that the survey data acquired by using randomized sampling is badly suited to explanatory studies that address social relations and various interactions among people. This is precisely because individuals are "randomly selected and thereby uprooted from their social environments" (Hedström 2005, 109). As mentioned above, the way in which structural equation models are used in causal analysis also poses quite severe restrictions to those "causal mechanisms" that can be modeled by using them.

For reasons of this kind, the aforementioned critics have argued that causal models in sociology should be explicitly based on sociological theories that aim to describe *concrete and recurrent social processes and mechanisms that consist of the interactions between individuals* (and sometimes also organized groups), not of the statistical associations between variables. In this view, the definition of the concept of causation is typically detached from empirical regularities as well as from the practices of experimentation and uses of specific statistical methods. Accordingly, causation is understood in terms of *generative processes* that bring about observable phenomena and exist independently of our models and theories about them (e.g. Little 1991; Goldthorpe 2001; Hedström 2005; Manicas 2006). The generative processes are in turn often explicated in terms of activities and interactions of *entities with causal powers, capacities, and tendencies* (e.g. Harré 1970; Harré and Madden 1975; Bhaskar 1975; Cartwright 1989). Advocates of this approach to causal modeling also often argue for a view that "[t]here is no such thing as pure social causation from macro-state to macro-state; instead, hypotheses about social causal mechanisms must be constructed on the basis of an account of the 'microfoundations' of the processes that are postulated" (Little 1998, 198). These microfoundations are often understood in terms of individuals (or typical individual actors) acting and interacting in structured social contexts, but sometimes organized groups may also be accepted as parts of microfoundations.

The theoretical modeling tradition has its roots in classical sociological theories, rational choice theories, and mathematical sociology. In the following, I will limit my attention to the most recent incarnation of theoretical modeling in the movement of analytical sociology. This movement focuses on building theoretical models[2] of social mechanisms that regularly bring about (or generate) certain type of outcomes in a certain range of conditions (Hedström and

Swedberg 1998; Hedström 2005; Hedström and Bearman 2009). Causal mechanisms of this kind are assumed to consist of entities and activities which, in the context of sociology, are typically considered as individuals and their actions (Elster 1998; Hedström 2005; Hedström and Ylikoski 2010). It is important to note that this view of causal mechanisms is different from the intervening variable account of causal mechanisms as well as from Woodward's (2003) and others' modular account of causal mechanisms that were discussed above. However, it should be added that, even though they criticize practices of statistical causal modeling in sociology, analytical sociologists do not deny that sociologists need statistical methods for establishing those social phenomena that require explanation as well as for empirical testing of the postulated theoretical models about social mechanisms (e.g. Hedström 2005; cf. Morgan and Winship 2007, ch. 8).

## Theoretical Models of Social Mechanisms and Causal Inference

In his book on the basic principles of analytical sociology, Hedström (2005, 232) states that "the core idea behind the mechanism approach is that we explain not by evoking universal laws, or by identifying statistically relevant factors, but by specifying mechanisms that show how phenomena are brought about." To this end sociologists need a *theoretical toolbox* of relatively general theoretical models about causal mechanisms of different kinds which they can adapt to different explanatory tasks, and it is the aim of analytical sociologists to build such a toolbox (e.g. Hedström and Ylikoski 2010, 61). Unlike advocates of statistical approaches to causal inference, analytical sociologists do not aim to provide a set of rules that can be applied in making causal inferences. Rather, analytical sociologists seem to hold that causal inferences in sociology are relatively context-dependent issues and, depending on the explanatory task at hand, different types of data and methods of analysis can be used in arriving at mechanism-based causal explanations of social phenomena (58). In this respect, analytical sociology appears to be more pluralist than the robust dependence and the potential outcome views of causal inference, where the possibility of making causal inferences is more or less tied to a specific method of analysis. For example, many analytical sociologists consider *agent-based simulations* as important tools for developing and testing theoretical models about social mechanisms (e.g. Hedström 2005; Hedström and Bearman 2009; Hedström and Ylikoski 2010). Hence, in contrast to the statistical approaches to causal inference, analytical sociologists "make a clear distinction between statistical analysis and sociological explanations" (Hedström 2005, 113; also Hedström and Swedberg 1998).

In analytical sociology, theoretical models are then assumed to open up the black boxes by detailing "the causal cogs and wheels" (Hedström and Ylikoski 2010, 54) through which certain types of social phenomena are regularly brought about. It is also emphasized, following Merton's (1968, ch. 2) ideas, that theoretical models about social mechanisms focus only on limited aspects of concrete social processes and that it is futile to aim to provide a comprehensive explanation of any social phenomena (Hedström and Ylikoski 2010, 61–62). Though the borders of the analytical sociology movement are somewhat vague, examples of commonly cited theoretical models about social mechanisms include the following:

- self-fulfilling prophecies (Robert Merton)
- the Matthew effect and the theory of cumulative advantage (Robert Merton)
- diffusion mechanisms (e.g. James Coleman)

- segregation mechanisms (e.g. Thomas Schelling)
- threshold mechanisms (e.g. Mark Granovetter).

This list is far from comprehensive, but all of these mechanisms not only involve complex social interactions but have also generated important theoretical discussions and empirical applications.

The strength of analytical sociology is that it has paid attention to the importance of sociological theories that cannot be reduced to statistical models. However, it has been claimed that the idea of generative mechanism as such does not provide us with a method for verifying theoretical models about mechanisms and that the generative account of causation is too metaphysical and vague for the purposes of empirical research (e.g. Morgan and Winship 2007, ch. 8). It has also been argued that analytical sociology is too individualistic and reductionist in approach, that it does not do full justice to the various institutions, organizations, and cultural contexts where social action is embedded (e.g. Little 2012). It is not clear, however, how fundamental these individualist and reductionist assumptions are to the program of analytical sociology.

## Conclusion

I made a distinction between three views of causation and causal inference that have all been influential in explanatory sociology. The first was the robust dependent view, according to which causal inferences can be made by using the method of elaboration (i.e. analyzing the observed correlations between two variables in the classes of some third variable). According to this view, causal relations are basically understood in terms of non-spurious correlations between variables. The second view was the potential outcome model of causal inferences that presupposes a manipulationist account of causation, which is an instance of counterfactual theories of causation. In this approach, the most rigorous way of making causal inferences is to conduct randomized controlled experiments and causation is understood, to use Woodward's (2003) phrasing, in terms of relations of dependence between the values of variables that remain invariant under interventions. This view also suggests that causal inferences in nonexperimental settings should be made by imitating the experimental designs as far as possible. Finally, the third approach is based on the generative theory of causation, and its understanding of causal mechanisms is different from those of the robust dependent and potential outcome views. Accordingly, this view makes a distinction between statistical analysis and causal analysis, even though it does not deny the importance of statistical methods for sociological research.

It is clear that these three views include incompatible assumptions about the nature of causation, causal inferences, and causal models. One way to react to these differences would be to say that they all include important ideas about causation that can be applied in restricted contexts but none of them is capable of providing a general theory of causation and causal inference that fits all social scientific contexts where causal inferences are made and causal explanations are formulated. These kinds of pluralist views on causation and causal inference have recently been defended, for example, by Cartwright (2007) and Reiss (2009). Other philosophers and social scientists nevertheless disagree and continue to defend their own favorite theories of causation and causal inference.[3]

# Notes

1 It can be also added that the variables X and Y should not be conceptually related, in the sense that they constitute each other, and that we have some reasonable idea why they are correlated.
2 For the sake of simplicity, I will use the term "theoretical model" broadly to cover mechanism schemes, middle-range theories about mechanisms, as well as formalized mechanism models.
3 I would like to thank Juho Härkönen and Julie Zahle for their helpful comments on an earlier draft of this chapter.

# References

Abbott, A. (1998) "The Causal Devolution," *Sociological Methods and Research* 27: 148–81.

Bhaskar, R. (1975) *A Realist Theory of Science*, Leeds: Leeds Books.

Blalock, H. M., Jr. (1961) *Causal Inferences in Nonexperimental Research*, Chapel Hill: The University of North Carolina Press.

Cartwright, N. (1989) *Nature's Capacities and Their Measurement*, Oxford: Oxford University Press.

Cartwright, N. (2007) *Hunting Causes and Using Them: Approaches in Philosophy and Economics*, Cambridge: Cambridge University Press.

Elster, J. (1998) *Nuts and Bolts for the Social Sciences*, Cambridge: Cambridge University Press.

Gangl, M. (2010) "Causal Inference in Sociological Research," *Annual Review of Sociology* 36: 21–47.

Goldthorpe, J. H. (2001) "Causation, Statistics, and Sociology," *European Sociological Review* 17(1): 1–20.

Goldthorpe, J. H. (2007) *On Sociology*, vol. 1, *Critique and Program*, Stanford: Stanford University Press, 2nd edn.

Harré, R. (1970) *The Principles of Scientific Thinking*, London: Macmillan.

Harré, R. and E. H. Madden (1975) *Causal Powers: A Theory of Natural Necessity*, Oxford: Basil Blackwell.

Hedström, P. (2005) *Dissecting the Social: On the Principles of Analytical Sociology*, Cambridge: Cambridge University Press.

Hedström, P. and P. Bearman (eds.) (2009) *The Oxford Handbook of Analytical Sociology*, Oxford: Oxford University Press.

Hedström, P. and R. Swedberg (1998) "Social Mechanisms: An Introductory Essay," in P. Hedström and R. Swedberg (eds.) *Social Mechanisms: An Analytical Approach to Social Theory*, Cambridge: Cambridge University Press.

Hedström, P. and P. Ylikoski (2010) "Causal Mechanisms in the Social Sciences," *Annual Review of Sociology* 36: 49–67.

Kincaid, H. (2012) "Mechanisms, Causal Modeling, and the Limitations of Traditional Multiple Regression," in H. Kincaid (ed.) *The Oxford Handbook of Philosophy of Social Science*, Oxford: Oxford University Press.

Manicas, P. (2006) *A Realist Philosophy of Social Science: Explanation and Understanding*, Cambridge: Cambridge University Press.

Merton, R. K. (1968) *Social Theory and Social Structure*, New York: The Free Press, 2nd extended edn.

Lazarsfeld, P. (1957) "Interpretation of Statistical Relations as a Research Operation," in P. A. Lazarsfeld and M. Rosenberg (eds.) *The Language of Social Research*, Glencoe, IL: The Free Press.

Little, D. (1991) *Varieties of Social Explanation: An Introduction to the Philosophy of Social Science*, Boulder, CO: Westview Press.

Little, D. (1998) *Microfoundations, Method, and Causation*, New York: Transaction Publishers.

Little, D. (2012) "Analytical Sociology and the Rest of Sociology," *Sociologica* 1(12): 1–47.

Morgan, S. L. and C. Winship (2007) *Counterfactuals and Causal Inferences: Methods and Principles for Social Research*, Cambridge: Cambridge University Press.

Pearl, J. (2000) *Causality: Models, Reasoning, an Inference*, Cambridge: Cambridge University Press.

Reiss, J. (2009) "Causation in the Social Sciences: Evidence, Inference and Purpose," *Philosophy of the Social Sciences* 39(1): 20–40.

Sobel, M. (1996) "An Introduction to Causal Inference," *Sociological Methods and Research* 24(3): 353–79.

Sobel, M. (2000) "Causal Inference in the Social Sciences," *Journal of the American Statistical Association* 95: 647–51.

Sørensen, A. B. (1998) "Theoretical Mechanisms and the Empirical Study of Social Processes," in P. Hedström and R. Swedberg (eds) *Social Mechanisms: An Analytical Approach to Social Theory*, Cambridge: Cambridge University Press.

Woodward, J. (2003) *Making Things Happen: A Theory of Causal Explanation*, Oxford: Oxford University Press.

## Further Reading

Goldthorpe, J. H. (2001) "Causation, Statistics, and Sociology," *European Sociological Review* 17(1): 1–20, is a non-technical discussion on statistical approaches to causal inference in sociology.

Hedström, P. (2005) *Dissecting the Social: On the Principles of Analytical Sociology*, Cambridge: Cambridge University Press, is an important textbook on analytical sociology.

Morgan, S. L. and C. Winship (2007) *Counterfactuals and Causal Inferences: Methods and Principles for Social Research*, Cambridge: Cambridge University Press, is a thorough exposition of the new counterfactual approaches to causal inference in sociology and related statistical techniques.

Woodward, J. (2003) *Making Things Happen: A Theory of Causal Explanation*, Oxford: Oxford University Press, develops in detail the manipulationist theory of causation and causal explanation.

# 19
# COLLECTIVE INTENTIONALITY
## Marija Jankovic and Kirk Ludwig

### 1 Introduction

Intentionality is the property of being about, or directed at, something. Your belief that Athens is the capital of Greece is about *Athens being the capital of Greece*. Your desire for another cup of coffee is about *your having a cup of coffee*. A state with intentionality is an intentional state. Paradigmatic intentional states are propositional attitudes such as beliefs, intentions, desires, and hopes. They have a psychological mode (belief, intention, desire, hope, etc.) and a propositional content (e.g., that Athens is the capital of Greece), which may match or fail to match the world.

Collective intentionality concerns intentionality *in the social context*. Its distinctive focus is the conceptual and psychological features of joint actions and attitudes, their relations to individual actions and attitudes, and the implications for the nature of social groups and their functioning. It subsumes the study of collective action, responsibility, reasoning, intention, emotion, phenomenology, knowledge, trust, rationality, responsibility, cooperation, and competition, and how these underpin social practices, norms, conventions, institutions, and ontology. Collective intentionality is a growing interdisciplinary area of research with contributions from philosophy, psychology, political science, legal theory, linguistics, cognitive science, sociology, anthropology, and computer science.

In this chapter, we focus on collective action and intention, and their relation to conventions, status functions, norms, institutions, and shared attitudes more generally. Collective action and shared intention play a foundational role in our understanding of the social.

The three central questions in the study of collective intentionality are:

1. What is the ontology of collective intentionality? In particular, are groups per se intentional agents, as opposed to just their individual members?
2. What is the psychology of collective intentionality? Do groups per se have psychological states, in particular propositional attitudes? What is the psychology of the individuals who participate in collective intentional behavior? What is special about their participatory

214

intentions, their we-intentions, as they are called (Tuomela and Miller 1988), as opposed to their I-intentions?

3. How is collective intentionality implicated in the construction of social reality? In particular, how does the content of we-intentions and the intentional activity of individual agents create social institutions, practices, and structures?

Section 2 discusses collective action and shared intention in informal groups. Section 3 discusses mechanisms for constructing institutional structures out of the conceptual and psychological resources made available by our understanding of informal joint intentional action. It extends the discussion of collective action and intention to institutional groups, such as the Supreme Court, and explains how concepts of such organizations are constructed out of the concepts of a rule, convention, and status function. Section 4 discusses collective attitudes beyond intention. Section 5 is a brief summary and conclusion.

## 2 Collective Action and Intention

### 2.1 Plural Agency

What is the difference between individual and collective action? We begin with actions attributed to informal groups picked out using plural referring terms. We call these *plural group agents*, without implying they are agents per se. We can sharpen our initial question by asking what the difference is between the truth conditions for [1] and [2].

[1] I moved a bench.
[2] We moved a bench.

The parallel forms of [1] and [2] seem to commit us to the subject in [2], a group, being the agent of a bench's moving, and so to group agents per se. However, initial appearances are misleading. To see this, we bring to bear the event analysis of singular action sentences like [1] (Davidson 2001) on the distributive/collective ambiguity of plural action sentences like [2] (Ludwig 2007a, 2010).

On the event analysis, [1] says its subject is the agent of an event. For present purposes, we ignore tense and some details about how verbs select determinate forms of the agency relation (Ludwig 2007a, 2016, ch. 6). We analyze [1] as in [1a] (where '$(\exists e)$' means 'there is an event $e$ such that').

[1a] $(\exists e)$(I am an agent of $e$ and $e$ is a bench's moving and only I am an agent of $e$).

[2] can be read distributively or collectively. Read distributively, it means that *each of us* moved a bench, as in [1d]. The collective reading derives from giving *each of us* narrow scope with respect to the event quantifier. [2] says that there is some event of which each of us is an agent and no one else is (thus adjusting the requirement of sole agency also) and it is a bench's moving, as in [1c].

[1d] [Each $x$ of us]$(\exists e)$($x$ is an agent of $e$ and $e$ is a bench's moving and only $x$ is an agent of $e$).
[1c] $(\exists e)$[Each $x$ of us]($x$ is an agent of $e$ and $e$ is a bench's moving and only we are agents of $e$).

The difference lies (to a first approximation) in whether we are saying each of us did something to bring about an event of a certain type *or* that there is an event of a certain type each of us contributed to bringing about. On this account of the collective reading of plural action sentences, then, we have no need for group agents per se. We still refer to groups, but only their members are agents.

## 2.2 Shared Intention

We act together intentionally when we successfully execute a shared intention. We attribute shared intentions with sentences like [3].

[3]  We intend to move a bench.

[3] has a distributive reading, [3d].

[3d]  Each of us intends (himself) to move a bench.

Our interest lies in the collective reading on which we intend to move a bench together. On the collective reading, [3] attributes a shared intention to move a bench. Some authors take shared intentions to be states of groups as such (Velleman 1997; List and Pettit 2011; Pettit 2003; Tollefsen 2002; Copp 2006; Stoutland 1997, 2008). But, *prima facie*, if we don't need group agents for collective action, we don't need them as subjects of shared intention (we turn to institutional agency below). We therefore treat the subject of [3] distributively even on the collective reading, as in [3c].

[3c]  Each of us intends that we move a bench together.

On this view, for us to share an intention is for each to have an appropriate intention to participate in our doing something, a we-intention as opposed to an I-intention. The problem of shared intention then reduces to the problem of we-intentions.

There are number of competing analyses of we-intentions.

John Searle (1990, 1995, 2010) holds that we-intentions are intentions to bring about a joint action by way of an individual contribution. (Searle is often said to hold that we-intending is primitive, but Ludwig argues that this is a misinterpretation [2007b].) This isn't sufficient, as each of us could intend to bring it about that we do something together but have it in mind to trick the other into doing his part. For example, suppose that each of us intends to go to NYC with the other and wants to take the more expensive fast train, but thinks that the other intends to take the slower train. Each could then plan to get the other to board the fast train by tricking her into thinking that the train currently on the platform is the slow one (by moving her clock forward). In this case, though each of us intends that we go to NYC by way of something she does, we don't share an intention to go to NYC.

Margaret Gilbert (2006) explains shared intention in terms of the primitive notion of joint commitment. When we share an intention, we jointly commit to doing something (e.g. moving a bench) *as a body*. This joint commitment entails *sui generis* obligations of each party to do her part. These obligations are owed to the other parties and cannot be unilaterally rescinded. The parties, however, need not have any particular individual intentions (contra Searle, Bratman, Ludwig). If Gilbert is right, all joint intentional action involves norms internal to its nature.

However, while it is widely accepted that obligations with the content Gilbert describes typically accompany collective intention, it is controversial whether they necessarily accompany it (Bratman 1999b).

David Velleman (1997) has argued that shared intentions are realized in interlocking speech acts—one person saying, e.g., *I will if you will*, and the other saying *I will*—which jointly cause their own conditions of satisfaction. But this cannot cover all cases of shared intention. Furthermore, it is motivated by the worry that if each group member intends that they do something, then counterintuitively each thinks he will *determine* what the others do—which has been shown to be incorrect (Bratman 1999a). Accounts of we-intentions have also been advanced in terms of a special sort of reasoning (team reasoning) leading to joint action (Gold and Sugden 2007). But team reasoning, although directed at a group interest, is reasoning of individuals who are deciding strategically in light of what others will do. It is therefore compatible with their having only I-intentions directed at that group interest. Raimo Tuomela (Tuomela and Miller 1988; Tuomela 2005, 2013) has championed a conception of we-intentions as intentions to do one's part in the group's doing something together, under conditions of mutual belief about others in the group so intending and the conditions for a reasonable chance of success being in place. However, Tuomela notes specifically (2005) that by 'the group's doing something together' he means 'the group's doing something together *intentionally*' (contra Searle's [1990] interpretation). Consequently, he does not aim to give a fully reductive account of we-intentions since the analysis uses a concept related to the concept it analyzes in giving the content of the intention.

In contrast, Michael Bratman's influential account of we-intentions gives a reductive account of their content (1992, 1993, 1999a, 1999b, 2006, 2014). He holds that a we-intention is an intention of an individual that a group she belongs to do something by way of meshing (i.e. compossible) subplans associated with each member's intention that the group do it. A virtue of this account is that it captures the idea that joint intentional action is fundamentally collaborative. This is implied by the requirement that each member of the group intend that the subplans they associate with their intentions mesh. This element rules out the case of mutually intended deception toward the same goal considered above. In this case, each intends that we go to NYC in part by way of the other's intentions that we go. But each intends to deceive the other into taking the fast train, rather than to arrive at compatible subplans. An important question is how much mesh of subplans is required (Ludwig 2015a): *all* seems too strict (one can intend not to be fully cooperative, but cooperative enough to get the job done); *some* seems not strict enough (we can intend to take advantage of the others' plans up to a point only).

A similar reductive approach, motivated by semantic considerations, is Ludwig's (2007a, 2016). He understands we-intentions as intentions to make a contribution to the group doing a particular thing in accordance with a shared plan (which need not be given ahead of time), where the shared plan incorporates a margin for error around a canonical plan conception. Modest deviations from the canonical plan are compatible with the group carrying out the plan successfully. This helps avoid the problem of degree of mesh that Bratman's account faces. It also rules out cases of mutual deception because in that case the agents do not intend there be a shared plan in accordance with which they both act. Both accounts accommodate joint intentional action involving competition. For the participants cooperate in bringing about an action type that specifies that they compete *within a framework of rules* to achieve an end that not all can attain.

Other important accounts, which we lack space to discuss, are those of Seumas Miller (2001) in terms of intentions directed at shared ends, and Sara Chant and Zach Ernst (2008) in terms of rationality conditions for joint action.

# 3 The Role of Collective Intentionality in Our Understanding of the Social

Joint intentional action is one of the basic building blocks for institutional reality. By institutional reality, we mean both institutions understood as networks of interconnected roles (that is, organizations), like the Supreme Court, and social customs or practices, like tipping, shaking hands, or speaking a language. Due to space constraints, we discuss in detail only the former. Institutions as organizations (henceforth 'institutions') we explain using the concepts of a status function and status role. These, in turn, we explain using the concepts of a constitutive rule and a convention. Status roles come with powers, rights, duties, and responsibilities. Many social norms can be understood as grounded in assignments of status functions and roles. The structure of status roles in an organization is particularly relevant to distributing individual responsibility when the group is held to blame (morally or legally) for its actions.

We begin by contrasting the language of institutional agency with that of informal (plural) group agency. Then we discuss conventions. Next we explain status functions and roles. We use these to explain the structure of institutions, and one sort of social norm.

## 3.1 Singular Group Agents

Institutional action sentences typically employ grammatically singular subject terms, as in [4].

[4]   The Supreme Court reversed its 1896 ruling that segregation is constitutional in *Brown* vs. *Board of Education* in 1954.

Call groups denoted with grammatically singular terms *singular group agents* (again, without implying they are agents per se). Singular group agents appear to differ from plural group agents in several important respects.

(a)  Singular group agents can perform actions that individuals cannot, even in principle.
(b)  Singular group agents retain their identity through changes in membership.
(c)  Singular group agents could have had different members than they do.
(d)  Membership in singular group agents is socially constructed.
(e)  Singular group agents often act through the agency of some subgroup, or individual member, as in the case of a spokesperson, so that the expression of group agency seems not to depend on all its members contributing to what it does.

These differences may suggest that we think of singular group agents (institutions in particular) as genuine group level agents.

However, as above, initial impressions are misleading (Ludwig 2014a, 2017b, chs. 3–5). First, many singular group action sentences, like [5], have both a distributive and collective reading.

[5] The Supreme Court went to lunch.

[5] may mean that the Supreme Court went to lunch together, or that they went to lunch separately. This parallel with plural group action sentences supports the multiple agents analysis of the collective reading. Second, when singular group action sentences do not have a distributive reading, as for [4], it is because the verb expresses an action type that by definition requires

contributions from multiple agents (this explains (a)). This is unrelated to the grammatical number of the subject. The same point applies to 'We met in the library'. Neither of us could do this alone, even in principle. This is because meeting requires at least two people. The same goes for Supreme Court rulings.

Third, (b) and (c) are explained by (d). To be a member of the Supreme Court is to accept an institutional role (on which more below) by being nominated by the President, accepting the nomination, and being confirmed by the Senate. This is different from merely being arbitrarily grouped with other things. Most importantly, it is a time-indexed condition, for the status that suffices for membership can be removed (by resigning, for example) and assigned to someone else. This allows us to talk about the members of the group at a time: when the group acts, its members *at that time* contribute to what it then does (Ludwig 2014a, 2017b, ch. 5, section 2). Thus, [4] says that the 1954 members of the Court reversed the ruling of its 1896 members. No super-agent is required.

Fourth, the fact that institutional membership is time-indexed and socially constructed also explains how it is possible for the institution to have had different members (Ludwig 2014a, 2017b, ch. 5, section 3). For it is possible for different individuals to have been assigned the relevant status. This no more requires an agent over and above its members than the fact that the president might have been someone else requires a super president to shadow the elected one (contra, e.g., Sheehy [2006]).

The explanation of (e) and (f) requires the concepts of a status function and a status role. First, we take up the concept of a convention, which we will employ in explaining status functions.

### 3.2 Conventions

'Convention' is used to express a number of related concepts. In one sense a convention is simply a custom, like what people wear, or whether they use chopsticks or forks. We focus on a narrower notion—which also concerned, e.g., Lewis in his (1969) classic—on which a convention rests on a (at least) tacit agreement in a group about how to solve a coordination problem. A simple example is a convention for driving on the right or left side of the road to avoid collisions. We want cars driving in opposite directions to consistently choose different sides. No one can solve the problem alone, so to solve it we must enter into a kind of agreement about which side to drive on. The problem is solved when everyone agrees to follow the same rule (idealizing a bit here). However, for this to be a genuine convention, more is required than that agents follow the same rule. This could happen even if each regards the others simply as states of nature in a strategic game. A convention is a solution to the problem that is understood as a joint solution. This happens when each member of the relevant group we-intends that whenever any of them are in the relevant sort of situation (driving with others on a public road), they act in accordance with the rule to drive, e.g., on the right (Jankovic 2011, 2014, ch. 6). This is a matter of them having appropriate conditional we-intentions to do their parts (realizing a tacit agreement). Conventions then are grounded in shared conditional intentions (Ludwig 2015b), which are a structure of conditional we-intentions of members of the group in which the convention is maintained.

### 3.3 Status Functions and Roles

A status function is assigned to objects, events, or persons (token or type) in social transactions. A status function is an agentive function. An agentive function is defined in relation to a use "to which agents intentionally put objects" (Searle 1995, 20), such as being a chair or a saw. What's special about status functions among agentive function is that they can perform their functions only in virtue of being collectively accepted as having them (Searle 1995, ch. 2). Examples are being a king in chess, a twenty-dollar bill, a royal seal, a judge, a ruling, or a border between countries. Thus, nothing can function as a twenty-dollar bill unless it is collectively accepted in the relevant community as a unit of exchange in monetary transactions. The physical characteristics are insufficient. In contrast, something with the right physical characteristics can saw a log in two, even if no one thinks of it as a saw.

How can collectively accepting something as having a certain function be crucial to its ability to perform the function? The answer is that the relevant function is defined in a way that leaves open what particular objects are to perform it (Ludwig 2014b, 2017b, chs. 6–10).

The rules that determine the function are constitutive rules—rules the intentional following of which partially constitutes the type of activity they govern (Searle 1969). The rules of chess, for example, are constitutive rules. In contrast, *Robert's Rules of Order* are regulative rules because they govern a kind of activity that exists independently of the rules being followed.

The rules of chess define functions for certain objects in its play. For example, the white king belongs to the player who makes the first move. Positioned four squares from the right, it can be moved one square in any direction, if the square is not occupied by white's pieces, and not threatened by black's; it takes any opposing piece occupying the square. If it is in check and cannot move, black wins.

While the rules define the role of the king, they do not fix what object is to be used in the role. Thus, two people who intend to play chess face a coordination problem. The solution consists in their accepting the same objects for the roles defined by the rules of chess. This coordination on particular things to play these roles is a convention, in the sense of the previous section. In the case of coordination on types to play roles in recurring social activities, collective acceptance amounts to adopting conditional we-intentions to use the relevant type of object in the roles in that activity type. Thus, a twenty-dollar bill has the status function it does because it is collectively accepted that things of its type are to be used in certain commercial transactions, even if it is never used.

A status role (or agent status role specifically) is a special sort of status function assigned to an agent where (a) the agent must be part of the group that collectively accepts the assignment, and (b) the function is partly defined in terms of how the agent in the role is to interact with other agents, events, and objects on the basis of their status roles and functions (Ludwig 2014b sec. 5; 2017b, ch. 10). Examples are being a judge, policemen, senator, professor, student, and so on.

Thus, membership in an institution is a status role, and this provides a precise sense in which membership in an institution is socially constructed (Ludwig 2017b, ch. 11).

### 3.4 Institutions as Networks of Status Roles

We can define institutions as networks of status roles designed for coordinating joint intentional action for certain purposes by their possessors (Ludwig 2017b, ch. 10–11). For example, to join the army is to be assigned (and to accept) a status function. Though it is presupposed that roles are occupied voluntarily, typically there will be provisions for how to treat someone who does not perform the duties associated with the role. In joining the army, one acquires the determinable status role of being soldier, and a determinate of that designated by rank and unit, as well as more specific status roles within organizations in the army. The effective functioning of the organization (its fulfilling the purposes for which it is designed) depends on enough of its members performing adequately in their roles vis-à-vis others. The roles in an organization are typically defined in terms both of how one is to interact with other members and how one is to interact with various non-members, since organizations typically have status roles in larger institutional settings. An organization can also assign status functions to others (without their acquiescence) to determine how its members are to treat them. For example, designating others as enemy soldiers or civilians assigns them status functions (though not status roles) that govern how they are to be treated.

The possibility of perpetual existence of institutions comes to the possibility of realization of the relevant organizational structures in successive (often overlapping) groups of agents. An institutional group may survive periods in which it lacks members when it has a place in a larger group. For example, the 22nd Regiment of the United States Army was initially formed in the war of 1812, but disbanded and then reconstituted for the Indian wars of the 1860s, and it has been disbanded and reconstituted a number of times since then.

### 3.5 Proxy Agency in Institutional Action

A distinctive feature of institutional agency is the capacity to do things through authorized agents. We call these proxy agents (Ludwig 2014b). How does this work? Take the case of the spokesperson. Both groups and individuals can have spokespersons. This shows that proxy agency is not limited to groups. However, in both cases, the possibility of proxy agency relies on a background social agreement focusing on the spokesperson playing a role, by the exercise of her agency, in a social transaction between one person or group and others. Being a spokesperson then is a status role.

The key to proxy agency is authorization. Authorization is the assignment of a status role. We consider the simplest case in which members of the group, e.g. a club, designate a member by consensus to serve as spokesperson, and agree on what message the spokesperson is to convey. The purpose is to *publicly* commit the group to acting in accordance with the message. Both audience and group understand the exchange involving a spokesperson as their engaging in a joint intentional action. The audience's role is to recognize the spokesperson as acting under her authority to represent the group and attend to her message in that capacity.

The spokesperson's role is to produce an utterance act whose content is the message that the group aims to convey to its audience. The utterance act itself then has a status function in the transaction with the audience. The name for this status function is *a group announcement*. In this we borrow the language of speech acts applied to individuals, but its significance is different, because it is not an announcement of the spokesperson, and it is not in the ordinary sense a speech act by the group because the group does not have an intention to assert something in the way an individual does.

A conceptually necessary condition on the spokesperson's act counting as the group's announcing something is her being designated as their spokesperson. Thus, when the group announces something through a spokesperson, every member of the group contributes constitutively to the group announcement. In this way, even the phenomenon of proxy agency is brought under the multiple agents account of institutional agency.

This simple structure may be complicated along at least two dimensions (Ludwig 2017a).

First, the group can give more autonomy to the proxy agent. The proxy may be authorized, to decide on the specific way in which to convey a policy, to answer questions about it, or even to determine policy, or to make decisions that commit the group to various projects. In this way decision-making may be officially delegated to a subgroup or individual. The notion of a group decision here (like that of a group announcement) is constructed out of the social arrangements that give it content.

Second, the power to authorize individuals or subgroups to act as proxy agents for the group may also be assigned to a status role. The authorizations made by those proxies are then authorizations by the group by proxy. And this may extend through a chain of proxy agents. In more complicated cases, the constitutive contribution of many members of an organization may come to little more than their roles in constitutively sustaining the structure of the organization within which these authorizations are made and exercised. Yet, the basic conceptual structure remains the same.

### 3.6 *Social Norms and Status Functions*

There is an important connection between social norms (in one sense) and status functions and roles (Ludwig 2017b, ch. 10, sections 1–3). In the relevant sense of social norm, to violate a social norm is to make a mistake or to do something wrong internal to the type of social action the norm governs. For example, a policeman who makes a false arrest under the color of law has violated a norm internal to the type of action he undertakes.

How are social norms in this sense grounded in status functions? Things with status functions have associated norms determined by their role in the action type for which they are designed. There are three kinds. First, there are norms derived from the constitutive rules governing the action type. These define what has to be done for the action type to be instantiated. Thus, the rules of chess provide norms for chess. Second, there are norms derived from the conventions that attach functions defined by constitutive rules to particular objects, states, or events. These are norms about what objects or types have functions in relevant social transactions. Third, there are norms that are derived from ideals for a type of action that can be instantiated without conforming to the ideal. For example, in many competitive sports there are expectations about how play is to go, violations of which are assigned a penalty. These rules provide norms for the activity, which are not constitutive, and not derived from conventions that attach status functions to particular objects, but rather are derived from a canonical conception of play. The canonical conception is a regulative ideal for play of the game. The same goes for many other types of essentially collective intentional action types. This extends to status roles. Status roles provide norms for their occupiers determined by their design function. These define the powers, rights, and duties of the role players vis-à-vis others given their roles. For example, in a class, a professor has the power and duty to assign grades and the duty to do so on the basis of student performance. Students have a right to expect that grades are assigned fairly. This provides one sense in which social norms are constitutive of social institutions and practices. They may of course conflict with each other and with others sorts of norms, such as moral norms. This is illustrated by the case of a guard at a concentration camp.

## 4 Collective Attitudes Other than Intention

The practice of ascribing psychological attitudes to groups is not limited to intentions. Ascriptions of beliefs, desires, and emotions to groups are commonplace in everyday talk, as illustrated in [6]–[8].

[6]  The Democratic Party believes that all Americans have the right to a fair wage.
[7]  North Korea wants to sign a peace treaty with the United States.
[8]  Russia is angry at Turkey.

Moreover, many social-scientific and philosophical explanations involve irreducible appeal to collective attitudes. For example, rational choice theory has to appeal to the notion of common knowledge, because the strategic situation of agents in an interdependent choice is sensitive to whether they have common (or just mutual) knowledge of certain facts (Halpern 1986; Schelling 1960; Lewis 1969). More controversially, group guilt is invoked to account for the feelings of guilt that members of a group may harbor regarding a group action that they took no part in (Gilbert 1997).

The main issues in this area are analogous to those for collective intentions. There are psychological and ontological questions. The psychological questions concern the nature and structure of collective attitudes and their connection with states of individuals that constitute the relevant collectives. For example, common knowledge is initially glossed as knowledge that is *public*, and public knowledge is explained as knowledge a group has just in case everyone in the group knows that everyone knows (and so on *ad infinitum*) that something is the case (Lewis 1969). Is the regress involved conceptually problematic? Is it psychologically plausible that regular people would have such attitudes? Does the regressive formulation give the correct explication of the relevant notion of publicity?

The ontological questions concern the ontological commitments of ascriptions like [6]–[8], specifically, whether they commit us to group entities with genuine psychological states. The major groups of views concerning this issue are eliminativist, singularist (or individualist), and pluralist. (It might be thought that each of these has its appropriate context of application, but below we consider them as purporting to give a uniform account.)

Eliminativists reject all talk of group attitudes. They may consider ascriptions of psychological attitudes to groups to be false or metaphorical. These accounts have not been explored much, but some remarks by Quinton (1975) may be interpreted in this way.

Singularist accounts (the term is due to Gilbert [1987, 1989, 2006]) hold that collective attitude ascriptions are true, but consider them to be making claims about states of individuals, such as individual beliefs, desires, and intentions.

Eliminativist and singularist accounts are both compatible with methodological individualism, understood as the conjunction of the following two theses:

1. We can understand and explain individual action on the basis of the individual's own attitudes and reasons (which may refer to other agents and their attitudes and reasons, and to reducible group attitudes and reasons) together with physical and nonsocial facts.
2. Social ontology consists solely of the actions and activities of individuals and their relations and interactions, and reference to groups and group properties is reducible to the bases in (1) and (2).

Within the singularist camp, we may distinguish between summative and non-summative accounts (following Quinton). Summative accounts hold that a logically necessary condition of the truth of an ascription of the form

Group G $\psi$-s that $p$ (or to $P$)

is that

all (or most or enough) members of G $\psi$ that $p$ (or $\psi$ to $P$),

where "$\psi$" stands in for a propositional attitude verb, "$p$" a sentence, "$P$" a verb phrase. Call this condition the *summation condition*. For example, we might say the curriculum committee wants to change the distribution requirements only if all (or most or enough) members of the curriculum committee want to change the distribution requirements. Gilbert (1987) criticizes summative accounts that hold the appropriate summation condition to be both necessary and sufficient for the truth of the collective attitude ascription (Quinton 1975), as well as those that also require that it be common knowledge in the group that the summation condition holds; Corlett (2007) has responded to a number of Gilbert's criticisms.

Summative accounts of both kinds appear to be subject to counterexamples. First, they appear to be too weak. Suppose that each member of Congress believes that the minimum wage should be raised and that this is common knowledge, but that Congress has not taken a vote on the issue, and, for various reasons, is not going to do so. In this case, it would be odd to say that *Congress* believes that the minimum wage should be raised.

Summative accounts also appear to be too strong. We can use the discursive dilemma (described by Pettit [2001, 2003, 2007]) to illustrate how it can appear that a group may believe/want/intend that $p$ even though none if its members believe/want/intend that $p$. (Schmitt [1994] gives a similar argument.) Suppose that a company (call it "All-for-Safety") is deciding whether to institute pay cuts in order to introduce several safety measures. For simplicity, suppose All-for-Safety is a cooperative so that the employees own it. The decision is made by the employees on the basis of three considerations: (1) whether the danger is serious enough to justify the cut; (2) whether the measures to be introduced are effective enough to justify the cut; (3) whether the employees can bear the pay sacrifice. Suppose that an individual employee will vote for the pay cut just in case she votes yes on all three considerations. The company may employ two decision procedures. It may employ a *conclusion-centered* procedure, which consists in aggregating individual employees' votes on whether they will take the pay cut. Or it may employ a *premise-centered* procedure, which consists in aggregating individual votes on the three considerations, and adopting the pay cut if the majority of the employees vote *yes* on each individual consideration. Suppose that All-for-Safety adopts a premise-centered approach and that the employees vote as follows.

|  | Dangerous | Effective | Bearable | Conclusion-centered |
|---|---|---|---|---|
| ⅓ | Yes | Yes | No | No |
| ⅓ | Yes | No | Yes | No |
| ⅓ | No | Yes | Yes | No |
| Premise-centered | Yes | Yes | Yes | Yes (P) / No (C) |

In this case, it appears that (9) is true and (10) false.

[9] All-for-Safety believes that the employees should accept a pay cut.

[10] All/most/some members of All-for-Safety believe that the employees should accept a pay cut.

One may reject summative accounts without rejecting singularism. For example, the discursive dilemma plausibly shows that a group belief ascription can be true when the corresponding summation conditions are false. If that's right, an ascription of a collective belief that $p$ cannot be reduced to some configuration of individual beliefs that $p$. But the individual intentional states to which an ascription of collective attitude reduces do not have to match the psychological mode and content of the collective attitude, as postulated by the summation condition. For example, one may hold that group G believes that $p$ if members of the group jointly accept the judgment-aggregating procedure according to which, if most members of the group believe $p$ and $q$, and $r$ follows from $p$ and $q$, then G believes $r$.

Finally, on pluralist accounts, collective attitude ascriptions cannot be understood solely using the concepts drawn from individual theory of mind and action. For example, Gilbert (2006) explains collective attitudes (in general) in terms of the basic notion of joint commitment. In general, in joint commitment, we commit to holding a certain attitude as a body. For example, if we jointly commit to believing, as a body, that democracy is the best form of government, we collectively believe this. If we jointly commit as a body to feeling guilty about a certain action, we feel collective guilt over that action. And so on.

In contrast to eliminativist and singularist accounts, pluralist accounts are not compatible with methodological individualism.

Philosophers have discussed collective belief (Gilbert and Pilchman 2014; Gilbert 1987, 1989, 1994, 1996; Pettit 2003; List and Pettit 2011; Tollefsen 2007; Tuomela 1992; Schmitt 2016), collective memory (Wertsch 2009; Roediger and Abel 2015; Olick, Vinitzky-Seroussi, and Levy 2011; Michaelian and Sutton 2013; Hirst and Stone 2015), and collective moral attitudes such as guilt, pride, remorse, and shame (Gilbert 1997, 2002, 2001; Kutz 2000; May 1992; Tollefsen 2006), as well as collective emotions more generally (Huebner 2011; Wilson 2001).

## 5  Summary and Conclusion

Attributions of intentionality to collectives play a central role in our understanding of the social world. Our focus has been on collective intention and action. These are among the fundamental building blocks of the social world. They are implicated in our understanding of agreements, conventions, status functions, institutions, and social norms. We have suggested that collective intention and action rest on the capacity of individuals to form intentions with a distinctively cooperative content. An account of these we-intentions contributes not only to our understanding of the fundamental structure of the social world, but also of the capacities of mind that allow us to have the kinds of sociality we have. The self-conscious deployment of the concept of joint intentional activity patterns gives rise to the concept of a constitutive rule for social behavior, which prepares the way for the concepts of a status function, and of a status role, networks of which form the fabric of institutional reality. In addition to social ontology, the study of collective intentionality has implications on further areas of traditional interest to philosophers and social scientists such as cooperation, collective attitudes, responsibility, rationality, problem solving, attention, memory, and emotion. A further discussion of these and other topics can be found in Jankovic and Ludwig 2017.

## References

Bratman, Michael. 1992. Shared Cooperative Activity. *Philosophical Review* 101(2): 327–41.
———. 1993. Shared Intention. *Ethics* 104(1): 97–113.
———. 1999a. I Intend that We J. In *Faces of Intention: Selected Essays on Intention and Agency.* Cambridge: Cambridge University Press.
———. 1999b. Shared Intention and Mutual Obligation. In *Faces of Intention: Selected Essays on Intention and Agency.* Cambridge: Cambridge University Press.
———. 2006. Dynamics of Sociality. *Midwest Studies in Philosophy: Shared Intentions and Collective Responsibility* 30(1): 1–15.

———. 2014. *Shared Agency: A Planning Theory of Acting Together*. Oxford: Oxford University Press.

Chant, Sara, and Zachary Ernst. 2008. Epistemic Conditions for Collective Action. *Mind* 117(467): 549–73.

Copp, David. 2006. On the Agency of Certain Collective Entities: An Argument from 'Normative Autonomy'. *Midwest Studies in Philosophy: Shared Intentions and Collective Responsibility* 30(1): 194–221.

Corlett, J. Angelo. 2007. Analyzing Social Knowledge. *Social Epistemology* 21(3): 231–47.

Davidson, Donald. 2001. The Logical Form of Action Sentences. In *Essays on Actions and Events*. New York: Clarendon Press. Original edition, 1967.

Gilbert, Margaret. 1987. Modelling Collective Belief. *Synthese* 73: 185–204.

———. 1989. *On Social Facts*. London: Routledge.

———. 1994. Remarks on Collective Belief. In *Socializing Epistemology: The Social Dimensions of Knowledge*, ed. Frederick F Schmitt. Lanham, MD: Rowman and Littlefield.

———. 1996. Concerning Sociality: The Plural Subject as Paradigm. In *The Mark of the Social*, ed. J. Greenwood. Lanham, MD: Rowman and Littlefield.

———. 1997. Group Wrongs and Guilt Feelings. *Journal of Ethics* 1(1): 65–84.

———. 2001. Collective Remorse. In *War Crimes and Collective Wrongdoing: A Reader*. Malden, MA: Blackwell Publishing.

———. 2002. Collective Guilt and Collective Guilt Feelings. *Journal of Ethics* 6(2): 115–43.

———. 2006. *A Theory of Political Obligation: Membership, Commitment, and the Bonds of Society*. Oxford: Clarendon Press.

Gilbert, Margaret, and Daniel Pilchman. 2014. Belief, Acceptance, and What Happens in Groups. In *Essays in Collective Epistemology*, ed. J. Lackey. Oxford: Oxford University Press.

Gold, Natalie, and Robert Sugden. 2007. Collective Intentions and Team Agency. *Journal of Philosophy* 103(3): 109–37.

Halpern, Joseph Y. 1986. Reasoning about Knowledge: An Overview. In *Theoretical Aspects of Reasoning about Knowledge*, ed. J. Y. Halpern. Los Altos, CA: M. Kaufmann Publishers.

Hirst, W., and C. B. Stone. 2015. A Unified Approach to Collective Memory: Sociology, Psychology, and the Extended Mind. In *Ashgate Research Companion to Memory Studies*, ed. S. Kattego. Farnham. UK: Ashgate.

Huebner, Bryce. 2011. Genuinely Collective Emotions. *European Journal for Philosophy of Science* 1(1): 89–118.

Jankovic, Marija. 2011. The Intentional Underpinnings of Convention. Presented at *Pacific Division of the American Philosophical Association*, San Diego, CA, April 20–23.

———. 2014. Conventional Meaning. Ph.D. Dissertation, Department of Philosophy, Indiana University.

Jankovic, Marija, and Kirk Ludwig, eds. 2017. *The Routledge Handbook on Collective Intentionality*. New York: Routledge.

Kutz, Christopher. 2000. *Complicity: Ethics and Law for a Collective Age*. Cambridge: Cambridge University Press.

Lewis, David. 1969. *Convention: A Philosophical Study*. Cambridge. MA: Harvard University Press.

List, Christian, and Philip Pettit. 2011. *Group Agency: The Possibility, Design, and Status of Corporate Agents*. Oxford: Oxford University Press.

Ludwig, Kirk. 2007a. Collective Intentional Behavior from the Standpoint of Semantics. *Noûs* 41(3): 355–93.

———. 2007b. Foundations of Social Reality in Collective Intentional Behavior. In *Intentional Acts and Institutional Facts: Essays on John Searle's Social Ontology*, ed. S. L. Tsohatzidis. Dordrecht: Springer.

———. 2010. Adverbs of Action. In *Blackwell Companion to the Philosophy of Action*, ed. T. O'Connor and C. Sandis. Oxford: Wiley-Blackwell.

———. 2014a. The Ontology of Collective Action. In *From Individual to Collective Intentionality*, ed. S. Chant, F. Hindriks, and G. Preyer. Oxford: Oxford University Press.

———. 2014b. Proxy Agency in Collective Action. *Noûs* 48(1): 75–105.

———. 2015a. Shared Agency in Modest Sociality. *Journal of Social Ontology* 1(1): 7–15.

———. 2015b. What are Conditional Intentions? *Methode: Analytic Perspectives* 4(6): 30–60.

———. 2016. *From Individual to Plural Agency: Collective Action I*. 2 vols. Oxford: Oxford University Press.

————. 2017a. Proxy Agency. In *The Routledge Handbook on Collective Intentionality*, ed. M. Jankovic and K. Ludwig. New York: Routledge.

————. 2017b. *From Plural to Institutional Agency: Collective Action II*. 2 vols. Oxford: Oxford University Press.

May, L. 1992. *Sharing responsibility*. Chicago: University of Chicago Press.

Michaelian, Kourken, and John Sutton. 2013. Distributed Cognition and Memory Research: History and Current Directions. *Review of Philosophy and Psychology* 4(1): 1–24.

Miller, S. 2001. *Social Action: A Teleological Account*. Cambridge: Cambridge University Press.

Olick, J. K., Vered Vinitzky-Seroussi, and D. Levy, eds. 2011. *The Collective Memory Reader*. Oxford: Oxford University Press.

Pettit, Philip. 2001. Deliberative Democracy and the Discursive Dilemma. *Noûs Supplement: Philosophical Issues* 11: 268–99.

————. 2003. Groups with Minds of their Own. In *Socializing Metaphysics*, ed. F. Schmitt. Lanham, MD: Rowman and Littlefield.

————. 2007. Responsibility Incorporated. *Ethics* 117(2): 171–201.

Quinton, A. 1975. Social Objects. *Proceedings of the Aristotelian Society* 75: 67–87.

Roediger, H. L., and M. Abel. 2015. Collective Memory: A New Arena of Cognitive Study. *Trends in Cognitive Sciences* 19(7): 365–71.

Schelling, Thomas C. 1960. *The Strategy of Conflict*. Cambridge, MA: Harvard University Press.

Schmitt, Fred. 2016. Collective Belief and Acceptance. In *The Routledge Handbook on Collective Intentionality*, ed. M. Jankovic and K. Ludwig. New York: Routledge.

Schmitt, Frederick F. 1994. The Justification of Group Beliefs. In *Socializing Epistemology: The Social Dimensions of Knowledge*, ed. Frederick F. Schmitt. Lanham, MD: Rowman & Littlefield.

Searle, John. 1969. *Speech Acts: An Essay in the Philosophy of Language*. London: Cambridge University Press.

————. 1990. Collective Intentions and Actions. In *Intentions in Communication*, ed. P. R. Cohen, J. Morgan, and M. E. Pollack. Cambridge, MA: MIT Press.

————. 1995. *The Construction of Social Reality*. New York: Free Press.

————. 2010. *Making the Social World: The Structure of Human Civilization*. Oxford: Oxford University Press.

Sheehy, Paul. 2006. *The Reality of Social Groups, Ashgate New Critical Thinking in Philosophy*. Aldershot: Ashgate.

Stoutland, Frederick. 1997. Why are Philosophers of Action so Anti-Social? In *Commonality and Particularity in Ethics*, ed. L. Alanen, S. Heinamaa, and T. Wallgren. New York: St. Martin's Press.

————. 2008. The Ontology of Social Agency. *Analyse & Kritik* 30: 533–51.

Tollefsen, Deborah. 2002. Collective Intentionality and the Social Sciences. *Philosophy of the Social Sciences* 32(1): 25–50.

————. 2006. The Rationality of Collective Guilt. *Midwest Studies in Philosophy: Shared Intentions and Collective Responsibility* 30(1): 222–39.

————. 2007. Group Testimony. *Social Epistemology: A Journal of Knowledge, Culture, and Policy* 21(3): 299–311.

Tuomela, Raimo. 1992. Group Beliefs. *Synthese* 91: 285–318.

————. 2005. We-Intentions Revisited. *Philosophical Studies* 125: 327–69.

————. 2013. *Social Ontology: Collective Intentionality and Group Agents*. New York: Oxford University Press.

Tuomela, Raimo, and Kaarlo Miller. 1988. We-Intentions. *Philosophical Studies* 53(3): 367–89.

Velleman, David. 1997. How to Share an Intention. *Philosophy and Phenomenological Research* 57(1): 29–49.

Wertsch, J. V. 2009. Collective Memory. In *Memory in Mind and Culture*, ed. P. Boyer and J. V. Wertsch. Cambridge: Cambridge University Press.

Wilson, Robert A. 2001. Group-Level Cognition. *Philosophy of Science* 68(3): S262–S273.

# 20
# MICROFOUNDATIONS

## *Daniel Little*

A large amount of debate in the philosophy of social science is devoted to the question of how to understand the relations across levels of the social world. Are higher levels generated by lower levels? Are higher levels emergent with respect to lower levels? Are higher levels supervenient upon lower levels? It is promising to think that the idea of microfoundations can be invoked to trace out the relations among these various inter-level concepts. The call for microfoundations is an assertion that the lower levels of individual and social behavior are more fundamental than the higher levels. Consider Figure 20.1.

The diagram represents the social world as a laminated set of layers of entities, processes, powers, and laws. We might think of these levels as "individuals," "organization, value communities, social networks," "large aggregate institutions like states," etc. Entities at $L_2$ are composed of or caused by some set of entities and forces at $L_1$. Likewise $L_3$ and $L_4$. Arrows designated by $\Omega$ indicate microfoundations for $L_n$ facts based on $L_{n-1}$ facts. Diamond-tipped arrows indicate the relation of generative dependence from one level to another. Square-tipped lines indicate the presence of strongly emergent facts at the higher level relative to the lower level. The solid line ($L_4$) represents the possibility of a level of social fact that is not generatively dependent upon lower levels. The vertical ellipse at the right indicates the possibility of microfoundations narratives involving elements at different levels of the social world (individual and organizational, for example).

Here are preliminary definitions for several of the primary concepts mentioned here.

*Microfoundations* of facts in $L_2$ based on facts in $L_1$: accounts of the causal pathways through which entities, processes, powers, and laws of $L_1$ bring about specific outcomes in $L_2$. Microfoundations are small causal theories linking lower-level entities to higher-level outcomes.

*Generative dependence* of $L_2$ upon $L_1$: the entities, processes, powers, and laws of $L_2$ are generated by the properties and powers of level $L_1$ and nothing else. Alternatively, the entities, processes, powers, and laws of A suffice to generate all the properties of $L_2$. A full theory of $L_1$ suffices to derive the entities, processes, powers, and laws of $L_2$.

*Reducibility* of y to x: it is possible to provide a theoretical or formal derivation of the properties of y based solely on facts about x.

*Strong emergence* of properties in $L_2$ with respect to the properties of $L_1$: $L_2$ possesses some properties that do not depend wholly upon the properties of $L_1$.

*Weak emergence* of properties in $L_2$ with respect to the properties of $L_1$: $L_2$ possesses some properties for which we cannot (now or in the future) provide derivations based wholly upon the properties of $L_1$.

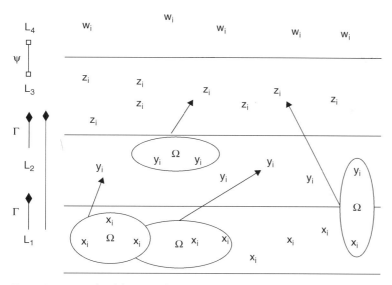

*Figure 20.1* Levels of the Social: Generation, Microfoundation, Emergence.

*Supervenience* of $L_2$ with respect to properties of $L_1$: all the properties of $L_2$ depend strictly upon the properties of $L_1$ and nothing else.

I will return to the question of how the concept of microfoundations permits us to discover the relations among these concepts in the final section.

## What Is a Microfoundation?

A microfoundation for a higher-level social fact is something like this:

An account of the mechanisms at the individual actor level (and perhaps at levels intermediate between actors and the current level—e.g. institutions) that work to create the structural and causal properties that we observe at the meso or macro levels.

A fully specified microfoundational account of a meso-level feature consists of an account that traces out (1) the features of the actors and (2) the characteristics of the action environment (including norms and institutions) which jointly lead to (3) the social structure or causal power we are interested in. A microfoundation specifies the individual-level mechanisms that lead to the macro- or meso-level social fact. This is the kind of account that Thomas Schelling illustrates so well in *Micromotives and Macrobehavior* (Schelling 1978). For example, the microfoundation for an observed failure to carry off a successful tiger hunt is the set of circumstances of recruitment through which eligible participants are enabled to "free-ride" on the participation of others.

The idea that hypotheses about social structures and forces require microfoundations has been around for at least forty years. Maarten Janssen's *New Palgrave* essay on microfoundations documents the history of the concept in economics (Janssen 2008). E. Roy Weintraub was among the first to emphasize the term within economics, with his *Microfoundations: The Compatibility of Microeconomics and Macroeconomics* (Weintraub 1979). During the early 1980s the contributors to analytical Marxism used the idea to attempt to give greater grip to some of Marx's key explanations (falling rate of profit, industrial reserve army, tendency towards crisis). Several such strategies are represented in John Roemer's *Analytical Marxism* (Roemer 1986). My own work (Little 1986, 1991) took up the topic of microfoundations in detail and relied on it as a basic tenet of social research strategy. The concept is consonant with Jon Elster's approach to social explanation in *Nuts and Bolts for the Social Sciences* (Elster 1989), though the term itself does not appear in this book or in the 2007 revised edition (Elster 2007). Most recently the literature surrounding analytical sociology has adopted an approach to social analysis and explanation that is equivalent to a methodological commitment to microfoundations (Hedström 2005; Hedström and Udehn 2009).

The concept of microfoundations relates to a specific understanding of social ontology. Social entities are understood to be compositional; they are assemblages constituted and maintained by the mentality and actions of individuals. So providing an account of the microfoundations of a structure or causal connection—say a paramilitary organization or of the causal connection between high interest rates and the incidence of alcohol abuse—is a specification of the composition of the social-level fact. It is a description of the agent-level relationships and patterns of behavior that cohere in such a way as to bring about the higher-level structure or causal relationship.

Key within the microfoundations approach is the question of the theory of the actor with which we want to work. Advocates for microfoundations have most often fallen within the broad confines of rational choice theory. This is particularly true of the efforts within economics to discover the microfoundations of macroeconomics in microeconomics. It is also true of the field of analytical sociology (Coleman 1990; Hedström 2005; Little 2012a). However, a microfoundations approach is not logically committed to a rational choice theory of the actor; it would be possible to make use of substantially richer assumptions about the agent's behavior within a microfoundational approach. In particular, the assumptions about agency associated with the new pragmatism are compatible with the microfoundational approach (Little 2014).

## The Appeal of the Microfoundations Approach

One reason why the microfoundations concept was appealing in application to Marx's social theories in the 1970s is the fact that great advances were being made in the field of collective action theory. Then-current interpretations of Marx's theories were couched at a highly structural level; but it seemed clear that it was necessary to identify the lower-level social processes through which class interest, class conflict, ideologies, or states emerged in concrete terms at the individual level. (This is one reason many found E. P. Thompson's *The Making of the English Working Class* [Thompson 1966] so enlightening.) Advances in game theory (assurance games, prisoners' dilemmas), Mancur Olson's demonstration of the gap between group interest and individual interest (Olson 1965), Thomas Schelling's brilliant unpacking of puzzling collective behavior onto underlying individual behavior (Schelling 1978), Russell Hardin's further exposition of collective action problems (Hardin 1982), and Robert Axelrod's discovery of the underlying individual behaviors that produce cooperation (Axelrod 1984) provided social scientists with new tools for reconstructing complex collective phenomena based on simple assumptions about individual actors. These provided concrete analytical resources that promised to help further explanations of complex social behavior. They provided a degree of confidence that important sociological questions could be addressed using a microfoundations framework.

There is another reason why the microfoundations idea was appealing—the ontological discipline it imposed with respect to theories and hypotheses at the higher level of social structure and causation. The requirement of providing microfoundations was an antidote to lazy thinking in the realm of social theory. Elster's critique of G. A. Cohen's functionalism in his treatment of Marx's theory of historical materialism is a case in point (Cohen 1978); Elster argued convincingly that a claim that "X exists because it brings about Y benefits for the system in which it exists" can only be supported if we can demonstrate the lower-level causal processes that allow the prospect of future system benefits to influence X (Elster 1982). Careless functionalism is unsupportable. More generally, the idea that there are social properties that are fundamental and emergent is flawed in the same way that vitalist biology is flawed. Biological facts are embedded within the material biochemistry of the cell and the gene, and claims that postulate a "something extra" over and above biochemistry involve magical thinking. Likewise, social facts are somehow or other embedded within and created by a substratum of individual action.

Part of the appeal of the concept of microfoundations derived from a very simple and logical way of understanding certain kinds of social explanation. This was the idea that slightly mysterious holistic claims about macro-level phenomena can often be given very clear explanations at the micro level. Marx's claim that capitalism is prone to crises arising from a tendency for the rate of profit to fall is a good example. Marx himself specifies the incentives facing the capitalist that lead him or her to make investment decisions aimed at increasing profits; he shows that these incentives lead to a substitution of fixed capital for variable capital (machines for labor); profits are created by labor; so the ratio of profit to total capital investment will tend to fall (Marx 1977 [1867]). This is a microfoundational explanation, in that it demonstrates the individual-level decision making and action that lead to the macro-level result.

This approach is appealing because it is a very natural way of formulating a core scientific question about the social world: "How does it work?" To provide microfoundations for a high-level social process or structure (for example, the falling rate of profit), we are looking for a set of mechanisms at the level of a set of actors within a set of social arrangements that result in the observed social-level fact. A call for microfoundations is a call for mechanisms at a lower level, answering the question, "How does this process work?"

These observations suggest that the microfoundations approach might serve as a general requirement about the nature of social explanation: explanations of social phenomena should always take the form of detailed accounts of the pathways that bring them about at the level of individual socially situated actors. This position suggests a research strategy along the lines of Coleman's boat (Coleman 1990; Little 2012b). However, careful reflection demonstrates that the principle should not be understood as a general prescription about social explanation. The microfoundations approach is a perfectly legitimate explanatory strategy; but it is only one approach out of many. So searching for microfoundations ought to be considered an explanatory heuristic rather than a methodological necessity. Microfoundational accounts represent one legitimate form of social explanation (micro-to-meso); but so do "lateral" accounts (meso-to-meso explanations) or even "descending" accounts (macro-to-meso explanations). So a search for microfoundations is only one among a number of valid explanatory approaches we might take. Analytical sociology is one legitimate approach to social research; but there are other legitimate approaches as well (Little 2012a).

## Microfoundations as Social Ontology

A microfoundation is a kind of causal story. By itself the concept has no methodological impli‐
cations. So what prescriptive ideas are commonly associated with the concept? The most basic
imperative associated with the microfoundations approach is ontological; it serves to constrain
the ways we conceptualize the social world. It can be understood as an ontological requirement
about acceptable social constructs; higher-level social constructs must be such that it is credible
that they are constituted by patterns of individual-level activity. This is a strategy of disaggre‐
gation, a "dissecting" strategy, and a non-threatening strategy of reduction. (William Wimsatt
takes much of the fury out of the debate over the scientific status of reduction advanced in
"Reductive Explanation: A Functional Account" [Wimsatt 1976].)

The emphasis on the need for microfoundations is a very logical implication of the position of
"ontological individualism"—the idea that social entities and powers depend upon facts about
individual actors in social interactions and nothing else (Epstein 2007). This is the view that
social entities, powers, and conditions are all constituted by the actions and thoughts of individ‐
ual human beings, and nothing else. The social world is constituted by the socially situated indi‐
viduals who make it up. Brian Epstein articulates this requirement in these terms: "Ontological
individualism is the thesis that facts about individuals exhaustively determine social facts" (187).
It is unsupportable to postulate disembodied social entities, powers, or properties for which we
cannot imagine an individual-level substrate. So it is natural to infer that claims about social
entities need to be accompanied in some fashion by an account of how they are embodied at the
individual level; and this is a call for microfoundations. This formulation makes it evident that
individualism and microfoundations are closely linked. When we provide microfoundations for
a given social entity or power, we show how the entity depends upon the thoughts and actions
of the individuals who make it up. Ontological individualism is distinct from methodological
individualism; it does not require a sharp distinction between purely individual characteristics
and social characteristics. (My own version of this idea is the notion of methodological local‐
ism; Little 2006.) (It should be noted that Epstein has mounted challenging arguments against
ontological individualism; Epstein 2007, 2015.)

So the ontological principle is that social entities are wholly fixed by the properties and
dynamics of the actions of the actors that constitute them. The requirement of microfounda‐
tions simply reproduces the ontological principle, ruling out ontologically impossible rela‐
tions among social entities. On this interpretation, the requirement of microfoundations
is not a requirement on what an explanation needs to look like; rather, it is a requirement
about certain beliefs we need to be justified in accepting when we advance a claim about
social entities. So the requirement of microfoundations is also valuable as heuristics for social
research: microfoundations provide intellectual resources that help social researchers decide
where to look for explanatory links, and what kinds of mechanisms might turn out to be
relevant.

Construed as an ontological principle for social theory, the microfoundations principle can be
formulated at a range of levels. The strong version of the principle requires that microfounda‐
tions should actually be provided for the chief social entities and causes in a given social theory.
An intermediate version requires that the researcher should have a fairly good sketch of what
those microfoundations look like, but doesn't need to actually provide them. The weak version
requires merely that the researcher should be confident that microfoundations exist for his or her
central social claims, but is not obligated to specify or sketch them.

Important challenges have emerged to the concept of microfoundations as an ontological condition on social theory and explanation. First, some sociologists have maintained that social entities are emergent in a strong sense, and have properties that cannot be derived from facts at the level of individuals (Elder-Vass 2010; Bhaskar 1975). Second, there is the view that some social entities have stable causal properties that do not require explicit microfoundations in order to be scientifically useful (Little 2012b). Third, there is the idea that there is a specifiable range of social facts that inherently lack individual-level microfoundations (Searle 2010). Fourth, there are theorists who doubt that the level of the intentional individual agent is the right level for grounding the microfoundations of all social entities and forces. These theorists sometimes argue that there are higher-level cognitive agents (e.g. organizations) which function as actors, and sometimes argue that it is necessary to go below the level of the deliberating human individual to the underlying cognitive and practical mental processes that underlie deliberation (Kaidesoja 2013). And finally, there is Brian Epstein's general critique of the assumptions of ontological individualism as a whole (Epstein 2007, 2015). Each of these positions raises significant problems for existing formulations of the ontology of microfoundations.

## Technical Practices

Let us now consider a few hard cases—social phenomena for which it may seem difficult to provide microfoundations. Let us begin with social practices such as etiquette or crafts.

Do social practices possess microfoundations at the local level? By a practice I mean such things as agricultural techniques, craft technologies, and customs of ordinary life—how to greet a neighbor, how to discipline one's children, how to decorate the home for a holiday, how to brew beer. A practice is a combination of concrete knowledge, a string of practical techniques, and a set of attitudes and judgments. Do social practices have "microfoundations"?

First, consider the social reality of a practice like wine-making. Pre-modern artisanal wine makers possess an ensemble of techniques through which they grow grapes and transform them into wine. These ensembles are complex and developed; different wine "traditions" handle the tasks of cultivation and fermentation differently, and the results are different as well (fine and ordinary burgundies, the sweet *Gewurztraminers* of Alsace versus Germany). The novice artisan does not reinvent the art of wine-making; instead, he/she learns the techniques and traditions of the elders. But at the same time, the artisan wine-maker may also introduce innovations into his/her practice—a wrinkle in the cultivation techniques, a different timing in the fermentation process, the introduction of a novel ingredient into the mix.

So the practice of Alsatian wine-making in the seventeenth century has a complex social reality. There are elements of knowledge and practice common among many wine growers in the region; there are differentiating changes over space and time; and the whole tradition has a history that extends backward in time and space. We might imagine that the geo-history of the wine-making traditions of Alsace would track the continuity, change, and transformation of the complex of practices across time and space—perhaps in the form of a set of dynamic maps illustrating the diffusion of the tradition, and the diffusion of variants and modifications, over space and time.

Now we can come back to the question of microfoundations. There are at least two aspects of this story that require microfoundations, corresponding to persistence and change: the social mechanisms of reproduction of the practice from generation to generation (persistence) and the social mechanisms of transmission of innovation across space and time (change). If we committed the error of reification and imagined that there is one unique and extended social practice that is "Alsatian wine-making wherever it occurs," we would have missed a crucial part of the story just told; there is *no* essential social practice of wine-making (or greeting a neighbor or decorating the house for Passover). Rather, there are bundles of bits of knowledge, assumptions, judgments, and behaviors that are embodied in the thoughts and actions of individuals at a certain time; and there are social mechanisms through which these bundles of knowledge are transmitted across generations and across space and time.

Seen from this point of view, the study of the persistence, change, and brachiation of a social practice or traditional technology is a window into patterns of human activity over time. If it were possible to trace the travel of an innovation in the fermentation process from its origin in a given village, along the circuits of the periodic markets, across a jump to a more distant place (by long-distance ship, for example) we would have a "marker" of the routes of social interaction and travel that were characteristic of seventeenth-century rural Alsace. The logic of this investigation would be similar to that pursued by historical linguistics, observing the gradual transformation of the syntax, phonology, or vocabulary of a language over several centuries and an extended region.

It is clear that the topic of microfoundations is an important question in this story. It invites us to ask several foundational questions:

- What are the social processes within which the complex social practice is embodied in human behavior and knowledge at a certain time?
- What are the social processes through which this body of knowledge is transmitted relatively intact from one generation to the next?
- What are the social mechanisms of transmission through which these clusters of human knowledge and their variations are conveyed across space and across social groups (from village to village)?

Much of the work of ethnography and micro-sociology goes into providing answers to questions like these. In general, it is clear that there are microfoundations for social practices, and that it is a valuable sociological project to uncover them.

## Do Social Structures Have Microfoundations?

In ordinary sociological theorizing, social structures have enduring properties that are largely independent of the individuals whom they encompass; they affect the behavior of individuals within them, and they affect the outcomes that individuals achieve through their efforts; and they are causally influential in large processes of social change and social stability. Workers enter a labor market that is largely independent of their own choices and actions. Structures are *things* with sufficient fixity over time and sufficient firmness to permit them to be regarded as social entities. Do social structures possess microfoundations at the level of socially situated individuals?

It is clear that social structures exist with reasonably stable properties and that they influence the behavior of individuals. Examples include the government of the state of California, the system of labor organization and representation in the United States, and the vertically organized corporation. In each case the social entity consists of a set of roles, regulations, and actors, along with a set of physical and financial resources, that confront the citizens and consumers who interact with them as objective realities. Developers go to the appropriate agencies for permits and conform to the requirements of state law and state and local inspectors. Criminals conform to the requirements of their organizations as well. Institutions and organizations regulate and constrain the lives of individuals.

It is also evident that structures are populated and constituted by individuals. So whatever causal powers the structures may have and whatever persistent features they possess must somehow be embodied in the actions and states of mind of those individuals. The effects of the structure on individuals and other social entities and processes depend on the coordinated actions of individuals within the structure. Individual actions within the structure are constrained by the meanings, rules, meanings, and enforcement mechanisms that exist within the structure. And external individual actions and social arrangements are affected by the knowledge and representations that these external players have of the workings of the structure. Structures rest upon microfoundations. And there must be specific processes of inculcation, coordination, and enforcement through which the required forms of action transpire at the level of the actors. Anthony Giddens puts the point this way:

> The term 'social structure' thus tends to include two elements, not clearly distinguished from one another: the patterning of interaction, as implying relations between actors or groups; and the continuity of interaction in time.
>
> (Giddens 1979, 62)

Further, structures are plastic. Zygmunt Bauman makes this point in a particularly provocative way by insisting the social world is "liquid" (Bauman 2000). The metaphor overstates the case, since many structures have significantly more stability than the image of liquidity implies; but the fundamental notion that social structures and other entities are subject to change is certainly a valid one. We can observe the drift in the functioning and roles of institutions in every aspect of life—political, economic, educational, and ideological.

Several fundamental kinds of questions must be answered when we contemplate the idea of structures and organizations possessing persistent properties over time. First is the question of the conformant behavior of role players within the organization at various points of time. What are the microfoundations of compliance? Individuals do not conform simply because the employee handbook specifies that they should. Rather, they need to be incentivized, trained, motivated, supervised, and disciplined, in order to bring about the forms of orderly behavior that the organization requires. And this means that an organization depends on the existence of roles presenting incentives and constraints for supervisors and trainers as well.

Second is a larger question of accounting for the stability of the rules and roles themselves. What factors work against entropy and the conflicting interests of various internal actors, each of which tends to undermine the stability of the rules and roles? Are there forms of weak homeostasis that work to restore a social structure in face of minor deviations? The "entropic" forces that should be expected to push organizations towards incessant change are fairly obvious; most evidently, individuals in strategic positions within an organization often have interests that are well served by adapting, reconceptualizing, or disregarding the rules. (Michel Crozier and Erhard Friedberg make this point in their analysis of organizations as strategic site; Crozier and Friedberg 1980.) So a large question for the theory of organizations and institutions is that of stability. What are the features of an organization in an environment that lends stability to its current constitution? Kathleen Thelen considers both aspects of this question in much of her work (Mahoney and Thelen 2010; Thelen 2004).

## Coleman's "House of Cards"

James Coleman offers a skeptical position on the question of the reality of social structures (Coleman 1990), and his analysis contributes to a better understanding of the microfoundations that social structures may have. Coleman advocates for a view of research and theory in sociology that emphasizes the actions of situated purposive individuals, and he deliberately avoids the idea of persistent social structures within which actors make choices. His focus is on the relations among actors and the higher-level patterns that arise from these relations. He refers to a social structure in these terms: "The structure is like a house of cards, with extensive interdependence among the different relations of which it is composed" (43–44).

Here Coleman provides a sketch of how we might conceive of a social ontology that suffices without reference to structures as independent entities. We are advised to think of social structures and norms as no more than coordinated and mutually reinforcing patterns of individual behavior. The emphasis is on individual behavior within the context of the actions of others. As he puts the point later in the book, "The elementary actor is the wellspring of action, no matter how complex are the structures through which action takes place" (503).

Anyone who accepts that social entities and forces rest upon microfoundations must agree that something like Coleman's recursive story of self-reinforcing patterns of behavior must be correct. But this does not imply that higher-level social structures do not possess stable causal properties nonetheless. The "house-of-cards" pattern of interdependency between auditor and worker, or between server and client, helps to explain how the stable patterns of the organization are maintained; but it does not render superfluous the idea that the structure itself has causal properties or powers. The microfoundations thesis does not entail reductionism. (David Lewis provides a different approach to social interdependency in his analysis of convention. He shows how conventions emerge from intentional behavior at the individual level; *Convention: A Philosophical Study* [Lewis 1969].)

## Reformulation

It is possible to summarize the theory of microfoundations as a philosophy of social science into a series of assertions:

1. All social forces, powers, structures, processes, and laws (social features) are ultimately constituted by mechanisms at the level of individual actors (*ontological principle*).
2. A description of the microfoundations of a social entity S is an account of the circumstances and individual mechanisms that bring about patterns of individual activity resulting in the properties of S.
3. When we assert the reality or causal powers of a social entity, we need to be confident that there are microfoundations that cause this social entity to have the properties we attribute to it (*microfoundations principle*).

   a. Strong version: we must provide a credible statement of the microfoundations.

   b. Intermediate version: we must have a back-of-envelope sketch of possible microfoundations.

   c. Weak version: we must have confidence that there are microfoundations, but we do not have to have any specific ideas about what they are.

4. Providing microfoundations for a given social outcome is a particularly direct form of explanation of the outcome's properties (*explanatory principle*).

Taking these assertions together, this position amounts to a fairly specific view of the social world and the ways in which we can best investigate it. It is a specific orientation to social research, more at home with analytical sociology than Durkheimian holism. But broad swathes of sociological theory can be understood as being compatible with the requirements of the microfoundations approach, including Margaret Archer's theory of morphogenesis (Archer 2013, Archer 2014).

Above we noted that there are a number of inter-related concepts used to describe the relations of higher-level and lower-level social entities. The question of the availability of microfoundations for social facts can be understood to be central to all the other issues: reducibility, emergence, generativity, and supervenience. There are several positions that we can take with respect to the availability of microfoundations for higher-level social facts.

1. If we have convincing reason to believe that all social facts possess microfoundations at a lower level (known or unknown) then we know that the social world supervenes upon the micro level; strong emergence is ruled out; weak emergence is true only so long as some microfoundations remain unknown; and higher-level social facts are generatively dependent upon the micro level.

2. If we take a pragmatic view of the social sciences and conclude that any given stage of knowledge provides information about only a subset of possible microfoundations for higher-level facts, then we are at liberty to take the view that each level of social ontology is at least weakly emergent from lower levels—basically, the point of view advocated under the banner of "relative explanatory autonomy" (Little 2012b). This also appears to be roughly the position taken by Herbert Simon (Simon 1996 [1969]).

3. If we believe that it is impossible in principle to fully specify the microfoundations of some social facts, then weak emergence is true; supervenience is false; and generativity is false. (For example, we might believe this to be true because of the difficulty of modeling and calculating a sufficiently large and complex domain of units.) This is the situation that Fodor believes to be the case for many of the special sciences.

4. If we have reason to believe that some higher-level facts simply do not possess microfoundations at a lower level at all, then strong emergence is true; the social world is not generatively dependent upon the micro world; and the social world does not supervene upon the micro world.

In other words, each of the concepts of supervenience, reduction, emergence, and generative dependence can be defined in terms of the availability or unavailability of microfoundations for some or all of the facts at a higher level based on facts at the lower level. Strong emergence and generative dependence turn out to be logical contraries.

# References

Archer, Margaret S., ed. 2013. *Social Morphogenesis*. New York: Springer.

———. 2014. *Late Modernity: Trajectories towards Morphogenic Society*. Cham and New York: Springer.

Axelrod, Robert M. 1984. *The Evolution of Cooperation*. New York: Basic Books.

Bauman, Zygmunt. 2000. *Liquid Modernity*. Cambridge and Malden, MA: Polity Press/Blackwell.

Bhaskar, Roy. 1975. *A Realist Theory of Science*. Leeds: Leeds Books.

Cohen, G. A. 1978. *Karl Marx's Theory of History: A Defence*. Princeton, NJ: Princeton University Press.

Coleman, James S. 1990. *Foundations of Social Theory*. Cambridge, MA: Harvard University Press.

Crozier, Michel, and Erhard Friedberg. 1980. *Actors and Systems: The Politics of Collective Action*. Chicago: University of Chicago Press.

Elder-Vass, David. 2010. *The Causal Power of Social Structures: Emergence, Structure and Agency*. Cambridge: Cambridge University Press.

Elster, Jon. 1982. "Marxism, Functionalism, and Game Theory." *Theory and Society* 11: 453–82.

———. 1989. *Nuts and Bolts for the Social Sciences*. Cambridge: Cambridge University Press.

———. 2007. *Explaining Social Behavior: More Nuts and Bolts for the Social Sciences*. Cambridge and New York: Cambridge University Press.

Epstein, Brian. 2007. "Ontological Individualism Reconsidered." *Synthese* 166(1): 187–213.

———. 2015. *The Ant Trap: Rebuilding the Foundations of the Social Sciences*. Oxford Studies in Philosophy of Science. New York: Oxford University Press.

Giddens, Anthony. 1979. *Central Problems in Social Theory: Action, Structure and Contradiction in Social Analysis*. Berkeley: University of California Press.

Hardin, Russell. 1982. *Collective Action*. Baltimore: The Johns Hopkins University Press.

Hedström, Peter. 2005. *Dissecting the Social: On the Principles of Analytical Sociology*. Cambridge and New York: Cambridge University Press.

Hedström, Peter, and Lars Udehn. 2009. "Analytical Sociology and Theories of the Middle Range." In *The Oxford Handbook of Analytical Sociology*, ed. Peter Hedström and Peter Bearman. Oxford: Oxford University Press, 25–47.

Janssen, Maarten C. W. 2008. "Microfoundations." In *The New Palgrave Dictionary of Economics*, ed. Steven N. Durlauf and Lawrence E. Blume. London: Palgrave Macmillan.

Kaidesoja, Tuukka. 2013. "Overcoming the Biases of Microfoundationalism: Social Mechanisms and Collective Agents." *Philosophy of the Social Sciences* 43(3): 301–22.

Lewis, David K. 1969. *Convention: A Philosophical Study*. Cambridge, MA: Harvard University Press.

Little, Daniel. 1986. *The Scientific Marx*. Minneapolis: University of Minnesota Press.

———. 1991. *Varieties of Social Explanation: An Introduction to the Philosophy of Social Science*. Boulder, CO: Westview Press.

———. 2006. "Levels of the Social." In *Handbook for Philosophy of Anthropology and Sociology*, ed. Stephen Turner and Mark Risjord. Amsterdam and New York: Elsevier Publishing, 343–71.

———. 2012a. "Analytical Sociology and the Rest of Sociology." *Sociologica* 1/2012. Accessed June 2, 2014. www.sociologica.mulino.it/doi/10.2383/36894.

———. 2012b. "Explanatory Autonomy and Coleman's Boat." *Theoria* 74: 137–52.

———. 2014. "Actor-Centered Sociology and the New Pragmatism." In *Individualism, Holism, Explanation and Emergence*, ed. Julie Zahle and Finn Collin. Dordrecht, London, and New York: Springer, 55–75.

Mahoney, James, and Kathleen Ann Thelen. 2010. *Explaining Institutional Change: Ambiguity, Agency, and Power*. Cambridge and New York: Cambridge University Press.

Marx, Karl. 1977 [1867]. *Capital*. Vol. 1. New York: Vintage Books.

Olson, Mancur. 1965. *The Logic of Collective Action: Public Goods and the Theory of Groups*. Cambridge, MA: Harvard University Press.

Roemer, John. 1986. *Analytical Marxism*. Cambridge: Cambridge University Press.

Schelling, Thomas C. 1978. *Micromotives and Macrobehavior*. New York: Norton.

Searle, John R. 2010. *Making the Social World: The Structure of Human Civilization*. Oxford and New York: Oxford University Press.

Simon, Herbert A. 1996 [1969]. *The Sciences of the Artificial*, 3rd edn. Cambridge, MA: MIT Press.

Thelen, Kathleen Ann. 2004. *How Institutions Evolve: The Political Economy of Skills in Germany, Britain, the United States, and Japan.* Cambridge Studies in Comparative Politics. Cambridge and New York: Cambridge University Press.

Thompson, E. P. 1966. *The Making of the English Working Class.* New York: Vintage Books.

Weintraub, E. 1979. *Microfoundations.* Cambridge: Cambridge University Press.

Wimsatt, William C. 1976. "Reductive Explanation: A Functional Account." In *PSA 1974*, ed. R. S. Cohen, C. A. Hooker, A. C. Michalos, and J. W. Van Evra. Dordrecht: Springer Netherlands, 671–710.

# 21

# SOCIAL ONTOLOGY

## Brian Epstein

The social sciences are unusual, as compared to the other sciences, with respect to how they investigate the objects they work on. Chemists, for instance, take it to be an ordinary part of the job to figure out the building blocks of molecules. Cell biologists spend a good chunk of their time investigating the parts of cells, and climatologists the composition of atmosphere, oceans, and landmasses. It is a common and well-established task for scientists to work out the building blocks of objects and phenomena. Social scientists, on the other hand, tend to skip this task: with few exceptions, publications are devoted to models and empirical investigations, without inquiring into building blocks. Occasionally a brief controversy will flare up about the nature of social entities—the topic that is now starting to be called "social ontology"—but it has received little attention in the course of scientific practice.

For much of the twentieth century, work on the nature of the social world was stifled by the widespread rejection of metaphysics. Behaviorists, for instance, argued that the proper goal of the social sciences was to systematize observable human behavior. This perspective was a product of three complementary ideas. Inherited from logical positivism was the idea that the only meaningful statements are those that are observable, testable, or verifiable. From behaviorist psychology came the idea that what is observable about humans is their outward behaviors. And inherited from nineteenth-century social science was the assumption that the social sciences are a kind of psychology of society, that their topic is the mind of the group, which is built out of the minds of the individual members of the group. Together, these ideas led to a social science devoted to generalizing about the behaviors of individual people in large numbers. And they implied that there is not much to investigate about the social world: we already know that it is the aggregate of individual behaviors.

Even among the opponents of behaviorism, it has often remained more important to establish anti-metaphysical credentials than to take social objects seriously. Perhaps as a consequence of anxieties about whether the social sciences are appropriately scientific, the tendency to "operationalize" concepts in the social sciences lingers today, long after it disappeared from broader scientific practice. And in the philosophy of social science, scant attention has been paid to ontological questions. Jarvie (2011) has cataloged the topics addressed in fourteen anthologies in the field from 1953 through 2007, finding that questions of ontology were confined only to a single topic—individualism versus holism. And even this topic only shows up in a third of the anthologies.

The situation may now be poised for change. Social scientists increasingly recognize that their models continue to be built on highly idealized and questionable pictures of the social world, pictures that were locked in place in the 1950s with little change since. Standard models in economics, for instance, have long treated firms and institutions as black boxes. In recent years, it has become apparent that we need to develop more sophisticated pictures of these in order to model the economy, so theorists are increasingly concerned with their nature. Other momentum is coming from philosophers. The last quarter of the twentieth century saw a renaissance in metaphysics, with rapid advances in theories of causation, modality, space and time, objects and events, personal identity, individual agency, and more. Initially, the social was largely left out of these philosophical inquiries, but in the last few years it has become clear that the tools of metaphysics can help untangle longstanding puzzles about the social world, and conversely that investigating social phenomena is particularly fruitful for advancing metaphysics.

In this chapter, I address topics in recent social ontology that are most closely connected to the social sciences. I start in section 1 with a brief discussion of the different things theorists mean when they examine how the social world is "built." In section 2, I take up individualism versus holism, starting with traditional debates and then turning to recent contributions from metaphysics. Section 3 addresses theories of how social kinds and categories are set up or "anchored." Sections 4 and 5 discuss specific problems in the ontology of the social world. Section 4 addresses work on organizations and institutions. And section 5 introduces the collective intentionality literature.

# 1 Building the Social World

The term "ontology" has traditionally been understood as the study of which objects exist (Quine 1948). This aligns with the traditional way of thinking of the project of the nature of the social world: to assess whether social entities are "fundamental" or else are derivative in some way. For instance, some theorists argue that individual people are the fundamental building blocks in the domain of the social sciences, and the social world is built of individual people. Others argue that social entities are fundamental in some way: that they are irreducible to individuals, or that they operate autonomously of individuals, or that individual people are themselves constructed out of social parts. Still others advocate different building blocks altogether for the social, such as social practices, or routines, or collective attitudes, or ecosystems.

These are all important to examine, but it is increasingly clear in metaphysics that it is difficult to resolve these arguments, or even to make good sense of them, without addressing a different question first. What is meant by "building" the world in the first place (Bennett 2011)? If one argues that social entities are "built out of" individual people, or conversely, that individuals are constructed from the social, how are these to be understood? One way of thinking of "building" is as composition or the putting together of parts, as a house is built out of bricks or lumber. But this is not the only way we can conceive of building: for instance, if we are to make sense of the social construction of the individual, it seems unlikely that we should think of it as an assembly from parts.

I propose that we sharply distinguish two kinds of building to make sense of what we are talking about when we investigate the social world, and its relation to other parts of the world. One kind of building, "grounding," I draw from recent work in metaphysics. The other, "anchoring," I use as a new label for a kind of building that has been implicitly discussed in the literature for a long time but without being clearly distinguished (Epstein 2015).

To see the difference between these two kinds of building, it is helpful to think about two different paradigmatic types of social entities. Think on the one hand about a crowd of people, or about a bustling bazaar. And think on the other hand about a dollar bill, or about the spaces marked out in a parking lot, or a piece of land that is my property. All of these are "social things." There is, however, an obvious difference between crowds and bazaars on the one hand and dollars, parking spaces, and property on the other. Crowds and bazaars have individual people as their parts. They are composed of people. A bazaar at least partly consists of people transacting with other people; individuals are parts of the bazaar much as bricks are parts of a house. Dollar bills, on the other hand, do not have people as parts at all. Among the parts of a dollar bill are paper fibers and patterns of ink. People of course play an important role in "building" dollar bills, but the way people are the building blocks of dollars is different from the way they are the building blocks of crowds.

Thinking about the role of people in making up a crowd helps identify one sense of "building": the people are what the crowd is made of, or composed of. Facts about the crowd are, at least in part, facts about the arrangements of people. Facts about the crowd are *grounded* by facts about the arrangements of people. For dollars, on the other hand, the bodily and mental states of people play a very different role. They are part of an answer to the question: *what sets up these pieces of paper with certain characteristics and histories to be dollar bills? What puts the category* dollar bill *in place the way it is?* The role of people in "building" dollar bills is not to be parts or components. Instead, people are involved in setting up the way facts about dollars are grounded. Here, facts about people are part of what *anchor* the category dollar bill.

Once we have made the distinction, we see that we can investigate both grounding and anchoring for *all* social entities. We can ask questions about grounding: What grounds the fact that I have a dollar in my pocket? What grounds the fact that I own that piece of property? What grounds the fact that there is a crowd in the plaza? And we can ask questions about anchoring: what anchors the conditions for something to be a dollar? What anchors the conditions for something to be my property? What anchors the conditions for something to be a crowd?

With the distinction between grounding and anchoring, it becomes apparent that some theories attempt to answer questions about grounding, and some about anchoring. Work in social ontology can be divided into these two inquiries. In the following sections, I focus on the portions of each of these that are most closely connected to the practice of the social sciences.

## 2  The Individualism–Holism Debates

The longest-running debate over the nature of the social world has been between holism—the view that there are real social entities that are in some way autonomous or independent of individual people—and individualism—the view that all social facts are exhaustively determined by facts about individual people. For many years, these debates were tangled up by confusion of questions about the *ontology of the social* from questions about *methodology and explanation* in the social sciences. Watkins (1953), for instance, argues that social phenomena are built entirely out of the actions of individual people, and with no additional argument concludes that social scientists should *explain* social phenomena in terms of individuals. Other theorists, such as Popper (1962) and Coleman (1990), make slightly more modest claims about individualistic explanation of the social: they hold that the appropriate way to perform social explanation is to fix the institutional context and then within that context to ensure that all explanations are in terms of individuals. But they too mix up ontological arguments with explanatory ones: they take their conclusions about the building blocks of social phenomena to be equivalent to conclusions about how explanation should be performed. In recent years, those confusions have been largely cleared up, but important problems remain. Most importantly, it is now being questioned whether the dichotomy between individualism and holism is even the correct one to make.

Philosophers in the 1970s and 1980s made key advances in understanding how to formulate claims about the relation between different "levels" of entities. Much of this work was done in connection with debates over dualism in the philosophy of mind, with philosophers of social science quickly following their lead. In the philosophy of mind, Putnam (1967), Fodor (1974), Davidson (1980), and Kim (1978) laid the foundations for "nonreductive physicalism." This view effectively divides questions of the nature of mental states from questions about how to explain mental phenomena. Nonreductive physicalism holds that mental states are nothing more than physical states (and explains how to understand this). But it also holds that there may be no way to explain mental phenomena in terms of physical laws. The reason is that *types* or *kinds* of mental states cannot necessarily be identified with corresponding *types* or *kinds* of physical states. It is not that mental states are non-physical, but just that their natural categorizations do not line up with those at the physical level. Nonreductive physicalism, in short, gives a way to understand the mind "nonmystically," even for those who are skeptical about the reductive explanation of mental phenomena in terms of physics or neuroscience.

The key tool developed by nonreductive physicalists was the "supervenience" relation. Supervenience is a relation between two sets of properties, and is typically applied between a high-level set of properties like mental properties and a low-level set of properties like neural properties. The high-level properties supervene on the low-level properties just in case there can't be any changes in the high-level properties without there also being changes in the low-level properties. As applied to the mind, mental properties supervene on physical properties just in case any changes in mental properties (such as forming a thought or coming to perceive something) must be accompanied by changes in physical properties. (On supervenience, see McLaughlin and Bennett 2005.)

This strategy was quickly taken up by philosophers of social science to account for the relation between social entities and individual people and their interactions. Macdonald and Pettit (1981) describe what we might call "nonreductive *individualism*": the thesis that social entities are nothing more than individual people and their interactions, even though it may be impossible to identify types or kinds of social entities with corresponding types or kinds of individualistic entities. Following the philosophers of mind, they and others understood nonreductive individualism in terms of supervenience. Social properties supervene on individualistic properties: any changes in social properties must be accompanied by changes in individualistic properties. To many, this has seemed to be the best of both sides of the debate. There is no need to take on a worrisome ontology of social wholes, thinking that they somehow occupy a separate sphere of existence from individuals. On this view, it is possible that social types or kinds are indispensable to explanation, even though they do not have a separate reality. (For a recent statement of this, see Sawyer 2002.)

In recent years, this approach has begun to show cracks, some minor and some serious. It turns out to be important just how we understand the supervenience relation: there are many different varieties of supervenience, and not all of them are even good candidates. Currie (1984) already pointed out that only a very weak version of supervenience—"global supervenience"— plausibly holds between the social and the individualistic, and that stronger varieties do not. And philosophers have worried in recent years about just how useful global superveni-ence is (Sider 1999; Shagrir 2002; Bennett 2004).

Another worry is that some philosophers have argued that the best-of-both-worlds position is actually incoherent. Kim (1998), for instance, argues that supervenience entails reducibility. His argument is specifically in the philosophy of mind, but the argument is easily applied to the social: if correct, his argument would rule out nonreductive physicalism, and a similar argument would rule out nonreductive individualism in social science.

It also has recently become clear that supervenience of any sort is only a rough approximation of what we want to say when we assert that one set of properties is "nothing more than" another. To say that the social supervenes on the individualistic means only that they co-vary in certain ways. But we do not just want co-variation: we want to say that the individualistic *exhaustively determines* the social, or that the social *ontologically depends on* the individualistic. Recent work on the relation between entities at different levels tends to treat supervenience as a diagnostic tool for the presence of a more intimate determination or dependence relation. Recently, theo-rists have proposed that "determination" and "dependence" ought to be understood in terms of a more fundamental metaphysical relation: the grounding relation (Fine 1995; Correia 2005). To say that fact G grounds fact F is to say that G is the metaphysical explanation for F (Schaffer 2009; Rosen 2010; Audi 2012; Fine 2012). Thus if the debate over individualism and holism is to get clearer, this strategy suggests that it be recast in terms of grounding. (For more detailed discussion of these issues, see Epstein 2015.)

Even more serious are worries about individualism. *Which properties are the individualistic ones?* Over the last several generations, many proposals have been floated regarding how to under-stand individuals and their properties, for them to serve as the building blocks of the social (see Udehn 2001 for an interesting book-length presentation). Epstein (2009, 2015) challenges the workability of any of these in principle. This argument grants the starting assumptions of individualism—that social entities are not ontologically fundamental, and that we can separate the individualistic properties from the non-individualistic ones. But it argues that even if we reject holism, still there is no plausible interpretation of individualism that makes it correct. (See Little 2015 for recent discussion of this.)

Other theorists do not even grant the individualist this much, but instead reject individualism on more radical grounds. An extensive tradition, for instance, argues for the social construction of the self (Foucault 1978; Vygotsky 1978; Bakhtin 1981; Gergen and Davis 1985; Taylor 1989). Davis (2003) argues a version of this from the perspective of economics: that the conception of the individual in economic theory is a social one. A related but slightly different argument is to deny the separation between individualistic facts and the social ones. In other words, one strat-egy for the social constructionist is to retain the separation between social and individualistic facts, and reverse the order of dependence, so that the individual ontologically depends on the social. A different strategy is to deny the distinction.

Although these debates have been going on for years, the recent approaches present new avenues for clarifying and rethinking them. Many theorists continue to defend or assume various sorts of individualism, and work needs to be done in clarifying and assessing these arguments. In addition, there is much work to be done on the connections between these ontological issues and the methodology of social science. Even if we do clearly separate questions of ontology from those of explanation, there still are links between the two: a natural way to model social phenomena is to model its building blocks and the causal networks of which they are a part. Many social scientists advocate the search for "microfoundations" and other individualistic methodologies (Lucas 1976; Kydland and Prescott 1982; Coleman 1987; Lucas et al. 1989; Cook 1991; Rizvi 1994). Clarifying the ontology of the social and the relation between ontology and explanatory methods may have a bearing on these programs.

## 3 Approaches to Anchoring

The traditional individualism/holism debates address the "building blocks" of the social in the sense of grounding. Are social facts exhaustively grounded by individualistic facts? They do not address the other general question regarding the "building" of the social world: namely, to explain what puts in place the social categories we have. There is, however, an extensive tradition that addresses this question. These are the theories of *anchoring*.

Most theories of anchoring social categories take a common approach: that social categories are a product of human cognition. Ways that people think or believe, or other cognitive states we have, are the things that put social categories in place. I will describe some versions of this, and then turn to alternative accounts of anchoring that reject the idea that anchors are typically cognitive states.

John Searle's theory (Searle 1995, 2010) is the most familiar to philosophers. The subject matter of Searle's theory is the creation of entities like money, corporations, private property, and national boundaries. Somewhat oddly, he calls these "institutional facts"; as he uses it, the term refers to what are more typically understood as social objects or social kinds. His account, in brief, is this: institutional facts exist in virtue of the community's *collective acceptance* of *constitutive rules*, which is invariably generated by *declarative speech acts*. Constitutive rules consist of the assignment of certain kinds of powers, such as rights and obligations, to objects. Collective acceptance is an aggregate mental state of members of the community. According to Searle, for community C to collectively accept rule R is for all the members of the community individually to have the "we-accept" attitude toward R. (See below for more on collective attitudes.) And declarative speech acts are linguistic utterances the performance of which has an effect on the world. When a minister declares a couple to be married, the minister produces a we-attitude in the members of the congregation to the effect that couple has a particular status, i.e. certain rights and responsibilities.

In all the details of Searle's account, it is important not to overlook his central thesis, which is about the sorts of facts that are the metaphysical anchors of the social world; i.e. the facts that put social categories in place. According to Searle, the social world exists in virtue of the community's ongoing collective acceptance of a rule. His theory is an instance of a *cognitive theory of anchoring*: social categories are put in place exclusively by human cognitive states. Moreover, his particular version is that they are put in place by a strikingly uniform sort of cognitive state. That is, that all members of the community we-accept the rule. Searle's version is innovative in the sense that he puts collective attitudes at the center of the existence of the social world, while most other cognitive theories of anchoring do not draw on collective attitudes. But it is very traditional in the sense that his theory of anchoring makes high demands of individual cognitive states, and requires a high degree of uniformity.

Many theories of social categories in anthropology and sociology provide different cognitive theories of anchoring. Mid-century structuralism, for instance, is another clear example. Lévi-Strauss (1963, 1966) discusses systems of kinship, totemic classification, caste systems, and other sets of social categories. Each of these, according to Lévi-Strauss, is a product of symbolic structures in the minds of society members. These structures are unconscious, much as our knowledge of the rules of linguistic syntax are unconscious. It is not necessary, on this view, that any member of society has attitudes toward categories or rules, or has made declarations regarding them. Nonetheless, the basis of social categorization is still wholly cognitive. It is a matter of mental structures.

A glimmer that anchoring may not be an entirely cognitive matter comes in certain post-structuralist approaches to the social. The sociologist Pierre Bourdieu, for instance, puts forward a "theory of practice," which may be in part regarded as a theory of the anchors of social categories (Bourdieu 1977, 1990). Practices, for Bourdieu, are embodied routines in the social world. These routines include cognitive states among their building blocks, but also include patterns of physical action and infrastructure in the world that encode our systems of meaning and understanding. If it is a community's practices that anchors the social categories for that community, then those anchors are more than just cognitive states. However, other features of Bourdieu's view make it difficult to say whether it can genuinely be regarded as a non-cognitive theory of anchoring. In particular, a centerpiece of his account is what he calls the "habitus," which is the community's internalization of the patterns of practice in that community. How mentalistic Bourdieu's theory ends up being depends on how we interpret the nature and role of the habitus in setting up social categories. Other theories of practice may be better candidates for non-cognitive theories of anchoring. Theories of "structuration" (Giddens 1984; Sewell 2005), for instance, make it clearer how individual practices are intertwined with features of our constructed environments in setting up social institutions.

A different promising strategy for incorporating external facts in anchoring comes from work on kinds in the philosophy of science. This work largely focuses on biological and chemical kinds, but has been applied to social kinds as well, and is suggestive of other strategies that could be developed. Particularly innovative is the work of Ruth Millikan. Millikan (1984) develops a naturalistic approach to the notion of biological functions and biological categories. According to Millikan, kinds are present where there are lineages or families of objects that are copied or reproduced. The reason that explains why their characteristics are reproduced is their "Proper function." In her account, then, what sets up a kind includes the actual tokens, their features, and the factors that explain their reproduction. Millikan's account does not need to involve any cognition at all. In certain cases, tokens of social kinds may be reproduced because of human intentions, but intentions or other cognitive states need not be part of the story at all (Millikan 1999, 2005). Richard Boyd also advances a non-cognitive theory of kinds (Boyd 1999b, 1999a). On his theory, it is the presence of a "homeostatic mechanism," rather than a history of reproduction, that figures into grouping a set of characteristics into a kind. Like Millikan's theory, Boyd's accommodates a potential role for cognitive states in his mechanism but does not require it.

## 4 Institutions and Organizations

In this section and the next, I turn to a couple of specific applications of social ontology and their connections to the social sciences. Herbert Simon imagines a Martian gazing down on Earth with a telescope that could pick out social structures. He comments that the dominant features of the landscape the Martian would observe would not be markets or nations, but organizations (Simon 1991). Organizations and institutions have long been a central topic in sociology, and have had a recent renaissance in the economics literature as well. Yet to date, they have largely been neglected by philosophers, particularly in the English-speaking world. This has left it largely to social scientists to theorize about the nature of institutions and organizations. These questions, however, should be an area of interest for people working in social ontology; they offer a potentially fruitful point of connection between philosophy and the social sciences.

The terms 'institution' and 'organization' denote somewhat vague categories. In general, institutions are understood to be large-scale and general features of a society, including things as varied as units of government, systems of contracting and enforcement, marriage and family structures, educational systems, and more. Organizations are understood as either a subset of institutions involving groups of people organized into cohesive units of some sort or else as particular instances. I will discuss just one important family of theories: those based on the idea that institutions and organizations are the rational solutions to strategic problems of interaction and coordination. These views are not exhaustive; very different approaches to firms and institutions come from sociology and political science, including approaches that see institutions as fundamentally arising from social norms, or else from cultural structures. Most influential in economics is the "New Institutional Economics" program, spearheaded by Douglas North, Oliver Williamson, Elinor Ostrom, and others. Among the topics examined in this literature is the theory of firms or corporations. The literature was pioneered by Ronald Coase (Coase 1937, 1960), in which he examined the question of why firms exist at all. Firms are mid-sized organizations governed by authority, within the market as a whole. Why are there these "islands of conscious power"? Why not just use market price mechanisms to assign value to the contributions of individuals to production? Coase argued that the problem arises from the fact that the use of the price mechanism comes with costs. It is costly to discover prices, to negotiate contracts, and there are costs associated with the difficulty of forecasting the proper duration of contracts. If it were costless to perform transactions between individual actors, Coase argued, then it would be inefficient to organize in firms. But since transactions are costly, organizing into firms helps minimize these costs and increase overall efficiency.

Williamson took up and popularized this topic in the 1970s with theories of how various institutional structures such as markets, hierarchies, multidivisional corporations, and alliances solve different problems of transaction costs (Williamson 1979, 1981, 1996). Williamson took from Herbert Simon the idea of "bounded rationality," arguing that these bounds gave rise to key sources of transaction costs, in particular to the incompleteness of contracts. (That is, to the fact that no contract can foresee or specify all eventualities that may occur.) Firms, Williamson argued, have different authority structures than markets. Conflicts in the marketplace sometimes appeal to the court system. But disputes internal to a firm are rarely regarded as being subject to judicial adjudication outside the firm. Rather, managerial authority is a sort of private legal institution (Williamson 2002; Foss and Klein 2008).

Another group of theorists developed related thoughts about the role of firms but arrived at a different conclusion: they rejected Coase's claim that there is a genuine line between firms and markets altogether. Alchian and Demsetz argue that there is no significant difference between authority mechanisms and price mechanisms for allocating resources: a conceptually similar process takes place whether one decides to fire one's employee or to "fire" one's grocer (Alchian and Demsetz 1972, 777). Jensen and Meckling assert that the "the private enterprise or firm is simply one form of legal fiction which serves as a nexus for contracting relationships" (Jensen and Meckling 1976, 311). This view has come to be known as the "nexus of contracts" view of the firm.

The "new property rights" view is a related approach to the nature of the firm that shares much with Williamson, especially regarding the incompleteness of contracts. But instead of regarding the role of the firm to be in resolving disputes beyond the bounds of contracts, this approach regards the firm as generating authority through the possession of property ownership rights. A firm owner has power over the assets of the firm, so can control employee behavior through the threat of withdrawing access to those assets. The firm, on this view, is a collection of property rights (Grossman and Hart 1986; Hart and Moore 1990). And a fourth view of the firm is the "resource view." This view takes firms to be collections of assets or resources, including human capital as well as technologies, raw materials, etc. Regardless of what transaction cost problems a firm may have been designed to solve, what distinguishes one firm from another is the resources and capabilities the firm has accumulated over time (Penrose 1959; Barney 1991; Conner and Prahalad 1996).

It is interesting to consider the extent to which these views can be considered accounts of the nature or ontology of organizations or institutions. Although Coase's 1937 paper is titled "The Nature of the Firm," it is principally a discussion of what he takes to be the primary *function* that firms play in an economy. He only gives a rough statement of what a firm is: "A firm, therefore, consists of the system of relationships which comes into existence when the direction of resources is dependent on an entrepreneur" (Coase 1937, 393). And the relationships in question are the "master and servant" or "employer and employee" relationship, in which in exchange for a fixed wage, the employee grants to the employer the right to control or interfere with the way the work is to be done.

Williamson takes a slightly different approach. He follows Coase in his development of the firm's function and reason for existence, but relies more on the work of John Commons for his ontology. The basic elements of an economic system, according to Commons, are the transaction, which is built on the principles of conflict, mutuality, and order; and rules of governance for reconciling these three principles. Institutions, then, consist of a set of rights and duties, an authority for enforcing them, and some degree of adherence to collective norms of reasonable behavior (Commons 1924; Van de Ven 1993).

The other views appear to make more explicit claims about the nature of firms: a nexus of contracts, a collection of property rights, a collection of resources. It is not obvious, however, that these are genuinely competing views or alternatives to one another. One question to ask about all of these approaches is the relation between accounts of the function of institutions and organizations and accounts of their nature. Relatedly, it may be useful to clarify the parts of these accounts that explain how the conditions for being a firm or other kind of organization are set up or anchored, and those that serve as the grounds for being a firm or organization. As yet there has been little engagement with this literature by philosophers, but the claims and questions in this area overlap with the concerns of social ontology.

## 5 Collective Intentionality

The dominant topic in the social ontology literature is the actions of groups or collectives and their intentional states (knowledge, belief, judgment, intention, reasoning, etc.). The idea that a group can act or have intentional states was out of favor for the bulk of the twentieth century, but has had a recent resurgence through the efforts of Margaret Gilbert, Michael Bratman, John Searle, and Raimo Tuomela since the late 1980s. Gilbert's *On Social Facts* (Gilbert 1989) and "Walking Together" (Gilbert 1990) set out important desiderata for a theory of collective actions and intentionality. Prior to this work, theories of collective intentionality typically took what Tollefsen (2015) calls "summative" approaches. Inasmuch as we can make sense of group G having a particular attitude A (for instance, having the attitude *intending to walk to the bank*), this approach analyzes it as merely the aggregate of all the members of G having that same attitude A.

In "Walking Together," Gilbert argues against this approach. All of the members of G having attitude A, she points out, is neither necessary nor sufficient for the group G to have attitude A. Suppose Alice, Bob, and Carol are a group having the collective intention to walk to the bank. And suppose that partway there, Carol turns to the right and walks away without saying anything. According to Gilbert, Carol has violated a normative commitment that comes with being a member of the group and having that collective intention. Alice and Bob would be justified in criticizing Carol for her violation. But that criticism would not be justified on the simple aggregative approach. If we just have the three separate intentions—Alice has the intention to walk to the bank, Bob has the intention to walk to the bank, and Carol has the intention to walk to the bank—then they have no joint commitments as a group. If the collective intention does carry the normative commitments, then it cannot just be the simple aggregate of the individual intentions.

Instead, Gilbert proposes that it is joint commitment that is characteristic of the formation of social groups. A social group is formed when a group of people jointly commit to one another, and Gilbert (1989) gives an account of the process by which joint commitments are formed. Gilbert analyzes the collective attitudes in terms of joint commitments. (For instance, group G intending to J is analyzed in terms of G having the joint commitment to intend to J.)

Bratman (1993, 2014) takes off from similar observations about the inadequacy of the simple aggregative approach, but develops a different analysis of shared intention. Bratman approaches it from the perspective of the theory of intentions in individual agents, and develops an account of joint intention that is built out of simple intentional states of individuals. According to Bratman's analysis, group G intends J if and only if: (1) the members of G each have the individual intention *that the group J*; (2) the members of G intend to perform their part in J by way of the others' intentions; and (3) the members of G have common knowledge of (1) and (2). The idea is that shared intention is not a matter of each of the members intending to J on their own, but rather of all the members have interlocking intentions to do so as a group.

Searle (1990) and Tuomela and Miller (1988) take yet a different approach. Both propose that there are distinctively social attitudes in the minds of individual people. Searle distinguishes I-attitudes from we-attitudes. For group G to collectively intend J, on his view, is for all the members of G to have the we-attitude that J. His view is very much like a "summative" approach, except that instead of all the members simply having the I-attitude that J, they are each in a different mental state. Tuomela distinguishes attitudes in the I-mode from attitudes in the we-mode. For Tuomela, however, the we-mode attitudes are analyzed in terms of more standard attitudes. Thus Tuomela's account, when the analysis is fully spelled out, has closer affinity to Bratman's view than to Searle's. (Recent work in cognitive science is pursuing the idea that there are distinctively social attitudes. See Knoblich et al. 2011; Gallotti and Frith 2013; Tomasello 2014.) In addition to collective intentions, other philosophers have worked on the analysis of other attitudes, such as collective belief and judgment (Gilbert 1987; Wray 2001; Hakli 2006).

Other theorists have objected to the typical focus of this literature on small unstructured collectives of adults interacting with one another (see Epstein 2015), and instead have worked on the attitudes of corporations and more complex groups. Much of this work is concerned with moral agency and corporate responsibility (see French 1979; Tollefsen 2002; Hess 2010). Others have developed more holistic approaches to cognition in large-scale systems (Hutchins 1995; Huebner 2013).

Although collective intentionality is the most widely discussed topic in social ontology, it has had only modest connections with the social sciences. The collective responsibility literature has had some impact in the business literature, and Bratman's work has been applied to theories of coordination and planning in multi-agent computer systems (see Grosz and Kraus 1996; Jennings 1996) and to some extent to democratic theory (see Richardson 2003; Goodin 2008) and legal theory (Shapiro 2011). But so far the points of connection between collective intentionality and social science have been limited.

## 6 Looking Forward

This is only a small selection of topics in social ontology that are plausibly connected to the practice of the social sciences. There are many others as well, including the nature of race, gender, social classes, social structures, money, property, law, and more. To some extent it is obvious that current models in the social sciences are based on ontological assumptions, but little work has been done to make these explicit. In some areas, such as the study of institutions and organizations, there is crossover among disciplines in the social sciences, but this work has not yet profited much from collaboration with philosophers. To be sure, there are theoretical and cultural obstacles to such collaboration. However, recent innovation in social ontology, coupled with the theoretical needs of the social sciences, creates promising new opportunities on this front.

## References

Alchian, A. A. and H. Demsetz (1972). Production, Information Costs, and Economic Organization. *American Economic Review* 62(5): 777–95.

Audi, P. (2012). A Clarification and Defense of the Notion of Grounding. In F. Correia and B. Schnieder (eds.), *Metaphysical Grounding: Understanding the Structure of Reality* (101–21). Cambridge: Cambridge University Press.

Bakhtin, M. M. (1981). *The Dialogic Imagination: Four Essays.* Austin: University of Texas Press.

Barney, J. (1991). Firm Resources and Sustained Competitive Advantage. *Journal of Management* 17(1): 99–120.

Bennett, K. (2004). Global Supervenience and Dependence. *Philosophy and Phenomenological Research* 68(3): 510–29.

——— (2011). Construction Area: No Hard Hat Required. *Philosophical Studies* 154(1), 79–104.

Bourdieu, P. (1977). *Outline of a Theory of Practice.* Cambridge and New York: Cambridge University Press.

——— (1990). *The Logic of Practice.* Stanford: Stanford University Press.

Boyd, R. (1999a). Homeostasis, Species, and Higher Taxa. In R. Wilson (ed.), *Species: New Interdisciplinary Essays* (141–85). Cambridge, MA: MIT Press.

——— (1999b). Kinds, Complexity and Multiple Realization: Comments on Millikan's "Historical Kinds and the Special Sciences." *Philosophical Studies* 95(1–2): 67–98.

Bratman, M. (1993). Shared Intention. *Ethics* 104(1): 97–113.

——— (2014). *Shared Agency.* Oxford: Oxford University Press.

Coase, R. H. (1937). The Nature of the Firm. *Economica* 4: 386–405.

——— (1960). The Problem of Social Cost. *Journal of Law and Economics* 3: 1–44.

Coleman, J. (1987). Microfoundations and Macrosocial Behavior. in J. Alexander (ed.), *The Micro–Macro Link* (153–73). Berkeley: University of California Press.

Coleman, J. S. (1990). *Foundations of Social Theory*. Cambridge, MA: Belknap Press.

Commons, J. (1924). *Legal Foundations of Capitalism*. New York: Macmillan.

Conner, K. R. and C. K. Prahalad (1996). A Resource-Based Theory of the Firm: Knowledge versus Opportunism. *Organization Science* 7(5): 477–501.

Cook, K. S. (1991). The Microfoundations of Social Structure: An Exchange Perspective. In J. Huber (ed.), *Macro–Micro Linkages in Sociology* (29–45). Newbury Park, CA: Sage Publications.

Correia, F. (2005). *Existential Dependence and Cognate Notions*. Munich: Philosophia Verlag.

Currie, G. (1984). Individualism and Global Supervenience. *British Journal for the Philosophy of Science* 35(4): 345–58.

Davidson, D. (1980). Mental Events. *Readings in Philosophy of Psychology* 1: 107–19.

Davis, J. B. (2003). *The Theory of the Individual in Economics: Identity and Value*. London: Routledge.

Epstein, B. (2009). Ontological Individualism Reconsidered. *Synthese* 166(1): 187–213.

——— (2015). *The Ant Trap: Rebuilding the Foundations of the Social Sciences*. New York: Oxford University Press.

Fine, K. (1995). Ontological Dependence. *Proceedings of the Aristotelian Society* 95: 269–90.

——— (2012). Guide to Ground. In F. Correia and B. Schnieder (eds.), *Metaphysical Grounding: Understanding the Structure of Reality* (37–80). Cambridge: Cambridge University Press.

Fodor, J. A. (1974). Special Sciences (Or: The Disunity of Science as a Working Hypothesis). *Synthese* 28(2): 97–115.

Foss, N. and P. Klein (2008). Organizational Governance. In R. Wittek, T. Snijders, and V. Nee (eds.), *The Handbook of Rational Choice Social Research* (513–55). New York: Russell Sage Foundation.

Foucault, M. (1978). *The History of Sexuality, I. An Introduction*. New York: Pantheon.

French, P. A. (1979). The Corporation as a Moral Person. *American Philosophical Quarterly* 16(3): 207–15.

Gallotti, M. and C. D. Frith (2013). Social Cognition in the We-Mode. *Trends in Cognitive Sciences* 17(4): 160–65.

Gergen, K. J. and K. E. Davis (1985). *The Social Construction of the Person*. New York: Springer Science and Business Media.

Giddens, A. (1984). *The Constitution of Society: Outline of the Theory of Structuration*. Cambridge: Polity Press.

Gilbert, M. (1987). Modelling Collective Belief. *Synthese* 73(1): 185–204.

——— (1989). *On Social Facts*. Princeton, NJ: Princeton University Press.

——— (1990). Walking Together: A Paradigmatic Social Phenomenon. *Midwest Studies in Philosophy* 15: 1–14.

Goodin, R. E. (2008). *Innovating Democracy: Democratic Theory and Practice after the Deliberative Turn*. Oxford: Oxford University Press.

Grossman, S. J. and O. D. Hart (1986). The Costs and Benefits of Ownership: A Theory of Vertical and Lateral Integration. *Journal of Political Economy* 94(4): 691–719.

Grosz, B. J. and S. Kraus (1996). Collaborative Plans for Complex Group Action. *Artificial Intelligence* 86(2): 269–357.

Hakli, R. (2006). Group Beliefs and the Distinction between Belief and Acceptance. *Cognitive Systems Research* 7(2): 286–97.

Hart, O. and J. Moore (1990). Property Rights and the Nature of the Firm. *Journal of Political Economy* 98: 1119–158.

Hess, K. M. (2010). The Modern Corporation as Moral Agent. *Southwest Philosophy Review* 26(1): 61–69.

Huebner, B. (2013). *Macrocognition: A Theory of Distributed Minds and Collective Intentionality*. Oxford: Oxford University Press.

Hutchins, E. (1995). *Cognition in the Wild*. Cambridge, MA: MIT Press.

Jarvie, I. (2011). Philosophical Problems of the Social Sciences: Paradigms, Methodology, and Ontology. In I. Jarvie and J. Zamora-Bonilla (eds.), *The Sage Handbook of the Philosophy of Social Sciences* (1–36). London: Sage.

Jennings, N. R. (1996). Coordination Techniques for Distributed Artificial Intelligence. in G. M. P. O'Hare and N. R. Jennings (eds.), *Foundations of Distributed Artificial Intelligence* (187–210). New York: John Wiley & Sons.

Jensen, M. C. and W. H. Meckling (1976). Theory of the Firm: Managerial Behavior, Agency Costs and Ownership Structure. *Journal of Financial Economics* 3(4): 305–60.

Kim, J. (1978). Supervenience and Nomological Incommensurables. *American Philosophical Quarterly* 15: 149–56.

——— (1998). *Mind in a Physical World*. Cambridge, MA: MIT Press.

Knoblich, G.,S. Butterfill, and N. Sebanz (2011). Psychological Research on Joint Action: Theory and Data. *Psychology of Learning and Motivation: Advances in Research and Theory* 54: 59–101.

Kydland, F. E. and E. C. Prescott (1982). Time to Build and Aggregate Fluctuations. *Econometrica* 50(6): 1345–170.

Lévi-Strauss, C. (1963). *Structural Anthropology*. New York: Basic Books.

——— (1966). *The Savage Mind*. Chicago: University of Chicago Press.

Little, D. (2015). Supervenience and the Social World. *Metodo. International Studies in Phenomenology and Philosophy* 3(2): 125–45.

Lucas, R. E. (1976). Econometric Policy Evaluation: A Critique. in K. Brunner and A. H. Meltzer (eds.), *The Phillips Curve and Labor Markets* (19–45). Amsterdam: North-Holland.

Lucas, R. E., N. Stokey, and E. Prescott (1989). *Recursive Methods in Economic Dynamics*. Cambridge, MA: Harvard University Press.

Macdonald, G. and P. Pettit (1981). *Semantics and Social Science*. London: Routledge & Kegan Paul.

McLaughlin, B. and K. Bennett (2005). Supervenience. In E. Zalta (ed.), *Stanford Encyclopedia of Philosophy*. Fall 2005 edn.

Millikan, R. G. (1984). *Language, Thought, and Other Biological Categories: New Foundations for Realism*. Cambridge, MA: MIT Press.

——— (1999). Historical Kinds and the "Special Sciences." *Philosophical Studies* 95: 45–65.

——— (2005). *Language: A Biological Model*. Oxford: Oxford University Press.

Penrose, E. T. (1959). *The Theory of the Growth of the Firm*. New York: John Wiley and Sons.

Popper, K. (1962). The Logic of the Social Sciences. in T. W. Adorno et al., *The Positivist Dispute in German Sociology* (87–104). London: Heinemann.

Putnam, H. (1967). Psychological Predicates. In W. Capitan and D. D. Merrill (eds.), *Art, Mind, and Religion* (37–48). Pittsburgh: University of Pittsburgh Press.

Quine, W. V. (1948). On What There Is. *Review of Metaphysics* 2(5): 21–38.

Richardson, H. S. (2003). *Democratic Autonomy: Public Reasoning about the Ends of Policy*. Oxford: Oxford University Press.

Rizvi, A. T. (1994). The Microfoundations Project in General Equilibrium Theory. *Cambridge Journal of Economics* 18: 357–77.

Rosen, G. (2010). Metaphysical Dependence: Grounding and Reduction. In B. Hale and A. Hoffman (eds.), *Modality: Metaphysics, Logic, and Epistemology* (109–36). Oxford: Oxford University Press.

Sawyer, R. K. (2002). Nonreductive Individualism: Part I. *Philosophy of the Social Sciences* 32(4): 537–59.

Schaffer, J. (2009). On What Grounds What. In D. Manley, D. J. Chalmers, and R. Wasserman (eds.), *Metametaphysics: New Essays on the Foundations of Ontology* (347–83). Oxford: Oxford University Press.

Searle, J. R. (1990). Collective Intentions and Actions. In P. Cohen, J. Morgan, and M. E. Pollack (eds.), *Intentions in Communication* (401–15). Cambridge, MA: Bradford Books.

——— (1995). *The Construction of Social Reality*. New York: Free Press.

——— (2010). *Making the Social World: The Structure of Human Civilization*. Oxford: Oxford University Press.

Sewell, W. H. (2005). *Logics of history: Social Theory and Social Transformation*. University of Chicago Press.

Shagrir, O. (2002). Global Supervenience, Coincident Entities, and Anti-Individualism. *Philosophical Studies* 109: 171–96.

Shapiro, S. (2011). *Legality*. Cambridge, MA: Belknap Press.

Sider, T. (1999). Global Supervenience and Identity across Times and Worlds. *Philosophy and Phenomenological Research* 59; 913–37.

Simon, H. A. (1991). Organizations and Markets. *Journal of Economic Perspectives* 5(2): 25–44.

Taylor, C. (1989). *Sources of the Self: The Making of the Modern Identity*. Cambridge, MA: Harvard University Press.

Tollefsen, D. (2002). Organizations as True Believers. *Journal of Social Philosophy* 33(3): 395–411.

——— (2015). *Groups as Agents*. Cambridge: Polity.

Tomasello, M. (2014). *A Natural History of Human Thinking*. Cambridge, MA: Harvard University Press.

Tuomela, R. and K. Miller (1988). We-Intentions. *Philosophical Studies* 53(3): 367–89.

Udehn, L. (2001). *Methodological Individualism: Background, History, and Meaning*. London: Routledge.

Van de Ven, A. H. (1993). The Institutional Theory of John R. Commons: A Review and Commentary. *Academy of Management Review* 18(1): 139–52.

Vygotsky, L. S. (1978). *Mind in Society: The Development of Higher Psychological Processes*. Cambridge, MA: Harvard University Press.

Watkins, J. W. N. (1953). The Principle of Methodological Individualism. *British Journal for the Philosophy of Science* 3: 186–89.

Williamson, O. E. (1979). Transaction-Cost Economics: The Governance of Contractual Relations. *Journal of Law and Economics* 22(2): 233–61.

———— (1981). The Economics of Organization: The Transaction Cost Approach. *American Journal of Sociology* 87(3): 548–77.

———— (1996). *The Mechanisms of Governance*. Oxford: Oxford University Press.

———— (2002). The Lens of Contract: Private Ordering. *American Economic Review* 92(2): 438–43.

Wray, K. B. (2001). Collective Belief and Acceptance. *Synthese* 129(3): 319–33.

# 22
# REALISM AND ANTIREALISM
## Randall Harp and Kareem Khalifa[1]

## Introduction

Our best social scientific theories try to tell us something about the social world. But is talk of a "social world" a metaphor that we ought not take too seriously? In particular, do the denizens of the social world—cultural values like the Protestant work ethic, firms like ExxonMobil, norms like standards of dress and behavior, institutions like the legal system, teams like FC Barcelona, conventions like marriages—exist? The question is not merely academic. Social scientists use these different social entities to explain social phenomena such as the rise of capitalism, the decline in oil prices, or the effect of unions on the sports labor market. But how could these explanations possibly work if social entities don't exist?

Questions about the existence of social entities have implications for both philosophical and social-scientific inquiry. A central area of philosophy is ontology—the study of what exists. Social ontology is a relatively new field, and enriches older ontological debates with novel questions and broader concerns. But the realism debate is not exclusively (or even primarily) about ontology; rather, there is an intimate link between these ontological questions and epistemological concerns about how social-scientific explanations should proceed. For instance, whether social entities exist determines the extent to which these explanations should emulate their natural-scientific counterparts. Similar considerations determine the extent to which these explanations must appeal to individual actions.

To navigate this intellectual landscape, let's introduce a distinction. A *realist* is anyone who believes that social scientists are warranted in believing that social entities exist; an *antirealist* is anybody who disagrees. Different antirealists disagree with realists for different reasons. Consequently, we canvass five kinds of antirealism below: explanatory pessimism, fictionalism, eliminativism, reductionism, and constructivism.

Debates about realism in the social sciences tend to cluster into one of three categories. First, should we be realists about the *theoretical entities* appealed to in our best social-scientific theories? These debates parallel their counterparts in the philosophy of natural science. Realists in the natural sciences argue that the predictive, experimental, and technological success of natural-scientific explanations warrants belief in entities such as quarks and gravity. Similarly, our most empirically successful explanations of poverty, for example, invoke social strata, social structures, and economic policies. If such entities are necessary features of our best explanations, does that entail that we should be realists about such entities? Realists argue that the best way to account for the explanatory success of our social scientific theories is by being realists about the entities posited in our theories; anti-realists deny this claim.

Second are questions about whether we should be realists about *groups*, where we can understand groups roughly as a collection of individuals organized with some collective interest, goal, or characteristic. Groups can range from micro-groups consisting of a few individuals, to meso-groups such as corporations, all the way up to macro-groups such as nations. Realists about groups believe that groups cannot be reduced to mere collections of individuals; antirealists about groups think that groups can be explained without remainder in terms of the individuals who constitute the group.

Third are questions about whether we should be realists about *the things that groups create*. Entities such as money, laws, race, and gender are "socially constructed," in the sense that their most important properties depend on how we conceive of them. By contrast, natural properties— the charge of electrons, the height of mountains, and the atomic weight of chemical elements, for instance—are independent of how we conceive of them. We might wonder, then, whether the fact that groups create social entities means that they are not real. Realists about socially constructed entities (such as money or race) argue that these entities could not function in our lives and in the world without being real; antirealists about socially constructed entities argue the contrary. In what follows, we look at these three realist debates, canvassing arguments both for and against realist and antirealist positions.

## 1 Should We Believe What Social Science Tells Us?

Social scientists are scientists. As such, they advance theories with the aim of predicting, explaining, and controlling some part of the world. Let us say that theories that fulfill these aims are *empirically successful*. A theory's empirical success is the most compelling reason to believe that it is (mostly) true. If these slogans about science are correct, then, to the extent that a social-scientific theory succeeds in predicting, explaining, and controlling some part of the social world, we should be realists about the social entities that it posits. In what follows, we develop this line of thought by discussing the central argument used to vindicate the reality of scientific entities. We then rehearse two prominent objections to that argument.

### 1.1 The Explanatory Argument

A powerful argument for realism is that the staggering level of empirical success of modern science would be nothing short of a miracle if its theories were radically false. For this reason, many philosophers and scientists are realists about subatomic particles, curved space-time, cells, species, natural selection, continental plates, and so on. The central idea is that realism provides the best (if not the only) explanation of the relevant aspects of the domain. Indeed, realists about many other entities (mathematical objects, moral truths, etc.) invoke this same principle to defend their positions. This suggests the following "Explanatory Argument" for realism about social entities:

EA1    If the best explanation of the relevant facts posits social entities, then we should believe that social entities exist.
EA2    <u>The best explanation of the relevant facts posits social entities.</u>
EA3    Therefore, we should believe that social entities exist.

A few clarifications are in order. First, the conclusion (EA3) amounts to realism about social entities. Second, an explanation *posits* an entity just in case that entity exists if the explanation is true. The *relevant* facts are typically those that most parties to a debate agree are in need of explanation. A hypothesis is the *best explanation* of a fact if it optimizes the set of criteria typically associated with our best theories: simplicity, scope, fit with background knowledge, predictive power, and so on.

Indeed, with a little bit of reconstruction, we can see that social scientists frequently argue in this manner. This is particularly clear when we examine the extensive work on both qualitative (King, Keohane, and Verba 1994) and quantitative (Blalock 1971) causal inference in the social sciences. For instance, suppose that the chief cause of poverty is a federal policy that permits a very low minimum wage. Then that policy is the best explanation of poverty. Furthermore, this explanation assumes that policies have causal efficacy. However, non-existent things can't have causal efficacy. Consequently, policies exist.

What of non-causal explanations? Consider sociologists' observation that men born in lower socioeconomic strata have a higher chance of upward social mobility than those born in higher socioeconomic strata (Blau and Duncan 1967). Why is this? To appreciate the answer, consider Al, who is born at a lower socioeconomic stratum than Bob. If a socioeconomic stratum is higher than Bob's current stratum it is also higher than Al's, but not vice versa. Hence, there are more ways that Al can make an upward move. This explanation appears non-causal, as it only invokes probabilities that fall out of the "structure" of socioeconomic strata in the United States (Garfinkel 1981). Zooming back out to the larger philosophical picture, the best explanation of the observed correlations between social origins and social mobility posits social strata and social structures. According to the Explanatory Argument, this means that we should believe that social strata and social structures exist.

## 1.2  Explanatory Pessimism

While the Explanatory Argument nicely captures a prominent way in which philosophers and scientists (both social and natural) justify realism about theoretical posits, it has faced several objections. In particular, philosophers have questioned its first premise, i.e. that our best explanations are an effective guide to what exists. For ease of reference, we call anyone who raises this challenge an *explanatory pessimist*. Explanatorily pessimistic social scientists are somewhat rare, though they typically are motivated by empiricist concerns that we can know only correlations, but cannot have causal knowledge. Comte (1868) and Mill (1904) are early examples of this critical stance towards social explanation. Other authors criticize the reliability of certain kinds of explanations, e.g. functional explanations (Elster 2007), and hence might be interpreted as expressing qualified forms of explanatory pessimism.

By contrast, several natural scientists (and the philosophers who have studied their work) have argued that our best explanations are not a trustworthy guide to reality. For instance, Newtonian mechanics was the best explanation of many phenomena for nearly three centuries. However, the advent of Einsteinian and quantum mechanics in the early 20th century revealed that Newton's account was mistaken. Consequently, it would appear that the Explanatory Argument has given us bad advice: we should not have believed that Newtonian space, time, gravity, and energy exist.

Similar examples can be found in the social sciences. Consider Oscar Lewis's (1975) once-prominent explanation of poverty. Looking at five Mexican families with different socio-economic outcomes, Lewis reasoned that the poorer families have a different value system (a "culture of poverty") from their more affluent counterparts, and that this value system prevents them from taking the measures needed to improve their socioeconomic status. As the explanation gained further corroboration, it had a good deal of prominence by the end of the 1970s, and figured prominently in policy decisions about social assistance. Hence, it was taken by many to be the best explanation of poverty. As such, the Explanatory Argument counsels us to believe in the existence of a culture of poverty.

Yet, throughout the 1980s, as finer-grained empirical measures of culture developed, and a wider variety of impoverished populations were studied, it became clear that the cultural variation among the poor was too great for this explanation to be true. As before, it would appear that the Explanatory Argument has given us bad advice: we should not have believed in the culture of poverty. Nor is this example an outlier; many explanations in the social sciences enjoy some notoriety, only to face searching empirical difficulties at a later date.

Antirealists use examples such as this to critique the Explanatory Argument. On one version, the so-called "Pessimistic Induction" (Laudan 1981), the best explanation at any given time is frequently rejected at a subsequent point in history. Consequently, we should not believe that our best explanations posit real entities, since they are likely to be replaced in the future. Hence, on this view, "best explanation" means "best for its time." On this formulation, Lewis's explanation was the best, posited a social entity (the culture of poverty), but we should not believe that this social entity exists. This falsifies the first premise of the Explanatory Argument.

Alternatively, and closely related, some antirealists argue that our explanation may only be the best of a bad lot, in which case we should not believe that it posits real entities (Stanford 2006; van Fraassen 1989). This view can simply be a variant of the Pessimistic Induction. Alternatively, it may motivate skepticism about our ability to identify the best explanation, even if such an explanation justifies realism. On this view, the best explanation of poverty may posit a culture of poverty, but we cannot know that this explanation is better than the rest.

There are reasons to think that these objections to the Explanatory Argument are especially thorny in the philosophy of social science. For instance, many realists have responded to these pessimist challenges by claiming that our best explanations only entail belief in posits that are indispensable to novel predictions (Psillos 1999; Worrall 1989) or experimental interventions (Hacking 1983). Since these demanding kinds of empirical success are far less common in the social sciences than in the natural sciences, explanatory pessimism in the social sciences may be even more persuasive than its natural-scientific cousin. Having said this, some have suggested that social-scientific hypotheses also contain these high-grade posits (Kincaid 2008), and so realism about social entities is on par with realism about natural-scientific entities.

### 1.3 Fictionalism

Frequently, non-philosophers find these debates about realism to be "pointless" or "merely academic." On such a view, it simply does not matter if social entities exist or not. There are more and less principled ways to make this point. A fairly sophisticated one comes from *fictionalists*. Like explanatory pessimists, fictionalists object to the first premise of the Explanatory Argument. However, whereas explanatory pessimists are largely concerned with showing why we cannot *know* much on the basis of our best explanations, fictionalists emphasize that we can still *use* our best explanations in the absence of this knowledge. Fictionalists can thereby articulate the principles behind the complaint that the realism debate is "pointless": it does not matter if realism is true, for it is enough to treat social entities as useful fictions. More precisely, even if our best explanations posit social entities, we can still use those explanations without believing that posited social entities exist. Typical "uses" include explanation, prediction, control, and model construction. For instance, based on Blau and Duncan's work, subsequent scholars have found it useful to explain social mobility in terms of social strata and social structures. However, fictionalists point out that all of this is compatible with agnosticism about these social entities.

While many social scientists express fictionalist commitments (e.g. Friedman 1953; MacDonald 2003), only a few philosophers are fictionalists about social entities (Demeter [2013] and Turner [2003] present fictionalists accounts of psychological states and social entities, respectively). However, the resources for a more thoroughgoing fictionalism are easy to find. Van Fraassen's (1980) constructive empiricism is a fictionalism that appears to apply to all science, though its chief applications have been in the natural sciences. Van Fraassen is a fictionalist about *unobservable* entities in science: he holds that we can use or accept posits about unobservable entities without believing that those entities exist. In other words, we can treat posits about unobservables as useful fictions (e.g. for the purposes of prediction and explanation). This can be applied to the social sciences, for the unobservable–observable distinction cuts across the natural and social domains. For instance, subatomic particles, beliefs, and social norms all appear to resist any direct observation. However, fictionalists of this sort then inherit all of the challenges to van Fraassen's view. For instance, some have wondered whether a distinction between observable and unobservable entities is sustainable (Churchland 1985; Hacking 1985). Arguably, this distinction is even more vexed in the social sciences (Block 1976).

To summarize, we have seen that realists deploy the Explanatory Argument to justify their position. Such a view holds that we should be realists about entities posited by our best explanations. Antirealist criticisms come in two broad varieties. First, explanatory pessimists question the extent to which we can trust our best explanations as a guide to what is real. Second, fictionalists argue that it is enough to use the posits of our best explanations, even if we do not think that they are real.

Before proceeding, a word of caution is in order. The Explanatory Argument presupposes that the social sciences ought to emulate the natural sciences. Specifically, it presupposes that realism about social entities is justified (and perhaps only justified) by social-scientific theories' success in predicting, explaining, and controlling the empirically testable parts of the social world. Indeed, even the critics of the Explanatory Argument assume this much of the time.

However, there is a longstanding debate as to whether the social sciences have different aims than the natural sciences. On this view, successful social theories need not be highly explanatory or predictive, but should instead furnish fruitful interpretations and give us a richer understanding of the people studied. This has led some philosophers to argue that because different sciences have fundamentally different methodologies, the entities in those sciences' respective domains are real or exist in different ways (Dupré 1993; Root 2000; Sundstrom 2002). On such a view, our beliefs in social entities' existence are subject to different standards than our beliefs in the existence of natural-scientific objects. By contrast, others argue that precisely because interpretation and understanding are more inquirer-relative than the explanation, prediction, and control characteristic of the natural sciences, realism about social entities is more difficult to defend than its natural-scientific counterpart (Reed 2008).

## 2 Are Social Groups Real?

Both explanatory pessimists and fictionalists criticize the first premise of the Explanatory Argument (EA1), which states that if our best explanations posit social entities, then we should be realists about those entities. However, many philosophers and social scientists have also challenged the second premise of this argument (EA2), which states that our best explanations posit social entities. For instance, we might wonder whether our best explanations of poverty *really* posit policies, social strata, or a culture of poverty, or if instead they only posit the individuals who are described by these social terms.

This concern shows up most clearly in discussions about the reality of social groups. Some find the idea of social groups standing over and above the individuals that constitute them to be spooky, and also find the methods of studying these groups to be unscientific. While these sorts of concerns are at least as old as Mill (1904) and Weber (1978), there is also a long tradition of defending the integrity of social groups and the distinctive methodology of the social sciences, e.g. Durkheim (2013). Contemporary heirs to Mill and Weber argue that "macro-level" social explanations must be grounded in "micro-foundations" that appeal only to individuals (Elster 2007; Hedström 2005); others demur (Colander 1996).

To that end, let's assess the following "Group Variant" of the Explanatory Argument:

GV1   If the best explanation of the relevant facts posits social groups, then we should believe that social groups exist.
GV2   <u>The best explanation of the relevant facts posits social groups</u>.
GV3   Therefore, we should believe that social groups exist.

As an example, consider why democracies tend not to fight wars with each other. Suppose that two democracies are in a dispute. Because losing a war has dire electoral consequences, both can anticipate that going to war will lead each to allocate large amounts of resources to a risky situation. Because of this, engaging in war is an unattractive option, as neither democracy is assured an easy victory (de Mesquita et al. 1999). As should be clear, this explanation posits social groups (democracies or electorates). So, according to this argument, we should infer that these groups exist.

We will call those who subscribe to this argument *group realists*. Those opposed to group realism have two potential strategies. First, they can challenge GV1, in which case they pursue the explanatory pessimist and fictionalist strategies above. Alternatively, they can challenge GV2. To that end, it's useful to first consider the arguments in favor of GV2. (We address objections to GV2 below.)

First, group realists emphasize that talk of groups is pervasive in our ordinary discourse: we predicate things of groups ("Americans are materialistic"); we attribute mental states to groups ("the Cato Institute believes in free markets and individual liberty"); and we conceive of groups as unitary agents capable of acting in the world ("ExxonMobil intends to grow its worldwide crude and natural gas production by 7.5 percent"). Group membership figures in racial, ethnic, or religious group affiliation, and thereby plays a prominent role in our sense of identity. And groups need not be large, or institutional; some theorists argue that groups as small as two people are the fundamental elements of social reality (Gilbert 1989).

Moreover, the social sciences follow ordinary language in their use of groups as explanatory concepts. Sociologists appeal to group-based concepts such as social institutions, organizations, states, societies, and cultures, while economists appeal to such things as firms and networks. As should be clear from our discussion of democratic peace, social scientists use groups to explain individual and collective behavior. Some social scientists also use groups to account for the nature of social reality (Berger and Luckmann 1991). On a cursory examination of social scientific practice, it would appear that GV2 is clearly true.

However, while nearly everyone agrees that social scientists *appear* to make use of groups in their theories, some argue that this appearance is misleading. Certain critics of group realism, whom we will call *eliminativists*, hold that our talk of social groups is false when taken literally (Quinton 1975).[2] Other critics of realism, whom we will call *reductionists*, hold that the use of social groups in our theorizing is dispensable: talk of social groups can always be translated into talk of the individuals that constitute the group. If either of these positions is correct, then our best explanations do not require us to posit social entities, and so GV2 would be false. In what follows, we examine these two alternatives to group realism.

## 2.1 Eliminativism

Eliminativists think that there are no such things as groups; rather, there are only individuals interacting with other individuals. This claim was memorably stated by British Prime Minister Margaret Thatcher (1987), who said:

> [A]nd so they are casting their problems on society and who is society? There is no such thing! There are individual men and women and there are families.

(Of course, for Thatcher to be a proper eliminativist, she would also have to say that there are no families.)

While eliminativists hold that claims invoking group concepts are false, eliminativists also maintain that true statements about individuals can replace these falsehoods. Thus, the claim that Americans are materialistic would be replaced by a claim to the effect that most of the individuals who are American citizens are materialistic.

On the face of it, eliminativism is counterintuitive. After all, eliminativists would have to hold that a claim of the form "FC Barcelona won the Champions League in 2015" is, strictly speaking, false; to be true, the claim should be reinterpreted so that it has the form "Xavi and Iniesta and Messi and Neymar and etc. won the Champions League." But regardless of what we want to say about that second claim, it seems wrong to say that FC Barcelona did *not* win the Champions League, on the grounds that there is no such thing as FC Barcelona.

Why, then, is eliminativism a plausible view? Some think that methodological individualism entails eliminativism, and so they find eliminativism plausible because they find methodological individualism plausible (Tuomela 1990). That argument, however, appears unsound. Methodological individualism requires that claims about collective entities be grounded in claims about the actions and properties of individuals, but that is consistent with collective entities' existence. So, one can be a methodological individualist without also being an eliminativist. (For more on methodological individualism, read the chapter on methodological individualism in this volume.)

Eliminativists must hold a stronger view. First, eliminativists must hold that *only* those things that factor into our best explanations determine what exists; and second, that *none* of our best explanations appeal to groups. These claims are strong, because social groups are featured in legitimate explanations all the time. Consider the following explanation of why more committed sports fans are likelier to be violent after their team's loss than less committed fans: whereas wins by a sports team enhance the social identity and self-esteem of all fans, losses only decrease the psychological well-being of those fans who most strongly identify with the team. Strongly identified fans then act aggressively in order to regain that well-being (Wann et al. 2001). If we paraphrase away the football club to be instead about the individual members, the explanation no longer identifies the main causes of spectator aggression. After all, membership of a team can change without a change in fan identification, and some people can strongly identify with a team without knowing all of its individual members.

Eliminativist arguments might work for establishing that particular *kinds* of social groups are not real. Consider groups such as "unwed mothers between the ages of 18 and 30" and "individuals who self-identify as Jewish." These are examples of groups such that possessing some set of properties is necessary and sufficient for membership in the group. While these groups sometimes seem to contribute to social-scientific explanations, the eliminativist would argue that the group functions in an explanation only insofar as the membership in the group highlights the causal factors that actually play an explanatory role. Because each of the individuals who make up the group possesses the properties that define the group, it will be those properties that are doing the explanatory work; the group is doing no work at all.

## 2.2 Reductionism

A third position, *reductionism*, falls in between eliminativism and group realism. A quick note about the term "reductionism": in certain discussions, reductionism is synonymous with eliminativism. The reason for this conflation is understandable, as reductionists agree with eliminativists that our best explanations do not posit social groups, i.e. they also deny GV2. Specifically, any of our best explanations that purport to posit social groups are really just shorthand for individualistic explanations. Moreover, individualistic factors are doing the real work in these explanations. However, like group realists, reductionists hold that social groups exist. So, following the philosophical mainstream, we will distinguish reductionism from eliminativism.

Two crucial claims justify reductionists' claim that social groups exist. First, reductionists assume that individuals exist. Second, and more controversially, they argue that social groups are nothing over and above the individuals that comprise them. From these two claims, it follows *trivially* that social groups exist. The triviality of this inference means that social groups don't exist in any "robust" or "substantive" sense. Thus, social groups are dispensable or redundant given information about the individuals who comprise them. For this reason, reductionists are sometimes called "redundant realists" (List and Pettit 2011).

However, reductionists differ from group realists in the explanatory roles they accord to social groups. Reductionists hold that individuals are ontologically fundamental while also allowing that statements about groups need not be strictly speaking false. Since reductionists hold that groups are not essential to our explanatory aims, and since all statements about groups can be translated to statements about individuals but not vice versa, reductionists deny that the best explanation of social phenomena requires us to posit social entities—we can make do with individual entities instead.

Like eliminativism, reductionism faces several challenges. For one thing, reductionists must account for the functional structure of social institutions. Social institutions are multiply realized in the behavior of individuals, meaning the institution itself can act in the same way even when the behavior of the constituent individuals is different. Consider the explanation of democratic peace given earlier. When we try to understand how the electorate influences the decisions of democratic leaders, a description of individual votes doesn't matter; what matters is a description of the voting of the electorate as a whole. If this is so, then explanatory claims which appeal to the social institution at the group level will work differently than explanatory claims which appeal to the social institution at the individual level: group-level claims explain in virtue of the *structural relationship* between the members, while individual-level claims explain in virtue of the properties of the individuals themselves (Kincaid 1986).

Finally, reductionism fails to explain how social groups can act as unitary agents, i.e. how firms, institutions, and the like intend to do things, perform actions, and hold action-relevant beliefs and desires. Indeed, List and Pettit (2011) argue that group agents *necessarily* possess action-relevant mental states that cannot be reduced to individual mental states. Similarly, Gilbert (1989) argues that group mental states have a distinctive normative component that cannot be generated by individually held mental states.

## 3 Can Things be Real *and* "Constructed"?

Many social scientists (and some philosophers) describe themselves as "social constructivists" (e.g. Berger and Luckmann 1991). However, there is significant disagreement as to what this doctrine entails, whether it is defensible, and if it is incompatible with realism. For instance, many social scientists equivocate between *reality itself* depending on social conditions, interests, and the like, and the more modest claim that our *representations* of reality exhibit this social dependence. Any careful formulation of the former is very difficult to defend. By contrast, the latter is compatible with there being a world with a structure that is independent of these representations, i.e. it is compatible with realism (Boghossian 2006). More qualified forms of constructivism claim that social scientists, as the foremost experts on society, play a special role in constructing social entities. For instance, MacKenzie, Muniesa, and Siu (2007) claim that economists make (i.e. construct) the markets that they study.

For our purposes, we will treat constructivists as a distinct kind of antirealist. To get a sense of the debate between realists and constructivists, consider three statements:

*Vertebrate:* Chris and Pat are vertebrates.
*Marriage:* Chris and Pat are married.
*Cute:* Chris and Pat are cute.

Intuitively, *Vertebrate* is true in some "objective" sense, and *Cute* is only true in some "subjective" sense. In principle, moderate realists and moderate constructivists can agree on these points. The disagreement concerns claims such as *Marriage*. Are these contested claims more "objective" like *Vertebrate* or more "subjective" like *Cute*? To make any progress, we need to get clearer on what "objectivity" and "subjectivity" mean in these contexts. To do this, we first examine the constructivist's claim that social entities "depend" on us, and then turn to the kind of objectivity at stake in the realist-constructivist debates.

### 3.1 Kinds of Dependence

Regardless of any further differences, all social constructivists hold that a constructed entity "depends" on something social in some way for its existence. More precisely, constructivist claims always involve two entities. The first is what we will call the *dependent entity*. We will focus on cases in which the dependent entity is a social entity. In our example, Chris and Pat's marriage is the dependent entity. The second is the *constructing entity*, i.e. the entity on which the dependent entity depends. Necessarily, constructing entities have to be social or psychological entities. Presumably, the constructing entities in our example are the marriage laws in Chris and Pat's community.

It is precisely the dependence on constructing entities that is supposed to preclude dependent entities from being real. Consequently, we must specify what this dependence entails, and how it bears on realism. To that end, we must distinguish two central kinds of dependence that figure in the constructivist literature (though see Sveinsdóttir [forthcoming] for a more nuanced taxonomy of constructions). First, there is *causal dependence:*

*F causally* depends on an individualistic/social entity G if and only if F would never have come into existence, or would have been substantially different, had G not existed.

While our chief concern is with constructed *social* entities, many causally constructed entities are *not* social entities. For instance, some elements, such as Rutherfordium, can only be created in laboratories, and hence causally depend on scientists' intention to synthesize such elements. However, elements are paradigmatic examples of physical (non-social) entities. More broadly, all artifacts are causally constructed. For instance, a manufacturer's intending to produce a bicycle is a cause of that bicycle's existence.

There is widespread consensus that causally constructed entities are real. Bicycles are causally dependent entities, and we have no more reason to be antirealists about bicycles than Rutherfordium and other natural-scientific entities. Thus, insofar as social entities are simply the effects of people's mental states and actions, then there is no reason to treat them as any less real than other artifacts.

However, there is good reason to think that some social entities, such as marriage, are not merely causally constructed. This is because marriage exhibits a different kind of dependence:

*F constitutively* depends on individualistic/social entity G if and only if the continued existence of G is a necessary condition for the continued existence of F.

Causally dependent entities can continue to exist even after the entities that constructed them have ceased to exist. By contrast, constitutively dependent entities cannot. To make this vivid, consider the status of constructed entities if every human were to disappear spontaneously: bicycles would continue to exist; marriages would not.

While realism about causally constructed entities is generally accepted, realism about constitutively constructed entities is more controversial. Some authors are realists about these entities (Haslanger 2012). Their argument proceeds in two steps. First, against those who think that marriage is more like cuteness, they deny that there is a good inference from "x is mind-dependent" to "x is not real" (Haslanger 2012; Rosen 1994). Second, they use the Explanatory Argument from above, but the relevant posits are constitutively dependent entities. For instance, some hold that race and gender play prominent explanatory roles in social inquiry, and hence are real, even though they are constitutively dependent on certain social conditions. This would suggest the following "Constitutive Variant" of the Explanatory Argument:

CV1   If the best explanation of the relevant facts posits constitutively dependent entities, then we should believe that constitutively dependent entities exist.

CV2   The best explanation of the relevant facts posits constitutively dependent entities.

CV3   Therefore, we should believe that constitutively dependent entities exist.

Realists of this persuasion might argue in the following manner. Marriage is constitutively dependent. Moreover, our best explanations posit marriage as a central determinant of, e.g., psychological well-being (Gove, Hughes, and Style 1983). Consequently, we ought to believe that marriage exists.

However, there are at least three objections to this argument. First, since constitutively dependent entities are simply a kind of social entity, the same objections to the Explanatory Argument apply to its Constitutive Variant. Hence, if explanatory pessimism, fictionalism, eliminativism, or reductionism are correct about social entities in general, they also apply to constitutively dependent entities.

Second, the Constitutive Variant Argument might prove too much. For instance, it is unclear why cuteness is not constitutively dependent upon people's attitudes and emotions. Moreover, cuteness might well figure in some of our best explanations, e.g. of the popularity of puppy memes on the Internet. However, as we have already suggested, realism about cuteness is implausible. While some realists have bitten this bullet (Haslanger 2012), others would take this as evidence that the first premise of the argument (CV1) is incorrect.

Third, it appears that explanations only invoking constitutively *constructing* entities can always "screen off" or "preempt" any explanation of which their corresponding constitutively *dependent* entity is a part. As a result, the second premise (CV2) of this argument can be contested. For instance, puppies' cuteness is constitutively dependent upon our attitudes about them. Consequently, it seems as if we could just as well explain the prevalence of Internet puppy memes by appealing to these attitudes, rather than adding another property—cuteness—into our ontologies. Similarly, although *attitudes* about race and gender explain various social outcomes, this does not entail that race and gender are real or explanatory. In other words, to the extent that an entity is constitutively constructed, it is unlikely to play the kind of role in our best explanations that licenses ontological commitment.

### 3.2 Objectivity

Another way of refining the Explanatory Argument so that it underwrites realism about constitutively dependent entities is to identify further criteria that distinguish real constitutive constructions—such as race and gender—from other kinds of constitutively dependent entities—such as cuteness. Here, we might (loosely) follow John Searle's (1995) suggestion that even if the *existence* of certain social entities depends on attitudes and social conditions, our *judgments* about those entities might be no less objective than our judgments about natural-scientific entities.

For instance, consider once again the statement that Chris and Pat are married. Marriages are constitutively dependent entities: the marriage of two people only exists insofar as it is appropriately held to exist by the legal structures of the society in which the participants live. Nevertheless, there is a fact of the matter about whether Chris and Pat are married, such as the recognized laws about marriage, and whether the procedures required by those laws were properly followed. More generally,

F is *epistemically objective* if and only if it is possible to hold that something is an F and be wrong.

Here, the "holder" (i.e. constructing entities) can either be an individual or a group. As should be clear, some entities, such as vertebrates, are epistemically objective. It is possible for somebody to be mistaken about who or what is a vertebrate. Moreover, we can also see why some social entities are epistemically objective. For instance, suppose that Chris and Pat are a legally married same-sex couple. Because of his religious beliefs, Frank may believe that Chris and Pat are not married. However, Frank's religious beliefs do not nullify Chris and Pat's marriage. Similarly, at first remove, no single individual's beliefs about race, gender, marriage, employment, income, etc. are capable of nullifying empirical statements about these social entities.

By contrast, judgments about cuteness function differently in our cognitive lives. They are epistemically *subjective*. In particular, the truth of (nontrivial) judgments about cuteness depends on the mental states of the person judging something to be cute. In other words:

A group or person's holding that a puppy is cute entails that the puppy is cute.

The Searlean realist claims that cuteness is in the eye of the beholder, while many claims about social entities such as marriage are not. How does this bear on social constructivism? While accounts of epistemic objectivity claim that "holders" are either individuals or groups, social constructivists will typically favor an account of epistemic subjectivity that regards holders as social groups:

F is *epistemically subjective* if and only if some group's holding that something is an F entails its being an F.

(Note: our discussion of epistemic subjectivity and objectivity is indebted, but not identical, to Searle's account.) As noted above, it is implausible that an individual, such as Frank, can nullify a marriage. By contrast, certain social groups or their proxies—such as a legislature or a judge—can nullify a marriage. Hence, the constructivist's position poses an interesting challenge for realists about constitutively dependent entities.

To summarize, both realists and constructivists might agree that some social entity is constitutively constructed. However, realists will claim that the entity is epistemically objective (and hence more like *Vertebrate*), while constructivists will claim that it is epistemically subjective (and hence more like *Cute*). For instance, constructivists will claim that judgments about membership in racial groups depend on some social group making that judgment.

How do we adjudicate between these competing claims? In the context of the social sciences, the defensibility of this kind of constructivism hinges (in part) on the specific methods that are used to make judgments about the social entity in question. For instance, some interpretive methodologies are sufficiently reflexive that social scientists' intuitions, feelings, beliefs, etc. necessarily figure in their judgments about social entities (Bourdieu and Wacquant 1992; Denzin 2001; Wylie 1994). Insofar as these methods are the only or best means of acquiring knowledge about certain social entities, constructivism *cum* epistemic subjectivism is relatively straightforward.

By contrast, some methods—particularly those that are shared with the natural sciences—purport to be answerable to a set of mind-independent empirical facts. These include observation, measurement, statistical analysis, and causal inference. If these methods do what they purport to do, then constructivism about the judgments that they justify would appear misplaced. However, some have advanced this particularly ambitious brand of constructivism about social entities (Law 2004), by appealing to constructivists about natural-scientific entities who deny the objectivity of these methods (Bloor 1976; Kuhn 1996; Latour 1987; Latour and Woolgar 1986; Pickering 1984, 1995).

So, to summarize, the debate between constructivists and realists about social entities is not a debate about entities that are causally dependent on social conditions. Otherwise, Rutherfordium would be socially constructed. Rather, it is a debate about constitutively constructed entities. However, some constitutively constructed entities, such as cuteness, do not seem to warrant realist treatment. So, when realists and constructivists disagree about constitutively dependent entities, the real sticking point is whether such entities are epistemically objective or epistemically subjective, i.e. whether the means for making judgments about these entities suffices to make those judgments true.

## 4 Conclusion

In summary, whether one is discussing social groups, social constructions, or any other social entity, realists appeal first and foremost to the Explanatory Argument. According to this argument, if our best explanations posit social entities, then we ought to believe that these entities exist. However, explanatory pessimists cite science's history of failed explanations as evidence against this contention. Fictionalists also challenge this realist doctrine by claiming that we can use social entities in our best explanations without believing in their existence.

The Explanatory Argument also asserts that our best explanations posit social entities. Paying special attention to social groups reveals two challenges to this claim. First, eliminativists claim that statements about social groups are false, and should be replaced by statements about individuals. Second, reductionists claim that statements about social groups are trivially true, because they are really just shorthand for statements about individuals. In neither case do our best explanations posit social entities.

Yet another aspect of realism concerns the objectivity of social entities. As we saw, realists hold that social entities are epistemically objective, in the sense that a group's or person's ideas about a social entity could be wrong. Constructivists, by contrast, claim that (at least some) social entities are epistemically subjective, meaning that ideas about those entities determine what they are.

A number of options and questions suggest themselves. Can realism in the social sciences be justified without the Explanatory Argument? Can the challenges of eliminativism and reductionism extend to social entities other than groups? If social entities are not real, why bother studying them? What would social scientists lose by adopting one (or more) of the antirealist stances canvassed above? Given the variety of positions available, there is ample room for having nuanced ontological positions in the social sciences.

## Notes

1 We would like to thank Lee McIntyre, Gioia Pappalardo, Jeremy Read, and an anonymous referee for their assistance with this project.
2 While we are referring to eliminativism about social entities, "eliminativism" frequently refers to an analogous position about individual mental states (beliefs, desires, etc.) in the philosophy of psychology.

# References

Berger, Peter L., and Thomas Luckmann (1991), *The social construction of reality: A treatise in the sociology of knowledge*. London: Penguin UK.

Blalock, Hubert M. (1971), *Causal models in the social sciences*. Chicago: Aldine Atherton.

Blau, Peter, and Otis Dudley Duncan (1967), *The American occupational structure*. New York: Wiley.

Block, N. J. (1976), "Fictionalism, functionalism and factor analysis," in R. S. Cohen, C. A. Hooker, A. C. Michalos, and J. W. Van Evra (eds.), *PSA 1974*. Dordrecht: Springer Netherlands, 127–41.

Bloor, David (1976), *Knowledge and social imagery*. London and Boston: Routledge & Kegan Paul.

Boghossian, Paul (2006), *Fear of knowledge: Against relativism and constructivism*. Oxford: Clarendon Press.

Bourdieu, Pierre, and Loïc J. D. Wacquant (1992), *An invitation to reflexive sociology*. Chicago: University of Chicago Press.

Churchland, Paul M. (1985), "The ontological status of observables: In praise of the superempirical virtues," in P. M. Churchland and C. A. Hooker (eds.), *Images of science: Essays on realism and empiricism with a reply from Bas C. van Fraassen*. Chicago: University of Chicago Press, 35–47.

Colander, David, ed. (1996), *Beyond microfoundations: Post Walrasian economics*. Cambridge: Cambridge University Press.

Comte, Auguste (1868), *The positive philosophy of Auguste Comte*. New York: W. Gowans.

de Mesquita, Bruce Bueno, James D. Morrow, Randolph M. Siverson, and Alastair Smith (1999), "An institutional explanation of the democratic peace," *American Political Science Review* 93(4): 791–807.

Demeter, Tamás (2013), "Mental fictionalism," *The Monist* 96(4): 483–504.

Denzin, Norman K. (2001), "The reflexive interview and a performative social science," *Qualitative Research* 1(1): 23–46.

Dupré, John (1993), *The disorder of things: Metaphysical foundations for the disunity of science*. Cambridge, MA: Harvard University Press.

Durkheim, Emile (2013), *Durkheim: The rules of sociological method, and selected texts on sociology and its method*. Translated by W. D. Halls. 2nd edn. Basingstoke: Palgrave Macmillan.

Elster, Jon (2007), *Explaining social behavior: More nuts and bolts for the social sciences*. Cambridge: Cambridge University Press.

Friedman, Milton (1953), "The methodology of positive economics," in Milton Friedman (ed.), *Essays in positive economics*. Chicago: University of Chicago Press, 5–43.

Garfinkel, Alan (1981), *Forms of explanation: Rethinking the questions in social theory*. New Haven: Yale University Press.

Gilbert, Margaret (1989), *On social facts*. Princeton, NJ: Princeton University Press.

Gove, Walter R., Michael Hughes, and Carolyn Briggs Style (1983), "Does marriage have positive effects on the psychological well-being of the individual?" *Journal of Health and Social Behavior* 24(2): 122–31.

Hacking, Ian (1983), *Representing and intervening: Introductory topics in the philosophy of natural science*. Cambridge: Cambridge University Press.

——— (1985), "Do we see through a microscope?" in P. M. Churchland and C. A. Hooker (eds.), *Images of science: Essays on realism and empiricism, with a reply from Bas C. Van Fraassen*. Chicago: University of Chicago, 132–52.

Haslanger, Sally (2012), *Resisting reality: Social construction and social critique*. Oxford: Oxford University Press.

Hedström, Peter (2005), *Dissecting the social: On the principles of analytical sociology*. Cambridge: Cambridge University Press.

Kincaid, Harold (1986), "Reduction, explanation, and individualism," *Philosophy of Science* 53(4): 492–513.

——— (2008), "Structural realism and the social sciences," *Philosophy of Science* 75(5): 720–31.

King, Gary, Robert O. Keohane, and Sidney Verba (1994), *Designing social inquiry: Scientific inference in qualitative research*. Princeton, NJ: Princeton University Press.

Kuhn, Thomas S. (1996), *The structure of scientific revolutions*. 3rd edn. Chicago: University of Chicago Press. Original edition, 1962.

Latour, Bruno (1987), *Science in action: How to follow scientists and engineers through society*. Cambridge, MA: Harvard University Press.

Latour, Bruno, and Steve Woolgar (1986), *Laboratory life: The construction of scientific facts*. 2nd edn. Princeton, NJ: Princeton University Press. Original edition, Beverly Hills: Sage Publications, 1979.

Laudan, Larry (1981), "A confutation of convergent realism," *Philosophy of Science* 48(1): 19–49.

Law, John (2004), *After method: Mess in social science research*. New York: Routledge.

Lewis, Oscar (1975), *Five families: Mexican case studies in the culture of poverty*. New York: Basic Books.

List, Christian, and Philip Pettit (2011), *Group agency: The possibility, design, and status of corporate agents*. Oxford: Oxford University Press.

MacDonald, Paul (2003), "Useful fiction or miracle maker: The competing epistemological foundations of rational choice theory," *American Political Science Review* 97(04): 551–65.

MacKenzie, Donald A., Fabian Muniesa, and Lucia Siu (2007), *Do economists make markets? On the performativity of economics*. Princeton, NJ: Princeton University Press.

Mill, John Stuart (1904), *A system of logic, ratiocinative and inductive: Being a connected view of the principles of evidence and the methods of scientific investigation*. 8th edn. New York: Harper.

Pickering, Andrew (1984), *Constructing quarks: A sociological history of particle physics*. Chicago: University of Chicago Press.

——— (1995), *The mangle of practice: Time, agency, and science*. Chicago: University of Chicago Press.

Psillos, Stathis (1999), *Scientific realism: How science tracks truth*. London: Routledge.

Quinton, Anthony (1975), "The Presidential Address: Social objects," *Proceedings of the Aristotelian Society* 76: 1–27, viii.

Reed, Isaac (2008), "Justifying sociological knowledge: From realism to interpretation," *Sociological Theory* 26(2): 101–29.

Root, Michael (2000), "How we divide the world," *Philosophy of Science* 67: S628–S639.

Rosen, Gideon (1994), "Objectivity and modern idealism: What is the question?" in Michaelis Michael and John O'Leary-Hawthorne (eds.), *Philosophy in mind*, Dordrecht: Springer Netherlands, 277–319.

Searle, John R. (1995), *The construction of social reality*. New York: Free Press.

Stanford, P. Kyle (2006), *Exceeding our grasp: Science, history, and the problem of unconceived alternatives*. Oxford: Oxford University Press.

Sundstrom, Ronald R. (2002), "Race as a human kind," *Philosophy and Social Criticism* 28(1): 91–115.

Sveinsdóttir, Ásta (forthcoming), "Social construction," *Philosophy Compass*.

Thatcher, Margaret (2015), Interview for *Women's Own* magazine, October 31, 1987. Available from www.margaretthatcher.org/document/106689, accessed December 1, 2015.

Tuomela, Raimo (1990), "Methodological individualism and explanation," *Philosophy of Science* 57(1): 133–40.

Turner, Stephen P. (2003), "What do we mean by 'we'?" *Protosociology* 18–19: 139–62.

van Fraassen, Bas C. (1980), *The scientific image*. New York: Clarendon Press.

——— (1989), *Laws and symmetry*. Oxford: Oxford University Press.

Wann, Daniel L., Merrill J. Melnick, Gordon W. Russell, and Dale G. Pease (2001), *Sport fans: The psychology and social impact of spectators*. London: Routledge.

Weber, Max (1978), *Economy and society*. Berkeley: University of California Press.

Worrall, John (1989), "Structural realism: The best of both worlds?" *Dialectica* 43 (1–2): 99–124.

Wylie, Alison (1994), "Reasoning about ourselves: Feminist methodology in the social sciences," in Michael Martin and Lee C. McIntyre (eds.), *Readings in the philosophy of social science*, Cambridge, MA: MIT Press, 611–24.

# Further Reading

Brock, Stuart, and Edwin David Mares (2007), *Realism and anti-realism*. Montreal: McGill-Queen's University Press, esp. chs. 1–3. A lucid introduction to general issues about realism and antirealism.

Leplin, Jarrett, ed. (1984), *Scientific realism*. Berkeley: University of California Press. A relatively comprehensive survey of the realism–antirealism debate as it plays out in general philosophy of science, though the different contributors tend to use natural-scientific examples.

Lipton, Peter (2004), *Inference to the best explanation*. 2nd edn. New York: Routledge. Carefully presents the main explanatory pessimist arguments, and offers detailed responses to them.

Mäki, Uskali, ed. (2002), *Fact and fiction in economics: Models, realism and social construction.* Cambridge: Cambridge University Press. Discusses fictionalism with respect to economics.

Risjord, Mark (2000), *Woodcutters and witchcraft: Rationality and interpretive change in the social sciences.* Albany: State University of New York Press. Shows how ideas very similar to Lipton's can be applied to the social sciences.

Sainsbury, R. M. (2010), *Fiction and fictionalism.* New York: Routledge. A good introduction to fictionalism.

Further discussions of eliminativism, reductionism, and group realism include:

Ritchie, Katherine (2015), "The metaphysics of social groups," *Philosophy Compass* 10: 310–21.

Tuomela, Raimo (2013), *Social ontology: Collective intentionality and group agents.* Oxford: Oxford University Press.

Further discussions of social constructivism include:

Hacking, Ian (1999), *The social construction of what?* Cambridge, MA: Harvard University Press.

Mallon, Ron (2007), "A field guide to social construction," *Philosophy Compass* 2: 93–108.

Sismondo, Sergio (1993), "Some social constructions," *Social Studies of Science* 23: 515–53.

# 23
# CRITICAL REALISM
## *Justin Cruickshank*

### Introduction

In social science, realism often gets juxtaposed with positions deemed relativist, namely social constructionism, post-structuralism, and postmodernism, but the accurate distinctions are: relativism versus universalism and realism versus idealism. Idealism holds that reality consists entirely of minds and ideas. Realism, by contrast, stresses the independence of reality from us. While our ideas of reality are part of reality, reality exceeds those ideas and cannot exist in an isomorphic relation to them, with ideas being exact "copies" of objects. It is useful to distinguish between "metaphysical realism" and what is termed here "substantive realism".

Metaphysical realism turns on a dualism between our representations of reality and the reality beyond these, which is unknowable. Trigg (1989, 1993) is a major advocate of metaphysical realism. He argues that science cannot be a project that is ever finished because reality in itself cannot be known. For Trigg, the recognition of this is what motivates scientific research, with scientists seeking ever better approximations of reality.

So, with metaphysical realism, we get an empty definition of reality as that which we cannot know. By contrast, what is termed here "substantive realism" does seek to posit some defining features of reality. The term substantive realism is used to avoid confusion that may arise over different meanings of other names for this position, such as scientific or social realism. With substantive realism, the distinction is not between our ideas and representations on the one hand and an unknowable reality on the other, but between a surface level of appearances and a deeper level of unobservable—but potentially knowable—causal mechanisms. Such substantive realism has a long history in the social sciences. Durkheim's (1993) argument about the unobservable "suicidogenic currents" of "integration" and "regulation" causing fluctuations in the national suicide rate statistics, if either were too high or too low, was an early form of substantive realism.

Critical realism is a form of substantive realism and developed from the work of the philosopher Roy Bhaskar, whose books *A Realist Theory of Science* (1975/1997), *The Possibility of Naturalism* (1979/1998a), *Scientific Realism and Human Emancipation* (1986/2009), and *Reclaiming Reality* (1989/2011) established critical realism as a prominent contemporary intellectual movement. Bhaskar subsequently developed his position by developing a realist philosophy of dialectics and then spiritualism. The chapter here is concerned only with his earlier work because this exerted the most influence over the social sciences.

## Post-Positivist Naturalism

Naturalist positions argue for the unity of method between the natural and social sciences. Normally naturalism is taken to be a positivist position. Against this, Bhaskar developed a post-positivist naturalism.

Bhaskar (1997, 1998a, 2009, 2011) argues that positivism commits the "epistemic fallacy" of reducing ontological questions about defining *what* reality is to epistemological and methodological questions about *how* we know reality. This entails a fallacy because it misdefines reality. With positivism, this occurs because positivist methodologies, which are taken to be induction and the hypothetico-deductive (H-D) method, are premised on an empiricist epistemology which holds that knowledge of causality stems from direct observation of fixed empirical patterns. The use of an inductive method is premised on the view that relations of cause and effect are directly observable, which means that correlation is treated as causation. As for the H-D method, this presumes that while causes may be unobservable, their effects are manifest as fixed empirical patterns that can be directly observed. So, with both methods, the reliability of scientific explanatory knowledge is taken to stem from direct observation of fixed empirical patterns. While such positions eschew any explicit ontological commitment, they have an implicit commitment to a "closed systems ontology" which presumes that the causal processes at work in natural reality create empirical regularities that are closed to change. Thus the ontological question of *what* reality is becomes answered implicitly by the commitment to *how* we know the world through empiricism, with this leading to the presumption that reality is a closed system. As we can see empirical patterns, laws of nature and their effects (with induction), or just their effects (with the H-D method), come to be defined in terms of observable patterns. Against this, Bhaskar (1998a, 9) argues that while laboratories may create artificial closed systems, the natural world is an "open system," meaning it is open to change at the realm of observable events. In other words, the reduction of ontological questions about *what* reality is to epistemological questions about *how* we know reality via observed patterns, results in the misdefinition of reality and the misdefinition of science. For a positivist, who has to stay at the realm of the observable "surface," the acceptance of an open systems ontology would mean that science was no longer possible, because there would be no causal processes, if it was accepted that patterns broke down. Bhaskar, though, rejects such an outcome, because he does not hold that explanation of causality turns on observing fixed empirical—surface-level—patterns.

Having shown that positivism cannot account for how science operates, Bhaskar (1997, 1998a, 2009, 2011) poses a transcendental question concerning the condition of the possibility of science. To answer this, he argues that we need to look for the ontological assumptions within science that account for its explanatory success. It is ontology and not epistemology that can tell us why science gets reality right. The ontological assumptions he takes to obtain in science are that the natural world is a stratified open system. It is stratified because causal processes exist beneath the realm of observable events, so science has to go "beneath the surface" to theorize about the existence of unobservable mechanisms. Furthermore, natural reality is stratified into different levels of "emergent properties," with the domains of chemistry and biology emerging from and being irreducible to the domain of physics.

Bhaskar (1997, 36) argues that he engages in metaphysics as a "conceptual science." What this means is that instead of engaging in metaphysical speculation about the ultimate nature of reality he seeks to make explicit the hitherto implicit ontological assumptions in science, with philosophy then acting as an "underlabourer" to clear away any potential positivist confusion. The term "underlabourer" stems from John Locke (1961), who was an empiricist, but here it is empiricism (and positivism) and not metaphysics that is to be swept out of the path of progress. In making this case, Bhaskar draws a distinction between the intransitive domain of natural reality and the transitive domain of scientific theories. The latter is referred to as transitive because while science is held to be successful it is also recognized as fallible and thus scientific theories will replaced. This recognition of fallibilism leads Bhaskar to argue for "epistemological relativism" (1997, 249). The type of relativism supported here is not the view that truth is wholly relative to a perspective, for that would entail the epistemic fallacy. Instead, it is the recognition that all knowledge is relative to fallible theories. We cannot see the intransitive domain but instead seek approximations to it through fallible theories. Such theories are guided by the ontological assumptions that have worked in past scientific theories. The ontological assumptions in the transitive domain thus end up having an implicit inductive justification. They are not justified in terms of mirroring the intransitive domain but instead are justified as a set of ontological assumptions which worked in the past transitive domain and which are therefore held to work in the future transitive domain. To try and justify the ontological assumptions of science in terms of their mirroring the intransitive domain would commit the "ontic fallacy" (Bhaskar 1998b, 642) of holding that reality had spoken in its own infallible language. The implicit turn to inductive justification, though, does entail the logical problem concerning the attempt to predict future success based on events in the past being replicated.

Bhaskar (1998a) argues for a "contingent naturalism." He argues that for the social sciences to be successful they need to be based on the correct ontological assumptions for the social world, which may not necessarily be the same as those of the natural world. To address this he turns to the structure–agency problem. Structuralism is rejected for reifying structures, and methodological individualist positions are rejected for failing to account for how any explanation of what individuals do has to make reference to social factors (such as institutional rules, economic resources, gender norms, etc.). To solve the structure–agency problem, structures need to be conceptualized as mechanisms that condition but do not determine agency, with these mechanisms being unobservable in themselves and operating in open systems. Social reality is an open system because structures interact in contingent ways and agents can change structures (Bhaskar 1998a; Sayer 1992). The outcome of this is that the social sciences need to be based on the same approach as the natural sciences, namely that of explaining the operation of structures which are unobservable in themselves, in open systems. This naturalism is contingent on the reality of society, and is not a matter of dogmatically prescribing a natural scientific method for the social sciences if they seek to be scientific, which positivists do.

The philosophy of critical realism seeks to act as a "meta-theory." What this means is that it does not supply the definition of substantive specifics but general definitions of social reality, which specific theories, designed to tackle specific empirical research problems, will draw upon. In this way it will underlabor for the social sciences by sweeping aside structuralism, methodological individualism and positivist naturalism, and replacing them with a critical realist ontological vocabulary that will establish a post-positivist naturalism.

## Emergence and Morphogenesis

As induction and the H-D method are rejected for being positivist, critical realists advocate a retroductive method. This entails a "mode of inference in which events are explained by postulating (and identifying) mechanisms which are capable of producing them" (Sayer 1992, 107). Or, as Bhaskar puts it, it entails: the resolution of a complex event into its components; the redescription of the component causes; the retrodiction to possible antecedent causes; and the elimination of alternative possible causes (1998a, 129). So, one needs to start with the manifest complexity presented by an open system and then use abstractions to try and define the causal mechanisms at work. Archer's (1995) morphogentic method is one attempt to do this. This method stems from her revision of Bhaskar.

Bhaskar's naturalism was not just a contingent naturalism but also a "qualified naturalism." He was wary of defining structures as being the same as causal mechanisms in nature because this could entail determinism and reification, replacing the attempt to link structure and agency with a structuralist ontology. He therefore sought to qualify his naturalism by arguing that social structures, unlike natural structures are: dependent upon agents' conceptions of what they are doing; dependent upon agents' activity; and only relatively enduring (1998a, 38). So, capitalism, for example, may influence individuals but, unlike a law of nature, it was dependent upon what agents thought and did; and was time-limited.

Archer (1995) argued that the first two of these qualifications made Bhaskar's position similar to Giddens's "structuration theory." Giddens (1979, 1995) defined structures as rules (meaning intersubjective norms) and resources, holding that the former only had a "virtual existence" until "instantiated" (acted upon) by agents. This leads Archer to define Giddens's position as one of "central conflationism," because it conflates both structures into agents and agents into structures, by seeing structures as rules enacted by agents. For her this "ontology of the presence tense" erred by failing to recognize that structures have some autonomy from agents. (For a defense of Giddens, see Stones 2001, 2005.) To correct this, and Bhaskar's move to a similar position, she defined structures as emergent properties that are activity dependent in the past tense. What this means is that structures emerge from the actions of agents in the past and then attain causal powers in their own right. In addition to material structures, or "structural emergent properties" (SEPs), such as the economy, Archer also holds that agents are conditioned by "cultural emergent properties" (CEPs), such as religion and gender norms. The longevity of sets of ideas such as religious doctrines and gender norms can only be accounted for if they are seen not as relying on ideas in agents' heads but as emergent properties that have the power to condition agents. Both SEPs and CEPs are "structural" in a generic sense because they are both emergent properties. As regards the dependency of structures on agents' conceptions of what they are doing, Archer argues that is this only of limited relevance. Agents may get married because they have positive conceptions of this, but they may lack any conception of their act reproducing the institution of one type of family form and the CEP that informs that.

While structure and agency are always intertwined in practice, the study of their interplay has to take place over time, because agency cannot change emergent properties quickly given their relative autonomy from agents. If and when change occurs it will take time. Thus any empirical research based on critical realism needs to start by retroductively stating what structures are at work in a given situation, stating how agents and structures interact over time, and then stating whether agency leads to morphogenesis (change) or morphostasis (continuity). This is referred to by Archer (1995) as the "morphogenetic method." Carter's (2000) study of British post-war immigration policy provides an example of this. He started at the surface level of a changing economy and changing government policy. Rather than discuss the actions of individual agents, such as politicians, though, he retroductively went from the surface to the underlying emergent properties, which he defined as the SEP of a growing economy and the CEP of racism, with the SEP and CEP conditioning agents. This constituted the first phase of his morphogenetic method. He then studied the interaction between agents (politicians and trades unionists), SEPs, and CEPs, to see how morphogenesis occurred over time, with immigration being used to meet a demand for labor despite racism in many quarters.

Archer, in her later work (2000a, 2003, 2007, 2010, 2012), develops a detailed definition of agency. She argues that agency is defined by an "internal conversation" which is in turn shaped by the type of reflexivity an agent operates with. She identifies four types of reflexivity. Autonomous reflexives seek the most efficient means to follow a particular goal; meta-reflexives constantly question their goals; communicative reflexives need to discuss their goals with others and are open to their comments; and fractured reflexives experience cognitive and emotional problems in goal setting and attainment. These types of reflexivity shape how the agent responds to the enablements and constraints furnished by the prevailing emergent properties. In a review article which is positively disposed towards Archer's oeuvre, Vandenberghe (2005) does nonetheless take Archer to task for having an insufficiently social conception of agency. For him, Archer's account is too "internalist" and fails to pay heed to the linguistic turn and the "intrasubjective and intersubjective" nature of inner dialogue. Vandenberghe states that "[e]ven if one narrates one's self, the other remains present as an 'inner witness' of the personal identity to which I commit myself" (233).

## Is the Structure–Agency Problem a Real Problem?

Some social scientists argue that the structure–agency problem is a pseudo-problem. Fuller (1998) takes this view and argues that the problem is a replay of old philosophical debates about determinism and free will, which entail metaphysical speculation and which cannot therefore be translated into a social scientific language to assist empirical research. The critical realist rejoinder to this would hold that through the method of retroduction one could arrive at empirical knowledge of structures operating in open systems that condition agents by furnishing sets of constraints and enablements. For example, a recession will limit job opportunities and pay; and some businesses will survive by selling cheaper commodities.

Hay (2002, 90–91; 2006, 85–86) writes from a broadly realist perspective and takes issue with Fuller, in a way that would be different from a standard critical realist rejoinder. Hay argues that Fuller has misconstrued the issue because "seeing this as a 'problem' with a potential 'solution' is effectively to claim that the issue is an empirical one which can be resolved definitively" (Hay 2006, 86). Hay rejects this, arguing that all data are construed according to prior ontological assumptions. In other words, Hay in effect accuses Fuller of committing the epistemic fallacy by holding that the observation of empirical data can lead to one ontology, such as critical realism, being proved and another, such as structuralism, being disproved. Ontologies, though, are not manifest in the data. If we accept the case for what Hay (2002) terms the "directional dependence" of epistemology and methodology on ontology, that is, of *how* questions on *what* questions, then there is no ontologically neutral way to observe the data. So, for Fuller, the problem is a false one because it cannot be solved within social scientific research (or philosophical speculation) and for Hay the solution to the problem cannot reside in empirical testing to see which ontology is correct. Instead, for Hay, the focus has to be on which ontology is internally coherent and how useful an ontology is in framing a research problem.

While Hay argues that the structure–agency problem is a real problem, he does actually reject the critical realist concepts of "structure" and "agency." In other words, saying how agency is mediated by factors beyond individuals is a legitimate problem, but the concepts of "structure" and "agency" are objectionable. Hay argues that we should not "reify and ontologise an analytic distinction" (2002, 125). What this means is that while we need to avoid methodological individualism to say how the social context conditions agency with enablements and constraints, which means invoking "structural factors" in a generic sense to refer to that context, we need to avoid thinking that "structure" and "agency" are two separate chunks of reality. This leads Hay to criticize Archer's morphogenetic method, which is premised on the attempt to explain the inter-relationship between different chunks of reality. He argues that:

> The impression she seems to give is of structure as distant, external and long-enduring, while agency is conceptualised, in contrast, as an ephemeral or fleeting moment. This seems to imply a residual structuralism punctuated only periodically yet infrequently by a largely unexplicated conception of agency. This appears from the shadows and returns swiftly from whence it came, a perturbation or disruption in the otherwise pristine logic of structural reproduction.
>
> (Hay 2002, 126)

To address this Hay adapts Jessop's (1990) "strategic relational" ontology to solve the structure–agency problem by arguing that we need to replace the concepts of structure and agency with the concepts of "strategic action" and "strategically selective context" (Hay 2002, 127). Strategy is defined as "intentional conduct oriented towards the environment in which it is to occur" (Hay 2002, 129) and the strategic environment is "strategically selective," in that it "favours certain strategies over others to as a means to realize a given set of intentions or preferences" (Hay 2002, 129). So, an analytic distinction between agents and the context they are enmeshed within is not "ontologised" with the context being reified into a separate "thing," because the focus is on agents operating with rules and norms that are neither synonymous with agents' practices nor a separate chunk of reality.

## Two Critiques of the Critical Realist Solution to the Structure–Agency Problem

We can now consider two criticisms of the way critical realism approaches the structure–agency problem that stem from non-realist positions. First, there is the interactionist critique (see, for instance, King 1999a, 1999b; Reed 2011), which argues that individuals are always already embedded in networks of shared (or "intersubjective") meanings that furnish enablements and constraints. Unlike individualist positions, which would hold that agents' meanings and motives were wholly internal to the individual and easy to change, meanings are held to be social and have significant traction over individuals. This position leads interactionists to argue that talk of structures as separate entities from agents reifies them and that to understand how agency is conditioned socially, we need to turn to shared norms and not emergent properties. Archer (2000b) responded to this critique by arguing that it was a form of individualism, because it denied the existence of structural emergent properties, giving us just individuals and their ideas; and that it committed the epistemic fallacy, by defining *what* social reality was in terms of *how* it is known, via shared meanings.

Second, there is the "problem-solving" critique articulated by Holmwood (1996), which eschews any attempt to base empirical research on the categories of meta-theories like critical realism or general theories like functionalism. He argues that categories need to be revised in the course of empirical research and not used as an *a priori* grid that is applied to carve up the social world. Applying this to the structure–agency problem he argues thus. In order to avoid "derogating" the lay agent by adhering to some form of structuralist determinism, which would reduce agents to being mere structural puppets, agents are held to be "knowledgeable" and able to exercise free will. This concept of agency as knowledgeable free will is invoked when continuity, which is taken to be produced by structures, gives way to change. The problem here is that the concept of agency is actually empty and that it is used as a conceptual sleight of hand to try and mask explanatory break down. The concept of agency is empty because it is actually defined by what it is not: agency is not a matter of agents being determined puppets. Saying that agents are knowledgeable possessors of free will does not actually say anything substantive about how and what agents are and what leads them to act in some ways and not others. Instead, agents who are defined as not determined are invoked when continuity, which is taken to be produced by structures, is replaced by change. Holmwood argues that:

> [T]he behaviours at odds with what is expected on the basis of the schemes mobilized to account for them, should be taken seriously as an insight into what is "invalid" in those schemes, and not as something "valid" in its own right, but without implication for the "validity" of the social scientific scheme.
>
> (Holmwood 1996, 121)

This raises the question of whether Archer's elaborated conception of agency is able to meet this criticism. Archer certainly seeks to account for how the enablements and constraints furnished by structures are mediated by different types of reflexivity. Someone arguing from a problem-solving position such as Holmwood's, though, may argue that agency is too complex to be fitted into three conceptual boxes, and that the existence of "fractured reflexive" to explain everything that does not fit into the other boxes illustrates this. Furthermore, it could be argued, from such a perspective, that while agency was no longer an "empty box," it was nonetheless the case that social continuity (morphostasis) was a matter of structures reproducing themselves and that agency could only be invoked as a *post hoc* account of structures failing to reproduce themselves.

## The Role of Criticism

Why critical realism is realist has been explained and now we can consider why it is critical. There are two reasons why critical realism is "critical." First, any fallibilist position has to be critical in the sense that all ideas can be revised or replaced through criticism. Hence scientific theories constitute a transitive domain of changing knowledge. Second, some critical realists, including Bhaskar, argue that critical realism is located within the Marxist tradition of critical theory and ideology-critique.

Here critical realism would help Marxism to become a non-positivist science of capitalist structures. Thus the critique of positivism was not just part of developing a realist philosophy of natural science. Rather, it was also a way of separating science from positivism and then claiming scientific status for Marxism by holding that Marxism is in accord with a realist conception of science. Marxist realism can be a science that, as a science, gets reality right, because as a science it is based on the correct ontological assumptions (concerning unobservable structures operating in open systems), unlike positivist conceptions of science (based on a closed systems ontology stemming from the epistemic fallacy). Althusserian structuralist Marxism, which rejected the concept of agency, had sought to re-establish the scientific status of Marxism. "Analytical Marxism" was opposed to Althusserian Marxism, but, in applying the analytic philosophy of its day to Marxism, it undermined the normative aspect of Marxism. Critical realism, developed after the decline of Althusserianism and structuralism more generally, continued with the problem situation of re-interpreting Marxism in order to underpin its scientific status (Bhaskar 1991). Furthermore, unlike analytical Marxists, Bhaskar wanted to develop a science of capitalist structures that necessitated normative criticism via a fact-to-value argument.

Bhaskar sought to develop a form of ideology-critique which allowed negative value statements about capitalist structures to be derived with logical necessity from factual statements about their operation and, in so doing, he rejected the "naturalistic fallacy." The naturalistic fallacy is the fallacy of deriving normative—or value—statements about what *ought* to be the case from factual statements about what *is* the case, with the derivation being taken to be motivated by logical necessity. For many philosophers, such fact-to-value arguments are fallacious because to accept factual statement X is only to accept factual statement X, with it being a *non sequitur* to conclude on the basis of accepting factual statement X, about what *is* the case, that one *ought* therefore to accept value statement Y. To be clear, avoiding the logical derivation of *ought* from *is* does not necessarily preclude the use of normative statements. Some, such as positivists, may try to avoid normative statements, but others may not. So, for example, one could argue that if the facts of capitalism are X and one's personal values are Y, one's prior commitment to Y could motivate the criticism of X. Bhaskar, in rejecting the naturalistic fallacy, though, argues that normative statements about what *ought* to be the case can be logically derived from factual statements about what *is* the case. In other words, normative criticism can be logically necessitated. Therefore it is not a matter of subjective opinion about one's values, which would entail a value-to-value argument. To understand this we need to understand his conception of ideology.

Ideological beliefs for Bhaskar are beliefs which are not just erroneous, but erroneous and caused by structures to occlude exploitation and the extent of inequality. "Explanatory critiques" of ideology will be critical because in addition to explaining how a structure causes false beliefs, they will criticize those beliefs and the actions informed by them; lead with logical necessity to a negative value judgment about that structure; and lead with logical necessity to a positive value judgment about actions geared up to remove that structure (Bhaskar 1991, 151; 1998a, 63). That such criticism is logically necessitated stems from the view that a commitment to truth is the condition of possibility of any discourse. A commitment to truth is therefore not a value premise that leads to a value-to-value argument, with a value judgment about truth leading to a value judgment about ideology, because the commitment to truth is necessitated by all discourse. Thus a rejection of ideology is necessitated because it is contrary to the very condition of the possibility of rational communication (Bhaskar 1998a, 63). In addition to this fact-to-value argument, Bhaskar also develops a value-to-fact argument. The case here is that in the social sciences the subject matter "is in part constituted by, or indeed, just consists in, values or things to which the agents themselves ... attach value" (1998a, 58). As social reality is in part "valuey" we will move from values to facts because the values impregnated in social reality will shape the facts.

Collier argues that the value-to-fact argument

> raises a doubt as to whether [Bhaskar] may not be cutting off the branch he is sitting on. ... For if facts are already valuey it is no great matter that they entail values. ... Either the fact/value gap has not been bridged, since the whole argument is valuey, or it has not just been bridged, but the distinction abolished altogether.
>
> (Collier 1994, 175)

For Collier, this means we should just accept the fact-to-value argument and use critical realism to criticize structures which cause false beliefs in order to undermine the institutions causing those beliefs. Collier argues that:

> [P]articular institutions and false beliefs about them may be in a *functional* relation, such that the false beliefs serve to preserve the institutions they are about. ... In such cases, to propound the truth is not just to criticize, but to undermine the institution.
>
> (Collier 1994, 172)

One problem to note here is that functional explanations are teleological. A need for stability in the future pulls false beliefs into being in the past, with cause and effect becoming reversed.

We can now consider the relationship between ontology and epistemology, with regard to criticism. There is a general problem within Marxism about defining agents as passive with their beliefs (and behaviors based on them) determined by structures, with agents thus lacking knowledge as such. In the critical realist account of ideology, agents are passive with their beliefs determined by structures, which are pulled into being to meet a functional need for structural reproduction. This is problematic because teleological arguments are erroneous, and because it vitiates the attempt to construct a post-Althusserian science of capitalist structures that acknowledges the reality of agency. An alternative to deterministic Marxist accounts of ideology, which was developed before critical realism, was taken by the Centre for Contemporary Cultural Studies, who presented "popular culture" as resistance (see for instance Hall and Jefferson 2006). Another problem concerns the attempt to combine the two versions of "critical". Fay (1990), for example, holds that the commitment to fallibilism contradicts the commitment to explanatory critiques, because the acceptance of fallibilism undermines the attempt to seek certainty in arguing that normative judgments are logically necessitated.

Moving to the issue of defining structures, some Marxists criticize the critical realist definition of social reality. Gunn (1988), for example, rejects the attempt to use a meta-theory, arguing that it is inherently unMarxist. The reason for this is that Marxism is taken to have a conception of social reality that is substantive and holistic. What this means is that categories are generated in such a way as to reflect the substantive interconnections of the many aspects of society concerning, for instance, commodities, value, labor power, class, fetishism and alienation, crisis tendencies, exploitation and relative immiseration, etc. The complexity renders categories from within, so to speak. By contrast, concepts of "structure" and "agency" act as conceptual forms, or "cookie cutters," to cut up the data in an arbitrary way to fit the two abstractions that are external to that data. Everything is to be cut to fit the conceptual forms of "structure" and "agency," with the explanatory focus then being on these forms, rather than the empirical content.

For further discussion on the relationship of critical realism to Marxism and critical theory more generally see: Bhaskar (1991, 1994); Brown, Fleetwood, and Roberts (2002); Keat and Urry (2011); Magill (1994); Outhwaite (1987); Roberts (1999); and Sayer (1998, 2000).

In sum, critical realism is becoming increasingly prominent and the key debates concerning it focus on: what sort of abstractions can be used for social science, that is, whether meta-theory and the concepts of structure and agency add anything to substantive explanations; and what mode (if any) normative critique based on empirical research should take.

# References

Archer, M. S. (1995) *Realist Social Theory: The Morphogenetic Approach*, London: Routledge.

——— (2000a) *Being Human: The Problem of Agency*, Cambridge: Cambridge University Press.

——— (2000b) "For Structure, its Reality, Properties and Powers: A Reply to Anthony King," *Sociological Review* 48: 464–72.

——— (2003) *Structure, Agency and the Internal Conversation*, Cambridge: Cambridge University Press.

——— (2007) *Making Our Way through the World: Human Reflexivity and Social Mobility*, Cambridge: Cambridge University Press.

——— (ed.) (2010) *Conversations about Reflexivity*, Abingdon: Routledge.

——— (2012) *The Reflexive Imperative in Late Modernity*, Cambridge: Cambridge University Press.

Bhaskar, R. (1991) *Philosophy and the Idea of Freedom*, Oxford: Blackwell.

——— (1994) *Dialectic: The Pulse of Freedom*, London: Verso.

——— (1997 [1975]) *A Realist Theory of Science*, 2nd edn., London: Routledge.

——— (1998a [1979]) *The Possibility of Naturalism: A Philosophical Critique of the Contemporary Human Sciences*, 3rd edn., London: Routledge.

——— (1998b) "Dialectical Critical Realism and Ethics," in M. S. Archer, R. Bhaskar, A. Collier, T. Lawson, and A. Norrie (eds.) *Critical Realism: Essential Readings*, London: Routledge, 641–87.

——— (2009 [1986]) *Scientific Realism and Human Emancipation*, Abingdon: Routledge.

——— (2011 [1989]) *Reclaiming Reality: A Critical Introduction to Contemporary Philosophy*, Abingdon: Routledge.

Brown, Andrew, Fleetwood, Steve, and Roberts, John (eds.) (2002) *Critical Realism and Marxism*, London: Routledge.

Carter, B. (2000) *Realism and Racism: Concepts of Race in Sociological Research*, London: Routledge.

Collier, A. (1994) *Critical Realism: An Introduction to Roy Bhaskar's Philosophy*, London: Verso.

Durkheim, E. (1993) *Suicide: A Study in Sociology*, London: Routledge.

Fay, B. (1990) "Critical Realism?" *Journal for the Theory of Social Behaviour* 20: 33–41.

Fuller, S. (1998) "From Content to Context: A Social Epistemology of the Structure–Agency Craze," in A. Sica (ed.) *What is Wrong with Social Theory? The Philosophical Debates*, Oxford: Blackwell, 92–117.

Giddens, A. (1979) *Central Problems in Social Theory: Action, Structure and Contradiction in Social Analysis*, Basingstoke: Macmillan.

——— (1995) *The Constitution of Society*, Cambridge: Polity.

Gunn, R. (1988) "Marxism and Philosophy: A Critique of Critical Realism," *Capital and Class* 37: 87–116.

Hall, S. and Jefferson, T. (eds.) (2006 [1975]) *Resistance through Rituals: Youth Subcultures in Postwar Britain*, 2nd edn., Abingdon: Routledge (first published as *Working Papers in Cultural Studies* no. 7/8).

Hay, C. (2002) *Political Analysis: A Critical Introduction*, Basingstoke: Palgrave.

——— (2006) "Political Ontology," in R. E. Goodin and L. Tilly (eds.) *The Oxford Handbook of Contextual Political Analysis*, Oxford: Oxford University Press, 78–96.

Holmwood, J. (1996) *Founding Sociology? Talcott Parsons and the Idea of General Theory*, London: Routledge.

Jessop, Bob (1990) *State Theory: Putting the Capitalist State in its Place*, Cambridge: Polity Press.

Keat, R. and Urry, J. (2011 [1975]) *Social Theory as Science*, London: Routledge Revivals.

King, A. (1999a) "Against Structure: A Critique of Morphogenetic Social Theory," *Sociological Review* 47: 199–227.

—— (1999b) "The Impossibility of Naturalism: The Antinomies of Bhaskar's Realism," *Journal for the Theory of Social Behaviour* 29: 267–88.

Locke, J. (1961) *An Essay Concerning Human Understanding. An Abridgment*, London: Dent.

Magill, K. (1994) "Against Critical Realism," *Capital and Class* 54: 113–36.

Outhwaite, W. (1987) *New Philosophies of Social Science: Realism, Hermeneutics and Critical Theory*, Basingstoke: Palgrave Macmillan.

Reed, I. A. (2011) *Interpretation and Social Knowledge: On the Use of Theory in the Human Sciences*, London: University of Chicago Press.

Roberts, J. M. (1999) "Marxism and Critical Realism: The Same, Similar, or Just Plain Different?" *Capital and Class* 68: 21–49.

Sayer, A. (1992 [1984]) *Method in Social Science: A Realist Approach*, 2nd edn., London: Routledge.

—— (1998) "Critical Realism and the Limits to Critical Social Science," *Journal for the Theory of Social Behaviour* 27: 473–88.

—— (2000) *Realism and Social Science*, London: Sage.

Stones, R. (2001) "Refusing the Realism–Structuration Divide," *European Journal of Social Theory* 4: 177–97.

—— (2005) *Structuration Theory*, Basingstoke: Palgrave Macmillan.

Trigg, R. (1989 [1980]) *Reality at Risk: A Defence of Realism in Philosophy and the Sciences*, 2nd edn., Hemel Hempstead: Harvester Wheatsheaf.

—— (1993) *Rationality and Science: Can Science Explain Everything?* Oxford: Blackwell.

Vandenberghe, F. (2005) "The Archers. A Tale of Folk (Final Episode?)," *European Journal of Social Theory* 8: 227–37.

# 24
# OBJECTIVITY

## *Eleonora Montuschi*

If we look at the various contexts in which objectivity is pursued (scientific inquiry, social debates, policy decisions) we immediately realize that, by referring to this concept, there is often a chasm between what is ideally aimed at and what can be sensibly argued for and/or achieved in practice (different practices).

Traditional empiricist epistemology tells us that to be objective is to represent the world the way it really is. This is sometimes referred to as 'the view from nowhere' (Nagel 1986), which entails looking at the world in a way that transcends individual experience, perception, or perspective. The underlying assumption is that our mind is such that, by either association of ideas (e.g. Locke) or by means of innate rules of reasoning (Descartes), it is able 'mechanically' and without any creative additions to reproduce existing states of affairs. A crucial corollary to this assumption is, of course, that *there is a way* that the world is, independently of how we view it, or what we make of it—a way that our mind can faithfully capture.

The domain of inquiry that best suits this scenario has long appeared to be the natural sciences. There is a long tradition—from Bacon to Hume to Galileo and Descartes—that claims that there are facts in nature that natural science is well equipped to investigate. The empirical methods of science successfully lead to the discovery of the natural laws that describe those facts with accuracy and explain them. The results of scientific inquiry are then the closest kin to offering a 'view from nowhere'. So called 'mechanical objectivity' established itself as the ideal image of scientific representation: "the image, as standard bearer of objectivity, is tied to a relentless search to replace individual volition and discretion in depiction by the invariable routines of mechanical reproduction" (Daston and Galison 1992, 98). Mechanical objectivity also entailed a particular type of scientist: "long on diligence and self-restraint, scant on genial interpretation," someone who is willing to "let nature speak for itself" (Daston and Galison 2007, 120–21).

Historically, traditional empiricist epistemology and the natural sciences have become *the* models for defining objectivity in the sense just suggested, as well as for dictating the standards by which to assess whether, and how far, domains and procedures of inquiry are (or can be) objective. The social sciences—a later addition to the field of science[1]—are enmeshed in this joint scenario. They were evaluated in comparison with the natural sciences, and this portrayed them from the start as 'lesser' sciences, bound to imitate the well-established paradigm of the natural sciences. In particular, by modeling social facts on natural facts, they were asked to embrace an epistemological view of objectivity that does not necessarily or appropriately fit the social domain. Indeed, the social sciences, besides being penalized by this comparison, were also somehow cheated: the traditional epistemological framework of knowledge as embraced by scientific method was put under severe critical scrutiny in the second half of the 20th century, and at least by its most radical critics it was declared altogether untenable. The image of science that social science was meant to imitate gradually lost at least some of its paradigmatic appeal.

That the social sciences have been caught in this comparison, and with what consequences, can be seen from two of the main debates where the issue of objectivity has been traditionally raised and discussed: the real/constructed debate, and the fact/value debate. In this chapter I will first retrace the general features of these two traditional debates and bring out the meaning of a concept of objectivity for social science formulated within the epistemological limits and constraints set out by these debates.

However, it will also be pointed out that these debates illustrate attempts at readjusting the concept of objectivity in such a way that might better fit it to the social domain—enough of an admission that the ideal standard is at the very least insufficiently descriptive within this domain (and possibly more generally, across the board of scientific disciplines). Reflecting on objectivity along these readjusted lines makes us ponder on what of the traditional concept can be retained and what ought to be dropped—to the point of doubting whether any concept of objectivity can retain at all a meaning and purpose in contemporary discussions. As a matter of fact, a craving for objectivity still plays a central role, for example in the ongoing debate on the use of science, natural and social, in policy making (the so called 'evidence-based policy and practice' movement), or in the contentious disputes concerning the reliability of so-called expert opinion. In the second half of this chapter I will look into what is expected of a concept of objectivity when it enters these more practice-oriented debates, and whether it still makes sense to invoke such a concept. We will see that, *pace* traditional epistemology, if objectivity is believed to have some use in the realm of social practice, it cannot ignore contexts, interpretations of contexts, and human judgment.

## 1 Received Views and Issues Redressed

### 1.1 Objectivity and Man-Made Facts

One way of questioning the objectivity of social science is by questioning the reality of the facts and phenomena it investigates. Surely an objective science should deal with 'real facts', facts whose existence can be discovered by our theories, inquiries, experiments, etc. Ontological objectivity, taken in this sense, entails that the objects of the material world, the world of nature, ought to be 'out there' (in some way to be qualified), and that they do not need human intervention in order to exist. Social objects, instead, seem to exist precisely because humans make them what they are, in the forms and types that we are acquainted with in our societies: money, marriages, race, political leaders, etc. Social facts owe their existence to societal configurations and choices, not to natural law. It is our actions, our inquiries, our theories, or our history that contingently and contextually make up social facts. Sometimes this idea is expressed by saying that social facts are 'invented' by humans. Needless to say, if we follow this line of argument, a science of invented facts barely qualifies as being 'objective', let alone as being a science *tout court*.

The discovered/invented divide has been traditionally used to mark a substantial difference between the natural and the social sciences, and to claim that only the former can be objective, as they deal with real objects (objects that are not an effect of their own creation). As is well known, the argument concerning the invented nature of man-made facts was widened also to include the reality of natural facts. Natural facts are as invented as the social facts, it was claimed, therefore the objectivity of natural science is on a par with that of social science, i.e. itself an invention.[2] However, even if we are prepared to maintain a distinction between the two domains and argue for an ontological difference between natural and social facts, this does not entail that objectivity is an out-of-reach goal in the social domain of inquiry. It does, though, take some domain-specific further reflection. A few examples will point in this direction.

According to Searle (1995), there is indeed a significant ontological difference between natural and social facts (or 'brute' and 'institutional' facts, as he refers to each of the two categories). Natural facts, unlike social facts, exist even without us: mountains are there, whether we represent them or not, whether we climb them or not. Natural facts, as he puts it, are ontologically objective. Social facts, instead, exist only if we represent them: in this sense, they are ontologically subjective. Yet, they qualify as objective entities, though only in an epistemic sense. What Searle means is that such facts owe their 'objective existence' to a collectively sustained recognition of their existence, namely to human agreement. More specifically, he argues, these facts might have some physical or material existence (for example, a piece of green paper in my pocket) but this is not enough nor appropriate to grant objective existence as social facts (e.g. being a five-dollar bill). In order for these facts to be acknowledged as objective kinds of entities (e.g. money), their physical existence needs to be represented and used in a particular way by one/more classes of individuals who agree about their specific representation and use. In this way, an ontology of objective social facts becomes possible, and so—we might add—is an objective science that deals with this category of facts (facts that are at the same time ontologically subjective and epistemologically objective, in Searle's terminology).

But there is more. If we focus on the mechanism of representation, a further difference can be brought up as regards natural and social facts. In describing the objects of the natural and the social world, Ian Hacking famously made a distinction between 'indifferent' and 'interactive' kinds (Hacking 1999, 103–6). "The classification 'quark' is indifferent'," he explained, "in the sense that calling a quark 'quark' makes no difference to the quark." With social or human kinds, the situation changes. When, as it happens in the social sciences, people and people-related facts become an object of study—child TV viewers, criminals, women refugees, racism referred to black and white people, etc.—they 'interact' (accordingly or contrastively) with the ways they are classified, described, or represented. People themselves also often experience who they are and what they do in the world according to ongoing classifications and descriptions. There is a feedback, or 'looping' effect involved with classifying people, which does not occur in the case of natural kinds, and which typifies the representational mechanism of social-kind making. *Kinds* of people may change, because the *people* classified as being of certain kinds might themselves change as a consequence of being so classified. The targeted referents of social scientific inquiries are, so to speak, constantly (at least in principle) on the move.

What effects does the way we classify social kinds have on their reality? Where should we look for their reality, if they owe their existence to the way we represent them? Does, or can, a science of social kinds be objective? It has been argued that the reality of social kinds should be assessed at the level of the specific categories the social order proceeds from, and not by comparison with natural-kind categories. Michael Root (2000), for example, claimed that in the social sciences "real taxonomy is less about generalization and more about regulations: we divide ourselves not by discovering our differences but by requiring ourselves to be different." Social categories, in other words, are essentially normative: "extrapolation across all instances is not possible, but normalization is," in the sense that social categories may prescribe not so much how whatever is classified by means of a certain category is, but rather how it ought to be. This is why these categories are "well made for social regulation" (Root 2000, S633). This does not mean that social categories are 'less real' than natural categories. The social world, just as the natural one, is ordered, but the source of such order is different: as Jon Elster once pointed out, it is an order based on norms and regulations (Elster 1989, 287; also quoted in Root 2000, S635).

Root discusses the example of race. Race, he claims, is like crime. If we had not invented appropriate laws or drawn certain property distinctions, nobody would be guilty of theft. Yet, given that we did, social scientists can classify us along certain categories, provide descriptions and explanations by making use of them, and even try to predict or explain phenomena and trends by means of those categories. Race is biologically real: to be black is to be black, not just to be perceived as being black, or to be believed to be black. And yet, the reality of race as a social category depends "on what we (collectively) have made of race, and … whether we regulate or discipline each other by race. Should we divide but not regulate by race, we would retain the races but not conserve their reality." So Root concludes: "Laws of nature do not make race real, we do" (Root 2000, S635, S638). As Searle would also say, we add categories to the world, we make 'new things' exist in the world by means of our categories, and we then turn towards investigating these 'things' with the tools and techniques of any science. The real/invented divide is not necessarily a threat for an objective science of the social.

This divide was, however, also taken up from one side in this debate as a reason for doubting whether using science to describe and explain social facts is indeed altogether appropriate. The subject matter of social research is not, properly speaking, social 'facts', but rather human action—a category, or better a 'concept', it is here argued, that cannot be captured by an apparatus of laws and causes. In the late 1950s Peter Winch, informed by Wittgensteinian philosophy, argued that in order to understand what is at stake when individuals act in historical and social contexts we ought to appeal to socially shared rules, meanings, reasons, and interpretations. No social 'science' can achieve this type of understanding. This is a task for a social philosophy.

Asking whether social philosophy can be objective cannot then be answered by invoking scientific methods and their results. Social philosophy is objective when it can grasp the point of, say, a social action in the light of, and on the basis of, community-followed rules of behavior—rules that we all share (more or less critically, or contentiously) when we act, and/or that we try to unveil and understand when others act. To be objective here is a type of intersubjective intelligibility made possible by a domain-specific understanding of the ontology of the social world (Winch 1958).

### 1.2 Do Values Detract from Objectivity?

Separating out facts from evaluations was one of the epistemological obsessions of empiricist philosophy. Starting from Hume's famous distinction between 'is' and 'ought' (signaling statements of facts, pertaining to how things are, and statements of value, pertaining to how we view things), a long tradition has sedimented on the position that knowledge is objective (and so is the inquiry into knowledge) only if values are sidelined. Values entail perspectives, perspectives are by definition partial, and partiality easily leads to distortion.

Objective knowledge cannot distort how things are. It should instead describe them as they really are. Besides, in this tradition values, by belonging to the realm of subjectivity, express inclinations, attitudes and feelings that cannot be factually justified or rationally disputed.

Knowledge cannot be objective and evaluational at the same time, precisely because objectivity entails justification and rational resolution of conflict among viewpoints (only one out of a range of viewpoints can be the objective one, and for reasons that are both valid and factual).

Scientific knowledge has become the prototype of this position, along this tradition. Of course natural scientists have beliefs or make value-judgments. However, their scientific results are independent of those beliefs and values. There cannot be any connection (logical inference) between factual conclusions and the presence of evaluations in the premises of scientists' investigations (see, among others, Hempel 1965, 91). In this sense, value-freedom is at the very essence of 'scientific' inquiry proper, and when social science entered the debate on the status of science and objective knowledge, in the late 19th century, this was the consolidated view it had to confront with. How did social science score vis-à-vis this general perspective?

Objects such as marriages, racism, political leaders—unlike molecules, gas temperature, and chemical reactions—arguably entail the very viewpoints and values that identify them as the type of objects they are in the societies where they belong and where they are valued (or devalued). Take those viewpoints and values away (indeed, take humans away) and they would cease to exist altogether, as we saw in the previous section. Asking social science not to deal with values would be just like asking it to be a science with no objects to investigate. Aware of this impasse, supporters of empiricism pursued strategies to have it both ways: keep values at a manageable distance and declare social science something of a science. Here are some alternative ways of achieving this.

Ernest Nagel pointed out that, regarding the fact/value distinction, the social sciences are not in a very different position from the natural sciences. Take for example a sociologist of religion who, in order to analyze his subject matter (religion), is required to characterize a series of distinctions within and about religion—for instance, a distinction between a mercenary and non-mercenary attitude. A distinction of this sort is somehow value-dependent, in that a value-judgment is passed through the terminology here adopted (the term 'mercenary' is normally used with some pejorative overtone). However, this does not make the sociologist much different from a physicist who describes a particular chronometer as inaccurate, or from a biologist who describes anemia as an undesirable condition. In fact, the attitude, commonly shared by both kinds of scientists, of expressing an evaluation (approval/disapproval) of the objects they describe does not prevent, or take over, their capacity for characterizing those objects, that is for making "an estimate of the degree to which some commonly recognised type of action, object or institution is embodied in a given instance" (Nagel 1961, 493–94). In both cases we are able to detect that an evaluation has been imposed on the description of either object, and this shows how there is more than values in that description. Admittedly, says Nagel, isolating the evaluational input might prove more difficult in the case of the social sciences (values are here commonly attached not only to the ends but also to the means of social research; values are often embedded in the very terminology used by the social scientists, etc.), but this is a practical difficulty, not an impossibility in principle.

With this position, the social sciences are put on a par with the natural sciences vis-à-vis the distinction (at least in principle). However, even assuming that the evaluational content—despite practical difficulties—can be singled out and put on hold, we are still left with the problem of what to do with the 'exuberance' of values in the social domain. Max Weber gives an articulated answer to this problem by analyzing how and where values play their role in social scientific inquiries, and even before that, by questioning whether altogether different types of values are present in those inquiries.

An important distinction must be drawn, says Weber, between individual, practical evalua-tions or prejudices (what he calls *value-judgments*) and those values which attribute significance to, and reveal our interest in, what we investigate—that is, values, which make certain objects relevant for us to inquire about (*cultural values*) (Weber 1904). In choosing what to investigate in social inquiry *value relevance* is what social scientists appeal to (they use values, rather than fixed criteria). So, for example, what makes the emergence of capitalism in Europe an interesting 'object' of sociological investigation is, according to Weber, a particular feature of it, that is, the fact that capitalism has become a systematic attempt to organize human activities in an efficient, calculable, and impersonal way. This is the feature that Weber calls 'internal rationalization'. As a result, capitalism will be studied according to the features deemed *relevant* for an interesting sociological investigation. Or more generally, what qualifies an event as 'socio-economic' is not something that the event itself possesses objectively. Its identification is rather conditioned by "the specific cultural significance which we attribute to the particular event" (Weber 1904, 64).

Nonetheless, a value-dependent (or value-relevant) object of inquiry does not exclude the possibility of a value-free investigation. Indeed, once the object of a social inquiry has been identified by means of relevant values, the social scientist is free (and must be free) to proceed in the investigation of this object by making use of the empirical, testable methods of any science. Social science can, in other words, for Weber be 'objective' despite being informed by relevant values.

The problem for Weber is not only to distinguish facts and values, but to distinguish between different categories of values, and allow research to be driven (at least initially) by the 'right kind'. The objects of inquiry for Weber (partially informed by a Kantian viewpoint) are by necessity 'perspectival' objects (he names them 'ideal types'), assembled and identified according to what we value and what makes them interesting: "in the method of investigation, the guiding 'point of view' is of great importance for the *construction* of the conceptual scheme which will be used in the investigation" (Weber 1904, 84).

Weber's position is important not only in opening a more nuanced debate about the nature and role of values in science (Kincaid et al. 2007; Longino 1990), but also in allowing a re-evaluation of the concept of objectivity as traditionally constrained by empiricist epistemology. Against the backdrop of a strict fact/value distinction the default position is that of keeping facts separate from values. On a Weberian framework we should keep facts separate only from cer-tain types of values. This allows for a further step: deciding what values can stay in (e.g. how to define and control bias), and where in the scientific process they can exert their influence (e.g. "the construction of the conceptual scheme," as we have just read) without detracting from the objectivity of inquiry. At the end of the 1950s the Swedish economist G. Myrdal claimed that if there is a "value problem in social science," this should be made to work for us, and not against us. By this he meant that values should as far as possible be acknowledged in social research, and be given a strategically favorable position—that is, they ought to be turned into means of inquiry rather than being pictured as a detrimental by-product of it (Myrdal 1958).

This also entails that values, despite empiricist veto, can be exposed to rational discus-sion and to a better understanding of the issues involved. Consider for example some recent discussion in climate change literature concerning how 'to discount' future generations, and how much or how quickly to invest in reducing carbon emission. Here it was shown how dif-ferent value-laden premises lead to different figures of discount rate. A utilitarian (such as the economist Nicholas Stern) calculates a low rate, whereas someone supposedly driven by a prioritarian moral view (such as William Nordhaus or Richard Toll) projects a much higher rate (Broome 2008; Cartwright and Montuschi 2014, 131–33). Does this mean that there is no objective figure to attach to the discount rate in this discussion? Quite the contrary, acknowledging the 'guiding points of view' in research, to use Weber's terminology, rather than detracting from objectivity, could fruitfully open scientific inquiry to the advantages of a more inclusive and meaningful discussion.

One way of describing what form this type of inquiry might take is to adopt what Helen Longino calls 'transformative criticism', a methodological strategy that makes the process of scientific inquiry responsive to a plurality of views and criticisms (Longino 1990, 73–74). Objectivity, in a perspective like Longino's, is secured by subscribing to a view of scientific inquiry framed and controlled by public criteria of social scrutiny for the evaluation of evidence, methods, assumptions, and reasoning. It is from this context that objectivity, as the practical goal of a critically aware (as well as accountable) scientific community, can only thrive.

## 2 From Theory to Practice

### 2.1 The Objectivity of 'Evidence-Based' Policy

In the age of science, evidence is considered to be the benchmark of objective knowledge. If to know objectively is to prove that a hypothetical claim is true (or false), or to be able to form an undisputed belief concerning the hypothesis, then evidence is the means to achieve this. To know *that p* means that I have the required evidence (to support, to prove, to justify) *that p*. Of course, in order to achieve this, evidence itself is to be objective (that is based on objective knowledge of the facts used as evidence).

In practical contexts, such as the formulation or the implementation of a policy, this role of evidence extends to the realm of decision-making. If we can count on good evidence to prove that, say, a certain intervention will be effective (or stands a good chance to be so), then basing our decision to implement such an intervention on the evidence we have will make our decision 'objective'. Evidence is the means to objective decisions.

The increasingly influential evidence-based policy and practice (EBPP) movement subscribes to this view, and advocates that basing policy on the results of evidence coming from scientific knowledge, including social scientific knowledge, is the key to making policy decisions more objective. With this in mind, governments are more and more willing to fund evidence-based approaches to policy-making; and government funding is increasingly tied to the demand for evidence (Cartwright 2008). There is political interest in assessing, as well as testing "the extent to which policies are 'evidence-based'" ( Science and Technology Committee 2006). In discussing its Millennium Development Goals, the United Nations also recommended EBP because: "evidence-based policymaking refers to a policy process that helps planners make better informed decisions by putting the best available evidence at the centre of the policy process" (UNICEF 2008).

Who could be opposed to this agenda? Consulting well-established empirical facts based on reliable methods, measurements and experiments when we make policy surely makes policy decisions more credible, more reliable, more solid, more corroborated. It even becomes tempting to think that the objectivity of our decisions is a direct consequence of the objectivity of the knowledge used to establish the evidence: the more certain our methods of acquiring evidence, and the better the quality of evidence, the better the decisions. So, a considerable amount of work has been put into how to regulate the use of evidence in the domains of practice. New institutional rules, structures, and guidelines have been suggested with this aim in mind.[3] For example, there is a widespread recommendation in policy practice to evaluate evidence according to 'evidence-ranking schemes'.[4] The idea behind these schemes is that a fixed rank can be given to kinds of evidence, and then depending on how the kinds are ranked, they are positioned in a hierarchy within the scheme. The scheme then "adjudicates" evidence from the very best to the second best, all the way down to the worst (less/least reliable).

Interestingly, if we glance through these hierarchical schemes, it is often the case that best evidence is associated with one particular type of methodology: well-conducted RCTs (randomized control trials) and/or systematic reviews of good RCTs.[5] There are several reasons why RCTs are pointed at as the 'gold standards' for providing evidence. They have inbuilt assumptions which ensure the results from an ideal trial (their results can be directly deduced from the evidence provided) and control for confounders (i.e. those variables that could interfere with genuine causes). Also, they calculate evidence in terms of probability, so the higher the probability, the better the evidence (and given that all concepts are operationalized, bias is purportedly kept under check). They seem, in other words, to entail some of the features that are deemed essential to ensure an objective outcome: certainty, rigor, quantitative formulation, measurability of results, strict experimental protocols, and absence of subjective distortion. For these appealing reasons they are widely used (or at least invoked) in policy-making projects and pilot program across a large variety of fields of social intervention (education, crime, poverty, child welfare, etc.).

However, those very features, that might well depict objectivity in the controlled field of a trial, or indeed in the ideal realm of (social) scientific inquiry, do not necessarily or automatically translate into a matching effect of objectivity in practice. When scientific and social scientific methodological apparata such as RCTs are used in pursuits such as justifying a policy decision, or handling a dispute over a social cause, there is a danger that the meaning of objectivity that we ideally attach to scientific inquiry (and as intended by using those apparata) takes over. The result might be overly selective: complex and varied hosts of facts and factors that come from the social domain get ignored, as they do not naturally fit within the strict parameters of, say, an experimental design (e.g. in a trial the efficacy of an intervention is tested under very special conditions). Context, local conditions, individual and social biographies, anecdotal evidence, 'field' knowledge—despite often proving to have an important, if not crucial, role to play— might not receive adequate recognition as they might not be immediately recognized as being relevant, or 'treatable', by rigorous scientific methodology.

This has at least two consequences. In practice, a neglect to address them appropriately might result in poor implementation and meager outcomes.[6] In theory, a concept of objectivity obtained by sticking to such a restrictively conceived 'evidence base' fails to capture what is at stake in real-world circumstances.

## 2.2 Is Expert Judgment Objective?

As RCTs come on top of evidence-ranking schemes, almost unfailingly expert opinion appears at the very bottom of these schemes. Indeed, part of the appeal of RCTs is that they are 'mechanical' procedures, and as such they can avoid subjective judgment. Expert opinions, despite qualifications to the contrary, are still 'opinions', and as such they are viewed as the poorest providers of solid evidence. This might appear puzzling. We all do endorse 'expert culture'. For most decisions, actions, resolutions, estimates, choices, in both private and public life, we can and often do rely on, or at least refer to, some expert, or experts, in one or more relevant fields. Take for example the case of child welfare. In our society, governments delegate different figures of experts to assess children's needs, to evaluate the adequacy of families in meeting these needs and to measure children's development in the context of the institutions they have created. This is how a 'curriculum of childhood' becomes the standard by which children's 'normal' growth is systematized and evaluated (Saraceno 1984). Yet, we also live in an 'expert-wearied culture'—or even worse, in an 'expert-despondent culture'. We are surrounded by too many experts (and indeed by too many bad experts) and this is enough to make us suspicious across the board, and often unsympathetic towards the category in general. To use the same example, in child welfare expert opinion is often associated with 'clinical judgment', which is viewed as experience-laden, intuitive, synthetic, individual, and unsystematic.

All in all, what makes expert opinion appealing to us, and makes us resort to experts in the first place—for example the exercise and display of competent judgment on issues and problems that matter, and that we are not able to solve on our own—seems nonetheless to be what makes us most uneasy about those very opinions: a lack of objectivity, and an excess of subjective discretion in how they provide for closure in the search for reliable evidence and reliable answers based on that evidence.

Should experts be trusted, and under what circumstances? To answer this question we often find ourselves resorting to issues more complicated and open-ended than the question itself. Trust might depend on the *authority* of the expert, but as any argument from authority would show, authority is not *ipso facto* an indicator of reliable expertise. Arguments from authority are first of all inductive arguments: to demonstrate that someone has the claimed authority is an empirical question, and often a contested and controversial one. Further, these types of argument can often fall prey to a logical fallacy: the truth of a conclusion cannot be logically (necessarily) inferred from whoever asserts it. This does not entail that the conclusion in question is false, only that the person who asserts it is not a sufficient condition for its truth. What other conditions ought to be granted in view of trusting the authority of an expert? The authority of the field of knowledge an expert appeals to (for example, a well-established scientific paradigm for an expert scientist) certainly is a primary matching condition. But assessing the authority of science, and on what parameters (epistemological, social, pragmatic), is itself a notoriously tangled call. Besides, even after accepting the authority of a well-established paradigm, we are still left with the question of whether the purported expert has sufficient knowledge of the field he/she derives authority from, whether knowledge in that field is all is needed to address the specific problem he/she is asked to deal with, or whether the claims he/she makes on the basis of his/her knowledge are free from conflict of interest, biases, etc.

This last issue in particular brings us to consider a second complex issue: trust has a bearing on the *responsibility* of the expert. Trusting an expert entails trusting that he/she does his/her job according to the rules of the profession (more/other than the rules of scientific method) as well as to the rules of the society where he/she operates—and the two sets of rules do not necessarily comply with each other. 'To be responsible' changes connotation depending on what sets of rules are valued more: on one side it might be felt that the greatest responsibility is towards knowledge, no matter what the consequences (social, moral) of pursuing it might be; on the other, it might be argued that the first responsibility is to society, and that the value of scientific truth does not exclude any other value. What expert would we trust more, then? Answering this question presupposes accepting from the start a trade-off between scientific truth and social good, which is sometimes a difficult call to make when it comes to trust—and even more so when it comes to trusting experts to give an objective opinion (which is different from trusting the purportedly objective results of an experimental trial). Should experts be consulted at all, and for what reasons? What do they provide that other sources of knowledge and/or evidence do not?

If we look back at evidence-ranking schemes, expert opinions are listed among the means for producing evidence—on a par with methods such as RCTs, cohort studies, etc.—but, given that the standards for quality are settled by those methods, expert opinion by default scores badly for quality: it seems to lack the rigor, systematic design, and deductive structure of those methods. However, as pointed out in the previous section, in practical contexts all these features are rarely sufficient to secure objective results on their own. Once a decision has been formulated, say, to suspend sales of dairy products which contain an excess percentage of dioxin per mml that could be harmful to humans (Douglas 2004), we are still left with the problem of checking what entered into that decision in terms not only of facts and scientific knowledge, but also of how the information that made it to the list of possible evidence was weighed, selected, amalgamated.[7] Besides, what social effects are considered more relevant, more acceptable or unacceptable in formulating the decision in question (public health problems or economic repercussions) depend on value judgments, sensitive to social and/or ethical considerations. In 'putting it all together' we cannot count on unfailing, mechanical 'gold standards'. An authoritative and responsible expert (though with awareness of the problems of definition sketched out above) might be in a position to undertake this task. In this sense good experts are 'aggregators' of knowledge: this is what qualifies their 'expertise' besides and beyond competence in a field of knowledge (Turner 2013, 193).[8] And if an expert opinion is to prove its objectivity in practice it cannot but be sustained and enacted by reliable subjectivity.

The discussion in the last two sections has the purpose to illustrate that when we move from theory to social practice a concept of objectivity must prove to be up to the challenges posed by complex and often difficult to represent (let alone predict) social domains. The protocols of social scientific inquiry (though with all the qualifications highlighted in the first half of this chapter) fall short of what is needed to make objectivity not only a desideratum of scientific research, but also a practical, and as far as possible achievable, goal for the good of society.

## Notes

1  The social sciences started appearing in the 19th century, while the natural sciences emerged in the 17th century.
2  Supporters and detractors of his argument ignited what became famous in some philosophical and sociological literature of the early 1990s as 'the science wars' (see Koertge 1998; Kukla 2000; Ross 1996).
3  Among these institutions are the Cochrane Collaboration (evidence-based medicine) and, modeled on the former, the Campbell Collaboration, which expands the idea of being 'evidence-based' to the fields of education, crime and justice, and social welfare. For details of these two organizations see their webpages at www.cochrane.org/ and www.campbellcollaboration.org/.
4  Examples of these ranking schemes can be found in SIGN (2004); or the Oxford Centre for Evidence-Based Medicine Levels of Evidence (2007).
5  A randomized controlled trial is an experiment in which investigators randomly assign eligible subjects (or other units of study, e.g. classrooms, clinics, playgrounds) to two groups. One of the groups receives one or more interventions (e.g. a particular treatment). The other does not receive it. If the observed outcome in the group that received the intervention is observed as being statistically significant, then it is concluded that it has indeed been caused by the experimenters' manipulation, i.e. there is a high probability that the intervention actually works. A systematic review is a literature review of all the evidence found in studies dealing with a particular research question that has been screened and has passed the

test for quality (by means of criteria and procedures explicitly defined in advance). Systematic reviews of RCTs include the results of all well-conducted RCTs (according to the quality criteria established for RCTs).

6 For examples of the limits of programme implementation see Cartwright and Hardie 2012; Seckinelgin 2008; Dehue 2002.

7 Douglas's argument is intended to deal with cases when science provides for uncertain evidence (e.g. there is no conclusive evidence about the cancerogenic effects of dioxin on humans). A similar argument can be purportedly put forward any time science impacts on contexts of use, no matter how certain scientific evidence is.

8 There is a vast literature (literatures) on experts and expertise. For a sample of the issues involved see e.g. Crease and Selinger 2006; Collins and Evans 2007; Cooke and Probst 2006.

# References

Broome, J. (2008), "The Ethics of Climate Change," *Scientific American*, 298 (June): 69–73.

Cartwright, N. (2008), "Evidence-Based Policy: Where Is Our Theory of Evidence?" in A. Beckermann, H. Tetens, and S. Walter (eds.), *Philosophy: Foundations and Applications*, Paderborn: Mentis-Verlag.

Cartwright, N. and Hardie, J. (2012), *Evidence-Based Policy. A Practical Guide to Doing it Better*, Oxford: Oxford University Press.

Cartwright, N. and Montuschi, E. eds. (2014), *Philosophy of Social Science: A New Introduction*, Oxford: Oxford University Press.

Collins, H. M. and Evans, R. (2007), *Rethinking Expertise*, Chicago: University of Chicago Press.

Cooke, R. M. and Probst, K. N. (2006), *Highlights of the Expert Judgment Policy Symposium and Technical Workshop*, Washington, DC: Resources for the Future.

Crease, R. and Selinger, E. (2006), *The Philosophy of Expertise*, New York: Columbia University Press.

Daston, L. and Galison, P. (1992), "The Image of Objectivity," *Representations*, 40 (Special Issue: Seeing Science): 81–128.

Daston, L. and Galison P. (2007), *Objectivity*, New York: Zone Books.

Dehue, T. (2002), "A Dutch Treat: Randomised Controlled Experimentation and the Case of Heroin Maintenance in the Netherlands," *History of the Human Sciences*, 15(2): 75–98.

Douglas, H. (2004), "Prediction, Explanation, and Dioxin Biochemistry: Science in Public Policy," *Foundations of Chemistry*, 6(1): 49–63.

Elster, J. (1989), *The Cement of Society: A Study of Social Order*, Cambridge and New York: Cambridge University Press.

Kincaid, J., Dupré, J., and Wylie, A. (2007), *Value-Free Science? Ideals and Illusions*, New York: Oxford University Press.

Hacking, I. (1999), *The Social Construction of What?* Cambridge, MA: Harvard University Press.

Hempel, C. (1965), *Aspects of Scientific Explanation*, New York: The Free Press.

Koertge, N. (1998), *A House Built on Sand*, Oxford: Oxford University Press.

Kukla, A. (2000), *Social Constructivism and the Philosophy of Science*, London and New York: Routledge.

Longino, H. (1990), *Science as Social Knowledge. Values and Objectivity in Scientific Inquiry*, Princeton, NJ: Princeton University Press.

Myrdal, G. (1958), *Value in Social Theory: A Selection of Essays on Methodology*, ed. Paul Streeten, London: Harper.

Nagel, E. (1961), *The Structure of Science*, New York: Harcourt, Brace, and World.

Nagel, T. (1986), *The View from Nowhere*, Oxford: Oxford University Press.

Oxford Centre for Evidence-Based Medicine Levels of Evidence (2007), www.cebm.jr2.ox.ac.uk/docs/level.html.

Root, M. (2000), "How We Divide the World," *Philosophy of Science*, 67: S628–S639.

Ross, A. ed. (1996), *Science Wars*, Durham, NC and London: Duke University Press.

Saraceno, C. (1984), "The Social Construction of Childhood: Childcare and Education Policies in Italy and the United States," *Social Problems*, 31: 351–63.

Searle, J. (1995), *The Construction of Social Reality*, London: Allen Lane.

Seckinelgin, H. (2008), *The International Politics of HIV/AIDS: Global Disease, Local Pain*, London: Routledge.

Science and Technology Committee (2006), "Scientific Advice, Risk and Evidence: How Government Handles Them," Evidence Report, London: House of Commons. www.parliament.uk/parliamentary_committees/science_and_technology_committee/sag.cfm.

SIGN (Scottish Intercollegiate Guideline Network) (2004), www.sign.ac.uk/guidelines/fulltext/50/compevidence.html.

Turner, S. (2013), "What Can We Say about the Future of Social Science?" *Anthropological Theory* 13(3): 187–200.

UNICEF (2008), "Bridging the Gap. The Role of Monitoring and Evaluation in Evidence-Based Policy Making." www.unicef.org/ceecis/evidence based policy making.pdf.

Weber, M. (1904), "'Objectivity' in Social Science and Social Policy," in *The Methodology of the Social Sciences*, ed. E. Shils and H. Finch, New York: Free Press, 1949.

Winch, P. (1958), *The Idea of Social Science and its Relation to Philosophy*, London: Routledge & Kegan Paul.

# Part III
# DEBATES

# 25
# ARE THERE SOCIAL SCIENTIFIC LAWS?

## Julian Reiss

## 1 Introduction

For someone whose thoughts haven't been tainted by postwar analytical philosophy, the most plausible answer to this chapter's question must be "Yes, of course!" There are *tons* of laws in economics and elsewhere:

- *the law of supply and demand* ("As the price for a good rises [falls], its quantity supplied goes up [down] and its quantity demanded goes down [up]; as the demand [supply] for a good goes up, its price increases [decreases]"; cf. Kincaid 2004);
- *Okun's law* ("The change in the unemployment rate is inversely related to the growth rate of output"; cf. Knotek 2007);
- *Say's law* ("Supply creates its own demand"; cf. Chang 2014);
- *the iron law of wages* ("In the long run, real wages tend towards subsistence level"; cf. Baumol 1983);
- *the iron law of oligarchy* ("Any democratic organization will tend, in the long run, towards rule by an elite"; cf. Hyland 1995, 247);
- *Malthus's law of population* ("Population growth is exponential"; cf. Ariew 2007);
- *the law of superposition* ("In undeformed stratigraphic sequences, the upper units of stratification are younger and the lower older"; cf. Harris 1979);
- *Zipf's law* ("Given some corpus of natural language utterances, the frequency of any word is inversely proportional to its rank in the frequency table"; cf. Fagan and Gençay 2010);
- *Duverger's law* ("Plurality rule elections structured within single-member districts tend to favor a two-party system"; cf. Schlesinger and Schlesinger 2006);

and many more. So there are laws, QED. The chapter could end right here. But we are postwar analytical philosophers and must therefore endeavor to find a fly in the ointment. The fly is the claim that these aren't *real* laws. They may carry the name of laws—perhaps because they are particularly entrenched principles or their authors want to reify the principles they've discovered by calling them laws—but they are not genuine because they are ridden with exceptions, merely 'phenomenological', subject to vague '*ceteris paribus*' clauses and so on. So a better title for this chapter would be: "Are There *Real* Social Scientific Laws?"

What *real* social scientific laws are is, of course, highly controversial. One of the reasons for controversy is that lawhood is unobservable. At best, an instance of the law is observable, but never the law itself. Suppose Galileo's 'law' of falling bodies, according to which bodies fall on the surface of the earth at a constant acceleration, is indeed a law. What we can observe in this case is the behavior of bodies—their positions over time and thus their accelerations—but not whether the behavior of the bodies is governed by a law. For all we know, bodies may behave the way they do purely accidentally. An exacerbating circumstance is that the quantities related by the law are often themselves not observable. According to the democratic peace hypothesis, democracies don't go to war with one another, and let us suppose that it expresses a true law. But who is to say with certainty whether a given set of observations qualifies as a democracy? Or as war? Perhaps the law is true but only for *real* democracies. And the nature of democracy is just as controversial as the nature of law.

Whether there are real social scientific laws depends on what concept of scientific law one uses, and it is not easy to find a concept that commands universal or near universal assent among social scientists, is free of obvious counterexamples, and plays the right functional roles such as the use of laws in prediction, explanation, and underwriting policies.

All the laws mentioned above express regularities of one kind or another, however. So let's begin with this idea, then see how it can be refined so as to have a chance to qualify as law, and finally address this chapter's question.

## 2 Regularity Plus $X$

In the positivist tradition, a law is a statement of the form "Whenever F, then G," or, formulated in first-order logic, "For all $x$, $Fx \rightarrow Gx$." Clearly, this cannot be all there is to a law, as many regularities seem accidental rather than lawlike. For instance, it is a true generalization that no country has more than 1.5 billion inhabitants (F = "is a country," G = "has a population smaller than 1.5 billion people"). Given actual history and predicted population growth rates, we can suppose that this is not only true today but also in past and future. And yet, we would not expect several million people to instantly die if China annexed Indonesia tomorrow. On the other hand, if, with David Hume, we suppose that the money supply in Great Britain were doubled overnight by slipping everybody a certain amount of money into their pocket, we would expect prices to rise eventually (cf. Schabas 2008). The quantity theory of money seems true in a manner different from the generalization about population size. Thus, if laws are regularities, they must be something else on top. A variety of proposals have been made about what the additional characteristic is. Before considering them, let me introduce two problems any good account of laws has to solve: the identification problem and the inference problem (cf. van Fraassen 1985). The identification problem asks us to identify a marker of lawhood that allows us to distinguish genuine laws from accidents. It addresses the question: What is it that makes one think that the "No country has more than 1.5bn people" generalization is only accidentally true whereas the quantity theory of money captures something more fundamental? The inference problem asks us to be able to identify genuine laws empirically. It addresses the question: How can we make sure that our empirical tools (tend to) establish genuine laws as laws and accidents as accidents?

## 2.1 Systems

In the Humean tradition, there is nothing in the world other than the occurrent facts; according to David Lewis, "all there is in the world is a vast mosaic of local matters of particular fact, just one little thing and then another" (Lewis 1986, ix). A law that states, "Whenever $F$, then $G$" says nothing more than that: $F$ happens, then $G$ happens; there is no glue that ties $F$ and $G$ together and $G$ doesn't arise from or because of $F$. Laws are essentially summaries of these occurrent facts. According to the 'Mill–Ramsey–Lewis' view of laws,[1] facts are to be summarized in deductive systems which are individuated by their axioms. Now, one can summarize facts in more than one way. The curve-fitting problem can be used to illustrate the issue in a social science context. Quantitatively oriented scientists often use statistical methods to summarize their data ('particular facts'). When deciding which functional form to use, they often face a trade-off between simplicity and accuracy. If, as they often do, they use linear regression, at most two data points can lie exactly on the regression line. The resulting principle, given by the regression equation, is very simple, but hardly accurate for most large data sets. Going to the other extreme, it is always possible to find some function such that all data points lie exactly on that function. This will be perfectly accurate, at least for past data, but rarely very simple. A judgment must be made about how to best trade off the two desiderata.

David Lewis maintains that just those statements expressing regularities are laws, which are axioms (or theorems) in a deductive system that optimally trades off simplicity and strength (which is closely related to accuracy). This view has a variety of desirable qualities, especially for philosophers who are wary of non-Humean entities such as causal powers or universals. This approach provides a neat in-principle solution to the identification problem ("Those generations are laws that are axioms in our best systematization of the facts"). However, for social scientists it would mean that laws are not now and probably will never be known. No social science is neatly arranged as a formal system with axioms from which all truths in the given domain can be deduced. Even economics, sometimes said to be a formalistic enterprise, is not, in the relevant sense, axiomatized (see for instance Stigum 1990, 2003). Given the complexity of the field, and the fast pace with which research questions and interests change, chances are low that this situation will soon change fundamentally. So under a 'best systems' account of laws, there may well be social scientific laws, but we would never (or not too soon) know them. This is an untenable state of affairs for a naturalistically inclined philosopher of the social sciences who prefers a conception of law that allows at least some of the statements social scientists call and regard as laws to be laws. The inference problem is, therefore, not solved.

## 2.2 Universals

A rival view maintains that laws are relations between properties. Properties such as 'being a real wage' or 'being a subsistence level' are understood as universals; that is, as real qualities that particulars (such as individual economies) have in common. If it is a law that "All $F$s are $G$," then this means that the universals $F$-ness and $G$-ness stand in the relation of nomic (as opposed to logical) necessitation. An $F$, thus, must be a $G$, not because $G$ is contained in the concept of $F$ (as 'is unmarried' is contained in the concept 'bachelor') but rather because of the existence of a physical necessitation relation between the two properties (Armstrong 1983).

On the face of it, interpreting laws as relations between universals seems to solve the identification problem: presumably, 'money supply-ness' and 'price-ness' stand in the right kind of relation whereas 'country-ness' and 'smaller than 1.5 billion people-ness' do not. However, the relation of physical necessitation is not observable, and in the literature on the universals approach to laws (apart from those of David Armstrong, Fred Dretske's and Michael Tooley's contributions are also important; see Dretske 1977; Tooley 1977) the metaphysics appears entirely disconnected from methodology.[2] Thus, again, under the universals account of laws, there may well be social scientific laws, but we'd never know what they are. Specifically, we could not tell whether any of the above-mentioned claims which social scientists regard as laws are genuine laws or not. Realism about laws thus does not solve the inference problem either.

## 2.3 Induction

Nelson Goodman argued that the problem of distinguishing accidental from law-like generalizations is closely related to induction and the confirmation of hypotheses: law-like, but not accidental generalizations are confirmed by their instances (Goodman 1954, 73). The examples he uses to illustrate are the confirmation of conductivity of copper by an instance, on the one hand, and the lack of confirmation of the generalization that all men in this room are third sons by the observation of this man's being a third son on the other.

A little reflection shows, however, that things aren't quite this clear-cut. Frank Jackson and Robert Pargetter, for instance, have argued that taking a sample of 50 (out of 100) men in this room and finding them all to be third sons does indeed confirm the hypothesis that all men in this room are third sons, whether or not it is only accidentally so. Indeed, as Elliott Sober has pointed out, whether or not an instance confirms its generalization depends on background assumptions, and under the right kinds of background assumptions an instance confirms its generalization even though the background assumptions entail that it is accidental (Sober 1988).

If that is true, we cannot take the fact that a generalization is confirmed by its instances as evidence that the generalization is law-like. Therefore, we cannot use Goodman's proposal to distinguish among the generalizations social scientists call laws between genuine and mere pseudo-laws. If successful, this approach would solve the inference problem ("Genuine laws are those that are confirmed by their instances, and there are good empirical confirmation methods") but it is not successful in addressing the identification problem.

## 2.4 Causality

A final view that I want to discuss here maintains that genuine laws describe causal relations. If it is true that G always follows F, then this regularity obtains on account of a causal structure that may have F as cause and G as effect or relate the two in more complex ways. Market prices and quantities supplied and demanded, for instance, stand in a relation of mutual causation, and which variable is the cause and which the effect can only be determined for a given particular case.

Causality is able to distinguish genuine from accidental regularities. Many of the statements at the beginning of the chapter permit a causal interpretation, as we've just seen for the law of supply and demand. By contrast, the reason for supposing that the statement "There is no country that has more than 1.5 billion inhabitants" is accidental is exactly that we cannot imagine any causal mechanism that makes 1.5 billion a threshold beyond which no country can grow. Causal claims also permit of being tested. There are tons of methods of causal inference, many of which are widely used across the social sciences and well understood by philosophers of science (see for instance Reiss 2015). *Prima facie*, the causal approach seems to address both the identification and inference problems.

However, causal claims do not entail corresponding claims about regularities (Anscombe 1971). The claim "*F* causes G" is consistent with *F*'s never being followed by G,[3] *F*'s sometimes being followed by G, *F*'s raising the probability of G, and *F*'s always being followed by G. We solve the identification problem at the cost of severing the relation between that which distinguishes between the genuine and the accidental on the one hand, and regularity, on the other. As we will see, this move will introduce a number of new problems.

## 3 Qualified Regularities

The discussion so far has tacitly assumed that the problem of finding real laws in the social sciences is the problem of distinguishing law-like from accidental, albeit true, generalizations. This way of putting the issue overlooks that there are few if any strictly universal and scientifically significant generalizations (of the form, "Whenever *F*, then G") in the social sciences. That most or all laws in the social sciences, if understood as strict generalizations, have exceptions has been well known since the 19th century. Indeed, both great social science methodologists of the 19th century, John Stuart Mill and Carl Menger, developed their conceptions of a social scientific law in response to the observation that empirical generalizations are never strict (Mill 1874 [1843]; Menger 1963 [1887]). For both, the reason for the nonexistence of strict regularities was that empirical outcomes are produced by many factors, all of which fall under a law. But these laws issue in regularities only in highly idealized situations, namely when a single law (or a small number of laws) operates all on its own without being subject to disturbances. The result is a view of laws as 'qualified regularities', regularities that obtain only under certain conditions. The main differences between alternative proposals concern the interpretation of the qualifier. Let us now consider two of the main accounts along these lines.

### 3.1 Ceteris Paribus *Laws*

The use of the *ceteris paribus* clause to qualify a general principle in economics goes back to at least the 13th century (Kaufer 1997). Petrus Olivi, a Franciscan friar from Provence, wrote in his tractate *De emptionibus, et venditionibus, de usuris, de restitutionibus* (quoted from Kaye 2014, 65):

> The right to receive a thing that is actually present, and the actual possession itself, is worth more … *ceteris paribus* … than either the right to receive something in the future or the right alone without actual possession.

'*Ceteris paribus*' is often translated as 'other things being equal'. The idea is that the regularity obtains whenever factors not mentioned in the generalization are held fixed or, more generally, do not vary. Let us, from now on, regard all laws as *causal* laws. A *ceteris paribus* law in this sense omits factors that have a causal influence on the effect variable; 'other things being equal' means that holding fixed these omitted causal factors results in a regularity.

The law of supply and demand, for instance, is true at best only under such a proviso. Holding fixed demand and other factors such as efficiency, an increase in scarcity will cause the prices to rise. By and large, the problem is not that extraneous factors vary but that they are there to begin with. When prices are controlled, supply can vary all it wants (holding fixed demand), but prices will remain the same. The better reading of *ceteris paribus* may therefore be 'other factors being *absent*'.

But a moment's reflection shows that that won't do, either. Social scientific generalizations hold, if at all, against an array of background conditions without which social factors, to the extent that it makes sense to talk of social factors in the absence of the background conditions, do not produce any effects, not to mention regularly. For increased scarcity to drive up prices, there has to be a market, certain kinds of norms have to be in place, and people must have certain kinds of tastes. To explain briefly, it is obvious that for scarcity to have any effects on prices, there has to be a regular exchange of the type of good in question. What is perhaps less obvious is that for any exchange to take place, exchanges must be regulated by social (and legal) norms, and people must trust each other. No one would attempt to exchange goods in the market if he feared that every time he entered an exchange, the partner tried to defraud him (Arrow 1973). The quality of most goods is not perfectly observable, so if there weren't any mechanisms that helped to attenuate problems of informational asymmetries, markets would collapse (Akerlof 1970). Finally, if people had perfectly elastic demand schedules (i.e. if the price increases above their reservation price, they'd stop buying the good altogether), increased scarcity would not have an effect on the price, either.

For prices to change in regular ways, we not only require institutionalized and regulated (by legal and social norms) exchange, we also require the existence of money. The existence of money, in turn, requires a host of other institutions—at minimum agreement on the use of one good as numeraire and general acceptance of that good in exchanges.[4] Thus, instead of requiring other factors to be absent, we need the constellation of other factors to be *just right* in order for the regularity to emerge.

I do not think that any of the three readings of the *ceteris paribus* condition—other things being *equal*; other things being *absent*; other things being *just right*—is the only correct or most defensible one. Instead, it is better to think of social scientific laws as being qualified by all three kinds of proviso. Some factors not mentioned in the generalization have to be held fixed; others absent; and yet others just right for the regularity to obtain. In fact, we've already seen that the law of supply and demand is subject to all three types of conditions: with increased scarcity, prices will rise whenever (among other things): a) demand remains stable; b) price controls are absent; and c) there exist certain institutions as well as social and legal norms, and people have certain kinds of tastes. From now on, I will refer to any violation of one of the three kinds of conditions as *interference*. Thus, demand not being stable, price controls, and relevant changes in (or simply absence of) background social norms and tastes are all kinds of interferences.

It is sometimes argued that including such provisos in the description of the regularity risks rendering a law empty (Hempel 1988). Essentially, including a proviso leads to the following dilemma. Either the conditions under which the generalization holds can be included in the description, or they can't (because they are unknown, say). If they can be included, the law isn't a *ceteris paribus* law after all; we may in some situations prefer a simplifying description, but at bottom, the law is just a statement of a regularity, albeit with a complex antecedent. If they can't be included, the law will essentially assert "Y regularly follows X, unless there is a reason for it not to" (see Roberts 2004, 159 for this formulation). The conditions under which a social scientific generalization holds can rarely be made explicit completely, so the first horn of the dilemma is unavailable. Accepting the second horn would mean that there are many social scientific laws indeed, but they would hardly be useful to know.

The situation isn't quite as dire as it sounds, however. The clause "unless there is a reason for Y not to follow X" can be read as "unless there is a *good* reason." As long as social scientists have some standards that distinguish between permissible and impermissible reasons; that is, as long as there are possible situations social scientists will regard as being incompatible with the law rather than a legitimate interference, the law has some empirical content.[5] How useful such a highly qualified generalization is for predictions and explanations depends on the frequency and character of the interferences that prevent the generalization from holding.

The main problem with *ceteris paribus* laws lies somewhere else. So far, we have understood the *ceteris paribus* clause as providing, essentially, a list of conditions under which the generalization holds. What we have omitted so far is to ask what happens when the conditions are *not* fulfilled. Does the generalization hold *approximately?* Or is the ensuing sequence of events entirely unpredictable? Does knowledge of generalizations concerning interfering factors help? As far as I can see there is nothing in the concept of a *ceteris paribus* law that addresses these questions. *Prima facie*, we have to allow the possibility that the law is simply silent about what happens when other things are not equal, disturbing factors are not absent, and structural conditions are not just right.

### 3.2  Causal Tendencies

John Stuart Mill thought it was a mistake to think of laws as being subject to exceptions. This is because *laws do not state regularities* (Mill 1874 [1843], book 6, ch. 10):

> Thus if it were stated to be a law of nature, that all heavy bodies fall to the ground, it would probably be said that the resistance of the atmosphere, which prevents a balloon from falling, constitutes the balloon an exception to that pretended law of nature.
>
> But the real law is, that all heavy bodies tend to fall.

What does it mean for a regularity to tend to obtain? Three things, in my view (Reiss 2013). First, the factor of interest *causally affects* the outcome. Tendency laws are causal laws. Second, regularities obtain only under highly idealized circumstances. Tendency laws express hypothetical or counterfactual regularities: "If such-and-such were the case, then X would regularly cause Y." The kinds of circumstances under which a regularity obtains have been discussed above. Third, and this is what makes a causal tendency different from a *ceteris paribus* law, the causal factor of interest *continues to make a systematic contribution to the outcome* when the circumstances are not ideal, in the presence of interferences.

This last point needs some elaboration. What Mill thinks is that the causal factor of interest makes a systematic difference to the outcome when interferences prevent it from realizing the outcome that is stated in the law. Helium-filled balloons don't fall but rise. What Mill means saying that all bodies tend to fall is that gravity makes a difference to its rate of fall; that is, its rate of fall is different from an otherwise identical situation in which gravity is not present.

How do causal factors combine? Mill, unfortunately, offers us only two highly simplified models: the physical (more precisely: the mechanical) and the chemical. In the mechanical model, causes combine additively. Since forces are vectors, when two forces combine, the result is the vector sum of its parts. In the chemical model, causal factors interact. If we regard the properties of individual elements as the causes of a chemical reaction, say, and the properties of the reaction product as the effect, it is often hard to see how the former make a systematic contribution to the latter; instead, something entirely new seems to emerge.

For some reason, Mill thinks that the social world is mechanical rather than chemical (Mill 1874 [1843], book 6, ch. 7):

> Men are not, when brought together, converted into another kind of substance, with different properties: as hydrogen and oxygen are different from water, or as hydrogen, oxygen, carbon and azote are different from nerves, muscles, and tendons. Human beings in society have no properties but those which are derived from, and may be resolved into, the laws of nature of individual man. In social phenomena the Composition of Causes is the universal law.

Under this model, then, the contributions from different factors affecting an outcome simply add up. If, say, scarcity exerts an upward pressure on prices, and increased competition a downward pressure, the result of the combined action of the two factors is something in between. If we knew the various elasticities involved, we could make a very exact numerical prediction of the combined effect.

Mill's mechanical and chemical models of the combination of causal laws are the two end points on a continuous spectrum. It is certainly conceivable and probably quite frequent that causal factors combine interactively but without complete annihilation of the individual contributions, as Mill describes chemical combination. This is why I would speak of a causal tendency whenever the causal factor makes a *systematic contribution* to the outcome; that is, whenever it is in principle possible to make a prediction about what happens in the presence of interferences or when there is a (meta) law of combination, even if that law is not as simple as vector addition.

## 4 In Favor of Tendency Laws

As mentioned in the introduction to this chapter, lawhood is unobservable. Thus, even if we can establish empirically that it is true that "X tends to cause Y," we could not establish empirically that it is a law that "X tends to cause Y." I nevertheless want to argue that tendencies have a special claim to being regarded as laws. There are a number of considerations in favor of doing so.

First, many statements in the social sciences called laws explicitly statements about tendencies. This is true of three of the nine laws mentioned at the beginning of this chapter: the iron law of wages, the iron law of oligarchy, and Duverger's law.[6]

Second, social scientists often talk as though they maintained a tendency account. Consider the following passage from Gunnar Heinsohn, a German/Polish sociologist and economist (Heinsohn 2012; my translation):

> Accordingly, the claim that deflation does not occur is as untenable as the claim that inflation does not occur. The former is invisible only as long as one looks at the prices for a pound of butter. But the ordinary butter buyer does not go to the central bank counter where he can find money for zero interest. The commercial banks, however, which guzzle there, buy shares or bonds and cause strong inflation in these markets which is in turn praised as 'added value'. For the statistician the deflation remains invisible because it is covered by artificial inflation, while he misses the inflation

because it is neutralized by the deflationary pull. Inflation is not only existent, but it is deliberately exploited for the retardation of deflation.

The relevant law here is 'increases in the money stock tend to raise prices'. Recall that there were three characteristics of a tendency law: (a) Factors cause outcomes. Heinsohn explicitly uses causal language. (b) A regularity obtains only in ideal circumstances. Heinsohn says that the inflation caused by the money glut remains invisible due to an interference, the 'deflationary pull' from other factors. Thus, if the deflationary pull had been absent, there would have been (visible) inflation. Just as a helium-filled balloon would fall if it were released in a vacuum. (c) The causal factor makes a systematic contribution to the outcome in the absence of interferences. Clearly, Heinsohn argues that there would be deflation if it wasn't for the artificial inflation brought about by the banks' guzzling at the central bank for zero interest rates.

To give a second example, consider a passage from a recent article in *The Economist* (2015):

> Europe's open economy is most exposed to a cooling in emerging-market demand, which is why more monetary easing there looks likely. But America's policy dilemma is more acute. The divergence in monetary policy between it and the rest of the world will put upward pressure on the dollar, hurting exports and earnings. And waves of capital may again seek out the American consumer as the borrower of choice. If so, the world's debt crisis may end up right back where it started.

Divergent monetary policies at home and abroad will put upward pressure on the US dollar. The outcome may be an increase of the dollar relative to other currencies, a decrease, or no change. What matters is that the exchange rate of the dollar will be higher than it would have been in the absence of the said divergences.

Third, important social scientific methods and analytic tools presuppose a tendency account. A clear example is multiple regression. If there were no stable tendency for $X$ to cause $Y$, it would not make sense to regress $Y$ on $X$ and a set of possible confounders $Z$. No stable tendency would mean that the effect of $X$ on $Y$ could in principle be different for any combination of values of the $Z$'s. The coefficient on $X$ would then represent an average effect over all the combinations of values of the $Z$'s. Such a quantity would hardly be meaningful and certainly not useful for policy. It would predict the correct value of the effect of an intervention on $X$ to change $Y$ only for a population that is characterized by the exact same combination of values for all $Z$'s.

Moreover, most regressions are linear. So not only does regression presuppose a tendency account of laws, it assumes a particularly simple law of combination—Mill's.

Fourth, tendency laws are useful for social scientists' endeavors to predict and explain outcomes. Only if there is a stable tendency for monetary policy to affect the exchange rate can *The Economist* predict that a divergent policy will lead to upward pressure on the dollar. While the prediction is not a categorical one—'the dollar *will* rise'—but rather a contrastive one—'the dollar will be higher than it would be in the absence of the policy divergence'—this is useful information, certainly in policy contexts (see also the Heinsohn quote above). The same can be said for explanation. Past divergences of policy have resulted in pressures on exchange rates, and the tendency law can explain the outcome relative to a hypothetical situation in which other factors are the same but the policy or policy change was absent. That explanation is always contrastive has been argued many times (van Fraassen 1980; Weber et al. 2013).

Fifth, laws are often said to be closely related to counterfactual statements. A law 'supports' a counterfactual or licenses a counterfactual inference. Thus, if it is a law that "Whenever $F$, then $G$," and some $x$ is not $F$, then I can infer that if $x$ had been $F$, it would have been $G$ as well (for example). The tendency account of laws fares better than the *ceteris paribus* laws account with such counterfactual inferences. This is because *ceteris paribus* laws remain silent about what happens when the *ceteris paribus* conditions are not fulfilled. So we cannot generally infer what would have happened if things had been different. Because of their degree of independence from interferences, tendency laws are not subject to this limitation.

## 5  Are There Social Scientific Laws?

This chapter's question, under the proposed reading, boils down to: "Are there causal factors that have an effect on outcomes relatively independently from possible interferences?" Before attempting to answer, let me make a couple of remarks. First, this is obviously an empirical question that cannot be addressed without paying detailed attention to social scientific evidence. Second, lawhood comes in degrees. With strict price controls, no change in the money stock will affect prices. Similarly, when the required social and legal norms are all absent, we'll be hard-pressed to meaningfully talk about 'changes in the money stock', even if physical analogues such as coins and bills can be found. There are, thus, interferences that make the regularity go away completely. On the other hand, minor changes in the organization of exchange may have a quantitative effect on money's effectiveness in changing prices without completely undermining it. For other regularities, all possible interferences may be of the former, qualitative kind so that the regularity only obtains in the absence of all interferences.

A first thing to note is that social scientific generalizations tend to be very highly context-dependent. If, say, we were looking for micro laws of the form, "When individuals are placed in a situation of type $S$, they will do $A$," we see that a great number of interferences can affect individuals' behavior in $S$ in ways that are quite unpredictable. Experimental economics is an enormous source of empirical results concerning these kinds of laws. Among the aims of experimental economics is the establishment of generalizations of this kind and the investigation of the conditions under which they hold. Situations can be market or strategic situations such as buying and selling good or making decisions in games such as ultimatum, dictator, and public games. '$S$' then may refer to 'being a proposer in an ultimatum game'. Here are some of the factors that influence what people do when they find themselves in situations of type $S$ (Reiss 2008, 92–96):

- the size and kind of the incentives;
- the availability and distribution of information;
- the experience of the participants;
- cultural and environmental factors;
- minute details of the experimental set up;

and others. The problem with these results is not that there are factors that interfere with an experimentally established regularity but rather that these factors affect results in highly unsystematic ways. While it is true, for instance, that people tend to think harder as the monetary incentives rise (Wilcox 1993), this doesn't always make them behave more rationally in the economists' sense. One study has shown that preference reversals increase rather than decrease with higher monetary incentives (Grether and Plott 1979). Henrich et al.'s 2001 study is famous for demonstrating the effect of customs and social norms on people's behavior in ultimatum games. Once more, that such factors should influence results is hardly surprising, but how a new group of people will behave is difficult to predict from knowledge about other people's behavior and their social norms.

What these experimental results demonstrate, in my view, is that it is hard to interpret behavioral generalizations as tendency laws. It is not the case that some factor—say, greed—has an effect on behavior in certain kinds of situations that persists despite interferences. Instead, what people do seems to depend on the entire constellation of background factors within which the behavior obtains. If all generalizations were like this—highly local and context-dependent—I would answer the chapter's question with "No" or "Social scientists haven't found any laws yet."

This phenomenon is not confined to microeconomics. In the 1990s there was a view—the 'Washington Consensus'—among policy makers that the following list of factors provides a desirable policy framework for economic growth (Rodrik 2007, 17):

1. fiscal discipline
2. reorientation of public expenditures
3. tax reform
4. interest rate liberalization
5. unified and competitive exchange rates
6. trade liberalization
7. openness to foreign direct investment
8. privatization
9. deregulation
10. secure property rights.

It would be mistaken to assume, however, that this list states a set of tendency laws of the form: "Fiscal discipline contributes positively to economic growth, relatively independently of context" and so on. Empirical evidence suggests the contrary: there is, if anything, a negative correlation between adherence to the list and economic success: many countries that did exceptionally well (such as the Asian tigers) score low on the list and many of those who closely followed the Washington policies did quite poorly (such as some of the Latin American countries post 1980). Instead, what matters is that the *mix* of economic policies is right. This is not to say that the factors on the list are not causes, triggers, or sustaining factors of economic growth. What it does say is that they need a constellation of other factors in order to exercise this function.

There are some examples that point in the other direction. Okun's law has relatively recently been tested in a cross-country study. Among the results are: (a) there is a relatively stable negative qualitative relationship between changes in unemployment and growth; (b) this relationship varies considerably across countries. What is noteworthy is that the variation in (b) appears to be systematic (Moosa 1997, 353):

> [E]mployment is more responsive to economic growth in the United States and Canada than in Europe and Japan. ... This finding can be explained in terms of some institutional differences that determine the rigidity or flexibility of the labor market. More

specifically, employment is more responsive to economic growth in the United States and Canada because of the lack of job security provisions and restrictions on layoffs. These provisions inhibit employers from reducing their workforce during recessions and hiring more workers during expansions.

This is at least consistent with a tendency law interpretation of Okun's law: there is a stable tendency of growth and changes in unemployment to co-vary that persists when disturbing factors are present. Specifically, job market rigidities affect the numerical rate of this relationship (like air resistance affects the rate of fall of bodies) but don't undermine it altogether.[7] This interpretation is further confirmed by longitudinal comparisons (ibid., 354–55):

> In the cases of Germany, France, and Japan, the steady increase in the absolute value of the coefficient may be attributed to labor market reform. Likewise, the stability of the coefficient in the cases of the United States and Canada may be attributed to lack of similar changes because the labor markets in these countries have been flexible throughout the sample period.

A final example is from political demography. Youth bulges, defined as excessive ratio of people aged 15–24 to the total adult population, have long been known to cause political violence (Moller 1968). In a recent study Henrik Urdal has looked at the effect of youth bulges on internal conflict, terrorism, and riots in particular as well as the role of intervening factors that affect this relationship (Urdal 2006). He can, first, confirm previous studies in that he finds that countries experiencing youth bulges of 35 percent run a risk of armed conflict which is more than twice higher than countries without youth bulge. More interesting are various (often, non-linear) interdependencies with other variables. The 'dependency ratio' is the ratio of 0–14-year-olds relative to 15–24-year-olds. It measures the degree to which a youth bulge is sustained or reduces over time. Sharply declining birth rates are often associated with economic development, which may help to lessen the effect of youth bulges on violence. Indeed, Urdal finds that (619):

> Youth bulges in the context of continued high fertility and high dependency make countries increasingly likely to experience armed conflict ... while countries that are well underway in their demographic transitions are likely to experience a "peace dividend."

Generally, higher levels of development reduce the risk of political conflict. The effect of youth bulges on political violence is lowest both in highly democratic and highly autocratic regimes; intermediary regimes are more conflict-prone. Again, this is just what we would expect: youths without opportunity in democratic countries will either voice their complaints in other ways or leave the country, and youths in highly autocratic regimes cannot express discontent violently (though there other forms of violence will be present).

There is a tendency, then, for youth bulges to cause political violence that persists in the presence of disturbing factors such as dependency burden and regime type. Youth bulges will cause violence also when the dependency burden goes down, but the relationship is attenuated. Youth bulges cause violence independently of regime type, but 'being strongly democratic/autocratic' is an interference that reduces incidents of rioting, terrorism, and civil conflict.

# 6 Conclusions

The most accurate answer to this chapter's question is "There is some evidence that there are social scientific laws." To give a more definite answer is difficult given the empirical nature of the question and the quantitative nature of lawhood. What we can know about the stability of causal factors depends obviously but crucially on the quality of the methods we use to establish causal claims, and the most frequently used method—multiple regression—is subject to various important limitations (Freedman 1997; Reiss 2016). Whatever results we find, these results are often not particularly stable under relevant specification changes, and so it is difficult to tell whether a factor that appears to make a stable contribution independently of the constellation of background factors can be replicated in a study that makes different background assumptions (for instance, about the statistical properties of the variables involved and their operationalization). It is well possible that factors that appear stable to us now, are in fact highly interactive. On the other hand, the behavior of at least some of the factors discussed here—youth bulges and changes in the money stock, for instance—has been investigated for long stretches of human history using multiple methods, and they come out as stable causal factors time and again, so I would suggest that the weight of evidence speaks in favor of the proponent of social scientific laws.

# Notes

1  A brief statement of the view can be found in Lewis 1973; Lewis 1983 elaborates on the earlier paper.

2  James Robert Brown proposes thought experiments as means to 'observe' laws understood as relations between universals (Brown 2004, 2010). Given the relative paucity of thought experiments in the social sciences and the ambiguity of their results, I don't think that Brown's epistemic Platonism is really an option for the social sciences (on thought experiments in economics, see Schabas 2008 and Reiss 2012). At any rate, his account explicitly addresses only the natural sciences and none of the law statements at the beginning of this chapter were established by means of a thought experiment.

3  Chris Hitchcock gives the following example: 'Swallowing 1kg of plutonium causes death', which is, presumably, a true causal claim, even if no one in world history ever swallows a kilo of plutonium. See Hitchcock 1995.

4  This is true on the standard, Mengerian, account of the origins of money. There are alternative (and more plausible) accounts that require a much larger number of institutions including strong property rights, individual freedom, enforceable debt contracts, and more. See Reiss 2012 for a discussion.

5  See for instance Kincaid 1990 and Hausman 1992 for a discussion of a number of criteria aimed to make *ceteris paribus* laws testable. With Kincaid and Hausman, I therefore disagree therefore with commentators such as Earman and Roberts 1999 who argue that hedged regularities cannot be discovered by science because they are not empirically testable. In particular, I disagree with their suggestion that under this reading there would be hedged regularities everywhere. For us to establish the hedged law, "*Ceteris paribus*, F causes G," we first have to establish that F does indeed cause G and then, in case F obtains but G doesn't (or doesn't obtain with the appropriate frequency), provide a good reason that despite the presence of F G does not obtain. That reason will very much depend on what F is. Earman and Roberts's criticism of Pietroski and Rey 1995 that under their proposal, *ceteris paribus* anything that is F is also G depends on specifics of their proposal that don't carry over to causal laws.

6  I should perhaps mention that I did not actively seek social scientific laws that explicitly express tendencies. Clearly, though, many social scientists do think that social scientific laws are really tendency laws and so one can find examples of attempts to make this explicit quite frequently.

7  I deliberately described the example in non-causal terms as most studies of Okun's law include only measures of unemployment and growth and I cannot imagine that there aren't common factors affecting both variables. Moosa assumes that causality runs from growth to changes in unemployment but the

opposite relationship is certainly conceivable. This does not change the interpretation of Okun's law as a tendency law, because no matter what the true causal relationship between these variables is, it seems to persist in the light of disturbing factors. I'd therefore speak of a tendency law here, albeit not a causal tendency from growth to changes in unemployment.

# References

Akerlof, George 1970, "The Market for 'Lemons': Quality Uncertainty and the Market Mechanism," *Quarterly Journal of Economics* 84(3): 488–500.

Anscombe, Elizabeth 1971, *Causality and Determination: An Inaugural Lecture*, Cambridge: Cambridge University Press.

Ariew, André 2007, "Under the Influence of Malthus's Law of Population Growth: Darwin Eschews the Statistical Techniques of Adolphe Quetelet," *Studies in History and Philosophy of Biological and Biomedical Sciences* 38(1): 1–19.

Armstrong, David 1983, *What Is a Law of Nature?* Cambridge: Cambridge University Press.

Arrow, Kenneth J. 1973, "Social Responsibility and Economic Efficiency," *Public Policy* 21: 303–17.

Baumol, William 1983, "Marx and the Iron Law of Wages," *American Economic Review* 73(2 [Papers and Proceedings]): 303–8.

Brown, James Robert 2004, "Peeking into Plato's Heaven," *Philosophy of Science* 71: 1126–138.

Brown, James Robert 2010, *The Laboratory of the Mind: Thought Experiments in the Natural Sciences*, London: Routledge.

Chang, Ha-Joon 2014, *Economics: The User's Guide*, London: Penguin.

Dretske, Fred 1977, "The Nature of Laws," *Philosophy of Science* 44: 248–68.

Earman, John and John Roberts 1999, "*Ceteris paribus*, There Is No Problem of Provisos," *Synthese* 118: 439–78.

Fagan, Stephen and Ramazan Gençay 2010. "An Introduction to Textual Econometrics," in *Handbook of Empirical Economics and Finance*. Aman Ullah and David Giles (eds.), Boca Raton, FL: CRC Press: 133–53.

Freedman, David 1997, "From Association to Causation via Regression," *Advances in Applied Mathematics* 18: 59–110.

Goodman, Nelson 1954, *Fact, Fiction and Forecast*, Atlantic Highlands, NJ: Athlone Press.

Grether, David and Charles Plott 1979, "Economic Theory of Choice and the Preference Reversal Phenomenon," *American Economic Review* 69: 623–38.

Harris, Edward 1979, "The Laws of Archaeological Stratigraphy," *World Archaeology* 11(1): 111–17.

Hausman, Daniel 1992, *The Inexact and Separate Science of Economics*, Cambridge: Cambridge University Press.

Heinsohn, Gunnar 2012, "Deflation und Inflation auch 2013 einträchtig beieinander." *Achse des Guten*. Accessed August 17, 2016. www.achgut.com/dadgdx/index.php/dadgd/article/deflation_und_inflation_auch_2013_eintraechtig_beieinander.

Hempel, Carl 1988, "Provisoes: A Problem Concerning the Inferential Function of Scientific Theories," *Erkenntnis* 28(2): 147–64.

Henrich, Joseph, Robert Boyd, Samuel Bowles, Colin Camerer, Ernst Fehr, Herbert Gintis, and Richard McElreath 2001, "In Search of Homo Economicus: Behavioral Experiments in 15 Small-Scale Societies," *American Economic Review* 91(2): 73–78.

Hitchcock, Christopher 1995, "Mishap at Reichenbach Fall: Singular vs. General Causation," *Philosophical Studies* 78(3): 257–91.

Hyland, James 1995, *Democratic Theory: The Philosophical Foundations*, Manchester: Manchester University Press.

Kaufer, Erich 1997, "Ceteris Paribus," *Journal of Economic Perspectives* 11(2): 190–91.

Kaye, Joel 2014, *A History of Balance 1250–1375: The Emergence of a New Model of Equilibrium and Its Impact on Thought*, Cambridge: Cambridge University Press.

Kincaid, Harold 1990, "Defending Laws in the Social Sciences," *Philosophy of the Social Sciences* 20(1): 56–83.

Kincaid, Harold 2004, "There Are Laws in the Social Sciences," in *Contemporary Debates in Philosophy of Science*. Christopher Hitchcock (ed.), Oxford: Blackwell: 168–85.

Knotek, Edward 2007, "How Useful Is Okun's Law?" *Economic Review of the Federal Reserve Bank of Kansas City* (Fourth Quarter): 73–103.

Lewis, David 1973, *Counterfactuals*, Cambridge, MA: Harvard University Press.

Lewis, David 1983, "New Work for a Theory of Universals," *Australasian Journal of Philosophy* 61: 343–77.

Lewis, David 1986, *Philosophical Papers*, vol. 2, New York: Oxford University Press.

Menger, Carl 1963 [1887], *Problems of Economics and Sociology*, Urbana, IL: University of Illinois Press.

Mill, John Stuart 1874 [1843], *A System of Logic*, New York: Harper.

Moller, Herbert 1968, "Youth as a Force in the Modern World," *Comparative Studies in Society and History* 10: 238–60.

Moosa, Imad 1997, "A Cross-country Comparison of Okun's Coefficient," *Journal of Comparative Economics* 24: 335–56.

Pietroski, Paul and Georges Rey 1995, "When Other Things Aren't Equal: Saving *Ceteris Paribus* Laws from Vacuity," *British Journal for Philosophy of Science* 46: 81–110.

Reiss, Julian 2008, *Error in Economics: Towards a More Evidence-Based Methodology*, London: Routledge.

Reiss, Julian 2012, "Genealogical Thought Experiments in Economics," in *Thought Experiments in Science, Philosophy, and the Arts*. James Robert Brown, Mélanie Frappier, and Letitia Maynell (eds.), New York: Routledge: 177–90.

Reiss, Julian 2013, *Philosophy of Economics: A Contemporary Introduction*, New York: Routledge.

Reiss, Julian 2015, *Causation, Evidence, and Inference*, New York: Routledge.

Reiss, Julian 2016, "Suppes' Probabilistic Theory of Causality and Causal Inference in Economics," *Journal of Economic Methodology* 23 (3): 289-304.

Roberts, John T. 2004, "There are no Laws of the Social Sciences," in *Contemporary Debates in Philosophy of Science*. Christopher Hitchcock (ed.), Oxford: Blackwell: 151–67.

Rodrik, Dani 2007, *One Economics, Many Recipes: Globalization, Institutions, and Economic Growth*, Princeton, NJ and Oxford: Princeton University Press.

Schabas, Margaret 2008, "Hume's Monetary Thought Experiments," *Studies In History and Philosophy of Science Part A* 29: 161–9.

Schlesinger, Joseph and Mildred Schlesinger 2006, "Maurice Duverger and the Study of Political Parties," *French Politics* 4(1): 58–68.

Sober, Elliott 1988, "Confirmation and Law-Likeliness," *Philosophical Review* 97(1): 93–98.

Stigum, Bernt 1990, *Toward a Formal Science in Economics*, Cambridge, MA: MIT Press.

Stigum, Bernt 2003, *Econometrics and the Philosophy of Economics: Theory-Data Confrontations in Economics*, Princeton, NJ: Princeton University Press.

The Economist 2015, "The Never-Ending Story," November 14, 2015.

Tooley, Michael 1977, "The Nature of Laws," *Canadian Journal of Philosophy* 7: 667–98.

Urdal, Henrik 2006, "A Clash of Generations? Youth Bulges and Political Violence," *International Studies Quarterly* 50: 607–22.

van Fraassen, Bas 1980, *The Scientific Image*, Oxford: Clarendon Press.

van Fraassen, Bas 1985, *Laws and Symmetry*, Oxford: Oxford University Press.

Weber, Erik, Jeroen Van Bouwel, and Leen De Vreese 2013, *Scientific Explanation*, Dordrecht: Springer.

Wilcox, Nathaniel 1993, "Lottery Choice: Incentives, Complexity and Decision Time," *Economic Journal* 103(421): 1397–417.

# 26

# BEHAVIORAL ECONOMICS

## Conrad Heilmann

### 1 Introduction

Anyone who has recently browsed in a bookstore's economics section and seen titles by Daniel Kahneman or Dan Ariely—or has read reviews of their books in newspapers or magazines—indeed anyone with a passing interest in economics at all—would be forgiven for coming away with the impression that behavioral economics is *brand new*. There is considerable buzz in popular media around the idea that economists might not be limited to building highly idealized models of rational agents after all. They are now, apparently, also modeling irrational behavior, investigating how individuals *really* make decisions, have dispensed with the assumption of perfectly rational maximizers, and are using a broad range of empirical tools, such as lab and field experiments. Behavioral economics, the "runaway success story in modern economics" (Angner 2015, 3557), is catching the attention of the general public, forms one of the most thriving sub-branches of the "economics made fun" genre (Vromen 2009), and has been building an influential branch of policy advice by implementing insights from behavioral economics in what is called "libertarian paternalism" or "nudge" (Thaler and Sunstein 2008).

Well-informed commentators know that the recent popularity of behavioral economics in- and outside of academia builds on scholarship that has been developing over several decades. As Erik Angner puts it in his textbook: "Behavioral economics can be said to have a short history but a long past" (Angner 2012, 5). Behavioral economics commonly refers to the study of individual decision-making in economics that has a particular focus on empirical methods and the goal of psychologically realistic explanation and prediction. It thus contrasts neoclassical economics and axiomatic rational choice theory, both of which often aim at a much more idealized account of individual behavior that is easier to trace mathematically, affording ease of economic modeling. Heukelom (2015) demonstrates in great detail that behavioral economics shares common roots with modern rational choice theory and has, by and large, developed in parallel to it, growing in significance and enjoying a surge in popularity especially in the past decades.

Where does behavioral economics stand today, and what is its status as a sub-discipline of economics? Many scholars have recently offered general reflections on this question. On the economics side, there are contributions by, for instance, Camerer and Loewenstein (2004), Fudenberg (2006), Pesendorfer (2006), and Mallard (2015). On the history of economic thought side, there are contributions by, amongst others, Sent (2004), Dow (2013), and Heukelom

(2015). On the methodology of economics side, there are contributions by, for instance, Mueller (2004), Nagatsu (2010), Angner and Loewenstein (2012), Reiss (2013), Ross (2015), and Angner (2015). These scholars discuss the history and prospects of behavioral economics as a sub-discipline of economics, asking to what extent and in what way exactly it is revolutionary or not, and advance arguments about the relation between behavioral economics and (core assumptions of) rational choice theory, neoclassical economics, mainstream economics more generally, psychology, experimental economics, as well as bounded rationality. While exact positions and arguments vary, the main consensus is that behavioral economics is, for all its importance and significance for economic theory, fairly close to mainstream economics in foundations, key concepts, and outlook. Heukelom (2014) has coined the term of "mainstreaming behavioral economics" for this perspective. On this consensus mainstreaming view, behavioral economics is thus not revolutionizing economics, or on the brink of doing so, but rather complementing it in significant ways, offering psychologically more realistic models of decision-making and an attention to empirical work, especially experiments. This, in turn, so the consensus view goes, means that behavioral economics is best understood as a diverse and growing collection of empirical results and theoretical contributions to economics, rather than a unified alternative to mainstream economics.

My aim in this chapter is to contribute to these discussions by underlining the current consensus view, albeit indirectly. I focus on two important areas of behavioral economics: nudge and hyperbolic discounting. In many ways, they are exemplary for the development of behavioral economics. Hyperbolic discounting has been amongst the most important topics in the development of behavioral economics, and still is a staple today, with renewed attention to the pioneering work by George Ainslie and its links to addiction, procrastination, and other problems of self-control. Nudge, on the other hand, a term coined by Richard Thaler and Cass Sunstein in their 2008 book, is a rather more recent phenomenon, relating findings from behavioral economics to applications in policy-making. Nudge and hyperbolic discounting also share the following trait: in both discussions, theoretical frameworks that are purported to unify and generalize insights of behavioral economics have been advanced. For hyperbolic discounting, the framework of multiple (or dual) selves has been proposed (notably by Ainslie 1992, 2001). Concerning nudge, the framework of dual process (or dual systems) has been used. Kahneman (e.g. 2003, 2011) also champions the dual process framework as a generalizing framework for all of behavioral economics. While these frameworks do not exhaust the options for advancing a more unified and generally relevant behavioral economics, many behavioral economists find them significant. I will argue that in both cases, these general frameworks—at least in their current form—neither contribute positively to a more unified behavioral economics, nor do they generalize the insights and findings of behavioral economics in relation to other fields or problems in tangible ways. Rather, the contribution of these frameworks is restricted to the tasks of developing the results and models within their original domains of application in nudge and hyperbolic discounting.

Section 2 reviews the main elements of behavioral economics. Sections 3 and 4 then go on to investigate the role of generalizing frameworks in discussions about hyperbolic discounting and nudge, respectively. Section 5 concludes.

## 2 Main Elements of Behavioral Economics

Behavioral economics can be understood as a sub-discipline of economics, which has used methods and insights from a range of other disciplines, in particular psychology, to investigate individual and interactive decision-making empirically, and contrast those findings to standard rational choice theory.

Given the focus on empirical work in behavioral economics, a first understanding of behavioral economics can be reached by compiling a list of its empirical findings. These often come in the form of choice patterns or stable phenomena surrounding choices of individuals, and can be suitably categorized under the following rubrics:

- *Other-regarding preferences.* Individuals are often motivated not only by gaining utility or resources for themselves, but also by considerations of altruism, envy, fairness, justice, reciprocity, and trust, to name but a few central concepts. In many experiments, individuals have been found to forsake personal gains in order to underline or enforce such motivations, such as when they "punish" non-cooperating or non-reciprocating opponents, or when they rather would waste resources than to have someone benefit more than others (Camerer and Loewenstein 2004, 27ff.; Camerer 2005; Angner 2012, 192ff.; Wilkinson and Klaes 2012, 393ff.).
- *Framing effects under certainty.* The presentation and context of a decision matters also in the absence of uncertainty. These so-called framing effects often have to do with loss aversion, the fact that individuals like gains less than they dislike losses of similar magnitude: equivalent choices lead to different results, depending on whether it is framed as a loss or as a win (Camerer and Loewenstein 2004, 15ff.; Angner 2012, 29ff.).
- *Judgments about probability.* Individuals often display systematic biases and commit fallacies when they assess probabilities, for instance not correctly calculating the probabilities of conjunctions and disjunctions, exhibiting confirmation bias (interpreting evidence in a way that supports prior beliefs), and base-rate neglect (assessing conditional probabilities incorrectly) (Camerer and Loewenstein 2004, 19ff.; Angner 2012, 81ff.; Wilkinson and Klaes 2012, 117ff.).
- *Framing effects in decisions under uncertainty.* Framing effects under uncertainty are more complex, as they often have to do with the interaction of utility and probability. From a theoretical point of view, it should not matter how such choices are bundled, yet individuals display a range of biases and heuristics that they use when faced with such decisions (Camerer and Loewenstein 2004, 19ff.; Angner 2012, 103ff.; Wilkinson and Klaes 2012, 148ff.).

There are two choices, the so-called Allais (1953) paradox and the Ellsberg (1954) paradox, that have been vital to the development of behavioral economics—not only in terms of cashing out the above framing effects in decisions under uncertainty, but also theoretically. The Ellsberg paradox has a similar structure to the Allais paradox, but poses bigger challenges concerning the evaluation of probabilities and uncertainty, and has led to a large literature on the problem of ambiguity aversion. Here, we simply focus on Allais (see Table 26.1). Consider the choice between Lottery A and Lottery B, and the choice between Lottery C and Lottery D.

Most individuals, when faced with this choice, choose A > B and D > C. Yet, rational choice theory prescribes choice patterns as rational that align Lottery A and C as well as B and D, since when disregarding the "Blue" column which gives the same outcomes in both choices (a "sure thing"), the latter are actually equivalent.

Two families of theories have emerged to provide predictions and explanations for why most individuals choose A > B and D > C. Prospect theory, initiated by Kahneman and Tversky (1979) and generalized by many contributors, notably Wakker (2010), maintains that individuals evaluate potential losses (in the first choice) differently from potential gains (in the second choice). Furthermore, individuals often over-represent small probabilities, which also explains

*Table 26.1* The Allais Paradox

| | Red p(*red*) = .01 | Green p(*green*) = .1 | Blue p(*blue*) = .89 |
|---|---|---|---|
| *Choice 1* | | | |
| Lottery A | $500 | $500 | $500 |
| Lottery B | $0 | $2,500 | $500 |
| *Choice 2* | | | |
| Lottery C | $500 | $500 | $0 |
| Lottery D | $0 | $2,500 | $0 |

choosing A in the first choice. Regret theory by Loomes and Sugden (1982) postulates that individuals evaluate the first choice as potentially losing the $500 outcome of A when choosing B and the Red outcome occurs, which would result in much regret, which is by and large absent in the case of losing out on winning when having chosen D. Starmer (2000) summarizes both aforementioned theories, but also many other such "non-expected utility theories" that have emerged in order to predict and explain Allais's choices and other choice patterns that deviate from rational choice theory in other examples and experiments. Prospect and regret theories can thus be understood in contrast to standard rational choice theory (von Neumann and Morgenstern 1944; Savage 1954).

In his historical account, Heukelom (2015) demonstrates in detail how rational choice theorists and their empirical challengers interacted. One key difference between the two has always been in method. Rational choice theory has focused on an axiomatic derivation of utility (and probability) functions from rational preference. In contrast, behavioral economics has sometimes fostered—and sometimes coincided with—a number of new ways to study human behavior in economics, including by lab experiments (such as with the Allais and Ellsberg problems), field study and field experiments (where experiments are set in real-world contexts), as well as process measures (process-tracing software and brain scans/brain imaging that is used mainly in lab experiments). For an introductory overview of these, see Angner (2012, 6f.) or Camerer and Loewenstein (2004), as well as Guala (2005) for a methodological critique of problems in experimental economics.

Scholarship that is now subsumed under the label "behavioral economics" has been marked by a fair share of scholarly controversies, such as the question of whether to interpret rational choice theory as descriptive or normative (Reiss 2013; Heukelom 2015); the sometimes fraught relationship between experimental and behavioral economists (see, for instance, comments in Camerer and Loewenstein 2004 and Ross 2011); the differences between the "Biases and Heuristics" research program of leading behavioral economists on the one hand (such as Kahneman 2003) and the "Simple Heuristics" research program of psychologists and economists on the other hand (such as Todd et al. 1999), reviewed in Katsikopoulos (2014) and Mallard (2015); the many attempts to make exact the notion of hyperbolic discounting (reviewed in Frederick et al. 2002); and debating whether the insights of behavioral economics should be exploited in public policy-making (such as Bovens 2008). I will now turn to analyze the latter two discussions.

## 3 Hyperbolic Discounting

Much of the early work in behavioral economics concerns intertemporal choice (e.g. Strotz 1955–56; Ainslie 1975), and it has remained an important area of research (Loewenstein and Elster 1992; Frederick et al. 2002; Loewenstein and Read 2003; Grüne-Yanhoff 2015). The key finding of behavioral economics consists of the idea of replacing exponential discounting of the future with hyperbolic discounting. Consider an agent who is presented with two choices. First, she is choosing between receiving one apple today and two apples tomorrow. Second, she is choosing between receiving one apple in 999 days and two apples in 1,000 days. Many individuals choose to receive one apple today and two apples in 1,000 days. Proponents of hyperbolic discounting hold that many intertemporal choices share the basic structure of the apple case: individuals choose a smaller, sooner reward over a larger, later one. Such patterns have been found in many cases where temptation and a lack of self-control are important, such as in procrastination, dieting, and addiction (O'Donoghue and Rabin 1999). Choosing a smaller, sooner reward over a larger, later one is often not consistent with exponential discounting, yet predicted by hyperbolic discounting.

The general idea of time discounting in economics entails that goods (such as apples, utility, or money) are multiplied with a discount factor that captures an individual's attitudes to the future. Exponential discounting gives a smoothly declining discount factor for every point in time, for instance by calculating it with the following formula $D(t) = \delta^t$, where $0 < \delta < 1$ is constant. Doing so has a number of modeling advantages. First, the model is simple and easy to track mathematically. Second, it also ensures dynamic consistency, as it preserves the integrity of the utility function through time: similar time intervals (of, say, one day) are treated in a similar way, irrespective of when they occur in time (for instance, the interval between now and tomorrow is treated in the same way as the time interval between 999 and 1,000 days from now). Samuelson (1937) proposed exponential discounting for the ease of modeling, whereas the prolonged popularity of exponential discounting is also due to it ensuring dynamic consistency. In the above example, exponential discounting recommends choosing the same number of apples in both choices, since the time interval is the same and the options are identical. Yet, many individuals choose differently: they exhibit present bias and choose one apple now and two apples in 1,000 days. After 999 days, they would then rather have one apple on that day, and thus have dynamically inconsistent preferences.

To model present bias, hyperbolic discounting assumes that $\delta$ is changing, and in fact declining. Roughly speaking, any hyperbolic discounting function characterizes three time horizons of a decision-maker: (i) the present and immediate, which is given full weight, (ii) the horizon, in which discounting factors are sharply declining between different periods, and (iii) the far future, in which discounting factors are very similar between different periods. The label "hyperbolic" discounting means to capture the idea that individuals tend to overemphasize time differences in the horizon, as witnessed by the numerical values, while not making differences between time points in the far future. As reviewed in Frederick et al. (2002), different hyperbolic discounting functions have been proposed that yield slightly different numerical values for the three time horizons. Yet, any hyperbolic discounting function will devalue receiving an additional apple tomorrow drastically, leaving the individual to choose the apple today. Furthermore, the hyperbolic discounting functions flatten out in the far future, so that both the one apple and the two apples in 999 and 1,000 days are discounted with similar factors, leaving the individual to select the two apples in the second choice.

The key problem in hyperbolic discounting is to make precise the shape of the discounting function. Apart from the general shape of hyperbolic discounting, described above, it remains unclear how exactly individuals discount the future hyperbolically (even though some models, such as Laibson's [1997] quasi-hyperbolic discounting are more generally accepted than others). The number of experiments is growing, but it is unclear how to arrive at a generally accepted theory of hyperbolic discounting that also specifies a specific discounting function.

Let us now turn to a more general theoretic framework that has often been argued to underlie hyperbolic discounting: that of multiple, or dual, selves. Theoretical approaches in behavioral economics have attempted to model these more complex cases of dynamic inconsistency by envisaging a decision-maker as composed of different "selves" which compete for influence on the behavior. Early treatments of such approaches are in Strotz (1955–56), Peleg and Yaari (1973), and Schelling (1980, 1984). In those models, as well as more recent ones (e.g. Thaler and Shefrin 1981; Benabou and Pycia 2002; Fudenberg and Levine 2006; and Read 2006), different selves embody the diverging evaluations of the decision-maker that lead to dynamically inconsistent preferences: a planner-self assesses the prospect, only to be undermined by a doer-self. Such "interactions" between selves are often modeled as dynamic games, modeling a wide range of types of dynamic inconsistency, including cases of lack of self-control in the face of temptation. They also allow them to outline how pre-commitment strategies can resolve dynamic inconsistency (for instance, when someone instructs a friend before dinner to order salad in order to prevent himself from choosing steak). The multi-selves models are mostly consistent with hyperbolic discounting—in fact, many accounts of both hyperbolic discounting and multi-selves show how the two modes of modeling can be formally equivalent (Fudenberg and Levine 2006; Xue 2008) and Ainslie (1992, 2001) combines aspects of hyperbolic discounting and multi-selves in his "picoeconomics" approach.

The dual-selves models thus offer a richer perspective on the inner dynamics of a decision-maker, and can in some cases be represented with hyperbolic discounting functions nevertheless. There are, however, two theoretical challenges that are associated with these theories. First, they have yet to be connected to standard pictures of rational choice theory—it seems that rational choice theory rests on a particular view of how to represent the agent that is undermined by the much richer structure that is offered in dual-selves models. There are recent contributions by Don Ross (2011, 2015) that take on these kinds of questions from a methodological point of view, but they are not yet related back to the question of how to generalize the empirical results of behavioral economics. Second, it is unclear what sort of entities dual or multiple selves are: some model them as sets of preferences (such that selves are competing preferences or values, e.g. Thaler and Shefrin 1981), while others model them just as time-slices of one agent (such that selves are competing time horizons, e.g. Fudenberg and Levine 2006). This, in turn, means that some models analyze dynamic inconsistency as a conflict between different personalities or values, while others just represent them as conflict between different temporal representatives, but others do not distinguish clearly between these two perspectives (e.g. Benabou and Pycia 2002). Yet, these three modeling choices offer radically different ways to capture dynamic inconsistency cases, and leave unclear what exactly is entailed in the understanding and explanation of, for instance, addiction, temptation, and procrastination that they offer.

It seems that while selves-models have been contributing to the development of hyperbolic discounting, they are not yet contributing to unifying perspectives on dynamic inconsistency. What is more, on the discussion presented here, the prospects for dual-selves models providing a conceptual foundation for behavioral economics that helps to unify and generalize it as a sub-discipline are slim. There are too many questions that are underspecified in the literature, and the metaphorical power of the idea of "selves" that accompanies the models of the inner dynamics of individual decision-makers is, so far, the only advantage of including dual or multiple selves in the theoretical accounts of intertemporal choice.

# 4 Nudge

The publication of Thaler and Sunstein's (2008) book has initiated an important phase in behavioral economics, and has considerably altered its influence. What started as a research program that subjected the axiomatic postulates of rational choice theory to empirical scrutiny did gradually mature into amassing insights into behavioral patterns. From there, Thaler and Sunstein (2008) argued, it is a small step to use these insights to devise policies that change the behavior of individuals. In a nutshell, the idea of nudge is to present choices in such a way that individuals' use of heuristics and biases leads them to make better choices; better, that is, by their own lights.

Thaler and Sunstein (2008) labeled policy advice based on such insights from behavioral economics as "Libertarian Paternalism," to reflect the idea that both freedom of choice as well as improvement of choices are inherent in nudges. More specifically, the choice architecture is designed so that a consumer is more likely to choose what is good for him or her, without limiting the range of available options. Classic examples of nudges include:

- Arranging food items for sale in a cafeteria such that fruits and vegetables are easier to reach than sweets, so that individuals eat healthier food (Thaler and Sunstein 2008, 1–4).
- Automatically enrolling individuals in saving and organ donation schemes, so that individuals who do not want to partake have to "opt out" (rather than making it the default that individuals are not enrolled and have to "opt in" to partake), in order to increase participation rates (Thaler and Sunstein 2008, 113–27).
- Incentivized smoking cessation programs, in which individuals deposit an amount of money in the beginning that they get back (in addition to a bonus) when successful abstaining from smoking for a period of time, in order to decrease smoking (Halpern et al. 2015).

Nudges thus aim to improve individual decision-making—without limiting freedom of choice—by using a variety of findings and insights from behavioral economics, including those concerning framing effects and reference points, loss aversion, and endowment effects. Nudges have been very influential in Western countries, with most governments implementing nudges on some level; but they have also been criticized extensively. It is useful to distinguish three types of criticism.

First, there is criticism from the perspective of ethics. Nudges have been criticized as manipulative and anti-liberal, not in line with basic tenets of democracy, not transparent enough, dangerous to citizens, nosy and a nuisance, and as a threat to the autonomous agency of individuals, amongst other criticisms (Bovens 2008; Grüne-Yanhoff 2012). Nudges interfere with a person's autonomy: choices formerly under a person's control, when nudged, are at least partly subject to the nudger's will (Hausman and Welch 2010). In the long run, nudges might infantilize people, who start to rely on external agencies with regards to their conception of the good (Bovens 2008).

Second, there is methodological criticism. Many commentators have investigated the question of how precisely to define nudges (e.g. Saghai 2013, but also in the articles just cited), since the original formulation was ambiguous in various ways. Heilmann (2014) points out that in order for a nudge to be implemented successfully, the policy-maker has to (i) correctly assess that most individuals in the target population are in conflict between what they really want and what they often end up choosing, (ii) design a particular intervention on the basis of findings from behavioral economics that lead an individual to select the better option, (iii) ensure that any individual can resist the nudge if they are so inclined, (iv) eventually lead a majority of individuals in the population to make the better choice. Fulfilling these conditions is a tall order. In similar vein, Grüne-Yanhoff (2016) argues that nudges should be based on the identification of stable mechanisms, and that the evidence for these mechanisms needs to be robust in order for nudges to be implemented faithfully.

A third type of criticism concerns the scope of nudges. Recently, many commentators have pointed out that there are many ways to base policies on behavioral insights, arguing that a broader range of behaviorally sophisticated public policies should replace nudges. For instance, so-called "Boosts" (Grüne-Yanhoff and Hertwig 2015) that aim to educate individuals about their mistakes and biases, and about (statistical) reasoning are often better. So-called "Budges" (Oliver 2013) are regulations that are informed by behavioral research (for instance, by requiring that consumers are informed about products without manipulation). There is thus a call to understand behavioral public policy in a much broader way.

One way to tackle these criticisms would be to turn to the broader theoretical foundations of nudges. Perhaps the most obvious candidate for a theoretical foundation for nudge is "dual process" or "dual systems" theory. There are two reasons for this: first, that has been the main theoretical framework by those who advocated nudge (see the references to dual systems in the Thaler and Sunstein [2008] book). Second, there are also some key proponents of behavioral economics (notably Kahneman 2003, 2011) who have recently advanced dual-systems views as the main conceptual foundation of behavioral economics.

The dual-system approach holds that there are two different kinds of capacities to human decision-making. On the one hand, there is the reflective system that is responsible for deliberation, and governs rational and conscious decision-making, which requires time and resources. On the other hand, there is the automatic system that is responsible for quick reactions and snap judgments, which requires less effort. In a nutshell, individuals succumb to biases because the automatic system governs the decisions, and the reflective system is not activated. Dual process/systems accounts are severely criticized as not providing an adequate picture of decision-making (Keren and Schul 2009; Frankish 2010 for overviews). In particular, Sahlin et al. (2010) provide a detailed critique against dual systems not corresponding to any other account of human behavior.

Moreover, basing nudges on a dual-systems view, as in Heilmann (2014), raises two main problems: first, nudges need to be defined in a very narrow way in order to adhere to a dual-systems characterization. There are many kinds of nudges that fall outside a strict definition of nudges as a manipulation of the interaction between the two systems. Second, nudges are very hard to implement in this way, as what is required is to identify a stable and general way in which for the population in question, the two systems interact when responding to the nudge intervention.

The dual-systems view, advanced as a more general framework for nudges by Thaler and Sunstein (2008), but also more broadly for behavioral economics (Kahneman 2003, 2011), does not seem to help in addressing any of the critiques. Concerning the methodological critique, the dual-systems view does help to point out how demanding nudges are methodologically, but does not offer resources to mount a detailed defense. Likewise, concerning the ethical critique, the dual-systems view can help to make some of the ethical worries more precise, but does not seem to offer any resources to defend it further. Concerning the criticism of scope, the dual-systems view forces us into a very narrow definition of nudges, and does not allow for nudges to subsume other behavioral public policies under its umbrella.

## 5 Conclusions

I have investigated whether the general frameworks sometimes advanced within behavioral economics would have the potential for unifying and generalizing behavioral economics: in hyperbolic discounting, the general framework of "multiple/dual selves" has been advanced, and for nudge, the view of "dual systems/processes" has been invoked. Both frameworks provide a less sparse framework of economic agency than is inherent in standard rational choice theory, and they might therefore be assumed to play a unifying role for the less idealized picture of individual decision-making advanced in behavioral economics. Alos-Ferrer and Strack (2014) maintain that this feature of both frameworks makes them perfect candidates to change economics. Yet, for both frameworks, there are considerable ambiguities about the interpretation of the key concepts (selves and systems/processes), and how these relate to similar concepts in psychology, folk psychology, neuroeconomics, and standard rational choice theory. Furthermore, while the frameworks have been undeniably helpful in the development of the models, they are not helpful in addressing objections raised against them.

Behavioral economics has shaped economics in many crucial ways, and will continue to do so: this is true both substantively and methodologically, and both descriptively and normatively. Yet, commentators widely agree that behavioral economics may be less a case of a revolution in economics, than a contribution to the development of economics itself. Part of the reason for why behavioral economics may be less revolutionary than one might think at first glance is that its proponents widely accept rational choice theory as both the right normative standard for decision-making, but also as foil and background against which behavior or real-world agents should be investigated. Behavioral economics is likely to continue to shape economics in significant ways in the future: whether it can mount a fundamental and revolutionary challenge to core economic assumptions—and replace them—remains to be seen.

## References

Ainslie, G. (1975). Specious reward: A behavioral theory of impulsiveness and impulse control. *Psychological Bulletin*, 82(4), 463–96.

Ainslie, G. (1992). *Picoeconomics: The Interaction of Successive Motivational States within the Individual.* Cambridge University Press.

Ainslie, G. (2001). *Breakdown of Will.* Cambridge University Press.

Allais, M. (1953). Le comportement de l'homme rationnel devant le risque: critique des postulats et axiomes de l'école Américaine. *Econometrica*, 21, 503–46.

Alos-Ferrer, C., and Strack, F. (2014). From dual processes to multiple selves: Implications for economic behavior. *Journal of Economic Psychology*, 41, 1–11.

Angner, E. (2012). *A Course in Behavioral Economics.* New York: Palgrave Macmillan.

Angner, E. (2015). "To navigate safely in the vast sea of empirical facts." Ontology and methodology in behavioral economics. *Synthese* 192: 3557–575.

Angner, E., and Loewenstein, G. (2012). Behavioral economics. In U. Mäki (Ed.), *Handbook of the Philosophy of Science: Philosophy of Economics.* Amsterdam: Elsevier, 641–90.

Benabou, R., and Pycia, M. (2002). Dynamic inconsistency and self-control: A planner-doer interpretation. *Economics Letters*, 77(3), 419–24.

Bovens, L. (2008). The ethics of nudge. In T. Grüne-Yanoff and S. O. Hansson (Eds.), *Preference Change: Approaches from Philosophy, Economics and Psychology.* Berlin and New York: Springer, 207–19.

Camerer, C. F. (2005). *Behavioral Game Theory: Experiments in Strategic Interaction.* Princeton University Press.

Camerer, C. F., and Loewenstein, G. (2004). Behavioral economics: Past, present, future. In C. F. Camerer, G. Loewenstein, and M. Rabin (Eds.), *Advances in Behavioral Economics*. New York: Russell Sage Foundation, 3–51.

Dow, S. (2013). Formalism, rationality, and evidence: The case of behavioural economics. *Erasmus Journal for Philosophy and Economics*, 6(3), 26–43.

Ellsberg, D. (1954). Classic and current notions of "measurable utility." *Economic Journal*, 64(255), 528–56.

Frankish, K. (2010). Dual-process and dual-system theories of reasoning. *Philosophy Compass* 5(10), 914–26.

Frederick, S., Loewenstein, G., and O'Donoghue, T. (2002). Time discounting and time preference: A critical review. *Journal of Economic Literature*, 40(2), 351–401.

Fudenberg, D. (2006). Advancing beyond advances in behavioral economics. *Journal of Economic Literature* 44, 694–711.

Fudenberg, D., and Levine, D. K. (2006). A dual-self model of impulse control. *American Economic Review*, 96(5), 1449–476.

Grüne-Yanhoff, T. (2012). Old wine in new casks: Libertarian paternalism still violates liberal principles. *Social Choice and Welfare*, 38(4), 635–45.

Grüne-Yanoff, T. (2015). Models of temporal discounting 1937–2000: An interdisciplinary exchange between economics and psychology. *Science in Context*, 28(4), 675–713.

Grüne-Yanoff, T. (2016). Why behavioral policy needs mechanistic evidence. *Economics and Philosophy*, forthcoming. doi:10.1017/S0266267115000425.

Grüne-Yanoff, T., and Hertwig, R. (2015). Nudge versus boost: How coherent are policy and theory? *Minds and Machines*, 26(1), 1–35.

Guala, F. (2005). *The Methodology of Experimental Economics*. Cambridge University Press.

Halpern, S. D., French, B., Small, D. S., et al. (2015). Randomized trial of four financial-incentive programs for smoking cessation. *New England Journal of Medicine*, 372, 2108–117.

Hausman, D. M., and Welch, B. (2010). Debate: To nudge or not to nudge. *Journal of Political Philosophy*, 18(1), 123–36.

Heilmann, C. (2014). Success conditions for nudges: A methodological critique of libertarian paternalism. *European Journal for Philosophy of Science*, 4(1), 75–94.

Heukelom, F. (2014). Mainstreaming behavioral economics. *Journal of Economic Methodology*, 21(1), 92–95.

Heukelom, F. (2015). *Behavioral Economics: A History*. New York: Cambridge University Press.

Kahneman, D. (2003). Maps of bounded rationality: Psychology for behavioral economics. *American Economic Review*, 93(5), 1449–475.

Kahneman, D. (2011). *Thinking, Fast and Slow*. New York: Penguin Books.

Kahneman, D., and Tversky, A. (1979). Prospect theory: An analysis of decision under risk. *Econometrica*, 47(2), 263–91.

Katsikopoulos, K. V. (2014). Bounded rationality: The two cultures. *Journal of Economic Methodology*, 21(4), 361–74.

Keren, G., and Schul, Y. (2009). Two is not always better than one: A critical evaluation of two-system theories. *Perspectives on Psychological Science*, 4, 500–33.

Laibson, D. (1997). Golden eggs and hyperbolic discounting. *Quarterly Journal of Economics*, 112(2), 443–77.

Loewenstein, G., and Elster, J. (1992). *Choice over Time*. New York: Russell Sage Foundation.

Loewenstein, G., and Read, D. (2003). *Time and Decision: Economic and Psychological Perspectives on Intertemporal Choice*. New York: Russell Sage Foundation.

Loomes, G., and Sugden, R. (1982). Regret theory: An alternative theory of rational choice under uncertainty. *Economic Journal*, 92(368), 805–24.

Mallard, G. (2015). *Bounded Rationality and Behavioural Economics*. Abingdon: Routledge.

Mueller, D. (2004). Models of man: Neoclassical, behavioural, and evolutionary. *Politics, Philosophy and Economics*, 3(1), 59–76.

Nagatsu, M. (2010). Beyond circularity and normativity: Measurement and progress in behavioral economics. *Philosophy of the Social Sciences*, 40(2), 265–90.

O'Donoghue, T., and Rabin, M. (1999). Doing it now or later. *American Economic Review*, 89(1), 103–24.

Oliver, A. (2013). From nudging to budging: Using behavioural economics to inform public sector policy. *Journal of Social Policy*, 42(04), 685–700.

Peleg, B., and Yaari, M. E. (1973). On the existence of a consistent course of action when tastes are changing. *Review of Economic Studies*, 40(3), 391–401.

Pesendorfer, W. (2006). Behavioral economics comes of age: A review essay on advances in behavioral economics. *Journal of Economic Literature*, 44, 712–21.

Read, D. (2006). Which side are you on? The ethics of self-command. *Journal of Economic Psychology*, 27(5), 681–93.

Reiss, J. (2013). *Philosophy of Economics: A Contemporary Introduction*. Abingdon: Routledge.

Ross, D. (2011). Estranged parents and a schizophrenic child: Choice in economics, psychology and neuroeconomics. *Journal of Economic Methodology*, 18(3), 217–31.

Ross, D. (2015). *Philosophy of Economics*. Basingstoke: Palgrave Macmillan.

Saghai, Y. (2013). Salvaging the concept of nudge. *Journal of Medical Ethics*. doi:10.1136/medethics-2012–100727.

Sahlin, N.-E., Wallin, A., and Persson, J. (2010). Decision science: From Ramsey to dual process theories. *Synthese*, 172(1), 129–43.

Samuelson, P. (1937). A note on measurement of utility. *Review of Economic Studies*, 4, 155–61.

Savage, L. J. (1954). *The Foundations of Statistics*. New York: Dover Publications.

Schelling, T. C. (1980). The intimate contest for self-command. *Public Interest*, 60, 94–118.

Schelling, T. C. (1984). Self-command in practice, in policy, and in a theory of rational choice. *American Economic Review*, 74, 1–11.

Sent, E.-M. (2004). Behavioral economics: How psychology made its (limited) way back into economics. *History of Political Economy*, 36(4), 735–60.

Starmer, C. (2000). Developments in non-expected utility theory: The hunt for a descriptive theory of choice under risk. *Journal of Economic Literature*, 38, 332–82.

Strotz, R. H. (1955–56). Myopia and inconsistency in dynamic utility maximization. *Review of Economic Studies*, 23(3), 165–80.

Thaler, R. H., and Shefrin, H. M. (1981). An economic theory of self-control. *Journal of Political Economy*, 89(2), 392–406.

Thaler, R. H., and Sunstein, C. R. (2008). *Nudge*. London: Yale University Press.

Todd, P. M., Gigerenzer, G., and the ABC Research Group (1999). *Simple Heuristics That Make Us Smart*. Oxford University Press.

von Neumann, J., and Morgenstern, O. (1944). *Theory of Games and Economic Behavior*. Princeton University Press.

Vromen, J. (2009). The booming economics-made-fun genre: More than having fun, but less than economics imperialism. *Erasmus Journal for Philosophy and Economics*, 2(1), 70–99.

Wakker, P. (2010). *Prospect Theory: For Risk and Ambiguity*. Cambridge University Press.

Wilkinson, N., and Klaes, M. (2012). *An Introduction to Behavioral Economics*. Basingstoke: Palgrave Macmillan.

Xue, L. (2008). The bargaining within. *Economics Letters*, 101, 145–47.

# 27
# MACHINE EPISTEMOLOGY AND BIG DATA

## Gregory Wheeler

### 1

Here is a portrait of experimental science. A question arises, a hypothesis is proposed, experiments are devised, then performed, and a judgment is made on how well some or another implication of that hypothesis, supposing it were true, accords with the outcomes. Such was Charles Sanders Peirce's view of experimental inquiry at the end of the nineteenth century.[1] By the close of the twentieth, a spectacular store of methods were on hand to quantify the uncertainty an experimentalist confronts, along with a logic, broadly speaking, to assess its consequences. Just as the differential calculus swept to the margins ancient bewilderment over change and how to reason about quantities that change, so have the triumphs of modern statistics pushed aside Cartesian paralysis over error and how to reason with corrigible, uncertain quantities. It is not so much that Leibniz and Newton answered Parmenides, or that Peirce set the course for Pearson and Fisher to refute the academic skeptics, but rather that in each case a genuine obstacle to inquiry was plucked from confusion and paradox and a clear way to reason around those obstacles was shown. For those who wonder what philosophical progress looks like, look no further.

### 2

Statistics confronts two questions. The first asks what can be inferred from data, given modeling assumptions that you choose, while the second asks after the reliability of those inferences. Data, a product of ingenuity rather than a commodity of passive experience, is therefore—historically, at least—in short supply. Further, since data is won through deliberation and action, assessing the reliability of a statistical inference comes after such choices are made, not before.

Knowledge within this portrait is an answered question, a problem resolved, and settled judgments from prior investigations are tools for new inquiries rather than a normative standard against which all new conclusions are assessed. The modern experimental sciences, as Dewey remarked, are not the only kind of knowledge, but they magnify the essential ingredients for knowledge of every kind.[2]

This pragmatic view of experimental inquiry, where evidence is taken from the world rather than given, stands in contrast to a long tradition in philosophy that views the objects of knowledge as prior to, and unchanged by, the mental activity of coming to know them. Knowledge, this tradition tells us, is a stock of beliefs that hits on the truth and does so for a reason. The task for epistemology is to divine the nature of such beliefs and the principles governing such reasons. It is little surprise then that statistical methodology is viewed as a puzzle for traditional epistemology rather than a reservoir of answers. On what grounds ought you select modeling assumptions? What justifies viewing your data, so-parameterized, as a suitable guide for an unknown event? These are the problems of Duhem and Hume, respectively.

For a pragmatist, this is entirely the wrong way to proceed. Knowledge is a means of control, not a special state of mind. Uncertainty is to be exploited rather than extinguished, and epistemic notions ought to be derived from the roles that they play in inquiry rather than the other way around. The proceedings of contemporary epistemology are a record of what comes from a tradition that stands opposed to each of these tenets. It is a record as far removed from advancing knowledge as the confabulations of numerologists are from advancing higher arithmetic.

I bring up these two radically different conceptions of experimental inquiry because the rise of machine learning and big data are at once a bewildering mystery by the lights of traditional epistemology and a clear demonstration of the pragmatists' point. Hilary Putnam called for a *pragmatic enlightenment* in epistemology,[3] one that followed through on Dewey's observation that uncertainty is a practical matter. The short history of machine learning is the closest we have to a side-by-side comparison of how well the entrenched ideas of traditional, Enlightenment epistemology stand up to the 'primacy of practice' that is at the heart of pragmatic epistemology. What emerges, I contend, is the outlines of a machine epistemology.


# 3


Machine learning is a marriage of statistics and computer science that began in artificial intelligence. Statistics, as I remarked earlier, is concerned with the question of what may be inferred from data that we've chosen to model in a particular way, and it also addresses how to assess the reliability of those inferences. Computer science engages with a different set of questions. It is concerned with the design of algorithms that run on a machine to solve some or another problem of our choosing, and it further addresses the question of which problems are tractable enough to admit a computational solution and which are not. From a modern point of view, machine learning is a discipline that sits at the intersection of statistics and computer science. But the question machine learning asks is fundamentally different from both statistics and computer science. For the question machine learning asks is how to make a computer learn from data without explicitly programming it to do so.

Machine learning, like statistics, is interested in the question of what can be inferred from data. But unlike statistics, machine learning aims to circumvent the requirement to explicitly set modeling assumptions prior to drawing meaningful inferences or, when unavoidable, seeks to design algorithms that learn on their own what modeling assumptions are best to select. Here again we find not an answer to Duhem nor a solution to the problem of Hume's but ways to reason around them.

This focus on designing algorithms which are not told in advance how to solve a particular task has had the peculiar effect of vindicating an insight from statistics that modeling assumptions are necessary to get anything meaningful out of data, but undermining a canard of epistemology that the making of such assumptions invites a regress. The key, which any student of machine learning will recognize, is that one must understand the goal of inquiry in order to pick which features to extract from data and to assess how well one method manages against another. What is perhaps surprising, to traditional statisticians and traditional epistemologists alike, is the extent to which these value-laden judgments can be described in general terms and managed by a machine.

Here the historical role that artificial intelligence played in the rise of machine learning is instructive. The question that artificial intelligence addresses is how to design computer systems that think or act as humans do, or rationally ought to do, yet the disjunction between 'thinking' and 'acting' has divided the field, much as it continues to divide philosophy. For those interested in how an artificial intelligence ought to think, the explicit representation of *objects* perceived, *meanings* of sentences understood, or *beliefs* endorsed as true is of central importance, followed closely by the development of some or another set of rules for manipulating these representations to represent *perceiving*, *understanding*, or *reasoning*. Unfortunately, this project has gotten nowhere. Approaches that focus on intelligent behavior, on the other hand, focus on the successful completion of tasks—the parsing of speech, the recognition of hand-written addresses, the production of a new grammatically correct or contextually meaningful vocalization of speech—have been wildly successful. Behind these successes are machine learning techniques and, often enough, volumes of data whose scale in size is extraordinary.[4]

4

Consider an example. Suppose that you are interested in the time it takes a taxi cab to travel from John F. Kennedy International Airport to Grand Central Station in Manhattan, New York. The act of taking a particular taxi from JFK to Grand Central, at least according to one textbook approach, is conceived as the selection of a single trip from a large population of such trips, like a single ball drawn from many in a large urn. Naturally, the more you know about the composition of the urn, the better your position to predict what sort of ball you will draw. Similarly, the more you know about the population of JFK-to-Grand Central taxi trips, the better your position to predict how your particular trip will fare.

The first hitch in this line of reasoning is that there is no single canonical population that your trip belongs to. There is the population of trips from JFK to Grand Central that run on the same day of the week as yours, the population of trips that run at the same time of day as yours, the population of trips that run at the same time *and* on the same day, and countless others. Selecting which population your trip belongs to is a version of the *reference class problem*. I say a version of the reference class problem because the original reference class problem concerns how to reconcile conflicting statistical evidence that you already have on hand, whereas the problem here is one of choosing which categories to measure and which to ignore.

The original reference class problem is this: if one possesses statistical information about two or more classes that an uncertain event belongs to, where the parameters of interest—say the *mean* travel time of taxi trips and the *variance* in travel times—have different values within each of the classes, then the original problem of the reference class is how to resolve those conflicts in your evidence. Hans Reichenbach (1938) claimed that to resolve the problem of the reference class one ought to always pick the narrowest reference class for which there are 'adequate' statistics. But Reichenbach offered no account for assessing statistical adequacy, nor did he offer any reason for maintaining that adequate statistics must be unique. The definite description of a particular event, for instance, is the singleton class consisting solely of the event itself. This class is by definition both the narrowest possible class and unique. However, this class is hardly adequate for it merely summarizes your current state of uncertainty about the event in question and offers no guidance whatsoever. Henry Kyburg supplemented Reichenbach's specificity condition with a principle he called *richness* (Kyburg 1974; Kyburg and Teng 2001), which serves as a non-trivial adequacy condition, along with another he called *strength* to ensure uniqueness. But while Kyburg's system has some intuitive appeal, the proposal remains deeply controversial.[5]

The alternative version of the reference class problem comes one step before Reichenbach's problem, for we are faced with the problem of selecting which evidence to gather rather than how to adjudicate conflicts among the evidence we have on hand. In practice, background knowledge from prior experience is called on to select which categories to measure and which to ignore. But to many philosophers this appeal to prior experience and absence of general principles for guiding one in selecting which categories to control for and which to ignore has been a source of despair (Broad 1952, 143).

The second hitch in this line of reasoning is that for practically every population you might choose the mean and variance of travel times will be unknown to you. Traditionally, this problem is solved by measuring the travel times in a sample of taxi trips judged to be representative of the population with respect to these two parameters. This is where the background knowledge of an experimentalist enters the picture and where the misgivings of traditional philosophers take hold. For the success of this type of statistical inference will hinge on one's choice of which features of the sample to investigate and which to ignore. In effect, our experimentalist must provide an answer to the indirect version of the reference class problem that confronted us before.

From the point of view of traditional epistemology, the pragmatic conception of inquiry is hamstrung because each instance of knowledge seems to rest on a host of assumptions which are without justification. And for those *algorithmic* proposals that do offer a solution, such as Kyburg's, there is no clear *a priori* standard against which to judge its success yet plenty of *a priori* objections with which to contend. It would seem that we should not be able to even get started on this view.

Now imagine an alternative scenario where instead of planning and justifying the pick of a sample of taxi rides to observe, you are provided instead with a record of *every* taxi trip in New York City for the prior year. In fact, at the time of writing, there are six and a half years of complete yellow taxi trip records freely available to the public.[6] Here, then, one can simply compare various classes to see which give similar estimates, and which give different estimates, and then see whether background knowledge of your particular trip allows you to exploit these differences to yield a good estimate for your trip. One might cross-reference this data set with the weather conditions in the New York Area, for instance, to consider the effect of weather on travel times. If snow was forecast for the day of your trip, this information might be useful in yielding a better estimate of your travel time. Or, analogously, you might discover that rain has no appreciable effect on travel times and choose to ignore it.

This pattern of reasoning is intuitive even if not terribly clever. But the point is that a lot of ground can be covered without being clever, since much of this sort of reasoning can be automated and evaluated without supplying a justification for the selection of parameters prior to making an inference. A machine can plow through combinatorial combinations of features involving enormous volumes of data, the scale of which is impossible for humans to replicate.

5

Common sense, craft, and calculation are involved in judging whether a statistical sample should be judged representative of a population. What machine learning techniques have shown, particularly when paired with large volumes of data, is that the roles that craft and common sense play in statistical inference can be minimized or sidestepped altogether by reëngineering the problem so a system can learn hidden structure to use as a substitute for the background knowledge that we might bring to a problem.

There are three main types of machine learning.

*Supervised Learning*: In a supervised learning task, you are provided with a data set that tells you what a correct answer should look like. For example, in our NYC Taxi data set, one can look at each trip record that starts at JFK Airport and plot distance in miles traveled against the duration of the trip. One might then use this data to predict the duration of your trip based on the distance between JFK and Grand Central Station.

More generally, supervised learning problems are categorized into regression and classification problems. In a *regression* problem, the goal is to predict an outcome on a continuous scale; what a regression problem attempts to do is to map an input variable (distance in miles) to some continuous function that predicts a continuous outcome (time). In a *classification* problem, the goal is to predict results in a discrete output, such as 'Pass' or 'Fail', 'low', 'medium', or 'high', or some other discrete set of categories.

Supervised learning problems are thus a form of enumerative induction. However, instead of observing a finite number of input–output pairs of some kind in order to draw an inference about *all* pairs of that kind, as enumerative induction is conceived to do, a supervised learning problem typically observes a finite number of pairs to draw an inference about an unobserved but likewise finite set of pairs. There is no pretense to learning a universal law through supervised learning, and in fact basic results in the field suggest that a search for universality is entirely the wrong approach. For one thing, there are many different supervised learning algorithms that each enjoy different strengths and weaknesses. As a result, the selection of a learning algorithm will depend on the goal of a particular inquiry and the features of the data that one has to work with. In fact, the 'no free lunch' results of (Wolpert and Macready 1997) indicate that there is no single algorithm that can be applied to all supervised learning problems which will outperform the pragmatic strategy of matching the structure of an algorithm to the structure of the problem and the aim of inquiry.

*Unsupervised Learning*: In an unsupervised learning task, you are provided with little or no idea what the resulting answer ought to look like. Here the task is to derive structure from data where we do not necessarily know the effect of the variables we are learning. Returning to our NYC Taxi data set, one might look at a collection of 1 million trips originating from JFK and find a way to automatically group trips that are somehow similar. Much of the power of machine learning and most of the controversy over machine learning applications involves unsupervised learning algorithms.

Generally, unsupervised learning problems provide no feedback to the learner based on the predictive results it returns; there is no oracle to correct the learner as there is for supervised learning. Instead, the goal of unsupervised learning is *knowledge discovery*. There are several varieties of unsupervised learning problems.

- In a *clustering* problem, which is the most common form of unsupervised learning, the goal is to derive hidden structure in data based on relationships among variables in the data. Clustering is a means of partitioning a collection of objects into groups that resemble one another along one or more dimensions of comparison, where the categories are not predefined. Among a wide range of applications across the sciences and business, clustering has also been viewed as a model for concept formation.[7]
- In a *latent factors* learning problem, the goal is to reduce a high-dimensional data set with many variables to a smaller number of latent variables that are most responsible for variability. A common approach to dimensionality reduction is called *principal component analysis* or PCA, which may be thought of as the unsupervised version of a (multi-variate) linear regression.
- In a *graphical structure* learning problem, the goal is to say which variables are most correlated with others, where the edges of a graph represent direct dependence, or go further to say which variables stand in the relationship of cause and effect to one another (Spirtes, Glymour, and Scheines 2000).
- In a *matrix completion* learning problem, the goal is to deal with missing or incomplete data by inferring reasonable values for missing data values.[8]

*Reinforcement Learning*: A reinforcement learning problem is characterized by a learner confronted with a decision problem in which a number of acts yield various (numerical) rewards, and the task for the learner is to discover which act maximizes the numerical reward. Reinforcement learning resembles an unsupervised learning problem in the sense that it does not have a set of training examples of 'correct' behavior from which to learn, although it also has a specified reward structure that the learner 'understands' ought to be maximized. One feature of reinforcement learning problems is that the learner must confront a trade-off between exploration and exploitation. If an agent learns from several rounds of play that a particular strategy yields him a particular reward, in the next round he must weigh playing the same strategy and receiving the same reward against playing an alternative strategy that yields an unknown reward.[9]

# 6

Unlike a commodity that is consumed, data is an inexhaustible and renewable resource. Only recently has science transformed from a data-scarce enterprise, which I alluded to at the start, to a data-rich one. Data was once expensive, the product of a controlled experiment or some other careful measurement regime. Now we are flooded with the stuff. The sequencing of the first human genome in 2002 determined the order of approximately 3 billion nucleotides. That achievement took thirteen years, involved twenty institutions, and cost $3 billion. Thirteen years later the cost is now $1,000 to sequence a human genome and a lab can generate more than 300 a week.[10]

To be sure, these new sources of data do not replace the role of controlled experiments and careful measurement, but the era of big data does introduce new opportunities to empirically explore topics cheaply or to empirically explore a question that until recently was difficult, if not impossible, to address.

Martin Nowak and colleagues have looked at the evolutionary dynamics of language to figure out how the rate of verb regularization depends on the frequency of word usage. This is precisely the sort of claim that not too long ago was forwarded *a priori* rather than tackled empirically. Jean-Baptiste Michel, Nowak, and colleagues have looked at 4 percent of all the books ever published, a staggering 5,195,769 digitized books, to explore cultural trends recorded in the English language between 1800 and 2000. Of 'culturomics' they say:

> We show how this approach can provide insights about fields as diverse as lexicography, the evolution of grammar, collective memory, the adoption of technology, the pursuit of fame, censorship, and historical epidemiology. Culturomics extends the boundaries of rigorous quantitative inquiry to a wide array of new phenomena spanning the social sciences and the humanities.
>
> (Michel et al. 2011, 176)

All this brings to mind three points to consider. First, from the point of view of the philosophy of science, data science arguably does offer a new mode of inquiry insofar as we are now routinely handling population data sets directly or sample sizes so immense, such as in our NYC Taxi dataset, that they behave like population data. In this setting, inferential methods of statistical reasoning are used for an altogether different task, namely, as a form of quality control for the direct methods applied to these enormous data sets. Second, there is now a realignment of interests that will make for new collaboration between business and publicly funded science. The fundamental interests of business and science are more closely aligned than they have been in the past—with the exception of chemistry, perhaps—which means, among several things, that some scientific innovations will come from the business community. Already the leading figures in the emerging field of computational social science are in industry, and many breakthroughs of that field are the intellectual property of companies rather than goods of the commonwealth.

Finally, the collection and storage of society's 'data exhaust' by governments and private companies is easily repurposed for countless tasks, some for the public good, others less so. Big data and machine learning are the mother-of-all dual-use technologies, where 'dual' in this setting is a euphemism for 'countless'. To take one example, PredPol Inc. is a California-based company that took an algorithm used to predict earthquakes and modified it to predict where crime is likely to occur within a 500-square-foot radius. The same tool that allows WalMart to adjust shipments of items to its stores in anticipation of large weather events can now be used to anticipate criminal behavior and adjust police presence.[11] The software is used by the Los Angeles and Santa Cruz police departments.

# 7

Dewey observed that the legal and economic organization of societies places the knowledge of how to regulate activity in the hands of a small number of individuals, and that there is an inclination for those individuals to use that knowledge to benefit themselves rather than the general public. The question for him was how to share such knowledge more widely and how to effect a more equitable participation in their results.[12]

In the age of big data and a machine epistemology that can anticipate, predict, and intervene on events in our lives, the problem once again is that a few individuals possess the knowledge of how to regulate these activities. But the question we face now is not how to share such knowledge more widely, but rather of how to enjoy the public benefits bestowed by this knowledge without freely sharing it. It is not merely personal privacy that is at stake but a range of unsung benefits that come from ignorance and forgetting, traits that are inherently human and integral to the functioning of our society.

# Notes

1 See "Abduction and Induction," in Peirce 1955.
2 See Dewey 1929, 100 and 250–51.
3 See Putnam 2004.
4 To give some examples, there are currently approximately 45 billion indexed webpages in Google's pagerank (www.worldwidewebsize.com; accessed March 27, 2016); each person has a genome the length of $3.8 \times 10^9$ base pairs, and thousands of people have had their genomes sequenced; the American retailer Walmart receives 2.5 petabytes of unstructured data from 1 million customers every hour.
5 Although efficient algorithms exist for calculating Kyburgian solutions to reference class problems (Wheeler and Williamson 2011), outputs can violate fundamental coherence principles underpinning standard- as well as set-based Bayes methods (Levi 1977).
6 The New York City Taxi and Limousine Commission Trip Record Dataset (www.nyc.gov/html/tlc/html/about/trip_record_data.shtml; accessed March 27, 2016) includes all trip records completed in yellow taxis in New York City from January 1, 2009, to June 30, 2015. These records include pick-up and drop-off GPS coordinates, pick-up and drop-off times, trip distances, itemized fares, rate types, payment types, and driver-reported passenger counts.
7 See in particular Michalski 1980 and the special issue of *Machine Learning* that includes Fisher 1987.
8 See Laurent 2001 for an introduction.
9 See Sutton and Barto 1998.
10 See May 2015.
11 See Beck and McCue 2009.
12 See Dewey 1929, 80–81.

# References

Beck, C. and C. McCue (2009, November). Predictive policing: What can we learn from Walmart and Amazon about fighting crime in a recession? *Police Chief* 76(11), www.policechiefmagazine.org/magazine/index.cfm?fuseaction=display_arch&article_id=1942&issue_id=112009, accessed August 10, 2016.
Broad, C. D. (1952). *Ethics and The History of Philosophy*. London: Routledge.
Dewey, J. (1929). *The Quest for Certainty*. New York: Capricorn Books, 3rd edn., 1960.
Fisher, D. H. (1987). Knowledge acquisition via incremental conceptual clustering. *Machine Learning* 2(2), 139–172.
Kyburg, H. E., Jr. (1974). *The Logical Foundations of Statistical Inference*. Dordrecht: D. Reidel.
Kyburg, H. E., Jr. and C. M. Teng (2001). *Uncertain Inference*. Cambridge: Cambridge University Press.
Laurent, M. (2001). Matrix completion problems. In C. Floudas and P. Pardalos (Eds.), *The Encyclopedia of Optimization*, vol. 3, 221–29. Dordrecht: Kluwer.
Levi, I. (1977). Direct inference. *Journal of Philosophy* 74, 5–29.
May, M. (2015). Life science technologies: Big biological impacts from big data. *Science* 344(6189), 1298–300.

Michalski, R. S. (1980). Knowledge acquisition through conceptual clustering: A theoretical framework and an algorithm for partitioning data into conjunctive concepts. *International Journal of Policy Analysis and Information Systems* 4(3), 219–44.

Michel, J.-B., Yuan Kui Shen, A. P. Aiden, A. Veres, M. K. Gray, The Google Books Team, J. P. Pickett, D. Hoiberg, D. Clancy, P. Norvig, J. Orwant, S. Pinker, M. A. Nowak, and E. L. Aiden (2011). Quantitative analysis of culture using millions of digitized books. *Science* 331(6014, January 14), 176–82.

Peirce, C. S. (1955). *Philosophical Writings of Peirce*. New York: Dover.

Putnam, H. (2004). *Ethics without Ontology*. Cambridge, MA: Harvard University Press.

Reichenbach, H. (1938). On probability and induction. *Philosophy of Science* 5(1), 21–45.

Spirtes, P., C. Glymour, and R. Scheines (2000). *Causation, Prediction, and Search*. Cambridge, MA: MIT Press.

Sutton, R. S. and A. G. Barto (1998). *Reinforcement Learning: An Introduction*. Cambridge, MA: MIT Press.

Wheeler, G. and J. Williamson (2011). Evidential probability and objective Bayesian epistemology. In P. Bandyopadhyay and M. Forster (Eds.), *Handbook of the Philosophy of Statistics*, 307–31. Oxford, etc.: Elsevier Science.

Wolpert, D. H. and W. G. Macready (1997). No free lunch theorems for optimization. *IEEE Transactions on Evolutionary Computation* 1(1), 67–82.

# 28
# EVOLUTIONARY PSYCHOLOGY

## Stephen M. Downes

### Introduction

Evolutionary psychology is a research program in the social sciences that explains human behavior in terms of evolved mechanisms that underlie the relevant behavior. Evolutionary psychologists aim to account for a large range of human behavior in this way, ranging from the choice of sexual partners, parenting and violent conflict between individuals to social organization, cultural practices and the production and use of artifacts. Evolutionary psychologists present their approach as a necessary one for the social and behavioral sciences and often support the stronger view that their approach should supplant other social science research programs (cf. Rosenberg 1980 on sociobiology).

Clark Barrett, in his recent systematic presentation and defense of evolutionary psychology, says "There are few things more obvious than the fact that we are products of evolution" (2015, 1). He goes on to say that despite the fact that all modern-day scientists agree with this statement, in the social sciences "there are few things a scientist can do to generate more controversy than to make a claim that [a given] feature of human thought or behavior is the product of evolution" (ibid.). The evidence for this is the "barrage of criticism that is directed at the field of evolutionary psychology" (ibid.). In his view, as evolutionary psychology has become more visible and grown in stature, controversy about it has increased.

Debates about evolutionary psychology range from local and focused discussions about evolutionary theory to wider-scope discussions about culture and politics. Evolutionary psychologists have fielded criticism from cultural anthropologists, evolutionary anthropologists, evolutionary biologists, philosophers (including feminist philosophers, philosophers of biology and philosophers of mind), psychologists, and sociologists. In philosophy there are several books whose main focus is criticizing evolutionary psychology and associated approaches to explaining human behavior (see e.g. Barker 2015; Buller 2005; Dupre 2001; Prinz 2012; Richardson 2007). Some critics object to the idea that human behavior and culture are amenable to evolutionary explanation, but this line of criticism does not capture all dimensions of debates about evolutionary psychology. Evolutionary anthropologists are also in the business of providing evolutionary explanations of human behavior and culture, yet they are among the sharpest critics of evolutionary psychology (see e.g. S. Hrdy 1999). In what follows we review the key issues in some of the different debates about evolutionary psychology. First, we briefly introduce the evolutionary psychologists' research program.

## Evolutionary Psychology's Research Program

Evolutionary psychology is an outgrowth of sociobiology (cf. Griffiths 2006, 2011). Sociobiologists argued that human nature should be accounted for in evolutionary terms (see e.g. Wilson 1978). On this view, our nature, expressed in universal human behaviors and cultural practices, is a product of our genes. The reason the traits making up our nature are universal is that the genes underlying these traits have been fixed in the population by natural selection. In contrast with sociobiologists, evolutionary psychologists change the locus of explanation from genes to psychological mechanisms. On this view, human nature, again expressed in our universal behaviors and cultural practices, is best understood as a collection of evolved psychological mechanisms (Cosmides, Tooby, and Barkow 1992; Tooby and Cosmides 1990, 2005). These evolved psychological mechanisms are specialized. Evolutionary psychologists argue that we see all manner of specialized morphological traits that adapt us to specific features of our environment—livers remove toxins and lungs oxygenate the blood—and we should expect to see analogous differentiation in our psychological mechanisms (see e.g. Barrett 2015; Confer et al. 2010). Evolutionary psychologists resist the idea that what makes humans successful is a highly flexible mind that is a general processor. They argue that such a general processor is highly unlikely to be the product of an evolutionary process that allowed us to adapt to survive multiple distinct environmental challenges. Rather, evolution produces many special-purpose mechanisms that fit with specific aspects of the world (Barrett 2015; Confer et al. 2010). As Barrett puts it "There are many ways in which the mind is 'fitted,' or shaped, to the world in which it operates, and all aspects of mind-world fit must, ultimately, be the result of the evolutionary process" (2015, 7). Our flexibility is the result of many specialized mechanisms acting in concert rather than the result of one undifferentiated general-purpose mechanism.

Evolutionary psychologists test their hypotheses using methods shared with other psychologists, including observational techniques, questionnaires, and neural imaging. They also use methods not shared with other psychologists. For example, they borrow from archaeology, comparative biology, ethnography, and paleontology (cf. Confer et al. 2010, 112). Evolutionary psychologists widen the scope of hypothesis-testing methods because they have the double burden of testing both psychological and evolutionary hypotheses. Evolutionary hypotheses are claims about the evolutionary process that led to the representation of a given trait in a population. Such hypotheses cannot be tested by simply establishing the prevalence of the trait in a population or by establishing that some individuals have an underlying mechanism that reliably produces the relevant trait. Barrett emphasizes that evolutionary psychology must be guided by the logic and research methods of evolutionary biology if it is to live up to its name (2015, 12).

Throughout the 1990s evolutionary psychologists proposed a huge number of evolved psychological mechanisms. Such mechanisms were proposed to explain all manner of social phenomena and human behavior, including selection of mates, the institution of marriage, the prevalence of murder of stepchildren, incest taboos, and differential parental investment in male or female offspring. In the last ten years many in the field have required higher standards of test for proposed evolved psychological mechanisms (cf. Barrett 2015; Confer et al. 2010). As a result, fewer mechanisms are defended. Some argue that many hypotheses about evolved psychological mechanisms have been straightforwardly falsified (see e.g. Confer et al. 2010). For some time Devendra Singh's (1993; Singh and Luis 1995) hypothesis that men had an evolved mechanism for detecting optimal waist/hip ratios in women was presented as a textbook case of an evolved psychological mechanism. Now this specific hypothesis about women's waist/hip ratios has come under severe critical scrutiny as a result of conflicting empirical findings (see e.g. Yu and Shepard 1998). However, there is lots of interesting work on why there is variation in women's waist/hip ratios within and between cultures that does not invoke optimal waist/hip ratio detection mechanisms in men (see e.g. Cashdan 2008). The evolutionary psychology hypotheses that men have an evolved preference for virgins and that male homosexuals persist in human populations because of kin altruism have also both been falsified (cf. Confer et al. 2010).

Barrett claims that our theory of mind module is a classic example of an "evolved psychological adaptation" (2015, 211). On the dominant view in cognitive science, our ability to attribute beliefs to others and to interpret their behavior via these belief attributions results from an underlying psychological mechanism, our theory of mind, that "comes online" at a specific time during development. Cognitive psychologists refer to our interpretive capacity as "mindreading" (see Nichols and Stich 2003 for a clear presentation of this literature). Barrett presents a large amount of work that supports the hypothesis that mindreading is "an evolved capacity" (Barrett 2015, 153). Other evolutionary psychology hypotheses that have strong support include: evolved fear mechanisms underlying our avoidance of snakes and spiders; evolved mechanisms for avoiding toxic foods; and evolved social exchange cheat detection mechanisms (Barrett 2015; Confer et al. 2010). As we shall see, while some critics of evolutionary psychology focus on hypotheses that evolutionary psychologists agree lack support, others focus on hypotheses that evolutionary psychologists take to be well supported. We now turn to debates about evolutionary psychology.

## Debates about Evolutionary Psychology

Evolutionary psychology's predecessor, human sociobiology, was attacked on several fronts. Biologists and philosophers of biology argued that human sociobiologists did not practice biology as rigorously as their counterparts in animal behavioral biology. Critics also argued that sociobiologists were guided by a narrow view of evolutionary theory, referred to as adaptationism, and that the phenomena they attempted to account for could be better explained by appealing to a range of alternative hypotheses (see e.g. Gould 1978; Kitcher 1985; R. C. Lewontin 1979). Other critics argued that human sociobiology was sexist, genetically determinist, and ignored human diversity. Human sociobiologists were also accused of inadequately characterizing culture and underestimating cultural influences on our diverse behavior (cf. Fehr 2011; Segerstråle 2000). All these criticisms, in slightly varied form, have been carried over to evolutionary psychology and make up the "barrage of criticism" that Barrett refers to.

Barrett (cf. Confer et al. 2010) attempts to deflect some of the barrage of criticism by pointing out that "the rise of evolutionary psychology has led to rampant generation of evolution-flavored hypotheses throughout the social sciences, not all of which would pass basic tests of evolutionary plausibility" (Barrett 2015, 12). Barrett implies that if critics are focused on this kind of work, then he is their ally. He also rejects evolutionary psychology hypotheses that are not framed as they would be by animal biologists and other evolutionary theorists. However, this move of Barrett's only accounts for a portion of the barrage of criticism. The focus of many critics of evolutionary psychology is popular works (see e.g. Pinker 2002; Wright 1994) rather than "evolution-flavored hypotheses" found in the pages of social science journals. Sociologists worry that popular books championing evolutionary psychology leave the impression that the science about the evolutionary origins of our behavior and culture is settled. They go on to argue that this situation is further compounded by media presentations of such popular works as works of science (see e.g. Fuller 2006; Jackson and Rees 2007). Further, critics have sometimes assumed that their critical attacks on popular works championing evolutionary psychology are sufficient to undermine the evolutionary psychology research program. This situation is a bit of a mess and confusing for students of philosophy of social science. My recommendation is that we focus our attention on critical discussion of the work of practicing evolutionary psychology researchers. Discussion of the popularization of scientific practice and presentation of popularizations as if they were cutting-edge science by the media is important but will not be our focus here (Barker 2015 confronts some of these important issues). We first turn to the debate over evolutionary psychologists' notion of human nature.

## Evolutionary Psychology and Human Nature

Evolutionary psychologists propose that human nature is biologically based. Many critics challenge this view. Some reject the view on the grounds that our nature is culturally specified rather than biologically based (see e.g. Prinz 2012). This type of criticism is undermined by the unfounded presupposition that culture and biology can be clearly distinguished (cf. Buller 2005). Work on cultural evolution and on the complex co-evolutionary processes underlying many human traits reveals that to the extent that cultural factors and biological factors can be distinguished, they both play important roles in the evolution of human behavior, social organization, and artifact production (see e.g. Lewens 2015; Richerson and Boyd 2005; Sterelny 2012). Criticisms of evolutionary psychologists' concept of human nature with more bite invoke evolution. The charge is that evolutionary psychologists' concept of human nature is not consistent with evolutionary thought (cf. Buller 2005; Lewens 2015).

Evolutionary psychologists propose that human nature is expressed in cultural universals and its biological basis is the collection of evolved psychological mechanisms we share (Tooby and Cosmides 1990). Buller (2005, especially ch. 8) draws on Hull (1986) and Sober (1980) to argue that this notion of human nature presupposes a species concept that is not accepted by evolutionary biologists and fails to acknowledge or account for human variation. The first charge is that evolutionary psychologists take the species *Homo sapiens* to be characterized by a collection of shared traits. This is not how biologists characterize species. Rather, species are lineages, historical entities with beginnings and ends, in the case of extinction. The view that species are identified by a cluster of traits that their members share has the following consequence: we could go extinct and at another time a population could arise with the same defining cluster of traits in common. On the view of species presupposed by evolutionary psychologists, the new population would be the same species as us. This conclusion is not supported by the evolutionary view of species. On this view the only way to be part of the same species is to be part of the same lineage.

So the account of species presupposed in evolutionary psychologists' account of human nature is not an evolutionary one.

Buller's second charge is that evolutionary psychologists' account of human nature ignores or cannot account for human variation (cf. Lewens 2015; Ramsey 2013). Humans exhibit a huge amount of morphological, physiological, behavioral, and cultural variation; like all other organisms we exhibit within-species variation. To propose that our nature consists in universal traits, or the mechanisms underlying those universal traits, ignores all this variation. If evolutionary psychologists counter that their view accounts for variation in terms of what we have in common, they still face problems. Evolutionary biologists, such as population geneticists, are in the business of confronting and explaining variation. For them, variation is a property of populations and they strive to account for the distribution of variation in a given population in terms of the distribution of variation in earlier populations that gave rise to the one under study. Variation in the population can also be due to the range of responses organisms have to the different environments they confront (cf. Buller 2005; Hull 1986; Sober 1980). Evolutionary biologists do not propose an underlying set of mechanisms that organisms share whose expression is disrupted in different environments. This is how evolutionary psychologists appear to use their account of human nature to explain variation. If so, their account of human nature is not an evolutionary one.

Barrett responds to both of Buller's charges but first combines them as follows: "Some philosophers and biologists argue that the fuzzy and variable nature of species and populations means that treating any species as having a nature is a kind of category error—species just aren't that kind of thing" (2015, 320). Barrett agrees that other evolutionary psychologists have ignored or failed to account for human variation; further, he agrees that it is the job of any evolutionary approach to confront and account for variation. However, he objects to critics who suggest that we cannot present an evolutionarily sound notion of human nature. He says, "Whatever human nature is, it's a biological phenomenon, with all that implies" (321). What Barrett takes this to imply is that human nature is a thing that is "a big wobbly cloud that is different from the population clouds of squirrels and palm trees. To understand human minds and behaviors, we need to understand the properties of our own cloud, as messy as it might be" (332). So human nature is not a collection of traits we share but the collection of all of the traits expressed in our lineage.

Buller anticipates Barrett's alternate view and responds as follows: "one possibility is that the concept of human nature could refer to the totality of human behavior and psychology." He goes on to say that this version of human nature "has no particular theoretical meaning; it is merely an abbreviation for talking about the rich tapestry of human existence" (Buller 2005, 420). Tim Lewens characterizes a similar account of human nature to Barrett's as "simply a collection of informative truths about humans" (2015, 77). He goes on to say "Once an account of human nature is loosened up so as to make room for variation … there is no way to gain control of it" (79). According to Buller and Lewens, then, Barrett's attempt to salvage an evolutionarily viable account of human nature results in no account of human nature at all or, at best, results in what Lewens calls a "libertine" account of human nature, which is innocuous but does no explanatory work. There are several people currently attempting to defend accounts of human nature that both serve evolutionary psychology and are consistent with evolutionary thought in general (see e.g. Machery 2008). As a result, this debate about evolutionary psychology is ongoing. We now turn to issues surrounding evolutionary psychologists' adaptationist approach.

## Evolutionary Psychology and Adaptationism

Buller's (2005) critical work on evolutionary psychology is structurally similar to Philip Kitcher's (1985) critical work on human sociobiology. Buller argues that evolutionary psychologists' work can be challenged on evolutionary grounds and he also proposes alternate explanatory hypotheses for various phenomena that evolutionary psychologists take themselves to have accounted for. Buller's support for some of his alternate hypotheses has been questioned (see e.g. Machery and Barrett 2007) but his criticisms of evolutionary psychology on evolutionary grounds are supported and shared by many evolutionary biologists and philosophers of biology (see e.g. Coyne 2009; Downes 2015; Lewens 2015; R. Lewontin 1998; E. A. Lloyd 1999; E. A. Lloyd and Feldman 2002; Richardson 2007; Woodward and Cowie 2004). Here we focus on just one strand of Buller's evolutionary criticism, his attack on the type of adaptationism evolutionary psychologists adopt.

There are numerous versions of adaptationism (cf. Godfrey-Smith 2001; Lewens 2009) and here we focus just on the adaptationism defended by evolutionary psychologists. The term adaptationism was used as a pejorative by some biologists (see e.g. Gould and Lewontin 1979; R. C. Lewontin 1979), but subsequent work reveals that this charge does not discriminate well between distinct kinds of evolutionary hypotheses (cf. Downes 2015; R. C. Lewontin 1978; Seger and Stubblefield 1996). Evolutionary psychologists hold that psychological mechanisms of interest, such as our mechanism supporting snake avoidance, are adaptations. These mechanisms are products of natural selection as opposed to other evolutionary processes such as drift or meiotic drive (see Sober 2000 for a nice introduction to various alternate evolutionary processes to selection). An adaptation, in this sense, is a specialized mechanism that solves a specific problem that the organism faced in its environment. These adaptations are also universal in the population. Evolutionary biologists refer to such traits as "fixed" or "at fixation." Evolutionary psychologists take psychological adaptations to be most closely analogous to organs such as kidneys. On this account, the snake fear mechanism evolved to solve the problem of dangerous snakes in the environment just as the kidney evolved to solve the problem of balancing bodily fluids. Buller argues that this account of adaptation is incomplete or too narrow.

Lewens nicely summarizes one main thrust of Buller's criticism as follows: "there is no special significance attached to traits that are at, or near to, fixation, and the explanatory processes that evolutionists deal in are just as suited to accounting for traits that are present in different proportions" (2015, 66). Buller points out that phenotypic plasticity—the ability of an organism to change phenotype in response to its environment—is just as likely to be the result of natural selection as a fixed phenotype. Some features of environments are very stable and predictable and selection may favor one sure-fire mechanism that helps the organism deal with these features, but lots of environments are highly dynamic and unpredictable and produce more selection pressure for flexible response. Many biologists, philosophers, and social scientists emphasize that humans are highly flexible and all claim that it is this flexibility that is the product of natural selection in our case (see e.g. Buller 2005; Cashdan 2013; Godfrey-Smith 1996; Griffiths 2011; Ramsey 2013; Sterelny 2003). On this view, not only is flexibility of phenotypic response to our dynamic environments a product of natural selection, but variation at both the genetic and the phenotypic level is sustained by natural selection. For example, a lot of genetic diversity is maintained in the genes underlying our immune systems. What Buller and others point out here is that natural selection is not just a process that fixes traits in a population or fixes genes in a population.

Barrett responds to this line of criticism by saying that evolutionary psychologists acknowledge phenotypic plasticity and humans' flexible responses to changing environments. Critics still maintain that this acknowledgement is not enough. The idea here is that if evolutionary psychologists took on board a more encompassing notion of adaptationism, they would avail themselves of a wider range of evolutionary hypotheses about how humans deal with their dynamic environments. Instead, the critics say, evolutionary psychologists always resort to accounting for our flexibility in the same way: we have a collection of specialized psychological mechanisms, shaped by selection, that allow for our flexible response. This debate about adaptationism is also ongoing. Critics have yet to engage Barrett's discussion of phenotypic plasticity and our flexible response to dynamic environments. What we turn to now is an alternative proposal about the evolution of mindreading, which gives a sense of the kind of alternative hypotheses evolutionary psychologists rule out by considering only hypotheses about selected psychological mechanisms.

## Alternate Evolutionary Hypotheses about the Origin of Mindreading

As we saw above, cognitive and evolutionary psychologists refer to our ability to attribute beliefs and desires to others and to explain behavior in terms of these postulates as mindreading. We saw that Barrett claims that our mechanism underlying our mindreading ability is a classic adaptation in his sense of the term. Kim Sterelny (Sterelny 2003) argues that this is not the right approach to explaining mindreading at all. Sterelny says that the way evolutionary psychologists approach mindreading is modeled on the way psycholinguists account for language. On this account, our linguistic ability is explained in terms of an innate mechanism, or set of mechanisms, that we all have, which enables us to communicate in a language. Other language speakers provide the environmental triggers that bring the language mechanism on line. Sterelny argues that this line of reasoning, one that is widespread in developmental cognitive psychology, is perhaps only well suited to the case of language. Sterelny thinks that the extension of this explanatory approach to mindreading, moral judgment, and all manner of human capacities is misguided. The key to Sterelny's criticism of evolutionary psychology is his presentation of alternate evolutionary hypotheses.

Nativists like Noam Chomsky originally responded to behaviorists. Nativists argued that behaviorism did not have the resources to explain complex capacities such as our linguistic ability. Peter Godfrey-Smith (1996) characterizes this debate as one between proponents of internalist as opposed to externalist forms of explanation. Internalists' explanations invoke mechanisms inside us in explanations of behavior. Psycholinguists' innate grammar, invoked to account for our ability to learn and speak languages, is such a mechanism. Externalists' explanations rely on features of our environment. For example, behaviorist psychologists account for our behavior, even complex behavior such as learning and speaking a language, in terms of stimuli and responses to those stimuli. Sterelny is an externalist in this sense but his externalism gives him many more explanatory resources than behaviorists have. Sterelny's (2003) externalist approach to mindreading is evolutionary and emphasizes niche construction (see Laland, Oddling-Smee, and Feldman 2000 for an introduction to niche construction). Behaviorists construe our environment as a collection of stimuli. Sterelny invokes a highly structured environment that has a great deal of potential for shaping development. The basic idea of niche construction is that organisms create aspects of their own environment—rabbit burrows, termite mounds, human tools, and other artifacts—and these structured environments constrain development but also, crucially, produce different selection pressures. Applying all this to mindreading, we get the proposal that humans have various basic perceptual capacities, doubtless shared with our primate ancestors, which, in the relevantly structured environment, can support our interpretation of others. On this approach, there is no need to seek the selective regimen that produced one specialized mechanism for mindreading. Rather we specify the structured environment that would support the re-tuning of basic perceptual capacities for the task of interpreting others.

Sterelny's is not the only alternative hypotheses about the evolution of mindreading. Sarah Hrdy (S. B. Hrdy 2009) defends an interesting evolutionary approach that places the selectively relevant environment for our mindreading capacity in our infant life stage. The idea here is that mindreading is a product of several factors. First, we spend a long time completely dependent on the care of others relative to other animals, including our closest primate relatives. Second, one of the keys to surviving this life stage is to have a grasp on who is a caretaker and who is not and to make sure that we are in good hands. Third, Hrdy relies on life history theory, whose proponents differentiate between selection pressures at different life stages of organisms (see Roff 2002 for a comprehensive introduction to life history theory). For example, there are quite different selection pressures on adult frogs and tadpoles. According to Hrdy, our adult mindreading capacity is built upon this infant survival strategy. Neither Sterelny nor Hrdy proposes and defends specialized psychological mechanisms that evolved for mindreading, but both propose evolutionary hypotheses intended to account for our capacity of mindreading.

To date evolutionary psychologists have not responded directly to the challenges posed by alternative evolutionary hypotheses about mindreading such as Sterelny's and Hrdy's. Barrett discusses neither of these hypotheses and does not respond to the line of criticism of evolutionary psychology that accompanies them. Further productive debates about evolutionary psychology could begin here. The general issue at stake would be where the evolutionary psychologists favored approach is best used and where other evolutionary approaches do better (see Laland and Brown 2002 for a presentation of many of the alternate evolutionary approaches to explaining human behavior). If future debates headed in this direction, participants would have to be well versed in evolutionary theory, in all its guises, and prepared to have some of their cherished hypotheses subjected to careful scrutiny.

## Conclusion

These three debates (or potential debate in one case) are highlighted here because they exemplify the kind of productive philosophy of science discussions we can have about evolutionary psychology. As noted above, much of the controversy about evolutionary psychology is focused on popular presentations of work in the field. There is much work for socially engaged philosophers of science to do in assessing the impact of popular evolutionary psychology on policy and society in general and Gillian Barker (2015) has begun to make useful inroads here. One recommendation is that philosophers critically assess evolutionary psychology by focusing on research in the field rather than by focusing on popularizations of that work. The critical work of assessing the influence of popularizations of evolutionary psychology is properly focused on popular works.

# References

Barker, G. (2015). *Beyond Biofatalism: Human Nature for an Evolving World*. New York: Columbia University Press.

Barrett, H. C. (2015). *The Shape of Thought: How Mental Adaptations Evolve*. Oxford: Oxford University Press.

Buller, D. (2005). *Adapting Minds: Evolutionary Psychology and the Persistent Quest for Human Nature*. Cambridge, MA: MIT Press.

Cashdan, E. (2008). Waist-to-Hip Ratio across Cultures: Trade-offs between Androgen- and Estrogen-Dependent Traits. *Current Anthropology*, 49(6), 1099–107.

Cashdan, E. (2013). What is a Human Universal? Human Behavioral Ecology and Human Nature. In S. M. Downes and E. Machery (Eds.), *Arguing about Human Nature* (71–80). New York: Routledge.

Confer, J. C., Easton, J. A., Fleischman, D. S., Goetz, C. D., Lewis, D. M. G., Perilloux, C., et al. (2010). Evolutionary Psychology: Controversies, Questions, Prospects, and Limitations. *American Psychologist*, 65, 110–26.

Cosmides, L., Tooby, J., and Barkow, H. (1992). The Psychological Foundations of Culture. In H. Barkow, L. Cosmides, and J. Tooby (Eds.), *The Adapted Mind* (19–136). New York: Oxford University Press.

Coyne, J. A. (2009). *Why Evolution is True*. New York: Viking.

Downes, S. M. (2015). Evolutionary Psychology, Adaptation and Design. In T. Heams (Ed.), *Handbook of Evolutionary Thinking in the Sciences* (659–73). Dordrecht: Springer.

Dupre, J. (2001). *Human Nature and the Limits of Science*. Oxford: Clarendon Press.

Fehr, C. (2011). Feminist Philosophy of Biology. In E. N. Zalta (Ed.), *Stanford Encyclopedia of Philosophy*. Fall 2011 Edition.

Fuller, S. (2006). *The New Sociological Imagination*. London: Sage.

Godfrey-Smith, P. (1996). *Complexity and the Function of Mind in Nature*. Cambridge: Cambridge University Press.

Godfrey-Smith, P. (2001). Three Kinds of Adaptationism. In S. H. Orzack and E. Sober (Eds.), *Adaptationism and Optimality* (335–57). Cambridge: Cambridge University Press.

Gould, S. J. (1978). Sociobiology: The Art of Storytelling. *New Scientist*, 80(1129), 530–33.

Gould, S. J., and Lewontin, R. (1979). The Spandrels of San Marco and the Panglossian Paradigm: A Critique of the Adaptationist Programme. *Proceedings of the Royal Society London B*, 205, 581–98.

Griffiths, P. (2006). Evolutionary Psychology: History and Current Status. In S. Sarkar and J. Pfeifer (Eds.), *Philosophy of Science: An Encyclopedia* (vol. 1, 263–68). New York: Routledge.

Griffiths, P. (2011). Ethology, Sociobiology and Evolutionary Psychology. In S. Sarkar and A. Plutynski (Eds.), *A Companion to Philosophy of Biology* (393–414). Oxford: Wiley-Blackwell.

Hrdy, S. (1999). *Mother Nature: Maternal Instincts and How they Shape the Human Species*. New York: Ballantine Books.

Hrdy, S. B. (2009). *Mothers and Others: The Evolutionary Origins of Mutual Understanding*. Cambridge, MA: Belknap Press.

Hull, D. L. (1986). On Human Nature. *PSA: Proceedings of the Biennial Meeting of the Philosophy of Science Association*, 2, 3–13.

Jackson, S., and Rees, A. (2007). The Appalling Appeal of Nature: The Popular Influence of Evolutionary Psychology as a Problem for Sociology. *Sociology*, 41, 917–30.

Kitcher, P. (1985). *Vaulting Ambition: Sociobiology and the Quest for Human Nature*. Cambridge, MA: MIT Press.

Laland, K. N., and Brown, G. R. (2002). *Sense and Nonsense: Evolutionary Perspectives on Human Behavior*. Oxford: Oxford University Press.

Laland, K. N., Oddling-Smee, J., and Feldman, M. W. (2000). Niche Construction, Biological Evolution, and Cultural Change. *Behavioral and Brain Sciences*, 23, 131–75.

Lewens, T. (2009). Seven Types of Adaptationism. *Biology and Philosophy*, 24, 161–82.

Lewens, T. (2015). *Cultural Evolution*. Oxford: Oxford University Press.

Lewontin, R. (1998). The Evolution of Cognition: Questions We Will Never Answer. In D. Scarborough and S. Sternberg (Eds.), *Methods, Models, and Conceptual Issues* (107–32). Cambridge, MA: MIT Press.

Lewontin, R. C. (1978). Adaptation. *Scientific American*, 239(3), 212–30.

Lewontin, R. C. (1979). Sociobiology as an Adaptationist Program. *Behavioral Science*, 24(1), 5–14.

Lloyd, E. A. (1999). Evolutionary Psychology: The Burdens of Proof. *Biology and Philosophy*, 14, 211–33.

Lloyd, E. A., and Feldman, M. W. (2002). Evolutionary Psychology: A View from Evolutionary Biology. *Psychological Inquiry*, 13, 150–56.

Machery, E. (2008). A Plea for Human Nature. *Philosophical Psychology*, 21, 321–29.

Machery, E., and Barrett, H. C. (2007). Review of David Buller *Adapting Minds: Evolutionary Psychology and the Persistent Quest for Human Nature*. *Philosophy of Science*, 73, 232–46.

Nichols, S., and Stich, S. P. (2003). *Mindreading: An Integrated Account of Pretense, Self-Awareness, and Understanding Other Minds*. Oxford: Oxford University Press.

Pinker, S. (2002). *The Blank Slate: The Modern Denial of Human Nature*. New York: Viking.

Prinz, J. (2012). *Beyond Human Nature: How Culture and Experience Shape the Human Mind*. New York: W. W. Norton.

Ramsey, G. (2013). Human Nature in a Post-essentialist World. *Philosophy of Science*, 80, 983–93.

Richardson, R. (2007). *Evolutionary Psychology as Maladapted Psychology*. Cambridge, MA: MIT Press.

Richerson, P. J., and Boyd, R. (2005). *Not by Genes Alone: How Culture Transformed Human Evolution*. Chicago: University of Chicago Press.

Roff, D. A. (2002). *Life History Evolution*. Sunderland, MA: Sinauer.

Rosenberg, A. (1980). *Sociobiology and the Preemption of Social Science*. Baltimore: Johns Hopkins University Press.

Seger, J., and Stubblefield, J. W. (1996). Optimization and Adaptation. In M. R. Rose and G. V. Lauder (Eds.), *Adaptation* (93–123). San Diego: Academic Press.

Segerstråle, U. (2000). *Defenders of the Truth: The Battle for Science in the Sociology Debate and Beyond*. Oxford: Oxford University Press.

Singh, D. (1993). Adaptive Significance of Female Physical Attractiveness: Role of Waist-to-Hip Ratio. *Journal of Personality and Social Psychology*, 65, 293–307.

Singh, D., and Luis, S. (1995). Ethnic and Gender Consensus for the Effect of Waist-to-Hip Ratio on Judgments of Women's Attractiveness. *Human Nature*, 6, 51–65.

Sober, E. (1980). Evolution, Population Thinking and Essentialism. *Philosophy of Science*, 47, 350–83.

Sober, E. (2000). *Philosophy of Biology* (2nd edn.). Boulder, CO: Westview Press.

Sterelny, K. (2003). *Thought in a Hostile World: The Evolution of Human Cognition*. Oxford: Blackwell.

Sterelny, K. (2012). *The Evolved Apprentice: How Evolution Made Humans Unique*. Cambridge, MA: MIT Press.

Tooby, J., and Cosmides, L. (1990). On the Universality of Human Nature and the Uniqueness of the Individual. *Journal of Personality*, 58, 17–67.

Tooby, J., and Cosmides, L. (2005). Conceptual Foundations of Evolutionary Psychology. In D. Buss (Ed.), *The Handbook of Evolutionary Psychology* (5–67). Hoboken, NJ: Wiley.

Wilson, E. O. (1978). *On Human Nature*. Cambridge, MA: Harvard University Press.

Woodward, J., and Cowie, F. (2004). The Mind Is Not (Just) a System of Modules Shaped (Just) by Natural Selection. In C. Hitchcock (Ed.), *Contemporary Debates in Philosophy of Science* (312–34). Oxford: Blackwell.

Wright, R. (1994). *The Moral Animal. Why We Are the Way We Are: The New Science of Evolutionary Psychology*. New York: Vintage.

Yu, D. W., and Shepard, G. H. (1998). Is Beauty in the Eye of the Beholder? *Nature*, 396, 321–22.

# 29
# COGNITIVE SCIENCE

## David Eck and Stephen Turner

The relationship between the social sciences and the cognitive sciences is underdeveloped and complicated, for reasons we will explain in this chapter, and the philosophical discussion of this relationship has the same properties. Many reasons for the lack of development relate to a traditional philosophical issue: explanation. The explanatory structure of cognitive science reasoning and argumentation is unusual and difficult to fit into the traditional model of scientific explanation, though they do relate, in an odd way, to the traditional "reasons" explanations discussed in the philosophy of social science, through the notion of "folk psychology." The cognitive science explanations themselves, as they relate to traditional "social science" topics, involve additional problems. They depend on a strategy of reducing complexity by beginning with those aspects of mind that can be most readily simplified, such as perception and body movements. Therefore, traditional social science topics, such as social interaction, which cannot be readily simplified, are something of an afterthought.

Nevertheless, much can be said about these issues and about the challenges of attempts to bring cognitive science to bear on social science topics, and for social scientists attempting to frame topics in forms that cognitive science can be applied to. The developing field of social neuroscience approaches the relationship from the bottom up: from the identification of cognitive mechanisms grounded in neural processes with observable, measurable, correlates to known social phenomena, such as empathy or free-rider punishment. In contrast, social scientists typically are interested in validating and improving social science concepts which have long been assumed to have a basis in psychological mechanisms, such as charisma (Schjoedt et al. 2011) or group biases (Amodio 2014), by showing that they in fact do correlate to observable and measurable neural processes. Sometimes these approaches converge on common concepts, such as empathy (Decety and Jackson 2004) or political orientation (Graham et al. 2009); the number of these convergences is gradually increasing.

There is, however, a different aspect to the relationship between the social sciences and the cognitive sciences which is closer to the heart of the philosophy of cognitive science itself: the problem of the general model of the mind and the person and of their relationship to the environment. One's commitments on this topic have deep connections to the ideas one can have of the social world. What is possible to put into the category of "the social" depends on what one takes to be the properties of the persons who compose it and of the interactions that produce the contents of "the social." Most of the discussion of this aspect of the problem has been mediated through consideration of the important social fact of language. Arguments for the modularity of mind, for example, have appealed to the idea that language acquisition requires a universal language module. But language is a problematic model for social facts generally, and not a good surrogate for other kinds of social facts, such as institutions and practices.

Arguments over these topics are typically concerned with claims about the conditions for the possibility of some social fact, whether it is language or the institution of money, with the understanding that there needs to be a neuroscience basis for these institutions or practices—that there is at least something in the brain that corresponds to them, or makes them possible. The implication of this reasoning is that the neuroscience foundation for these things consists of highly general features of the mind itself, such as a distinctive capacity for intending collectively, rather than local "sociological" facts (see Searle 1995).

These extensions of standard models of cognition to account for social facts face serious difficulties—so serious that they call the standard model itself into question, and provide support for the radical alternative models that have been proposed (see Hutto 2004, 2005; Gallagher 2008; De Jaegher 2009; Chemero 2011). Of particular interest is how Daniel Kahneman's (2011) distinction between fast and slow thinking bears on social phenomena and on the notion of modularity. In this chapter we will trace the background of these explanatory problems to their roots in the standard model, discuss the kinds of revisions that the social, cultural, and developmental data seem to require, and briefly discuss what is entailed by the alternatives to the standard model.

## The Standard Computational Model and Its Logic

There is no consensus model of the mind, but there is a family of notions that fit together into something that approximates a single model. Each element is or can be construed to be logically independent, but in the course of constructing and grounding explanations of actual phenomena, the elements are difficult to separate. The core of the model is computationalism. It is claimed that "over 80 per cent of articles in theoretical cognitive science journals focus on computational modeling (Miłkowski 2013, 1; see also Busemeyer and Diederich 2010). In this tradition, cognition is information processing in the physical symbol system (Newell 1980) or it is computation over representations (Miłkowski 2013, 3). The strong form of this doctrine or strategy is that the brain is a computer that works on representations to produce everything mental, as well as perceiving, direct action, and so forth. The core idea is that

> our cognitive architecture resembles a confederation of hundreds or thousands of functionally dedicated computers (often called modules) designed to solve adaptive problems endemic to our hunter-gatherer ancestors. Each of these devices has its own agenda and imposes its own exotic organization on different fragments of the world. There are specialized systems for grammar induction, for face recognition, for dead reckoning, for construing objects, and for recognizing emotions from the face. There are mechanisms to detect animacy, eye direction, and cheating. There is a "theory of mind" module, and a multitude of other elegant machines.
> (Tooby and Cosmides 1995, xiii–xiv)

These computers operate on information, or representations, and these operations comprise cognition.

Computationalism comes in different forms with respect to representations: one view is minimalist and treats information and its processing as a causal process; the strong form of this argument, however, treats representations as complex inferential objects best modeled, even for animal cognition, as parts of syntactic systems. This and similar approaches put their emphasis on the properties of representations or the rules for processing representations. The minimalist view is that "representations" are merely data structures, and that they form a part of virtually every account of mind. The fact that an ant navigates by external points of reference but can continue its direction when these are obscured indicates that it has a "representation" of its position (Gallistel 1989, 56).

The motivation for rejecting a limited notion of representation, and its even more limited variants, is that the notion of combination is difficult to construct without something like computational rules to account for the combinatorial properties of the representations. The notion of possessing rules in general seems to be best modeled on syntactic rules. So discussions of these combinatorial properties, as they apply to representations, gradually slide into assuming a model in which rules are shared socially or collectively, as they are supposed to be in the case of language (see Brandom 2009).

The strong form of this argument is the idea that the brain implements a syntactic and semantic system that is in some sense pre-given rather than learned. The idea that there needs to be a syntactic system in advance of learning is a consequence of the commitment to the idea that the mind operates on representations: it is difficult to see what sorts of operations these might be unless they were in some sense similar to the logical "operations" of explicit reasoning. The idea that they are pre-given rests on the following consideration: "The only known explanation for the existence of complex functional design in organic systems is natural selection" (Cosmides and Tooby 1994, 86). The core computationalist model—consisting of a pre-given architecture in which complex modules have evolved from more rudimentary ones that ultimately bottom out in brute processes—sets the contours for how the standard model applies to social phenomena.

If we apply this general strategy of modeling to the problem of how it is that people understand that other people have thoughts, beliefs, make errors, and so forth, and are able to more or less predict the actions of others and interact with them successfully, we get the following: that we tacitly represent thoughts, beliefs, and so forth in such a way as to make tacit inferences about them, and that there is a module devoted to this complex but specific task, which amounts to having a "theory of mind."

The modularization thesis lends itself to the idea that at some point in the journey to a fully calculative being, one activates a theory of mind module—learning is difficult for these kinds of computational models, which assume a large set of fixed rules—that does what representations do, namely allow combinations, or inferences. So representing the mind of another becomes the core to the explanation of social interaction, of understanding others, and so forth. Accordingly, this putative ToM (theory of mind) module leans on folk psychology intuitions—namely that the ubiquitous attribution of beliefs and motivations to others captures a fundamental element of their mental life.

So we are, for the major questions that concern us, still very much at the stage of entertaining hypotheses in terms of their plausibility, and attempting to extend by analogy our limited understanding of a few simple topics to areas we do not understand. But considerations of plausibility tug in different directions: what is phenomenologically plausible may not be computationally plausible, and vice versa. This is especially important in considering the extension of the standard model to "social" topics. What seems plausible for an account of language may become very implausible for an account of something like the skilled performances of a chess master. And it becomes a question of whether social life resembles a skilled performance or the mechanical following of inferential or syntactic rules, or something else (or many other things) entirely. Moreover, there is a problem integrating the computational model with much that is known about the brain—the role of various chemicals, such as dopamine, in emotion, and the relation between emotion and cognitive processes.

There are alternatives to the ToM approach, notably simulation theory, and there are known mechanisms in the brain—mirror neurons—that point to an alternative basis for mindreading. There are also new findings that make the older interpretation of the false belief experiments untenable, or at least in need of radical revision (Baillargeon et al. 2010; Choi and Luo 2015). These point to some significantly different approaches not only to the usual ToM approach, but to the standard model as a whole, and the alternatives cohere with some important "social science" considerations. In what follows, we will examine the social science issues with the ToM model, and discuss the ways in which the revisions to this model undermine the standard model itself.

## Beyond the Standard Model?

The difficulties with the standard model are many, but there is no comparably developed alternative: critiques are typically partial, and many of the explanatory practices that make up the model are employed by critics of the model as part of their own larger account. One ongoing issue is this: the ideas of representation and computation are defined so broadly and ambiguously it is possible to argue that the supposed alternatives are also forms of computationalism and representationalism. The differences in approach are nevertheless substantial. The core of the issues is summarized by Anthony Chemero under two headings: mental gymnastics and the kind of arguments from explanatory necessity which identify supposed "conditions for the possibility of" capacities.

By mental gymnastics Chemero means that most of the models of representational cum computational processes require an astonishing amount of computational activity to reproduce, through reverse engineering, the kinds of activities that are being explained. A case in point is the problem of animal navigation. Here the question is, first, do animals, such as ants and bees, have representational systems. The same considerations underlying the standard model apply: animals have quite astonishing capacities to orient themselves, communicate position to other animals in some cases, and to recover from errors. To model these capacities representationally and computationally requires a lot of complex mathematics and a lot of computational power to make these capacities operate in real time, though it is unclear what "a lot" means in this context (Gallistel 1989, 2011). Is it plausible that the ant brain works in this way? And if not, is it plausible that our brains also might work in some other way? It is also claimed that some mental activities are "representation hungry," that is to say that to construct a model of them requires us to attribute a lot of representing to the mind performing these activities. These claims serve to justify attributing "mental gymnastics" to their subjects.

As applied to humans, the argument, as Chemero summarizes it, is a "conditions for the possibility" argument: that "it will be impossible to explain truly cognitive phenomena without mental gymnastics" (2011, 33). There is a second, related argument, which is a *tu quoque* argument: that not only are these matters of explanatory necessity, the supposed alternatives, which we will discuss below, also "actually do attribute representations to cognitive systems" (ibid.). And as we can see even in the case of ants, it is difficult to separate the notion of representation from the notion of combinatorial processes—whatever is combined in mental processes turns out to look like a representation. A data structure which has combinatorial properties, for example, is representing something with special properties mimicked by the mental properties that allow for combination, and is thus, more or less by definition, a representation.

The problem of mental gymnastics is, however, a self-created problem: if we assume that the brain is a computer-like system with programs and rule-following calculations, even the apparently simplest activities, such as an ant returning to its nest, turn out to require a massive amount of computing power and complex mathematics. Modularity is a kind of solution: modularization makes increased speed plausible.

## The Theory of Mind Module

Social relations involve, centrally, the understanding of other people. The standard view models this understanding by the notion that people possess a theory of mind, which they use to make inferences about people's beliefs and desires from their actions. The empirical basis for this line of argument has been the facts about the development of children's capacity to solve the "false belief problem." The experiments that established the phenomenon worked like this. Children are presented with a story, with props, in which they are able to observe that a person hides an object in a basket and leaves; another person comes in and moves the object, hiding it elsewhere. The child would then be asked where the first person would look for the object. Children under age four typically would answer by saying that the person would look where the object had been moved to; at about age four children began to answer that the person would look where they had left the object originally. In short, they reasoned that the person had a false belief and would act on it. This requires a "theory" about false belief and its relation to action, and thus about mind, or, to put it differently, if they were reasoning explicitly (or slow reasoning), step by step, justifying each usage of every term, it would be like them having a theory. In this form, the results fit the idea that there is a theory of mind module that is activated, that this was not a matter of learning, because the capacity is not associated with intelligence, or any apparent outward stimulus, but merely appears at a certain age, and, moreover, is more or less universal across cultures.

But there is a problem with the experimental protocol that produced these results, and there are findings that conflict with it. The verbal interactions involved in answering the relevant questions—"elicited response tasks"—are complex and require abilities beyond merely recognizing false beliefs. Experiments that do not involve eliciting verbal responses, but measure spontaneous non-verbal responses, turn out to produce different results. Indeed, they show that fifteen-month-olds had expectations consistent with an understanding of false beliefs. The Sally-Anne test was similar. The measurements involved what the child paid attention to in different scenarios depicted for the child. Children reliably paid more attention—looked longer—when they were watching cases in which the unaware agent reached for the box containing the toy, rather than for the box in which the agent last saw the toy (Baillargeon et al. 2010, 110–11). The special attention paid by the children suggests they were surprised and, in turn, suggests their expectations were consistent with the unaware agent possessing a false rather than true belief.

This undermines the neat distinction between two systems, one corresponding to verbal, elic-itable content, which looks more like a "theory" or a matter of "folk psychology," and the other a mere capacity shared with apes, and even with much of the rest of the animal kingdom. If we think such things as "only humans have concepts," however, the results are troublesome. This is how some theorists have accommodated them:

> Taken at face value the infant data suggests that very young children must have some command of the concept of belief in place very early on. This is so even though much older children lack the capacity to pass standard, verbally based, false belief tasks— tasks that were previously taken to be the litmus tests for possessing the concept of belief.
>
> (Hutto 2015, 6)

But this serves to indicate the extent to which the standard representational model can accom-modate any result; that it is immune from empirical refutation.

Here, however, the plausibility of the model begins to slip. Fodor (1987, xii), argues, and the standard model presumes, that folk psychology is more or less true—that there are real things like beliefs and reasons, that mental objects combine in more or less the way that linguistic ones do, and so forth. What exists in the tacit realm, in short, is close to and resembles what exists in the explicit realm. For the standard model, what we do when we explain our reasoning about other minds is just an explicit form of what we tacitly do when we interact normally with other people. But the evidence of infant responses to false belief situations tends to pry apart the tacit from the explicit. We cannot be quite so sure that the fifteen-month-old infant is thinking in terms of notions like belief and truth and falsity, much less that they have something resembling a theory. The evidence we have of their thinking in these terms comes from something they do much later, and as a result of learning fairly complex linguistic skills, the skills that enable them to answer these questions. These kinds of considerations undermine the plausibility of the model, on which it primarily depends.

## Fast and Slow

One distinction seems, on the surface, to map well onto the stages of development observed in the experiments. Daniel Kahneman made famous the idea that there are fast and slow kinds of thinking (2011). The idea is that there are two (or more) systems operating in cognition, at least one of which is fast and the other slow. The slow system is the one familiar from conscious reasoning and folk psychology, and involves reasons, beliefs, and ratiocination. The fast system or systems work in a different way, below consciousness, and with somewhat different means— heuristics, for example—and through automatic processes. The fast kinds, operating with heu-ristics, produce quick judgments that are biased in certain ways, if they are contrasted to slow reasoning, i.e. the kind of explicit or near-explicit reasoning that we might go through step by step in explaining such things as what we thought would justify the theory of mind conclusion that the person who was unaware that the object had been moved would look in the wrong place for it. The fast–slow distinction seems well based, and it is observable in a variety of places.

But considerations of speed tug in different directions. When we try to map the distinction on to the theory of mind problem, we run into trouble. It is assumed by the standard model that theory of mind is modular, and like all complex modules it can only be a product of long evolutionary processes. There is also a difference in the way that theory of mind statements are expressed and evaluated in different cultures and languages. Some of these differences are quite radical.

If we take the elements to be distinct, and the cultural (and variable) one to be added last, we get a model in which culture figures as a kind of data added to the pre-existing computational modules, which are fixed and not learned. But this is an odd way to think about culture, which is largely tacit and involves automatic responses. Another example made prominent in the literature by Hubert Dreyfus (2014) also causes trouble: skilled, expert performance by such people as chess grandmasters or expert skiers. The skilled performer has learned how to do something, but has surpassed anything that can be done with slow thinking. The performances require ultra-fast cognition but cannot be understood as modules: evolution does not give us a skiing or chess module to be activated.

Normally culture is taken to be tacit and part of the "fast" kind of thought—very often, though problematically, as presuppositions which are taken-for-granted conditions for social interaction and practice. Moreover, culture is thought to be learned, and at a very deep level, so that it is manifested in such things as techniques of the body, emotions, and so forth. Indeed, culture in general is experienced as fast thinking—moreover, we are unable to articulate its contents, or even identify them, without comparing them to cultures in which people fast-think differently. Considerations like this led some theory of mind thinkers to suggest that theory of mind was itself cultural (Carrithers et al. 1985).

This is part of a much larger muddle, which we have seen aspects of already. The key to computationalism, representationalism, and the many other elements of the standard model is analogical reasoning. The only way we can think of mental processes that are otherwise inaccessible to us is to think of them in terms of our own overt "folk" psychological and logical concepts. The only way we can make sense of mindreading is as a fast version of slow reasoning about the beliefs, motives, and so forth of the other mind we are reading. We think about the thoughts of others as thing-like, and "represent" them to ourselves explicitly by devices such as cartoon thought bubbles. We then reason that something like this representing goes on tacitly in fast mindreading, or in infant mindreading, and that this therefore implies "possession" of a collection of relevant concepts.

But how is cultural difference even possible on this account? One can argue that the concepts that differ are mere add-ons and enrichments of the inherited symbolic systems in question. As Dan Hutto explains, a key feature of these arguments

> is that basic conceptual primitives act as atomistic placeholders—they are stable linch-pins, mental items that denote, refer or pick out items about which we can come to weave a wider set of conceptually-grounded inferences. These conceptual primitives can therefore be built upon through a process of on-going enrichment. On this model, when this happens no new concepts are introduced—instead we acquire expanded conceptions, wider understandings and new inferential connections tethered to our old concepts.
>
> (Hutto 2015, 5; see Hutto 2005 for fuller discussion)

Hence there is—and can only be—one core mindreading theory that develops from childhood to adulthood, one theory that, as Ian Apperly (2013) puts it, "grows up" through the introduction of new principles and the expansion of inferential linkages. But the way this argument must be constructed raises questions about the whole strategy of attributing symbolic systems, representations, "content," and propositional thought to infants, ants, and bees.

The whole point of conceptual enrichment and the acquisition of new inferential capacities depend on the newly added stuff being of the same type as the pre-existing stuff—the stuff being representations or concepts, for example. And this opens a large door. There must be processes other than evolution by which this new stuff gets generated and acquired. The theory of mind of the ancient Greeks which imputed madness to divine intervention, for example, is not a product of genetics. But what is it a product of? Whatever story one tells about how these inferential links or this novel "enriched" concept of mind were generated and acquired has to work like this: it identifies a process. In short, by appealing to conceptual "enrichment" the defenders of theory of mind have introduced a novel, parallel process that they admit is necessary to account for certain kinds of development.

Conceding that there are other sources of concepts, and even of the elements of cultural or interpersonal fast thinking is an important concession, because with it we can ask what other things this process, whatever it turns out to be, explains or might explain. And one answer could be that it explains—by itself and without reference to evolution and modules—the mentalistic concepts that make up the various folk psychologies that appear in different cultures, or even the core folk psychology that we have and attribute, correctly or incorrectly, to the rest of the world.

A plausible version of the theory of mind story that was consistent with the fact that expressions of mental concepts must be learned might go like this: infants have various non-conceptual capacities for social interaction, including the capacity to form expectations (i.e. behavioral covariances) about what people will do involving knowledge about their past behavior—in the case of the false belief problem, placing the object in a particular location. They only come to be able to articulate this knowledge, which is entirely tacit, when they learn a culturally specific mentalistic language. They must learn this language behavioristically (perhaps in conjunction with mirror neuron responses) by its application to the overt manifestations by other people in behavior or speech, and then apply it to themselves. Much of the developmental psychology literature makes it clear that one learns the terms one applies to oneself only when one learns to apply them to others. And since the terms vary across languages and cultures, there is no question that this is a matter of learning.

## The Alternatives

But is there an alternative to the standard model of mind that fits with this approach? There are alternative strategies of explanation that avoid some of the rigidities of the computational/representational model and have the merit of being based on mechanisms or facts that relate more closely to actual brain and bodily processes. These include connectionist accounts of learning, which fit with the "neurons that fire together, wire together" aspect of the brain; mirror neurons, which fire relevant action or pain neurons when another's actions or pain is observed, or when another pays attention to some object (leading to gaze following and joint attention), and may be relevant to intentions, providing a core mechanism for empathy, and therefore understanding, apart from any need for a ToM.

Richard Menary (2010) refers to the 4Es of cognition: the embedded, embodied, extended, and enactive movements. These approaches reject the computationalist paradigm's treatment of the individual–environment relationship. For them the core idea is that cognition is embedded or situated, and that there is a dynamic relation between the environment and the individual in which meaning is constituted. As Clancy puts it in a much-quoted paper:

> Situated cognition research rejects the hypothesis that neurological structures and processes are similar in kind to the symbols we create and use in our everyday lives. The symbolic approach, as described by Vera and Simon (1993), conflates neurological structures and processes with physical representations that we perceive and manipulate in our environment (e.g., a journal article) and experiences of representing in our imagination (e.g., visualizing or talking to ourselves).
>
> (Clancy 1993, 87)

The idea of situated cognition is that cognition is connected to doing, and is paradigmatically represented by skilled activities in which skills increase and expand.

These approaches come into their own in relation to social interaction, especially the co-constitution of meaning between agents—what the sociologist John O'Neill called "making sense together" (1975) or what cognitive scientists call participatory sense making. Consider a standard social science explanation—Edward Banfield's account of "amoral familism" (1958) as an ethos that prevented economic development, which he found in southern Italy and which has parallels in other poor communities. To be raised in this ethos is to be exposed to actions by others that need to be understood, to communicate to others in terms they understand, to feel the emotions that go along with and are constitutive of their gut moral attitudes, and to do this without reflection and with a sense that this social world is natural and right. This study was particularly revealing because it tested how people imagined scenarios involving other people and interpreted their actions, and the feelings this involved. It also explains how the way people thought was reinforced by their actual experiences of other people and their actions. This mode of life was not constructed on a purely cognitive basis, and involved concepts and emotions distinct from the generic emotions that could be said to be modular. It also involved something comparable to a ToM, in the limited sense that the members of the community had expectations about the behavior of others, attributed motives to them in terms of their own local concepts of motivation, and reacted accordingly. It was embodied, in the sense that it was carried out through embodied practices of various kinds.

Embedded, embodied, enactive, and extended accounts allow one to make sense of how a person in this dynamic interactive environment responds and becomes wired to respond, how change is possible through changing the interactive environment, how practices sustain emotional responses, and how these responses can be more than merely cognitive, but deeply connect different parts of the brain and body. There is no obvious benefit to thinking of these dynamic processes in terms of representation. Indeed, rather than representation-hungry, as human interaction is sometimes claimed to be, these processes are "dynamic interaction" hungry.

The question is how far these dynamic processes extend back to the more primitive and fundamental elements of the mind—those usually explained by modularity. The deeply social character and extraordinary social capacities of infants, as testified to by their ability to solve false belief problems at fifteen months, and to detect and respond to intentions much earlier, are a sign that the computational/representational story, which tends to put off the achievement of capacities to understand people and interact with them to a point after they have activated an advanced ToM, show that the older model is wrong, and that something more like the dynamic account, in which the "adaptive recoordination that occurs with every behavior" (Clancy 1993, 93) is a basic process, is more plausible, and not fraught with the limitations of the standard account.

# References

Amodio, David. 2014. "The Neuroscience of Prejudice and Stereotyping," *Nature Reviews Neuroscience* 15: 670–82.

Apperly, Ian. 2013. "Can Theory of Mind Grow Up? Mindreading in Adults, and Its Implications for the Development and Neuroscience of Mindreading." Pp. 72–92 in *Understanding Other Minds: Perspectives from Developmental Social Neuroscience*. Ed. S. Baron-Cohen, H. Tager-Flusberg, and M. V. Lombardo. Oxford: Oxford University Press.

Baillargeon, Renée, Rose M. Scott, and Zijing He. 2010. "False-Belief Understanding in Infants," *Trends in Cognitive Sciences* 14(3): 110–18.

Banfield, Edward. 1958. *The Moral Basis of a Backward Society*. New York: The Free Press.

Brandom, Robert. 2009. "How Analytic Philosophy Has Failed Cognitive Science." Pp. 197–226 in *Reason in Philosophy: Animating Ideas*. Cambridge, MA: Harvard University Press. https://docs.google.com/file/d/0B0xb4crOvCgTbXNBWlFXSERGNkU/edit (accessed June 9, 2015).

Busemeyer, Jerome and Adele Diederich. 2010. *Cognitive Modeling*. Thousand Oaks, CA: Sage.

Carrithers, Michael, Steven Collins, and Steven Lukes. 1985. *The Category of the Person*. Cambridge: Cambridge University Press.

Chemero, Anthony. 2011. *Radical Embodied Cognitive Science*. Cambridge, MA: MIT Press.

Choi, You-jung and Yuyan Luo. 2015. "13-Month-Olds' Understanding of Social Interactions," *Psychological Science* 26(3): 274–83.

Clancy, William J. 1993. "Situated Action: A Neuropsychological Interpretation Response to Vera and Simon," *Cognitive Science* 17: 87–116.

Cosmides, Leda and John Tooby. 1994. "Origins of Domain-Specificity: The Evolution of Functional Organization." Pp. 85–116 in *Mapping the Mind: Domain-Specificity in Cognition and Culture*. Ed. L. Hirschfeld and S. Gelman. New York: Cambridge University Press.

Decety, Jean and Philip L. Jackson. 2004. "The Functional Architecture of Human Empathy," *Behavioral and Cognitive Science Reviews* 3(2): 71–100.

De Jaegher, Hanne. 2009. "Social Understanding through Direct Perception? Yes, by Interacting," *Consciousness and Cognition* 18: 535–42.

Dreyfus, Hubert. 2014. *Skillful Coping: Essays on the Phenomenology of Everyday Perception and Action*. Oxford: Oxford University Press.

Fodor, Jerry. 1987. *Psychosemantics*. Cambridge, MA: MIT Press.

Gallagher, Shaun. 2008. "Inference or Interaction: Social Cognition without Precursors," *Philosophical Explorations* 11(3): 163–74.

Gallistel, C. R. 1989. "Animal Cognition: The Representation of Space, Time, and Number," *Annual Review of Psychology* 40: 155–89.

Gallistel, C. R. 2011. "Prelinguistic Thought," *Language Learning and Development* 7(4): 253–62. http://dx.doi.org/10.1080/15475441.2011.578548 (accessed June 9, 2015).

Graham, Jesse, Jonathan Haidt, and Brian Nosek. 2009. "Liberals and Conservatives Rely on Different Sets of Moral Foundations," *Journal of Personality and Social Psychology* 96: 1029–46.

Hutto, Daniel D. 2004. "The Limits of Spectatorial Folk Psychology," *Mind and Language* 19 (5): 548–73.

Hutto, Daniel D. 2005. "Starting without Theory: Confronting the Paradox of Conceptual Development." Pp. 56–72 in *Other Minds*. Ed. B. Malle and S. Hodges. New York: Guilford.

Hutto, Daniel D. 2015. "Basic Social Cognition without Mindreading: Minding Minds without Attributing Contents." *Synthese* online July. doi:10.1007/s11229-015-0831-0.

Kahneman, Daniel. 2011. *Thinking Fast and Slow*. New York: Macmillan.

Menary, Richard. 2010. *The Extended Mind*. Cambridge, MA: MIT Press.

Miłkowski, Marcin. 2013. *Explaining the Computational Mind*. Cambridge, MA: MIT Press.

Newell, A. 1980. "Physical Symbol Systems," *Cognitive Science*, 4, 135–83.

O'Neill, John. 1975. *Making Sense Together: An Introduction to Wild Sociology*. London: Heinemann Educational Books.

Schjoedt, Uffe, Hans Stødkilde-Jørgensen, Armin W. Geertz, Torben E. Lund, and Andreas Roepstorff. 2011. "The Power of Charisma: Perceived Charisma Inhibits the Frontal Executive Network of Believers in Intercessory Prayer," *Synthese* 6: 119–27.

Searle, John. 1995. *The Construction of Social Reality*. New York and London: The Free Press.

Tooby, John and Leda Cosmides. 1995. "Foreword." Pp. xi–xvii in Simon Baron-Cohen, *Mindblindness: An Essay on Autism and Theory of Mind*. Cambridge, MA: MIT Press.

# 30

# THE SOCIAL CONSTRUCTION OF KNOWLEDGE

## *Steve Fuller*

The social constructivist holds that society is nothing more—and nothing less—than the organized activities of living individuals, among whom may exist various asymmetrical relations which enable some individuals to exert a disproportionate influence over the social construction process for long periods of time. This, in turn, explains the impression of a stable 'social structure' in terms of which social life is then interpreted and explained. Social constructivism is itself neutral with regard to the significance of these asymmetrical relations, but as we shall see below they can be regarded positively or negatively, which is usually expressed as an attitude towards 'the state'. It would be easy to think that something called 'the social construction of knowledge' is most naturally distinguished from something called 'the individual construction of knowledge'. While some epistemologists (e.g. Goldman 1999) operate on this assumption, they misunderstand the spirit behind this influential movement in social science. In particular, they mistakenly focus on the *social* part instead of the *construction* part of 'social construction'. The natural antagonist of the social constructivist is the *social determinist*, namely, someone who holds that society as such exercises causal power over the character of social life independently of the individuals who constitute the society. In premodern times, 'tradition' would be invoked to justify this sense of society, but in the modern era the preferred theoretical term is 'social structure', which is something reproduced by default across generations unless explicitly interrupted.

This chapter consists of three parts, each of which captures a philosophical strand in the genealogy of social constructivism. The first presents the ultimate philosophical sources as Francis Bacon and Immanuel Kant. Their constructivism is founded on treating the systematic pursuit of knowledge through the lens of an inquisitorial approach to the law, which Kant called 'critical'. The second part deals with the metaphysics that underlies constructivism, which is closer to classical discussions about the unity of form and matter than to modern ones about the relation of epistemology and ontology. This observation is then used to frame an account of the failure of the history and philosophy of science to become a unified metascience in the late twentieth century. The third part locates social constructivism in the history of sociology, where it has been prominent yet quite distinctive. In particular, the dominant form of social constructivism has been aligned with a bottom-up, methodological individualist perspective, which has gone against the grain of sociology's development as a scientific discipline. This part ends by suggesting that Bacon would probably align more easily today with sociology's scientific defenders than its constructivist critics.

## 1 Back to Bacon: The Legal Origins of Social Constructivism

Although Kant is generally treated as the source of constructivism as a modern philosophical sensibility, in fact all of early modern philosophy is shot through with constructivism. The writings of Kant and many of his predecessors are full of legal references, both literal and metaphorical, related to the ongoing struggle to forge civil law traditions from the remnants of Roman law in the wake of the Protestant Reformation. In the case of England, this included whether the record of decisions taken in past cases—the 'common law'—might by themselves provide sufficient grounds for legitimacy. (Kelley [1990] provides a knowing wealth of insight into this backdrop, while Turner [2010] is nearly alone in pursuing this lead into the present.) These early modern discussions covered the main topics of any general theory of norms: the nature of the law's coercive power (where the scope of 'law' may include 'nature' in the sense of the patterns that are regularly on display as well as some more specifically 'divine' sense of ends, which would underwrite exceptional juridical interventions into the natural order), the identity and role of persons (where the scope of 'person' may not be restricted to humans, let alone include all of them), as well as the nature of trials over contested claims, the evidence mobilized in such cases, and the jurisdiction over which the verdicts in these cases apply.

All of these ideas translate easily into the discourse of modern philosophy: Common law's respect for precedent becomes the rule of induction; juridical interventions become experimental ones, now made in the name of finding hidden powers rather than restoring the natural order (but both interventions are dubbed 'causal'); personhood gets translated into mechanical agency with clear functional specifications; evidence is some appropriately processed version of personal experience for public consumption, in which 'cognitive' effectively naturalizes 'juridical', and so forth. In this respect, the intellectual frisson of social constructivism may be seen as resulting from its partial unearthing of the historical roots of these transformations, with, say, 'laws (of nature)' better rendered as 'rules (of inference)', especially after the later Wittgenstein (e.g. Winch 1958). The historian of modern ethics Jerome Schneewind (1984) has characterized these shifts as the devolution of the 'divine corporation', the process by which powers previously reserved to the deity are—fitfully, to be sure—diffused to the populace. In effect, whatever struggles God may have confronted in creating the natural world from recalcitrant matter are now faced by humans dealing with each other in the social world. The created world of theology thus becomes the negotiated world of social constructivism.

One Calvinist innovation—one which Hobbes, Locke and Rousseau variously secularized in their versions of the 'social contract'—stands out in mediating this transformation. It involved shifting the ground of political legitimation from the orderly confirmation of succession in a line of descent to a self-recognizing and self-confirming 'communion' of free agents in continual need of renewal. While this was originally seen as marking the passage from a Catholic to a Protestant default mode of religiosity, in the history of politics it appears in secular guise as a shift in presumption from a dynastic to an electoral basis for regime reproduction. Social constructivism universalizes this shift in sensibility. Ethnomethodology in the 1960s and 70s marked a watershed for this turn of thought in the social sciences, as it drew attention to the relative ease with which virtually any social convention could be 'breached' and thereby be in need of 'repair', typically by the negotiation of closure on the episode in the manner of an on-the-spot mutually binding agreement (Garfinkel 1967). This was the flipside of the later Wittgensteinian insight—associated with the continuation of a number series (*Philosophical Investigations*, 187–88)—that a rule may be followed in any number of ways, depending on, so to speak, who is in the room when closure needs to be reached and the features of past practice that they take to be salient in deciding how to go forward collectively (Bloor 1983).

I say that social constructivism 'universalizes' social contract theory because it is not clear from the early modern philosophers that the sort of explicit construction associated with the social contract was supposed to apply across all spheres of life, *à la* ethnomethodology. Indeed, with the possible exception of Hobbes (whose argument for the social contract has been alternatively read as a mere thought experiment or a subversive call to reboot the human condition), the capacity of people to tolerate the precarious relations implied in an overarching 'social contract' was normally predicated on the rest of their lives being governed by 'custom', which is to say, locally observed habits.

Thus, when Descartes's great contemporary Pascal famously twisted the ancient aphorism that custom is 'second nature' by explaining that it *destroys* 'first nature' (*Pensées* 93), he was saying something much less radical than at first it might appear. He was grouping the two natures together—perhaps as a sociobiologist or evolutionary psychologist might do today. Both natures operate largely in the same fashion, such that the second 'destroys' the first in the specific sense of 'replaces' it. (This sentiment informed the continuity of natural and civil histories in the Scottish Enlightenment prior to the Darwinian revolution.) Implied by contrast was some ultimately rational basis for society which might be brought about on a more explicit basis—from first principles, as it were, not simply by capitalizing on the default patterns of behavior represented by 'custom'. From this standpoint, social contract theory was radical because it promised just this explicit basis which Pascal himself was inclined to think that God alone could provide. However, over the next century Calvinists finessed this concern by allowing for a resolute 'communion in the faith' to be guided by what came to be called 'Providence', a kind of invisible divine hand which enabled the faithful who transited from Europe to the Americas to frame their journey not as a leap into the unknown but as an opportunity to re-enact divine creation in a 'new world'. It is the sensibility which Benjamin Franklin wittily captured as "God helps those who help themselves." Thus, the colonists' 'perseverance' in the face of resistance from the environment (including the recalcitrant indigenes) marked them as the sort of properly 'self-legislating' beings that Kant would subsequently universalize in the 'categorical imperative' (Passmore 1970, ch. 10).

Unfortunately these legal roots of social constructivism have been occluded by Kant's influential framing of the history of philosophy in the final section of the *Critique of Pure Reason* (Kuklick 1984). Here Kant is read as having installed a clear-cut distinction between those who believed that knowledge comes primarily from the senses (aka 'empiricists') and those who hold it derives from the intellect (aka 'rationalists'). This left the impression that the problem of knowledge is about getting these two principal faculties of the mind in the right order for human cognitive purposes, as we remain agnostic on the nature of reality itself. However, as we shall see in the next section, this distinction is better seen as more explicitly about the construction of reality itself. Put another way, the clarity of the modern distinction in metaphysical disciplines between *epistemology* and *ontology* depends on adopting a realist standpoint that is alien to Kantian constructivism. Indeed, 'epistemology' is a 19th-century neologism and 'ontology', itself a neologism of Kant's time, is treated in the *Critique* in purely formal terms, namely, as whatever objects satisfy the transcendental principles of reason as constructed through the categories of understanding.

To recover the legal roots of Kant's constructivism, we need to turn both to the very end of his potted history of philosophy and back to the very beginning of the *Critique of Pure Reason*. After dividing the senses and the intellect as sources of knowledge, Kant ends the book by drawing a somewhat orthogonal distinction between 'naturalistic' and 'scientific' approaches to the world. Lest today's Anglo-American readers find the very naming of this distinction odd (since nowadays the 'naturalistic' is associated with the 'scientific'), what Kant had in mind is rather like what social science methodologists mean when they distinguish 'naturalistic' and 'experimental' observation (cf. Fuller 1993, ch. 3). The former is roughly aligned with the Epicurean tradition, which Kant associates with an emphasis on the senses, and which on his reading stands accused of placing a superstitious trust in nature and custom. In contrast, the 'scientific' approach adopts a more focused and systematic attitude as it realizes reason's "ardent desire for knowledge." That reason has such a desire is confirmed at the start of the *Critique* in the dedication to Francis Bacon, who may be regarded as the godfather of social constructivism. In light of what follows, we may understand Kant's self-understanding as a 'critical' philosopher to be in the footsteps of Bacon's 'inquisitorial' method.

Bacon was, of course, not himself a scientist but Lord Chancellor—that is, the personal lawyer—to King James I of England. In that capacity, he imported the inquisitorial approach to judicial activity from the European continent (Franklin 2001, ch. 8). In popular history, this innovation is closely associated with "witch trials," on the basis of which general feminist critiques of the modern scientific attitude were launched (e.g. Merchant 1980). In inquisitorial legal systems, the state is in charge of framing the case and directing its prosecution. Thus, the judge calls the witnesses and sets the standards by which their testimony is evaluated as 'evidence'. Moreover, once a defendant is identified, he or she is presumed guilty and the point of the trial is to overturn that presumption. There are anticipations here of Karl Popper's *experimentum crucis*, which he explicitly adapted from Bacon. In any case, the experimental method of science consists in the leveraging of the inquisitorial approach to the study of nature. In both the case of the trial and the experiment, strict procedure is imposed on the actions of both the inquisitor and the defendant. The idea is to constrain the natural tendencies of both: in the former case, to find what one is looking for too easily; in the latter, to evade one's standing with regard to the charge. This helps to explain Bacon's famous opening of *The Great Instauration*: "the nature of things betrays itself more readily under vexations of art than in its natural freedom." By "the nature of things," Bacon does not mean 'thing' in some unprocessed sense of reality. On the contrary, he means it in the legal sense of *res*, the fact of the matter that results from a judicial proceeding and provides the basis for the judge's verdict. This is the original sense of 'fact' (literally, 'something made', in this case by the judge) which ties Bacon's inquisitorial approach to the 'social construction of scientific facts', to recall the subtitle of Latour and Woolgar (1979).

For Bacon nature is not naturally useful but needs to be made into something useful (Desroches 2006, ch. 2). Here he was influenced by two early modern trends: the revival of ancient atomism as a metaphysical doctrine and the conceptualization of nature as one of the two books through which God communicates (the other being the Bible, of course). He took both trends quite literally. Thus, Bacon envisaged the 'analysis' (literally the 'breaking down' or perhaps even 'deconstruction') of nature through the inquisitorial method to extract the grammar of the natural world, which can then be redeployed to enhance the human condition. Each trial would be designed to discover one or more of the relevant lexical or syntactic elements, which when recombined would yield increments in human welfare. This *modus operandi* was based on his approach to the English common law tradition. Rather than have the judge simply look for superficial resemblances with past cases, Bacon would have him directly interrogate the accused in ways that would result in discovering one or more elements common to many past cases. In this way, case-based law might be used—'abductively', as Charles Sanders Peirce would put it— to infer underlying general principles of governance which could in turn become the basis for a legal regime, perhaps one not so different from what his private secretary Thomas Hobbes would later present in the *Leviathan*. In short, once we see that Bacon would treat natural history as he treated common law, the constructivist spirit in which he originally proposed the experimental method becomes clear.

## 2 Kant's Constructivist Metaphysics and the History and Philosophy of Science

What must the world be like for 'social construction' to make sense? First, the world must be 'constructible', which implies a distinction between something that can construct and something that can be constructed. This is a more concrete version of the classical metaphysical distinction of 'form' versus 'matter'. However, the concreteness makes a difference. The sense of 'matter' is raw material, that is, without inherent form yet open to the reception of form; and the sense of 'form' is open-ended, that is, without a prior sense of its own limits yet in need of setting limits. Thus, for the constructivist there is none of the ideal matter-to-form ratio much beloved of classical aestheticians, whereby one aims to produce something that brings out a preconceived idea through an optimal deployment of a well-understood medium. Constructivism implies neither so much forethought on the part of the constructor nor such privileged access to whatever inherent properties the construction materials might possess.

Thus, as a movement in the history of art, 'constructivism' is generally understood to be 'non-representational', in the sense that it denies that there is an already existing version of whatever moves the artist to work in a particular medium. Rather, the artist operates in a more exploratory vein, either by trying to express the same idea in different media or exploiting a single medium for the different ideas it might express. In neither case does one presume that there is an ideal expression of some subject matter. Rather, there is literally a 'co-instruction' of form and matter: that is, each instructs the other. The modern starting point for this general sensibility is *Laocoön* by the Enlightenment critic and dramatist Gotthold Lessing, Germany's answer to Voltaire. Lessing argued that it made no sense to rank the arts in terms of their inherent expressive power, nor topics in terms of worthiness of expression. Rather, an artwork should be judged by how the artist enables the medium to express something distinctive about the topic. This in turn would establish the 'individuality' of the artwork. This sensibility provided the most obvious cultural backdrop for Kant's introduction of 'constructivism' in the sense we understand it today.

Put in terms favored by the idealist followers of Kant: The constructor and the constructible are originally unknown both to themselves and to each other. Knowledge only begins with action, the giving of form to matter and giving of matter to form. This is the 'co-instruction' implied by 'construction'. (A downstream, policy-oriented version of this idea is 'co-production', which Sheila Jasanoff [2004] has popularized in the more policy-oriented circles of science and technology studies.) The result is 'reality', but not in the sense of a discovery of some pre-existing state of being that is indifferent to our efforts. Rather, reality is the realization of a world that we recognize as our own, which is to say, meaningful. Art is this process of giving meaning to the world. (The *locus classicus* for this way of seeing things is Friedrich Schiller, *The Aesthetic Education of Man*, Letter XI.) Social constructivism may be seen as extending this general mind-set to all of social life in a manner quite unlike that of the original social contract theorists, who typically operated with a fixed conception of 'human nature', however defined.

Kant himself expressed this broad metaphysical idea of construction in more epistemological terms, which proved to be inspirational for subsequent discussions:

> Thoughts without content are empty, intuitions without concepts are blind. The understanding can intuit nothing, the senses can think nothing. Only through their unison can knowledge arise.
>
> (*Critique of Pure Reason* A 51, B 75)

The commonplace statement of this idea in contemporary philosophy of science is that 'theory without data is empty, data without theory blind'. However, in the 1960s, the idea had begun to acquire more momentous import as a thesis about the relationship between the history and the philosophy of science. Two versions stand out from the period. The first, by Russell Hanson, stressed the 'theory without data is empty' side; the second, by Imre Lakatos, stressed the 'data without theory is blind' side.

For his part, Hanson (1962) was reacting to the tendency of philosophers of science and professional scientists after World War II—both under the influence of US-style logical positivism—to pursue their inquiries without reference to history, often (as in the case of Thomas Kuhn) with the implicit acceptance that this separation of interests would enable historians of science to become a profession in their own right, without having to account for their activities to the scientific community. Nevertheless, Hanson said that the positivist consensus amounted to the proposition that because one can already use one's head, there is no point to learn how to use one's head better. In contrast, rather than simply carry on and repeat the mistakes of the past and alter one's methods in a piecemeal and individual manner, Hanson argued that with the aid of history one can draw on the collective experience of past philosophers and scientists to progress more systematically. Here Hanson was influenced by Charles Sanders Peirce, who in turn influenced a range of other broadly 'constructivist' thinkers in systems theory, developmental psychology, and education—all of whom argue that science can increase its rate of progress by incorporating its history as a feedback loop to orient future research. This 'second-order' or 'reflexive' approach to inquiry ('learning how to learn') would be facilitated by the emerging field of 'history and philosophy of science', or so Hanson believed. Moreover, it would permit a 'progressive' sense of historicity to science that was different from the much derided 'Whig' approach, in which the past was used simply to justify present-day scientific activities.

Interestingly, Hanson's proposal failed to take substantial root, despite its having been first presented as a vice-presidential address to the American Association for the Advancement of Science and then published in both *Science* and the leading US philosophy journal. This may have been due to his own premature death in 1967 or the overall impact that Kuhn (1970) had in demarcating the history and philosophy of science from the practice of science. Indeed, the latter 'boundary work', as social constructivists in science and technology studies call it, informed the launch of 'social epistemology' as a dedicated research program (Fuller 1988, ch. 7). To be sure, Hanson-friendly thinkers such as Dudley Shapere and Larry Laudan continued to promote his proposal into the 1980s, culminating in Donovan et al. (1988). However, by that time the argument had come to be seen as being more about the relationship of the history and the philosophy of science than about the relationship of those two fields and science itself, which fitted into the intellectual comfort zone of those influenced by Kuhn (1970). However, Will (1988) remains a still worthwhile attempt to provide a philosophical grounding for the original Hanson program.

For his part, Lakatos (1971) proposed something better suited to a post-Kuhn (1970) generation, namely, that all history of science is informed by some sort of philosophy of science, which basically provides the conceptual framework through which matters are included or excluded, evaluated, and provided with an overarching plotline. This is the respect in which one might speak of 'Whig', 'Tory', and what I have called 'Prig' historiographies of science (Fuller 2000, Introduction): namely, history from the standpoint of, respectively, the scientific winners, the scientific losers, and the history of science profession itself. In the rhetorical context of the time, Lakatos's move was meant to signal that there is no such thing as a 'value-neutral' history of science: The historian was always complicit in some normative narrative, one which either supported or opposed the status quo—to varying degrees. But as we shall shortly see, this was not quite how his thesis was taken forward by constructivists in the history and sociology of science who constituted the 'Prig' party.

Lakatos's own distinctive spin on his thesis was to suggest that the historian may be pro-science in its overall aims and methods but believe that they could have been executed much more efficiently, thereby avoiding some of the errors of the past, which may continue to be affecting science's ability to make progress today. Lakatos called this alternative, counterfactual historiography 'rational reconstruction', but it was clear that he believed that this should be the main business of the philosophy of science, especially if it was to be useful to science. While he did not believe that philosophers could prescribe science's future (a sin which he attributed to the idealist followers of Kant and the materialist followers of Hegel), he did hold that philosophers could deal with science retrospectively in terms of what worked, what did not work, and what and how things could have been done better, thereby generating data (not theory) for future science policymakers. Lakatos's idea remains worth exploring (e.g. Fuller 2015, ch. 6). However, it was originally criticized for its paradoxical implication that science may be heading in the generally right direction *in spite of* a succession of theory choices that were wrong in many crucial respects. To be sure, this conclusion comports with Lakatos's Popperian orientation, yet it has been generally seen as too counterintuitive to be taken seriously.

Moreover, Lakatos failed to anticipate the emergence of a third way between historians writing either in support ('Whig') or in opposition ('Tory') to science's dominant tendencies. This would be the standpoint of the history of science profession itself, which is led not by some overarching normative vision of science but simply by an interest in representing all the historical evidence equally well. This would reflect the historian's own investment in the 'archive' as a repository of the past as it actually happened. To be sure, this is a value commitment too, but one that enables the historian to stand above the fray of competing normative philosophies of science. The self-styled 'sociologist of scientific knowledge', David Bloor (1976) generalized this argument to cover all empirically based studies of science, be they historical, ethnographic or experimental. His term for this approach to inquiry, 'symmetry', has proved to be very influential in science and technology studies. The 'symmetry' in question pertains to the historian's, sociologist's, or psychologist's attitude to the truth-value of scientific claims. In good constructivist fashion, Bloor argues that the appropriate attitude should be one of agnosticism, if not classical skepticism (i.e. indifferent to truth or falsehood), given that scientists—like the rest of us—make truth claims without foreknowledge of their ultimate significance. Thus, the best explanation for why and how such claims get made will turn on the intellectual and material resources available to the scientists making them. No doubt, 'symmetry' in this sense encourages the full exploitation of the empirical record. But equally, it renders the historian, sociologist, or psychologist effectively 'value-neutral' in that she registers no stake in what the outcome of all this construction. It may help to explain the increasing deployment of science and technology studies researchers in policy-relevant contexts (Fuller 2000, ch. 5).

## 3 Social Constructivism Becomes Sociology: The Legacy of Berger and Luckmann

According to a 1998 poll of the membership of the International Sociological Association, *The Social Construction of Reality* by Peter Berger and Thomas Luckmann (1966) was voted the fifth most influential work of sociology in the twentieth century. Berger and Luckmann were careful to observe that 'sociological' refers to properties not of collective psychology but of the relations in which people are systematically engaged with one another (ch. 3). It follows that the 'sociological' is not especially concerned with the mindsets of individuals—including whatever common beliefs they might share—but rather with the mutually oriented actions of those individuals which result in relatively stable patterns of behavior. These patterns may be interpreted quite differently by the individuals involved in them. Nevertheless the 'sociologist' can discover the larger significance of such patterns for the overall functioning of society, an interest which the individuals themselves may or may not have.

Moreover, writing under the influence of the phenomenologist Alfred Schutz, Berger and Luckmann presume that individuals normally do *not* have such an interest, which in turn underwrites the need for 'sociology' as a distinct form of social knowledge. Schutz's most famous American publication in his lifetime, "The Well-Informed Citizen" (1946), was understood—not incorrectly—in the spirit of leading US journalist Walter Lippmann, as justifying the emergence of expertise in complex societies, a 'distribution of knowledge' comparable to the 'division of labor', given the range of options open to individuals in various aspects of their lives. However, Berger and Luckmann also read it as an implicit argument for sociology itself as a distinct expertise concerned with the second-order effects of the various decisions that people take—including their delegation of those decisions. Here it is worth recalling Schutz's training in international finance law, a field which highlights the specifically fiduciary character of complex social relations, according to which value may be gained or lost simply in the very maintenance of forms of those relations, the *modus operandi* of which may remain opaque to those dependent on them. In terms of Schutz's own professional training, this applied specifically to the trust invested in bank accounts, stocks, and insurance policies. However, he can be seen as having extended this idea to cover the role of sociology in securitizing the existence of society itself (Prendergast 1986).

Put somewhat paradoxically, sociology is the science dedicated to the construction of 'society' as a second-order object by its interpretive understanding of the set of social relations constituted by a group of individuals across a region of space-time. In this respect, society literally does not exist without the work of sociologists—only social relations exist. Notwithstanding its counterintuitive character, Berger and Luckmann read this proposal as an alternative gloss on Emile Durkheim's founding sociological insight that society is *sui generis*. However, for Durkheim himself, this meant that sociology must rely on methods, such as government statistics, which normally elude the comprehension of social agents and could be used as the basis for diagnosing and addressing 'social problems', which are invariably caused by some sort of 'deviation' from a statistically derived norm.

In contrast, Schutz, who shared the socio-economic orientation of his Viennese contemporaries Ludwig von Mises and Friedrich Hayek, was skeptical about the sense of misplaced trust and uninformed power that might be invested as a result of reducing 'the state of society' to a clutch of statistical indicators that abstract heroically from the full range of human interactions. (This is the deepest sense in which Schutz is a 'phenomenologist'.) Indeed, Schutz (1946) is usefully read alongside Hayek (1945), which treats 'price' not as a confluence of supply and demand curves to settle value but as a distillation of communications to coordinate action. On this basis, Schutz was one of the original people invited to join the Mont Pèlèrin Society established by Hayek in 1945 to promote liberal values in the spirit of Walter Lippmann (Kurrild-Klitgaard 2003). It would be another twenty years before the ethnomethodologist Aaron Cicourel (1964) applied a Schutz-inspired critique to sociology itself in a wide-ranging critique of official statistics, but Berger and Luckmann extended the critique still further to suggest that virtually all macro-level constructions of society threatened to become "reifications" if they were accorded a sense of reality on par with the life experiences of individuals engaged in social relations.

To be sure, sociology may enhance the human condition, if it enables people to come to a deeper understanding of why their lives are the way they are. Indeed, most of Peter Berger's subsequent career has been devoted to Max Weber-inflected questions about how people find meaning in life in a 'disenchanted' secular age. However, sociology may detract from the human condition, if it persuades people that their lives are governed by principles other than they had imagined. These two sociological prospects correspond to the two epistemological sides of the Marxist project: the former to the emancipatory power that comes from the realization of class consciousness; the latter to the alienation that comes from understanding that the world does not proceed as one had thought. Berger and Luckmann's twist was to turn Marx to much more socio-economically liberal purposes than Marx himself would have allowed.

In his mature work, Marx conceptualized alienation as a visceral feeling that workers had in response to the lack of control they had over both the disposition and the products of their labor. The point of Marxism, then, was to channel and sublimate that visceral feeling into 'class consciousness' by informing the workers of the causes of their plight in a way that would enable them to take matters into their own hands. However, following Schutz, Berger and Luckmann imagine alienation also to arise from people coming to have a second-order understanding of their condition. In other words, alienation may result from possessing a theory of social life as well as from social life itself. Indeed, this was the sense of alienation that Marx himself experienced, when he began to theorize about class consciousness in his youthful 'humanist' writings, which were translated into English in the 1960s and helped to inform the student movement of Berger and Luckmann's day.

The question which Berger and Luckmann left radically open—and marked them as liberals rather than socialists—was whether alienated people benefit more from possessing theoretical knowledge of alienation than simply possessing visceral knowledge of it. Implied here is that dealing with alienation on the level in which it is most immediately experienced may serve to stabilize society, whereas dealing with it on a level which involves thinking of society as a whole may be destabilizing. As the economists would say, first-order alienation can be dealt with at the level of 'local adjustments' (i.e. the shift of consumer preference curves) whereas second-order alienation would require 'global adjustments' (i.e. grounding the economy on a new set of principles). The argument for keeping alienation visceral and dealing with it locally is that more people already on the ground are likely to benefit with minimal disruption to their lives. In contrast, as alienation is rendered more theoretically self-conscious and hence symptomatic of the need for systemic change, society's welfare function tends to expand to include future generations as potential beneficiaries, as if to concede that harms greater than the alienation itself are likely to be generated in the course of the proposed societal transformation, which in turn would justify the need for a dummy variable ('future generations') to balance the moral ledger.

Berger and Luckmann's version of social constructivism remains the dominant one in sociology a half-century after its first publication. It is distinctly bottom-up in its approach, as Schutz's original links to the Austrian school of economics would suggest. However, there is a more 'top-down' way of thinking about 'social construction'. The example of markets illustrates the intended contrast. For followers of the Austrian school, including Berger and Luckmann, a market is simply an abstract representation of ordinary social interaction, whereby multiple individuals are trying to achieve their aims simultaneously. On this view, markets do not need to be created either in reality or in theory; rather they appear as part of the natural order of human relations. To be sure, certain markets may need to be regulated based on the concrete effects they have on the individuals involved in them, either directly or indirectly. Or, of course, markets may be arrested or thwarted altogether. However, these extreme acts would be regarded as a fundamental violation of human liberty.

A quite different approach to the matter is to suppose that a market is a second-order social construction which imposes a specific frame of reference on the conduct of social life that would otherwise not exist. Indeed, according to the economic historian Emma Rothschild (2001), who writes in the spirit of Albert Hirschman and Hayek's great Viennese nemesis, Joseph Schumpeter, markets in this sense are an invention of the early modern state in its attempt to exercise a subtler but more pervasive sense of social control through the promotion of wealth production. This was the sense in which markets were regarded as political innovations in the eighteenth century, by both Adam Smith and the marquis de Condorcet. In this context, the state's creation of a market in particular goods or services amounts to a delegation of its own authority to a prescribed novel form of social interaction, the outcomes of which are then taken as authoritative. Whereas in the past the Crown would have granted monopoly licenses in particular trades, the right to trade would now be open to multiple bidders whose worthiness would be proven by their results. Put in terms of principal-agent theory in political science, markets were thus socially constructed as mechanical agencies of the Crown which possessed their own sphere of autonomy as long as their outputs could be inserted into the socio-economic system as if the Crown had made the decision itself. Moreover, as both Smith and Condorcet would have realized, this is the sense of 'market' that carries forward Bacon's original program into the heartland of humanity. We are called to treat each other as Bacon would have scientists treat nature in experiment: not as useful in itself but useful only under mutually constrained conditions.

## References

Berger, P. and Luckmann, T. (1966). *The Social Construction of Reality*. Garden City, NY: Doubleday.
Bloor, D. (1976). *Knowledge and Social Imagery*. London: Routledge & Kegan Paul.
Bloor, D. (1983). *Wittgenstein and the Social Theory of Knowledge*. Oxford: Blackwell.
Cicourel, A. (1964). *Method and Measurement in Sociology*. Glencoe, IL: Free Press.

Desroches, D. (2006). *Francis Bacon and the Limits of Scientific Knowledge*. New York: Continuum.

Donovan, A., Laudan, L., and Laudan, R., eds. (1988). *Scrutinizing Science*. Dordrecht: Kluwer.

Franklin, J. (2001). *The Science of Conjecture*. Baltimore: Johns Hopkins University Press.

Fuller, S. (1988). *Social Epistemology*. Bloomington, IN: Indiana University Press.

Fuller, S. (1993). *Philosophy of Science and Its Discontents*, 2nd edn. (first pub. 1989). New York: Guilford.

Fuller, S. (2000). *Thomas Kuhn: A Philosophical History for Our Times*. Chicago: University of Chicago Press.

Fuller, S. (2015). *Knowledge: The Philosophical Quest in History*. London: Routledge.

Garfinkel, H. (1967). *Studies in Ethnomethodology*. Englewood Cliffs, NJ: Prentice Hall.

Goldman, A. (1999). *Knowledge in a Social World*. Oxford: Oxford University Press.

Hanson, N. R. (1962). "The Irrelevance of History of Science to Philosophy of Science." *Journal of Philosophy* 59: 574–86.

Hayek, F. (1945). "The Use of Knowledge in Society." *American Economic Review* 35: 519–30.

Jasanoff, S. (2004). "The Idiom of Co-production." in S. Jasanoff, ed., *States of Knowledge: The Co-production of Science and Social Order* (1–12). London: Routledge.

Kelley, D. (1990). *The Human Measure: Social Thought in the Western Legal Tradition*. Cambridge, MA: Harvard University Press.

Kuhn, T. (1970). *The Structure of Scientific Revolutions*, 2nd edn. (first pub. 1962). Chicago: University of Chicago Press.

Kuklick, B. (1984). "Seven Thinkers and How They Grew'. In R. Rorty, J. Schneewind, and Q. Skinner, eds., *Philosophy in History: Essays on the Historiography of Philosophy* (125–40). Cambridge: Cambridge University Press.

Kurrild-Klitgaard, P. (2003). "The Viennese Connection: Alfred Schutz and the Austrian School." *Quarterly Journal of Austrian Economics* 6(2): 35–66.

Lakatos, I. (1971). "History of Science and Its Rational Reconstructions." in R. Buck and R. Cohen, eds., *PSA 1970. Boston Studies in the Philosophy of Science*, vol. 8 (91–108). Dordrecht: D. Reidel.

Latour, B. and Woolgar, S. (1979). *Laboratory Life: The Social Construction of Scientific Facts*. London: Sage.

Merchant, C. (1980). *The Death of Nature: Women, Ecology and the Scientific Revolution*. New York: Harper & Row.

Passmore, J. (1970). *The Perfectibility of Man*. London: Duckworth.

Prendergast, C. (1986). "Alfred Schutz and the Austrian School of Economics." *American Journal of Sociology* 92: 1–26.

Rothschild, E. (2001). *Economic Sentiments: Adam Smith, Condorcet and the Enlightenment*. Cambridge, MA: Harvard University Press.

Schneewind, J. (1984). "The Divine Corporation and the History of Ethics." in R. Rorty, J. Schneewind, and Q. Skinner, eds., *Philosophy in History: Essays on the Historiography of Philosophy* (173–92). Cambridge: Cambridge University Press.

Schutz, A. (1946). "The Well-Informed Citizen: An Essay on the Social Distribution of Knowledge." *Social Research* 13: 463–78.

Turner, S. (2010). *Explaining the Normative*. Cambridge: Polity.

Will, F. (1988). *Beyond Deduction: Ampliative Aspects of Philosophical Reflections*. London: Routledge & Kegan Paul.

Winch, P. (1958). *The Idea of a Social Science*. London: Routledge & Kegan Paul.

# 31
# FEMINISM IN SOCIAL RESEARCH

## Marianne Janack

In season three of the show *Portlandia*, Candace's son Bob (played by Bobby Moynihan) comes to the feminist bookstore where Candace (played by Fred Armisen) and Toni (played by Carrie Brownstein) try to sell him a vagina pillow. He objects that he has too many of them already, and asks Candace to watch the baby while he shops in another store for a gift for his partner. In this exchange, Toni and Candace tell Bob that they don't want to know the gender or sex of the baby. Then Toni tells Bob this about gender:

Toni:     I don't know your gender. I don't know Candace's. I don't know mine.
Bob:      You don't know my gender?
Toni:     I don't.
Bob:      Do I look like a woman?
Toni:     I don't know what a woman looks like.
Candace:  Do you?
Bob:      I just feel like I'm good at recognizing a woman when I see one.

Later, when Bob complains about how confusing his gender upbringing has been, Candace comments that lots of brilliant people were confused, including Einstein. Toni asks: "Was Einstein a man or a woman?" Candace replies, "He turned out to be a man—because of the mustache. That was a big giveaway. Even a woman could not have a mustache that … thick."

The feminist bookstore scenes with Candace and Toni can be uncomfortable to watch as a feminist. There is a sense of lampooning, especially as Toni insists, in this scene, on a type of theoretical dogma that seems to be absurd in the face of the facts of gender difference. Simone de Beauvoir said, "In truth, to go for a walk with one's eyes open is enough to demonstrate that humanity is divided into two classes of individuals whose clothes, faces, bodies, smiles, gaits, interests, and occupations are manifestly different. Perhaps these differences are superficial, perhaps they are destined to disappear. What is certain is that right now they do most obviously exist."[1] Though she made this observation in 1949, the *Portlandia* sketch implies that it is still true. And though we might say that androgyny has become more acceptable than it was sixty-five years ago, there is nevertheless the sense that people who are gender ambiguous have some truth that could be revealed if we saw them without all the artificiality. Everyone is a man or a woman, and we can pretty much tell by looking at them, as Bob says. But of course the truth—even as we see it in *Portlandia*, where Toni and Candace are rather ambiguous, and Candace is played by a male actor—is more complicated.

One of the things that the social sciences can help us understand is the way in which human beings—beings that are embodied in particular kinds of ways, and beings immersed in the rich environment of culture—become what we are. The sciences do not just describe us—they also give us new ways of understanding ourselves, and present repeated challenges to those understandings.

Ian Hacking distinguishes natural kinds from human kinds on the basis of the latter's looping effects.[2] Rocks, he says, do not care what we say about them. But human beings are self-interpreting entities, and social scientific theories, which are meant to describe human activities and the people who participate in them, end up influencing those activities and those people. As new descriptions of human beings and their activities are generated, the way that the subjects of those descriptions come to understand themselves—and their behavior—changes, sometimes resisting those descriptions, sometimes reinforcing them, and sometimes creating an ambiguous relationship between resistance and reinforcement. In Risjord's words, "in an important sense … the phenomena of the social sciences are always just out of reach" (Risjord 2014, 52). Social scientific theories do not merely describe humans and the social world—they also shape it.

The looping effects of theories of gender are complicated by the assumed basis of gender in biological sex. We might say that when it comes to sex and gender, the line between a natural kind and a social kind is quite vague, if it exists at all. In fact, the relationships between these categories has given rise to a three-part distinction in gender studies: 'Sex' is the term used to refer to the category (male or female) assigned at a child's birth (or, sometimes, surgically acquired); 'sex category' refers to the category to which a person is recognized as belonging (which, needless to say, might be different from the first category); 'gender' comes about when one is recognized as a member of a sex category, and it involves accountability—that is, one becomes accountable to the norms of behavior that are thought to be incumbent upon, or acceptable for the class of 'women' or 'men' (and can thus be seen as norms of femininity or masculinity) (West and Zimmerman 1987). The normative aspect of gender spills over into sex and sex category, while sex and sex category are often taken to constitute the grounds of the normative force of gender. The biological becomes the grounds for the social, even though the biological is interpreted (and often reinterpreted) in terms of the social. The looping effects we see in the relationship between sex and gender influence not only what we think of as "social categories"—they also reverberate out into the "natural" categories of male and female.

I opened this chapter with a dialogue from a popular television show; I will also draw from articles published in *People* magazine, *Vanity Fair*, and an op-ed from *The New York Times*. Because of the extent to which the social sciences permeate popular culture and can come to serve as "intuitive" truths about a topic, I think these sources, though not traditionally scholarly, give us important data about the ways in which the looping effects of social kinds show up in subjects' self-understandings (and, I will argue, the ways in which those looping effects also show up in our understanding of putative natural kinds, like biological sex).

Another caveat: much feminist writing has focused on the concept of "intersectionality"—the idea that gender, race, sexuality, and class intersect in ways that give particular and relatively distinct textures to each of these categories as we encounter them interwoven with the other categories. And we always encounter them interwoven. But the scope of this paper does not admit of a detailed examination of the ways in which race, class, and sexuality intersect with gender and sex in the cases I discuss. Nevertheless, we should recognize that these, too, are human kinds that have their own looping effects (and that these categories, too, have been taken to have some basis in the natural kinds of biology). For an excellent example of a detailed working through of the concept of intersectionality, see Alcoff (2005) and the classic Crenshaw (1989), among others.

## Counting Women

Anne Fausto-Sterling begins her book *Sexing the Body* with a story of a female athlete. Or perhaps we should say that it begins with the story of an athlete who thought she was female, but whose femaleness was called into question by science. Did this make her male instead? That seems to be an open question. If we assume that these categories cover the biological terrain—that all human beings are either female or male—then by the law of excluded middle, if the person (she? he?) is not female, then he must be male.

Maria Patiño, a Spanish hurdler, failed the sex test administered by the International Olympic Committee's "femininity control head office" in 1988. Though she looked like a woman, and never had any reason to suspect that she wasn't a woman, Patiño learned that she was "really" a man, because she had a Y chromosome, and her labia contained testes. An examination also revealed that she had no ovaries or a uterus. She lost her boyfriend, her athletic scholarship, her national athletic residence, and all of the titles she'd won (Fausto-Sterling 2000, 1). We may be tempted to think that people like Patiño are unusual. But Fausto-Sterling's quarry is larger than the examination of the statistical frequency of "intersex" people: her larger point is that ideas about gender and sex category can be used to reconstruct biology and biological categories.

The treatment of intersex as a type of pathology, and the ways in which medical interventions are evaluated in those situations are examples, Fausto-Sterling says, of the normal dictating the natural: "From the viewpoint of medical practitioners, progress in the handling of intersexuality involves maintaining the normal. Accordingly, there ought to be only two sexes: male and female" (Fausto-Sterling 2000, 8). But what cases like this show is that the norms of gender (and heterosexuality) are not so easily distinguishable from the data of biology. Babies born with genitalia that are too long to be an "acceptable" clitoris or too short to be an "acceptable" penis are often the targets of reconstructive surgery. The determination about what counts as "acceptable" lengths shows, Fausto-Sterling says, the extent to which gender norms and their cousin, heteronormativity, come to animate biological facts. An acceptable clitoris is one that is not long enough to penetrate the vagina of another woman; an acceptable penis is one that is potentially long enough to do so. But, Fausto-Sterling points out, most intersex males are infertile (58–59), leaving us to wonder: what, then, is the motivation for defining genitalia in those terms?

But, to return to Maria Patiño: here was someone who had lived as a woman for all of her life; who appeared to all—including herself—to be a woman. But her claim that she was a woman was overruled by the data of biology.

Consider another story, this one taken from *People* magazine. Bruce Jenner, the American track and field Olympic star, was featured in a *Vanity Fair* magazine write-up in the summer of 2015. But Bruce was no longer Bruce: in a white bustier and glamorous make-up and jewelry, Caitlyn Jenner made her debut. Some women were taken aback by the fact that Caitlyn would embrace such a vampish persona, and that she seemed to reinforce all the stereotypes of women as being vain and rather silly creatures, too concerned about manicures, clothes, shoes, and hair. In an op-ed to the *New York Times*, Elinor Burkett gave voice to the frustration that many feminists felt about Jenner's claim that "my brain is much more female than it is male" and what seemed to be her idea of womanhood: the sexy bustier, "sultry poses, thick mascara, and the prospect of regular 'girls' nights' of banter about hair and makeup." Burkett worries that the talk of women and men having different brains, or the trope of a woman trapped in a man's body reinforces gender stereotypes that the feminist movement has been working to overturn for more than fifty years. "Nail polish does not a woman make," Burkett says at the end of her piece. Bruce Jenner lived a life filled with white male privilege prior to his transition, Burkett points out; this is hard to reconcile with what it is to be a woman: "By defining womanhood the way he did ... Mr. Jenner and the many advocates for transgender rights who take a similar tack ... undermine almost a century of hard-fought arguments that the very definition of female is a social construct that has subordinated us" (Burkett 2015). She is outraged that performances of the *Vagina Monologues* have been cancelled because of objections on the part of the transcommunity. A vagina does not a woman make, either, they object. But Burkett is stunned that tying womanhood to the possession of a vagina is characterized as exclusionary.

The *People* magazine article gives an account of the process that Bruce went through to become Caitlyn, starting with cross-dressing as a young man, and culminating in hormone treatments and plastic surgery in her sixties to "feminize" her face (and, of course, her figure), the addition of hair extensions, and the continued attempt to make her voice sound more like that of a woman. One of the most disconcerting things about the article, though, is the way that the author decided to deal with the challenges of pronoun use. In giving us a history of Caitlyn Jenner, the author refers to Bruce—the winner of the Olympic medals, the young father, the cast member on CHIPS—as 'she'. According to GLAAD, a person's current name and pronoun should be used when talking about them prior to their transition, so this usage is the one they recommend. Nevertheless, looking at Bruce Jenner, circa 1976, shirtless and sitting by a pool, and reading the captions, which use the pronoun 'she' and 'her', is an exercise in being confronted by the artificiality (or instability) of our concepts of sex and gender. According to this usage, 'he' and 'she' are not indexical, but are renegotiated in light of a person's present sex or gender identity. This, perhaps, gives us a clue about how gender is being understood: as an essential and unchanging element of a person's character. Thus, one can look, to all appearances, to be a man, and one might have, at the time of the picture, recognized oneself as the appropriate bearer of the term 'he'. But, it can turn out, one was mistaken about the proper pronoun.

Note that one way of thinking about pronoun use would be to think that it could shift after certain life events: one could spend part of one's life as a 'he' and another part as a 'she'. The pronoun usage that is recommended by GLAAD seems to point to a conception of gender identity that is invariant. But, as we will see below, that conception is at odds with one of the most prominent theories of gender as performance—the idea of "doing gender"—that we find in the social scientific literature.

The big question that arose on the Internet after Caitlyn's debut in *Vanity Fair* was the question about her genitalia: Had she had the "full genital reconstruction"? We might dismiss some of this as prurient, but what was more interesting is that several commentators emphasized that whether Caitlyn had had, or was going to have, surgery on her genitalia was irrelevant to her gender. "For all intents and purposes, I am a woman," Caitlyn Jenner told Diane Sawyer in an interview. She was a woman, even if she had a penis. Or didn't have a vagina. The information page in *People* explained it this way: "a person's gender identity refers to the deeply felt, core sense of who they are, and it may not match the sex organs they were born with" (Petrow 2015, 94).

This account of gender is in tension with several other uses of the term, not just with the theory of gender as performance. In her article about theories of gender in sociology, Reneé Hoogland lists the following different ways in which scholars use the term 'gender': "Some regard it as an attribute of individuals, as interpersonal relation, or as a mode of social organization. Others emphasize the gendered aspects of social status, sex roles, and sexual stereotypes. Yet others consider gender a structure of consciousness, as internalized ideology, or as performative practice" (2007, 629). Thinking of the ways in which gender and sex constitute looping kinds, it seems that gender has become, among the subjects who are studied by the social sciences, something more like sex: an aspect of one's true self; a structure of consciousness; an aspect of one's character or "true self." And in that respect, it has also become an element in stories about authenticity. We might ask: to what extent, and how, should theories of gender take this into account?

## "Doing" Gender

Candace West and Donald Zimmerman, studying conversational practices, introduced the idea of "doing gender." Their analyses emphasized the extent to which gender is an achievement, and furthermore an achievement that was context-dependent:

> [T]he 'doing' of gender is undertaken by women and men whose competence as members of society is hostage to its production. Doing gender involves a complex of socially guided perceptual, interactional, and micropolitical activities that cast particular pursuits as expressions of masculine and feminine 'natures'.
>
> (West and Zimmerman 1987, 126)

Gender, they claim, is an institutional and interactive undertaking; at its core is the notion of accountability, and this, they point out, is a fundamentally social ideal. To be accountable to an expectation or norm is to take myself to be a member of a group which has explicit or tacit understandings of what one is supposed to do or refrain from doing, and to take myself to be answerable to those expectations. So, for instance, if I am a practicing Catholic, I might not take Communion when I go to Mass because I have not been to confession and have recently lied to a friend, so I am really not in a state of grace. No one will know, of course, that I have not been to confession and have this mortal sin on my soul, but nonetheless I recognize myself as accountable to that norm, and I recognize myself both as a member of the community and as accountable by following the rule, even though, technically, no one would know whether I'd abided by the rule or not. My friend the Episcopalian may see herself as accountable to other norms governing the taking of Communion. So norms and accountability are ways of understanding intentional social action, and the doing of gender is a particularly ubiquitous form of accountability.

Gender is not a property of individuals, according to West and Zimmerman. It is, in essence, an emergent property of interactions. Nevertheless it is obligatory, and it legitimates the distinction between male and female; man and woman. It makes that division seem to be both a difference in essential characteristics and a difference that is neither arbitrary nor malleable. In West and Zimmerman's words: "Insofar as a society is partitioned by 'essential' differences between women and men and placement in a sex category is both relevant and enforced, doing gender is unavoidable" (1987, 137). And though not all social situations require sex categorization,

West and Zimmerman claim that any social encounter can be an opportunity to "do gender." Furthermore, they say: "Gender is a powerful ideological device, which produces, reproduces, and legitimates the choices and limits that are predicated on sex category. An understanding of how gender is produced in social situations will afford clarification of the interactional scaffolding of social structure and the social control processes that sustain it" (147).[3] We have in these two cases, though, an odd doing of gender: in Patiño's case the biological facts trump her claim to be a woman; in Jenner's case, they are ignored, and her self-ascription is allowed to stand. It may be that the time that separates the cases (some fifteen years) marks conceptual progress on the part of the public actors whose behavior and self-understandings are the basis for research into gender. However, it might also be that people who do gender in ways that accord with stereotypical ideas of womanliness, as Jenner appears to do, are extended a form of courtesy about their self-reported gender identity that women who are less stereotypically feminine do not receive. Alternatively, we could see these shifts as shifts toward the "undoing" of gender.

## Measuring Change: Thinking about Progress

The approach to the study of gender that understands it as a form of accountability in social interactions—as an achievement—has, according to Francine Deutsch (2007) and others, provided sociologists with excellent tools for examining the ways in which gendered behavior can change over time, and the ways in which it emerges as a norm that can provide structure to social interactions. Earlier theories that took gendered behavior to be a set of internalized social norms—that, in essence, took gender to be part of the psychological structure of individuals—operated with a static conception of gendered behavior; understanding gender as a context-dependent performance better accounts for the ways in which gender norms could be reworked and changed as contemporary cultural expectations changed. This, Deutsch says, meant that it was possible that large changes in gender relations could be made in a relatively short period of time, since it didn't require waiting for a new generation to internalize new norms (2007, 107). Understanding gender as a project, as an achievement, as a doing, also opened up the prospects for understanding the ways in which race, class, ethnicity, or heteronormativity could enter into the context of a gender performance, showing the ways in which 'men' and 'women' are fractured categories whose appearance of naturalness is itself part of the performance.

But Deutsch worries that the research program dictated by "doing gender" tends to focus not on how gender norms and gender itself is disrupted or displaced, but rather on the ways in which gender's malleability means that it can be constantly reconstituted, even as dramatic changes in the social and cultural landscape seem to challenge the naturalness and desirability of maintaining the categories of "men" and "women." Doing gender, Deutsch says, has made the forms of resistance to gender invisible, since the theory tends to focus on the ways in which gender conformity is retained through changing contexts.

In her survey of articles published in 2005 that draw on the model of gender as performance, Deutsch says that most of those articles focus on women and men in unconventional gender situations (for instance, women working in STEM fields), but they tend to emphasize the ways in which gender is stabilized and maintained rather than challenged in those contexts. Ways of interacting that could be understood as unconventional (women entering the workforce in large numbers, for instance; or becoming the majority of students at formerly all-male colleges and universities) or as making gender irrelevant come to be redescribed as gender performances, rather than sites of resistance to gendering. So as women enter bastions of maleness, their activities can be understood as being new forms of performing their "womanliness" if those activities are differently described. But Deutsch says that the questions we should ask in these cases might be different. Rather than asking "how, even in the face of what looks like the erosion of gender differences, is gender difference maintained?" she suggests that researchers ask: "even if difference is maintained, is it reduced? How does the entry of women and men into nontraditional jobs and occupations affect the perception of difference between men and women?" (2007, 115).

## Authenticity, Self-Expression, and Gendered Choices

In "Indulging Our Gendered Selves? Sex Segregation by Field of Study in 44 Countries," Maria Charles and Karen Bradley (2009) report that data from a variety of countries at different developmental levels show that the progress that was expected as a result of increasing material security in modernizing societies didn't really come along. The evolutionary approach, as they call it, thought of sex segregation as "a traditional relict that will decline under modern competitive pressures, or as egalitarian values are institutionalized and become manifest in attitudes and career aspirations" (925). However, what their study found was that some forms of sex segregation became more pronounced, not less, in the most socially or culturally modern societies (ibid.). Though women now constitute the majority of college and university graduates in the USA and other industrial societies, apparently this has not led to a degendering of the work force. Women tend to be clustered in public and nonprofit fields like education, health and social services, public administration, home economics, and library sciences, where they received 75 percent of the bachelor's degrees in the USA in 2001 (when women received 57 percent of all bachelor's degrees in the USA). Only 18 percent of US bachelor's degrees in engineering were awarded to women in 2001; only 28 percent of US bachelor's degrees in computer and information science were awarded to women that year (Roksa 2005, 208–9).

Charles and Bradley argue that different sex segregation schemes seem to operate in "materialist" and "postmaterialist" societies: the latter have many female-labeled service jobs and postsecondary curriculum options that link to those jobs (2009, 926). Women in postmaterialist societies (such as the USA, Britain, Australia, Denmark, Germany, etc.) may end up in those sectors of the economy as a result of their sense that job and career choice are, and should be, forms of self-expression. Colombia, Bulgaria, and Tunisia have the lowest overall levels of sex segregation in fields of study; Finland, Hong Kong, South Africa, and Switzerland the highest (940–2). In essence, modernization and increased prosperity is strongly correlated with increased sex segregation in fields of study.[4]

Charles and Bradley claim that the differences they observed in sex-segregation in fields of study in modern (postmaterialist) and developing or transitional (materialist) countries may be explained by two large-scale norms: (1) gender-essentialist ideology (the idea that men and women have essentially different, and innate, characteristics) and (2) the extent to which one is expected to choose a job that one loves, and so a job that is a form of self-expression (see Cech 2013). Countries in which one is not expected to love one's job, but rather to choose a job for its potential to provide financial security are countries that show weaker segregating effects. In those countries, they argue, it is less legitimate to choose a lower-paying job that accords with one's sense of oneself, and so the paths that women take tend to be less influenced by the ideal of self-expression and gender essentialism than in societies where jobs are relatively plentiful and students are expected to choose educational and vocational tracks that they find meaningful and fulfilling. In Charles and Bradley's words:

> [T]he liberal individualistic variety of egalitarianism that predominates today in advanced industrial societies emphasizes formal procedural equality, a principle that can exist quite comfortably alongside essentialist representations of gender difference. Sex segregation by field of study is ideologically compatible with liberal egalitarianism because it appears to reflect the naturally distinct preferences and aspirations of formally equal men and women.
>
> (Charles and Bradley 2009, 961)

Sex segregation is thus, in postmaterialist societies, a function of the free choices of people who are "autonomous but fundamentally gendered" (ibid.).

Chardie Baird argues that when we look at intraoccupational sex segregation, we see that when women entered fields that were previously the domain of men, they tended to cluster in sub-fields that were lower paid, or had less prestige: "more women entered medicine, but they were resegregated into subspecialties … such as pediatrics, gynecology, and family practice" (Baird 2012, 989). Looking at men and women's occupational choices, Baird's data show that 80 percent of men express a desire early in life to work in male-dominated occupations[5] and 56 percent do, while 36 percent of men work in sex-integrated jobs,[6] and 7 percent work in female-dominated occupations.[7] Fifty-two percent of women express a preference early in life to work in male-dominated fields, but the data for 1998 showed that only 15 percent did so. In 1998, 47 percent of women worked in female-dominated fields.

We might ask, though: if Charles and Bradley are right about the extent to which national prosperity and ideals of individual self-expression end up reinforcing sex-segregation in jobs, should we be worried? Similarly, is the fact that women constitute the majority of liberal arts college students something to be addressed with different admission policies and selection procedures, to ensure that they do not become too large a majority? But the question that seems most pressing, given the discussion of Patiño and Jenner, and which gets at the fundamental research practices that address these issues is: "how do we count women?"

## Gender and Sex

One thing to notice in these studies is that the data collected about segregation in occupations and fields of study is about sex segregation, not necessarily about gender segregation. Certain skills or occupations are "gendered," which means either that they have a majority of women in them, or that they are thought to be the kinds of fields that depend heavily on skills and interests that are thought to be differentially appropriate for men and women. Though 'gender' and 'sex' are sometimes used interchangeably, if Baird and Charles and Bradley had used the terms in that way, their studies would presumably be fairly uninteresting: it would simply mean that the occupations that had the most women in them had the most women in them. So part of the research model for studies of this kind is a distinction between sex and gender. But exactly how gender is distinguished from sex, and how the categories are thought to relate to each other, is a complicated story, as we saw from the Patiño case and the case of Bruce/Caitlyn Jenner's transition and ideals of authenticity.

The looping effects for gender and sex seem to show that, in some cases, biology is relevant to whether one is a man or woman, and sometimes it is not. One might argue that in pursuits that depend on physical strength or athletic abilities, as in the Olympics case, sex must be tracked "biologically" in order to guarantee fairness—even if different biological measures give different answers to the question "what sex is this person?" However, the sex category into which a person fits does not mean that he or she will be suitably and fairly matched physically with others in the same category. Renee Richards, though born a man, did not dominate women's tennis after her sex change. Fausto-Sterling shows that the interest in determining what sex an Olympic competitor "really" is goes back to the turn of the century, since there was a widespread belief that the very act of competing in sports was dangerous to women's womanhood (2000, 2 and 257, nn. 7 and 8). Cold War politics added to the paranoia, as Eastern Bloc countries were suspected of cheating by disguising male athletes as female athletes to give them an unfair advantage over other female competitors (2). Until 1968, women competitors were asked to appear naked in front of an IOC examining board to show that they had the appropriate equipment. But concerns about privacy, and the scientific advances that made chromosomal tests possible, led to the more "scientific" tests that involved cheek scrapings and allowed the IOC to sort people by whether they were XX or XY. These tests, however, cannot do the work that the IOC wants them to do, according to Fausto-Sterling: "A body's sex is simply too complex. There is no either/or. Rather, there are shades of difference ... labeling someone a man or a woman is a social decision" (3). She suggests that the data of biology in such cases might more reasonably be taken to point toward the abandonment of a system that distinguishes just two sexes.

But much social scientific research, even that which seeks to overturn sexism and gender essentialism, depends on being able to count women and men, and the subjects of the social sciences seem still to hold on to a gender and sex binary. We might want to move the public discourse beyond this; we might think that the results of social scientific research will eventually show that this binary is based on bad biology, or a bad theory of gender identity. But to the extent that those who are not feminist or gender scholars hold on to that theory, presumably it must be retained in the research frame. In their write-up of their research methods, Charles and Bradley and Baird do not tell us how they counted women: if it was an answer to a survey question (e.g. check one: male or female—or would it be man or woman?), were the respondents' self-reports taken as settling the question? Or did the survey administrator make a determination, on the basis of questions or observable traits, about whether the respondent was to count as a man or a woman, male or female?

As Sally Haslanger (2000) argues, gender, like race, is a category of analysis that can be and should be subjected to the pragmatic question: what do we want these categories to do? What function do we want them to perform? If we want to determine if women are subjected to unequal treatment or opportunity compared with men, that should be reflected in the constraints on the category's identity conditions. If, however, we are concerned that certain gendered traits or undertakings are devalued, that should be reflected in the way we define the category. If, however, we want to describe the ways in which gender categories themselves function, that will probably dictate yet another way of understanding and defining categories.

The result of this is that it seems that social scientific research into gender cannot abjure responsibility for its role in self-interpretations, nor can it avoid addressing questions about what social scientific research should be trying to do. Furthermore, the "biologization" of gender (the appeal to chromosomal identity, or "brain sex") does not show that gender can be translated into the terminology of natural kinds. Instead, what it seems to show is that the natural kinds of biology are, in fact, human kinds, showing the same looping effects that characterize more commonly recognized natural kinds terms. Social scientific research informs our interpretations of others' biological and psychological facts, as well as that of our own biology, and our own psychology: whether we find those biological facts or that psychological profile to be an irrelevant and unfortunate fact about us, or whether we embrace it, and think of it as an important element of who we are. How we count women is not just a matter of whether they look like women, or have two X chromosomes, or have vaginas, or think of themselves as women, because another part of this discourse is an irreducibly normative discourse. It is the discourse of authenticity, which also informs how we hear the claims of those who wish to be identified in particular ways, and how we understand those if we have only a binary system of gender and sex.

Maybe Candace and Toni were right after all. Maybe who is a woman is more complicated than it looks to be. Or maybe it should be.

## Notes

1 *Second Sex*, Introduction: http://netage.org/2010/05/17/the-second-sex-author%E2%80%99s-introduction/, accessed November 7, 2015.
2 This is also referred to as 'reflexivity'.
3 Readers might recognize affinities between West and Zimmerman's concept of "doing gender" and Judith Butler's understanding of gender as a repeated and obligatory performance. For a discussion of the common ground—and the differences—between these approaches, see Fenstermaker and West (2002).
4 Charles and Bradley differentiate between girls' and women's affinity for science and math (the extent to which they agree with the claim that they like science or math) and their achievement. Achievement in science and math does not seem to have the same robust explanatory power for the sex segregation they find in postindustrial societies that affinity does.
5 Those in which women constitute 30 percent or less of the workers.
6 Those in which women constitute 31 percent to 69 percent of the workers
7 Those in which women constitute 70 percent or more of the workers.

## References

Alcoff, Linda Martín. 2005. *Visible Identities: Race, Gender and the Self.* New York: Oxford University Press.
Baird, Chardie L. 2012. Going against the flow: A longitudinal study of the effects of cognitive skills and gender beliefs on occupational aspirations and outcomes. *Sociological Forum* 27(4): 986–1009. Accessed November 23, 2015. http://search.ebscohost.com/login.aspx?direct=true&db=aph&AN=83306193&site=ehost-live&scope=site.
Burkett, Elinor. 2015. What makes a woman? *New York Times*, Sunday Review, June 6. Accessed June 7, 2015. www.nytimes.com/2015/06/07/opinion/sunday/what-makes-a-woman.html?_r=0.
Cech, Erin A. 2013. The self-expressive edge of occupational sex segregation. *American Journal of Sociology* 119(3) (November): 747–89. Accessed November 23, 2015. www.jstor.org/stable/10.1086/673969.
Charles, Maria and Karen Bradley. 2009. Indulging our gendered selves? Sex segregation by field of study in 44 countries. *American Journal of Sociology* 114(4) (January): 924–76. Accessed November 23, 2015. www.jstor.org/stable/10.1086/595942.
Crenshaw, Kimberlé. 1989. Demarginalizing the intersection of race and sex: A black feminist critique of antidiscrimination doctrine, feminist theory and antiracist politics. *University of Chicago Legal Forum* 140: 139–68.
Deutsch, Francine. 2007. Undoing gender. *Gender and Society* 21(1): 106–27.
Fausto-Sterling, Anne. 2000. *Sexing the Body: Gender Politics and the Construction of Sexuality.* New York: Basic Books.

Fenstermaker, Sarah and Candace West. 2002. *Doing Gender, Doing Difference: Inequality, Power, and Institutional Change*. New York: Routledge.

Haslanger, Sally. 2000. Gender and race: (What) are they? (What) do we want them to be? *Noûs* 34(1): 31–55.

Hoogland, R. C. 2007. Gender, theories of. In F. Malti-Douglas (Ed.), *Encyclopedia of Sex and Gender*. Detroit: Macmillan Reference USA, vol. 2, 628–32.

Petrow, Steven. 2015. Let's talk transgender. In *The Caitlyn Jenner Story: From Olympic Icon to Transgender Hero*. *People* Special Edition. New York: Time Inc. Books, 94–95.

Risjord, Mark. 2014. *Philosophy of Social Science: A Contemporary Introduction*. New York: Routledge.

Roksa, Josipa. 2005. Double disadvantage or blessing in disguise? Understanding the relationship between college major and employment sector. *Sociology of Education* 78(3): 207–32.

West, Candace and Donald Zimmerman. 1987. Doing gender. *Gender and Society* 1: 125–51.

# 32
# RACE IN SOCIAL RESEARCH
## Michael Root

## 1 Introduction

Social scientists, when studying variations within the US population in a range of economic, political, social and health-related variables, routinely classify members by race, but, in their dealings with one another, they classify each other by race as well. Race is a tool social scientists use to describe their subjects, but race is also a badge social scientists wear, and, like their subjects, they are colored by race, marked as Black or White, as Asian or American-Indian; their racial attitudes or antipathies shape them, influence their practice, no less than they shape or influence the people they study.

My primary interest is the use of race as a descriptive and analytic variable in population-level studies in the social and biomedical (notably epidemiology) sciences, but I also discuss how race marks differences within the social sciences in professional opportunity and achievement.

## 2 Racial Categories

The term "race" first appeared in English in the 16th century and was used to divide people by origin or ancestry based on how they looked, their physical features, but on their culture or customs as well. A race was a breed, stock, tribe, or clan. People were routinely sorted by race but in a variety of different and ever-changing ways (Blanton 1977). Though widely used in the 16th and 17th centuries to mark off or identify groups of people by looks or behavior, race was not primarily a biological category.

In the 18th and 19th centuries, "race" acquired a more biologic meaning, and the groups picked out as different races came to be seen as different subspecies or lineages of man. In addition, members of some races were taken to be superior in ability or virtue to others, and race was often invoked to justify the control of one group of people by another and, in particular, to defend the Atlantic slave trade and the colonization of Africa and Asia by the countries of Europe.

Biological conceptions of race persist but have been widely contested in both the social and biological sciences. American anthropologists were among the first to raise doubts. Ashley Montague argued in a number of popular books and articles (Montague 1980) that race is a social rather than biological category, and Franz Boas debunked many of the claims of 19th-century racial science (Boas 1982) and showed that the cross-cultural generalizations advanced by proponents of the biological conception of race were mistaken. Many biologists came to adopt a similar view; the genetic differences between Blacks in the USA, they suggested, are as great as those between Blacks and Whites (Lewontin 1972); at the level of genes, Blacks do not differ from Whites any more than they differ from one another, and, in this respect, race is not biological.

## 3 Race in the USA

People in the United States have classified each other by race since the founding of the country, but not always in the same way. The Federal government has classified people in the USA by race since the first Census in 1790, but the racial groups into which people were placed changed from one decade to another. There were nine census races in 1930 and five in 2000, and six of the nine races in 1930 were not races at all in the 2000 Census (Bennett 2000).

In 1930, ethnic Japanese and ethnic Koreans in the United States were members of different races; in 2000, they were members of the same. Many Blacks in 2000 would have been mulattos had they lived in 1880. To the extent that race is a social rather than biological category, an individual's race can change with time and place even if his skin color and ancestry remain the same.

## 4 Defining Race

Some philosophers have attempted to define race. They asked a Socratic question, what makes one person White and another Black, and they sought a Platonic answer; they looked for necessary and sufficient conditions for a person to have one race rather than another and searched for a racial essence. They turned to an old tool, conceptual analysis, to clarify the concept of race and racial categories, and they tested their analysis against speaker intuitions or, most often, their own judgments of individual cases, on their confidence that this man is Black but that one White.

Terms like "White" and "Black" are terms of ordinary language, labels used in everyday talk-exchanges, but they are also employed in the social and biomedical sciences. Whatever virtue conceptual analysis might have, it does not serve any of the sciences, social or biological, very well for, in the sciences, few categories have essences or necessary and sufficient conditions to define them.

Social scientists use race as a descriptive or analytic variable to describe or explain differences in social and economic status. They routinely classify Americans by race in order to describe or explain differences in income, employment, health care, crime, school performance, home ownership, drug addiction, or marriage and divorce within the population.

When studying the US population, social scientists find significant differences between the races in each of a number of social or economic variables or traits. In particular, they find that the values of these variables differ more between racial groups than within them. Moreover, the differences between racial groups, their studies show, are persistent; year after year, the median or average value of a given social or economic variable for one racial group falls below or above the median or average value for another (Smelser et al. 2001).

Racial terms, whatever their meaning in ordinary language, have become naturalized; in the social sciences, their meaning is given by their use in studies of racial inequality and explanations of differences in educational achievement, political participation, housing, income, wealth, and health rather than any necessary and sufficient conditions for the application of terms like "Black," "White," "Asian," or "Native American" to members of a population.

In the USA, race is often used by social scientists in their population studies because their subjects, members of the US population, decide how to treat people based on the race they take them to be; they classify each other by race and decide how to treat someone based on the race they assign him; the differences in treatment have consequences, and the consequences are an object of study within the social sciences.

## 5  Official Racial Categories

In order to classify members of a population by race, each member has to be assigned to one or more of a fixed number of racial categories. Most social and biomedical scientists, when classifying members of the US population by race, rely on the classification system and standards for the collection and presentation of data on race adopted by an agency of the Federal government, the Office of Management and Budget (OMB).

According to an OMB directive (Directive 15, adopted in 1997), there are five races, five racial categories (Black; White; American-Indian or Alaskan Native; Asian; Native-Hawaiian or Other Pacific Islander) into which members of the U.S. population are to be classified or grouped whenever their race is counted or reported. These five categories provide a minimum standard for maintaining, collecting, and presenting data on race for Federal reporting purposes and are used to code all social, economic, and health data collected by an agency of the US government.

Social science and biomedical researchers rely on these government data in their studies of the US population and, as a result, routinely use the Federal government's five racial categories in describing or explaining how the risk or rate of poverty and homelessness or rates of political participation, incarceration, school graduation, employment, morbidity and mortality in the population vary with race.

Most social and biomedical scientists follow the Federal government and treat race and ethnicity as different categories. A member of the US population, according to the OMB, can be Hispanic and a member of any of five races, and a person classified as White can belong to any one of a number of a variety of different ethnic groups. As a result, Hispanics in the USA can be either Black or White, and the social or economic status of Black and White Hispanics can be different. While most epidemiologists follow the lead of the OMB in treating the category "Hispanic" as an ethnic rather than a racial category, they seldom study how rates of morbidity or mortality are different between Black and White Hispanics and, in most of their research, seem to assume the Hispanics that they study are White.

## 6  Assigning Race

The current OMB standard for collecting and reporting data on race lists five categories but is silent on how members of the population should be assigned a race and how to decide whether a member is one race, e.g. Black, rather than another, e.g. White, and one government agency can assign race in a way different from another. While the US Bureau of Census assigns members an OMB race based on the race they report themselves to be, the National Center for Health Statistics assigns them a race based on the race on their birth or death certificate. However, a member's self-reported race can be different from the race on his birth or death certificate. As a result, he can be assigned one race at birth, a different race as a young adult and a different one again when he dies (Hahn 1992).

When measuring errors in mortality statistics, researchers routinely treat a decedent's race on his death certificate as his "apparent" race and his race on an earlier population survey or birth certificate as his "actual" one if the two are different. They assume that a member's race can't change, but his race can be misreported.

In the USA, self-reported race has become the most common way of assigning race ("the gold standard") to members of a population in social science and biomedical research (Friedman et al. 2000). Assigning a member the race he assigns himself is often the easiest or most respectful way to assign him to a racial category. By allowing each individual to be the arbiter of his or her own race, the researcher displays the subjective and social nature of our system of racial classification and gives individuals control over their own identity. Nevertheless, the easiest or most respectful way to identify someone's race might not give race as much descriptive or explanatory power as a less easy or respectful way.

A workshop at the National Academy of Sciences concluded that research is needed to compare the race members of the US population assign themselves and the race they are most likely to be assigned by others (Edmonston 1996). Studies conducted since suggest that self-reports and other-reports of a member's race are sometimes different, and many foreign-born and Hispanic members of the population do not take themselves to be the race they are most often taken to be by others (Harris 2002). Other studies show that the self- and other-reported race of mixed-race members of the population (the offspring of parents of different OMB races) are often different or that the race of many members of the population report themselves to be varies with how, when, and by whom they are asked to name their race (Waters 2000).

Many members of the population seem to have a variety of context-specific self-identities, but, despite their self-identities, if many are consistently identified as Black by others, then researchers interested in how access to housing, education, mortgage lending, employment opportunities, or morbidity and mortality vary with race have a reason to take other-reports rather than self-reports as the best measure of the person's race, and officials who decide social or health policy have a reason to take other-reports rather then self-reports to measure the actual race of members of the population.

## 7 Actual Race

Race cannot be measured like age, weight, or height, but a member of the U.S. population is not whatever race he takes himself to be. There is a difference between being and appearing to be Black or being White and passing as White (Root 2000). But what is the difference based on and how should a social or biomedical researcher decide whether a member's actual race is his self-reported race, mother's race, or other-reported race if they are not the same?

Which race is a member's actual race, some have argued, can vary from one risk to another. A member's self-reported race can be his actual race in relation to his risk of depression and his other-reported race in relation to his risk of unemployment or his mother's race in relation to his risk of homelessness (Root 2009).

Other-reported race measures differences in risk better than self-reported race if the risk varies with a member's exposure to discrimination, since his exposure to discrimination is not based on the category he assigns to himself but the one he is most often assigned by others. As a result, whenever differences between groups in risk are primarily due to racial discrimination, a member's self-reported race, some suggest, should be routinely counted as his actual race in social and biomedical research only if his self- and other-reported race are the same.

No matter which way social or biomedical scientists distinguish between Blacks and Whites, the variation within each racial group in social and economic status or the risk of morbidity or mortality within the U.S. population is great. Nevertheless, the degree of intra- and inter-group difference in status or risk can vary with how race is assigned, and, given an interest in describing or explaining differences within the population in the risk of unemployment, homelessness, educational achievement, poverty, morbidity or mortality, the best way to assign race, some suggest, is whichever results in the largest difference between the groups in status or risk since where there is little or no difference, the categories won't describe or explain any variation in status or risk within the population, and race won't be a useful category in the study of population differences (Root 2005).

## 8  Pluralism

Race seems to be more like poverty or unemployment than age, weight, or height; though the category is real enough, how best to measure it is a subject of debate. There are many ways to measure poverty and unemployed in a population, and a count of the poor or unemployed can change with the measure chosen. According to the US Bureau of Census, the US poverty rate rose from 11.7 percent in 2001 to 12.1 percent in 2002. The statistics are based on a measure of poverty adopted by the Federal government in 1965. The measure has two parts: first, a set of income thresholds (poverty lines) for families of different sizes, and, second, a definition of family income to be compared to the threshold. The 1965 measure is what economists call absolute and objective, objective in the sense that poverty is measured by a family's income rather than perceptions and absolute in the sense that whether one family is poor is independent of how other families are doing. As a result, given the official measure, every family in the USA could have been living in poverty in 2001 or 2002; the income of every family could have been below the threshold.

The official US measure is one of many ways poverty can be measured (Ruggles 1990). Many international organizations take a family to be poor if and only if the family's income is less than one half the country's median income: this is an objective but relative (comparative) measure of poverty. According to this measure, not every family in the USA can be living in poverty. Poverty could also be measured by a family's consumption rather than income or measured by what members think they need in order to keep up with their neighbors; this is a subjective measure. Families can feel poor no matter what their wealth or income.

Given a variety of measures, a researcher who wishes to study how a social or biomedical risk within a population varies with poverty has to choose between them. Moreover, any estimate of the error in a poverty statistic will rely on his or her choice, since any error in a measurement of the number of poor is the difference between the number of members of the population who are taken to be poor and the number who are actually poor, and the number who are actually poor depends on the poverty measure.

Which measure a researcher should choose depends on his or her interest. An absolute measure of poverty might better describe or explain the risk of malnutrition, while a relative measure might better describe or explain the risk of depression. No one measure describes or explains every risk better than all the others.

We cannot capture something as complex as poverty with a single measure of poverty, most researchers agree, but we cannot capture something as complex as race with a single measure, either. Race, like poverty, has a number of dimensions and one measure of race can be a better measure of one and a worse measure of another. To allow the methods of assigning race to vary follows a recommendation of the National Research Council that reports on race should rely on multiple methods of measurement rather than one, since no one measure can capture all the different ways race can affect the health or well-being of members of a population (Blank et al. 2004).

## 9 Ancestry

Race is often associated with ancestry. The races are often taken to be descent groups and the members of each race to be the descendants of the original people of a geographical region of the world like Europe, Asia, or Africa. According to OMB Directive 15, Blacks have origins in any of the black racial groups of Africa and Whites in any of the original peoples of Europe, the Middle East, or North Africa. However, the directive is silent on how a member's ancestry should be used to assign him an OMB race or whether members of mixed European and African ancestry are Black, White, both, or neither.

Between 20 percent and 30 percent of self-reported Blacks and Whites, according to some estimates, have mixed African and European ancestry (Parra et al. 1998). The median proportion of European ancestry among self-reported Blacks is 18.5 percent, and the average proportion is 14 percent (Tishkoff et al. 2009).

Admixture rates vary from region to region of the USA, and self-reported Blacks in California have the highest percentage of European ancestry and in Georgia the lowest (Parra et al. 1998). However, in every region of the USA, many people who identify themselves as Black have both African and European ancestors, as do many Whites as well. According to one estimate, going back seven generations, self-reported Blacks in the USA have on average 128 African and 22 European ancestors.

If a small percentage of African ancestry is enough to count as Black (the "one-drop" rule), then many members of the US population who take themselves to be White are Black (apparently White but actually Black) since between 20 percent and 30 percent of self-reported Whites in the USA are estimated to have between 2 percent and 20 percent African ancestry.

If 20 percent to 30 percent of self-reported Whites are Black or between 20 percent and 30 percent of self-reported Blacks are White, then the US Bureau of Census over-counted the number of Whites or Blacks in the US in 2000 by between 20 percent and 30 percent.

But why should a member with a small or even large percentage of European ancestry count as White if he has always identified himself or been identified by others as Black or someone with a small or even large percentage of African ancestry count as Black if he has always identified himself or been identified by others as White? If the self-reported and other-reported race of a member is White, why isn't his actual race White whatever his percentage of European or African ancestry?

No matter what his percentage of African ancestry, researchers have no reason to take his race to be other than his self-reported or other-reported race unless, by assigning him a different race, they can better describe or explain how differences in social or economic status vary with race. The issue isn't what percentage of African or European ancestors makes a member Black rather than White but how or whether a member's ancestry should be taken into account when assigning him a race in studies of social, economic, and biomedical disparities.

## 10  Mixed Race

Some members of the US population would report themselves to be mixed race, rather than one or more of the five OMB races, if "Mixed" were one of the racial categories they were able to choose from. Between 1990 and 1997, many individuals and groups lobbied Congress and the OMB to alter the list of official races to include a stand-alone multiracial classification and include "Mixed" as an option in the 2000 Census.

However, if "Mixed" was an official option, on what basis should a member of the population be assigned to that category: on the basis of a self-report, the race of his parents, or the race others take him to be? Moreover, should a member be counted as mixed if one of his parents is mixed or only if his parents belong to two different OMB races?

"Mixed" is not a racial category in the US Census but neither is "Mixed" used in most studies of racial differences in social and economic status or health outcomes. In most studies of differences in infant mortality, for example, an infant's mother's OMB race is usually taken to be his actual race, whatever the race of his father, and no infant is taken to be mixed race rather than one of the five OMB races (Kleinman and Kessel 1987). If "Mixed" was a category in infant mortality studies, the rate of Black infant death would decrease, but the amount of decrease would depend on how "Mixed" was assigned to infants.

Using his mother's race to predict an infant's risk of poverty, homelessness, morbidity, or mortality (the current practice) biases the estimate of Black–White differences in risk if infants with parents of different races have different risks than infants with same-race parents.

## 11  Genetics

Humans originated in Africa 200,000 years ago; however, many years later, some left and established settlements in Europe and Asia. The different settlements, isolated from one other, evolved independently, and genetic differences between them grew; in time, genes common to one became rare in another. As a result, today, some genetic differences are greater between than within the people of Africa, East Asia, and Europe. The differences are small (in the frequency of a some genes [alleles]) but are not random and some are medically significant. Hemochromatosis (iron overload), for example, is associated with a mutant allele found in all European groups but virtually absent in East Asians and Africans, and another, thromboembolic disease (blockage of the blood vessels) is associated with an allele present in approximately 5 percent of Europeans but rarely found in East Asians or Africans.

According to some studies of human genetic variation within the US population, some alleles are more common in one self-reported OMB race than others (Risch et al. 2002). The frequency of an allele affecting the metabolism of some heart drugs, for example, is reported to be different in self-reported Blacks and self-reported Whites, while the frequency of an allele associated with alcohol metabolism is reported to be different in self-reported Whites and self-reported American-Indians.

Though race might be a useful category in measuring the risk of a genetically linked trait within the population, genes are not useful in measuring the race of the members. Were members of the US population assigned an OMB race based on a gene (allele), even one that occurs more often in one (self-reported) race than the others, the size of each OMB race would shrink significantly since the allelic variation within the (self-reported) races is great.

Though there is some disagreement among population biologists over the usefulness of race as a biological category and some maintain that the races differ in allelic frequencies, few if any maintain that a member of the US population should be assigned an OMB race based on his genes. While social scientists have reason to assign members of the US population to one of the OMB races based on other-reports, self-reports, or parents' race, they have no reason to assign them one race rather than another based on the presence or absence of a gene.

Members of the US population do not assign themselves or each other a race based on their genes or gene frequencies, and race describes and explains differences in their socio-economic status better if assigned based on self or other reports than genes. Genes are not an objective and self/other reports a subjective measure of race, as they might be with sex, for race, more than sex, is a social rather than biological category.

## 12 Race within the Social Sciences

Social scientists classify their subjects by race, but they classify each other by race as well; they are no more likely to be blind to race than anyone else, and they are no more likely to ignore an individual's race when deciding how to treat her than their subjects are in deciding how to treat each other. Racial discrimination marks education, employment, funding, and promotion inside no less than outside the social sciences. Blacks are underrepresented in the social sciences as they are in other professions, and their underrepresentation within the social sciences is sometimes due to overt and institutional or statistical discrimination much as they are elsewhere.

In 2006, Blacks comprised 12.5 percent of the US population, but earned only 7.9 percent of the bachelor and 8.8 percent of the master degrees in science and engineering; in 2007 Blacks earned only 2.5 percent of all science and engineering doctoral degrees. Though, at the doctoral level, Blacks are better represented in the social than the natural sciences, their representation in the social sciences, relative to Whites, is low and varies significantly between fields; they are better represented in sociology than economics and better represented in qualitative than quantitative subfields. Approximately 15 percent of sociology Ph.D. recipients are Black or Hispanic, compared to 13.1 percent in political science, 8.3 percent in economics, and 12.8 percent in psychology (National Academy of Sciences et al. 2011).

According to a 2007 study of the representation of minorities in sociology, Blacks who earn doctorates are more likely to receive tenure-track jobs than Whites, 71.8 to 57.6 percent, and Black full-professors earn $1.30 for every dollar earned by White full-professors, but Blacks, though overrepresented at the junior level, are underrepresented at the senior. In sociology, Blacks disproportionately "leak" from the pipeline as they move up the ranks, and the relative proportion of Blacks, in contrast to Whites, decreases as they move closer to the top (Spalter-Roth and Erskine 2007).

There are few studies of minority underrepresentation in US economics departments, but, according to one frequently cited study, in 1995, Blacks, Hispanics, and Native Americans accounted for 3 percent of the economic doctorates employed by four-year colleges and medical institutions, and, among all colleges and universities, Blacks accounted for 1.6 percent of tenured faculty; among universities with doctoral programs in economics, the underrepresentation was even more severe, with Blacks only .08 percent of tenured faculty (Collins 2000).

In 2012, Blacks and Hispanics together occupied only 5.6 percent of all full-time tenured and tenure-track economics positions across all institutions. In Ph.D.-granting economics departments, Black economists represented 1.8 percent of assistant professors, 2.8 percent of associate professors, and 1.2 percent of full professors (Scott and Siegfried 2013).

The underrepresentation of Blacks and other racial minorities in the social sciences, and within college and university departments in particular, can be explained in different ways. According to one explanation, the underrepresentation is due to demand-side factors, e.g. discrimination in hiring or promotion and, according to another, supply-side factors, e.g. too few Blacks earning a required academic credential. According to one study, an increase in the number of Black doctorates in economics has an inelastic effect on the share of Black faculty due to high non-academic wages/salaries for Blacks with an economics Ph.D. (Myers and Turner 2004).

Discrimination can occur anywhere in the course of an academic career, in the beginning, in the middle, or at the end. In a survey of newly minted sociology Ph.D.s, when asked whether they received faculty help in publishing, a key measure of academic productivity, 33 percent of Blacks while 56 percent of Whites answered "yes" (Spalter-Roth and Erskine 2007).

Racial discrimination is often subtle and difficult to measure; however, more than one hundred years after W. E. B. Du Bois spoke of the "color line," many studies of the academic labor market suggest that the line continues to hold Blacks back in the social sciences and especially as they near the top of a field or subfield (Price 2009). The line appears in each of the social sciences, but seems to be drawn at a somewhat different place in each of them.

## 13 Conclusion

Race is routinely used in social science research to describe and explain differences in socio-economic status as well as in the risk of morbidity and mortality within the US population. However, race can be used to describe and explain differences in status within the social science population as well. The issue, when doing social research, is how best to assign race to members of the US population and not whether race is real. Race is real for a social scientist's subjects and within his professional or academic life as well.

## References

Bennett, Claudette (2000), "Racial Categories Used in the Decennial Censuses, 1790 to Present," *Government Information Quarterly*, 17: 161–80.

Blank, Rebecca M., Marilyn Dabady and Constance F. Crito (Eds.), Panel on Methods for Assessing Discrimination (2004), *Measuring Racial Discrimination*. Committee on National Statistics, Division of Behavioral and Social Sciences and Education. Washington, DC: The National Academies Press.

Blanton, Michael (1977), *The Idea of Race*. London: Tavistock.

Boas, Franz (1982), *Language and Culture*. Chicago: University of Chicago Press.

Collins, Susan M. (2000), "Minority Groups in the Economics Profession," *Journal of Economic Perspectives*, 14(3): 133–48.

Edmonston, Barry, Joshua Goldstein, and Juanita Tamayo (Eds.) (1996), *Spotlight on Heterogeneity: The Federal Standards for Racial and Ethnic Classification*. Washington, DC: The National Academies Press.

Friedman, Daniel, Bruce Cohen, Abigail Averbach, and Jennifer Norton (2000), "Race/Ethnicity and OMB Directive 15: Implication for State Public Health Practice," *American Journal of Public Health*, 90: 1714–719.

Gravlee, Clarence C. (2009), "How Race Becomes Biology: Embodiment of Social Inequality," *American Journal of Physical Anthropology*, 139: 47–57.

Hahn, R. A. (1992), "The State and Federal Health Statistics on Racial and Ethnic Groups," *Journal of the American Medical Association*, 267: 268–71.

Harris, David, R. and Jeremiah Joseph Sim (2002), "Who is Multiracial? Assessing the Complexity of Lived Race," *American Sociological Review*, 67: 614–27.

Kleinman, Joel C. and S. S. Kessel (1987), "Racial Differences in Low Birth Weight: Trends and Risk Factors," *New England Journal of Medicine*, 317: 749–53.

Lewontin, Richard (1972), "The Apportionment of Human Diversity," *Evolutionary Biology*, 6: 381–98.

Montague, Ashley (1980), *The Concept of Race*. Westport, CT: Greenwood.

Myers, Samuel L. and Caroline S. Turner (2004), "The Effects of Ph.D. Supply on Minority Faculty Representation," *American Economic Review*, 92(2): 296–301.

National Academy of Sciences (US), National Academy of Engineering (US), and Institute of Medicine (US) Committee on Underrepresented Groups and the Expansion of the Science and Engineering Workforce Pipeline (2011), *Expanding Underrepresented Minority Participation*. Washington, DC: The National Academies Press.

Office of Management and Budget (1997), "Revisions to the Standards for the Classification of Federal Data on Race and Ethnicity," at www.whitehouse.gov/omb/fedreg/1997standards.html (accessed August 18, 2016).

Parra, E. J., A. Marcini, J. Akey, J. Martinson, M. A. Balzer, R. Cooper, et al. (2009), "Estimating African American Admixture Proportion by the Use of Population Specific Alleles," *American Journal of Human Genetics*, 63: 1839–851.

Price, Gregory N. (2009), "The Problem of the 21st Century: Economics Faculty and the Color Line," *Journal of Socio-Economics*, 38: 331–43.

Risch, Neil, Esteban Burchard, Elad Ziv, and Hua Tang (2002), "Categorization of Humans in Biomedical Research: Genes, Race and Disease," *Genome Biology*, 3: 1–13.

Root, Michael (2000), "How We Divide the World," *Philosophy of Science*, 67 (Proceedings): S628–S639.

Root, Michael (2005), "The Number of Black Widows in the National Academy of Sciences," *Philosophy of Science*, 72: 1197–208.

Root, Michael (2009), "Measurement Error in Racial and Ethnic Statistics," *Biology and Philosophy*, 24: 375–85.

Ruggles, Patricia (1990), *Drawing the Line: Alternative Poverty Measures and Their Implications for Public Policy*. Washington, DC: The Urban Institute.

Scott, Charles E. and John J. Siegfried (2013), "American Economic Association Universal Academic Questionnaire Summary Statistics," *American Economic Review*, 103(3): 678–82.

Smelser, Neil, William Julius Wilson, and Faith Mitchell (Eds.) (2001), *American Becoming: Racial Trends and Their Consequences*, vol. 2. Washington, DC: The National Academies Press.

Splater-Roth, Robert and William Erskin (2007), "Race and Ethnicity in the Sociological Pipeline," *ASA Research Brief*, American Sociological Association Research and Development Department, at www.asanet.org/images/research/docs/pdf/Race%20and%20Ethnicity%20in%20Soc%20Pipeline.pdf (accessed August 18, 2016).

Tishkoff, S. A., F. A. Reed, F. R. Friedlaender, C. Ehret, A. Ranciaro, A. Froment, et al. (2009), "The Genetic Structure and History of African and African Americans," *Science*, 324: 1035–44.

Waters, Mary C. (2000), "Immigration, Intermarriage, and the Challenges of Measuring Racial/Ethnic Identities," *American Journal of Public Health*, 90: 1735–737.

# Part IV
# INDIVIDUAL SCIENCES

# 33
# PHILOSOPHY OF ECONOMICS

## *Don Ross*

Like most disciplines, economics grew out of origins in what we now regard as philosophy. Three of the most important early economists, Adam Smith, John Stuart Mill, and Karl Marx, are regarded as contributors to the philosophical canon. Others, such as Jean-Baptiste Say, Antoine Augustin Cournot, and David Ricardo, have been assigned by intellectual history strictly to the roster of economists. As one might expect, this reflects the wider breadth of interests of the former group. In the present age a few economists, notably Ken Binmore and Amartya Sen, regard themselves and are acknowledged as philosophers; but most economists would resist such an attribution, as implying that they tend to wander outside the boundaries of professionalism.

I open with these remarks as a way of expressing my view that the boundaries between philosophy of *x* and *x*, where *x* is an academic discipline, are institutional rather than grounded in sound methodological or ontological principles. Some work in economics is simply estimation of magnitudes or calculation of probable movements in variables given manipulation of other variables, and is of little philosophical interest except as a source of examples of practice. But all economics that involves theoretical or modeling innovation has a philosophical aspect. And much philosophical work, in decision theory and formalized political philosophy, does not differ greatly from what might be presented at an economics conference or published in an economics journal.

Institutionally, when philosophers write about economics this is called 'philosophy of economics', and when economists write reflectively and self-consciously about their own discipline it is called 'economic methodology'. Increasingly, contributors to these literatures are expected to be aware of the same bodies of prior work, which is to say that the two literatures are fusing into a single one. This is as we should want things.

The domains of the philosophy of economics can be clustered into three broad bodies of inquiry, which overlap on their boundaries.

Cluster #1 is philosophy of science applied to economics. The set of questions probed in this cluster includes the following:

(1) Which aspects of the world is economics *about*?
(2) Which assumptions about the structure of reality do economists tend to take for granted?
(3) Are there distinctive economic methods, and if so are they justified by the nature of economists' subject matter?
(4) What features that are not strictly institutional and historical distinguish economics from neighboring disciplines, particularly the psychology of valuation, and sociology?

(5) Are there distinctive ways in which economists try to explain phenomena, and if so how well and how reliably do they succeed?

(6) The rhetoric of economics places considerable emphasis on empirical prediction. In light of this, how impressive is economists' track record of successful forecasting? What, in general, can economists typically predict successfully and what can they not?

(7) Most economists aim to design, promote, and criticize policy. In this respect economics resembles engineering. What, if anything, stands in the relationship to economic policy design that physics occupies with respect to physical engineering?

Mapped onto the grand sub-disciplines of philosophy, questions (1) and (2) are mainly *onto-logical*, questions (3) and (6) are mainly *epistemological*, and the others combine ontological and epistemological inquiry.

Cluster #2 studies the moral and ethical presuppositions and implications of economics. Leading questions debated within this cluster include the following:

(1) Do economic theories cope, and cope successfully, with the broad range of values that motivate people and that people valorize in themselves and others? To the extent that the answer is 'no'—implying that economists model only a sub-set of human normative drivers—does this lead to moral and ethical distortion in the policy advice that economists and others derive from their work?

(2) To what extent is economics motivated by, and to what extent does it motivate, political ideology?

(3) To what extent does work by economists tend to shore up status quo values, both political and moral?

(4) Much of economics is concerned with discovering ways of fostering the growth and spread of human material well-being. To what extent is this in tension with human well-being more broadly considered? To what extent does economists' emphasis on growth undermine efforts to preserve long-run sustainable environments, both natural and artificial?

(5) Economists typically favor using market mechanisms to solve allocation and distribution problems (though the mechanisms in question are often to be chosen and put in place by governments). To what extent does this tend to undermine community values that markets tend to erode, and to what extent is that something that should be resisted?

(6) To what extent is economics *imperialistic*? That is, to what extent does it privilege a cer-tain way of considering problems and solutions that is characteristic to specific professional guild, class, gender, or cultural roles and values?

Cluster #3 groups work that interrogates the meaning and consistency of economists' *concepts*. Historically, the most important of these concepts by far has been *rationality*. To what extent do economists presuppose that people *actually are*, or *should be*, rational in ways that actual people are not, or perhaps should not strive to be? To what extent are economists' ideas about rationality—particularly as incorporated in the formal theories of decision and choice on which they rely—narrow or misguided norms by comparison with wider standards considered by phi-losophers? A second economic concept that has preoccupied philosophers of economics is *wel-fare*. To what extent do the notions of welfare that figure in economists' analyses and policy proposals involve a pinched, unduly materialistic, or unduly individualistic, understanding of human flourishing?

The above schema sets the organization principle for the present chapter; I will comment on each cluster that makes up the philosophy of economics in sequence. I will devote most space to cluster #3, because that has been the dominant cluster in the literature. The thrust of my critical argument, however, will be that the attention devoted to this cluster has been seriously out of proportion to its importance. I will conclude hopefully, however, by pointing the reader toward some of the emerging work in clusters #1 and #2 that shows promise of dominating the future philosophy of economics.

## Core Economic Concepts

### *Rationality*

All of economics is concerned with how some *agent* could do something better or best. I refer to 'agents' rather than 'people', because in many economic models the agents are firms, or households, or governments, or teams. In some recent economic models they are parts of people's brains that have goals of their own (Montague and Berns 2002), or time slices of people that have temporary priorities (O'Donoghue and Rabin 1999, 2001; Bénabou and Tirole 2004; Benhabib and Bisin 2004). (As an example of such a property, a smoker in withdrawal wants a cigarette more than anything else, but once she has it she might experience regret and wish she hadn't had it. Most temporary priorities are not pathological. In the early flush of love a person wants to be with their lover and scarcely cares about anything else by comparison; but the secret to long and happy marriages is managing the transition *out* of that transient state of preference, and most people would choose, if they could, to be in that kind of state only from time to time.) And there is a thriving literature that applies economic modeling to the behavior of non-human animals (Noë, van Hoof, and Hammerstein 2001).

An agent is by definition an entity that chooses among different alternative courses of action, and does so by reference to her assessment of their comparative values to her. Such assessments must be based on information, which might or might not be accurate. The agent must also have beliefs about which courses of action are likely to lead to which outcomes; and some of her beliefs might be false. In general, then, we cannot assume that whatever an agent does is what she *preferred* to do. On the other hand, if there is not a general *probabilistic* relationship between these things, we have no basis for regarding the agent as an agent at all. Since my mother entered into the most advanced stage of Alzheimer's several years ago she remains a human being but is no longer an economic agent, because her behavior reveals nothing about her preferences, if it even makes sense to say that she has preferences.

Both economists and philosophers gloss all this by saying that an economic agent is *rational*. The economist assesses rationality with respect only to whether chosen means tend reliably to bring about the agent's preferred outcomes. Some philosophers, however, in the tradition of Aristotle, also address themselves to the question of whether goals are rational in themselves. Other philosophers, followers of Immanuel Kant, hold that it can never be rational to prefer to do moral harm. Economists, however, are almost united in declining to pronounce on what preferences an agent ought to have. A Bond villain who wants to destroy the Earth with a death ray is rational to want to eliminate Bond, less rational in bringing the live Bond within proximity of his HQ's self-destruct button, more irrational still in having a self-destruct mechanism in the first place; but the economist does not call him irrational for preferring a devastated Earth. So insofar as philosophers inquire into what sort of life is best for a person, they are not doing philosophy of economics. In this respect John Rawls (1971), in maintaining that a just society should accommodate a plurality of conceptions of the good, sides with the economists.

The idea that rational agency consists in always choosing what is best for her from within the set of options made available by her budget usually fails to apply to real people (or real firms, or real households) for two general reasons. First, people (etc.) change their minds about what they want. Sometimes they are never quite sure what they want, or like to pretend to themselves that they want something other than what they really do. Such inconsistency is most manifest when choices are spread out over time. And certainly no one thinks that a ten-year-old has, or should be expected to have, the same preferences as her forty-year-old self. Second, economists often build into their applications of what they call 'rationality' that an agent uses all of the information available to her in assessing the course of action that is most likely to optimize her preferences. But few agents, including even very sophisticated and highly incentivized ones like hedge fund managers, actually do this.

It has recently been fashionable for *behavioral* economists to call for a revolution in economics that, they say, would arise if economists put agents based on real, less-than-fully rational, people into their models (Thaler 1992; Camerer et al. 2005; Ariely 2008). Under what circumstances would this actually be revolutionary? Economists model agents as rational by attributing *utility functions* to them. The key property of a utility function is that its output is either an ordered list of states of the world that ranks them from most preferred to least preferred, or that assigns relative magnitudes of desirability to them in some measurable units. Utility functions actually used by economists vary widely with respect to their inputs. What is critical is that utility functions must be integrable, because what economists mainly want to do with them is ask: If every one of a group of interacting agents are all trying to optimize their utility functions under conditions of scarcity they face collectively, what will happen? The answer to that question is what economists call an *equilibrium*. If the utility functions that describe the behavior of real, less-than-fully rational people can't be integrated—if, for example, as one adds new behavioral observations the functions jump from being concave to convex or vice versa—then we would need to stop doing economics and guide economic policy choice entirely on the basis of other sciences, particularly the psychology of valuation. But various methods are available for constructing usable utility functions for representing complicated human behavioral patterns. For my own preferred general strategy, see Andersen et al. (2010).

A very large proportion—perhaps the majority—of publications in the philosophy of economics have in one way or another been about the extent to which people are, or should be, rational in the sense that economists need them to be in order to apply the mathematics of joint optimization to them. In my view this has mainly resulted from the heavy normative load carried by the word 'rational'. To call someone 'irrational' is, after all, a serious criticism. But the question of how to make real behavior representable by utility functions is a technical question, not a philosophical one; as the Andersen et al. (2010) solution referred to above illustrates, it is largely a matter of clever econometrics, that is, of finding ways of writing down descriptive equations that can be solved to generate optimizable output. Admittedly, for most of the history of economics, before economists had easy access to very powerful computers, they were forced to resort to simplifications in their modeling that left most individual human behavior beyond their powers of representation. Worse, since economists are generally interested in the consequences of the *interaction* of utility functions in groups of agents, they have been forced to represent all interacting functions in a given model as having the same structure. McFadden (1974) showed in principle how to solve this problem, but the solution in question still required imposition of strong simplifying restrictions given the computational power then within most economists' reach. (For readers who have studied advanced economics: in the 1970s using McFadden's solution required assuming that everyone's utility function could be estimated with minimal bias using a conditional logit procedure.) The nearly limitless power of contemporary econometric estimation packages has largely banished this constraint.

I do not think that we should expect to make much progress in the philosophy of economics by debating how 'rational' people are. It matters a great deal in economic applications how people's preferences are structured, and how these structures are conditioned on variables in their environments, including parts of their own brains that are like external variables in being beyond individuals' direct power to influence. This takes us into issues of methodology, epistemology, and ontology that are the subjects of the philosophy of science. They will not be solved by analyzing the concept of rationality, or any other concept.

It also matters a great deal in economic applications how much information agents use, and how accurately they represent information, when they make choices. Economists sometimes say that 'expectations' are 'rational' when and only when agents soundly bring *all* information that is in principle available to them to bear in making economic choices. This is so bizarre a use of the concept of rationality that philosophers can be forgiven for wondering if economists are actually acquainted with human beings. In fact, the point of promoting 'rational expectations' can be rendered into a simple, and thoroughly sensible, methodological principle, stated as follows by Xavier Ragot (2012, 187–88): "If the economist builds a theory or model in which the agents fail to do something that it is in their interests to do, then the economist must justify why they did not do it." Note that Ragot's formulation requires no reference to rationality. The soundness of the principle lies in the fact that the economist who doesn't use it is arbitrarily supposing that agents are just exactly as lazy in gathering or computing information as her model requires. Of course that would be bad scientific procedure and we shouldn't need to rely on philosophers to point it out.

### Welfare

If debates about the concept of rationality have been a red herring that has massively distracted writers on the philosophy of economics, the similar situation that prevails where the concept of welfare is concerned is still more serious in its consequences. Obsessing over the concept of rationality imperils sound appreciation of the value of economics. Obsessing over the concept of welfare can distract us from devoting attention to some of the worst barriers to dignified and enjoyable human lives.

Economists are motivated by the ambition to recommend policies that allow societies, or firms, or households, or (only very occasionally) individual people to be *efficient*, that is, to avoid choices that gratuitously throw away welfare. Imagine, for example, that a government decided that house prices should reflect only 'intrinsic' consumption values of houses, rather than all the contingencies embodied in market-driven prices, and so decreed that all house prices should be set as a function of floorspace. Any economist could tell us what would result. Prices of houses in big cities would be fixed below market prices relative to prices of country houses, so existing owners of city houses would stop selling them, instead planning to keep them for their children to inherit. Prices of country houses would be fixed above market prices, so their occupants would be unable to sell them. City dwellers who wanted to move to the country would face a penalty, so many would stay in the city against their preferences;

and country dwellers who wanted to move to the city would be forced to stay in the country. The construction industry would respond by building only urban rental blocks and large houses in cities that only the wealthy could afford, and country houses that were smaller than what people who wanted to live in the country actually preferred. No government in its right mind would ever pass a law of this type because it pointlessly throws away welfare in the following sense: most people would no longer be able to choose the size of house they prefer in the location they prefer. There would be a few winners, namely people with unusually large suburban houses. Few would think that their gains could possibly outweigh the widespread losses.

Economists tend to treat all welfare calculations in the spirit of the fanciful example above: a society or household optimizes its welfare to the extent that its individual members can optimize the vector of values in their utility functions subject to their budget constraints. Room is immediately opened for asking how this concept of welfare is related to other concepts that feature in broader understandings of human flourishing. Standard economic welfare measurement that doesn't attempt to estimate so-called 'shadow prices' ignores the value of sources of well-being that can't be directly or indirectly exchanged on markets. This includes important goods that markets tend to under-supply because their consumption can't typically be restricted to those who paid for them. A pressing example of such a public good in many countries is efficient urban transport infrastructure; the most urgent example at the global scale is control of carbon emissions. Welfare as economic efficiency also ignores the historical processes that produced the status quo distributions of assets in the markets that do exist. In the real world, where house prices are driven by the interaction of supply and demand, changes in the structure of labor markets are pushing up relative house prices in large cities with well-educated populations and depressing them elsewhere. This is an unearned windfall for people who already owned urban real estate and an undeserved source of exclusion for those whose investments are tied up in the countryside or in peripheral cities. According to the standard welfare criteria of economists, the dynamics are welfare-improving just in case the urban winners are enjoying large enough gains that they *could* compensate the rural and peripheral losers, though whether changes in taxation will be introduced to actually bring about this compensation is a separate matter.

Questions about how societies should negotiate inequality, or provide people with access to sources of well-being they can't—or that most can't—buy in the marketplace, or fund public goods are among the most important of all human political and cultural problems. However, it is implausible to think that an important part of their solution lies in revising *concepts* of welfare and flourishing. The economist's concept of welfare is sensible and important; policies that gratuitously waste it should almost always be avoided. But such policies are far from rare; every economist could produce a list of the ones that most annoy her. To the extent that attention to economic welfare tends to crowd out other aspects of human flourishing in policy evaluation and implementation processes, we are led to consider the issues identified above as falling into cluster #2.

I have devoted most of the space available to me in this chapter to cluster #3 issues, only to reach the negative conclusion that they aren't very important. This reflects the fact that most of the literature in the philosophy of economics has been preoccupied with them. Fortunately there are signs that a new philosophy of economics, one much more closely anchored in the details of everyday economic practice, is gaining institutional strength. To these hopeful indicators I now turn (beginning with cluster #1).

## Economic Science

Since the eruption of the global financial crisis in late 2008 it has been fashionable for critics to cast doubt on the claims by economists that they are actually experts on anything. One frequently hears it said that economists failed to predict the problems in the US housing market that spread into the global banking industry and through that channel caused the most serious contraction of global wealth since the Great Depression. Some sophisticated critics—e.g. Orlean (2014)—have gone so far as to blame economists for the crisis. Economists, according to such critics, encouraged both bankers and their regulators to complacently assume that diversification of risk across markets was sufficient to contain it. It was not noticed, this critic continues, that diversification of risk implied *correlation* of risk, so that as soon as a few big banks were seen to be holding more debt than they could bear, it would be instantly obvious that *all* were over-geared, thus triggering a generalized collapse of confidence. Economists' emphasis on the efficiency of global markets in allocating risk and distributing responsibility to those who were best placed to measure it, the critic concludes, led those outside the industry to discount the danger that those same agents might be 'greedy' and 'irrational', prone to destabilize the overall system in pursuit of ever-higher profits and then to panic the moment their over-exposure to unrecoverable housing loans was exposed (Akerlof and Shiller 2009).

This populist attack on economics squares poorly with the actual record. Skeptics about the value of economics might, for example, be referred to Edward Leamer's (2008) study of the history of the US business cycle since World War II, written for non-specialists on the very eve of disaster. Through careful sifting of data, undistracted by any grand, over-arching theoretical bias, but alert to the multiple interacting network of causal relationships in the national-scale market for goods, services, real estate, and financial assets, Leamer identifies the indicators of looming trouble, particularly the huge expansion in the housing stock relative to increases in overall GDP, that were then flashing red. His review echoes the numerous conversations among economists that I remember from as early as 2005, which were strongly picked up by the mainstream economics media. *The Economist*, for example, produced repeated warnings for over three years that mortgage debt levels threatened 'Main Street' through the channel of 'Wall Street', a point illustrated on one front-cover cartoon that showed houses falling out of the sky onto bank towers and factories (Posner 2009; Ross 2010). The journalists at *The Economist* get their economic forecasts by talking with broad samples of economists.

The philosophy of science literature that has focused on economics has long emphasized the predictive power—and problems with it—associated with economic models. This has closely reflected the actual rhetoric of economists.

The last comment is best framed by taking a step back. Prior to World War II the closest economists came to having a single 'establishment' approach to their subject matter—and it wasn't very close—was reflected in the evolution through various editions of Alfred Marshall's *Principles of Economics* (1890/2013). Marshall emphasizes piecemeal systematization of observations of the practices of businesses. By 'systematization' (which isn't Marshall's word) I refer to representing these practices in a simplified way by a universally applicable framework of pricing and rates of production and investment in capital stock. Such systematization, Marshall argues, can allow the economist to identify recurrent *trends* in commercial activity by directing her attention to variables that tend to shift together and portend what we would now call 'macro-scale' inflections and shocks. However, Marshall cautions, the economist is generally not in a position to predict the timing of economic events on a scale that would allow short-run investors to profit from the knowledge. Note carefully the emphasis on 'short-run'. Anyone could have benefited from Leamer's, or *The Economist's*, analysis in 2008 or earlier by selling their house and signing a rental lease. By contrast, only a tiny number of (lucky) investors were able to make spectacular profits by shorting Goldman Sachs and other large investment banks at exactly the right moment just before the crash. This says more about the (standard) relationship between very large risks and very large profits than it does about the expertise of economists. In one of the most astute general polemics in recent philosophy of economics, Sutton (2000) defends Marshall's view of economic prediction as still conforming, in fact, to the understanding most working economists share concerning the value they add for their clients in industry and government.

The loose Marshallian dominance at the apex of the profession, however, ended decisively after World War II. The landmark of the transition was the publication of Paul Samuelson's *Foundations of Economic Analysis* (1947/1983). As Samuelson made clear in the prefaces he wrote to successive editions of the book, he aimed to make economics 'scientific' by reconstructing what he took to be the sound economics of his day (by which he mainly meant a rough synthesis of then standard marginalist and ordinalist microeconomics with Keynesian macroeconomics as interpreted by John Hicks) on the basis of "operationally meaningful theorems." Though he did not cite the philosopher of science Karl Popper, by 'meaningful' Samuelson meant 'falsifiable'. What rendered a theorem falsifiable, according to him, was precision. This he equated with mathematical formalization.

Samuelson's plea for, and demonstration of, the mathematical turn was a resounding institutional success. Before the 1950s, most articles in leading economics journals were merely decorated with smatterings of mathematics. Beginning in the mid-1960s, an economist could not expect to publish in the discipline's leading journals unless the core of his or her paper consisted of a mathematical model accompanied by a proof of a unique stationary equilibrium. Samuelson's accompanying falsificationist philosophy of science was equally successful, at least rhetorically.

Economists' writings on methodology during the decades after the *Foundations* were sparse. Philosophers of science at that time devoted almost no attention to economics, their preoccupations being either abstracted away from actual science altogether, or focused almost exclusively on physics. However, almost all such remarks on methodology as economists vouchsafed in those years were Popperian in character. Later this was supplemented by nods in the direction of the philosopher Imre Lakatos, who revised Popper's stringent falsificationism by adding the significant qualification that sound scientific theory typically included a 'hard core' of assumptions that are not directly subject to empirical test. The historian of economics Mark Blaug (1980) stated the Popperian rhetorical orthodoxy in one of the few book-length methodological treatises that economists noticed, while also sternly taking his fellow economists to task for failing to live up to it. Economists, Blaug argued, professed adherence to falsificationism despite being preoccupied with formal models and showing little interest in testing them against data.

Some economists during the years under consideration defended their lack of interest in testing theory by appealing to a discipline-specific form of operationalism rather than to Lakatos. In one of the few methodological texts that the majority of economists have actually read, Milton Friedman (1953) opened this line of defense. Friedman argues that economics is pursued for the sake of practical policy rather than scientific explanation. In consequence, the theoretical propositions that constrain it are to be understood not as empirical generalizations but simply as tools for constructing models of specific relationships. This view has affinities with some versions of logical empiricism that also disavow explanation or concern for the truth, as opposed to the consistency and power in generating predictions, of general propositions. However, as Mäki (2009) points out, empiricist skittishness about endorsing the truth of theoretical generalizations in sciences such as physics has been based on the alleged unobservability of the central entities figuring in the generalizations; whereas Friedman follows the tradition of Robbins (1935) in taking the subject matter of economics to be accessible to everyday observation. Friedman might respond by disassociating his view from the positions in general philosophy of science which, as Mäki argues, it fits awkwardly amongst, on grounds that economics doesn't pretend to be a science. This response would anticipate a recently popular view among economists (e.g. Leamer 2012) according to which economics is a 'craft' rather than a science. Ross (2016) argues that this attitude depends on a simplistic philosophical interpretation of paradigmatic sciences such as physics. In any event, even if Friedman were thought to provide a sound defense of economists' unconcern with testing their core theories, he clearly must assign very great weight to empirical testing of economic predictions. Blaug would respond that economists—or at least the economists of his day—are no more inclined in fact to test their predictions than they are to test their theories.

Blaug's charge of insincere empiricism was typically repeated by the few philosophers of science who were interested in economics in the later twentieth century. Alexander Rosenberg (1992), though no Popperian himself, echoed Blaug's theme that economists, despite their Samuelsonian rhetoric, showed little interest in testing their theories against empirical data. The Lakatosian dodge impressed neither Blaug nor Rosenberg; it is one thing for scientists to allow a hard core of theory to go untested, but quite another thing to operate a science that seemed to consist of nothing *but* a hard core. In the economics of the 1960s through the 1980s this was particularly manifest in the prestige accorded to discovering properties of economies in general equilibrium, that is, in which *all* consumption and production are represented simultaneously and no consumer or producer is failing to do the best they can. As the conditions for general equilibrium never prevail in any real economy, and as states that are formally 'close' to general equilibrium do not predict economic conditions similar to those that would be predicted in general equilibrium (Lipsey and Lancaster 1956), much of the economics published by the discipline's leading figures of the period resembled the purest philosophy, in being investigation of a wholly abstract, *merely* possible world that was interesting only for what it showed about the technical concept of efficiency.

In retrospect we can see what was missing from both Samuelson's understanding of economics and that of the skeptics just considered: recognition of the fact that most empirical science, notably including physics (Morgan and Morrison 1999), consists in testing statistical estimations of models constructed and interpreted under the guidance of theories. This allows for clearer identification of the Lakatosian hard core than Lakatos achieved: economists typically test models informed by theory, and almost never directly test background axioms. We can now also see, from the contemporary vantage point, why economists seemed overly focused on their hard core until the 1980s. First there was the problem, noted earlier in connection with McFadden's work, that they lacked the computational power or the statistical technology to often perform the identifications on which model discriminations that matter really turn. Second, and equally important, they had not yet fully absorbed game theory into their basic tool-kit.

Ross (2014) is among a number of philosophers of economics who view the importation of game theory into economics as having been fundamentally transformative (see also Sutton

2001). The Nash equilibrium concept and its relatives—particularly Bayes-Nash equilibrium, which allows for players to hold uncertain beliefs (Harsanyi 1967)—generalized the traditional economic equilibrium and allowed it to be applied to agents who hold less than complete information, and differ from one another in the information available to them. This in turn has facilitated the following crucial advances:

(1) Economists are no longer restricted to modeling industries as either monopolistic or perfectly competitive. Most actual industries are oligopolies, that is, dominated by a small number of major firms. Thus game theory allows economists to give strategic advice to businesspeople, in the sense of allowing them to identify strategies that imply dangerous unpredictability because they are not equilibrium strategies, or that, equally dangerously, depend on competitors failing to work out their best responses. No one should invest in a business model that depends on suboptimal behavior by competitors—here we see a sound application of Ragot's formulation of 'rational' expectations.

(2) Once economists could model specific strategic situations and treat them as partially isolated from the larger economy—which is to say, from a *fictitious* larger economy in general equilibrium—then the philosophical issues associated with isolation in economics came to resemble those observed in other sciences, including physics (Cartwright 1983, 1989; Mäki 1992, 2009)

(3) The game-theoretic context brought into technical economics a point that had been made by Friedrich Hayek (1945) years before, but never cleanly exemplified in disciplinary practice: that markets are fundamentally *information-processing* phenomena; so if economics is the science that studies markets, then economics is among the sciences of information (Martens 2004; Herrmann-Pillath 2013; Ross 2014).

Game theory, I contend, along with Sutton (2000), has allowed economists to return to the sensible practices advocated by Marshall, and has rendered economics no longer peculiar among the empirical sciences, as one more devoted to proving formal theorems than identifying and estimating empirical relationships.

## Economic and Other Valuation

Space limitations prevent a systematic review of the issues I identified a falling into cluster #2. Fortunately most of the questions associated with cluster #2 can be understood by readers who have not yet studied economics, or philosophy of economics, even if one needs to know something of both fields to provide fully sophisticated answers to them. We can note merely that rhetorically posing the questions listed under cluster #2 does not constitute a critique of economics in itself, because sophisticated answers *have* been provided to all of them, even if these answers are always incomplete in the sense of being open to further cycles of criticism and refinement. For an outstanding but highly accessible tour through these answers, the reader is referred to Heath (2009).

Here I will confine myself to one very general theme. Many of the tensions over politics and ethics that tend to divide economists from other opinionated commentators are traced to the *individualism* that economists often espouse, and to their supposed faith in *unregulated* markets. The second attributed allegiance is something of a caricature. Though some economists, especially those associated with the University of Chicago in the second part of the twentieth century, indeed promoted the ideology of political libertarianism, only a small minority of the profession actually holds that freedom from state interference is the dominant political value. The majority of economists *do* think that governments under-use market *mechanisms*, in that they frequently try to achieve outcomes by simply issuing orders under circumstances where objectives would more likely be achieved, and at lower costs, if the orders in question were combined with structures that aligned people's incentives to seek positive rewards. For example, governments often ration scarce goods without setting up markets that would allow those who attach most value to the scarce goods in question to buy the access rights of those who value them less. An economist who calls for a 'market solution' of this kind does not thereby express disagreement with the social value served by the regulation in question; rather, she criticizes the efficiency of the way in which the regulation is designed and implemented.

Where individualism is concerned, economists might be said to have confused their critics because they have philosophically confused *themselves*. Most economists think, and say, that macroeconomics—the study of large-scale, aggregate phenomena such as inflation, unemployment, public expenditure, and interest rate determination—should have *microfoundations*. This is not unnaturally read by non-economists as meaning that all aggregate economic variables should be analyzed into, or derived from, variables that range over the behaviors, preferences, and beliefs of individual people. In fact, very little economics conforms to this attributed 'ideal'; most relationships statistically estimated by economists are, and always have been, irreducibly aggregate in character. What economists mean by 'microfoundations' in practice is simply conformity to Ragot's dictum: economic models should not feature groups or classes of agents who in principle do not learn better responses to changes in economic conditions or policies if any are available.

Ross (2014) argues that economists' rhetorical espousal of very casually formulated statements of 'individualism' typically stems from widespread failure on their part to distinguish *normative* individualism from *descriptive* individualism. The former refers to the Enlightenment conviction that individuals, not groups, are the centers of human dignity and valuation that most *deserve* valorization. In modern democracies this is a normative, philosophical premise that liberals and conservatives generally share. Descriptive individualism, on the other hand, refers to the view that people acquire their preferences asocially. Descriptive individualism is, in general, false: most human preferences, and almost all of the most important ones, are copied from other people or shaped under their guidance and tutelage. Indeed it can be among the reasons for valuing distinctive features of individuals that distinctiveness—particularly distinctiveness in virtue and depth of wisdom—is a person's most significant achievement in the context of the mighty information-processing and behavior-coordinating machines, modern markets, that economists mainly study.

# References

Akerlof, G., and Shiller, R. (2009). *Animal Spirits*. Princeton, NJ: Princeton University Press.

Andersen, S., Harrison, G., Lau, M., and Rutström, E. (2010). Behavioural econometrics for psychologists. *Journal of Economic Psychology* 31: 553–76.

Ariely, D. (2008). *Predictably Irrational*. New York: HarperCollins.

Bénabou, R., and Tirole, J. (2004). Willpower and personal rules. *Journal of Political Economy* 112: 848–86.

Benhabib, J., and Bisin, A. (2004). Modeling internal commitment mechanisms and self-control: A neuro-economics approach to consumption-saving decisions. *Games and Economic Behavior* 52: 460–92.

Blaug, M. (1980). *The Methodology of Economics*. Cambridge: Cambridge University Press.

Camerer, C., Loewenstein, G., and Prelec, D. (2005). Neuroeconomics: How neuroscience can inform economics. *Journal of Economic Literature* 43: 9–64.

Cartwright, N. (1983). *How the Laws of Physics Lie*. Oxford: Oxford University Press.

Cartwright, N. (1989). *Nature's Capacities and their Measurement*. Oxford: Oxford University Press.

Friedman, M. (1953). *Essays in Positive Economics*. Chicago: University of Chicago Press.

Harsanyi, J. (1967). Games with incomplete information played by 'Bayesian' players, Parts I–III. *Management Science* 14: 159–82.

Hayek, F. (1945). The use of knowledge in society. *American Economic Review* 35: 519–30.

Heath, J. (2009). *Filthy Lucre*. Toronto: HarperCollins Canada.

Herrmann-Pillath, C. (2013). *Foundations of Economic Evolution*. Cheltenham: Edward Elgar.

Leamer, E. (2008). *Macroeconomic Patterns and Stories*. Berlin: Springer.

Leamer, E. (2012). *The Craft of Economics*. Cambridge, MA: MIT Press.

Lipsey, R., and Lancaster, K. (1956). The general theory of second best. *Review of Economic Studies* 24: 11–32.

McFadden, D. (1974). Conditional logit analysis of qualitative choice behavior. In P. Zarembka, ed., *Frontiers in Econometrics*, 105–42. New York: Academic Press.

Mäki, U. (1992). On the method of isolation in economics. In C. Dilworth, ed., *Idealization IV: Intelligibility in Science*. Special issue of *Poznan Studies in the Philosophy of the Sciences and the Humanities* 26: 319–54.

Mäki, U. (2009). Realistic realism about unrealistic models. In H. Kincaid and D. Ross, eds., *The Oxford Handbook of Philosophy of Economics*, 68–98. Oxford: Oxford University Press.

Marshall, A. (1890/2013). *The Principles of Economics*, 8th edn. London: Macmillan.

Martens, B. (2004). *The Cognitive Mechanics of Economic Development and Institutional Change*. London: Routledge.

Montague, P. R., and Berns, G. (2002). Neural economics and the biological substrates of valuation. *Neuron* 36: 265–84.

Morgan, M., and Morrison, M. (1999). Models as mediating instruments. In M. Morgan and M. Morrison, eds., *Models as Mediators*, 10–37. Cambridge: Cambridge University Press.

Noë, R., van Hoof, J., and Hammerstein, P., eds. (2001). *Economics in Nature*. Cambridge: Cambridge University Press.

O'Donoghue, T., and Rabin, M. (1999). Incentives for procrastinators. *Quarterly Journal of Economics* 114: 769–816.

O'Donoghue, T., and Rabin, M. (2001). Choice and procrastination. *Quarterly Journal of Economics* 116: 121–60.

Orlean, A. (2014). *The Empire of Value*. Cambridge, MA: MIT Press.

Posner, R. (2009). *A Failure of Capitalism*. Cambridge, MA: Harvard University Press.

Ragot, X. (2012). The economics of the laboratory mouse: Where do we go from here? in R. Solow and J.-P. Touffut, eds., *What's Right with Macroeconomics?* 181–94. Cheltenham: Edward Elgar.

Rawls, J. (1971). *A Theory of Justice*. Cambridge, MA: Harvard University Press.

Robbins, L. (1935). *An Essay on the Nature and Significance of Economic Science*, 2nd edn. London: Macmillan.

Rosenberg, A. (1992). *Economics: Mathematical Politics or Science of Diminishing Returns?* Chicago: University of Chicago Press.

Ross, D. (2010). Should the financial crisis inspire normative revision? *Journal of Economic Methodology* 17: 399–418.

Ross, D. (2014). *Philosophy of Economics*. Houndmills, Basingstoke: Palgrave Macmillan.

Ross, D. (2016). Economics and allegations of scientism. In M. Pigliucci and M. Boudry, eds., *Science Unlimited?* University of Chicago Press, forthcoming.

Samuelson, P. (1947/1983). *Foundations of Economic Analysis*, enlarged edn. Cambridge, MA: Harvard University Press.

Sutton, J. (2000). *Marshall's Tendencies*. Cambridge, MA: MIT Press.

Sutton, J. (2001). *Technology and Market Structure*, 2nd edn. Cambridge, MA: MIT Press.

Thaler, R. (1992). *The Winner's Curse*. New York: Free Press.

# 34
# PHILOSOPHY OF HISTORY

## *Paul A. Roth*

### In the Beginning

If one were to construct a type of genealogical chart, it would show analytic philosophy of history as the runt of a litter of topics sprung from philosophy of science in its youth.[1] Birth could plausibly be dated with the publication of Carl Hempel's classic article, "The Function of General Laws in History" (Hempel 1942). There Hempel stipulates as a condition for the scientific/logical adequacy of historical explanations that they contain a covering law. Absent some law or law-like connection between the explanandum statement and those serving as explanantia, historical explanations constitute at best "explanation sketches." Notoriously, this did not just imply that historians simply needed to logically tidy up their presentations. Rather, inasmuch as historians had no laws to insert, they had no genuine explanations on offer.

Hempelian and related models of (scientific) explanation result in a *de facto* exile of academic history from the realm of legitimate sciences. An ensuing debate about explanatory form thus initially serves as an important impetus for analytic philosophers to examine what counts as explanation in histories. As Louis O. Mink notes, "It could be said without exaggeration that until about 1965 the critical [i.e. analytic] philosophy of history was the controversy over the covering-law model" (Mink 1987a, 169). Since that time sea changes have ensued in philosophical fashion regarding accounts of explanation and all of those related topics that at first estrange historiography from consideration within philosophy of science. As it happens, an almost total neglect of historical explanation within philosophy of science turns out to accompany these philosophical shifts, a neglect that persists largely unabated to this day (see especially Danto 1995).

But why does philosophy of history suffer this peculiar fate? Consideration of some of the epistemological concerns that underlay debates inspired by Hempel's models suggests a reason that helps account for its persistent orphaned status. Exercises in analysis such as Hempel's focus on identifying formal criteria that would also be normative for what could count as an explanation. But as debates around Hempelian models lapse into epicycles in the 1960s, emphasis in historiography comes to fall on narrative form as *the* salient characteristic of historical explanation. (For a canonical overview, see Salmon 1990.) By the mid-1970s there had been a basic shift *away* from consideration of Hempel-like models of explanation and a movement towards consideration of narrative as the *sui generis* form of historical explanation. Indeed, discussion of narrative achieves in that moment an ascendency within historical theory under the powerful influence exerted by Hayden White's work that it has yet to relinquish.[2] But this focus on narrative *form* proves inhospitable to *epistemic* analysis. For narrative theory does not yield criteria, formal or otherwise, that holds any promise of providing what analytic philosophers desire—normative benchmarks for goodness of explanation (see Vann 1995 and Mink 1987a). Thus the "rise of narrative" and its related seeming resistance or indifference to epistemic interests accounts for, I suggest, the "parting of the ways" between philosophy of science and historiography.

However, this timing proves to be quite ironic. For just as discussion of historical explanation within philosophy of science effectively ceases, Thomas S. Kuhn's *The Structure of Scientific Revolutions* begins to exert its important and ongoing influence on philosophical views about science (see Roth 2013). The irony concerns the fact that inasmuch as history did not achieve even *prima facie* scientific status by the philosophical standards prevailing in the early 1960s, it should have been impossible for a history of science to challenge accounts of scientific rationality. Nonetheless, Kuhn's historical practice here trumps philosophical dogma. Indeed, Kuhn helps create within philosophy a powerful and (for some) unsettling historicized view of scientific (and ultimately philosophical) rationality. Alan Richardson aptly characterizes subsequent debates as offering competing "histories of reason," albeit non-Hegelian and non-Whiggish ones (see Richardson 2002 and 2003; Domski and Dickson 2010; and Zammito 2004).

More generally, while disputes about the nature of science and logic based on differing histories prove ongoing, what makes for the goodness of historical argument remains unexamined and unexplicated. But this continuing neglect of historical explanation imperils and impedes philosophical self-understanding. For a concern with history as a systematic form of empirical inquiry inevitably links analytic philosophy of history and philosophy of science. And inasmuch as philosophical developments starting in the 1960s fundamentally alter the relationship between history and philosophy of science, a dilemma arises. If philosophers of science deny explanatory legitimacy to narratives, they fail to account for why differing histories of science exert a critical influence on a *philosophical* understanding of science. If philosophers of science accept narratives as explanatory, they still owe an account of why. In short, failure to accommodate narrative explanations marks an important deficit in philosophical self-understanding. There needs then to be a refounding of how philosophy of history and philosophy of science interconnect, one that recognizes if not a priority of the former vis-à-vis the latter, then at least their near parity. Moreover, this dilemma holds *a fortiori* for how philosophy of history relates to other areas of philosophy as well (see Roth 2011 and Kuukkanen 2015).

If philosophy of science cannot escape engagement with philosophy of history and the topic of historical explanation, then that means taking up once again narrative as a form of explanation. For narrative must be recognized as not simply a characteristic form of histories, but also an inescapable one as well (Little 2010). And any philosophic quest regarding the epistemic and explanatory characteristics of narrative best begins, I suggest, by taking a renewed look at what Arthur Danto and Louis Mink had to say decades ago about narrative form and its role in historical explanation. Each identifies epistemic factors unique to narrative form. In addition, Mink long insisted that history ought to serve as a test case for any theory of knowledge. Specifically, he maintained that history cannot be assimilated to any other discipline that claims to provide empirical knowledge due to its characteristic form as narrative.

The claim of a narrative history is that its structure is a contribution, not just a literary artifice for the presentation of a series of factual descriptions. Yet classical theories of knowledge have never even formulated the problem of the relation of statements of fact to narrative structure, as they have formulated and discussed in detail the relation of statements of fact to the structure of scientific theories.

(Mink 1987a, 168)

But given the philosophical *Zeitgeist* prevailing when they wrote, neither Danto nor Mink were paid any heed.[3] And indeed philosophical orthodoxy remains wedded to the view that analyses of narrative prove orthogonal to epistemic interests.[4] Yet as shall be shown, their insights remain invaluable to any serious consideration of this topic.

## The Logic of Narratives: Three Theses

This sets a basic philosophical challenge for those interested in the "logic" or "form" of narrative explanations. Daniel Little offers the following helpful gloss of what 'narrative' means: "it is an account of the unfolding of a series of events, along with an effort to explain how and why these processes and events came to be. A narrative is intended to provide an account of how a complex historical event unfolded and why. ... So a narrative seeks to provide hermeneutic understanding of the outcome ... and causal explanation" (Little 2010, 29). Mink helps fill out what this holistic characterization of narrative implies by what I shall call the *non-detachability thesis*. "But despite the fact that an historian may 'summarize' conclusions in his final chapter, it seems clear that these are seldom or never detachable conclusions .... The significant conclusions ... are ingredient in the argument itself ... in the sense that they are *represented by the narrative order itself*. As ingredient conclusions they are *exhibited* rather than *demonstrated*" (Mink 1987b, 79; see also Mink 1987a, 172; Fay et al. 1987, 11). In a sense elaborated below, events explained by histories exist *qua* events only as constructions of those histories. Primarily as a consequence of this feature narratives explain only by virtue of the narrative order itself.

Danto, I believe, coins the phrase 'narrative explanation' (Danto 1965, 237).[5] Subsequently it comes to name that form of explanation specific to history, and has come to capture those differences already in play prior to Hempel's article. What makes 'narrative explanation' something other than an oxymoron by Danto's own lights concerns how the term 'narrative' figures in his justly famous *Gedankenexperiment* regarding an Ideal Chronicle and so the role Danto attributes to narrative sentences (another Danto coinage) (see Danto 1962). Danto's narrative sentences demonstrate that all statements true of a time *t* could *not* be known true at time *t*, even by a being with perfect apprehension of all that happens as it happens. For truths about *t* continue to accrue after *t*; e.g. (A): "The Thirty Years War began in 1618." Danto observes that (A) is true *of* 1618 but not knowable as true *then* even by a being with perfect knowledge of all that happens at each moment in 1618. Knowledge of this truth has *nothing* to do with some notion of correspondence between statements and states of affairs, since *ex hypothesi* no "facts" alter regarding any moment in question. So much the worse then for any hope of an Ideal Chronicle.

Danto terms sentences like (A) 'narrative' because they relate a later event to an earlier one in a way that indicates a *conceptual/theoretical* connection. Narrative sentences reveal something known true of an earlier time *in light of* a later. Additional truths continue to accrue to past times just because the passage of time reveals what *antecedents* of later happenings were latent in earlier ones.

Put another way, narrative sentences create new events under novel descriptions.[6] *Historical events only exist as events under a description, and descriptions continuously emerge and change retrospectively*. In short, historians look to explain an event as it exists under a particular description, a description that ties to a retrospective and so what I am here terming a "narrative perspective." As Danto puts it:

> Completely to describe an event is to locate it in all the right stories, and this we cannot do. We cannot because we are temporally provincial with regard to the future. … The complete description then presupposes a narrative organization, and narrative organization is something that we do. Not merely that, but the imposition of a narrative organization logically involves us with an inexpungeable subjective factor. There is an element of sheer arbitrariness in it.
>
> (Danto 1965, 142)

Here we find the beginnings of a philosophical rationale for the metaphysical plurality and epistemic legitimacy of *competing* narratives. (For a development of this view, see Roth 2012.)

Narrative *sentences* do *not* constitute a *narrative* in any theoretically relevant sense of that term, but typically they imply one. Danto takes such "antecedents revealed in retrospect" as a defining mark of the historical. The *implied* narrative would develop an account of how that later time shapes our understanding and significance of earlier, one that that period of time has now but could not be known to have then.

Moreover, narrative *sentences* do not determine the *content* of an implied connection, but only broadly demarcate events for narrative fashioning. As Mink observes (Mink 1987c, 184), Huizinga's *The Waning of the Middle Ages* by its very title adumbrates a narrative sentence, i.e. one that creates an event by postulating a conceptual connection between earlier and later points. Put in the context of the theory of narrative explanation that I am elaborating, Huizinga's title conjures into existence a large-scale event, one naming a historical transition about which more can then be known. Fashioning this macro-event then makes it possible to specify truths about some earlier times knowable only as a result of later developments.

Yet Danto's use of the term 'narrative' invites confusion between, on the one hand, *conceptually* relating an earlier time to some later one and, on the other hand, offering an *actual* narrative that develops that relation. Only the latter counts as what theorists in this area think of as a narrative. Even more, Danto's still important analysis of temporal language and his coinage of the term 'narrative explanation' does *not* signal any interest or basis in his own work for a defense of narrative as itself a legitimate form of historical explanation. Rather, his notion of a narrative sentence makes vivid and compelling a reason why our human relationship to history will always be dynamic and not static. For the passage of time inevitably reveals truths about the significance of past times not knowable at those moments. In short, *Danto contributes importantly and insightfully to an epistemic and not any narratological understanding of histories*.

Mink expands and enhances some basic insights regarding the metaphysics and epistemology of histories left implicit and unrecognized in Danto's own account of narrative sentences and the attendant impossibility argument regarding an Ideal Chronicle. His elucidations underwrite the previously noted "non-detachability" thesis regarding historical explanations in connection with those narratives that present them. Mink's reflections also tell against any assumption that human history has a natural or intrinsic structure and so against any idea that there exists just one human past. More specifically, in addition to the aforementioned "non-detachability thesis," I add two others as defining characteristics of narrative as a form of explanation. One of these I term the non-standardization thesis and the other the non-aggregativity thesis.

Regarding the non-standardization thesis, Mink introduces a version of this idea when he notes:

> And such 'narrative sentences' belong to stories which historians alone can tell. ... A present event may belong to indefinitely many stories, none of which can be told until it is completed. The description of the past does not come closer and closer to an Ideal Chronicle but departs further and further from it as more descriptions become available which were not earlier available even in principle.
>
> (Mink 1987d, 138–39)

This brings to the fore two striking disanalogies between historical events and those that scientific theories target for purposes of explanation. One is that historical events do not exist as constructs within some articulated theory. Indeed, on rough analogy with Davidson's discussion of anomalous monism, there exists at present no reason to believe that the sort of events that interest humans for purposes of historical elucidation will be captured by any theory that utilizes anything like laws.

In short, there exists no analog in history to what permits "normal science" in Kuhn's sense. Nothing answers to normal history, because there exists no theory that normalizes historical events in this respect. "Danto's argument depends on bringing out with maximum forcefulness the point that there are many descriptions of an event, and no standard or complete description" (Mink 1987d, 139). Indeed, non-standardization underwrites non-detachability at least in the following way. Because there exists no standardized way of demarcating either event types—e.g. revolutions—or specific historical events—e.g. The American Civil War—these become non-detachable from histories that discuss them. No prior theories function to "standardize" such events, and neither do they constitute natural kinds. Thus, historical events "exist" only as part of some narrative or other.

The other disanalogy that Mink discerns emerges with regard to what he terms a conceptual asymmetry. By "conceptual asymmetry" Mink means "Descriptions possible only after the event because they depend on later conceptual modes of interpretation and analysis, e.g., 'the unpropertied citizens of Rome constituted the first urban proletariat'" (Mink 1987d, 140) This importantly complicates any understanding of the process just noted by which historical events become constituted for purposes of inquiry. Conceptual asymmetries represent a further principled barrier to any hope of normalizing descriptions of historical events. Danto emphasizes the *temporal* asymmetries that narrative sentences produce and how these frustrate any hypothesized Ideal Chronicle. But he does not comment upon conceptual asymmetries, and so overlooks a related critical limitation on historical knowledge. Critical race theory and feminist perspectives serve as examples here. Later concepts do not standardize events, but bring to light relations previously unobservable.[7]

But in addition to the non-standardization thesis, Mink also brings into view what I term the non-aggregativity thesis. This builds on observations that Mink makes regarding the very intelligibility of Danto's thought experiment. Mink notes that Danto's setup for the Ideal Chronicle seems plausible because one finds nothing obviously unimaginable in the initial suggestion of an

Ideal Chronicle as a totality of the historical record. "To say that we still presuppose … a concept of universal history, means: we assume that everything that has happened belongs to a single and determinate realm of unchanging actuality" (Mink 1987c, 194). So while Danto offers a *reductio* of the possibility of any such chronicle, Mink discerns an additional important epistemological consequence. This involves an assumption that histories can or should *aggregate*. Aggregation presupposes that all the events could belong to some one narrative, an implied unifying perspective. But there can no more be a single story than there can be an Ideal Chronicle, for new and different events and new and different stories constantly come into being (Mink 1987c, 197). Moreover, in order to aggregate, events would have to be detachable and standardized, but narratives allow for neither.

"The Past" cannot as a result exist as a static object about which one may hope to know more and more, as in Kuhn's image of normal science. For nothing now licenses an assumption of The Past conceived as an untold or partially told story, but always nonetheless the *same* story, a human past narratable *sub specie aeternitatis*. Rather, one confronts the fact that what these various histories "have in common is *the impossibility of being gathered together under any rubric of 'universal history.'* … Instead of the belief that there is a single story embracing the ensemble of human events, we believe that there are many stories, not only different stories about different events, but even different stories about the same event" (Mink 1987c, 193–94, emphasis mine). Absent a "master narrative," no One True History lies waiting to be discovered in what evidence provides (see also Roth 2008 and Roth 2012). As the non-standardization thesis implies, histories rather create pasts by the way in which particular events come to be fashioned and accounted for. Non-aggregativity adds that these histories cannot therefore be expected to cohere, to theoretically aggregate into one seamless account of The Past.

## Histories of Reason

A case for taking narrative as a form of explanation thus builds on the fact—and it is a fact—that philosophers pervasively use narratives to explain and that these exhibit the three previously noted defining features of historical narratives—the non-detachability of conclusions, the non-standardization of events explained, and the non-aggregativity of narrative explanations. Absent, then, some demarcation criterion, it would be more plausible to simply admit narrative histories to any list of legitimate forms of explanation rather than to continue to exclude them in theory while honoring them in practice. Examining some well-known "histories of reason" provides test cases illustrating how narratives function as a *sui generis* type explanation. In this regard, I briefly consider some well-known work by Thomas Kuhn and Michael Friedman, including as well writing by Friedman on the history of analytic philosophy.

Kuhn's work generates disputes persisting to this day regarding the relation of the history of science and the philosophy of science. A great if unintended irony regarding philosophical reception of *Structure* can be glimpsed in the following remark by Danto: "Kuhn advanced a view of history so powerful that, rather than being an applied science as Hempel holds history to be, history came to be the matrix for viewing all the sciences" (Danto 1995, 72). *Danto's remark gives voice to the important albeit still unacknowledged fact the Kuhn's great work effectively reverses the received order of epistemic authority.* In particular, Kuhn can be read as upending philosophical views that true science moves by an inexorable logic that transcends time and place. He replaces this with a history of reason, where what counts as good reasoning even within science will vary with the theory in disciplinary ascendance.

Kuhn worries about how history relates to science, but never satisfactorily resolves his concerns on this score (see Roth 2013). The title of Kuhn's famous book adumbrates a narrative sentence, inasmuch as what counts as a revolution (scientific or otherwise) appears only in retrospect. One can attempt to date its beginning after the fact, but that becomes a fact true of the earlier time only when seen in retrospect. The title is of course also ironic, since Kuhn's argument shows that changes in theoretical fashion have a "structure" only in a somewhat hand-waving sense of the term. This follows from his challenges to both Hempelian and Popperian orthodoxies regarding the rationality of scientific change insofar as neither verification nor falsification can explain historically significant theoretical transitions in what passes as a science.

What persistently escapes notice, however, involves just how Kuhn's book itself embodies a form of explanation that neither Hempel nor Popper could accommodate. Note in this regard that even what to count as a science appears known retrospectively. That a discipline has successive paradigms related in a certain ways—has a particular history—creates a lineage for physics and chemistry as sciences but not, e.g., for astrology and alchemy. Kuhn's narrative also exhibits that what passes as scientific rationality has a history. The "argument" for his history of reason consists in showing how different cases of theoretical transition also alter what makes for proper procedures within a science. Kuhn's emplotment of these successive transitions shows them resistant to any over-arching analysis of scientific rationality.

Indeed, *Structure* manifests exactly those characteristics of a narrative explanation sketched above. For the argument regarding the *general* significance of paradigm shifts cannot be detached from how Kuhn narrates key episodes within his history of science. The events discussed do not exist in any standardized form, and so the endless complaints regarding how Kuhn uses the term 'paradigm'. And one of the most notorious consequences he draws from his argument—the inability to make clear sense of any notion of scientific progress—instantiates the inability of histories to aggregate, at least with respect to some story of progress. (Kuhn endorses Mink's work here. See Roth 2013 for details.) In addition, his narrative does not aggregate either as a history of a stable something known as "science," or with traditional histories in this area.

In important work over the last fifteen years, Michael Friedman challenges Kuhn's history of science but has done so using specifically narrative means. Commenting on Friedman's *The Dynamics of Reason*, Richard Creath remarks, "Friedman's historical narrative is, in effect, an explication of the role of reason within the particular historical context in which these [mathematical and scientific] revolutions take place. ... So the historical narrative does real work for Friedman's account. The history is not an illustration of his argument ... it *is* the argument itself—a powerful one" (Creath 2010, 504). Friedman emphatically endorses this characterization of his "argument" (Friedman 2010, 792, n. 317; see also 712ff.). "Whatever the fate of this new philosophy of science may be, it is clear beyond the shadow of a doubt, I think, that careful and sensitive attention to the history of science must remain absolutely central in any serious philosophical consideration of science" (Friedman 1993, 37). Friedman also did early and well-known work on explanation. Like Kuhn, he cannot be charged in this regard with a lack of familiarity with philosophical debates about explanation, or an ignorance of scientific theories and mathematics, or an inability to work in those terms. Yet, also like Kuhn, although Friedman self-consciously uses historical narrative to reshape thinking about what science is, he does not explicitly reflect on how narratives explain.

Such contested histories of reason extend as well to questions about the status of logic and mathematics. Consider in this light Friedman's *A Parting of the Ways* (Friedman 2000). For Friedman offers there a specifically historical narrative explanation in the sense rehearsed above. For the purpose at hand, his explanation holds important implications for contemporary debate regarding the state and content of what has come to be called analytic philosophy (itself, of course, now the topic of multiple conflicting histories). Here what is at stake is nothing less than how analytic philosophy should be understood. This essay does not answer the question of which history to accept. What matters is that Friedman provides a *narrative* explanation, one that shapes and influences not only how one conceives of what philosophers did and but also what they ought to do.

Although not a necessary feature of a narrative explanation on my configuration of that term, Friedman's title connotes the sort of narrative sentence that Danto teaches us to attend to. For on Friedman's telling, the conference at Davos comes to mark a parting of the ways. Friedman roots his tale of that encounter in two very different and influential ways in which the Kantian project has been appropriated at that time. Having thus situated his narrative, he can then locate the confrontation at Davos between Cassirer and Heidegger as a critical moment in a much broader intellectual story. But these "facts" can be apprehended only retrospectively; those at Davos could not have used some model of explanation available then or now (or ever, I would venture to speculate) to explain what happens then as marking the origins of a "continental divide" (see Gordon 2010).

This narrative proves fraught with great significance regarding how to understand those who gave our discipline much of its current shape, and so determinative of our own professional self-understanding. As Friedman puts it, he proposes to "show" (his term, having in context the connotation of 'prove' or 'explain')

> that the Davos encounter between Carnap, Cassirer, and Heidegger has particular importance for our understanding of the ensuing split between what we now call the analytic and continental philosophical traditions. Before this encounter there was no such split …. I further hope to show that carefully attending to the very different ways in which the thought of all three philosophers evolved in sharply diverging directions from a common neo-Kantian core can greatly illuminate the nature and sources of the analytic/continental divide.
>
> (Friedman 2000, xi)

Friedman means to account for how a present unanticipatible in the past nonetheless came to be the intellectual and professional space that we inhabit.

This conforms, I take it, with exactly the points on which Danto and Mink insist. Historical explanation *qua* narrative explanation concerns itself with a *developmental* or *innovative* process that emerges only in retrospect, and that the purpose of a narrative is to trace that path of development, a path not defined or marked by any known laws or the like. The event emerges as an event only because our interests call it into being; events so constituted do not represent or embody some natural kind. Following that path might well and perhaps even should change our perception of how to proceed on the basis of an altered understanding of that past. As Friedman writes, "We have now arrived at the beginning of our own particular story, and also at a fundamental intellectual crossroads" (Friedman 2000, 147). One need not agree with Friedman in all the particulars to share his sense that philosophy does stand at a crossroads, one rooted in divergent and deeply contested ways of understanding the legacies of Frege, Russell, Carnap, Wittgenstein, Quine, and Sellars. As another distinguished historian of analytic philosophy has put it, "On the story I tell, the central strand of the analytic tradition in philosophy decisively shaped by our three figures [Frege, Carnap, and Quine] has, I think it is fair to say, no salient continuation among those who name themselves the heirs of that tradition" (Ricketts 2004, 182). No less than the history of science, the history of analytic philosophy has given rise to deeply conflicting narratives, ones that cannot aggregate or be made to agree. Indeed, these competing narratives prove unrecognizable as histories of the same topic to contending authors.

As noted earlier, the complexities and complication manifest in the relationship of the philosophy of history and the philosophy of science can be readily extended to other areas of philosophy as well. Histories of reason exemplify why philosophy of history ought to be regarded as both important to and unavoidable for any ongoing effort to understand the role and scope of philosophical inquiry. The issue cannot be whether or not to consider attending to the nature of historical explanation, but rather why philosophers have for so long avoided doing so.

# Notes

1 A terminology specific to debates about historical explanation invokes a distinction between nomothetic and idiographic modes of explanation. The former explains by regimenting statements of fact into explanatory patterns so as to reveal how such patterns instantiate laws or law-like connections. The latter mode explains by elaborating those contexts in which things happen; on this account, the specifics of a situation provide what is needed by way of explanation. A distinction between explanation and understanding evolves in tandem with these differing notions of explanation, the suggestion being that nomothetic explanations provide causes, and idiographic accounts engender understanding. That is, causal explanatory accounts imply underlying scientific laws or at least their simulacra, and so do not depend on time and context. Understanding ties to context typically by seeking to comprehend what counts in a particular situation as good or sufficient reasons for action. No claim is made that the goodness of the reasons generalizes; such matters will be specific to time and place. For good summary overviews of this aspect of the debate, see Habermas 1988. For an updated extension of this traditional debate, see Stueber 2006. For an account of how "critical" or "analytic" philosophy of history evolves, see Mink 1987a.

2 The absence of discussion of Hayden White's work in this chapter in no way implies a lack of appreciation of it regarding the development and discussion of philosophical issues attached to historical narratives. See especially his importantly innovative and enduringly influential 1973 or any of the volumes of his collected essays. But as I have elsewhere elaborated, White does not directly engage the issues of narrative *qua* explanation; see Roth 1992. For helpful overviews of the impact of White's works, see Vann 1995 and Vann 1998.

3 For example, Salmon 1990 provides only the briefest mention of the controversy occasioned by Hempel 1942. He does cite in his bibliography an early and still interesting article by Danto defending narrative for purposes of historical explanation. See Danto 1956. But narrative as a possible counter-example to Hempel receives no consideration.

4 In a recent survey article, Kosso 2011 begins by observing, "The philosophical issues in the analysis of knowledge are almost entirely epistemological" (9) and concludes by stating flatly, "Narrative explanation suits the situation of historiography, but not science" (24). Velleman 2003 offers a quite negative assessment for the prospects of epistemically disciplining narrative. Survey articles by historians manifest the dissociation of discussions of narrative and epistemic concerns inasmuch as epistemic issues simply receive no mention. See, e.g., Rigney 2013.

5 The context suggests that it is Danto's own coinage. *Inter alia*, his use of this term occurs as part of his explicit defense of narrative as a form of explanation. Close anticipations of Danto's term can be found

in Popper and Gallie, and one might well read Collingwood as suggesting this as well (Gallie 1964, 113–24, but esp. 124; Popper, 1957, 143–44. Hayden White brought these to my attention.

6 Danto borrows G. E. M. Anscombe's celebrated phrase "under a description" to characterize what makes random facts into an event of a certain sort, e.g. one described as "the beginning of the Thirty Years War." I term a connection formed by a narrative sentence "conceptual" in order to highlight the point that while "the facts" (however one wishes to understand what those are) may not be of human making, events comprised by them are.

7 Hacking in effect rediscovers this point and exploits it in his own work. Regarding the philosophical significance that Hacking attaches to the notion of events as existing under a description, see Hacking 1995, esp. ch. 17. For a discussion of Hacking on this point, see Roth 2002 and Roth 2013, n. 1.

# References

Creath, R. (2010) "The Construction of Reason: Kant, Carnap, Kuhn, and Beyond," in M. Domski and M. Dickson (Eds.) Discourse on a New Method: Reinvigorating the Marriage of History and Philosophy of Science, Chicago: Open Court.

Danto, A. C. (1956) "On Explanations in History," Philosophy of Science 23: 15–30

—— (1962) "Narrative Sentences," History and Theory 2: 146–79.

—— (1965) Analytical Philosophy of History, Cambridge: Cambridge University Press.

—— (1995) "The Decline and Fall of Analytical Philosophy of History," in F. Ankersmit and H. Kellner (Eds.) A New Philosophy of History, Chicago: University of Chicago Press.

Domski, M. and M. Dickson (2010) "Introduction," in M. Domski and M. Dickson (Eds.) Discourse on a New Method: Reinvigorating the Marriage of History and Philosophy of Science, Chicago: Open Court.

Fay, B., E. O. Golob, and R. T. Vann (1987) "Introduction," in B. Fay, E. O. Golob, and R. T. Vann (Eds.) Historical Understanding, Ithaca, NY: Cornell University Press.

Friedman, M. (1993) "Remarks on the History of Science and the History of Philosophy," in P. Horwich (Ed.) World Changes: Thomas Kuhn and the Nature of Science, Cambridge, MA: MIT Press.

—— (2000) A Parting of the Ways, Chicago: Open Court.

—— (2010) "Synthetic History Reconsidered," in M. Domski and M. Dickson (Eds.) Discourse on a New Method: Reinvigorating the Marriage of History and Philosophy of Science, Chicago: Open Court.

Gallie, W. B. (1964) Philosophy and the Historical Understanding, London: Chatto & Windus.

Gordon, P. (2010) Continental Divide: Heidegger, Cassirer, Davos, Cambridge, MA: Harvard University Press.

Habermas, J. (1988) On the Logic of the Social Sciences, Cambridge, MA: MIT Press.

Hacking, I. (1995) Rewriting the Soul, Princeton, NJ: Princeton University Press.

Hempel, C. G. (1942) "The Function of General Laws in History," Journal of Philosophy 39: 35–48.

Kosso, P. (2011) "Philosophy as Historiography," in A. Tucker (Ed.) A Companion to the Philosophy of History and Historiography, Malden, MA: Wiley-Blackwell.

Kuukkanen, J.-M. (2015) Postnarrativist Philosophy of Historiography, New York: Palgrave Macmillan.

Little, D. (2010) New Contributions to the Philosophy of History, New York: Springer.

Mink, L. O. (1987a) "The Divergence of History and Sociology in Recent Philosophy of History," in B. Fay, E. O. Golob, and R. T. Vann (Eds.) Historical Understanding, Ithaca, NY: Cornell University Press.

—— (1987b) "The Autonomy of Historical Understanding," in B. Fay, E. O. Golob, and R. T. Vann (Eds.) Historical Understanding, Ithaca, NY: Cornell University Press.

—— (1987c) "Narrative Form as a Cognitive Instrument," in B. Fay, E. O. Golob, and R. T. Vann (Eds.) Historical Understanding, Ithaca, NY: Cornell University Press.

—— (1987d) "Philosophical Analysis and Historical Understanding," in B. Fay, E. O. Golob, and R. T. Vann (Eds.) Historical Understanding, Ithaca, NY: Cornell University Press.

Popper, K. (1957) The Poverty of Historicism, London: Routledge and Kegan Paul.

Richardson, A. (2002) "Narrating the History of Reason Itself: Friedman, Kuhn, and a Constitutive A Priori for the Twenty-First Century," Perspectives on Science 10: 253–74.

—— (2003) "Conceiving, Experiencing, and Conceiving Experiencing: Neo-Kantianism and the History of the Concept of Experience," Topoi 22: 55–67.

Ricketts, T. (2004) "Frege, Carnap, and Quine: Continuities and Discontinuities," in S. Awodey and C. Klein (ed) *Carnap Brought Home*, La Salle, IL: Open Court.

Rigney, A. (2013) "History as Text: Narrative Theory and History," in N. Partner and S. Foot (Eds.) *The Sage Handbook of Historical Theory*, Thousand Oaks, CA: Sage.

Roth, P. A. (1992) "Hayden White and the Aesthetics of Historiography," *History of the Human Sciences* 5: 17–35.

———— (2002) "Ways of Pastmaking," *History of the Human Sciences* 15: 125–43.

———— (2008) "Philosophy of Science after Quine," in S. Psillos and M. Curd (Eds.) *The Routledge Companion to the Philosophy of Science*, New York: Routledge.

———— (ed.) (2011) "What Does History Matter to …" *Journal of the Philosophy of History* 5(3) [whole issue].

———— (2012) "The Pasts," *History and Theory* 51(October): 313–39.

———— (2013) "The Silence of the Norms: The Missing Historiography of *The Structure of Scientific Revolutions*," *Studies in History and Philosophy of Science* 44: 545–52.

Salmon, W. C. (1990) *Four Decades of Scientific Explanation*, Minneapolis: University of Minnesota Press.

Stueber, K. R. (2006) *Rediscovering Empathy*, Cambridge, MA: Bradford.

Vann, R. T. (1995) "Turning Linguistic: History and Theory and *History and Theory*, 1960–1975," in F. R. Ankersmit and H. Kellner (Eds.) *A New Philosophy of History*, London: Reaktion.

———— (1998) "The Reception of Hayden White," *History and Theory* 37: 143–61.

Velleman, D. (2003) "Narrative Explanation," *Philosophical Review* 112: 1–25.

White, H. (1973) *Metahistory*, Baltimore, MD: Johns Hopkins University Press.

Zammito, J. H. (2004) *A Nice Derangement of Epistemes: Post-Positivism in the Study of Science from Quine to Latour*, Chicago: University of Chicago Press.

# 35
# PHILOSOPHY OF PSYCHOLOGY

## *Nico Orlandi and Janette Dinishak*

Writing a short introduction to the philosophy of psychology is a difficult task. This is so for at least two reasons. First, psychology is a vast discipline. It includes social psychology, behavioral psychology, cognitive psychology, comparative psychology, artificial intelligence, neuropsychology, and clinical psychology. Whether there is a common thread to these different areas of research is itself a philosophical question (Hatfield 2002).

Second, it is not clear that there is a unique subject matter to the philosophy of psychology, and whether there is a difference, for example, between the philosophy of psychology and the philosophy of mind. Some consider "philosophy of mind" and "philosophy of psychology" two labels for the same general area of inquiry (Jackson and Rey 1998). Others suggest that the philosophy of psychology differs from the philosophy of mind not in subject matter, but in being closer to current empirical research (Bermúdez 2005; Mason et al. 2008).

To give a coherent, if partial, glimpse of the field, we propose to view the philosophy of psychology as a reflection on the question of *how* to study the mind—that is, on the question of how to do psychology. This is a somewhat different, although related, question from the question of what the mind is, which we take to be central to the philosophy of mind.

To further restrict our subject matter, we focus primarily on the methodology of *cognitive* psychology. We understand cognitive psychology as the branch of psychology that aims to map cognitive states and processes for the purpose of predicting and explaining human behavior.

In what follows, we examine how this area of scientific psychology should be done. We start by asking whether the folk psychological categories of belief, desire, and intention should be part of scientific psychology. This question is what José Bermúdez calls the 'interface problem' (2005). After introducing the problem, we consider how it plays out in two fields of empirical research: mindreading and rationality. Then we illustrate some other ways of approaching the question of how to study the mind by sketching some recent discussions in the philosophy of psychiatry.

## 1 Common-Sense Psychology: Reductionism, Realism, Eliminativism, and Instrumentalism

Cognitive psychology is a relatively new scientific enterprise, having developed in its more rigorous form only since the 20th century. While the initial focus of this discipline was consciousness, and a description of conscious mental life, modern times have seen a shift in focus towards prediction and explanation (Hatfield 2002). Cognitive psychologists aim to understand mental states and processes for predictive purposes. But how should cognitive psychology be done?

To begin addressing this question, we can compare common-sense psychology (or folk psychology) and neuroscience. Both common sense and neuroscience aim to make sense of people's behavior, but they do so by using different tools. Folk psychology takes people to have beliefs, desires, intentions, and fears that partly determine what they do. Neuroscientists, on the other hand, focus on neurological and physiological states and processes. What is the relation between these different ways of predicting and explaining behavior? Is one better than the other from a scientific point of view?

In metaphysics and the philosophy of science, these questions are sometimes usefully framed in terms of levels of description (Putnam 1987; Heil 2003). We can construe common-sense psychology and neuroscience as theories that describe people at different levels. Common sense describes people in 'macroscopic' terms, as subjects that have psychological states that relate to each other in various (rational) ways. Neuroscience, by contrast, thinks of people in 'microscopic', physical terms—that is, in terms of synapses, neuron firings, and chemical secretions. Both of these descriptions are presumably good in some way, but both are also 'partisan'. Each description assumes the existence of certain objects and properties that are *unique* to that description. As a result, the two descriptions may also differ in predictive power.

One central question is whether these descriptions are equally good from a scientific point of view. Should we reduce the first kind of talk to the second? Should we eliminate one in favor of the other when we do scientific psychology? If the folk description is ineliminable, is this because it picks out something over and above what is picked out at the micro level?

When one entertains these questions, one can think of four main positions that seem to cover the spectrum of possible answers. The positions are reductionism, (intentional) realism,[1] eliminativism, and instrumentalism.

### *1.1 Reductionism*

Reductionism comes in different forms, but one way to understand it is to suppose that the description at the macro or common-sense level is an *abbreviation* of a much more complex neurological description. When we describe a human subject in common-sense, psychological terms we are referring to microphysical and microphysiological entities and properties. Because the micro description is too complex, we use vulgar (in the sense of non-scientific) terms. Ultimately, however, all common-sense descriptions should be translatable into the language of neurophysiology (Carnap 1932/1959; Hempel 1935/1949). Carnap famously says: "Every psychological sentence refers to physical occurrences in the body of the person (or persons) in question" (Carnap 1932/1959, 197, quoted in Hatfield 2002). In this view, there is an ontological asymmetry between the common-sense and neurophysiological descriptions in that the former does not reflect the existence of entities and properties over and above the ones at the neurological level.

In psychology, early behaviorists are sometimes interpreted as adopting a reductionist position (Watson 1913). Behaviorism itself comes in different guises. Some of its proponents are known to subscribe to the *methodological* claim that a science of the mind should only concern what is observable—for example, observable stimuli, behaviors, and intervening physiological states (Skinner 1938). In other versions, behaviorism is understood as a view of the nature of mental states and processes, namely that they reduce to behavioral dispositions. Believing that it is raining, for example, amounts to being disposed to assert that it is raining, grabbing an umbrella, and having other behavioral and physiological manifestations (Skinner 1938; Tolman 1932). In yet other versions, behaviorists seem to adopt the reductionist idea that all talk of hidden mental states and processes should be translated into—or understood in terms of—talk of behavioral and physiological dispositions (Watson 1913; Ryle 1949/2009).[2]

Despite their ontological parsimony, both behaviorism and reductionism have been criticized on multiple counts. First, the kind of translation that some reductionists and behaviorists advocate either fails to capture and explain mental life, or reintroduces mentalistic talk (Chomsky 1967). Mental states and processes are better understood as hidden *causes* of behavior. They do not *reduce* to behavior.

Such states and processes also do not reduce to physiological and neurological states and processes. Reductionism suggests that if we describe a person as believing something, and then also a cat as believing the same thing, then there should be a microphysiological property that the person and the cat share. This is because, according to reductionists, the expression 'believing something' picks out a microphysiological state. Various subjects can be correctly described as having a given belief *in virtue* of a certain microphysical state that they are in.

Mental states and processes, however, are often thought to be *multiply realizable* (Putnam 1967). Different neurophysiological and brain states can implement a belief in different creatures. This means that a correct ascription of belief does not depend on sharing a particular physiology.

Partly because of these problems, reductionist paradigms have been largely abandoned in psychology. A natural alternative is intentional realism.

### 1.2 Realism

According to intentional realism, mentalistic talk is not an abbreviation of behavioral or neurophysiological talk. Common-sense psychological terms pick out *real* psychological entities that are not reducible to neurophysiological or otherwise physical entities. Discovering the lawful ways in which beliefs, desires, and intentions correlate and in which they affect behavior is the primary goal of cognitive psychology.[3]

In this paradigm, psychology is not reducible to neuroscience. The two are independent in a similar way to how the study of the software of a computer is independent from the study of its hardware—an analogy to which we will return.

An immediate challenge for this type of realism is of course to specify the nature of the psychological states and processes that are introduced. Are psychological states abstract entities? Are they non-material, purely mental entities? Are they functional entities? Depending on the specification, a realist may be able to preserve a materialist outlook while not giving in to reductionism.

A second challenge for this kind of realist view is explicating the relation between the psychological entities and the neurophysiological ones. Intuitively, the former depend on the latter for causal efficacy. A belief affects behavior through its physical realization in the brain. The causal powers of the entities and properties at the macro level seem to depend on what goes on at the micro level. Thus, there seems to be a tension between the causal dependence of macro-level entities and their ontological independence. This has given rise to a healthy debate concerning the causal efficacy of the mental (Heil 2003; Kim 1993).

René Descartes can be regarded as an early realist whose position raises both of the challenges just sketched. Descartes believes that the mental constitutes an independent and immaterial realm, not reducible to the realm of the physical and the mechanistic (Descartes 1641/1996).[4]

Understanding the causal efficacy of the mental is one of the main problems brought up against the Cartesian Doctrine by early behaviorists. Gilbert Ryle, in particular, points out that it is mysterious how an immaterial substance could cause anything physical to happen. According to Ryle, adopting the kind of realism recommended by Descartes amounts to giving up the hope for a scientific understanding of the mind (Ryle 1949/2009).

More recently, Jerry Fodor defends a different type of intentional realism (Fodor 1987). In line with a number of other philosophers of mind, Fodor understands mental states and processes in functional terms—that is (roughly) as defined by the function they perform within an organism (Putnam 1967; Armstrong 1981/2002). Someone believes that it is raining, for instance, when she is in an internal state that is usually caused by the perception of—and refers to—rain in the world, and that causes certain behaviors.

With this understanding of mental states, Fodor argues for the usefulness and indispensability of 'belief-desire' psychology (Fodor 1987). Belief-desire psychology is, according to Fodor, very successful at predicting and explaining behavior, both in experimental and in everyday circumstances. It resembles the hard sciences in having a deductive structure—where predictions are deduced from its generalizations—and in positing un-observables (hidden mental states) that play an explanatory function.

Further, by using multiple-realizability considerations, Fodor argues that belief-desire psychology is indispensable. It posits entities that are multiply realizable at the neurological level, and it explains behaviors that are themselves multiply realizable by physical movements. The generalizations of common-sense psychology concern a level of reality that cross-classifies the level described by the physiological and neurological sciences. Psychology is not about bodily movements. It is about kinds of actions. It is not about how specifically one grabbed an umbrella. It is about the general fact that one did and why.

Importantly, Fodor points out that these considerations are strengthened by the fact that belief-desire psychology accords with the work already done in scientific cognitive psychology. This branch of psychology, according to Fodor, is committed to both the Representational (RTM) and the Computational Theory of Mind (CTM).

As the names suggest, these theories emerged from the collaboration of psychology (and philosophy) with computer science—the basic idea being that the mind is analogous to a digital computer (Turing 1950). RTM and CTM hold that mental states and processes are functional states and processes that can be understood as relations, and operations over, mental representations, or symbols. Mindful creatures have internal symbolic states akin to the states of the software of a digital computer. When one believes that it is raining, one is in an internal symbolic state that refers to rain in the world. This state is typically caused by the presence of rain, and it typically causes certain predictable behaviors. Fodor famously calls the internal symbolic arsenal of mindful creatures a *language of thought*, initiating a long-standing dispute concerning whether this language is innate or acquired.

Introducing this language, according to Fodor, commits psychological theories to entities that are relevantly similar to the entities introduced by belief-desire psychology. RTM and CTM posit the existence of internal, unobservable states that have meaning, and that do not reduce to physiological and neurological states. Such states have the features that propositional attitudes (beliefs, desires, hopes, etc.) also have. They are semantically evaluable, they have causal powers, and they interact in various complicated ways that psychology is supposed to describe. Belief-desire psychology, then, garners support by aligning with computational, scientific psychology.

Intentional realism has been a fertile ground for a number of central debates in the philosophy of mind. One debate concerns how best to understand the computational processes that presumably constitute mental activity. Fodor distinguished two types of computational processes—*modular* and *non-modular* (Fodor 1987). The former, according to Fodor, have some distinctive properties: they are fast, automatic, not influenced by information coming from other processes, generally innate, localizable in specific brain areas, manifesting characteristic break-downs, having shallow or non-conceptual outputs, and taking only a restricted and characteristic set of inputs. Perceptual processes like vision and audition, and some linguistic capacities are modular.

Non-modular processes tend not to have these features. They are inferentially promiscuous, acquired, conceptual, and not as well localized in the brain. The capacity to reason and in general the higher cognitive abilities of humans are regarded as non-modular by Fodor.

There is ongoing debate concerning whether the mind contains anything like a module, whether this is a useful distinction at all, and whether Fodor is right concerning what is modular and what is not (Machery 2010). Some psychologists and philosophers have argued both that perception is not modular (Churchland 1989) and that reasoning capacities are underwritten by modules (Carruthers 2006; Sperber 1994).

Another debate within the realist, computational paradigm concerns how best to understand the semantic aspect of mental states. Beliefs, desires, intentions, and fears are understood as functional states that have semantic *content*. A belief that it is raining has accuracy conditions given by whether it is, in fact, raining. One question is what gives beliefs and other mental states their content. *Externalists* tend to suppose that mental states have content in virtue of some relation that individuals have to the social and natural environment in which they are situated (Burge 1979, 1986; Putnam 1975). *Internalists*, by contrast, suppose that mental content can be given by the internal organization of cognizers, for example by the relation that one belief has to others in a network (Harman 1987).

The issue of how to understand the relationship between individuals and their environments in a realist/computational framework has also given rise to new forms of externalism that concern not just content, but also the location and composition of mental states and processes. One particularly active debate is about whether mental states and processes extend outside the skin of individuals (Clark and Chalmers 1998). Opponents argue for preserving the traditional idea that mental life is internal to cognizers (Rupert 2004).

Despite ongoing disagreement on these issues, the general consensus among intentional realists is that psychological states are real entities that do not reduce to neurophysiological and behavioral entities. This commits the realist to a certain ontological exuberance. Those who dislike this aspect of realism—and perhaps also dislike its dubious claims to predictive success—may adopt an alternative called 'eliminativism'.

### 1.3 Eliminativism

As we saw in section 1.1, one of the problems with reductionism is that the terms used at the common-sense level do not seem to refer to microphysical states and processes. They seem to pick out irreducible entities and properties. But if one thinks that all that there is, ontologically speaking, are the entities and properties admitted by the physical and neurophysiological sciences, then one might be inclined to take this as a sign that the terms and predicates at the common-sense level do not refer *at all*. Or better, they are terms of our language like "Santa Claus." They do not refer to any existing entities.

This is the core claim of eliminativism. Our common-sense description of people in psychological terms does not pick out microphysical states and processes, and such description cannot pick out anything over and above those states and processes, because there is nothing over and above them. So, the description at the macro level is, strictly speaking, false. When it comes to psychology, our vocabulary of beliefs, desires, and intentions could and should be substituted with the more precise vocabulary of neuroscience. Common-sense psychology—and perhaps also cognitive psychology as it is currently done –should ultimately be eliminated.

Eliminativism, like reductionism, comes in different varieties. Some eliminativists stress the centrality of syntax and the dispensability of content in explaining mental processes (Stich 1996). Other forms of eliminativism are developed in tandem with non-classical and non-Fodorian computational models of mental activity—for example, connectionism (Rumelhart et al. 1988). Paul Churchland famously argues that the emergence of artificial neutral networks as models of mentality supports the abandonment of belief-desire psychology. Such a psychology, according to Churchland, is akin to alchemy in being false, stagnant, and far from indispensable (Churchland 1981).

Connectionism helps Churchland's case by introducing a way of understanding mental life that does not rely on symbolic states. Artificial neural networks are nets of connected units that spread information by spreading levels of activation, simulating a biological brain. There are different ways of building networks, but some can learn to perform cognitive functions (such as playing chess, or recognizing faces) by using simple units and connections, rather than more sophisticated symbolic and representational structures.

There is ongoing disagreement concerning whether connectionist networks make use of representations *at all*. Compared to classical, artificial models of intelligence, they are more prone to non-representational interpretations (Ramsey 1997; Ramsey et al. 1991). At the very least, connectionist nets do not use a language of thought in Fodor's sense. They do not introduce symbolic structures that are similar to common-sense beliefs and desires. The units in a network—unlike the words and other syntactic units in a language—have no comfortable semantic interpretation. It is then hard to identify what a belief would be like in a connectionist network. It would seem to be just a tendency for the network to do certain things, which is reminiscent of a certain kind of behaviorism.

Similar eliminativist tendencies are shared by *dynamics*, a recent approach to the study of the mind based on a branch of statistical mechanics that studies the evolution of bodies through time. Dynamicists regard minds as dynamical physical systems whose behavior can be predicted by the differential equations of dynamical systems theory with no reference to unobservables such as beliefs and desires (van Gelder 1995).

While keeping our ontology respectable, eliminativism contrasts with the deep-seated intuition that talk of psychological states is explanatory, and not analogous to talk of Santa Claus. Instrumentalism tries to preserve this intuition.

### 1.4 Instrumentalism

So far we have described intentional realism, eliminativism, and reductionism as three major competitors in the philosophy of psychology. Daniel Dennett (1981) develops a fourth position. According to Dennett, whether beliefs, desires, intentions, and other psychological states exist is neither a completely objective matter of fact—akin to whether someone has a virus—nor a completely fictitious matter of taste. Rather, whether someone has a belief depends on what we are interested in.

Dennett holds that while mental states are perfectly objective phenomena, they can be discerned only from the point of view of one who adopts a certain predictive strategy. Further, the existence of these psychological states can be confirmed only by an assessment of the success of the strategy. This means that, if in predicting what humans do, we need to consider them as intentional agents—ascribing beliefs, desires, and intentions to them—then the reality of these states is as real as it gets. We should not hope to find psychological states of this kind if we adopt a purely physical outlook. Adopting such a stance would prevent us from discerning anything psychological.

It is a matter of dispute whether this instrumentalist position is coherent and stable, or whether it dissolves into its realist and eliminativist competitors. A more recent version of this debate arises in connection with the notion of mental content (Neander 2015; Egan 2014). As we saw, mental states are thought to have content and it is a question how, if at all, this content originates. Eliminativists about content hold that this notion should have no place in our scientific theories, while realists claim that it should. Intentional realists of different stripes disagree on whether content is reducible to natural facts about the world.

Like instrumentalists, pragmatists about content aim to formulate an alternative. According to pragmatism, whether content exists is not an entirely objective matter of fact, but something that depends on pragmatic considerations, for example on the usefulness of content ascription for explanatory and predictive purposes. And just as for instrumentalism, it is not clear whether pragmatism constitutes a genuine alternative.

With the four main competitors on the table we now briefly turn to two branches of empirical cognitive psychology, and see how the debate concerning folk psychology plays out there.

## 2 Mindreading

The arguments that we have looked at so far are of a quite general and normative nature. They concern whether we *should* keep folk psychological notions in scientific psychology. It is a further question, however, whether and how we actually *do* use these notions in our everyday ability to predict and explain what others do.

When we attribute to ourselves and others desires, intentions, emotions, and beliefs, we are 'mindreading'[5] or 'mentalizing'. The capacity to mindread presumably makes social coordination possible. But how should we describe and explain mindreading?

To a large extent, two approaches have dominated inquiry into the nature of mindreading: 'theory-theory' (TT) (Churchland 1979; Dennett 1987; Gopnik and Meltzoff 1997) and 'simulation theory' (ST) (Davies 1994; Goldman 2006; Gordon 1986; Heal 1998). TT explains the human capacity to predict behavior in terms of the possession and use of a *theory of mind*. A theory of mind—not unlike folk psychology—is a set of generalizations about how humans' mental states and behaviors are usually connected. It allows one to infer mental states from observable behavior and to, in turn, predict behavior on the basis of mental state ascriptions. One may, for example, infer a certain umbrella-grabbing behavior from the ascription of a belief in rain, and a desire to stay dry.

According to ST, TT misrepresents what we do when we exercise our mindreading capacities. TT overemphasizes theoretical inference and the need for a theory. ST says that mindreading involves imaginatively adopting the perspective of another and using one's own mind as a model to simulate what another would do.

Simulation theorists often distinguish simple and complex forms of simulation. Low-level simulation is a largely automatic form of "mental mimicry" that is prompted by observation. High-level simulation is conscious and more effortful: one adopts the perspective of the target and reflects on the target's situation. One also constructs how things are, were, or will be "playing out" for the person, and imagines what one would do if one were in that person's shoes. Although ST does not require the possession of a theory, high-level simulation presumes substantive psychological sophistication.

For some time, TT and ST were considered the only two games in town, and were treated as mutually exclusive. More recently, there is growing consensus that some combination of theoretical approaches is needed. This is partly due to the fact that mindreading has been found to be a complex phenomenon that does not just concern prediction and explanation, but also the ascription of praise and blame (Knobe 2007). The ascription of intentions, for example, is sensitive to whether one wants to blame the subject of the ascription.

Hybrids of TT and ST and 'third' alternatives are currently being developed. Approaches inspired by the phenomenological and hermeneutic traditions have been particularly generative. For example, proponents of 'direct perception views' (DPV) (Zahavi 2010; Krueger and Overgaard 2012) reject what they take to be a common assumption of TT and ST, namely that minds cannot be perceived. According to DPV, in some cases, others' emotions can be directly perceived within their patterns of expressive behavior. One objection to this view is that its advocates are required to embrace a form of crude behaviorism (Jacob 2011).

The Narrative Practice Hypothesis (Gallagher 2012; Gallagher and Hutto 2008; Hutto 2008) is also an emerging alternative. According to this view, mature mindreading is better understood as a form of narrative competency. Such competency is the intersubjective practice of producing and interpreting narratives that recount one's actions within shared socio-cultural norms.

## 3 Rationality

Common-sense psychology presumes that human beings are—to a certain extent—rational beings. To be a believer is to be rational. Believers do not just respond to physical forces like rocks do. Their actions can result from what they *believe* to be the case, rather than from what *is* the case.

As such, believers respond to what they *should* do, not just to what they cannot help but do (Plato 1992). Beliefs, desires, and intentions are related to each other, and to behavior, in a rational way. If one believes that it is raining, then one is expected to have both a certain type of behavior, and a certain set of other beliefs. Having a belief in rain means that one should also believe that there is water in the world. It seems strange to ascribe a "rain belief" of this kind to someone who does not hold *any* of the beliefs that are logically related to it, and to someone who exhibits *none* of the corresponding behaviors. A massively contradictory being is, arguably, not a believer (Aristotle 1998, IV).

Recent empirical research puts the folk psychological presumption of rationality into question. Human beings are found to be skewed by biases and heuristics (Kahneman 2011; Tversky and Kahneman 1974; Piattelli-Palmarini 1994). This is particularly true when notions of probability are involved, for example when subjects are asked to judge the probability of a certain event given some background story. People commonly ignore base-rates, and they overlook well-known statistical facts—for instance, the fact that a conjunction of events is always less probable than a single event no matter how plausible a "conjunction story" sounds.

Further, even outside the realm of probability, people are found to engage in contradictory thinking, in wishful thinking, and in confirmation bias, seeing only evidence that confirms their views (Mandelbaum 2013).

What this body of evidence shows is a matter of contention. While one could argue that the assumption of rationality—and the folk psychology that comes with it—should be given up in favor of an instrumentalist or eliminativist position, a viable option is to redefine rationality in a way that does not impose an unrealistic requirement on human subjects (Cherniak 1990). The idea would be to find a minimal sense of rationality that allows ascription of belief, while being compatible with the evidence. Either way, it seems that the folk psychological notion of rationality needs some reconsideration.

# 4 Philosophy of Psychiatry

In sections 1–3 we focused on the interface problem. Here we briefly note some other ways the question of how to study the mind plays out in the philosophy of psychiatry. We focus, in particular, on the methodological question of whether and how the study of the "abnormal" can illuminate our understanding of the "normal."

Empirical research on atypical development and on forms of psychopathology—for example, autism, schizophrenia, and addiction—provides philosophers with real-life examples of deviations from typical human experience. Such deviations can expose assumptions that are based on excessive focus on "normal" cases. For example, some philosophers (e.g. Sass et al. 2000; Overgaard 2007; Fuchs 2009) have argued that the experiential anomalies associated with schizophrenia—such as thought-insertion—function as counter-examples to the philosophical claim of "mineness." "Mineness" is the sense of first-personal ownership that is presumably essential to human experience. Thought insertion, by contrast, is the sense that someone else is thinking through one's mind, such that one denies that the "inserted" thoughts are one's own. As Overgaard (2007) suggests, when faced with the insertion evidence, the philosopher has to chose "to either adopt the extremely unconvincing view that schizophrenics have no (human) experience, or else do what is right, and abandon the original claim" (39–40).

Cases of deviation can thus serve to revise our assumptions concerning the mind. In most instances, however, deviations are used in a different manner. They are used as a *contrast class*. Particular psychopathologies are taken to show what is present in "normal" instances of cognitive functioning and, vice versa "normal" instances are taken to shed light on what is missing in the pathologies.

In the first instance, pathologies are used to build models of typical cognitive architecture. For example, the patterns of sparing in the linguistic capacities of individuals with Williams syndrome are taken as evidence for particular models of the typical cognitive architecture of linguistic creatures (see Karmiloff-Smith 1992; Bellugi et al. 1994; Clahsen and Almazan 1998; Karmiloff-Smith et al. 1997 for discussion).

In the second instance, typical cognitive development is used to draw conclusions concerning what is missing in the individuals affected by the psychopathologies. The dominant approach that follows this methodology is the deficit-based model of psychopathology. One starts with a proposal about how cognition operates in the typical case, and explains phenomena associated with the pathological condition by citing ways normal cognition is selectively impaired (Cratsley and Samuels 2013). For example, Simon Baron-Cohen and others have claimed that the social and communicative difficulties associated with autism are due to a selective impairment of a "theory of mind" module that is present in typical subjects (Baron-Cohen et al. 1985, 44).

Recently, this use of developmental psychopathologies has been challenged. Karmiloff-Smith (1992, 2002) argues that such a use relies on the false assumption that atypical development can produce selective deficits while the rest of the system develops normally (Thomas and Karmiloff-Smith 2002). The mature brains of those with atypical development may be so different that one must model them directly, in their own right. Using a model of typical cognitive structure to infer conclusions about the existence of specific cognitive deficits is problematic.[6]

## 5 Conclusion

In this chapter, we introduced the philosophy of psychology as a reflection on how to study the mind. We first discussed this question in relation to whether folk psychological notions, such as beliefs, should be preserved in a scientific psychology. After surveying the main positions on this topic, we looked at two areas of current empirical research where debates about the nature and status of folk psychology loom large. We concluded with some further methodological considerations, this time concerning interactions between the study of the "normal" mind and the study of the "abnormal" mind (psychopathology). These considerations arise in the philosophy of psychiatry, an emerging field that promises further developments in our understanding of how best to do psychology.

## Notes

1 The label 'realism' is used in a variety of ways to characterize a variety of positions. 'Scientific realism', for example, is a general view concerning scientific theories and their ontological commitments. In this chapter, we focus on 'intentional realism', which is a view specific to the philosophy of psychology. According to intentional realism—as described and named by one of its main proponents (Fodor 1987)—folk psychology is a starting point for the development of a scientific psychology, and its posits are real and irreducible psychological entities. Although different in scope, intentional realism and scientific realism share the intuition that if a theory is successful in a certain domain, then it likely picks out real entities and properties. In what follows, when we use the label 'realism' we mean 'intentional realism'.

2 See Hatfield 2002 for a different interpretation of classical behaviorists like Tolman and Watson. Ryle himself is hard to classify as a reductionist. His work can be read as an attempt to analyze the *concept* of mental states—that is, what people actually mean when they use talk of mental states.

3 There is a complex issue here concerning the nature of the claims made by the intentional realist. When the realist says that beliefs and desires are real, she can make an ontological or an epistemic claim (or both). An epistemic reading of the realist position would be that beliefs and desires are real just in the sense of being needed for explanation. In this chapter, we take intentional realists to hold both that folk psychology is epistemically useful and that it is ontologically real. Thanks to Lee McIntyre for raising this issue.

4 Whether and how Descartes can be read as a realist is a matter of interpretive debate. Part of the challenge concerns the interplay between his ontological and epistemic commitments. For a helpful discussion of how Descartes can be read as a realist about the mental, see Hatfield 2014.

5 'Mindreading' as it is used here and in the psychological sciences is a technical term and should not be confused with uses of 'mindreading' that refer to telepathic thought-transference.
6 For a detailed critique of Karmiloff-Smith's arguments see Machery 2011. Machery distinguishes the claim that atypical development may affect many (perhaps all) cognitive systems from the claim that atypical development produces different kinds of systems, and argues that one may grant the first claim, without thereby having to accept the second, stronger claim.

# References

Aristotle. 1998 *The Metaphysics*, trans. and ed. H. Lawson-Tancred, H. London: Penguin Books.

Armstrong, D. 1981/2002. "The causal theory of the mind." In *Philosophy of Mind: Classical and Contemporary Readings*, ed. David J. Chalmers, 80–87. Oxford: Oxford University Press.

Baron-Cohen, S., Leslie, A. M., and Frith, U. 1985. "Does the autistic child have a 'theory of mind'?" *Cognition* 21: 37–46.

Bellugi, U., Wang, P., Jernigan, T. 1994. "Williams syndrome: An unusual neuropsychological profile." In *Atypical Cognitive Deficits in Developmental Disorders: Implications for Brain Function*, ed. Sarah Broman and Jordan Grafman, 23–56. Hillsdale, NJ: Erlbaum Press.

Bermúdez, J. L. 2005. *Philosophy of Psychology: A Contemporary Introduction*. New York: Routledge.

Burge, T. 1979. "Individualism and the mental." In *Midwest Studies in Philosophy*, IV, ed. Peter French, Edward Uehling, and Howard Wettstein, 73–121. Minneapolis: University of Minnesota Press.

Burge, T. 1986. "Individualism and psychology." *Philosophical Review* 95: 3–45.

Carnap, R. 1932/1959. "Psychologie in physikalischer Sprache." *Erkenntnis*, 3: 10–42. Trans. George Schick as "Psychology in physical language." In *Logical Positivism*, ed. A. J. Ayer, 165–97. New York: Free Press.

Carruthers, P. 2006. *The Architecture of the Mind*. Oxford: Oxford University Press.

Cherniak, C. 1990. *Minimal Rationality*. Cambridge, MA: MIT Press.

Chomsky, N. 1967. "A review of B. F. Skinner's *Verbal Behavior*." In *Readings in the Psychology of Language*, ed. Leon A. Jakobovits and Murray S. Miron, 142–43. Englewood Cliffs, NJ: Prentice Hall.

Churchland, P. M. 1979. *Scientific Realism and the Plasticity of Mind*. Cambridge: Cambridge University Press.

Churchland, P. M. 1981. "Eliminative materialism and the propositional attitudes." *Journal of Philosophy* 78(2): 67–90.

Churchland, P. M. 1989. *A Neurocomputational Perspective*. Cambridge, MA: MIT Press.

Clahsen, H. and Almazan, M. 1998. "Syntax and morphology in Williams syndrome." *Cognition* 68(3): 167–98.

Clark, A. and Chalmers, D. 1998. "The extended mind." *Analysis* 58(1): 7–19.

Cratsley, K. and Samuels, R. 2013. "Cognitive science and explanations of psychopathology." In *The Oxford Handbook of Philosophy and Psychiatry*, ed. K. W. M. Fulford, Martin Davies, Richard Gipps, George Graham, John Sadler, Tim Thornton, and Giovanni Stanghellini, 413–33. Oxford: Oxford University Press.

Davies, M. 1994. "The mental simulation debate." In *Objectivity, Simulation and the Unity of Consciousness*, ed. Christopher Peacocke, 99–127. Oxford: Oxford University Press.

Dennett, D. 1981. "True believers: The intentional strategy and why it works." In *Scientific Explanation: Papers Based on Herbert Spencer Lectures Given in the University of Oxford*, ed. A. F. Heath, 150–167. Oxford: Clarendon Press.

Dennett, D. 1987. *The Intentional Stance*. Cambridge, MA: MIT Press.

Descartes, R. 1641/1996. *Meditations on First Philosophy*, trans. John Cottingham. Cambridge: Cambridge University Press.

Egan, F. 2014. "How to think about mental content." *Philosophical Studies* 170: 115–35.

Fodor, J. A. 1987. *Psychosemantics: The Problem of Meaning in the Philosophy of Mind*. Cambridge, MA: MIT Press.

Fuchs, T. 2009. "Phenomenology and psychopathology." In *Handbook of Phenomenology and Cognitive Science*, ed. Daniel Schmicking and Shaun Gallagher, 547–73. Dordrecht, New York, Heidelberg, and London: Springer Science and Business Media.

Gallagher, S. 2012. "Empathy, simulation, and narrative." *Science in Context* 25(3): 355–81.

Gallagher, S. and Hutto, D. 2008. "Primary interaction and narrative practice." In *The Shared Mind: Perspectives on Intersubjectivity*, ed. Jordan Zlatev, Timothy P. Racine, Chris Sinha, and Esa Itkonen, 17–38. Amsterdam: John Benjamins.

Goldman, A. 2006. *Simulating Minds: The Philosophy, Psychology, and Neuroscience of Mindreading*. Oxford: Oxford University Press.

Gordon, R. 1986. "Folk psychology as simulation." *Mind and Language* 1: 158–71.

Gopnik, A. and Meltzoff, A. N. 1997. *Words, Thoughts and Theories*. Cambridge, MA: MIT Press.

Harman, G. 1987. "(Non-solipsistic) conceptual role semantics." In *New Directions in Semantics*, ed. Ernest Lepore, 55–82. London: Academic Press.

Hatfield, G. 2002. "Psychology, philosophy, and cognitive science: Reflections on the history and philosophy of experimental psychology." *Mind and Language* 17(3): 207–32.

Hatfield, G. 2014. *The Routledge Philosophy GuideBook to Descartes and the "Meditations."* New York: Routledge.

Heal, J. 1998. "Co-cognition and off-line simulation: two ways of understanding the simulation approach." *Mind and Language* 13(4): 477–98.

Heil, J. 2003. *From an Ontological Point of View*. Oxford: Clarendon Press.

Hempel, C. 1935/1949. "Analyse logique de la psychologie." *Revue de Synthèse* 10: 27–42. Trans. Wilfrid Sellars as "Logical analysis of psychology." In *Readings in Philosophical Analysis*, ed. Herbert Feigl and Wilfrid Sellars, 373–84. New York: Appleton-Century-Crofts.

Hutto, D. 2008. *Folk Psychological Narratives: The Socio-Cultural Basis of Understanding Reasons*. Cambridge MA: MIT Press.

Jackson, F. and Rey, G. 1998. "Mind, philosophy of." In *Routledge Encyclopedia of Philosophy*, ed. T. Crane. Accessed November 15, 2015. www.rep.routledge.com/articles/mind-philosophy-of/v-1/.

Jacob, P. 2011. "The direct-perception model of empathy: A critique." *Review of Philosophy and Psychology* 2: 519–40.

Kahneman, D. 2011. *Thinking, Fast and Slow*. New York: Farrar, Straus and Giroux.

Karmiloff-Smith, A. 1992. *Beyond Modularity: A Developmental Perspective on Cognitive Science*. Cambridge MA: MIT Press.

Karmiloff-Smith, A., Grant, J., Berthoud, I., Davies, M., Howlin, P., and Udwin, O. 1997. Language and Williams syndrome: How intact is 'intact'?" *Child Development* 68: 274–90

Kim, J. 1993. *Supervenience and Mind: Selected Philosophical Essays*. Cambridge: Cambridge University Press.

Knobe, J. 2007. "Folk psychology: Science and morals." In *Folk Psychology Re-Assessed*, ed. Daniel Hutto and Matthew Ratcliffe, 157–73. Dordrecht and London: Springer.

Krueger, J. and Overgaard, S. 2012. "Seeing subjectivity: Defending a perceptual account of other minds." *Protosociology* 47: 239–62.

Machery, E. 2010. "Philosophy of psychology." In *Philosophies of the Sciences: A Guide*, ed. Fritz Allhoff, 262–92. Oxford: Wiley-Blackwell.

Machery, E. 2011. "Developmental disorders and cognitive architecture." In *Maladapting Minds: Philosophy, Psychiatry, and Evolutionary Theory*, ed. Pieter R. Adriaens and Andreas De Block, 91–116. Oxford: Oxford University Press.

Mandelbaum, E. 2013. "Thinking is believing." *Inquiry* 57(1): 55–93.

Mason, K., Sripada, C. S., and Stich, S. 2008. "The philosophy of psychology." In *The Routledge Companion to Twentieth-Century Philosophy*, ed. Dermot Moran, 583–617. London: Routledge.

Neander, K. 2015. "Why I am not a content pragmatist." Available online at the 2015 Minds Online conference. Accessed August 12, 2016. Originally accessed September 2015. http://mindsonline.philosophyofbrains.com/wp-content/uploads/2015/09/Why-I%E2%80%99m-not-a-Content-Pragmatist.pdf.

Overgaard, S. 2007. "What, if anything, can phenomenology teach psychopathology (and vice versa)?" First Conference for Applied Phenomenology, University of Tokyo, Japan. Accessed August 12, 2016. Originally accessed September 2015. www2.ipcku.kansai-u.ac.jp/~t980020/Husserl/appliedPhenomenology/overgaard.pdf.

Piattelli-Palmarini, M. 1994. *Inevitable Illusions: How Mistakes of Reason Rule Our Minds*. New York: John Wiley and Sons.

Plato. 1992. *Republic*, trans. G. M. A. Grube, rev. C. D. C. Reeve. Indianapolis: Hackett.

Putnam, H. 1967. "Psychological predicates." In *Art, Mind, and Religion*, ed. W. H. Capitan and D. D. Merrill, 37–48. Pittsburgh, PA: University of Pittsburgh Press. Repr. in Putnam 1975 as "The nature of mental states," 150–61.

Putnam, H. 1975. "The meaning of meaning." In *Philosophical Papers*, vol. 2, *Mind, Language, and Reality*, 215–71. Cambridge: Cambridge University Press.

Putnam, H. 1987. *The Many Faces of Realism*. Paul Carus Lectures. La Salle, IL: Open Court.

Ramsey, W. 1997. "Do connectionist representations earn their explanatory keep?" *Mind and Language* 12: 34–66.

Ramsey, W., Stich, S., and Garon, J. 1991. "Connectionism, eliminativism, and the future of folk psychology." In *Philosophy and Connectionist Theory*, ed. William Ramsey, David Rumelhart, and Stephen Stich, 199–228. Hillsdale, NJ: Erlbaum.

Ramsey, W., Stich, S., and Rumelhart, D., eds. 1991. *Philosophy and Connectionist Theory*. Hillsdale, NJ: Erlbaum. Rupert, R. 2004. "Challenging the hypothesis of extended cognition." *Journal of Philosophy* 101: 389–428.

Rumelhart, D. E., McClelland, J. L., P. R. Group, et al. 1988. "Parallel distributed processing," vol. 1. IEEE.

Ryle, G. 1949/2009. *The Concept of Mind*. London and New York: Routledge.

Sass, L., Whiting, J., and Parnas, J. 2000. "Mind, self and psychopathology: Reflections on philosophy, theory and the study of mental illness." *Theory and Psychology* 10(1): 87–98.

Skinner, B. F. 1938. *Behavior of Organisms: An Experimental Analysis*. New York: Appleton-Century.

Sperber, D. 1994. "The modularity of thought and the epidemiology of representations." In *Mapping the Mind*, ed. Lawrence A. Hirschfeld and Susan A. Gelman, 39–67. Cambridge: Cambridge University Press.

Stich, S. 1996. *Deconstructing the Mind*. New York: Oxford University Press.

Thomas, M. and Karmiloff-Smith, A. 2002. "Are developmental disorders like cases of adult brain damage? Implications from connectionist modelling." *Behavioral and Brain Sciences* 25: 727–88.

Tolman, E. C. 1932. *Purposive Behavior in Animals and Men*. New York: Century.

Turing, A. 1950. "Computing machinery and intelligence." *Mind* 59(236): 433–60.

Tversky, A. and Kahneman, D. 1974. "Judgment under uncertainty: Heuristics and biases." *Science* 185(4157): 1124–131.

Van Gelder, T. 1995. "What might cognition be, if not computation?" *Journal of Philosophy* 92(7): 345–81.

Watson, J. B. 1913. "Psychology as the behaviorist views it." *Psychological Review* 20: 158–77.

Zahavi, D. 2010. "Empathy, embodiment and interpersonal understanding: From Lipps to Schutz." *Inquiry* 53: 285–306.

# 36
# PHILOSOPHY OF SOCIOLOGY AND ANTHROPOLOGY

## Mark Risjord

### 1 Introduction

Myriad philosophical issues arise from the disciplines of sociology and anthropology. Depending on how your university has chosen to carve itself into departments, the faculty members of an Anthropology Department may study symbolism, economic relationships, language, institutional structures, politics, history, and more. Members of the Sociology Department will study these topics with an additional emphasis on institutions, large-scale societies, urban settings, and social change. There are, of course differences. Anthropology, especially in the USA, has traditionally included archeology, human evolution, and the biological variation among humans (physical anthropology) within its scope, while the sociological concern with social structure overlaps with topics studied in psychology, political science, and economics. Indeed, it is difficult to find any topic in the social sciences that anthropologists or sociologists do not study. As a result, almost every chapter of this volume raises an issue in the philosophy of sociology and anthropology. The definitive issues in the philosophy of sociology and anthropology arise from concepts that play distinctive roles in sociology and anthropology. This chapter will discuss two: culture and norm.

The concept of culture has traditionally provided a unifying theme for the discipline of anthropology, and appeal to culture is a common part of anthropological analyses. Anthropologists have typically treated institutions, kinship relationships, political arrangements and other elements of social structure as a *part* of culture. Sociologists have often distinguished between culture and social structure (or sometimes "the cultural system" and "the social system"). Culture, on this view, is a realm of values, meanings, or symbols, while the social structure concerns the way in which individuals are related. By making this distinction, sociologists isolate the social system for study in ways that many anthropologists would resist. In our discussion here, we will gloss over these differences between sociology and anthropology, focusing on their shared notion of culture.

The use of "culture" in anthropological and sociological theories raises three important philosophical questions: What kind of thing is a culture? How is it related to the beliefs and behavior of individuals? And how do we come to know about cultures? The first two questions are meta-physical, and they touch on issues of reductionism (see Chapters 10, 12, and 21 of this volume), functionalism (Chapter 13), social ontology (Chapter 22), and realism (Chapter 23). The third is an epistemological question. While it is important (and Chapters 2, 3, 4, 7, and 9 of this volume discuss aspects of it), this essay will consider epistemological issues only as they bear on the two metaphysical questions. The debates we will discuss are not just philosophical. As a consequence of these ongoing debates, the concept of culture evolved in significant ways during the twentieth century. We will inquire into these questions in sections 2 and 3.

Norms are an aspect of both culture and social structure. Many questions asked in the study of a particular social group are about norms: Who is permitted (or required) to marry whom? What foods are appropriate (or forbidden) to eat? What forms of decoration are considered beautiful (or ugly)? Who may speak at public assemblies? Who may own property? These are "normative" in the sense that they invoke, explicitly or implicitly, the ideas of permission and prohibition, entitlement and exclusion. Rules or laws are explicit norms, and sociologists often invoke explicit norms in their explanations of institutions and other forms of social structure. Cultural norms, such as norms of dress or etiquette, may have important roles among a group of people even if they remain unspoken.

The central philosophical issue about norms in the social sciences concerns their relation to the thoughts and actions of the members of a group. It is almost a dogma of modern philosophy that statements about what *ought to be* (what we are here calling norms) cannot be reduced to or defined by statements about what *is*. There is no contradiction between saying that "drivers ought to be polite" and pointing out that most drivers are not polite. Norms present us with a dilemma. If norms are identified with patterns of behavior (as many social scientists do), then it is difficult to see how they can be truly normative. Talk of "norms" is just a misleading way of describing regularities in what people, in fact, do. On the other hand, if norms are taken to have a special ontological status over and above the thoughts and actions of individuals, it is difficult to see how they could have any use in scientific explanations. For explanatory purposes, one might say, it does not matter what people *ought* to do; it only matters what they *actually* do, and why. We will examine this issue in sections 4 and 5.

## 2 The Reification of Culture

To get a feel for the ways in which the concept of culture has figured in social explanation and understanding, let us begin with an example: Renato Rosaldo's ethnographic classic *Ilongot Headhunting 1883–1974* (1980). The Ilongot are a group that traditionally lived in the highland areas of the northern Philippines Islands. As the title of the book suggests, one of their distinctive practices was "headhunting." Rosaldo lived among the Ilongot, collecting many stories about headhunting raids in which his interlocutors participated. Some of these raids were part of longstanding feuds between communities of Ilongot. Other raids were against non-Ilongot communities in the lowland areas of the island. One common form for such raids was for a small group of unmarried, young adult men to form a raiding party. Experienced headhunters would lead the novices. The raid often took the form of an ambush. When the victim was killed, his (or her) head was severed and thrown into the forest.

Viewed from the perspective of the twenty-first century, this practice is unimaginably grue-some. The brutal beheadings by militant groups in Iraq and Syria have shocked and appalled the rest of the world. Can we understand the Ilongot practices differently? Should we? The anthropological and sociological approach to such matters has been to try to attain an "internal" or "emic" perspective on such events. That is, they try to understand the activities of a group as the members of the group understand it. In Malinowski's memorable phrase, "The goal is, briefly, to grasp the native's point of view, his relation to life, *his* vision of *his* world" (Malinowski 1922, 25).

Rosaldo discusses several ways in which headhunting was integrated into Ilongot life. Participation in headhunting raids was part of the way that young men came to have the status of full adults in the community. Those who had successfully "taken a head" were permitted to wear special forms of decoration. The status made it more likely for a man to marry and start a household. In addition, the raids were part of a system of feuds and alliance-building among Ilongot communities. Raids were justified on the basis of "anger" about past attacks or other insults. Covenants would stop the cycles of violence and retaliation, and intermarriage between the groups might strengthen the relationship. Headhunting raids could continue against *other* groups, but a covenant suspended raiding among allies.

This very brief sketch illustrates several ways in which the concept of culture is important for understanding human behavior. First, to speak of the culture of a group is to make a generalization about it: they conduct retaliatory headhunting raids, they form binding agreements not to raid each other, and so on. Such generalizations identify patterns that transcend individual difference; they are not exceptionless, nor are they averages. Their generalizing power arises partly from their normative character. That is, while not every young man who becomes an adult participates in a headhunting raid, the Ilongot regarded raiding as valuable and important, something a young man should do. Even when generalizations about culture are not so explicitly normative—e.g. that the Ilongot practiced swidden agriculture and hunted in the forest—they capture patterns that are locally salient.

A second feature of the way culture figures in social explanation is that to understand a culture is to understand how its different elements are integrated. Having identified different patterns, the anthropologist or sociologist tries to show how they fit together. In his account, Rosaldo fits the practice of headhunting into Ilongot settlement practices and inter-community relationships, as well as their expectations about the typical life cycle, attributions of status, and conceptualization of kin relations. We understand something about why headhunting persisted by showing how it fit with other aspects of the culture. To understand why some of these patterns change over time, we look for change in other parts of the culture.

The holistic character of culture helps anthropologists and sociologists explain both social events and individual actions. Contextualization is one form that such explanations take. Why did this young man lie in ambush and kill another? The answer is that he was participating in a headhunting raid. If we want to know something more specific, such as the individual's actual motives or reasons, we may appeal to commonly held beliefs and values. We might point out that the young man was courting a specific woman, and he believed that the social status brought by a successful headhunting raid would improve his chances. These are culturally specific beliefs, and their ability to explain the action depends on the cultural context. After all, if a young man in your university ambushed and killed another just to gain the admiration of a woman, we would treat him as criminally insane.

Appealing to culture in explaining action appears to treat culture as a kind of thing, distinct from the beliefs and actions of the individuals. Should we think of cultures as having this kind of ontological status? In the sciences, it is common to postulate the existence of entities that cannot be directly experienced; think of dark matter or space-time. At first, these theoretical entities may seem ontologically extravagant. We become more comfortable with them as they demonstrate their value in explanations or for unifying different theories. One might make the same argument for the existence of culture. By supposing that groups of people have cultures we can explain social phenomena that we could not otherwise understand; hence we should suppose that cultures exist. Let us call this view a "realist" conception of culture.

Some of the most important arguments against treating culture as a kind of thing (or, as we will say, reifying it) have come from within sociology and anthropology. These arguments have been partly empirical and partly philosophical. As mentioned above, holism is one of the key features of the way culture is used in explanation. Many have argued, however, that cultures are much less integrated than the ethnographic studies portray them to be. Even in very small societies with clear geographic boundaries—like the Ilongot—there are important differences among individuals and over time. Individuals within a single group may have conflicting views about what one "ought" to do, or how social practices "normally" proceed. Such differences and conflicts within the group may be very important mechanisms for both social change and the reproduction of the very patterns that the anthropologist or sociologist is trying to explain. This general point has been supported by both theoretical argument and empirical evidence (Bourdieu 1977; Archer 1988).

Further problems arise around the idea of cultural boundaries. In its classic form, the concept of culture cleanly divided human populations into a world-wide patchwork quilt. Each group had a culture, and each culture was distinct from its neighbors'. In practice, things were never quite so tidy. Rosaldo describes episodes where some Ilongots moved to the lowlands, integrated into the culture there, then later returned to the highlands. While living in the lowlands, having adopted new forms of behavior, were they Ilongot? The question does not have a clear answer, because people often move fluidly among groups, even when those groups have different languages or religions. More importantly, cultures may overlap and share members. In some cases, such coincidence means that whether a single individual is a member of this or that culture depends on the immediate context. In other cases, it may be indeterminate. The idea that cultures have clear boundaries seems to arise from a combination of geographical accident—studying groups who inhabit islands or are otherwise isolated—and the conventions of ethnographic writing (Clifford and Marcus 1986).

These two problems, the lack of holistic integration and the lack of clear boundaries, undermine the explanatory power of culture. If we seek to show that a form of behavior conforms to the culture, a critic may ask "which part?" or "which culture?" The behavior may conform or fail to conform to more than one possible generalization about the group. And if cultural patterns are not determinate, then showing how the action fits a pattern has little explanatory value.

We might respond to the foregoing issue by admitting that merely showing that an action fits a pattern is not much of an explanation. It does not really tell us *why* the agent acted as he or she did. Culture *determines* action, at least in part. This raises an issue that is sometimes called the problem of structure and agency. If culture or social structure fully explains action, then the particular motivations (beliefs, values, emotions, and so on) of the individuals become irrelevant to explanation. People are treated as mere cogs in a social machine. While this may feel uncanny, the deeper problem is that it ignores the way in which individuals often resist aspects of their culture. Indeed, because cultures are not homogeneous and perfectly coherent, individual agents may use one aspect of culture against another, exploiting contradictions and incoherencies. The challenge is to find some way to treat the cultural (or social) level as explanatory and at the same time recognize the importance of individual agency. It is not clear that a realist conception of culture can meet this challenge.

## 3  Alternative Conceptions of Culture

If culture is not a kind of thing, then what is it? As a result of the arguments we have just canvassed, anthropologists and sociologists have tried to re-think the idea of culture. While there are many different suggestions, we will discuss two prominent ones. The first takes a reductionist or individualist approach. On this view, cultures do not exist over and above individual humans. Humans *represent* the world around them by forming beliefs, concepts, and values. They act and make choices on the basis of these representations. The concept of culture is a rough way of identifying groups of people who have similar, but not identical, representations. The similarity among members of a culture is analogous to the similarity among recipes. If you search online for "the" recipe for fruitcake, you will find dozens of different recipes. These recipes will use flour, eggs, dried fruit, spices, and some kind of liquor. But the kinds and amounts will vary; some ingredients will be omitted. Like generalizations about culture, we can make generalizations about recipes: fruitcake recipes include dried fruit. While the boundaries are vague, at some point the differences are so great that we stop recognizing the recipe as a fruitcake recipe. A cake made from liver, dried fruit, flour, and brandy might be tasty (or not!), but it wouldn't be a fruitcake. Similarly, members of a social group will have overlapping, but not identical, representations. There is no clear boundary between those who are in the culture and those who are not, but at some point the differences become so great that generalizations about the group break down entirely.

An individualist conception of culture changes the way culture figures in explanation, as well as the questions we can ask about culture. To explain an individual's actions, we must appeal to his or her representations. To explain why s/he has those representations, we must appeal to his or her particular experiences. This means that generalizations about a group do very little to help understand individual action. Moreover, the questions of cultural analysis change. Treating culture as homogeneous and integrated presupposes that members of a group share representations. On an individualist conception, by contrast, the fact that members of a group have similar representations is something to be explained. Why do such clusters of similar representations arise and why are they stable? Why do some representations catch on and spread quickly while others fade away? Sperber (1996) has argued that cognitive psychology must figure in the answers to these questions, thus linking anthropology and sociology to psychology.

Not all anthropologists and sociologists have been satisfied with an individualist account of culture. Treating culture as nothing but patterns of individual representation seems to lose the explanatory power of the original idea of culture. For example, we might wonder why headhunting persists among the Ilongot. After all, it perpetuates brutal cycles of violence among neighbors. Why don't the parties simply eliminate headhunting? The answer based on Rosaldo's ethnography would involve the role of headhunting in the male lifecycle, status in the community, and so on. These patterns are not easily translated into individual beliefs. Indeed, many anthropologists and sociologists emphasize that members of a social group may have inaccurate beliefs about their own culture. One of the reasons anthropologists, in particular, study people very different from themselves is precisely that features of the culture or social system may be more visible to an outsider than they are to an insider. On an individualist approach, the members of the group must represent all elements of the culture.

An alternative to both the realist and individualist approach to culture is often called "practice theory." This is something of a misnomer, because there is no specific theory shared by those who adopt this view. Rather, it is a general approach to thinking about culture and social structure with philosophical roots in Wittgenstein (1953). It was prominently developed by Bourdieu (1977), Giddens (1984), and Ortner (1984). "Practices" sit in the middle between individual actions and the abstractions of reified culture. Like the individualists, the practice theorists see cultural forms as the result of individual interactions. But unlike the individualists, they do not try to reduce cultural forms to individual actions. As a first pass, practices can be thought of as recurring patterns of coordinated action. Practices are like a dialogue or conversation insofar as they unfold as agents respond to prior moves by others. Practice theory comfortably accommodates Rosaldo's analysis of headhunting. It is a recurring pattern of action, reproduced through the response of agents to each other. The Ilongot also have practices of treating some young men as full adults, others as eligible (or desirable) for marriage, and so on. A culture is a group of agents who participate in overlapping and interlocking practices.

Practice theory preserves the holism of earlier conceptions of culture insofar as the practices coexist and influence each other. It also permits the anthropologist or sociologist to make generalizations about the culture and use these in explanations. There are, however, two important differences between practice theory and a realist concept of culture. First, the realist treats culture as largely independent of the actions of individuals. Practice theorists, by contrast, see all practices as reproduced through the agency of community members. Practices are something that people enact. This does not mean that practices are all the result of deliberate calculation. Many practices are habitual and unreflective. Think, for example, about the patterns of behavior in your college cafeteria—the way people do (or do not) form lines, how gender, race, and other affiliations pattern how people move, where they sit, and so on. As freshmen, these practices were quite foreign to you. You may have had to think about them and figure them out. Now you engage with them unreflectively. When practices are habitual, we are capable of reflecting on them. We can, and do, deliberately violate them. Sometimes, such deliberate violations lead to social change, as when during the American civil rights movement, Black students deliberately sat in areas designated "Whites only."

The possibility of disrupting practices through deliberate action highlights the second difference between practice theory and the realist concept of culture. Practice theorists agree with the criticism that culture is rarely well integrated. Practices will often be in tension or outright conflict with one another. Agents can use these conflicts strategically. In Rosaldo's analysis, for example, he notes the tension between the need to retaliate in a feud, and the various relations by marriage that are reasons against feuding. An individual agent may be at the nexus of these practices, able to invoke kinship as a reason for peace, or to invoke insult as a reason for war. For practice theorists, the *lack* of integration among practices is an important resource for understanding the mechanisms by which cultural forms change and reproduce.

Practice theory is not without its philosophical difficulties. Practices are often treated as if they were nothing more than patterns of behavior. Conceived in this way, they have many of the same defects as the realist concept of culture. Similar to the realist, generalizing about a practice goes beyond the actual behavior. Just as two data points on a graph can be made to lie on an infinite variety of possible curves, a pair of actions can be described as fitting indefinitely many patterns of practice. Since no evidence can discriminate among them, the choice among patterns seems arbitrary. Some practice theorists address this difficulty by postulating that agents internalize the practices of their group. The actions of two agents are part of the same practice when the actions arise from the same internal source. This solution simply pushes the difficulty inside the agent (Turner 1994). If practices are reproduced through the transmission of some internalized disposition, we must ask "in virtue of what are these internal dispositions the same?" The practice theorist seems forced to admit that such dispositions need not be the same, only similar. Having made this move, practice theory seems to collapse into individualism: practices are nothing more than patterns of action produced by agents with similar representations.

Practice theorists respond to the potential collapse of practices into individual actions by highlighting the *normativity* of practice. To say that a number of people participate in a practice is to say that they regard doing so as appropriate, or even obligatory. Practice theorists argue that when we try to reduce correct and incorrect ways of acting to individual beliefs about what it is right to do, the normativity—the sense that one ought to act in a certain way—gets lost. This response opens a new debate: can there be a scientific study of what one *ought* to do?

## 4 Social Norms

Appeals to social norms have been a staple of anthropological and sociological analysis. But what do we mean by a "norm"? Let us begin with some examples:

- Conversational distance. When two people speak, they put a comfortable distance between themselves. Stand too close and it feels creepy; too far apart makes you self-conscious. Anthropologists and linguists have shown that the preferred distance varies among cultures, and within a culture it may vary with gender and social status.
- Status and role. It is common for introductory sociology textbooks to distinguish between statuses and roles. A social status is a recognized social position, such as teacher, student, or police officer. A social status typically is a place within the larger social order. A person who occupies a status is expected to act in particular ways. A teacher, for instance, ought to answer questions, provide explanations, and grade fairly. A teacher is also often expected to give advice and professional mentorship. These are different roles attached to the status of being a teacher.
- Taboo. In many cultures anthropologists have found strong prohibitions against doing certain actions, talking to a particular person, touching certain kinds of object, or eating specific foods. These prohibitions are often limited to a time or context, and violation of the taboo is thought to invoke misfortune or spiritual punishment.
- Institutional rules. Organizations, especially in literate, modern societies, govern themselves with explicitly stated rules and regulations.

These examples illustrate several important features of norms as discussed in anthropology and sociology. First, there is a difference between *descriptive* norms and *prescriptive* norms. A descriptive norm is a generalization about what most or many people in a society do. In today's universities, for example, very few students dye their hair purple. In most cases, this pattern is a descriptive norm. There is no rule demanding undyed hair, and while the other students might think purple hair is eccentric or interesting, they do not judge it wrong or inappropriate. Of course, a school could adopt a rule against dyeing one's hair purple, and then the norm would be prescriptive. Each of the four examples, above, illustrates a kind of prescriptive norm that has played a role in sociology and anthropology.

Prescriptive norms say what ought or ought not be done. They articulate permissions, prohibitions, entitlements, and binding obligations. Notice that norms may be positive or negative; they can permit or forbid. Notice also that they come in a variety of strengths. Some norms say that you *may* do something, but you *need* not do so: enrolled students are permitted to use the library. Other norms express what you must (or must not) do: if you check out a library book, you must return it. Failure to follow a norm invites judgment or criticism, but not all norms invite sanction or punishment. Because you are an enrolled student, for example, the librarian *ought* to let you check out a book. If he or she does not, then you can rightly complain. When you fail to return that library book, by contrast, the library will not just complain, it will fine you.

Prescriptive norms may be more or less *explicit*. Your university probably has a written policy about who can use the library. Institutional policies, rules, and regulations are examples of explicit norms. They are either written down for all to see or they are announced in public contexts. Some taboos and social roles are explicit. Parents formulate some of these norms for their children; religious texts express others. But not all norms are explicit. Behavior, not words, expresses implicit norms. When someone violates an implicit norm, those around the violator typically respond in some way. The behavior may attract mild forms of sanction, such as frowns or "the hairy eyeball." If the violation is significant enough, it may attract a rebuke or stronger punishment. Because implicit norms are easiest to see when they are violated, travelers often notice the difference between the norms of their community and the local norms. For example you may never have noticed the norms governing conversational distance. When you travel, and you find your conversational partners uncomfortably close, the difference in norms becomes obvious.

The possibility of implicit norms can obscure the difference between descriptive and prescriptive norms. In the absence of an explicitly stated rule, one might well wonder whether there really is a difference between "most people do it" and "everybody ought to do it." For example, is maintaining a particular conversational distance really a *norm*? Or is it just something that most people do? The possibility of making a mistake grounds one commonly accepted criterion for the difference: if $x$ is a norm, then there must be a difference between something seeming right (permissible, required) according to $x$ and something being right according to $x$. If maintaining a particular conversational distance is a norm, then it must be possible for an individual to think that he or she is acting properly, but be mistaken. On the other hand, if maintaining a particular conversational distance is only a common behavior, a person cannot make a mistake. The reactions of other people to a deviation from the common pattern are thus important indicators[1] of whether a pattern is a descriptive or prescriptive norm. If there are no reactions, or if the reactions are only of surprise, then the pattern is likely to be a descriptive norm. Conversational distance is normative because people regard those who behave differently as making mistakes. Standing too close or too far away invites responses tinged with disapproval, if not outright censure.

Two philosophical issues arise from the use of norms in anthropological and sociological explanations. The first is epistemic. A longstanding issue in the philosophy of the social sciences is whether the social sciences should (or must) adopt the methods and forms of theorizing found in the natural sciences. Let us call the doctrine that the social sciences can be "scientific" only insofar as they emulate the natural sciences *methodological naturalism*.[2] From a naturalistic point of view, the appeal to prescriptive norms in anthropology and sociology is problematic. Natural science is based on systematic observation and testing, and theories in the natural sciences take the form of generalizations about what has been observed. The natural scientific explanation of an event proceeds either by showing how the event follows natural laws or by displaying the event's causes. The appeal to prescriptive norms in the understanding of culture and society does not obviously fit this form. Norms do *not* characterize what people actually do. It is entirely possible for norms to exist in a culture, and yet they may be routinely violated. And if norms are explanatory, they do not explain by showing the causes of behavior. We have, then, a dilemma: either we reject methodological naturalism and present an alternative account of the epistemology of sociology and anthropology, or we accept methodological naturalism and treat all social norms as descriptive norms.

The second issue arising from the appeal to norms in explanation is metaphysical. Many philosophers and scientists hold that there is one natural world. It is a world of causes and mechanisms, and it does not include any entities like souls or values. This position is also sometimes called "naturalism," so let us distinguish this doctrine from the first by calling it *ontological naturalism*. In the history of philosophy, it has been common to argue that "ought" cannot be reduced to "is," and one possible conclusion of such arguments is that the domain of right and wrong must be metaphysically different from the domain of is and is not. If these arguments are correct, then norms cannot be part of the "natural" world and ontological naturalism must be rejected. Social scientists, however, have not generally rejected ontological naturalism. They have offered many accounts of norms and normativity that try to show how they fit with or grow out of the causal mechanisms of human evolution, psychology, and social relationships. The question, then, is whether it is possible to provide a satisfactory account of norms within a causal and mechanistic metaphysical framework.

## 5 Concepts of Culture and their Consequences for Normativity

The metaphysics of normativity and the metaphysics of culture have similar, if not the same, roots. This means that the different conceptions of culture have distinct resources for meeting the challenges presented by ontological and methodological forms of naturalism. In sections 2 and 3 we discussed three different conceptions of culture: a realist conception that treated culture as a kind of thing, an individualist conception that reduced culture to the representations of individuals, and a practice-theoretic conception that treated cultures as clusters of interlocking practices. Let us consider the consequences of each of these for the problem of naturalism and normativity articulated at the end of section 4.

Anthropologists and sociologists who are realists about culture treat it as something distinct from the beliefs, attitudes, and actions of individuals. Culture is the home of symbols, meanings, values, and rules. Proponents of this kind of view are likely to reject both ontological and methodological naturalism. Culture, they will argue, does not reduce to a material realm of causes and law. Laws and causal generalizations must describe what is the case. To understand human action, we must describe what is *not* the case. Humans act for the sake of goals that do not yet exist. Humans create and act on norms that say what ought to be, not what is. Our ability to give ourselves norms and rules and to abide by them is a crucial part of what it means to be human. If ontological naturalism is inconsistent with normativity, then naturalism means giving up on understanding humans. Therefore, we must treat culture and normativity as distinct from the physical or biological basis of human life. Rejecting ontological naturalism in this way requires rejecting methodological naturalism as well. Insofar as the methods of the natural sciences cannot reveal prescriptive (as opposed to descriptive) norms, they are inadequate for a science of culture. Sociology and anthropology must have their own methods.[3]

An individualist can respond, of course, by reminding the realist of the difficulties that arise from reifying culture. The problem of structure and agency is particularly pressing when we consider norms. Suppose we want to explain why a particular Ilongot young man went headhunting. To say that there is a norm in his culture for young men to headhunt does not explain his action. Norms say what ought to happen, and they are not always followed. If the young man acted *because* of the norm, then he must have had some representation of the norm. He must have believed that he ought to go headhunting. Once we postulate the belief, the existence of the norm becomes irrelevant for the explanation. A realm of norms that is distinct from the world of causes and laws is scientifically unnecessary; all we need is to postulate the belief that there is a norm. A culture, the individualist will conclude, is just a population of individual humans with similar representations of norms, symbols, values, and so on.

An individualist conception of culture can thus accept both ontological and methodological naturalism. Ontologically, the elements of culture—norms, symbols, values, meaning—are all treated as individual representations. These shared beliefs are the basis for action, and insofar as the beliefs are similar, the actions will be too. Cultural generalizations and explanations are thus nothing more than characterizations of common beliefs. Epistemologically, studies of culture do not need any special methods because the goal is to identify patterns and causes. There will be differences between the natural and the social sciences, of course, since the subjects' language must figure in the methods (e.g. surveys will need translation, and interviews are a good way to identify subjects' beliefs). But this difference is no greater than the difference in method between chemistry and biology.

An opponent of an individualist conception of culture will object that an individualist conception of norms has two serious defects. First, it collapses the distinction between descriptive and prescriptive norms. To say that there is a norm among the Ilongot that one ought not conduct headhunting raids against kin, on an individualist view, is simply to say that many Ilongot believe that one ought not conduct such raids. But the statement about common belief describes a pattern. It does not articulate how people ought to behave in this culture. Hence it does not express a norm. In response, the individualist might accept this point, but insist that it is no objection. Normativity is not found in the pattern of beliefs; it is found in their content. The belief that one ought not conduct raids against kin is distinct from the belief that some, many, or most people do not. To say that there is such a norm in Ilongot culture is to point to beliefs about what ought to be done, not beliefs about what is done.

The individualist response to the first challenge runs right into the second challenge. Any account of normativity must leave room for a distinction between something *seeming* correct and something *being* correct according to the norm. If normativity is found in the content of the individual belief that one ought to do such-and-such, the difference between seeming right and being right collapses. Suppose an Ilongot man conducted a raid against a distantly related kinsman. He could insist that the relation was too distant to really count as "kin." Since this is a matter of his belief, he gets to construe the norm any way he likes. But that means anything he does is in conformity to the norm and there is no sense in which he is making a mistake. The same problem can be seen from another angle if we consider two Ilongot with different beliefs about when raids are appropriate. If there is nothing that makes one right and the other wrong, any argument between them about what ought to be done is empty. Whatever seems right to each individual is right. Arguing about what ought to be done would be as pointless as arguing about whether vanilla ice cream tastes better than chocolate ice cream. Presumably, participants to such debates presuppose that there is something at stake—something to get right—in their discussion. Individualism forces us to misrepresent the attitudes of those we seek to understand.

One of the motivations for practice theory is that it can address individualism's difficulties with norms without falling back into a realist conception of culture. For practice theory, normativity is not contained in individual representations. Normativity arises from the responses of individuals to each other. If an Ilongot man conducted a raid against his kin, others would respond to him. The kinsmen would demand restitution of some kind, and it is likely that these claims would be supported by members of the man's own household. Notice the structure here: (1) an individual does an action, (2) others take the attitude that (1) is correct or incorrect, and (3) still others take the attitude that (2) is correct or incorrect. The correctness or incorrectness of an action, then, is determined by the attitudes others take towards it. And these attitudes are themselves taken to be appropriate or inappropriate. To say that there is a norm that "one ought to do A" in a culture, then is to say that a group of people is responsive to performances of A, greeting it with attitudes of approval and perhaps reward which are themselves subject to assessment. It is clear that, on this conception of normativity, an individual can believe that his action is correct, and yet be mistaken.

The question of how a practice-theoretic account of norms squares with ontological or methodological naturalism is currently a question of great debate among philosophers of social science.[4] Practice theory is not reductionist, because practices cannot be identified with individuals or individual attitudes. The relationships among individuals constitute practices. Yet, unlike a realist conception of culture, the practice-theoretic account does not appeal to a non-material realm of norms. Norms are constituted by the attitudes and responses of individuals toward each other, and the materials of cognitive psychology fully account for such attitudes. In this way, practice theory seems consistent with ontological naturalism. In response, some argue that if practice theory really is committed only to a world of causes and laws, then it captures normativity no better than the individualist does. At the end of the day, practice theory just describes a more sophisticated pattern than does individualism. Both are just descriptions, and neither expresses a proper prescription.

## 6 Conclusion

Anthropological and sociological appeals to culture and normativity form the basis of an active field of philosophical inquiry. In this chapter, we have discussed only a small part of a larger set of questions. We have focused on the metaphysical questions about cultures and norms: What sorts of thing are they, and how are cultures and norms related to the thoughts and actions of individual humans? We have identified three philosophical positions—realism, individualism, and practice theory—and we have discussed *some* of the debate among these views. From the vantage point of this chapter, you can see some of the other interesting issues that arise in this area. We briefly touched on issues of explanation. How can a norm, which says what *ought* to be, not what *is*, explain individual actions or group events? Are such explanations causal, or is there a form of explanation specific to norms? We briefly touched on the need for translation, and interesting issues arise here too. When translating an unfamiliar language, must we assume that what the speakers say is largely true and rational? Or is it possible to find that their norms of rationality are different from the translator's? Finally, we had occasion to briefly mention the relationship between psychology, norms, and culture. How does culture and normativity fit with contemporary work on the evolution of cooperation, behavioral economics, and cognitive neuroscience? Should these research programs constrain our concepts of culture and norm, or should they remain distinct realms of inquiry? Having reached this waypoint in our philosophical tour, I can only recommend that you explore further.

## Notes

1 Reactions cannot be definitive, because there may be something that interferes with the reactions. For example, there may be other norms in play that suppress negative reactions from the onlookers.
2 For a thorough discussion of the different forms of naturalism, see Chapter 14 of this volume.
3 For a sense of what these methods might be like, see Chapters 3 and 7 of this volume.
4 See the essays in Risjord 2016.

## References

Archer, Margaret S. 1988. *Culture and Agency: The Place of Culture in Social Theory*. Cambridge: Cambridge University Press.

Bourdieu, Pierre. 1977. *Outline of a Theory of Practice*. Cambridge: Cambridge University Press.

Clifford, James, and George Marcus, eds. 1986. *Writing Culture: The Poetics and Politics of Ethnography*. Berkeley: University of California Press.

Giddens, Anthony. 1984. *Constitution of Society: Outline of the Theory of Structuration*. Cambridge: Polity Press.

Malinowski, Bronislaw. 1922. *Argonauts of the Western Pacific*. New York: E. P. Dutton & Co.

Ortner, Sherry. 1984. "Theory In Anthropology since the Sixties." *Comparative Studies in Society and History* 26(1): 126–66.

Risjord, Mark, ed. 2016. *Normativity and Naturalism in the Philosophy of the Social Sciences*. New York: Routledge.

Rosaldo, Renato. 1980. *Ilongot Headhunting 1883–1974*. Stanford: Stanford University Press.

Sperber, Daniel. 1996. *Explaining Culture*. Oxford: Blackwell.

Turner, Stephen. 1994. *The Social Theory of Practices*. Chicago: University of Chicago Press.

Wittgenstein, Ludwig. 1953. *Philosophical Investigations*. Trans. G. E. M. Anscombe. New York: Macmillan Publishing Company.

# 37

# WHY IS THERE NO PHILOSOPHY OF POLITICAL SCIENCE?

## Bruno Verbeek and Lee McIntyre

When looking at the field of philosophy of social science, it is striking that there are so many common questions across the disciplines that are concerned with explaining human behavior. Questions about the nature of explanation, the proper unit of analysis, reductionism, social ontology, methodological individualism—as well as other various questions about methodology—all seem to bubble up.

When we turn to the individual social sciences, however, something remarkable appears—or rather does *not* appear. While most disciplines have room for systematic reflection on the philosophical dimensions of their own particular field, not all of them exist. There is a well-established body of literature referred to as "philosophy of economics" which deals with fundamental concepts, methods, and problems that economic thought unearths. Similarly, there is a small but thriving field of philosophy of history (not to be confused with the large and thriving field of history of philosophy). There is philosophy of psychology, and even a budding philosophy of (Western and non-Western) sociology and anthropology. To a large extent these fields have their own journals, conferences, professional associations, and students. This is not the case, however, for one of the commonly recognized "big six" of the social sciences—economics, psychology, sociology, anthropology, history, and political science. And so we ask why, so far, has there been no field recognized as the "philosophy of political science"?

Now to say this does not mean that there has been no work in this area. Although this may sound like a contradiction, it is important to point out that a remarkably similar situation once existed in the philosophy of chemistry. Although there were a few scholars doing excellent work on relevant questions, there was no formally recognized discipline called the "philosophy of chemistry" until about 1997. Then everything changed. The field saw a sudden explosion of interest, resulting in two journals, an annual international conference, various research symposia, and several anthologies. And along with self-conscious recognition came a wealth of opportunities.[1]

Does a similar situation now exist for the philosophy of political science? In asking this, it is important to do an assessment of the current standing of the field. For one thing, there is a Master's Degree program in the philosophy of political science offered at the University of

Leiden. How can it possibly be that there is a graduate program in a subject when there is no subject? The answer is that of course there is a subject, but perhaps it has just not gotten enough philosophical attention or recognition. Either the philosophy of political science already exists (but is just not called that), or it doesn't exist (because it shouldn't), or it should exist (but doesn't). Whichever of these possibilities explains the fact that there has so far been no formally recognized discipline that goes by this name—making it the longest-standing "missing tooth" in the philosophy of social science—it is beyond dispute that work in this field has at least been neglected by most philosophers of science.

If one looks at the table of contents for the spate of recent handbooks, guides, and companions that have cropped up in the philosophy of social science over the last fifteen years (Turner and Roth 2003; Jarvie and Zamora-Bonilla 2011; Kincaid 2012) there is a discernible pattern. Although most feature ample coverage of issues in the philosophy of economics, history, and psychology, only one of them (Kincaid 2012) features an article with more than passing mention of political science. The situation is apparently no better at the biennial meeting of the Philosophy of Science Association (PSA), which showcases work throughout the philosophy of science (including both the philosophy of chemistry and the philosophy of social science). In a recent blog post Eric Schliesser asks "why the lack of philosophical interest in so many social sciences?"[2] He goes on to point out that at the 2014 PSA meeting in Chicago, there was ample representation of the philosophy of economics, but almost no coverage of any issues that could be said to fall within the philosophy of sociology, anthropology, or political science "despite the 'naturalistic' turn of the last four decades." The same is true if one looks for research symposia, books, papers, and most anything else with "philosophy of political science" in its title.

So has the philosophy of political science—insofar as it exists—at least been neglected?

Perhaps the answer to this oversight has more to do with institutional forces than with scholarship. Political science arrived relatively late as an academic discipline. Before the mid-1800s there was a lot of scholarly work on politics done by historians and philosophers. In addition, there was more applied work done by the German *Polizeiwissenschaft* and the French *Écoles d'Administration*. Political science made its official debut in the American academic arena around 1860 and for a long time it was really an American discipline. From its very inception as political *science* practitioners placed far less emphasis on normative political theory than their intellectual predecessors. Instead, they sought to come up with a positive science of politics. Initially, they used historical methods.[3] Later generations of political scientists abandoned for a large part the historical approach and tried to model the discipline after the natural sciences.[4]

This had a strong boost with the arrival of behaviorism and later with the adoption of new institutionalism after World War II. The political scientists of those days were anxious to distinguish themselves from political theorists. Political scientists sought to create a positive science and shed the fascination with normative speculation and ideal theory, which one of them—William Riker—characterized as "belles lettres, criticism, and philosophical speculation" as well as "phenomenology and hermeneutics" to distance his preferred branch of science from those approaches. Thus the self-image of those political scientists was that of a new science, unburdened with the "journalism" of earlier scholars, engaged in some hard-nosed inquiries about political behavior modeled after some ideal vista of (natural) science. (In this way, the methodological history of political science seems to have taken a page from economics, which underwent a similar change during the "marginal revolution" of Jevons and Walras.) The discipline was simply too busy distancing itself from more philosophical approaches to engage in much philosophical reflection on its core concepts, methods, and theories. As an explanation for the absence of such reflection this is not very convincing, however, since similar processes occurred in the establishment of the other branches of social science (notably psychology and economics) and this did not stop them from developing a systematic philosophical reflection on their disciplines. So the question remains: why is there no philosophy of political science?

Another possible explanation is that the label 'political science' as it is understood these days covers a plethora of approaches, theories, methods, objects of study, and intellectual traditions. It is natural to conclude that there is no single discipline of political science. If one looks at the various sub-disciplines that are traditionally included in political science this impression gets stronger. What do political theory, comparative politics, public administration, international relations, public law, and political economy have in common? This impression of a hodge-podge of disciplinary methodology is enhanced if one reflects on the approaches political scientists use: positivism, interpretivism, rational choice theory, behaviorism, structuralism, post-structuralism, realism, institutionalism, and pluralism. Perhaps the best we can say is that there is a set of topics and concerns that "political scientists" share, typically referred to as "politics". In this regard, political science is not unlike, say, the study of marketing or area studies. That is, there is no political science as a unified discipline, what unites political scientists is a common topic of study. No wonder there is no philosophy of political science.

However, this explanation will not do either. First, because it is unclear what the common topic is.[5] Political scientists study wildly diverging topics ranging from parliamentary history to comparative political psychology, voting and elections, political movements, etc. The only thing these topics have in common is that they are in the domain of political science—and not even exclusively so, as people working in sociology, history, and anthropology concern themselves with these things as well. More importantly, the situation is not that different from the other special sciences. There too, an overabundance of ideas, approaches, theories, objects of study, and traditions shape the self-image of the field. And, once again, these sciences have their own 'philosophy of' so why would political science be so different?

Still another explanation for the absence of a philosophy of political science says that there are no *special* philosophical problems raised by the research of political scientists. That is, the philosophy of political science is just a run of the mill application of the philosophy of social science to the activities and concerns of political scientists. The philosophical problems political scientists face are no different from those, say, an economist or a psychologist might face. Could this be why there is no philosophy of political science? We note again a relevant similarity here to the debate over the founding of the philosophy of chemistry, when some initially said that the reason there was no such discipline was that all of the interesting questions in it were already taken up in the philosophy of physics. Had this been true, however, one would have expected the philosophy of physics to consider more questions that were of actual interest to chemists, rather than being almost exclusively concerned with relativity, quantum mechanics, and space-time. There did turn out to be some good philosophical questions in the philosophy of chemistry that were irreducible to the philosophy of physics, the first of which was whether chemistry itself was in fact completely reducible to physics. Similarly, one might now ask the question: if the philosophy of political science does not exist because it is reducible to some other discipline, what would that discipline be?

Some might argue that the successful introduction of formal economic methodology in political science shows that political science, understood as a positive science, basically is economics applied to the study of politics.[6] Certainly, if one looks at the bulk of publications from the last decade of the previous century in the *American Political Science Review* (by many considered to be *the* journal in political science) this argument has some merit. Most publications consisted either of detailed survey comparisons or of formal models of certain aspects of political processes (often without any empirical testing) inspired by the sort of work done by the best economic modelers. However, by the beginning of the 21st century, there was a lot of resistance to this kind of one-sided methodological approach and when in 2000 the so-called "Perestroika" movement emerged, it became clear that many, if not most, political scientists would not support this reduction of political science to economics, either substantially or formally.[7]

At this point, the question in our title may seem a bit odd, for if none of these aforementioned factors could explain, let alone justify, the absence of a philosophy of political science, one might feel moved to ask: "should it exist?" or "doesn't it already?" After all, perhaps the work is just being done under the name of political theory by philosophers and political scientists alike. In what follows we will suggest that there are in fact some fundamental philosophical questions that are specific to the study of human political behavior. What is more, practitioners of political science are often aware of these results. In other words, we will suggest that there is (and should be) a philosophy of political science. However, unlike the other disciplines in the social sciences, there has as yet been no separate field of study commonly referred to as the "philosophy of political science."

A lot of philosophical analysis of political behavior is being done under the heading of political theory, yet political theorists do not have a monopoly on all philosophically interesting aspects of political science. For one thing, we would take it as a virtue that if a field called "the philosophy of political science" comes forward, it would be recognized—like its brethren "the philosophy of economics" and "the philosophy of psychology"—as a branch of the philosophy of social science, which is itself a branch of the philosophy of science. Here it seems important to draw a potential distinction between the "philosophy of political science" and "political theory." Obviously, the latter field has existed for thousands of years, and traces its roots back to Aristotle, Hobbes, Locke, Rousseau, Machiavelli, and Condorcet, roots that are intertwined with the roots of philosophy itself. This does not mean, however, that the only philosophical interest here concerns theory, for, as we have seen, political science at its incipience put itself forward as an *empirical* discipline. This should put at least some questions in the philosophical study of political science squarely in the wheelhouse of the philosophy of social science (and so the philosophy of science), where we may be rightly concerned with explanation, laws, reductionism, and other methodological issues in the scientific study of human behavior. Indeed, if the distinction between theory and behavior does not exist in the social sciences, then why hasn't there been more debate over whether economics deserved its own "philosophy of" designation and could have been better handled as "economic theory?" Why did political science, along with economics, psychology, and certain branches of sociology, long ago come forward as a quantitative discipline with a laser-like focus on the scientific explanation of human behavior? Because they recognized that in the actual world, we do not always behave as rationally or consistently as we do in theory. And, even if the earliest economic models had difficulties with its own simplifying assumptions about "perfect information" and "perfect rationality," the philosophy of economics was nonetheless born of an interest in seeing how, in comparison with actual behavior, we might make our explanations better. In fact, one wonders whether all of the previous philosophical criticism over the inadequate methodology of neoclassical economics is what has led, in recent years, to the much more rigorous (experimental) research program of behavioral economics. Might a similar methodological revolution be on the horizon if we turned the attention of more philosophers of science toward political science?

In what follows, we will give three more or less interdependent examples of current work done by political scientists that is distinctively philosophical in nature and of particular interest to the concerns of empirical political scientists. Of course these three examples do not exhaust the philosophical questions within political science, nor are they completely representative of such questions, but they do support our assertion that a more self-conscious focus on the issues that may arise from the "philosophy of political science" might yield many benefits.[8]

## Voting

Perhaps the most distinctive act of political activity in all contemporary states is the act of voting. Political scientists have studied voting behavior systematically since the 1940s, focusing on the determinants of voting behavior, the interplay between institutional rules, and strategies of political candidates. Often they have attempted to predict election results, thus living up to the self-image of political science as a positive discipline.

However, the practice of voting raises all kinds of fundamental philosophical questions about the activity and its coherence. First, there are fundamental questions as to why people vote in the first place. As Downs(1957) and others have remarked, in many circumstances it makes no sense to vote.[9] An example can bring home the point. Suppose all that matters to a typical voter is that her preferred candidate, A, wins the district seat in a winner-take-all, single-vote system. Suppose furthermore that there are ninety-nine voters in this district and that there are only two candidates, A and B. Then either her vote is the deciding vote that gets candidate A the win or it is not. This is the case only if the vote is completely tied. That is, if A has exactly forty-nine supporters and B has the remaining forty-nine votes. Even if we assume that for each typical voter in this group the probability that they support A equals 0.5, then the probability that her vote will be the deciding one is 0.01. For any other distribution that probability rapidly approaches 0. Since most actual elections have more than two candidates, and the probability with which candidates are supported varies, the chance that one's vote is decisive is negligible. Given that voting requires some effort and that other things besides the outcome of the election will matter to voters, it is unlikely that voting is actually worth the effort—it is irrational. Yet, paradoxically, people vote.[10]

This initial conclusion has raised a lot of discussion about the motivation of voters. Downs's theory is an example of the so-called public choice school in political science, which takes its inspiration from economic theory.[11] Public choice theory models political agents as self-interested preference maximizers whose behavior is rational relative to those preferences. In doing so, it proposes a very particular and somewhat restricted view of voting behavior. It leaves out expressive or intrinsic reasons for voting that motivate voters to express their political preferences. If those are taken into account, voting once again seems to make sense.[12] However, it does so at a cost, for it abandons the elegant—if somewhat unrealistic—picture of political man as a rational preference maximizer and imbues her with drives and motives that seem puzzling from the point of view of the public choice approach.[13] More generally, discussions such as these have flagged a fundamental concern about the plausibility of the implicit picture of the citizen in empirically oriented political theory.[14]

It is not just the motivation of individual voters that seems paradoxical; it has long been observed that common democratic voting procedures are problematic as well. Nicolas de Condorcet (1743–94) already proved that simple majority rule could result in incoherent overall social preferences.[15] For example, suppose one third of the electorate prefers candidate A to B to C; another third B to C to A, and a final third C to A to B. Then the majority of this electorate prefers A to B; B to C and C to A. Thus, even if individual political preferences are perfectly coherent and rational, the overall ranking of alternatives need not be. Two hundred years later, Nobel Prize winner Kenneth Arrow generalized this observation and proved that any voting procedure that meets some very weak and plausible requirements can generate such results. His proof is one of the central results of social choice theory—the formal theory of collective decision processes and procedures.[16]

A quick discussion of Arrow's impossibility result may be helpful to illustrate this. Let $N = \{1, 2, ..., n\}$ (with $n > 2$) be the set of voters and $X = \{x, y, z, ....\}$ be the set of alternatives submitted to the vote (these can be candidates, policies, proposals, etc.). Suppose that each individual $i$ has a preference ordering $R_i$ over these alternatives. Let the function $F$ be a voting rule that gives an overall ordering of the alternatives $R$. Then these are the requirements that Arrow proposed:

- *Universal domain*: F takes as its domain the set of all logically possible profiles of complete and transitive individual preference orderings. In other words, a plausible voting rule works for all possible electoral preference rankings of alternatives.
- *Ordering*: For any profile of individual rankings $< R_1, R_2, ..., R_n >$ in the domain of $F$, the overall ordering $R$ is complete and transitive. So the overall ordering that $F$ gives, will include all the alternatives and is non-cyclical.
- *Weak Pareto principle*: For any profile $< R_1, R_2, ..., R_n >$ in the domain of $F$, if all individuals rank $x$ over $y$, then $F$ ranks $x$ over $y$. This is a weak unanimity requirement.
- *Independence of irrelevant alternatives*: For any two profiles $< R_1, R_2, ..., R_n >$ and $< R^*_1, R^*_2, ..., R^*_n >$ in the domain of $F$ and any $x, y \in X$, if for all $i \in N$ $R_i$'s ranking between $x$ and $y$ coincides with $R^*_i$'s ranking between $x$ and $y$, then $xRy$ if and only if $xR^*y$. This just means that the overall order between $x$ and $y$ will not change if other alternatives are added to $X$.
- *Non-dictatorship*: There does not exist an individual $i \in N$ such that, for all $< R_1, R_2, ..., R_n >$ in the domain of $F$ and all $x, y \in X$, $xP_iy$ implies $xPy$.

Notice that these requirements are indeed plausible and seemingly innocent. We already saw that simple majority rule does not satisfy these requirements. Condorcet's theorem illustrates this: in the example above there was no clear 'winner'. Arrow proved that there is no voting rule $F$ that satisfies these conditions.

There is enormous variety in voting procedures: majoritarian rules, rank-dependent systems (e.g., Borda rule), winner-take-all, etc. Arrow's formalization gives the theorist the tools to characterize any possible voting procedure. However, the importance of Arrow's work is not just theoretical. It gave focus to a lot of research in real-world electoral systems and their problems. For example, it is well confirmed that voting procedures tend to co-vary with electoral constellations and political outcomes. For example, a much-discussed observation is 'Duverger's law', which says that plurality rule voting in a single member district system favors two-party systems as is the case in the USA and the UK.[17] Social choice theory gave researchers tools to put Duverger's law to the test and improve upon it.[18]

Arrow's impossibility theorem has been regarded as a challenge for political scientists who are interested in voting procedures. William Riker argued that the theorem shows that populist democracy is incoherent.[19] He also argued that there is at least one historical example of a radical failure of the sort that Arrow's theorem predicts: the voting in the United States House of Representatives that led to the start of the American Civil War resulted in a non-transitive ordering. Others have taken issue with his claim that democracy is incoherent.[20] Still others have taken issue with the requirements of Arrow. For example, Duncan Black has shown that if one restricts the universal domain condition in such a way that only well-behaved 'single-peaked' rankings are in the domain of $F$, then the overall ordering will be complete and transitive.[21] Others have taken issue with the Pareto requirement since it can imply that individual rights will be violated, rendering it less attractive as a requirement.[22]

Similarly, the requirement of the independence of irrelevant alternatives has attracted some scrutiny.[23] It turns out that rules that violate this requirement are vulnerable to strategic voting. Strategic voting is voting behavior where voters do not vote according to their real preference, but instead vote in such a manner that the overall result will be more to their preference. A well-known example concerns the voting by supporters of Ralph Nader in the 2000 presidential election who voted for Al Gore rather than Nader so as to prevent George Bush from winning—their least preferred alternative. Alan Gibbard and William Sattertwaite have shown that voting rules that result in unique winners that satisfy universal domain and non-dictatorship conditions (and have at least three alternatives) can be manipulated in that way.[24] This then again raises questions about the motivation of voters to vote in a particular way: to what extent can one be sure that these reflect actual political preferences? Since many actually used voting procedures (such as the Borda rule or the plurality rule) violate this requirement, one also wonders to what extent the resulting collective outcome reflects the political preferences of voters.

The important thing to realize is that these results are the outcome of meticulous theoretical thought about voting as well as empirical research. They provoke intense debate about the nature of voting, the role of institutional rules about voting, as well as questions of institutional design. Here then is one example of a range of philosophical questions that have been considered primarily—but of course not exclusively—within circles of political scientists, that are ripe for more philosophical work.

## Democracy

Voting is the quintessential political act that most adults in modern liberal democracies will ever perform. It is no coincidence then that many political scientists interested in voting are concerned with democracy as well. Democracy, in its most general and abstract meaning, refers to those methods of collective decision making that are characterized by a kind of equality among the participants. This requirement of equality can be conceived in purely formal terms in that every vote counts equally towards the result, as is the case in many representational systems. It can be more substantial in that all voters have an equal say in substantive matters, as is the case in participatory democracies, or it can be interpreted as a constraint on the legitimacy of outcomes according to which a political decision is legitimate or authoritative only if the interests of all those concerned were considered, or indeed, anything in between. The diversity of democratic regimes and institutions requires a theory of democracy that does justice to the variety of democracies and their accompanying systems of participation and representation, but also explains what all democratic systems have in common.

If one thinks of voting as a form of expressing one's political preferences and judgments—that a voting procedure is supposed to transform into a more or less coherent collective judgment, as is the case in public choice and social choice theory—then it seems obvious to think of democracy as a kind of preference aggregation procedure where the political preferences of the citizens are more or less given and the political result, e.g., the winner of elections, is to be evaluated against these. Politics, in this conception of democracy, is the institution that aims to satisfy the (political) preferences of citizens, much like markets aim to satisfy the economic preferences of consumers. Democracies then are those political aggregation systems where everyone's preference has an equal weight resulting in a fair compromise between these preferences, much as equal purchasing power of consumers in the market would lead to fair market outcomes. In this light, the concern of social choice theorists for incoherent and manipulable overall collective judgments becomes quite relevant. If it can be shown that under real-world conditions specific democratic institutions thwart the "fair" outcomes, then so much the worse for those institutions. Manipulation of democratic processes, similarly, will be a major worry as these too can thwart such 'fair' outcomes.

However, democracy's potential virtues as a fair form of institutional preference aggregation have not played a dominant role in any alternative school of thinking. In the same writings in which the marquis de Condorcet argues that simple majority rule could render aggregative results incoherent, he recommends trial by jury using a simple probability calculus. Suppose that a jury has to decide whether or not a defendant is guilty. Suppose that for each juror individually the probability that he or she gives the right verdict upon examining the evidence equals $p$ and $p > 0.5$. Then the probability that the majority of the jury will reach the correct decision approaches 1 as the number of jurors on the jury increases.[25] Extrapolating this rather simple argument to actual juries and actual electorates (as well as actual organizations), these authors argue that democratically organized collectives are more likely to 'get it right'. That is, the reason why democracy is preferable to other forms of governance is epistemic, rather than that the resulting decision will be a fair compromise of the preferences of all citizens.[26]

Others, however, reject both these ways of thinking about democracy and indeed of politics. They emphasize that politics is not just a more or less passive process of preference aggregation where political institutions, like markets, simply function to "translate" these preferences into a more or less coherent result. Neither is politics an institutional way of consulting the wisdom of crowds. Crucial to politics is the formation of those preferences and beliefs. Political debate is not just a collective bargaining process, where agents try to maximize their political preferences or consult others' beliefs, rather it is the very place where those preferences and beliefs are formed. That is, these authors contrast democracy conceived as a market of preferences or beliefs with democracy conceived of as a "forum"—a place of debate and deliberation.[27] For these theorists, voting is but one form of democratic participation and not the most interesting one for that matter. Furthermore, democratic deliberation that shapes political preferences is massively important for the acceptance and legitimacy of the decisions thus reached.[28] This emphasis on the formative and legitimizing aspects of democratic institutions has spawned a lot of research into the efficacy of alternative deliberative institutions. Citizen juries, deliberative panels, and many alternative forms of consultation and deliberation have been proposed and investigated.[29]

Here, therefore, we have another example of philosophical reflection on political scientific research into the nature of democracy. A lot of this work is done under the heading of "political theory" but it is crucial to see and understand that it is born from the cross-fertilization of philosophical and empirical work in political science.

## Freedom

Historically, the interest in democracies comes from a view of political freedom. Democracies, it is thought, are free societies. This imprecise claim raises conceptual, methodological, as well as empirical questions.

Consider the conceptual issue of freedom. What is it? In 1819 Benjamin Constant wrote his famous essay comparing the freedom of the "ancients" with that of the "moderns".[30] "Ancient" freedom is republican, participatory freedom. On this view, a state is free if it is free from outside influences and interference and enjoys self-rule. Citizens have a burdensome moral obligation to participate in the governing of the state. This notion of freedom, then, is primarily concerned with the question "who rules?". "Modern" freedom on the other hand is the freedom one enjoys in the absence of the state. A state is free if its citizens have civil liberties and the state is absent in some private areas of life. Isaiah Berlin, in his famous inaugural lecture, echoed this distinction and traced the historical roots of either notion.[31] He distinguished "negative" from "positive" freedom. A person is free in the negative sense, if she is free from external limits on her options. (This is similar to Constant's "modern" sense of freedom.) This view of freedom can be traced back to Hobbes.[32] Negative freedom then is only impaired by the presence of something. A person is free in the "positive" sense, if she is master of her own life; when it is "up to her" what she will do. Notice that one can be free in this positive sense, even if there are very few options available to the agent. Berlin, like Constant before him, criticized the ancient tradition and endorsed the liberal, "negative" version of freedom.

Contemporary authors, however, have a very different understanding of positive freedom. Rather than the freedom to self-rule, they think of positive freedom as the presence of the means to utilize one's negative freedom. For example, if there is no access to the Internet in a society because of legal prohibitions, that society lacks important negative freedoms. Suppose that these prohibitions are lifted and access to the Internet becomes available in this society, but that it is prohibitively expensive to use. In that case, there is more negative freedom than before in this society, but the positive freedom to utilize this option is lacking. In other words, supporters of negative freedom claim that one can only be robbed of one's freedom by the presence of some obstacle; supporters of positive freedom on the other hand hold that one can also be robbed of one's freedom by the absence of something (e.g., sufficient income).

Gerald MacCallum has pointed out that if this is how one understands positive and negative freedom, then it is relatively straightforward to combine the two notions in one triadic formula: $x$ is free from $y$ to $z$, where $x$ ranges over individuals, $y$ over obstacles, and $z$ over actions.[33] The disagreement between supporters of negative freedom and those of positive freedom then is not a disagreement as to what the "real" or "true" conception of freedom is. Rather, it is a disagreement about the extension of $y$ and $z$. This unified conception of freedom is important for the theory of the measurement of freedom.

Before we get to the methodological issues at stake in that debate, we need to consider one important contemporary third way of understanding freedom. This is the neo-republican theory of freedom, which in many ways goes back to the old republican tradition that was rejected by Constant. Neo-republicans hold that to be free means that one is free from arbitrary and non-controllable power.[34] This third way shares with the "ancient" understanding of freedom that external influences are seen as something undesirable. It shares with the unified triadic formulation of freedom that one can be unfree when one is subjected to external obstacles or internal compulsions (for then one is not free to do $z$), but only when these are the result of arbitrary and uncontrollable factors. What is more, these factors need not even be active to result in a loss of freedom. For example, imagine a benevolent dictator who rules with absolute authority over his subjects. He does so with their wishes and well-being in mind. He imposes minimal constraints on their daily activities and indeed on their political activities. His subjects are free from coercion and interference by him and they are free to do (most of) the things they want to do. However, should this dictator decide to take away these freedoms and impose fierce constraints simply because he feels like it, his subjects are completely at his mercy. It is not unlikely that the subjects of our dictator will adapt their behavior so as not to displease him and avoid attracting his ire and ill feeling. Neo-republicans argue that this constitutes a loss of freedom. Note that the loss is not the result of (actual) coercion and state interference. Nor is it the result of somebody other than the subjects determining here and now what they are going to do (i.e., they are free in the positive sense as Berlin distinguished it), yet these people lack robust control of their own lives. For this reason neo-republicans favor strong constitutions that bind authorities as well as certain forms of social support that enable people to be independent and have control over their own lives.[35]

Having distinguished these three ways of thinking about freedom, one might wonder how one determines whether one is free. Similarly, one could compare regimes in terms of how much freedom they allow their citizens. That is, with the conceptual work out of the way for now, one could start to wonder about the measurement of freedom. It is here that the techniques of social choice theory once again become relevant.

Some have argued that the idea of measuring freedom is nonsensical. One reason for this can be found in what the value of freedom is in the first place. For example, Ronald Dworkin has argued that freedom as such does not have any value—only specific freedoms are valuable.[36] The freedom to buy fifty kinds of soda is irrelevant, whereas freedom of speech is relevant. Therefore, the idea that one can attach a value to freedom as such is nonsensical, as are comparisons of freedom. However, it is an open debate whether freedom only has such specific value. Ian Carter has argued that freedom has non-specific value.[37] That is, one's freedom has increased with the addition of feasible options. If before one could only get one kind of soda and now fifty kinds of soda, that is an enlargement of one's soda-buying liberty from no liberty to a lot of liberty even though there is nothing specifically valuable in the freedom to buy a particular brand of, say, root beer.

Using very weak and plausible assumptions, Pattanaik and Xu have constructed a metric of freedom that reflects this non-specific value of freedom. It entails that as one's feasible options increase, one is more free—a result they deem to be 'naïve and trivial' in that it throws out all kinds of other information one may have about the options.[38] Taking their lead, others have tried to construct measurements of freedom that avoid naïveté and triviality. However, in doing so, several difficult problems arise, most notably the problem of how to individuate the feasible options open to the agent. If freedom consists, *inter alia*, in the lack of constraints an agent faces, removal of constraints enlarges one's freedom. So suppose that one makes driving an automobile much cheaper. Then one has removed a constraint on driving. How many constraints has one removed? Just one, or has one removed a constraint on driving to this or that specific destination? What should we count? Moreover, how should the individual options be weighed? Does the freedom to kill other human beings count for as much as the freedom to borrow books from the library? Another problem concerns the comparability of the different ways of constraining freedom. Does the unfreedom created by coercion and state interference count for as much as the unfreedom created by natural events?

Traditionally, these questions were objects of abstract theorizing by political theorists and political philosophers. More and more, however, they are raised by actual empirical work, for example, in the methodology of the various rankings that organizations like Freedom House and others publish.[39] These questions are not just of concern to political philosophers and theorists but have important ramifications for comparative empirical work. It should be clear that this work is relevant for how we think of freedom, of its value, of its place in democracies, or indeed, of the freedom to vote. In other words, here too we find an example of philosophical reflection on research done by political scientists that merits the label 'philosophy of political science'.

## Conclusion

In this chapter, we have tried to illustrate that, contrary to the question in our title, there already *is* a philosophy of political science. Much of it is done by political scientists as well as political theorists, but not exclusively so. This means that the situation of political science, in spite of the details of its emergence on the academic scene or the somewhat chaotic cornucopia of methodology and topics, is not much different from the situation of the other special disciplines. So does it matter much what we call it or insist that it be recognized as a branch of the philosophy of social science? If political theory and the philosophy of political science are largely extensionally equivalent, how much advantage is there in trying to create the philosophy of political science? Or at least to bring it in out of the shadows and call it what it is?

If the only role that philosophers had in this debate were to say "we should pay more attention to what they're doing in political science" the effect would be minimal. For—as we have shown—there are those who are already paying attention. Likewise if the conclusion of most philosophers turned out to be "there are no current issues in political science that are worthy of much philosophical attention; let the political theorists have it," we would be loath to impose interest where there was none. But neither seems to be the case. Rather the content of a legitimately recognized philosophical study of the *science* of human political behavior seems to already be there, as it has been for some time, and has merely not bothered to do the work to claim a new title.

Why should it? We think that the payoff could be great. By embracing the idea that the philosophy of political science is part of the philosophy of social science, it will open new doors, as those who are schooled in the particular interests and expertise of philosophers of science will bring fresh insight to the methodological and explanatory questions that concern political science. The establishment of political science a century and a half ago sought its break from the study of politics and its pre-scientific history, and took up questions that could only be answered by an empirical approach. Doesn't philosophical concern with this discipline therefore deserve its own break from political theory?

Is this to presume that all of political science is (or should be) quantitative? That the war with qualitative methods has been won? Some would argue that the reason the philosophy of economics and the philosophy of psychology have been able to come forward so robustly is that their underlying fields are more scientific, so their 'philosophy of' designation is less problematic. Sociology, anthropology, and history, however, are less empirical, so their standing as branches of the philosophy of social science is more suspect. But note that even the latter have their own 'philosophy of' designations. Of course, this does not presume an answer to the debate over the usefulness or status of positivism, interpretivism, or any of the other methodological approaches in political science, any more than in anthropology or sociology. There are quantitative and qualitative methods in all of the social sciences. But the focus of all of them is nonetheless explanatory and so, finally, empirical. As such, especially given the speed of its recent turn toward quantitative methods, as well as the fierce organized resistance to it, political science seems long overdue for its own 'philosophy of'.

The philosophical study of economics and psychology has thrived under this arrangement. So has the philosophy of chemistry. We believe that the philosophical questions raised by political science will receive more and better-focused attention—and more scholarship devoted to the specific questions raised by its methodology—as a result of this self-conscious shift in focus. Philosophers of science are well attuned to the explanatory and methodological issues in scientific fields. We bring something that historians of political thought—or what has been called "political philosophy"—have not self-consciously wrought, which is the acceptance and consideration of political science as an empirical examination, *inter alia*, of our ideas about democracy and freedom as revealed in our voting behavior.

There are, of course, institutional benefits too: conferences, symposia, anthologies, and with them more scholarship. Just as in the philosophy of chemistry, one expects that the good work done so far will be followed by an avalanche of good work to come. Thus do we feel that the philosophy of political science should take its rightful place alongside the philosophy of economics, the philosophy of history, and the philosophies of psychology, sociology, and anthropology as a branch of the philosophy of social science, devoted to the explanatory questions that arise in the empirical study of human political behavior.

So what's in a name? In itself nothing. Unless you use it to signal others who might have missed it that you're here and worthy of renewed attention. Then it can be extraordinary.

## Notes

1 For more on the history of this transformation see Scerri and McIntyre 1997. For an excellent compendium of work in the philosophy of chemistry before it was called that, see Scerri 1997.
2 Schliesser 2014.
3 Thus, for example, the motto of the seminar room of the Political Science Department at Johns Hopkins University, one of the early powerhouses of the newly established political science, was "History is past politics and politics present history."
4 On this most authoritative histories of the discipline concur. For a good overview, see Farr 1988.
5 The question as to what constitutes 'politics' is itself a question of ongoing concern and disagreement, as can be seen if one compares, for example, Lasswell 1936; Arendt 1958; Easton 1965; Crick 2000; Leftwich 2004.
6 This is one way in which so-called 'economic imperialism' is manifested (Mäki 2009).
7 Monroe 2015.
8 It is important to point out here, however, that all of our examples focus more or less on the increasing use of formal methods (especially social choice theory) in political science, as well as some of the reactions to this trend. We do not mean to take sides in the debate about the merits of these methods. They are certainly not the only game in town. However, they are illustrative of our claim that there is a case for the existence of a philosophy of political science.
9 But see Riker and Ordeshook 1968 for a contrary result.
10 What is more, if this line of reasoning is correct, it is also paradoxical that voters take the effort to inform themselves about political issues and what each candidate stands for. In this connection the rise of voting advice applications is remarkable, e.g., Fossen and Anderson 2014.
11 A nice overview of the theory and its main results is Mueller 1997.
12 Brennan and Lomasky 1993.

13 Some authors have concluded that voters are irrational and that, therefore, politics is intrinsically irrational, e.g. Caplan 2007, 2008. Again, the potential for experimental work on this assumption, by analogy with behavioral economics, seems ripe.

14 See for example Elster 1983, 1989. Of course, there are concerns about the adoption of such ideal types in social science that are relevant for all social sciences alike.

15 Condorcet 1785.

16 Arrow 1950.

17 Duverger 1959.

18 See Riker 1982b for an overview.

19 Riker 1982a.

20 For example, Mackie 2003.

21 Black 1948. A ranking profile is 'single peaked' if one can order the alternatives $x$, $y$, $z$, from 'left to right', such that each individual's ranking will have a most preferred alternative on that line with decreasing preference as alternatives get more distant (in either direction) from the most preferred position. In the example of Condorcet, the preferences of the electorate are not single peaked.

22 For example, Sen 1970.

23 One can't here resist sharing an old joke about the irrationality of considering irrelevant alternatives. A philosopher walks into a diner to order a piece of pie. The waiter says "We have cherry and apple." The philosopher orders a slice of apple pie. The waiter then says "Oh wait, we also have pumpkin," to which the philosopher replies "In that case I'll take the cherry."

24 Gibbard 1973; Satterthwaite 1975. It is, of course, unclear to what extent that is a bad thing: Dowding and Hees 2008.

25 Here is an arithmetical example. Suppose a typical juror has a probability of $p = 0.6$ to arrive at the right answer. A jury consisting of one juror then will return the correct verdict with $p = 0.6$. Suppose we expand the jury to three members, then the probability that the majority of the jury will reach a correct verdict then equals $p = 0.6^3 + 3(0.6 \cdot 0.6 \cdot 0.4) = 0.648$. It is crucial, however, that for this to work the jurors must not be influenced by one another before they have made their decision. For more on the intricacies of the Condorcet Jury Theorem see Sunstein 2008.

26 For example, Estlund 2008.

27 Elster 1997.

28 Rawls 1971; Habermas 1976; Rawls 1993; Habermas 1998.

29 The work of John Dryzek is a good example of this trend to test philosophically inspired claims about deliberative institutions empirically: J. Dryzek 1999, 1999; J. S. Dryzek 2006, 2010.

30 Repr. in Constant 1988.

31 Berlin 1969.

32 Hobbes 1991, ch. 21.

33 MacCallum 1967.

34 Pettit 1997, 2012.

35 See also Pettit 2014.

36 Dworkin 1978, 268–74.

37 Carter 1999.

38 Pattanaik and Xu 1990.

39 For example, the kinds of comparisons that are made in "Freedom House" 2015; "Country Rankings: World and Global Economy Rankings on Economic Freedom" 2015; "How Free Is Your State?" 2015.

# References

Arendt, Hannah. 1958. *The Human Condition*. Chicago: University of Chicago Press.

Arrow, Kenneth J. 1950. "A Difficulty in the Concept of Social Welfare." *Journal of Political Economy* 58(4): 328–46.

Berlin, Isaiah. 1969. "Two Concepts of Liberty." In *Four Essays on Liberty*, 118–72. Oxford: Oxford University Press.

Black, Duncan. 1948. "On the Rationale of Group Decision-Making." *Journal of Political Economy* 56(1): 23–34.

Brennan, Geoffrey, and Loren Lomasky. 1993. *Democracy and Decision: The Pure Theory of Electoral Preference*. Cambridge: Cambridge University Press.

Caplan, Bryan. 2007. *The Myth of the Rational Voter: Why Democracies Choose Bad Policies*. Princeton, NJ: Princeton University Press.

———. 2008. "Reply to My Critics." *Critical Review* 20(3): 377–413.

Carter, Ian. 1999. *A Measure of Freedom*. Oxford, etc: Oxford University Press.

Condorcet, Jean-Antoine-Nicolas de Caritat. 1785. *Essai sur l'application de l'analyse à la probabilité des décisions rendues à la pluralité des voix*. Paris: Imprimerie royale.

Constant, Benjamin. 1988. *Political Writings*. Cambridge: Cambridge University Press.

"Country Rankings: World and Global Economy Rankings on Economic Freedom." 2015. Accessed December 17, 2015. www.heritage.org/index/ranking.

Crick, Bernard. 2000. *In Defence of Politics*. London: Continuum.

Dowding, Keith, and Martin Van Hees. 2008. "In Praise of Manipulation." *British Journal of Political Science* 38(1): 1–15.

Downs, Anthony. 1957. *An Economic Theory of Democracy*. New York: Harper & Row.

Dryzek, John. 1999. "Transnational Democracy." *Journal of Political Philosophy* 7(1): 30–51.

Dryzek, John S. 2006. *Deliberative Global Politics: Discourse and Democracy in a Divided World*. Cambridge: Polity.

———. 2010. *Foundations and Frontiers of Deliberative Governance*. Oxford: Oxford University Press.

Duverger, Maurice. 1959. *Political Parties: Their Organization and Activity in the Modern State*. New York: Wiley.

Dworkin, Ronald Myles. 1978. *Taking Rights Seriously*. London: Duckworth.

Easton, David. 1965. *The Political System: An Inquiry into the State of Political Science*. New York: Alfred A. Knopf.

Elster, Jon. 1983. *Explaining Technical Change: A Case Study in the Philosophy of Science*. Cambridge: Cambridge University Press.

———. 1989. "Rationality and Social Norms." In *Logic, Methodology and Philosophy of Science*. New York: Elsevier Science.

———. 1997. "The Market and the Forum: Three Varieties of Political Theory." In *Deliberative Democracy*. Cambridge, MA: MIT Press.

Estlund, David M. 2008. *Democratic Authority: A Philosophical Framework*. Princeton, NJ: Princeton University Press.

Farr, J. 1988. "The History of Political-Science." *American Journal of Political Science* 32(4): 1175–195.

Fossen, Thomas, and Joel Anderson. 2014. "What's the Point of Voting Advice Applications? Competing Perspectives on Democracy and Citizenship." *Electoral Studies* 36: 244–51.

"Freedom House." 2015. Accessed December 17, 2015. https://freedomhouse.org/report/freedom-world/freedom-world-2015#.VnKXQb_oTtI.

Gibbard, Allan. 1973. "Manipulation of Voting Schemes: A General Result." *Econometrica* 41(4): 587–601.

Habermas, Jürgen. 1976. *Legitimation Crisis*. Trans. Thomas MacCarthy. London: Heinemann Educational.

———. 1998. *Between Facts and Norms: Contributions to a Discourse Theory of Law and Democracy*. Cambridge, MA: MIT Press.

Hobbes, Thomas. 1991. *Leviathan*, ed. Richard Tuck. Cambridge Texts in the History of Political Thought. Cambridge: Cambridge University Press.

"How Free Is Your State?" 2015. Accessed December 17, 2015. http://freedominthe50states.org/.

Jarvie, Ian, and Jesus Zamora-Bonilla, eds. 2011. *The Sage Handbook of the Philosophy of Social Sciences*. London, etc: Sage.

Kincaid, Harold, ed. 2012. *The Oxford Handbook of Philosophy of Social Science*. Oxford University Press.

Lasswell, Harold D. 1936. *Politics; Who Gets What, When, How*. New York: Whittlesey house.

Leftwich, Adrian. 2004. *What Is Politics? The Activity and Its Study*. Cambridge and Malden, MA: Polity Press.

MacCallum, Gerald C. 1967. "Negative and Positive Freedom." *Philosophical Review* 76(3): 312–34.

Mackie, Gerry. 2003. *Democracy Defended*. Cambridge: Cambridge University Press.

Mäki, Uskali. 2009. "Economics Imperialism: Concept and Constraints." *Philosophy of the Social Sciences* 39(3): 351–80.

Monroe, Kristen R., ed. 2015. *Perestroika! The Raucous Rebellion in Political Science*. London: Yale University Press.

Mueller, Dennis C., ed. 1997. *Perspectives on Public Choice: A Handbook*. Cambridge: Cambridge University Press.

Pattanaik, Prasanta, and Yongsheng Xu. 1990. "On Ranking Opportunity Sets in Terms of Freedom of Choice." *Recherches Economiques de Louvain* 54: 383–90.

Pettit, Philip. 1997. *Republicanism: A Theory of Freedom and Government*. Oxford Political Theory. Oxford: Clarendon Press.

———. 2012. *On the People's Terms: A Republican Theory and Model of Democracy*. Cambridge: Cambridge University Press.

———. 2014. *Just Freedom: A Moral Compass for a Complex World*. New York: W. W. Norton & Company, Inc.

Rawls, John. 1971. *A Theory of Justice*. Cambridge, MA: Harvard University Press.

———. 1993. *Political Liberalism*. New York: Columbia University Press.

Riker, William H. 1982a. *Liberalism against Populism: A Confrontation between the Theory of Democracy and the Theory of Social Choice*. San Francisco: Freeman.

———. 1982b. "The Two-Party System and Duverger's Law: An Essay on the History of Political Science." *American Political Science Review* 76(4): 753–66.

Riker, William H., and Peter C. Ordeshook. 1968. "A Theory of the Calculus of Voting." *American Political Science Review* 62(1): 25–42.

Satterthwaite, Mark Allen. 1975. "Strategy-Proofness and Arrow's Conditions: Existence and Correspondence Theorems for Voting Procedures and Social Welfare Functions." *Journal of Economic Theory* 10(2): 187–217.

Scerri, E. R. 1997. "Bibliography on Philosophy of Chemistry." *Synthese* 111(3): 305–24.

Scerri, Eric R., and Lee McIntyre. 1997. "The Case for the Philosophy of Chemistry." *Synthese* 111(3): 213–32.

Schliesser, Eric. 2014. "Why the Lack of Philosophical Interest in So Many Social Sciences?" *Digressions & Impressions*. November 12. Accessed December 21, 2015. http://digressionsnimpressions.typepad.com/digressionsimpressions/2014/11/why-the-lack-of-philosophical-interest-in-so-many-social-sciences.html.

Sen, Amartya. 1970. "The Impossibility of a Paretian Liberal." *Journal of Political Economy* 78(1): 152–57.

Sunstein, Cass R. 2008. *Infotopia: How Many Minds Produce Knowledge*, 1st edn. Oxford: Oxford University Press.

Turner, Stephen P., and Paul A. Roth. 2003. *The Blackwell Guide to the Philosophy of the Social Sciences*. Blackwell Philosophy Guides. Malden, MA, etc: Blackwell.

447

# INDEX

Made in United States
Orlando, FL
13 January 2022